WILDMEN
OF CRICKET

VOL 1

Ken Piesse
& Brian Hansen

Brian Hansen Publications

Viv Richards calls for help after Australian Peter Toohey is downed by an Andy Roberts bouncer on a greentop at Port-of-Spain in 1978. Bowled out for 90 on the first day, the Australians lost by an innings inside three days.

PUBLISHER'S NOTE

Bradman – Botham – Lillee- Lara – Imran – Miller – Richards – Hughes – Warne – Barnes – Marsh.

There's a word for each them. No two of them are alike.

Invincible – Violent – Volatile – Arrogant – Ambitious – Flamboyant – Explosive – Humorous – Unplayable – Unmanageable – Determined.

These are the greats of cricket. Temperamental, provocative, even disturbing. They dared to be different and that's what set them apart. They yielded to no man and triumphed against adversity, sharing the wild times to write cricket's most romantic and adventurous stories.

Other than the mighty Khan, who was born with a silver spoon and schooled at Oxford, this mob did it tough, clawing their way to the top, their only weapons their unique skills and fierce spirit.

There is a story of sporting magic in every one of them and those stories are told in this publication as they have never been told before. These are the inside stories of their glories and catastrophes. Their hatred and feuds. The humor and the dramas. Never a dull word.

Some will question the inclusion of Don Bradman amongst the Wildmen. My co-author certainly did – and with considerable feeling. But I believe the story of Bradman in this publication will justify his selection.

Brian Hansen Publications takes pride in publishing the first volume of Wildmen of Cricket with such a noted international cricket authority as Ken Piesse. I invited Ken to partner me in this publication because of his encyclopaedic knowledge of the game, his writing skills and his meticulous attention to detail. We selected our own subjects for the Wildmen of Cricket series and do not necessarily share the same opinions.

Ken makes it clear he has an admiration for Sir Donald Bradman that borders on religion and I too, who played junior and suburban cricket with a Don Bradman autograph on a Don Bradman bat, have worshipped at the Bradman shrine of cricket then and now.

But The Don has another facet to his character which led to friction both on and off the field. He was the spark that ignited the wildest and most passionate times in all cricket history. Nor did controversy and hostility begin and end with his flailing bat – he was a provocative captain, a ruthless selector and a harsh ruler. Some of his own players hated him.

Sir Donald is revered throughout Australia and the older he gets the more revered he becomes; that's one of the virtues of age but does not mean we should bury the darker side of his story and only remember the scores themselves. They came at a price.
–Brian Hansen.

Patrick Eagar

THE AUTHORS

Ever since KEN PIESSE was old enough to realise that "Sundries" wasn't a player's surname, he's been a cricket buff with a particular love of the Australian X1 and its diverse range of characters.

Having edited cricket magazines for 20 years, Ken is well versed with the game's greatest and wildest characters of recent decades from Rod Marsh and Dennis Lillee through to Merv Hughes and Shane Warne.

A noted cricket journalist and author, Ken has written almost 20 cricket books, including the best-selling, *Warne, Sultan of Spin* and *The Great Australian Book of Cricket Stories* which went into several editions.

Australian Cricket magazine, which he has edited since 1994-95, is published six times a year from October to March.

BRIAN HANSEN has long been regarded as one of Australia's foremost sports writers and editors and author of many fine books.

From the time he saw Don Bradman's farewell innings in Melbourne and shared in the jubilation for his 117th and final century in December, 1948, he has been a cricket devotee with a leaning towards the game's more outspoken and flamboyant. Brian covered countless Tests and for years associated with the great Keith Miller.

This is his first cricket book with Ken Piesse.

ACKNOWLEDGEMENTS

The authors thank Greg Chappell for his foreword and gratefully acknowledge the assistance of Tony Crafter, Col Dawson, Tony Dodemaide, Ross Dundas, Craig Dunshea, 3AW's David Mann, Bob Parish snr., Susan Piesse, Jack Pollard, Terry Prue, the ICC's David Richards, photographers Sergio Dionisio, Patrick Eagar, David Munden/Sportsline and Ken Rainsbury and all the players who made it possible, especially the great Keith Miller, Rod Marsh, Dennis Lillee and David Hookes.

Published by Brian Hansen Nominees Pty Ltd
First published 1997
ISBN 1 876151 14 5
Designed and produced by Publishing Solutions, Melbourne
Printed in Australia
Wildmen of Cricket Vol 1. is proudly supported by 3AW.

Front cover illustrations – top left and then going clockwise: Merv Hughes, Brian Lara, Don Bradman, Shane Warne and Dennis Lillee/Javed Miandad. Back cover – from top to bottom: Viv Richards, Keith Miller, Ian Botham and Jeff Thomson.

CONTENTS

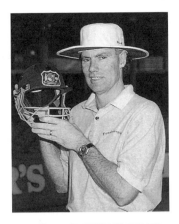

FOREWORD

THE POWER & THE PASSION

One of the endearing qualities of the game of cricket is that, by its very nature, it breeds people with character. The pages of *Wisden* abound with characters such as W.G. Grace from the early days of Test cricket through to Shane Warne of the modern era.

Despite the introduction of the shortened game more recently, the game itself is basically the same.

To succeed at the top level for any length of time, a player must have character, courage, resilience, a sense of humor and be more than a touch crazy, because the capricious nature of the game tests everyone many times over. Any personality flaws or weaknesses will be explored by the game, the opposition and, not infrequently, by one's own teammates.

As a young lad I remember going to the Adelaide Oval to watch a Test match between Australia and England. Traditionally the Adelaide Test was played on the Australia Day weekend, as it was on this occasion, in January '63. Australia Day was celebrated with a 21-gun salute from the Torrens Parade ground adjacent to the oval.

Play had just commenced on this morning with Fred Trueman bowling to Australia's Alan Davidson, who was not out overnight. If my memory serves me correctly, Trueman stopped in his run-up as the first salvo was fired and then endured a round or two through each of his next seven deliveries.

By the 15th round, Trueman had a big, white handkerchief out of his pocket waving surrender! Despite the tension of the moment, all concerned, on and off the field, were amused and marvelled at Trueman's sense of fun and timing.

Not many years later I played for Somerset against Trueman and his beloved Yorkshire. It was my first county game, in what turned out to be his last season of first-class cricket. Well past his prime at 37, he was still a formidable sight as he ran up to the wicket on a cold, rainy day in Taunton.

Having gone in to bat on a hat-trick in the dark and damp conditions, I was nervous enough without having to face one of the legends of the game. I proceeded to be made to look foolish as Fred hooped his outswinger past my groping forward defence time and time again.

Much to my embarassment, I got off the mark with an outside edge, waist-high through the slip cordon and proceeded to score from both outside and inside edge, as Fred tried a few inswingers to break up the monotony of my thick outside edges.

After what seemed an eternity Fred could stand it no longer and as I jogged through for yet another single to third man, he stood right in front of me and gave me an icy glare as he pronounced, "I know where thee learnt thy cricket son, Edge-Baston!"

For the next few overs he gave me a verbal barrage like I had never had before. Liberally laced with expletives and libelous remarks, it seemed fairly serious until, in exasperation, he attempted a bouncer which seemed to stick in the slow, soft surface of the pitch before sitting up invitingly in front of my face.

Instinctively I hooked and finally, hit one in the middle. As the ball raced away to the square leg boundary, Fred snorted to no one in particular, "This is like bowlin' a bloody doughnut on a bloody muckheap."

As I came to a halt right in front of him, he stood feet astride with his hands on hips and looking me in the eye said, "Wait 'til I get thee at Scarborough lud. I'll knock thy bloody head off!"

With that, everyone within hearing distance burst out laughing at the ageing quick, past his best, still giving the young buck a temperament-testing tongue-lashing. Eventually even I saw the funny side of it.

Cricket at the top-level is a passionate game, thankfully so for, if it wasn't and the players not passionate about what they were doing, it wouldn't be worth watching.

Crowds appear to be down for Test matches in many parts of the world, but if you take into consideration the television audience for the game worldwide it has never been more keenly watched.

Television is a two-edged sword for, while it helps promote the game and the players, the umpires have never been under more scrutiny as to performance. The umpires have always made mistakes – and always will – and while television tends to highlight the mistakes, I believe it also underlines how many good decisions are made.

Equally, while television and the media generally, is quick to jump on the sensational incident, what it does show, but perhaps doesn't highlight enough, is how well the players conduct themselves in the main.

What Ken Piesse and Brian Hansen have set out to do in WILDMEN OF CRICKET is not to denigrate some of the great names of the game, but to show they are not one-dimensional, but are passionate, committed and proud human beings who, like all of us, have made the odd mistake – some bigger than others – in a highly-charged and emotion-packed arena.

Of the many champions included in either detailed or cameo fashion in this, Volume One of WILDMEN, I have played with or against the majority of them at some time or the other. The one I have known the longest is my elder brother Ian. Growing up in Adelaide we often played our make-believe test matches in the backyard. These tests were always between Australia and England and therein lay the rub for me as Ian, being the eldest, was always Australia and I had to be England!

Now I wasn't too keen on being beaten by my older brother but I can't say I had my heart set on winning for England either!

These tests were always hard-fought and as Dad insisted we use a hard ball, but only supplied us with a bat for protection, we had to learn to take a few blows and get on with the game. While we did our own umpiring, we were years ahead of our time in that we had own match referee in our mother Jeanne. If things got too noisy, Mum would come out and to see what it was about and generally found us arguing about whether I was out or not.

What I learnt early on was if I didn't think I was out, or didn't want to go out, I just made enough noise until Mum appeared, knowing she would always insist Ian give me another chance, me being younger and smaller!

This usually brought quick retribution as Ian would then let fly with a barrage of bouncers off the ridge, where the black soil was laid on the top of our back lawn, accompanied by a volley of abuse that singed the leaves on the lemon tree adjacant to the end of his follow-through.

All this was valuable experience for by the time I got to play real Test cricket there was nothing they could throw at me I hadn't already experienced, in spadefuls, in the backyard. When Ian moved onto higher levels of cricket, I became Australia and Trevor, England, and I was able to pass on much of what Ian had taught me.

The characters of the game are the ones who have left their indelible mark as players and catalysts for change and controversy. I have no doubt you will enjoy reading WILDMEN OF CRICKET and whether you're experiencing some of the more celebrated incidents for the first time or being reminded of them now, it goes to show that all the greatest cricketers had passion with a capital "P!"

Greg Chappell

GREG CHAPPELL
Canberra, September, 1997.

PREFACE

FIRST OF THE WILDMEN

A Time of Grace

T he giant nestled his thick, luxuriant beard into his chest, gave a hitch to the knotted school tie that served as a belt for his cricket creams. He settled at the crease, waggled his bat and fixed his eye on the man at the other end of the strip of turf.

At that end the self-styled King of Speed adjusted his monocle, flexed his right arm, fastened a seaming grip on the ball and began his charge to the wicket, rhythmic, menacing, building up steam and speed with every stride of his 25 yard run... the gentlest of breezes trailing at his back.

The batsman, Dr. W. G. Grace, *(pictured left)*, was well settled – the great man of cricket, seemingly invincible ... but not totally.

The bowler unleashed a thunderbolt, the perfect seamer. It struck the pitch just outside the line of off stump and cut back venomously inside the great man's downswinging drive of the bat. The off bail duly clipped, fell to earth beside the Doctor's wicket. No need to appeal – the great man was out! Or so they thought.

Totally unfazed, Grace bent down, picked up the errant bail and replaced it on the stumps before beaming down the wicket to the umpire who was only now contemplating the raising of his right forefinger...

"Windy isn't it?" boomed the Doctor, a master of gamesmanship.

"Yes," said the umpire, "But I'm not. You're OUT!"

Grace doffed his cap and departed.

When he was comprehensively bowled in another match, the doctor replaced the bails and declined to leave the wicket. He gestured to the crowd and the bowler, "They have come to see me bat, not you get wickets."

The umpire mumbled "No-ball" and Grace batted on!

He seldom gave his wicket away without a fight. The greatest pace bowler of his time Charles Jesse Kortwright of Essex believed he had the great man lbw several times before finally whipping a fast yorker under the Grace bat to cartwheel his middle and leg stumps out of the ground. The Doctor pondered the carnage but still waited for the decision that he was out. It could have been a no-ball.

The deadly finger pointed skywards and "W. G." moved towards the pavilion in resignation. Charlie called after him, "Hey... you're not really going Doctor? There's still one stump standing."

No doubt about it, Grace set the ethic for this game of games.

Dr. William Gilbert Grace (1848-1915) cricketer for England, Gloucestershire and London County. Undisputed Father of the game. Captain in almost every game he played. The Daddy of them all.

This large and bearded man towers above all, even Sir Donald Bradman, as the progenitor of the great game of cricket. His ethic was not of the proudest English traditions, more of the Bodyline strain. No doubt he would have warmly approved that philosophy had he lived to see it applied by his successors Douglas Jardine and Harold Larwood. Then again, perhaps not.

Beneath it all Grace was a humorist with a genuine love for the noble character of cricket, he couldn't help it if his sense of the outrageous outweighed his sense of proprietary.

Grace was the original wildman of cricket. The key Grace brothers, county coroner Dr. Edward Mills Grace (1841-1911) and W. G. were the two finest cricketers of their time. A third Grace brother (G. F.) also played Tests, with his brothers.

E. M. Grace confounded his contemporaries with unorthodox batting such as stepping across his wicket and pulling balls outside his off stump to the legside boundary – preceding Bradman's Bodyline batting technique by six decades. Not only did he wield an unorthodox willow but he was also prone to pursue unruly barrackers through the crowds and out into the suburbs.

Because of his vocation, he was known universally as "The Coroner." A right-hand batsman who bowled "floaters," he was the best allrounder in England and in 1862 made a first-class century for the Marylebone Cricket Club against The Gentleman, scoring 192 not out and taking 10 wickets. He was the outstanding fieldsmen of his time patrolling point when that was the elite fielding position.

Younger brother George Frederick Grace (1850-80) died in the midst of a promising career after catching a cold during a three day match.

Fred was tall, handsome and charming, a thrashing right hand batsman who W. G. believed would have been the greatest of the Graces. The three brothers played together in the first Test against Australia at The Oval. Fred made a pair but took a spectacular catch to end the innings of Australia's "Colonial Hercules," George Bonnor. .. a catch recorded as one of the legendary takes in first-class cricket. Bonnor hit the ball so hard and high that the batsmen were on their third run when Fred gathered in the catch after a long sprint around the boundary. Fourteen days later he was dead.

There were five Grace brothers; the other two did not make it into first-class records.

We can trace the eccentricities of the Grace Bros. back to their grandfather on the mother's side, George Pocock, organist at Portland Wesleyan church, Kingsdown via Bristol. He gave up playing for the church after a physical aside with fellow organists and deacons. Thereafter the Wesleyans prayed without the background comfort of the organ. Mr. Pocock owned the instrument and took it with him on departure, thus setting the precedent for getting the sulks, taking his ball and going home.

The Coroner, Edward Mills Grace had a long cricket career punctuated by explosive incidents. When given out lbw, unjustly, while batting as a schoolboy at Long Ashton he simply nodded to the umpire pulled up the stumps and walked from the oval with bat and stumps under his arm – upholding the family tradition set by Grandfather George. Even then he cut a commanding figure and none dared wrest the stumps away from him. We are given to understand the game continued by transporting the three remaining stumps from end to end as each over expired.

It is a brave man who would strike four successive sixes off such a man – bearing in mind he was also a qualified Coroner. F. L. Cole stole a single off the first ball of a Dr. E. M. Grace over. Mr. F. A. Leeston-Smith smote the next ball over the pickets for six; and the next; and the next; and the next! The umpire said, "That's over Doctor."

"Shut up," snapped E. M. "I'm going to have another ball."

He trundled down his delivery which the batsman swung at, missed and was stumped. Honor satisfied, Grace strode from the crease as the umpire's digit finger indicated Leeston-Smith should retire to the pavilion!

It was little wonder that his contemporaries elected not to argue or debate the issues with him. He was appointed secretary of his county club and the minutes of one meeting of Gloucestershire in 1873 was brief and to the point:

> *Committee meeting held at the White Lion Hotel, Bristol, on Thursday, November 25 at 3 o'clock. Present E. M. Grace – "And that's all."*

The two brothers presented a pre-possessing front with W. G. being much the bigger. Huge-framed and towering over all other cricketers of their time by many inches, they had thick waistlines, heavy shoulders and faces shrouded in thick, luxuriant black growths of facial fungus.

Cricket evolved over several centuries but most enthusiasts believed the modern game began with the accession of W. G. to the throne – a throne he refuses to vacate even in after-life. He will reign forever as the King of Cricket. Not necessarily a just and righteous monarch, but certainly regal and commanding.

W. G. began his senior cricketing career in his earliest youth. He struck his initial first-class century aged 16 when he scored 170 for South Wales against the Gentlemen of Sussex. He played his last Test aged 50. More than any man, he oversaw the transition of the game from roughshod uneven strips of village turf to the manicured first-class wickets that prevail today. It was Grace who popularised the game to the extent vast crowds began to surround the playing ovals. He was the first great cult figure and was feted throughout England and the colonies. W. G was the first entertainer.

How he played his audience. No thespian has ever done it better. He had the bearing and appearance of a Shakespearian actor – the eyebrow wickedly thick and angled could have been inherited from Old Nick himself. He had a devilish smile and a perpetual glint in the eye. The only blemish on this awesome figure was his voice. It was high and squeaky. Incongruous.

He was also something of an adventurer. Planes were yet to take to the air when Dr. Grace went ballooning over the Avon Gorge.

County cricket was the launching pad for England's expansion into international cricket. The county competition took shape from the 1860s as the teenage William Gilbert Grace set his own stage in the midst of this sporting revolution. English cricket and Dr. Grace grew up together.

Through these formation years, England's cricket evolved to the ultimate contest. The Gentlemen v. The Players – this was the blue riband event that captivated England. The war of the classes being fought on the village green.

W.G. Grace batting against Victoria, November, 1891. It cost the organisers 3000 pounds to bring him to Australia for only the second time in his illustrious career.

Dr. Grace was the only personality the public was interested in and he commanded their attention for 30 tempestuous years. He scored massively season after season and was an outstanding allrounder and fieldsman despite his great bulk. He matched his batting with his wicket taking and catches. For every 14.6 runs scored, he matched it with a wicket or a catch.

There was never any question of the quality of the man. His timing was incredible. Arch rival James Shaw commented on the Grace defence: "Oh yes, he blocks the shooters, but he blocks 'em to the boundary."

The 1873 season saw him record the first 2000 runs and 100 wickets in a season (2139 and 106). He repeated the allround double for six successive seasons. Dr. Grace was as prolific as he was consistent. He hit triple centuries including 344 for the MCC against Kent and 318 not out against Yorkshire in 1876. *Wisden* pointed out that his incredible batting feats were recorded on dangerous and unpredictable wickets countering any suggestion that he faced inferior bowlers to those faced by the latter day heroes.

All players have a stellar year – 1876 was Grace's. He scored 2622 runs and took 129 wickets.

On August 10, he was in a hurry after his MCC team had been forced to follow on against Kent. He belted 344 from 546. A couple of days later he made 177 of 262 against Nottinghamshire and with his brother took 17 of the 20 wickets to fall.

He left that team in tatters to travel to Yorkshire where the locals swore they would shoot him before allowing him to continue his rampage. They must have been crook shots because he stayed at the crease all day without being hit and slammed 318 not out. He had scored 839 runs in eight days for twice out!

His skirmishes with umpires are legend, but in truth it seems most of them were of a jocular nature as most umpires were former cricketers and firm friends. "I do not dispute with umpires," he liked to say. "I merely educate them."

He was a ruthless captain and never failed to work an edge. Before one Gloucestershire match, the young captain of the opposing side was so determined to have his team sharp for the encounter with the Graces he had them in the nets for an hour before the match. He gave them sharp fielding practice until a bell clanged the imminent start to the match. The skipper and his players hastened back to the pavilion to be greeted by Dr. Grace and The Coroner, padded up and striding to the wicket. Hastily the captain set his field and tossed the ball to his bowler. At lunch the brothers had reached 0-150, only then the young captain realised he hadn't tossed the coin and Dr. Grace had opened on a perfect strip!

In 1895, he became the first man to amass 100 centuries in first-class cricket. In the same year he became the first batsman to compile 1000 runs in May, the first month of the season. During his last serious season in 1898, he suddenly declared his team's innings closed for no apparent reason – he was 93 not out at the time. When asked for an explanation, he waved a dismissive hand, "Oh I suddenly remembered that throughout my career I had scored everything from 0 to 100 with the exception of a 93!"

He toured Australia twice, once as captain, but only after his terms of 3000 pounds plus expenses were met! Not bad money if you can make it; especially for a declared amateur!

All up it's estimated he grossed more than 120,000 pounds from cricket.

He delighted in strutting his stufff for the colonials – even to the extent of inviting the public to bowl to him in the nets. One afternoon in Melbourne he was crashing the public bowling all over the place when a young man took the ball, bowled a couple of looseners before bowling the Doctor neck and crop. "Who did that? Who did that?" squeaked W. G. as the young "Demon," Fred Spofforth disappeared into the crowd. Grace rubbed his hand through his beard and pondered that delivery – and well he should.

The Demon became a legend in Australian cricket and was the man who finally humbled Dr. Grace. In May 1878, he took 6-4 and 5-16 at Lord's to rout England. He's also the only man in history to take all 20 wickets in a match, all bowled! Admittedly it was a minor match, in 1881.

W. G. made 54,896 runs in senior cricket, 126 centuries, took 2876 wickets and 871 catches. The Doctor made another 95 centuries in minor cricket. His 152 at the Oval in 1880 was the first Test century recorded against Australia in England. He led England in 13 series. The great man died of a heart attack when he suffered a seizure during an air raid in 1915, aged 67.

The Graces were Grace by name alone. As a cricketing combination they were doubly formidable, prone never to waste an opportunity to unnerve a batsman or bowler. When Australia's big-hitting George Bonnor was peeved at being dismissed at Clifton, he declared the Grace Bros. had nagged him out with their incessant needling.

Bonnor was somewhat of a rebel himself. When playing for the Non-Smokers against The Smokers at Lord's in 1894 he strode to the wicket with a large cigar clamped between his teeth and batted with a cloud of smoke rings floating above his stumps! The Anti-Smoking campaign was set back 100 years as he puffed his way to 124 of the 156 runs scored by the Non-Smokers.

Bonnor was a massive striker of the ball who made five biennial tours of England for Australia. In 1880 he struck 26 sixers on tour. Most memorable amongst these were three sensational straight drives from the Australian legend, Spofforth, then playing in England.

Dr. Grace described the 198cm Bonnor as a "model of physical beauty." He was recorded as having thrown the cricket ball 119 yards without hardly a warm-up.

Bonnor's greatest moment in Test cricket came at the Sydney Cricket Ground in the fourth Test of the 1884-85 series when he scored 113 in a session before reaching 128 in 115 minutes to set up an Australian win. Yet who remembers the Colonial Hercules?

Dr. Grace was wickedly unconventional. He once stormed the hallowed Lord's pavilion to hijack Australian tourist William Midwinter and took him to the Oval for an important match. Although born in England, Midwinter had been taken to Australia when nine years old. He learned his cricket on the Bendigo goldfields and furnished into a superb spin bowler and free-scoring batsman. He made the Victorian XXII and played the English tourists in 1873-74 taking the wickets of both the Grace brothers.

Midwinter won selection in Australia's first Test team and took 5-78 in the first

W. G's allround feats over five decades on uncovered wickets were extraordinary.

innings. At 26, he returned to England and played for his native Gloucestershire. Australia selected him in its 1878 touring team, saving the boat fare to England. Midwinter was padded up at Lord's ready to bat when W. G. burst into the Australian rooms and thundered loyalty at the cowering Midwinter. Within minutes Australia had an empty set of pads on their hands as W. G. trundled their star off to play and win with Gloucestershire. Thereafter W. G. toasted the victory by sinking a magnum of champagne in a single swallow and balancing the bottle on his head!

Australia finished their tour with only 11 players. Three years later Midwinter toured Australia with the English team and played four Tests against Australia. A year later he declared he was Australian "through and through" and played the last Test against Ivo Bligh's English team. Thus from 1876-82, he represented Australia-England-Australia.

Billy Midwinter was to die tragically, aged only 39. His wife and two children died in quick succession and left the unfortunate man paralysed mentally and physically from the trauma. He had lost the will to live and soon died.

Wildmen come in all hues, shapes and sizes. The one thing they have in common is a volatile trigger point. When ignited, hell hath no fire like it...

Legend is built around Yorkshire's Fred Trueman, a great bowler who loved a riotous, beer-swilling living. There was a Yorkshire precedent for Fred. Bobby Peel was a Yorkshire lad who loved his drink before, after or during a match. This was prone to make him a little erratic and unreliable. One day he took up the new ball and made a long fierce run before delivering the ball at the pavilion. He had forgotten to turn around after measuring his run. Lord Hawke led him to the gate pointed out to the distant hills and told him to keep going.

Who would have imagined that Dennis Lillee could kick a Pakistani or that Javed Miandad would contemplate removing the Lillee cranium with his bat? ... That John Snow would fell Terry Jenner with a bouncer and then invite an irate Sydney lynch mob to do their worst? An incredible scene developed in the first Test in Sydney on the 1970-71 tour when Snow was warned by umpire Lou Rowan to desist from intimidating bowling. Ray Illingworth, England's captain, made matters worse as he argued. This led to the crowd erupting. They hurled missiles onto the ground. Illingworth inflamed the situation by sending Snow to field on the boundary at fine-leg – at the very hot spot of crowd anger. A spectator reached over the fence and dragged Snow by the arm. Illingworth led his team from the field where he was cautioned by the umpires England would forfeit the Test if he did not return to play. Illingworth realised the severity of his decision and the likely implications for his career and the Poms returned to the field.

Illingworth was by no means the most inflammatory skipper to captain England in Australia. The hated Douglas Jardine created the worst scene in all cricket history when he was so rash as to call for a legside Bodyline attack from Harold Larwood. This immediately after all but killing Australian skipper Bill Woodfull with a blow to the heart from a Larwood delivery to an orthodox field.

Little Indian amasser of runs Sunny Gavaskar set a high price on his wicket. When given out lbw in Melbourne on the Indian 1980-81 tour he claimed a nick on to his pads and ordered his batting partner Chetan Chauhan to walk off the MCG in protest. The pair were approaching the point of no return – the players gate – when team manager Wing Commander Durani ordered Chauhan back to the centre. Rather than risk being beheaded as a mutineer Chauhan returned to the crease.

Australia's Rodney Hogg, equally bad tempered after bowling seven no-balls in five overs in the previous series against India at Bangalore, kicked down the stumps. Skipper Kim Hughes was forced to rebuke him and apologise to the umpire. Almost at the same time West Indies pace man Michael Holding kicked down the batsman's stumps after having an lbw appeal rejected in Dunedin.

Which wasn't nearly as nasty as West Indies pace bowler Sylvester Clarke who got sick of being pelted with missiles during a clash with Pakistan at Multan in the 1980-81 series. Fielding on the fine leg boundary, he hurled a brick back into the crowd badly injuring an innocent student. The West Indies captain Alvin Kallicharran averted a mob lynching by going down to the fence, dropping to his knee and beseeching forgiveness from the angry crowd. Clarke was suspended for three matches.

Passion ran hot during the West Indies tour of New Zealand in 1979-80 when Colin Croft was repeatedly no-balled during a tense stage of a Test. Croft was furious as he went back to his marker. This time he took a running line directly through the umpire to the batsman. The batsman could not see Croft on the run-up as he maintained his line and crashed into the umpire Fred Goodall. Croft was later suspended but not before the West Indies went on strike. They refused to return to the field after tea and the bewildered crowd waited almost quarter of an hour before the West Indies re-emerged.

There seems little doubt the wildest Australian team to tour was the mob of 1893 under the captaincy of wicketkeeper-batsman Jack Blackham – a trip fouled by allegations of drunkenness, brawling and financial disputes.

Blackham kept in gloves that offered no more protection than light gardening gloves and suffered many painful blows to hands, face and body in the line of duty. Being nervous, agitated and prone to anxiety attacks, he wasn't the ideal leader for a group of wild Colonial boys. This highly-strung and unpredictable skipper was inclined to abuse his players publicly for their failures. If the team suffered a bad day his players were likely to find him hiding in a corner with his head hidden under a blanket or stalking back and forth wringing his hands and predicting disaster. It is little wonder his team turned to the demon drink to cope with the stress!

There were other problems, too. The players hated the tour manager Victor Cohen who they accused of being little more than a spy for the Australian Cricket Council. The players also resented that the world's No. 1 allrounder George Giffen had been able to force a tour passage for his inept brother Walter Giffen. Walter had played two Tests against Lord Sheffield's team in 1891-92, scoring only 1, 3, 3 and 2. Although Australia won that series 2-1, Giffen's performances were hardly the form to suggest he would be able to score runs in England. And he didn't, with just 170 runs in 14 completed innings. Enough to drive a team to drink, which it did.

But the wildman of this tour was a man who didn't drink. One player who didn't succumb to the demon grog was Victorian allrounder Arthur Coningham. Arthur could do a few more things than left-arm pace bowling and rapid fire batting. He was a marksman, athlete, rugby star and elite billiards player. He didn't mind a practical joke. He had a most unusual farewell as he set sail for England with the team. That morning the striking athlete dressed up, went to church and married his glamorous girlfriend before sailing off without her. He was a superbly proportioned and handsome athlete of the Keith Miller mould and had his dalliances, sometimes taking leave without notice from the cricket field to attend to his affairs.

Never was he far from the centre of attraction. He just happened to be sightseeing when he dived into the Thames and saved a drowning boy. England was too cold for Arthur and he created considerable aggro when he gathered up some grass and twigs and lit a fire when freezing in the outfield during one game at Blackpool. After cricket he became a bookmaker and caused a stir when he defended a court action with a revolver strapped to his waist.

Coningham featured prominently in Cyril Pearl's famous book *Wildmen of Sydney* and the Protestant Coningham made raging national headlines when he sued a Catholic priest Father O'Haran. Arthur accused the priest of having an affair with his wife. The case stirred up a remarkable religious controversy. Coningham conducted his own case with remarkable polish after his solicitor quit in the midst of the emotional upheaval – he lost.

Australia gave back the Ashes on the 1893 tour, lost 10 matches and didn't win a Test. The ACC spy Victor Cohen reported back to the Council that he had to physically defend himself against assaults by his players. After one train trip the Australians closed ranks and nobody would explain why one of their carriages was saturated in blood.

They did draw the Lord's Test. Lost the second and drew the third. Manager Cohen said the Australians had been a total embarrassment at Lord's. The players were unmanageable, swore at him publicly and were drunk all the time. Which isn't the way you are expected to behave at Lord's even though the ground may not be quite as regal as many enthusiasts believe. Lord's is the world's most famous ground yet many people believe its name comes from its blueblood connections. Not so, it is Lord's not Lords.

The ground is named after Thomas Lord and has been situated on its site in St. John's Wood since 1814. It is the third of the Lord's grounds – the first (1787-1810) was where Dorset Square now stands. The second (1809-13) at North Bank made way for Regent's Canal. Third time lucky, Lord's hosted its first Test match in 1884.

The unhappy tourists were angry at the miserly payments they received on tour and on the way home raided Cohen's cabin and sized his account books. They were able to use the information gleaned from these books to force an increase in payments from 50 pounds a player to 190 pounds. The players alleged Cohen was lining his own pockets at the expense of themselves and the impoverished ACC.

The greatest blot on that trip apart from the inept leadership of Cohen and Blackham was Australia's loss to Philadelphia on a short tour of the United States. The inexperienced Americans beat them by an innings and 77 runs.

Cohen responded to accusations levelled against him by declaring he had been assaulted by players who were continually drunk. Victorian batsman Bill Bruce was one who broke the code of silence to admit he threatened to pull Blackham's nose. Blackham said he was more than willing to reciprocate. Coningham, the non-drinker said, "When a man is full of champagne overnight, he is not fit for much the next day. One morning coming down the stairs we found one of them asleep with his clothes on, his head on the stair mat."

The summary of the tour was that of a team in total disarray, devoid of loyalty, friendship and discipline. An unpleasant group of sulking individuals who on return to Australia were greeted by an empty wharf and the contempt of a nation. That was not Australian cricket's greatest hour.

The 1893 Australians..."a team in total disarray, devoid of loyalty, friendship and discipline. An unpleasant group of sulking individuals..." At least they posed for the team photo! Manager Cohen is second from the left sporting the top hat, while captain Jack Blackham is easily distinguished by his beard. The wild one Arthur Coningham is seated at Jack's feet.

THE WILD TIMES

TIMELINE OF TROUBLE

1879: England X1 captain Lord Harris is attacked by a larrikin with a stick during a wild melee when spectators invade the field in Sydney after NSW X1 opener Billy Murdoch is given run-out by a Victorian, George Coulthard. Teammate A. N. "Monkey" Hornby is punched in the face and has his shirt torn while trying to protect Harris. Play is abandoned for the day, big betting punters unhappy at the local team's position.

1893: Arthur Coningham, an Australian allrounder with a firebrand personality, lights a fire with twigs and fallen branches at Blackpool to keep himself warm while fielding in a corner of the outfield during Australia's tour. He later headlines in an adultery case against his wife, conducting his own defence complete with a loaded revolver in his pocket.

1897: The great Bobby Peel, in his final county year, is sent from the field by his Yorkshire captain Lord Hawke at Bramall Lane for reporting for play drunk. He expressed his readiness to bowl but proposed to do so facing the pavilion rather than the stumps.

1906-07: Eleven New South Wales cricketers, including Victor Trumper, are placed under temporary suspension for being party to the Melbourne Cricket Club's plans to host an English tour.

1908: The Melbourne Cricket Club sponsors a visit to Australia by a Fijian side. The Australian Cricket Board of Control had refused the Fijian's initial request, saying it was against The White Australia Policy. The games are excluded from first-class status.

1912: Australian captain Clem Hill is involved in an extraordinary fist fight with selector and longtime adversary Peter McAlister in the Sydney offices of the New South Wales Cricket Association. A table is upturned during the 20 minute brawl, McAlister claiming that Hill, after a disagreement over the composition of Australia's third Test team, had thrown the first punch before wrestling him to the ground. Hill said he had acted under high provocation, after McAlister referred to him as the "worst captain" in Australian cricket history. Industrial action is threatened by Australian trade unions against the staging of the fourth Test in Melbourne if Australia names Queensland fast bowler John McLaren who'd acted as a special constable in a strike earlier that year. He's omitted from the X1 for Melbourne and plays his one and only Test a fortnight later in Sydney.

1921: With the Ashes retained, Australian captain Warwick Armstrong ambles off to the boundary and defiantly reads a newspaper which had blown in his direction in the closing stages of the final Test at The Oval. "I wanted to know who we were playing," he says. In the previous Test, following a break in play at rainy Manchester, he'd become the first man to bowl two overs in a row at Test level.

1922: Hampshire stalwart John Newman is ordered from the field at Trent Bridge by his captain Lionel Tennyson for refusing to bowl while the crowd was barracking. He kicks down the stumps in his anger on his way to the pavilion.

1923: Victoria's Arthur Liddicutt sends down an underam in exasperation in Melbourne after English pair Geoffrey Wilson and Wilfred Hill-Wood bat through the entire third and final day's play.

1932-33: England captain Douglas Jardine orders his battery of pacemen to bowl deliberate leg theory at the Australians. G. O. "Gubby" Allen, an amateur, refuses and dares Jardine to send him home. The Bodyline controversy comes to a head in Adelaide when Australian captain Bill Woodfull, struck earlier in the game by Harold Larwood, tells the MCC management, that "only one team out there is playing cricket. " For a time Anglo-Australian relations are strained after Australian Board of Control issue a telegram saying that Bodyline bowling contradicts the spirit of cricket.

1945: Umpire Jack Scott asks for an apology from colorful Australian Services allrounder Cec Pepper who remonstrates with him after an lbw appeal against Don Bradman in his home town Adelaide is rejected. Cricket writer Dick Whitington helps Pepper compose the apology, but the Australian Cricket Board of Control say the letter is never received and Pepper, a Test prospect, refuses to send another, instead severing all ties with Australian cricket.

1946: In a controversial resumption to Test cricket after the war, Don Bradman refuses to walk in Brisbane after Englishmen Jack Ikin at second slip claims a catch. "We were stunned and felt a great injustice had been done," says Englishman Denis Compton. Touring captain Walter Hammond walks past Bradman at the change of ends and says, "A fine. . . . . way to start a series. "

1947: Australian X1 opener Bill Brown is run out in Melbourne while backing up too far at the bowler's end by Indian spin bowler Vinoo Mankad. A month later, Brown again wanders out of his crease and Mankad runs him out, this time without offering a warning.

1948: Don Bradman is accused of upsetting Royalty by walking with his hands in his pockets with King George V at Balmoral at the conclusion of the all-conquering '48 tour. Sid Barnes upsets Australian officials by filming matches during the tour.

1951-52: Prompted by some fiery spells from New South Wales paceman Alan Walker, Australian authorities move to outlaw intimidatory bowling at Sheffield Shield level by recommending a change of laws empowering umpires to intervene in the case of "unfair bowling" pitching in line with a batsman in his normal stance. Walker had struck South Australia's Bruce Bowley on the head and also upset Victorians with short-pitched bowling in an earlier game.

Sid Barnes sues the Australian Cricket Board of Control after it vetoes his selection in the third Test against the touring West Indians for reasons "other than cricket. "

1954: Frank Tyson is sconed by a Ray Lindwall bouncer in Sydney; having bounced his fellow fast bowler previously in the opening Test in Brisbane. A shower of bottles, boxes and other debris thrown onto the ground halts play during the West Indies-England Test at Georgetown. England captain Len Hutton refuses to take his team from the ground, saying, "We want another wicket or two this evening. "

1960: Trinidadians riot mid-way through the Test against England, disappointed by their own team's performance at Port-of-Spain. Peter May and his English players remain on the field, huddled around the pitch. Seeing all the bottles and debris on the field, next man in Wes Hall turns back to the pavilion, saying, "I'm not going out there for anybody's money, man!"

1963: Ian Meckiff is no-balled out of cricket in the summer's opening Springbok Test in Brisbane, the central victim in a clean-up campaign against thowing. Years later he concedes, "The more I hear, the more I believe it was got up to put me out of business." Popular England batsman Ken Barrington accuses West Indian express Charlie Griffith of throwing.

1967: Spectators riot at Calcutta, several trying to damage the pitch during the India-West Indies Test and others hurtling chairs and benches onto a midfield blaze.

1969: Australian captain Bill Lawry is accused of striking an Indian photographer in mid-pitch during a break in play at Eden Gardens with Australia tantalisingly close to victory. Hundreds of fans had spilled onto Eden Gardens having been pelted by oranges and fruit from upstairs stands.

1970: Apartheid demonstrations stop the 1970 South African tour of England. Twelve months later widespread demonstrations force the Australian Board of Control to also bow to political pressure and call off the scheduled South African tour of Australia.

1971: Bill Lawry is sacked as Australia's captain with one Ashes Test to play, the climax of his controversial leadership period, after which several of his teammates to India and South Africa expressed misgivings about his leadership.

Ray Illingworth leads England from the Sydney Cricket Ground following a wild demonstration during which beer cans are thrown onto the field and fast bowler John Snow manhandled by a spectator after earlier being warned for intimidatory bowling.

Snow is suspended for a Test after shouldering India's Sunil Gavaskar at Lord's. He relays a message to the English selection hierachy: "Tell them they can stuff themselves. "

1973: Having conceded 19 runs from one of his wayward overs, Derbyshire's Alan Ward is sent off the field by his county captain Brian Bolus at Chesterfield after refusing to bowl again on the final day of the county game against Yorkshire.

1975: Ewan Chatfield's heart stops beating after he deflects a bouncer from England's Peter Lever onto his temple in Auckland. His life is saved by England's physiotherapist Bernard Thomas who runs onto Eden Park and helps revives the stricken New Zealander, who suffers a hairline fracture of the skull. As Chatfield lies motionless, Lever slumps to his knees in disbelief and starts crying. "I thought I'd killed him," he says.

1976: Indian captain Bishen Bedi accuses England new ball pair Bob Willis and John Lever of using vaseline to help shine the ball during England's winning tour, their first to India in more than 30 years. Within 48 hours, the International Cricket Conference replies to Bedi's official complaint, clearing the two Englishmen of any "sharp practice" and saying the vaseline-fastened gauze strips used by Lever and Willis to keep the sweat from their eyes were totally appropriate to the sweltering conditions.

1978: Umpire Ralph Gosein and stand-by umpire John Gayle refuse to stand on an unscheduled sixth day to allow a finish to the fifth Test between the West Indies and Australia at Kingston. Play had been abandoned the night before after a crowd disturbance with the West Indies facing likely defeat, at nine wickets down, with 6.2 overs still to be bowled.

At the height of the World Series conflict, many nations refuse to follow the lead of England and Australia and continued to allow their Packer-contract players to figure in traditional cricket. Among Pakistan's WSC Testmen for the first series against India in 17 years are captain Mushtaq Mohammad and champion fast bowler Imran Khan.

1979: Rick Darling is carried unconscious from the Adelaide Oval after blacking out having been hit under the heart by Bob Willis' fifth delivery of the Australian first innings. In the same game, a furious Australian captain Graham Yallop confronts Rodney Hogg as the fast bowler heads for the dressing rooms having bowled just four overs on the third morning. "At one stage Hogg suggested we survey the back of the Adelaide Oval – and I don't think he had a tennis match on his mind," says Yallop.

In the two-Test series against Pakistan which follows, Hogg bashes down his stumps in anger in Melbourne after Javed Miandad runs him out with an unaware Hogg shuffling up the wicket in-between balls to complete a spot of gardening. In the following Test in Perth, relations between the two sides deteriorate further when Alan Hurst "mankads" Sikander Bakht and Sarfraz Nawaz successfully appeals against Andrew Hilditch after the Australian retrieves a wayward return and hands the ball to Sarfraz.

Ian Chappell, in his farewell first-class season, is suspended for 21 days for abusive language against umpires in a Sheffield Shield game in Devonport. Later in the summer, in South Australia's international against England, he again runs foul of the umpires and receives a suspended sentence.

1981: Australian captain Greg Chappell instructs his brother Trevor to bowl an underarm to New Zealand No. 11 Brian McKechnie to finish a one-day international in Melbourne. Chappell admits later he was

mentally exhausted and not fit to captain Australia that day.

Indian captain Sunil Gavaskar motions his batting partner Chetan Chauhan to also walk off with him in protest against an lbw decision against him in Melbourne. Chauhan is stopped at the gate by Indian manager Wing Commander S. K. Durrani who tells him to resume his place at the wicket for fear of the Indians forfeiting the game.

West Indian paceman Michael Holding kicks down the stumps in anger after having a caught behind appeal against New Zealand's John Parker disallowed at Dunedin. In the next Test at Christchurch, Colin Croft, having become frustrated after no-ball calls, deliberately runs into umpire Fred Goodall and flattens him.

Dennis Lillee kicks Pakistani Javed Miandad after a mid-pitch collision in Perth. Lillee claims he was only retaliating after Javed jabbed him with his bat. He is later suspended from two one-day internationals.

Imran Khan uses a bottle top to scuff the ball in a game between Sussex and Hampshire.

Dennis Lillee and Rod Marsh bet against Australia winning the Leeds Test – and win $A15,000 after an astonishing second innings collapse. Future contracts are to forbid any Australian player or associate gambling on games.

1984: Rodney Hogg defuses speculation of a rift between him and captain Kim Hughes despite almost punching Hughes after he'd taken Gordon Greenidge's wicket at Port-of-Spain. "I was off the planet, my eyes were spinning. I was that glad to take the wicket," says Hogg. "I didn't know who was next to me even though I almost knocked his head off."

Kim Hughes, in tears, resigns the Australian captaincy in Brisbane, saying, "the constant criticism, speculation and innuendo by former players and a section of the media over the last four or five years have finally taken their toll."

Australia's Geoff Lawson is fined $500 and bonded $1500 for his on-field behaviour after an incident with West Indian Gordon Greenidge serious enough to warrant an official protest from the tourists during the Christmas Test in Melbourne.

1985: Viv Richards threatens to fight Allan Border behind the back of the Sydney member's stand after Border joins in a verbal row between King Viv and Steve Rixon in Sydney.

1987: Ian Botham has to be separated from Pakistani wicketkeeper Salim Yousuf by umpire Ken Palmer after Yousuf had picked up a juggled ball from the ground and claimed a catch during the third Test at Leeds.

1990: Wasim Akram cannons into Merv Hughes in mid-pitch in Adelaide, prompting a furious war of words and intervention from umpire Tony Crafter. "It was a clash of the heavyweights," said Crafter. "I was stuck in the middle of them."

1992: Former Pakistan fast bowler Sarfraz Nawaz sues Allan Lamb for libel following the English Testman's accusations that Pakistani pacemen were known "ball tamperers. " Lamb's explosive revelations follow the acrimonious Lord's Test when umpires are forced to change the ball during the English innings. Denying that he is going public for his own monetary gain, Lamb donates his 5000 pound fee received from a London newspaper to charity.

1993: Merv Hughes triggers fury in the New Zealand camp after spitting at opening batsman Mark Greatbatch at Eden Park. "If it was within the rules to get physical, Merv would have done it," says Greatbatch.

1994: Champion leg-spinner Shane Warne repeatedly tells South Africa's Andrew Hudson to "F. . . off" after bowling him behind his legs during the third Test at Johannesburg. He admits to having become a victim of pressure, his mood not being improved after a shocked ACB fined him his entire match fee of $4400. Merv Hughes is fined a similar amount after separate misdemeanours.

Pakistan captain Salim Malik is central in bribery accusations brought against him by Australian trio Shane Warne, Tim May and Mark Waugh. Australian Cricket Board executive director Graham Halbish dubs it "cricket's greatest crisis in 20 years."

England captain Mike Atherton admits to storing dirt in his pocket and rubbing it across the ball to help dry it during the first Test against South Africa at Lord's. He's fined 2000 pounds but maintains that he was ignorant of the law and had never knowingly cheated at cricket.

New Zealanders Matthew Hart, Dion Nash and Stephen Fleming are suspended by the NZ Board for smoking cannabis during the tour of South Africa. A fourth player, Chris Pringle, is also disciplined for "unspecified behaviour."

1995: Viv Richards accuses Steve Waugh of cheating in that he claimed a juggling catch at Bridgetown to dismiss Brian Lara which he knew had hit the ground. "If I had doubts," says Waugh, "I would have called him back."

Brian Lara walks out, briefly, on the West Indian tour of England saying cricket has ruined his life.

1997: Shane Warne is given police protection after a county game in which Australia's acting captain Steve Waugh halts play and asks security men to stop a torrent of abusive barracking. In the Trent Bridge Test which follows, a rowdy element continue their Warne baiting asking, "Everyone who hates Shane Warne, stand up."

Warne celebrates Australia's Ashes win with an impromptu jig of delight and a one-finger gesture which draws a "please explain" from the Australian Cricket Board.

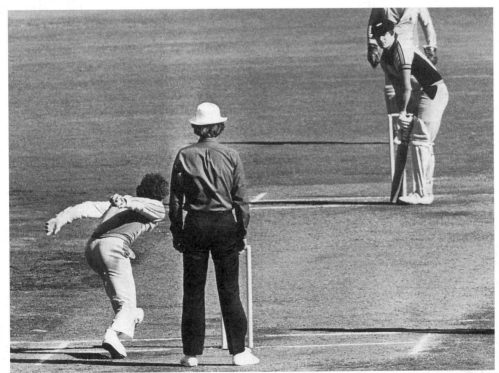

The Trevor Chappell underarm to Brian McKechnie which caused trans-Tasman ripples.

Peter Bull

1
THE
FLIPPERMAN

"I hope I don't get hung for it for the rest of my life because I stuffed up once." – SHANE WARNE

The fast-tracking into Test cricket of Shane Warne, the chubby leg spinner with the larrikin streak, was a stroke of genius, as important a selection as Don Bradman in 1928-29 and Dennis Lillee in 1970-71. Within 12 months, the bottle-blond from seaside Black Rock was the toast of Australian cricket. . .

EVERYONE HAS A darkest moment they regret, even spin bowlers noted for their affability. For all of Shane Warne's catapulting fame and fortune, the nightmare of Johannesburg '94 still scalds like a branding iron.

For a second or two on Black Sunday, Warne snapped. By losing control and telling South African opening batsman Andrew Hudson to "F... off," having taken his wicket during the opening Test, a vehement Warne committed cricketing treason.

Not only did he bring the game into disrepute with his vitriol, he alienated many of his fans worldwide and tarnished a fairytale story which, except for a bust-up at the Cricket Academy, had been straight from Boys' Own.

Despite his resultant years of good behaviour, bar the cackling sendoff of Paul Adams during the '97 tour of South Africa, many cricketing purists still haven't forgiven him. They regard Warne as too immature for higher office, especially the captaincy of the Australian cricket team.

Others recognise that snowballing travel and playing schedules, combined with exhausting off-field responsibilities, can create a mental and physical fatigue which triggers occasional out-of-character behaviour. With television cameras following a player's every move around the world, sometimes there seems no escape, especially for players who are so openly combative.

Warne admits to being haunted by the Hudson incident. It's the only time over his

David Munden/Sportsline

whole career he'd like to have over again. "I'll stand by everything else," he says.

Sometimes it's difficult not to overstep the fine line between being a natural showman and over exuberance. Soon after being hit in the centre of his back by a large orange at Johannesburg, Warne blew a fuse big-time

For weeks, ever since Australia's arrival for its first official tour of the Republic in 23 years, Warne had been beseiged everywhere he turned. Not only was he the man who could spin the ball on ice – to borrow one of Richie Benaud's famous lines – he had the spiked blond hair, ear-ring and flamboyant, new-age personality to match.

Australian vice-captain Ian Healy likened the incredible attention reserved for the charismatic Victorian to Elvis rising from the dead. Girls staked out the Australian team motel hoping to catch a closer look. Revellers knocked on his door well after midnight to ask for autographs.

Sections of the partisan matchday crowds took delight in baiting him. Often the abuse crossed the line between fun and something more serious. The barracking of the Africaaners was particularly unsettling. At Wanderers where the players must make an extraordinarily-long walk from the playing arena into the dressing rooms, many were treated like clay pigeons, being pelted with missiles, from oranges and drink cans to large stones. The Australians called it the Bull Ring.

On the few occasions when an autograph request was refused, even when players were in the middle of a restaurant meal or at practice, some South African fans turned feral.

The Australians and particularly Warne, found the exposure overwhelming. Some of the abuse was out of left field.

Warne had nursed a sore shoulder, the result of over bowling, into the tour and was still to satisfy his own high standards in either the Test preliminaries or in the nets. Hansie Cronje, the leading South African batsman, had punished him unmercifully in several of the one-day internationals. On the eve of the first Test, he made 44 and 251 for Orange Free State against the Australians at Bloemfontein. Crowd cries of "Warne's a wanker," first heard during the opening one-day international in Johannesburg continued. When Cronje came in at the fall of the first wicket, several in the crowd asked for Warne to be brought on so Cronje could continue his mastery.

Since his heady days in England in 1993, Warne was used to being the lynchpin in the Australian attack. He expected to take three and four wickets an innings and when he didn't, became frustrated. Normally happy-go-lucky, he was tense and uptight as the players warmed up on the morning of the first Test. He even snapped at 12th man Paul Reiffel, a fellow Victorian and one of his good mates.

Teammate David Boon says he missed the warning signs pre-match. Had he been more inquisitive, he believes the explosion early on the fourth afternoon could have been averted. "There had been so much pressure on Warnie to take wickets and dominate the Test, that it had built up within him," he said.

"We failed to pick up how quiet he was during the morning practice, which is unlike him. Fielding at fine-leg when the Test began, he was again quiet, not calling out to encourage his teammates – which is a feature of his game."

Held back until the 44th over of the South African second innings, when his spinning partner Tim May had already bowled 15 overs, Warne sensed the match fortunes could well depend on his opening overs. "We need you Warnie," captain Allan Border told him. "Come on, get us a wicket."

Hudson and Cronje were well set and South Africa was eyeing a matchwinning lead.

Breathing deeply, part of his now-familiar ritual in helping compose himself before

Trouble in the Bull Ring as Andrew Hudson is bowled. "The guy in the footage is not the real me," says Shane Warne.

a new spell, he had immediate success, bowling Hudson around his legs with his third delivery of the day.

As the South African lingered momentarily, assessing his mistake, Warne ran down the pitch abusing him.

"Hudson was just in the wrong place at the wrong time," said Boon. "Shane exploded immediately after that dismissal, hurling a torrent of abuse at the outgoing batsman, and although no-one can ever sanction or excuse what he did or said, I have always felt that I should have apologised to Shane. As a team man and senior player, I shouldn't have missed the signs that something was wrong and should have been able to prevent what happened."

Warne says it was a totally out-of-character action. "I was pumped up to do well. We needed a wicket and it just happened with the third ball. When things aren't going your way, you tend to let it get to you."

As the bails flew, Warne ran down the wicket and abused Hudson, before being re-strained by wicketkeeper Ian Healy. "F... off. Go on Hudson, f... off out of here!" he said.

Umpire David Shepherd immediately conferred with counterpart Barry Lambsen and called Border to mid-pitch. At the end of the over Border appeared to lecture Warne and at the next break in play, Warne apologised to Border, the umpires and later to Hudson.

"By my own actions I let a lot of people down – my teammates, all those who have helped me over the years and in particular those who follow and support Australian cricket," Warne said.

"For a moment I let everything get to me. The film of that incident is pretty awful and the guy in the footage is not the real me.

"It was a mistake I deeply regret and one that I will never repeat. It was a mistake I hope won't be taken too far from the context of the game. In order to perform at my best, I need to be aggressive. It's the same for all players. It's just as important for a spin bowler to be aggressive, as it is for a fast bowler. We play at a very high level of arousal, on the edge of fury if you like. I hope those sitting calmly at home in their armchairs will try to understand this. I hope I don't get hung for it for the rest of my life because I stuffed up once. I want to win people over again if I've lost them and I'd like to be given that chance."

The International Cricket Council's match referee Donald Carr issued $440 fines for Warne and his room-mate for much of the tour, fast bowler Merv Hughes, who had also been found guilty for verbal abuse in mid-match.

Carr had the power to fine each player $3000, or 75 per cent of their match fees.

Instead, he opted to penalise them just 10 per cent. The fines was widely regarded with contempt, everywhere but in the Australian dressing room. Warne, being a first offender, could have hoped for a more lenient penalty than Hughes, who had been cited twice previously. The world press believed the two in-trouble Australians had been whipped with the force of a feather. Others dismissed it as yet another ICC failure to take responsible control of player behaviour at the highest level.

The Australian Cricket Board was clearly unhappy at the level of the fines and imposed additional $4000 penalties.

Just weeks earlier, during the second Test in Sydney, Warne had given Daryll Cullinan a colorful send-off and when Hughes was found guilty of swearing at Gary Kirsten, ACB chairman Alan Crompton issued a warning that such behaviour was "totally unacceptable and detrimental to the interests of Australian cricket."

A PATHETIC SIGHT

In a scathing editorial, "The Age," Warne's hometown newspaper in Melbourne commented: "There are few more pathetic sights in sport than grown men throwing temper tantrums on the cricket field.

"The Australian cricketers seem to be making a habit of this sort of boorish behaviour and it is no coincidence that it reached a crescendo whenever Australia is being beaten. . .

"The sight of the young and gifted Warne snarling, swearing and virtually frothing at the mouth after dismissing a batsmen who scored freely from his bowling, was ugly and offensive."

Furthermore, send-offs were "cowardly and unAustralian" and the example of Warne and Hughes "totally inappropriate for young Australians to follow."

In the original incident with Cullinan, Warne said he had become incensed after Cullinan grinned at him. The South African had hit two 4s earlier in the cover before being deceived by a flipper. No action was taken by the umpires.

Australian team coach Bob Simpson said Warne would again be cautioned to temper his aggression. As a second-time offender, he was on notice to immediately improve his behaviour, or face the consequences. "There is very little to be gained by telling the batsman what you think of him after you've dismissed him," Simpson said. "You have already won the battle by getting him out. Players must be aware of their actions. They come under close scrutiny and are seen by a wider audience off the field."

One commentator, Peter Roebuck, believed Warne should be sent home should he transgress again. "If he arrived here as a saint, he is rapidly losing his halo," he said.

At the end of the Test as Australia was sliding to a comprehensive defeat, Warne was booed from the field, having fallen lbw to Brian McMillan. It was a rude awakening for Australian cricket's starlet, who said later he had been heckled and from the opening day of the game had had oranges and rocks thrown at him while fielding at fine-leg.

Condemnation of his actions raged back in Australia and around the cricketing world, many asking if his heady highpoints of previous campaigns had affected his judgement.

In-between Tests, at Stellenbosch, Warne had a heart-to-heart on the team bus with vice-captain Mark Taylor and admitted the pressure had got to him and he'd developed "a short fuse."

"I'm letting everything get to me when I shouldn't. I feel myself snapping," he said. "Maybe my expectations are too high after everything that has happened in the last year. The continual ride over the last 18 months has got to me and I'm just burning up. I feel angry all the time, but I haven't been reported before and don't want to carry a 'bad boy' reputation for doing one stupid thing. I know I did the wrong thing, but the people who know me know that it's not me. I don't intend to ever again do on the cricket field what I did in the first Test."

A WARNING FOR WARNE

During South Africa's 1993-94 tour of Australia, the Australians dubbed competitive allrounder Brian McMillan "Inspector Depardeau" believing him to be a dead-ringer for the French actor.

In Adelaide, Warne kept referring to McMillan as "Inspector." After the game, just as the Australians were about to fly out to South Africa, McMillan sent a note into the Australian rooms: "Hey Warne, hundreds of people go missing every day in South Africa. One more won't make any difference."

Warne conceded he had allowed his frustrations to bubble over and had not considered his actions, or the goodwill built by the Australians since their arrival in South Africa. As a key member of the side, he had to be prepared to be in the public eye. Every action was important. He was sorry, but he had been unable to relax away from the game.

Taylor told Warne he was not acting like the Shane Warne the players liked and respected. Every player of international quality went through a rough patch. Knowing how to handle it was crucial in returning to top form. He had to consider all his responsibilities as an ambassador, as well as a player.

Warne admitted he'd become carried away with all his publicity. He'd become cocky and big-headed. He wanted to do something about it.

Sport had always been Shane Warne's consuming passion. As a kid growing up in the affluent beachside suburbs of Melbourne, he had figured prominently at little athletics, could hold up a corner in doubles and loved cricket and particularly Australian Rules football. Like many of his mates, he idolised Dennis Lillee and practised sprinting to the wicket, trying to bowl as swiftly as "The Tiger." After junior practices, Warne would often stay behind and watch the seniors work out.

Of particular fascination were the guys who bowled wrist spin. He loved to see the ball spin and bounce past the outside edge of the bat and batsmen become all tangled after failing to spot the mysterious googly. Asking his under-age coach, Ron Cantlon to demonstrate the basic grip for the leg-break, Warne listened intently as Cantlon explained how the grip not only was suitable for the leg-break, but fine also for the googly and the top spinner – the only variance being the position of the wrist at the point of delivery. Depending on how the wrist was cocked, the ball would turn from the leg, go straight through or maybe even track back into the right-hander. The key was to flick the ball hard and hear the ball ripping out of the fingers.

With anyone else so young, Cantlon probably wouldn't have bothered with so much detail but in Warne, realised he had a gifted student capable of not only absorbing the knowledge, but putting it into practice.

"Shane was able to impart spin on the ball right from the start," said Cantlon. "They didn't always land for him, but he knew what he was doing. Even then, he had a good feel for it. He had a natural action and was clearly a talent ready to blossom.

"Seeing any kid spinning the ball was a surprise as it just wasn't on the agenda at all in those days. Everyone would run in like Dennis Lillee with the wrist cocked and try to bowl it as fast as they could."

Cantlon coached Warne for four years and regards him as the most eager-to-please young player he's ever met. "He was happy to do whatever you asked. He thought it important to be nice to you. He loved life and was a good kid. We talked about how there mightn't be too many good spinners around right now, but even world champion teams like the West Indies had a weakness against quality spin. I told him to keep at it, because in 10 year's time, the national selectors would be searching the country for a leggie. Of course, no-one ever dreamed it would be Shane."

According to his principal at Sandringham state school, noted former footballer Neil Roberts, Warne was "a natural at ballsports, "very obliging and popular."

"He was very competitive and invariably red in the face through effort," he said. "Shane loved and was very good at physical education. He was a natural ballhandler, moved with grace and could read and track a moving ball as well as any student I've seen. He was a very energetic student, well-mannered, vitally interested and a delight to teach."

The opportunity to attend Mentone Grammar on a sporting scholarship in years 10, 11 and 12 was important in Warne's rapid development. Not only was he playing turf cricket against some of the best kids for their age in the state, his promise was spotted by sportsmaster Andrew Lynch, who recommended him to district cricket club St Kilda, where he played at first X1 level as an opening batsman.

He was flamboyant even then, schoolmates remembering him for his strawberry blond hair, affable nature and fetish for fast food and strawberry milkshakes.

Before joining St Kilda as a lower X1 batsman and change bowler, he had a season with his mates at sub-district club Brighton, a year most notable for second X1 captain, Mike Tamblyn, recommending he should concentrate on his batting rather than bowling!

"Down at Brighton, they never considered me a good judge of anything," said Tamblyn. "I was more impressed with Shane's batting, however. He always stuck around when I wanted him too. He'd only just turned 17 and didn't bowl the same stuff as he bowls now. He'd flick them across his fingers, but he'd also bowl an occasional offie and even a slow-medium pacer thrown in there as well."

His beginnings at St Kilda were equally humble. He played thirds and fourths cricket, as well as several Colt's matches on a Sunday.

St Kilda captain-coach Shaun Graf, an ex-Australian one-day representative, thought him "a fat little fella" with lots of natural ability who at that stage badly lacked the necessary work ethic. He felt his batting too loose and while he could spin his leg-break, he was pretty laid back about his bowling. In his first match in the fourths he didn't even get a bowl.

Throughout his late teen years, Warne mixed football with cricket and in 1988, his first year out of school, had a season with St Kilda under 19s. Playing at full-forward, he earnt the princely wage of $30 per match. He had the skills, too, and won promotion to the reserves only to dragged after half-time in his solitary match having twice failed to chase his direct opponent. When the Saints suggested he'd be better off continuing his football elsewhere in 1989, he was genuinely hurt. It was the first major rebuff he'd ever had in his sporting career.

Rather than attempt to continue playing, he went to England for some league cricket with his St Kilda clubmate Ricky Gough. While it was more of a summer-long party than anything else, his cricket developed and he made some great friends, several of whom were to attend his wedding six years later.

For transportation, the pair paid 10 pounds for an old yellow Cortina which they thrashed. They lost count of the times they were stopped by police, but they were never fined even once, despite the car being unregistered. "We just talked cricket to the policemen and they loved it. We didn't come across one bad copper. That was the year the Australians were touring. They were the flavor of the month," said Gough.

After making almost 1000 runs, including his career-best score of 139 and taking 90 wickets with one "nine-for" analysis, Warne returned to Melbourne keen to play either firsts or seconds. He was stunned when Graf and the St Kilda selectors started him in the third X1 for the opening game against Ringwood. Unimpressed by the prospect of again spending his Saturday afternoons playing anonymously in the park, he genuinely considered returning to his old friends at East Sandringham.

"Graffy probably didn't realise what Shane had done in England," said Gough. "Shane thought he was better than that. He had expected to start in the seconds."

The first two games were washed-out and when the sides were re-selected for round three, the first of the two-day games, he was in the seconds.

All aspects of his game had improved and he worked hard to shed at least some of his excess weight, with regular runs of the Albert Park Lake and sprint work with second's captain Stephen Maddocks. "I was doing some extra running work one night with Peter Chambers, jogging the ends and striding out on the straights when Shane joined in," said Maddocks. "It was a muggy night and he was hating it. We said to him how he needed to improve his fitness. It was a fairly solid session and he moaned and groaned but he stuck at it and was still there at the end. He didn't drop off. He just kept going. It was a good sign that he wanted to go on and really do it."

During that season he took his first "five-for" and started to bowl regularly in the nets usually reserved for just the first and second X1 players.

Shane Warne has always demanded the spotlight with his extrovert ways. On his first representative tour, with an Australian youth team to the West Indies, teammates dubbed him "Billy Idol" after he had his hair dyed jet-white.

He also had an ear-ring and invariably cornered much of the attention, whether it was disco-dancing poolside at the team motel in Montego Bay, or lying prostate pretending to be asleep among the luggage on the airport's baggage conveyor belt system in Barbados!

His eating habits were notorious, particularly his liking for "chip" rolls, smothered in tomato sauce! He was also big on tin spaghetti and toasted cheese sandwiches. Rarely did he eat any fruit or touch a vegetable.

At the end of the tour, the West Indians presented him with a tie for being the most sociable and friendly opponent.

His playful sense of fun was not appreciated by everyone, however, particularly during his stint at the Government-funded AIS Australian Cricket Academy in 1990.

A few at the Academy resented his presence, mistaking his boyish, good humor for something darker and more rebellious. While many worked part-time to supplement a weekly Academy handout, Warne existed mainly on the money sent him by his parents. Others were jealous of his skill, particularly when it became obvious that he was the favored wrist spinner in the squad. The standout games of the Academy season were the back-to-back one-dayers against the visiting Englishmen at Prince Alfred College. Warne was the only Academy player to reach double figures (11 & 11) in both innings. He also claimed his first "major" wicket, Robin Smith caught behind.

From his earliest days at the Academy, he was known as a lovable larrikin with a liking for loud music, x-rated videos and night-clubbing. He was one of only two in the squad who smoked and answered to the nickname "Showbags" – his mates reckoned he looked good, but there was nothing of substance inside!

He had been a wildcard selection for the Academy, having bypassed the normal representative carnivals for the elite under 17 and under 19 cricketers in the country. The previous winter he'd played league cricket in England and had stacked on so much weight, particularly around the face, that his own father hardly recognised him when he came to pick him up from Tullamarine Airport!

Midway through his Academy stint, Warne, Greg Blewett and Warwick Adlam were sent home early, by bus, after an incident at the hotel swimming pool in Darwin. Warne was said to be the ring-leader and that he'd upset a guest by allegedly exposing his backside.

It was never meant to be anything but a boyish lark, but as cricket was in its infancy as an AIS-funded sport and there was a constant fear of Government support suddenly being withdrawn, head coach Jack Potter and the AIS administration manager Brendan Flynn had to be seen to be taking strong action, especially as the misdemeanour had been bought to the attention of the AIS's Canberra-based administrator Robert De Castella.

"Shane was a lovable larrikin," said Flynn. "But in my shoes as the person representing the government, what happened shouldn't have happened."

Potter believed the extended bus trip back through the heart of Australia was punishment enough and on return from the Top End, declared the matter closed. He had a good rapport with Warne and hoped the incident would remain "in-house."

He was to resign soon afterwards, when the Australian Cricket Board picked their own coach, Steve Bernard, for the youth tour of the West Indies, despite the majority of those chosen having been coached by Potter at the Academy. On Warne's return from the West Indies, it was clear some wounds still festered, on both sides.

With Potter off the scene running a sandwich kiosk, Warne lost his major ally and resented the stern discipline imposed by Potter's successor, stand-in coach Barry Causby.

After a Sunday morning session running the sandhills at nearby Henley Beach during which Warne apparently upset a female photographer, it was decided he had stepped out of line once too often. He'd already lost his weekly allowance. Now the selectors would re-consider their team for Sri Lanka and leave him home.

He loaded his belongings into his hotted-up Cortina and headed back to Melbourne and in a bizarre twist, within a month had been named for his Sheffield Shield debut. "I was longing to come back to Melbourne and when I was left out of the Sri Lankan tour, thought there was no point hanging around the Academy anymore," Warne said.

In essence, he had forfeited his choice. While he was to become the Academy's first Test player, he was also the first to be expelled.

When Shane Warne was first shown how to bowl his now-famous flipper, it opened another dimension in his understanding of leg-spin bowling.

Academy head coach Jack Potter had an indoor session with Warne the day he arrived, in May, 1990. Potter had never seen Warne bowl and they stood at opposing ends of the Adelaide indoor nets. "Show me what you've got," said Potter.

"Immediately I knew he was a young bowler of uncommon promise. The ball fizzed effortlessly out of his hand. I thought if he could ever control this stuff, he's a real chance. He had a big-looping leg-break and a bit of a wrong-un. He could also make the ball bounce quite a height.

"I said to him, 'You've got a lot of stuff here Shane, but you have to have a ball which comes through straight, or skids through, to help you get the lbws.'

"I mentioned how Richie Benaud had developed his flipper and immediately become a better bowler for it and how the great Englishman Jim Laker used to bowl the last over before lunch from the pavilion end in county cricket, turn the ball two feet and come on the other end afterwards and bowl arm balls.

"'Please yourself,' I said, 'But if I was playing against you and I knew that's all you could bowl and didn't have something which hurried through, I'd just wait and try and pick you off. You only have to land it once or twice or spread a rumor that you've got one and people will start wondering and it'll help get you wickets. ' " While Warne was overweight and still keen to live the good life, Potter warmed to his self-assurance and positive attitude to life. He could also bowl. "You could hear the ball come out of his hand. He wasn't rolling them, he was ripping them," said Potter.

At one of their first sessions, he showed Warne how to bowl a flipper, the deceptively-fast skidding delivery which darts in towards the off and middle stumps like a quicker off-break, with only the slightest change of action. Warne immediately determined to master the delivery, which even the coaching manuals shy away from, believing it too difficult for fledglings to control.

"For the next three or four weeks, that's all Shane bowled," said Potter. "It used to hit the side of the net, the roof, everything. At one stage he said to me, 'I'll never be able to bowl this.'

"If anyone from the media had seen him in the first three weeks hitting the roof and hitting the square leg net while practising his flipper, they would have wondered what was going on. We kept it really quiet. But when he realised there was a sniff of success, he worked and worked at it.

"He was lucky of course. He's been recognised by higher powers that he had loads of talent. Lots of people were pulling for him and when he started to get wickets, he realised he had a future in cricket. Australia was screaming out for a spin bowler. He hardly had a wicket for Victoria and he was in the Test team."

THEY BOWLED THE FLIPPER
Australia's three leading exponents of the flipper, pre-Warne, were Bruce Dooland, Doug Ring and Richie Benaud.

While Dooland played most of his career in England and remains underrated for his feats in Australia, Ring and particularly Benaud helped swing Test matches with some outstanding displays.

Ring utilised his flipper as a variation for his leg-break. It was often mistakenly referred to as a wrong-un, a ball he was unable to bowl without discomfort after hurting his back during the war.

Benaud had a more classic side-on action and worked for hours, bowling at a handkerchief on a good length.

With 248 Test wickets, he was Australia's most successful spin bowler before Warne passed the mark during Australia's 1997 tour of England.

Shane Warne had taken just 26 first-class wickets when plucked from the pack for his Test debut, against Mohammad Azharuddin's Indians at Christmas time, 1991-92. He was Australia's 350th Test cricketer – and lucky to be there. His leg-spinning predecessor, Trevor Hohns, who was no longer available for Test cricket, had played 133 games before his maiden international. Warne had played just seven! It was a remarkable, meteoric rise, coming just 12 months after his hasty exit from the Cricket Academy.

At the start of the summer, Warne had contemplated a shift to Sydney, being unsure of securing a regular game with Victoria given the presence in the squad of more-experienced pair Peter McIntyre and Paul Jackson, who had been picked ahead of him for the 1990-91 Shield final.

Just a fortnight before his Test call-up, he'd even been omitted from Victoria's X1 for the match against Queensland in Brisbane.

As thrilled as he was at his selection, deep down he knew he hadn't paid his dues. While he batted ably and was thrilled by the warm reception accorded him by the Sydney crowd, he bowled like the rookie he was, unused to such responsibility. Bruce

Reid's breakdown just four overs into the game had greatly reduced Allan Border's options. Introduced into the attack the over before tea on day two, he bowled only leg-breaks, with an occasional flipper, but held back his wrong-un for fear of embarrassing himself. Outwardly, he seemed composed, but inside he was burning, especially early on day three when he fumbled a sharp caught and bowled chance from Ravi Shastri in his 22nd over when the Indian opener had made just 66.

He was into his 41st over when he finally broke through, Shastri, who'd gone onto a double-century, holing out to outrider Dean Jones running in from the extra cover fence.

Warne's figures on a placid, batsman-friendly wicket were an unflattering 1-150. Shastri made 206 and teenage starlet Sachin Tendulkar, 148 not out.

Warne had bowled mechanically, without great variation and run into an array of quick-footed well-balanced batsmen, expert at taking the attack to spinners.

With his roly-poly figure and bleached blond hair which protruded past his collar, he didn't look the part either. It had been a humbling experience. If he was to last as a Test cricketer, he'd have to go back to school.

Having failed to take a wicket in Adelaide, he was 12th man in the final Test in Perth and was convinced by new Cricket Academy head coach Rod Marsh to return for a further stint in the off-season, rather than returning to England for another year of Lancashire League.

Warne was on trial. He'd been earmarked for higher honors and while he promised much, his commitment was questionable. After one of his first sessions back at the Academy in April, Warne was at Terry Jenner's house talking cricket and life in general, in between flicking cricket balls to one another. Suddenly Jenner stopped and asked what sacrifices Warne had made to play Test cricket.

There was an embarrassed silence before finally Warne answered.

"None," he said.

He was still a smoker and a drinker and one for the late nights, being a regular in the bayside and boutique hotels in and around Melbourne. He lived on junk food and had never been absolutely serious about his fitness, even in his year of League football at St Kilda.

Jenner, who'd represented Australia 20 years previously, told him of his own missed opportunities and how he regretted not having the maturity or the tunnel vision to have made cricket his priority.

Ever since they'd been introduced two years previously, in Adelaide, they'd struck up a genuine friendship. Both had a larrikin streak in them, liked a laugh, a few beers and a punt. In Jenner's case, he'd gone to jail for embezzlement. Working with the kids at the Academy was part of his rehabilitation.

Warne was immediately taken by Jenner's knowledge and his down-to-earth manner. Even now when Warne needs advice about his bowling, he turns to Jenner and refers to him as his "spin doctor."

He thought long and hard about what Jenner had said and resolved to be the best, he had to radically change his lifestyle and make the sacrifices. He regards this conversation as a key in his reformation.

Returning to Melbourne, he embarked on an exhaustive fitness campaign with one of his mates from the St Kilda football club, Craig Devonport. The pair weren't working and everyday for weeks, would train in the gymnasium, play golf, have a net at a park in Sandringham, shop or simply play pool.

In just four months from April to the start of Australia's tour of Sri Lanka in August, Warne lost 12 kilograms, lopped his long hair and re-shaped his wardrobe. At the airport, Australian captain Allan Border wanted to know who the svelte "new boy" was. "When he came back having lost so much weight, it showed me he really wanted to be a Test cricketer," said Border.

Only two spinners had been chosen in Australia's 13-man Sri Lankan squad, Warne and NSW's Greg Matthews. While Warne didn't play in either of Australia's two lead-up games, an indicator that he may have been in the party only for experience, he was unexpectedly named for the first Test in Colombo after Border assessed the flint-hard Sinhalese Sports Club wicket as being a fast bowling graveyard.

The Sri Lankans dominated much of the game, establishing a 291 run first innings lead, Warne's leg-breaks being savaged by the left-handers Asanka Gurusinha and Arjuna Ranatunga. In just 22 overs he conceded 107 runs, without taking a wicket.

While the Australians fought back courageously, scoring 471, including 35 from Warne and the lion's share of a 40 run last wicket stand with Mike Whitney, Sri Lanka seemed destined to breakthough for a historic first Test win, especially after careering to 2-127, just 54 runs short of victory.

Warne's important innings had bucked his spirits, as had motivating conversations with "Mo" Matthews and Border.

The night before, hardly believing the punishment reserved for him by Ranatunga and Co., he had gone downcast to Matthews and asked what was going wrong with his bowling. For all of Matthews' eccentricities, he's never been anything but a committed and passionate team-man. He called Warne "Suicide" after the INXS song, Suicide Blonde. Over a plate of pasta he told Warne that he was good enough and wouldn't have been named in the first place if the selectors didn't think he could bowl. "*Go down fighting, Suicide,*" he said. "*If it bounces twice, who cares? If you're spinning it hard, you're a chance.*"

Border had also consistently urged Warne to remain positive and enjoy the challenge of Test cricket. As a rookie Test captain he'd let his performances do the talking and infrequently consulted with his younger men. Buoyed by Australia's revival in the late '80s, he was now far more worldly and wise and a genuine leader. In Warne, he saw a kid of infinite promise who only needed encouragement and one or two good performances to make it bigtime.

"One day it'll click for you, Shane, if you keep hanging in there," Border said. "I'm a big believer in guys who keep trying, keep putting in hard work and keep working hard."

Warne was the sixth bowler used in the Sri Lankan second innings and after being hit for consecutive 4s by the aggressive Aravinda De Silva, was immediately withdrawn from the attack.

But with victory within sight, Aravinda, on 37, miscalculated a reckless, on-the-up drive from the bowling of Craig McDermott and skied a catch to Border running back from the in-field and Warne was re-summoned.

It was a huge, out of character gamble by Border. The Sri Lankans were 6-137, just 36 from victory. Warne's Test average had blown to more than 350. Reaching the top of his run-up, he allowed himself a glance at the scoreboard, took in some deep breaths and remembering what Matthews had said the night before, resolved to rip the ball as far as he possibly could. "Spin up, spin up," he kept on saying to himself, a reminder to take the batsman on and not bowl too flat. Matthews was also calling out. "Come on, Suicide," he said. "Spin 'em hard, spin 'em up. C'mon, let's go."

Twenty minutes later, in an amazing change of fortunes, the game was over and Warne the unlikely hero after he'd claimed 3-0 in 11 deliveries. Pramodya Wickrema-singhe and Don Anurasiri drove with a leading edge to hole out in the covers while

Sri Lankan No. 11 Ranjith Madurasinghe tentatively lifted a drive straight to a jubilant Matthews.

It had been a remarkable collapse. Sri Lanka had been bowled out for 164, just 17 short of a first-ever victory against Australia.

The celebration was a rip-roaring affair, the Australians realising they'd stolen a game they had no right to win. Cans of beer were being thrown and splashed everywhere and David Boon, standing on a table, belted out the team anthem, "Under the Southern Cross" as joyously as at any time in his career. Next door, some of the Sri Lankans were crying, from bewilderment, disappointment and shock.

Tony Dodemaide, Australia's 12th man, said Warne's "force of personality" had been crucial in the dramatic ending. "He'd been belted all around the park in the first dig and just to be able to land them was a test. The odds were stacked against him but in his own relaxed way, he kept his cool, even though he must have been in turmoil. He landed them really well. Looking back, I thought, 'Gees this kid really has got a chance, he's going to make it.'"

"If ever it was all going to come undone and the big questions asked, it was going to be on that afternoon."

Warne was to miss the next Test with a foot injury and play the last, both games being drawn, ensuring Australia a 1-0 series win, one of its few series victories overseas in recent years. Warne's frontline role in Colombo had been all-important. Yet he wasn't even sure if he should have been there.

Shane Warne's career turning point wasn't his Academy axing, the realisation he had to make sacrifices to last or his prime hand in the Great Colombo Heist.

It came on the final day of his debut Test in hometown Melbourne in 1992-93 when he helped skittle the mighty West Indies. The flipper which castled Calypso captain Richie Richardson remains the most satisfying of his career and brought long-lasting ecstacy to those purists who had feared the much-admired art of wrist spinning had become obsolete.

Not only did it help swing the Test match and give Australia its solitary win of the summer by 139 runs, it also eased Warne's own self-doubts, which had been so apparent the night before during his conversation with vice-captain Ian Healy.

His career average of 90-plus was a damning indicator of how poorly he'd made the transition from State cricket onto the Test scene. He'd missed selection for Brisbane, instead playing an up-country Puma Cup slogathon in Bendigo.

While he'd been reinstated for Melbourne and taken a wicket in the West Indian first innings, it was only their No. 10 batsman Curtly Ambrose. He felt vulnerable and it showed.

As the Australians walked from the Hilton through Yarra Park down to the dressing rooms on the fifth morning, Ian Healy, a willing and supportive ally, sensed Warne's nervousness and asked, as casually as he could, what he was thinking about. "I'm thinking about bowling badly and being belted out all over the place and people questioning why I was ever picked in the first place."

Healy immediately went into recovery mode. "You're making it too complicated for yourself," he said. "You know how well you can bowl. Take it ball-by-ball, over-by-over. Don't think about anything else. Be positive. Today is the day it's all going to change."

Few had given the Windies much hope of victory, especially without their greatest star Viv Richards, who had retired. They still needed 328 in three sessions; an improbable target on a wearing wicket.

But from their overnight 1-32, the Windies punished the Australians, Phil Simmons hitting two 6s during his 66 run session and Richardson also reaching his half-century in the final overs before lunch. At 1-143, just over 200 were needed when Warne began his ninth over of the morning.

All match he'd struggled with his flipper. He'd tried more than a dozen, but all had been wide or poorly pitched. Remembering Healy's advice to shut everything else out and concentrate only on the delivery in hand, Warne composed himself, walked in his four paces and produced the flipper of his life. Not only was it quicker, it was directed straight at off-stump and Richardson, playing back, sensed the danger too late and watched in horror as it skidded past his defensive bat and shattered his stumps. The Windies 2-143, last man 52.

All of Warne's self-doubts evaporated in the heady next seconds as he enjoyed the spoils of his finest moment of his embryonic Test career. Warne had always said his ambition was to take the important wicket which changed a match. He'd finally done it and in a Test match in front of his own adoring crowd against the game's world champion.

It was the start of a memorable spell which was to bring him six more wickets, three from the northern end, where he had operated from originally and four from the southern end when he wrapped up the match.

With 7-52 from 23.2 overs, Warne had produced the finest analysis by an Australian leg-spinner since Richie Benaud's 7-72 against India at Madras in 1956-57. In the rooms later, he kept on shaking his head. He couldn't believe what he'd done.

Writing in the *Sunday Age* newspaper, Warne said: "That day proved to me that if I bowled well and stuck to my game plan, I could do it at Test level. You don't forget those days."

In his autobiography, Warne says that one delivery had saved his Test career. "Looking back now, I can say definitely that that ball was the turning point in my career. All that practice with Jack Potter at the Academy trying to get the flipper right had paid off in one delivery."

He led the Australians from the field, stump in hand, to standing applause and was soon joined in a jubilant Australian dressing room by his father, Keith. To his satisfaction and relief, his career had been re-born. He'd virtually guaranteed his selection for the tours of tours, to England from April.

A BOUQUET FROM BORDER

Allan Border was one of the most enthusiastic in his praise of Shane Warne after his demolition of the West Indies in his Melbourne debut.

"His time was right today and he showed a lot of guts," Border told pressmen. "He's worked a lot on his technique and come up trumps. It's hard for him because there are so many expectations for a bloke who is only 23.

"He has lost more than 10 kg which is not easy for a good-time lad and he has sought advice from a lot of people. "His approach has been positive and with more cricket under his belt, he can only improve."

Shane Warne's spitting leg-break which castled Mike Gatting first-ball at Old Trafford in 1993 was an unforgettable way to start the young Victorian's Ashes career.
Yet only weeks before he had been collared by Graeme Hick in the very first major game of the tour at picturesque Worcester. In making 187, Hick cemented his status as England's most-dangerous batsman. He took 19 from one Warne over, including three 6s, one of which soared over the New St. entrance gates and into the surrounding streets. One local paper referred to it as SLAUGHTER AT THE CATHEDRAL.

As in New Zealand only weeks earlier when he was first confronted by the Kiwi's master batsman Martin Crowe, Australian captain Allan Border hadn't wanted Warne to show his full repertoire of deliveries to Hick, insisting his matchwinner concentrate only on refinding his rhythm and spinning his big leg-break. But with 1-122 from 23 overs, including 96 to Hick, Warne's first serious bowl in England had been a disaster. He had been mauled and didn't like it.

After his heady successes in New Zealand, coupled with his matchswinging 7-52 against the West Indies in Melbourne at Christmas time, it seemed Warne's honeymoon could be over. Even world renowned leg-spinners such as Richie Benaud had toiled without consistent result on the slower English wickets. Maybe Warne's flame was flickering.

Sensing his star bowler's fragile confidence, Border applied a little positive psychology, reinforcing Warne's worth and how, come the opening Test, he was likely to beat Hick by an inch, he'd be stumped by a yard and he could tell him to %$#* off.

"All spinners are going to get a bit of tap now and again," Border said. "I don't think he felt too badly about it. Hick was a danger man but he didn't get a chance to play Warnie much as Mervyn used to sort him out."

Being part of an Ashes-winning team in England will always be the proudest of moments for any Australian cricketer. Warne's contributions from day two at Manchester, when he castled Gatting, to the end of a triumphant tour, ensured his status as Australia's man of the series and catapulted him up the world rankings.

The Gatting delivery, perhaps the most famous ever bowled in Ashes history, has been known ever since as THAT BALL, THE BALL FROM HELL or, perhaps even more appropriately, THE BALL OF THE CENTURY. In reality, it was only ever meant to be a loosener, but Warne imparted so much spin on the ball that it drifted dramatically from a direction close to the off stump to wide outside leg, before jagging back and clipping the off stump bail.

As jubilant wicketkeeper Ian Healy jumped in delight, a pumped-up Warne raced down the wicket, fist clenched to be enveloped in a sea of congratulation. A thunderstruck Gatting stood beside his broken wicket for a full eight seconds, staring blankly at the pitch, hardly believing his fate. Initially, he wondered if the ball had ricocheted from Healy's pads onto the wicket. Finally he looked across to square leg umpire Ken Palmer for confirmation. Yes, he was out – bowled.

Gatting says he might have played it differently, had he been well set. "For once in my life, at least I didn't get myself out. It wasn't a bad shot," he said. "Now it's a nice thing to look back on and be a part of Test history. I'm glad Shane has gone on and got a lot of wickets, otherwise I would have been a bit upset about it.

"As Graham Gooch said, 'Had it been a cheese roll, Gatt would have charged down the wicket and given it a belt.'"

By lingering at the wicket for so long, Gatting also gave Warne and the Australians a psychological edge crucial in the series fortunes. Gatting was renowned as a fine player of spin bowling. If he couldn't lay bat on Warne, who could?

"Every ball bowled by Warne looked likely to take a wicket, including the full toss," said Richard Hutton in *The Cricketer International*.

The zooter which dismissed Alec Stewart in the second innings gave him almost as much pleasure as the Gatting dismissal. By taking 4-51 and 4-86 and 34 wickets in six Tests, Warne was the chief destroyer in Australia's commanding 4-1 victory, confirming his status as Australia's brightest bowling prospect since a young Dennis Lillee burst onto the scene so dramatically against England more than 20 years previously.

He'd also conceded less than two runs an over, a damning commentary on the attitude of the crease-bound English batsmen, who treated his deliveries like they were hand grenades.

Writing in the Melbourne *Age*, Peter McFarline said Warne's unhurried four-pace run-up was intrinsic to his appeal. "He ambles into the bowling crease with the haste of an old man going to check on his cauliflowers."

"In cricket there is no better sight than an innocuous slow bowler making total fools of big names with wide bats and respectable averages 22 yards down the pitch."

Warne's triumphant progress through England saw him take eight wickets at Old Trafford, eight at Lord's, six at Trent Bridge, one at Headingley, six at Edgbaston and five at The Oval. He often bowled in tandem with off-spinner Tim May, who took 21 wickets. Between them the pair claimed 55 wickets, the most by any Australian spin pair in a series in England.

Not long before Victorian coach Les Stillman had wondered if spin bowlers would ever enjoy the prominence of yesteryear. He genuinely doubted their places in the game. Yet in one tour of England, Warne had taken 34 wickets. In three tours, Benaud took 25.

Confronted by Warne's devastating side spin, the English seemed fearful of venturing even a step or two forward of their creases. Robin Smith, such a courageous and effective player of fast bowling, was dismissed by spin seven times out of 10 before losing his place at The Oval.

At Lord's, Warne finished the game in emphatic style, bowling Peter Such and Phil Tufnell with giant back breaks. His big-spinning leg-spinner, so admired by his earliest coaches, had become his signature ball.

At tour end, Robin Marlar wrote: "Warne arrived like the Belle of the Ball, indeed with a belle of the ball. To produce that in-ducking, overspun, ripped leg-break which pitched outside leg stump and hit the top of off is the impossible dream."

THAT BALL REACTIONS:

"The spirit of '56 rose from the footprints at Old Trafford yesterday when Shane Warne, in a moment of leg-spinning magic, swung the course of a Test match with arguably the best ball of his career." – ROBERT CRADDOCK, Sunday Herald Sun.

"It was one of the greatest balls I've ever seen bowled in Test cricket." – RICHIE BENAUD, News of the World.

"It was the Ball of the Century," – ROBIN MARLAR, Sunday Times.

"The best ball ever seen in Test cricket," – RICHARD WILLIAMS, Independent on Sunday.

Within weeks of his arrival in England for the tour of tours, Warne was as recogniseable as Kylie Monogue and Jason Donovan from the popular Australian tv soapie Neighbours. A management company was employed to field all his offers. He was asked to write a column for the *London Sun*, sign 100s of autographs and pose for photographs, including one in just his jockstrap for 25,000 pounds!

The tabloid press sought every possible angle, including insights into Warne's colorful romantic past. One woman was paid handsomely to reveal her brief romance with Warne when he was a virtual unknown playing league cricket.

Warne initially enjoyed the attention, but was unimpressed when the press followed his every off-field move, including cutting into his precious time-off with his attractive girlfriend, Simone, who had arrived in June with most of the other wives and partners.

Warne was to propose during a boat cruise to the Lake District. At the conclusion of the tour, the pair holidayed for two weeks in Europe. Their romance sparked new headlines, CAUGHT OUT BY CUPID and LOVE PUTS SHANE IN A SPIN.

They had met just over a year previously at a Victorian cricket celebrity day, where Simone was working as a hostess. They didn't date until six months afterwards, Warne having mistakenly thrown out the packet of cigarettes on which he had noted Simon's home number.

"I wasn't impressed as I didn't know where she worked or how to get in contact with her," he said. "It all faded out. Then I saw her again at the Saloon Bar five or six months later. It was the night I got 69 against the Wackers (Western Australia) at the Junction Oval and we all went back there for a drink.

"She was playing pool with a friend and they were winning. They wouldn't get off the table. I was trying to say hello and asked her for her phone number and she said, 'No way!'

"I said, well here's my phone number, please give me a ring," but she never did.

A month later, at another charity golf day, they met again. "We called it a truce. I rang up and we got together."

They now have a daughter, Brooke, and share a luxurious double-decker house right on the beach at one of Melbourne's trendiest south-of-the-Yarra addresses.

TWELVE OF THE BEST
Shane Warne's 12 most satisfying wickets

1   **Richie Richardson** (*West Indies*), bowled by a matchswinging flipper minutes before lunch on the final day, Melbourne, 1992-93.
2   **Mike Gatting** (*England*), bowled by a hypnotising leg-break, Warne's first in Anglo-Australian Test cricket, Old Trafford, 1993.
3   **Salim Malik** (*Pakistan*), caught at mid-off from a well-tossed leg-break in their first meeting since the bribery allegations become public, Brisbane, 1995-96.
4   **Devon Malcolm** (*England*), caught brilliantly by David Boon at short leg from an over-spinning leg-break, Warne's hat-trick ball, Melbourne, 1994-95.
5   **Shivnarine Chanderpaul** (West Indies), bowled by a prodigious leg-break delivered from around the wicket, wide into the opposing footmarks, Sydney 1996-97.
6   **Basit Ali** (*Pakistan*), bowled around his legs by a leg-break on the very last delivery of Saturday night's play, Sydney, 1995-96.
7   **Graham Gooch** (*England*), bowled around his legs by a leg-break, fulfilling a prediction Warne had made to friends the previous night, Edgbaston, 1993.
8   **Pat Symcox** (*South Africa*), bowled through his legs, the very next ball after he'd padded a ball away and hollered at Warne, "You'll never get me there, boy," Sydney, 1993-94.
9   **Alec Stewart** (*England*), caught at slip via a big turning leg- break which ripped out of the rough, took an edge and was held by Mark Taylor, Old Trafford, 1997.
10 **Brian Lara** (*West Indies*), caught at the wicket bat-pad by Ian Healy from an over-spinning leg-break which hurried on, Jamaica, 1995.
11 **Robin Smith** (*England*), caught at slip via a big-spinning, beautifully-pitched leg-break shortly after "that" ball, Old Trafford, 1993.
12. **Daryll Cullinan** (*South Africa*), bowled by a flipper after he'd hit Warne for two 4s earlier in the over, Sydney, 1993-94.

The much-awaited Ashes re-matches in 1994-95 when England hoped to repel the Warne bogey were preceded by Australia's explosive short-tour of Pakistan.

Pakistan won the series 1-0, but not before Warne and teammates Tim May and Mark Waugh were the central figures in stunning bribery allegations involving Pakistan's captain Salim Malik and the all-powerful Bombay-based gambling cartels synonymous with major sport on the sub-continent.

Warne and his Australian teammates claimed Malik, acting for the cartel, twice offered them bribes to play below their best.

In sworn declarations, Warne and May said the first inducement from Malik came during the first Test in Karachi when they were each offered $70,000 to bowl poorly. According to Warne's statement, he told the Pakistani to "f... off. That's not the way we do things in Australia."

Warne says he was invited to see Malik at his hotel room at the Pearl Continental after the fourth day of the first Test.

Malik was alone and allegedly told Warne, "Pakistan's pride is at stake... we cannot afford to lose the first Test. It means a lot to us not to lose. You and Maysie are the keys tomorrow. We don't want you to bowl well."

Malik then was alleged to have offered the big cash, which he said he could have at the hotel within an hour.

In his statement, Warne said, "I couldn't believe what I had heard and said, "You are f...... kidding."

When Warne asked Malik if he was serious, the Pakistani replied, "you must get back to me."

Later in the tour, before a one-day international at Rawalpindi, it was asserted Mark Waugh had received an even bigger bribe, again from Malik, who Waugh knew through his English county connection at Essex.

The Australians were shocked and amazed at the offers and as a group decided that they'd take no action fearing physical reprisals if they went public.

They also didn't want to drop their focus, not only for the Pakistani Tests, but for the big internationals against England back in Australia. Their conspiracy-of-silence was so effective that tour manager Col Egar didn't even find out about the scandal until the last days of the tour.

"No Australian is ever going to take any money for throwing a game," said May. "We have far too much pride in our country."

The Australians dubbed Malik "The Rat" and sledged him frequently during the series, causing him to complain to the umpires.

Once it was made public the bribery furore caused ructions around the cricket world and remains an embarrassment for the international game, especially after cricket's ruling authority, the International Cricket Council, declared under its present rules it was unable to even hear the case.

As the controversy meandered, the Australian Cricket Board was also criticised for not taking a stronger, supportive stand. In *Australian Cricket* magazine, May said, "I don't know what was lower – being offered the bribe in the first place, or the pathetic way the cricket administrators both here and internationally handled it.

"At the time I didn't think much of it. Warnie and I said, 'Alright, we know about it. Now let's forget about it.' The lowest moment came later when we were stuck out on a limb and told fend for yourself. I don't know how much the Australian public believed, but generally the press was writing stuff which virtually intimidated that May, Warne and Waugh were lying about the whole episode. That was particularly distressing. There wasn't too much defence coming from the administrators, which was terribly disappointing."

Pending an internal inquiry, Malik was stripped of his captaincy and barred from playing even at club level. Players had complained about his leadership during the tour of Zimbabwe, particularly opening batsman Aamir Sohail who accused Malik of having key involvements in match-fixing and game day betting offences.

Nine months after the allegations had first been made public, the Pakistanis finally conducted an inquiry, headed by Justice Fakhruddin Ebrahim.

After lengthy deliberations, Justice Ebrahim dismissed all of the Australian accusations, clearing Malik and allowing him to continue his international career. The three Australians were branded as "concocters" and the Australian Cricket Board criticised for refusing permission for the Australian trio to fly to Pakistan to attend the hearing.

Board chairman Denis Rogers said the ACB was unconvinced that the Pakistanis could guarantee the safety of the deputation. The Board had been prepared to fly them to London, but the ICC said they had no jurisdiction to become so closely involved.

Malik was immediately reinstated in time for Pakistan's 1995-96 Australian tour, prompting an angry backlash in Australia.

Suddenly the heat was back on Warne and he was ropable. "I'm not a liar. I didn't make up the stories. Why would I?" he said. "With the success of the Australian cricket team and myself in the last few years… why would I throw all that away? It hurts me to hear people say we might have made the story up."

Relations with Malik were icy throughout the return series in Australia, the Australians refusing to speak or even acknowledge him – on or off the field.

He played only two of the three Tests, having injured his hand while fielding early in Brisbane. He didn't bat until the second innings and when he did, at the fall of the sixth wicket, fell fourth ball playing across the line to a delighted Warne who punched the air in delight even before Craig McDermott had completed a simple catch.

It was an emotionally exhausting confrontation. Later Warne said, "It goes to show that there is justice in the game. I've been pretty down. Mum, Dad and my wife got me through. I'd like to dedicate the wicket to them especially."

Warne said it was one of the most satisfying wickets of his Test career, only marginally behind the Richie Richardson flipper and "that" ball which castled Mike Gatting at Old Trafford in '93.

The Australians won by an innings, featured by Warne's own 11 wicket haul. At the press conference, Warne openly criticised Malik for not batting in Pakistan's first innings. "I know if that had been one of the Australians he would have batted and would just about have gone out with a broken leg… I don't know if he'll play the next Test, but hopefully he'll get a duck in every innings he plays."

Throughout the first 15 years of his career, including his junior days at East Sandringham, Shane Warne had never taken a hat-trick.

When he did, against Mike Atherton's Englishmen in the Christmas Test in Melbourne, it continued his remarkable run of success which inspired one writer to call him "the greatest spin bowler on earth."

Ironically, he almost had two hat-tricks in successive Tests, his first-up wrong-un to England No. 11 Phil Tufnell in Brisbane shaving his off-stump during his remarkable 8-71, the finest-ever figures by an Australian in an Ashes Test at the 'Gabba.

Unlike the Pakistanis and Sri Lankans, who'd dance to Warne and try and take him on the half-volley whenever possible, the Englishmen were rooted to their crease and seemed unable to pick his deliveries, even his googly, which had always been only a minor variation and never as deadly as his flipper or big-spinning leg-break.

During the fourth day in Brisbane, England openers Atherton and Alec Stewart borrowed some field glasses and sat with the Channel Nine cameramen, intensely watching Warne operate from high-up behind his arm.

If they detected anything, putting their new theories into practice was easier said than done. Warne took 11 wickets in Brisbane and was equally menacing with nine in the next Test in Melbourne.

Having decimated the Englishmen with six first innings wickets, he grabbed three in three balls in the second: Phil DeFreitas (lbw), Darren Gough (caught behind) and Devon Malcolm (caught at short-leg).

As Malcolm, with a Test average of just six, ambled to the crease, the non-striker Stewart said to Warne, "You'll never ever have a better chance of a hat-trick!"

After consulting his Victorian teammate Damien Fleming, who'd taken a hat-trick only months previously in his debut Test in Pakistan, Warne opted against bowling a

The ball of dreams: Devon Malcolm is caught at short leg giving Shane Warne his first hat-trick in any form of cricket, Melbourne, 1994-95.

flipper or a wrong-un. Instead, he went with an over-spinning leg-break which he believed would widen his options. It bounced more than Malcolm had expected and ballooned off his gloves wide of David Boon, fielding in-close on the leg-side.

In a magnficent reflex effort, Boon threw himself to the right and picked up a remarkable catch before regaining his feet and flinging the ball up triumphantly.

Within seconds, he'd been buried in a scrum of delighted Aussies, Warne one of the first to get to him. "It's the quickest I've ever run," he said.

England hadn't even lasted an hour on the final day, being bowled out for 92 in yet another ineffectual, inept performance.

High-up in the MCC members, Warne's mentor Terry Jenner was as excited as his pupil. "One or two people didn't like Shane Warne's spiked hair or the fact that he smoked, but now they don't say a thing. They let him be Shane Warne," he said.

His parents, Keith and Brigitte, couldn't stop shaking their heads. "They couldn't believe it," said ex-international Shaun Graf, who was sitting with them. Like Jenner, he had been one of Warne's alltime major influences.

Test selector and former leg-spinner Jim Higgs said Warne's feats had added another dimension to cricket. Kids everywhere were wanting to experiment with leg-spin, an art which had become unfashionable to the point of extinction . "Warne has breathed new life into the game," Higgs said. "I can't see how anyone could have been better. He spins the ball as much as it is physically possible to do and he has as good as control as imaginable."

Warne said he had only wanted to "tie up an end" on the final day. "I got lucky," he said.

Afterwards Mark Taylor admitted he was just about to take Warne off, after he'd bowled six consecutive maidens to wicketkeeper Steve Rhodes. He'd even told Tim May to warm-up!

During the game, Warne's 31st in Test cricket, he passed 150 wickets, including 54 in just eight Ashes Tests. His strike-rate of a wicket every 63 deliveries was superior even to

Australia's most-revered spin bowlers, Clarrie Grimmett and Bill O'Reilly.

His hat-trick was the first by an Australian since Lindsay Kline at Capetown in 1957-58 and the first in an Ashes Test at the MCG since Hugh Trumble in 1903-04.

England had lost 13 of their 19 most-recent Tests to Australia, their worst losing sequence in history.

"I have always liked the way Shane bowls. He really gives the ball a rip," said the just-retired Allan Border, at the helm for much of that Ashes domination. "He has big strong hands. Other leg-spinners in recent years have bowled the ball out of the back of their hand but he tends to use more of his wrist and makes it come out of the side which increases the spin."

Writing in the London *Mirror*, Chris Lander said, "Four years ago Shane Warne was a beer-swilling beach bum, three-and-a-half stone (20 kg) overweight and remembered as the only player to be kicked out of the Australian Cricket Academy. Today he is being heralded as the greatest spin bowler on earth after a one-man demolition job on England's shellshocked Test stars."

In Warne's first four years and 43 Tests, home and away, only three were, by his own estimatations, less-than-satisfactory:
- England (at Headingley, 1993),
- New Zealand (Perth, 1993-94) and
- England (Sydney, 1994-95).

He'd become Australia's matchwinning bowler at both the Test and one-day game, sharing equal billing with West Indian batting starlet, Brian Lara, as the outstanding and most-magnetic cricket personality in the world. Their autumn duel in the Caribbean was billed as cricket's feature event of 1995.

Lara's recordbreaking Test and first-class scores had seen him advance from precocious wonderkid to the most irresistible batsmen in the world. His duel with Warne was clearly going to be one of the most important factors in the showdown for world cricket supremacy. It would be a classic case of master batsman against master bowler.

As can so often happen, however, it was never the central theme, Steve Waugh being the outstanding player and virtually single-handedly ensuring Australia a breakthrough series victory, despite the early-tour breakdowns of Craig McDermott and Damien Fleming.

After nearly two decades of domination, the Windies had finally been toppled from top place on the Test charts.

While Lara averaged 44, it was well short of his 99 the previous Caribbean summer against England, or even his 58 on Australian wickets in 1992-93. Beginning a brilliant run as his nemesis, Glenn McGrath produced the ball of the series, a spitting offcutter, in the opening Test at Bridgetown which induced a tickle to Ian Healy. While Lara made 88 in the second Test at St John's, he always appeared vulnerable, being out to the faster bowlers six times in seven completed innings.

While he had the best of their duels with Warne, he did, however, fall to him in the fourth Test at Jamaica when he had threatened to take charge.

With 15 wickets in the four Tests, Warne filled a valuable back-up role, without producing his matchwinning form of 1993-94 when he was the International Cricketer of the Year.

Critics pointed to his herculean work-load, saying it had robbed him of his old "edge." No longer was he spinning the ball as sharply or ripping the ball with as much vigor from his wrist and fingers. While new captain Mark Taylor had tried to lessen his responsibilities and asked him to radically reduce his net bowling, come the heat of the

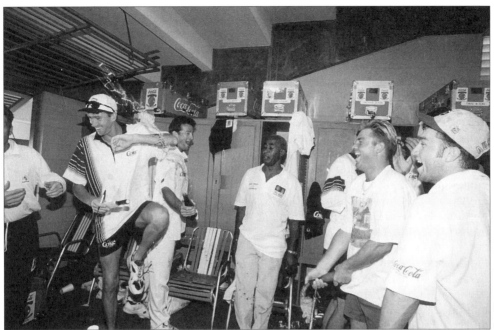

Ray Titus

Australia celebrate after winning the first Test against the West Indies in Barbados on its way to the world championship, 1995 tour.

battle, he believed it impossible not to turn to Warne, given his remarkable record and sheer appetite for bowling.

He was, however, consistently bowling one-third of Australia's overs and in all major cricket in 1993 and 1994, sent down an average of 1300 overs a year, for each 12 month period. Other world-class spinners like England's Phil Tufnell were bowling just 500.

The chance of an extended break, a rarity for the elite Australian players in the '90s, freshened him considerably. He had married Simone Callahan in a private service at Como House, one of Melbourne's oldest landmarks and, despite the ever-meandering bribery scandal which became headline news again from September, entered the re-matches with Pakistan full of expectation.

His dismissal of arch antagonist Salim Malik was the feature of his 11-wicket haul in Brisbane. With 7-23 and 4-54 he continued his love affair with the 'Gabba, which was rapidly becoming his most successful ground.

While his spinning finger was requiring pain-killing cortizone injections and his shoulder was becoming sorer from over-use, his performances were amazingly consistent.

Twelve more wickets in three Tests against the Sri Lankans, were more expensive than normal, but in Perth he passed 200 wickets in his 42nd Test – only four others had achieved the milestone in fewer matches – and in Melbourne, the controversial Test in which Sri Lanka's Muttiah Muralitharan was no-balled by Darrell Hair for throwing, he reached 50 Test wickets for the third consecutive calender year, another "first."

His first World Cup, a gripping contest which saw a giantkilling victory from Sri Lanka, underlined his importance to Taylor. With 12 wickets and the concession of less than four runs an over, he was again Australia's leading bowler, despite his worsening finger ligament injury which forced a wintertime operation. Specialists had also suggested shoulder surgery, but he declined, saying the shouder would repair naturally given regular physiotherapy and a longer-than-usual break which seemed likely to see him miss the short tour of Sri Lanka as well as the one-off Test against the Indians in New Delhi in September.

Having been a reluctant absentee from Australia's opening internationals of the extended summer on the sub-continent, Warne's 1996-97 season start was delayed until early October and the beginning of the Mercantile Mutual Cup one-day competition.

As Victoria's new captain, replacing the out-of-favor Dean Jones, Warne had set a sterling example at training camps in Darwin and at the outer-Melbourne naval base, *HMAS Cerberus*, where for two days Victorian squad members trained like commandoes before finishing with steak and soft drinks in a novel preparation aimed at increasing team togetherness and spirit.

Other than some casual overs of slow medium pace during the extrav-

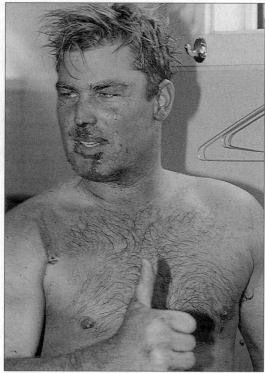

Hard yakka pre-season, HMAS Cerberus, August

Ken Rainsbury

agent Super 8s competitions in Darwin and far-north Queensland in July, Warne hardly even rolled his arm over until late September when he gingerly first tested his finger, rolling a maximum of five or six gentle leg-breaks as part of his daily fitness routine.

His finger, operated on by Melbourne-based orthapaedic surgeon Greg Hoy in May, had taken months to settle. It had been a long and painfully slow convalesence and several times he wondered about life without cricket.

As the finger finally showed signs of improvement, he was tempted to make himself available for the Test match in India, but realised he may be jeopardising his career. "I tried to look at the big picture, the long-term, not the short," Warne said in his column in the *Sunday Age*.

"If I came back too soon and ended up damaging the finger again that could be it. Finished as a cricketer at 27. No thanks."

By early October, Warne believed himself capable of bowling 15 overs, ideally in two different spells.

However, he said the swelling in his finger would make it impossible for him to bowl the next day, an unsatisfactory situation for both himself and the team.

Reluctantly withdrawing from the squad to India, he said the basic issue was whether his once-golden finger was fit enough to answer the every call of his captain.

"You can't say to your captain on the morning of a Test match that you'll be right to bowl 15 overs… you can't put conditions on playing in a Test match," he said.

"What would happen if the weather was hot, the pitch flat, dry and turning and doing nothing for the quicks?

"As the senior spin bowler, my job in that situation would be to bowl as long as the skipper wants. Unfortunately my finger is not good enough now and still wouldn't be when the Test against India starts."

Jack Pollard Collection

Injury maintenance, 1995-96 season.

He'd been looking forward to the challenge of playing against Indian starlet Sachin Tendulkar, who he rated, with Mark Waugh, as the finest batsman he'd ever opposed. There was also the small matter of reducing his Test average which stood at an embarrassing 228 after his only Tests against the Indians in his maiden international appearances in 1991-92.

It was the first Test Warne had missed since Brisbane, 1992-93. He may have been tempted to make himself available had there been another two month break following the Test, but with the Titan Cup one-day internationals against India and South Africa to come, it left no time for further rehabilitation.

He remained back in Melbourne, concentrating on his pre-season with the Victorians and playing his first comeback games in the lower-key atmosphere of the domestic one-day competition. He even played his first matches for almost two years with his old club St Kilda.

Overcoming the pain barrier was his major obstacle to returning to his best. Specialists had told him his finger was structurally sound and he could do no further damage; it was a matter of gradually getting it accustomed again to the stresses of bowling 25 overs on consecutive days.

At every opportunity, Warne would massage his finger with Exoplast, a soft plasticine substance, keeping it as mobile as possible. He wore a small brace on his finger at night and before and after bowling, he'd have massage on his finger, wrist, hand, forearm, elbow, tricep and shoulders.

As the Australians were tumbling to an embarrassing Test loss on a slow-and-low turner at New Delhi, Warne was making his first tentative comeback steps in Adelaide, for Victoria against South Australia. With 2-55 from 10 one-day overs, he was expensive, but importantly, he was slowly regaining his old confidence in the finger.

"It's taking longer than we hoped, but it's healing stronger and will last longer," he said.

While still well short of being able to impart maximum "work" on the ball, he believed he was improving with every performance, encouraging news with the world championship re-matches with the West Indies rapidly approaching.

Having a more leisurely build-up rather than playing at international level too quickly had suited him and the marketers, who heavily promoted his presence back in Australia. On the eve of Victoria's first home fixture, against Tasmania at Optus Oval, one advertisement read: WARNE PULLS HIS FINGER OUT TOMORROW and included an illustration of Warne's hand with the ring finger heavily bandaged.

Warne could not have hoped for a more-encouraging homecoming. With 5-35, his career-best figures at Mercantile Mutual Cup level, he helped decimate the Tasmanian middle-order in his most vigorous workout since the World Cup final.

Victoria's medical staff had suggested he should step up his program, with the opening Sheffield Shield games and the first Test starting from early November.

'I did start to wonder when it was going to come good," said Warne. "After the Tassie match, I felt 'phew, I'm nearly there.'"

He'd been able to bowl all his deliveries, even the big-spinning leg-break which requires most effort and flick from his fingers and was confident he could regain his best touch of early 1994-95 when he'd virtually ensured Australia the Ashes after two Tests.

Leading into the series with the Windies billed by the Australian Cricket Board as THE DECIDER, the ACB's chief executive Graeme Halbish announced that the Board's top six contracted players would all gross at least $300,000 from direct match payments alone in 1996-97. With his Channel Nine, Just Jeans, Oakley, Optus, Gunn & Moore and assorted other contracts, Warne's annual wage was closer to $1 mill. He'd moved with his wife Simone into a prestigious double-decker house on the esplanade at Brighton beach, his neighbours including some of Melbourne's richest businessmen and high-profile types such as football celebrity Sam Newman.

Workmanlike performances in Victoria's opening Shield games had satisfied the selectors and he was immediately reinstated for the first West Indian Test in Brisbane. He'd been particularly happy with his form against South Australia in Melbourne where he took 3-25 and 0-61 (from 40 overs). Several of his leg-breaks kicked enough to strike wicketkeeper Darren Berry high-up on the body. "The ball was dipping and turning... guys were playing and missing," he said.

On the eve of the Test, Warne told how delighted he was to be back. He said his high-profile rarely allowed him time to himself, but if it meant he was in the Test side and doing well, it was all worth it.

"I just love playing for Australia," he said. "I had a period around '93-'94 where I reckon I let it get to me, I got a bit cocky and a bit arrogant. I did a couple of things I was ashamed of in South Africa when I sledged Andrew Hudson. I just couldn't believe I did that. A couple of close friends had a word to me that I was getting a bit big-headed about it all. Since then I've made a conscious effort to just be myself. The one thing I have learned is that you can't please everybody, not everybody will like you.

"Some people will be jealous, some guys will think you carry on like a pork chop, others will read everything in the press and think they know you."

The mind games which so often surround the biggest sporting events were clearly evident in the lead-up to the Frank Worrell Trophy contests. With no leg-spinners in their squad, the touring West Indians called for local leg-spinners to come and give them practice on the eve of their confrontation with Shane Warne. However, no-one was forthcoming, other than a couple of military mediums.

Later it was learnt that senior Queensland clubs had been told not to supply any wrist spinners.

Relations between the two teams, which had often been heated in the past, appeared to be on the improve, however, with the West Indian team management, led by legends Clive Lloyd and Malcolm Marshall, asking the Australians to revive the old practice of mixing after-play in one another's dressing rooms.

With four wickets in a Test dominated by Ian Healy's magnificent double of 161 not out and 45 not out, Warne bowled for long periods with great economy without his normal side spin. Others benefited from his accuracy, as wickets fell rapidly at the other end, the Windies plummeting to a 123 run defeat.

Warne was clearly not putting as much "work" on the ball as in his glory years, but it had been only six months since a major operation and he was sure to improve.

Former captain Allan Border again suggested that Warne's workload be carefully monitored. "I thought Shane's comeback to Test cricket at the 'Gabba on the weekend

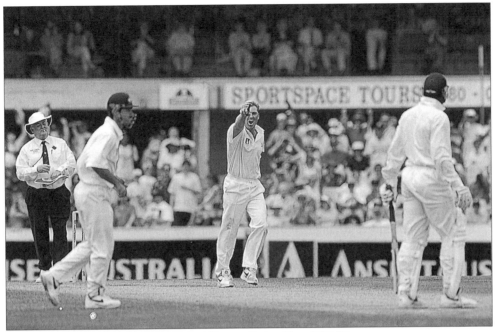

A not-so-subtle sendoff of West Indian Carl Hooper, Sydney Test, 1996-97

Shaun Botterill/All Sport

was promising but the last jump he has to make is a philosophical one. It seems he is still protecting his right shoulder, which like his finger, has been sore for some time," he said.

"It seems he hasn't quite got the confidence to give the ball the full rip. He is not following through as well as he can and is rolling the ball rather than ripping it.

"It must have been hard for Warne to come to terms with his injury knowing any ball he bowled could be his last. I don't think people realise how seriously damaged Warne's finger was. Finger surgery to a spinner is like knee surgery to a footballer. How many footballers do you see come back from knee surgery and immediately become the player they were? It can take 18 months."

Border believed Warne had developed more variety since his triumphant tour of England in 1993, partly to ease the intense pressure on his shoulder and finger in producing the big-spinning leg-break, which for so long had been his meal ticket. "The $64,000 question is will the late model Warne be more successful than the massive tweaker of 1993? Something tells me the freakish hauls of 7-23 will be more irregular, but who knows?" Border said.

"History says he was always going to have to modify his approach. How many giant turners of the ball can you name who have had long careers? The laws of science tell us the muscles and tendons which are strained by the unnatural pressures of such a delivery can stand up for only so long."

Less than a week separated the first and second Tests and Australia continued its early domination, this time with a 124 run win in Sydney. With seven wickets for the game, Warne was again a force. The spitting leg-break which cut back savagely to bowl Shivnarine Chanderpaul on the final delivery before lunch on day five was one of his finest, prompting Warne's now familiar two fist salute. So far outside the off stump did it pitch that it could have been called a wide, had it not darted back so wickedly. WIZARD WARNE BACK WITH A BITE was one of the headlines. The *Herald Sun*'s Robert Craddock said it was as fine a delivery as "that" ball at Old Trafford in '93. "With arguably the best ball of his career to dismiss Shivnarine Chanderpaul, Shane Warne yesterday convinced a doubting world he is ready to re-emerge as the most venemous strike force in Test cricket," he said. "The man who couldn't even shake hands with friends a few months ago after finger surgery, used the same dodge digit yesterday to turn the ball almost a metre and strike fear into West Indian hearts at the SCG."

Chanderpaul's cameo of 71 in 68 balls had been a gem. He'd even outshone Brian Lara, who was given out caught at the wicket having withdrawn too late from a pull shot and feathered it through to a tumbling Ian Healy.

Warne said until Sydney he had lacked confidence in his finger, but against Chanderpaul had decided to give the ball the biggest possible "rip."

"It worked and it very satisfying to see it come back so much. It's one of the best balls I've bowled."

He said his finger was still sore after a day's play and it could be six months before it was fully recovered.

With the West Indies trailing 2-0 after two Tests, any goodwill between the teams seemed superficial when it was learned Lara had barged into the Australian rooms upon his dismissal, telling Australian coach Geoff Marsh that Healy had caught the ball on the half-volley and saying he was not welcome in the West Indian room. The Australians believed Lara was just being petulant again and remained disappointed that the resultant apology came from team manager Lloyd rather than Lara himself.

While the Windies were to fight back with victory in three days on a Melbourne greentop, they were convincingly beaten in the decider in Adelaide, Australia winning by lunchtime on the fourth day having made 517 and established a lead of almost 400 on the first innings. Michael Bevan was the unlikely destroyer with 10 wickets for the match. Warne took six, all but one in the top-order.

The Windies won the "dead" Test in Perth, but with a 3-2 series victory, Australia had held the world championship and left for South Africa after barely a week's break with great expectations, especially with pace bowler Glenn McGrath in such rampaging form.

With 26 wickets in five Tests, he'd outbowled everybody, including the great West Indian pacemen Curtly Ambrose and Courtney Walsh. With 22 wickets, Warne had also been superb, considering his self-doubts leading into the summer.

The pair had often bowled in tandem and by maintaining peak pressure from both ends, had triggered wickets for each other. Warne had also fine-tuned his attack to again take maximum advantage of the roughage at the other end, just as he had when the 110 kg Merv Hughes was ploughing in in his hey-day.

With almost 20 Test matches and double the number of one-day games in 1996-97, Australia's schedule was tough and unrelenting. Vice-captain Ian Healy had predicted months earlier that there would be casualties leading into the English tour and afterwards given six more Tests back at home against New Zealand and South Africa in 1997-98 as well as a three-Test tour of India.

The exhausting demands of fast bowling had seen Craig McDermott retire at Christmas, while Paul Reiffel, having failed to play a Test and only four of the six one-dayers in South Africa, was initially left home when the English touring party was announced in April. Given that Reiffel had been one of the few success stories on the short Indian tour in September and had finished his Australian Test season with 5-73 and 0-24 against the Windies in February, it was the hardest-possible call, despite increasing suspicions about his battle-weary hamstrings.

Despite not having a five wicket haul in a Test for almost 18 months, Warne only had to stand-up to be an automatic selection for England. With 11 wickets in the three South African Tests and 10 in five one-day games, he remained Australia's matchwinning performer, this time in tandem with the greatly-improved McGrath, who was bowling as fast as old "White Lightning" himself, Allan Donald.

Not only did the Aussies win the Tests 2-1, they won the one-day series, too, 4-3, a mammoth effort considering South Africa's standing as the world's outstanding limited-over team of the previous 12 months.

The tour highlight came at Port Elizabeth where the Australians won by two wickets thanks to the finest innings of Mark Waugh's majestic career. With 116 out of 8-271, Waugh was peerless on a wicket tough for batting and against a keen and able bowling attack. Captain Mark Taylor was so chuffed after Ian Healy had hit a six for victory, that he called it Australia's finest win in his time as captain.

With five wickets for the game, Warne again made a considerable contribution. Rather than being frustrated by not taking the big bags of wickets as he had early in his career, he believed he was bowling as well as he ever. He was mentally tougher and more patient. "If I was bowling fairly poorly, but picking up flukey wickets and getting the odd five-for, I'd be unhappy," he said. "But I know I'm bowling well. In the end we are winning and I'm contributing which is all that matters."

In mid-match at Wanderers, Warne summoned his spin coach, Terry Jenner, to the nets, unhappy that his leg-break wasn't spinning as in the past. Jenner advised him that he was putting too much forward thrust on the ball, rather than sideways spin. He suggested he brace his leg more at delivery and bowl midway across the popping crease, rather than closer into the stumps so his shoulders could be put to best use. Warne tried one or two deliveries standing-still, before gradually increasing his run. "Warne's a genius because he can absorb advice and choose the good bits," said Jenner.

The advice clearly worked. With 4-43 from 28 overs in the South African second innings, Warne demolished the top-order, dismissing Gary Kirsten and Jacques Kallis (bowled), old adversary Daryll Cullinan (caught behind) and Jonty Rhodes (lbw). His variety was continuing to confound the South Africans and captain Hansie Cronje conceded his senior batsmen were as much at sea against Warne in '97 as they were in 1993-94.

They were unable to regularly turn the strike over against him and had fallen victim to his unrelenting pressure and Mark Taylor's field placings which included two close-in catchers, for everyone, bar Cronje, who was the surest of all the South Africans against Warne.

"Shane is a fine bowler but I do feel there are certain basic things that we did wrong against him this time around that we've got to rectify very quickly," Cronje said. "One way of judging if he's bowling well or not is the pace of his flipper and I thought the pace of the flipper was there this time around."

Cronje said the South Africans felt pressure every time Warne came onto bowl and it had been a bonus when he was unavailable for the triangular one-day tournament in India in October.

"The biggest difference between India and now is that Shane Warne didn't play in that series and is playing now," he said.

"I regard him as one of the best bowlers in the world at the moment, but he's certainly not unplayable. He does bowl certain unplayable deliveries, but he's not unplayable.

"Once you get on top of him and realise you can hold him out and score off him it's very important. He wasn't in India and it was a tremendous boost for the team when we went onto the field against an Australian side without Shane Warne."

Full-throated as normal: A Warne appeal, Lord's 1997,

David Munden/Sportsline

Despite several dropped catches, including two at Wanderers, Warne's strike-rate was again bordering around 70 balls per wicket. While he considered his tour an unqualified success, others weren't so sure.

At Port Elizabeth, after Warne laughed uproarously when South African No. 11 Paul Adams tried a reverse sweep only to embarrassingly deflect the ball to slipsman Mark Taylor, many said he had acted immaturely and unnecessarily ridiculed Adams, a young player in only his second international season.

South African coach Bob Woolmer felt the Australians shouldn't have mocked Adams. "There was no need. The guy's out."

Adams had played the reverse sweep in the first Test, too, during a cavalier stay at the crease in which he poked his tongue out at fast bowler Glenn McGrath after the Australians became irritated by his antics. They considered him an upstart. "Listen champ, you'd better be able to bowl," said Mark Waugh.

Woolmer had taught all the South Africans the technique required for the shot. Jonty Rhodes had played it particularly well against Warne in the one-day internationals and Woolmer felt it was a legitimate shot, played properly, to help break up the bowler's line.

Warne received several stern faxes, accusing him of acting in an unsportsmanlike manner. The most biting criticism came from Melbourne *Age* feature writer, Patrick Smith who claimed Warne was guilty of "the most childish and embarrassing acts committed by an Australian Test cricketer."

"It says so much about the lack of temperament and maturity of Warne that he could not allow the dismissal to go without resorting to such puerile and demeaning behaviour," Smith said.

Under pressure, Smith claimed Warne "turns into a boor" and "lacked the sustained dignity" to hold such a post as the Australian cricket captaincy.

"The pleasant young man of television interviews is easily interchangeable with an immature hothead when challenged on the cricket field. And Australian cricket suffers for it," he said.

He suggested Warne should be reprimanded, if not fined.

The criticism triggered a stinging response from Warne, who claimed Smith was grandstanding to help *The Age* lift its circulation. He did agree, however, that he needed more experience before he could contemplate any higher leadership roles than the Victorian cricket captaincy.

"I'm not ready yet and it is not part of my career plans," he said. "I need to get more used to the pressures and see how I go as Victoria's captain. I need that leadership experience before I think of taking on responsibilities at a higher level. There are others in the Australian team who are better qualified."

Warne said if it was straight case of on-field captaincy, he'd have no problem. It was all the other demands such as dealing with officials, writing reports, meeting with umpires and match referees and endless interviews with the media which were the complication.

Writing in the *Sunday Age*, he said, "I know this is part of the job and does lead to other opportunities after cricket, but I'm human and it does get to me, like it does to all of the players. At present I feel like I have enough to do maintaining my bowling form and playing well, without having to worry about the extra things a captain has to do."

He said life on tour could become a grind and while he was grateful for the opportunity to cement his future through playing a sport he loved, it had its drawbacks, especially when he was on the other side of the world away from his pregnant wife.

Answering Smith's criticism, he said, "Some people just don't like the way you play. I just go out and be myself. If people like me great. If not I am not going to lose sleep."

"Like every other person we have days when we are tired or get out of the wrong side of bed. The trouble is when that happens, we blow our top not in the kitchen or in the office, but in the middle of the crowded cricket ground with television cameras filming our every move.

Getting ready to bowl, Texaco Cup, 1997

Sergio Dionisio

"Sometimes you feel like you have no escape, that everything you do is watched and analysed and often criticised.

"Mark Taylor chews his gum the wrong way. Steve Waugh doesn't smile often enough and I appeal aggressively, or as some people say, arrogantly. I'm not arrogant. I have confidence in my ability. Yes, I'm emotional about my cricket. I'm competitive and aggressive. I have to be. I'm a bowler and I'm in the team to dismiss batsmen. That's what I'm paid to do."

Australia was endeavouring to win the Ashes for a record-breaking fifth consecutive time when the '97 series began. To counter the Warne menace, curators around England were urged to prepare greenish wickets suitable to seam and not spin.

While the form and renewed fitness of Glenn McGrath was crucial, key responsibility rested with Warne, the most experienced of a fledgling attack. "Everyone expects him to be a genius and take a wicket every ball," said newly-crowned vice-captain Steve Waugh.

With wife Simone expecting their first child in mid-tour, Warne was clearly distracted early and even toyed with the idea of returning briefly to Australia to be at the birth.

While he enjoyed some success at county level, his bowling disappointed at Edgbaston where he gained only marginal spin and England won easily, having seen Australia capitulate on the first morning.

When he was seen to be rubbing his shoulder in apparent discomfort, the English broadsheets questioned whether he'd have to have another operation at the end of the tour.

Asked by journalists what was different in 1997 compared with his previous Ashes campaign in 1993, he said, "About 10,000 overs and four years."

Mentally he was having problems setting himself for another gruelling series.

He'd received a lot of abuse in the first Test, too, the crowds sensing his frailty.

Unlike in 1993, when he bowled in tandem with the experienced Tim May, who did almost as well, Warne's spin partner, the left-handed Michael Bevan, struggled to find any of his Australian form and by July had been axed from the X1.

As if they needed the extra challenge, the Australians hit back superbly and after being denied victory at Lord's by inclement weather, won three Tests on end, at Old Trafford, Edgbaston and Trent Bridge to smother England's early hopes.

With 6-48 and 3-63 in the third Test on a dusty, pot-ridden pitch, Warne had been instrumental in squaring the series. The leg-break which ripped from the footprints and caught the edge of Alec Stewart's bat to be caught by Mark Taylor at slip was headlined in the *Mirror* as BALL FROM HELL II. A second headline screamed, WHO SAID THIS GUY IS FINISHED?

In answer to some jibes about his weight, Warne stood on the balcony, puffed out his stomach and raising a finger to the crowd. "I was just showing them the finger that did the damage," he said.

With three weeks in between the third and fourth Tests, he negotiated some time off and returned to Australia ever so briefly to see his wife and daughter before joining the tour again and celebrating the retention of the Ashes

While McGrath was again Australia's premier striker, relishing the wickets tailor-made for speed and seam, Warne had again been an undeniable frontliner. The Englishmen played him differently than in '93, enjoying the spinless tracks and playing shots against anything off-line. However, as they showed on the turner at Old Trafford, the old fears soon returned. Said Warne: "I can get wickets against these guys no matter how many videos they've watched or theories they've worked on. If the ball pitches around middle and leg and still turns, they are going to nick it."

Warne on the Fourth of July

(..who said this guy is finished)

BALL FROM HELL II

5-wicket Warne wrecks England

By MIKE WALTERS

SHANE WARNE conjured up the "Ball from Hell II" as England's worst Ashes nightmares came flooding back last night.

And Mike Atherton's men then walked into a blistering attack from coach David Lloyd after Warne sent them skidding to 181-8 at the close — 74 behind.

Lloyd accused his batsmen of "going down like a pack of cards".

Aussie spin-wizard Warne bamboozled Mike Gatting at Old Trafford four years ago — and he hit the bullseye with another monster

← Turn to Page 42

SUN, Tuesday, July 8, 1997

SunSport SunSport SunSport

I'VE GUT YOU BEAT

Warne belly laugh over England flop

By JOHN ETHERIDGE

SHANE WARNE got his own back on England — and had a real belly laugh about it.

The spin king took nine wickets in the match as Australia won the Third Test at Old Trafford by 268 runs.

And then he light-heartedly gave fans the bird after they taunted him about his weight.

Victory for Australia squared the six-match series at 1-1. But England skipper Mike Atherton reckons he will have the last laugh by regaining the Ashes.

Athers said: "We must hold up our hands — Australia outplayed us in this game.

"But I'm very confident we can bowl them out twice and win at least one of the last three Tests. Our mood is very optimistic. We have an extra week's break before the next

Turn to Page 39

HUGE SUCCESS .. Warne plays up to the crowd   Pictures: MARK TATTERSALL

FINGER OF FUN .. Warne's salute to fans

Headlines from the London tabloids, 1997 tour.

Shane Warne THE MAN & HIS RECORD

Born: September 13, 1969

Teams: Victoria & Australia

First-class debut: 1990-91

First-class record: Matches 109. Batting – Runs 1874, Average 15. 61, Highest score 74 not out, 50s 3. Bowling – Wickets 469, Average 24. 54, Best bowling 8-71, Five wickets in an Innings 20, Ten wickets in a Match 3. Fielding – Catches 67.

Test debut: 1991-92

Test record: Matches 58. Batting – Runs 1027, Average 14. 46, Highest score 74 not out, 50s 2. Bowling – Wickets 264, Average 23. 94, Best bowling 8-71, 5wl 11, 10wM 3. Fielding – Catches 42

One day international debut: 1992-93

One day international record: Matches 76. Batting – Runs 375, Average 12. 50, Highest score 55, 50s 1. Bowling – Wickets 129, Average 22. 17, Best bowling 5-33, 5wl 1. Fielding – Catches 25.

Tours: Zimbabwe 1991-92 (Australia B), Sri Lanka 1992-93; New Zealand 1992-93; England 1993 & 1997; South Africa 1993-94 & 1996-97; Sharjah 1993-94; Sri Lanka/Pakistan 1994-95; West Indies 1995; India/Pakistan (World Cup) 1996.

Sergio Dionisio

Shane Warne's Test record series by series:

BATTING & FIELDING

Season	Opponent	Mt	Inns	No	HS	Runs	Ave	50s	Ct.
1991-92	India (h)	2	4	1	20	28	9. 33	-	1
1992-93	Sri Lanka (a)	2	3	0	35	66	22. 00	-	1
	West Indies (h)	4	7	0	14	42	6. 00	-	3
	New Zealand (a)	3	4	2	22*	49	24. 50	-	1
1993	England (a)	6	5	2	37	113	37. 66	-	4
1993-94	New Zealand (h)	3	2	1	74*	85	85. 00	1	4
	South Africa (h)	3	4	1	11	16	5. 33	-	2
	South Africa (a)	3	5	0	15	41	8. 20	-	-
1994-95	Pakistan (a)	3	4	0	33	69	17. 25	-	2
	England (h)	5	10	1	36*	60	6. 66	-	5
1995	West Indies (a)	4	5	0	11	28	5. 60	-	2
1995-96	Pakistan (h)	3	4	1	27*	39	13. 00	-	1
	Sri Lanka (h)	3	1	0	33	33	33. 00	-	5
1996-97	West Indies (h)	5	7	0	30	128	18. 28	-	6
	South Africa (a)	3	5.	0	18	42	8. 40	-	3
1997	England (a)	6	6	0	53	188	18. 80	1	2
Totals		58	80	9	74*	1027	14. 46	2	42

BOWLING

Season	Opponent	Mts	Overs	Mds	Runs	Wicks	Ave	BB	5wl	10wM
1991-92	India (h)	2	68	9	228	1	228. 00	1-150	-	-
1992-93	Sri Lanka (a)	2	38. 1	8	158	3	52. 66	3-11	-	-
	West Indies (h)	4	108. 2	23	313	10	31. 30	7-52	1	-
	New Zealand (a)	3	159	73	256	17	15. 05	4-8	-	-
1993	England (a)	6	439. 5	178	877	34	25. 79	5-82	1	-
1993-94	New Zealand (h)	3	151. 3	49	305	18	16. 94	6-31	1	-
	South Africa (h)	3	175,1	63	307	18	17. 05	7-56	2	1
	South Africa (a)	3	190,5	69	336	15	22. 40	4-86	-	-
1994-95	Pakistan (a)	3	181,4	50	504	18	28. 00	6-136	2	-
	England (h)	5	256,1	84	549	27	20. 33	8-71	2	1
1995	West Indies (a)	4	138	35	406	15	27. 06	4-70	-	-
1995-96	Pakistan (h)	3	115	52	198	19	10. 42	7-23	1	1
	Sri Lanka (h)	3	164,4	43	433	12	36. 08	4-71	-	-

1996-97	West Indies (h)	5	217,1	57	594	22	27.00	4-95	-	-
	South Africa (a)	3	133	47	282	11	25.63	4-43		
1997	England (a)	6	237,1	69	577	24	24.04	6-48	1	-
Totals		58	2773,4	909	6323	264	23.94	8-71	11	3

COUNTRY BY COUNTRY RECORD

BATTING & FIELDING

Country	Mt	Inns	No	HS	Runs	Ave	50s	Ct.
v England	17	25	3	53	496	22.54	1	11
v India	2	4	1	20	28	9.33	-	1
v New Zealand	6	6	3	74*	134	44.66	1	5
v Pakistan	6	8	1	33	108	15.42	-	3
v South Africa	9	14	1	18	99	7.61	-	5
v Sri Lanka	5	4	0	35	99	24.75	-	6
v West Indies	13	19	0	30	198	10.42	-	11

HOME & ABROAD

	Mt	Inns	No	HS	Runs	Ave	50s	Ct.
Tests at home	28	39	5	74*	431	12.67	1	27
Tests abroad	30	41	4	53	596	16.05	1	15
Totals	58	80	9	74*	1027	14.46	2	42

BOWLING

Country	Mts	Overs	Mds	Runs	Wicks	Ave	BB	5wl	10wM
v England	17	933,1	331	2003	85	23.57	8-71	4	1
v India	2	68	9	228	1	228.00	1-150	-	-
v New Zealand	6	310,3	122	561	35	16.02	6-31	1	-
v Pakistan	6	296,4	102	702	37	18.97	7-23	3	1
v South Africa	9	499	179	925	44	21.02	4-43	-	-
v Sri Lanka	5	211,5	51	591	15	39.40	4-71	-	-
v West Indies	13	463,3	115	1313	47	27.93	7-52	1	-

HOME & ABROAD

	Mts	Overs	Mds	Runs	Wicks	Ave	BB	5wl	10wM
Tests at home	28	1256	380	2927	127	23.04	8-71	7	3
Tests abroad	30	1517,4	529	3396	137	24.78	6-136	4	-
Totals	58	2773,4	909	6323	264	23.95	8-71	11	3

HIS HIGHEST TEST SCORES

74*	v New Zealand, Brisbane, 1993-94
53	v England, Old Trafford, 1997
47	v England, Edgbaston, 1997
37	v England, The Oval, 1993
36*	v England, Sydney, 1994-95
35*	v England, Nottingham, 1993
35	v Sri Lanka, Colombo, 1992-93

HIS BEST TEST BOWLING

8-71	v England, Brisbane, 1994-95
7-23	v Pakistan, Brisbane, 1995-96
7-56	v South Africa, Sydney, 1993-94
7-52	v West Indies, Melbourne, 1992-93
6-31	v New Zealand, Hobart, 1993-94
6-48	v England, Old Trafford, 1997
6-64	v England, Melbourne, 1994-95
6-136	v Pakistan, Lahore, 1994-95

HIS HIGHEST ONE-DAY INTERNATIONAL SCORES

55	v South Africa, Port Elizabeth, 1993-94
30	v Pakistan, Colombo (PIS), 1994-95

HIS BEST ONE-DAY INTERNATIONAL BOWLING

5-33	v West Indies, Sydney, 1996-97
4-19	v New Zealand, Melbourne, 1993-94
4-25	v New Zealand, Adelaide, 1993-94
4-36	v South Africa, Port Elizabeth, 1993-94
4-36	v West Indies, Mohali, World Cup 1996
4-34	v New Zealand, Sharjah, 1993-94
4-34	v Zimbabwe, Nagpur, World Cup 1996
4-37	v Pakistan, Sydney, 1996-97
4-40	v South Africa, Faisalabad, 1994-95
4-52	v Pakistan, Adelaide, 1996-97

THE
ASSASSIN

"They said I was a killer with the ball. They didn't take into account that Bradman with a bat was the greatest killer of all." – Harold Larwood.

In an emotion-charged career which rewrote the record books, Don Bradman changed the laws of the game and established him, beyond argument, as the greatest batsman of them all. But there was a darker side that created enmity. Was he a career wrecker? Was he the power behind savage reprisals on Australian heroes?

ENGLAND – THE OVAL – fifth Test – final day, August 1930. Was this cricket? Or was it game hunting! Gathered behind the back of the small, lightly framed Australian was a flock of vultures, mouths drooling for the spoils of the kill.

Sweeping towards the victim was a lithe young animal, superbly balanced, gaining greater momentum with every step – the long-striding limbs a blur of symmetry as the speed demon made a final spring and unleashed a 100 mph thunderbolt.

The rock hard missile crashed into the treacherous pitch, well short of the Australian whose only defence was a shaft of willow. The ball reared off the turf and whipped at frightening speed at the unprotected head of the intended victim. He jumped high and the ball caught him just above the heart.

The batsman winced, grimaced with pain and took block again.

Harold Larwood gave that leather coated grenade a rub on his flannels and charged in again. Another thunderbolt flying at the head. A gimlet eye and incredible reflexes saw the head flick away from the flight path to allow the orb to rocket into the diving left glove of the English wicketkeeper. The Notts miner walked back to his mark and smiled at his captain, "He didn't like that one little bit."

BRADMAN A WILDMAN?

Sir Donald Bradman was too focused an athlete, too proud of his capacities and too resolute an opponent to have gone through life without enemies. Jealousy was undoubtedly his greatest enemy.

No matter how hard they fought the green-eyed master, great players were racked by jealousy and reduced to a standard of behaviour and resentment that made them dislike themselves and hate Bradman for the lowering of their self esteem as sportsmen and performers.

With vicious back biting, questionable playing ethic and subversive articles they created an image that Sir Donald clearly resented. History has remedied the injustice. Longevity has been Sir Don's ally. He has out-lived his detractors and all that remains are those who admire him for his accomplishments and his impeccable lifestyle. As in the playing field Sir Donald Bradman has batted through the innings and left his enemy at his feet.

Before Sir Donald Bradman ascended to the throne as undisputed monarch of all things cricket, he went through the fires of hell. He was central to the greatest storms the great game has endured.

Bradman wasn't a chest thumping, hairy extrovert of the Ian Botham mould. He was not a wild man in a theatrical sense – far from it. He has his place in Wildmen of Cricket folklore because he made his opponents wild; he made his own players wild and he made nations wild. He created the stormiest scenes in sport and dominated the wildest years of the game. Sir Donald slew his enemy with a flailing willow that had no edges.

Don did more than destroy the souls of the world's greatest bowlers; he also humbled nations and destroyed their self esteem. Great players hated him because he caused them to discard sportsmanship and make cheats out of champions.

Bradman was not to blame for Bodyline but he caused it. This embarrassed the pompous English autocrats who believed they ruled the game. They preached fair play and the spirit of "play up, play up and play the game." But in the end winning was more important to them. They resorted to tactics which destroyed the fabric of England's character – and all England hated Bradman for it.

They were suitably ashamed but angered that a single colonial could reduce them to shoddy practices. The austere Douglas Jardine was their instrument and a lowly Nottingham miner their scapegoat. Harold Larwood rose above the disgrace to win back world respect. Jardine never did.

The boy from Bowral was involved in more than the dreadful Bodyline saga – he had his own fights with cricket bureaucracy that threatened to terminate his career. He bucked the system and won. He was up to his neck in the chucking controversy when he intervened to restore honesty and credibility to the game. You don't clean out a game without making enemies and controversy. He served as Australia's head national selector and a member of cricket's Board of Control. Because he was Bradman he was seen as the absolute authority and when great players like Sid Barnes, Keith Miller, Ian Meckiff and their like were banished from the international scene, Bradman was blamed.

It is this side of the Bradman story we reveal in this publication and leave it to the reader to form their own opinions. We do not challenge his greatness nor his integrity. For we, too, believe Sir Donald Bradman is the greatest Australian of them all – he is our hero, too. There can be no question that whatever Sir Donald did in his cricketing life he did it for the well being of cricket and the benefit of the nation. Nor should any man be decried for pursuing his personal goals with unrelenting focus.

Welcome to Bodyline, Don Bradman. Little did The Don know, the worst was yet to come.

Larwood had been probing for a weakness, he thought he spotted one. He was a proud man and had no intention of being belted out of international cricket by the diminutive Australian.

This was England 1930. Bradman had been the hero of a magnificent Australian Ashes triumph. Larwood had a mixed series against the Aussies as he came into the fifth Test at The Oval. Having taken 2-21 in the first Test, he missed the Second with tonsillitis and returned for the Third to be battered by Bradman.

Bradman made 334 while Larwood took 1-139. He was infuriated. "I had him out for nought, caught behind. He was palpably out. Even the fairest of cricketers Jack Hobbs said he was out. The umpire said otherwise and instead of having the Aussies 2-1 he went on to make 334 and cost me my place in the fourth Test."

Larwood believed Bradman should have walked and a great enmity was born.

Larwood was reinstated for the Fifth and took another pasting (1- 132) but late in the Australian innings the weather turned dirty and transformed the pitch into a death-trap. The ball was flying viciously. Remember these were the days of uncovered pitches. Larwood hit both Bradman and Archie Jackson about the body with vicious deliveries.

"Archie Jackson and Bradman were batting and putting together a fantastic partnership when conditions changed. I had the ball flying around their chest and shoulders. I decided to give it everything I had. I pinked Archie a few times. He took it like a man and played the game of his life." He thought Bradman showed fear. "Don was a cruel man," he said. "He was cruel the way he flogged you. Nobody had any real idea of what he was like. Good length stuff he jumped down the pitch too – it went to the boundary like a rocket. He didn't break my heart in 1930, he just made me so very, very tired."

Larwood said he departed that Ashes losing Test with terrible figures but having claimed Bradman's wicket at 232. Bradman said he wasn't out, Larwood thought he was. It was small consolation for the earlier time he "knew" Bradman was out for 0 and The Don went on to a world record Test score of 334. Bradman won one, lost one with the umpires and finished with 568 runs for the two hands. Larwood had bowling figures of 2-271.

"It hadn't occurred to me that Don didn't like ball rising at his midriff. I'd always concentrated on putting the ball up to him – this was something to think about."

Larwood had four years to think about it and during those four years he had a talk with the man in the Harlequin cap – Douglas Robert Jardine.

Jardine made a study of Bradman. There was no fair way to get the man out – not fair within the spirit of the game. But to Jardine the spirit of the game was to win, no matter how. Harold Larwood was his vehicle. A little Notts miner with big, rough hands but the fluent, superbly-balanced run of a cheetah. A smooth, rolling swing of the hip and upper torso that was poetry itself. Quite the most devastating fast bowler the world had seen.

Used injudiciously, Larwood was a potential lethal weapon. Used fairly, he was a devastating bowler who could have rewritten the record books. It was a tragedy that in his obsession to destroy Bradman, Jardine destroyed Larwood and deprived the world of a classic head-to-head confrontation between the world's best batsman and greatest bowler.

Larwood said Bill Voce was the first to give Bodyline a thorough trial. It was in a county match against Somerset. "He felled an amateur named Cecil Case with a flier. Case dropped his bat. He was so groggy when he staggered off the field he walked off with the stump instead of his bat."

Jardine spent several years perfecting a bowling strategy that was designed to shatter the morale of Australia's wonder batsman. Jardine's secret weapon was dissembled after a few trial runs in England before being launched for one bitter series before it was outlawed.

Don Bradman returned from that triumphant 1930 tour a national hero – little did he know what the immediate future held for him. At that stage he could only marvel at how so much had been accomplished in so few years.

Unlike Superman, the extraordinary personality that was Don Bradman did not arrive as a meteor from outer space. Nor did any enemy power ever find the kryptonite weakness in his make-up although the supposed evil genius that was Douglas Jardine thought he had found such a weapon.

For a time it seemed Jardine had succeeded but the Superboy from Bowral responded as all super heroes do. He finally triumphed over the evil and restored the game to the Australian way. He simply used a slender slither of willow and super vision to thrash the enemy out of the attack.

Donald George Bradman was actually born at Cootamundra on August 27, 1908 at the time Dr. W. G. Grace elected to put his beard in curlers and retire. Don was the youngest of the Bradmans, his parents George and Emily of English "Bradnam" stock had three daughters and two sons. Don who was to become famed as the Boy from Bowral was saved from becoming the Coot from Cootamundra by a switch of residency to Bowral – aged three. Bowral then had a population of 1751.

The Bradman homestead was isolated and much too far from civilisation for the youngster to have regular playmates, his brother Victor was four years older and not inclined to join his kid brother in childish games. There was no radio, let alone television. Totally isolated and without suitable playmates, young Donald improvised. He had the best opposition in the world – himself.

On the other side of that world, a lad eight years his senior and infinitely better placed to be a cricketer was crisply stroking a ball to the Oxford boundary. A haughty young Englishman named Douglas Robert Jardine, son of former Oxford captain Malcolm Robert Jardine.

The young Jardine went about fulfilling his sporting destiny, blissfully unaware many, many miles away, on an isolated Australian farm was a ragamuffin (by Jardine standards) kid throwing a golf ball against a corrugated water tank, striking the flying and erratic rebounds with a cricket stump. This developed his wonderful footwork. The child's eye and timing was uncanny. His patience boundless as he perfected his skills hour after hour, day after day, month after month.

When he had sweetly struck the ball time after time with scarcely a miss, he would move on to his fielding, hurling the golf ball, sometimes a tennis ball, at an uneven fence and taking super catches as the ball flew off at varying speed and at all conceivable tangents. If it was within diving reach he claimed the catch every time, if it flew wide he tried to chase it down before it stopped.

By the time he was nine he graduated to a kerosene tin in the backyard and upon arrival home from school he would call on his mother to trundle down her left-arm slow-mediums. He also found time to become an accomplished pianist, an attribute he retained throughout his sporting and business career.

His father was a carpenter who played cricket and did work for Alf Stephens the Bowral Mayor, builder and captain – president of the Bowral Town Cricket Club.

Bowral could not provide him with cricket competition as he reached his mid-teens and this became a crisis time in his sporting career. He turned his hand to tennis with considerable success. Aged 15 and 16 Bradman could have changed direction for Wimbledon. He was a more than useful rugby player, a fine sprinter and with that eye an excellent marksman. Later in life he was a long hitting and accomplished golfer on scratch. He was always going to be great at something.

Fortunately for posterity he got back on the cricket trail when he turned 16 and joined the Bowral senior team with great effect. His first hand was a 66 not out. Aged 17 he was introduced to turf wickets in 1925 and immediately met up with a promising young bowler playing for the neighboring Wingello district – Bill "Tiger" O'Reilly, then 19.

Bradman scored 234 not out. O'Reilly was livid. "My captain dropped him off me twice in slips before he reached 30," he snorted. O'Reilly was still bemused that such a pocket-sized individual could give him such a lacing. When the game resumed the next week, O'Reilly ended the Bradman innings first ball.

We move swiftly through those foundation years noting that young Don Bradman swept and hooked all before him as a cricketing prodigy. Bradman made a couple of other centuries for Bowral that season 105 and 120 and a triple century; averaging 101.3 for the season. Now superior forces moved him to the Sydney domestic competition where he joined St. George and made 37 not out in a state trial – this didn't get him a state cap but he was trembling on the brink of bigger things.

A century for Combined Country was enough to put him in the NSW state second X1 against Victoria. He top scored with 63 and later made 320 as an opening bat for Bowral in the competition final against Moss Vale. The batting holocaust was well and truly launched.

Selection for the senior state team followed. His first season of serious first-class cricket, 1927-28, saw him launch a spectacular attack on Australian bowling legend Clarrie Grimmett. Surprising strength in one so supple took Grimmett by surprise. Confident front foot stroke play rifled the ball to the boundaries – the sharp, crisp echo of the cracking bat sounded a 22 gun salute. The dashing 118 against South Australia ended caught Norm Williams bowled Jack Scott. Grimmett picked him up in the second innings for 33, clean bowled.

The young prodigy was an automatic selection in the opening first-class game of the 1928-29 season. An Australian X1 opposed to The Rest was a preview of the Australian team to contest the Ashes series with the MCC team which toured Australia under "Percy" Chapman. Don, playing for The Rest, had a demoralising start to his international aspirations when he fell for 14 and 5 to the Australian X1.

Never one to tuck his tail between his legs, Bradman struck back with centuries in each innings against Queensland, 131 and 133 not out. NSW played the MCC and his first meeting with Maurice Tate and Larwood produced 87 and 132 not out. If the Australian selectors didn't realise an extraordinary phenomenon was unfolding before them they would be completely lacking in perception. The MCC made 7-734 and when Bradman went to bat NSW was 3-24. He saw out a desperate period to stumps and next day batted defiantly for 87 before being clean bowled by "Tich" Freeman. After he made a defiant 133 not out in the second dig, Walter Hammond was more than impressed and declared the youngster gave the air of being able to "bat forever."

It was no surprise he was included in an Australian X1 to face the MCC. Hands of 58 not out and 18 followed. That was enough to seal his place for his first Test against England, this being the first played in Brisbane. England amassed a big first innings before Australia batted and collapsed, they were 5-71 when he took block. He struck four superb boundaries before Tate nabbed him lbw at 18 with his slow ball. The youngster picked up just one run in his second hand on a sticky wicket.

England won by 675 runs and he was dumped to 12th man, setting a fierce resolve in the young man that the Poms would suffer damnation for this humiliation. Australia was trounced again in the second Test. Recalled for the Third after a brave 71 not out against Victoria, Bradman was grimly resolved to show the selectors his mettle – which he did with free wheeling hands of 79 and 112. Australia lost the Test and the series but it was clearly not young Don's fault.

He celebrated his second and permanent coming to the Australian team with a scintillating 340 not out for NSW against Victoria. The triple century, apart from being a state record, was so breathtaking in its quality that Bradman was elevated to immediate hero status the length and breadth of the land.

The Don was now well and truly founded in international cricket and giving England considerable cause for pause as he played the fourth Test and lost his wicket at 40 to a catch by Larwood off the veteran Tate.

The remaining two Tests saw him score 40 and run out for 58 in Adelaide; 123 and 37 not out in Melbourne as he steered the Aussies to victory. The MCC team went home with the Ashes and an uncomfortable foreboding about the new Aussie batting colossus. A batsman who had rewritten Australian records with 1690 in the season at an average of 93.88.

A colossus who stood less than 170 cm tall.

A boy just emerging from the bush was about to face his demons and few men have been confronted by so many demons, many from within his own ranks.

The 1929-30 season was almost an anti-climax as Australia played a domestic season without visitation. There was an early excursion by the MCC en route to New Zealand and he welcomed their brief visit with a sparkling season opening of 157 and followed this with 124 and 225 in an Australian trial match. Before anybody realised it, he had passed 500 runs in his first two matches of the season. The rest of the season was occupied with Shield cricket and he relieved the tedium by belting a second innings world record 452 not out against Queensland. The 400 came up in 377 minutes. The Queenslanders chaired him off the field when Alan Kippax declared the NSW innings closed, one assumes they wanted to make sure he left.

He had another 139 in an Australian X1 against Tasmania to wind up that season with an average of 113.28 and Australia was agog at the prospects as the Australian team headed to England to launch 1930 challenge for the Ashes.

Automatically selected for the English tour, he was embarking on his first overseas adventure and the Poms were waiting for him on and off the field. He signed his first touring contract and there was a clause that prohibited the tourists, Bradman included, from writing or commentating on the tour. In exchange, he received a tour payment of 600 pounds; a king's ransom as Australia and the world was in the grip of a devastating depression.

The Australians boarded the *Orford* in Perth and the great adventure began. The Don was soon embroiled in his first controversy. A literary agent persuaded him to write a book which Bradman said could not be published until he returned to Australia, as per his contract. Not a young man to involve himself unduly in the social swirl of the tour, he spent a considerable amount of his spare time writing the book.

The first tour match for the Australians was against Worcestershire and the county side surrendered for a meek 131. Bradman was soon at the wicket and on foreign soil took his time to study bounce, atmosphere, ball movement and every other peculiarity that set the English turf and atmosphere apart from Australian. He and Bill Woodfull scored centuries. Bradman went on to score 236 the first double-century by an Australian on debut. That was food for thought for the home team and their media. Next match he had another 185 not out against Leicester before the game was rained out. His average was 421 when he went to Yorkshire for the third match of tour and by the time he scored 78 he was in the unique position of needing just one run to bring up 500 runs and no matter how briefly an average of 500. Instead he was caught and bowled by Macaulay and his average plummeted … to 249.5!

His batting over the next three tour games was not quite so spectacular but he threw aside the modest 40s and 60s to slam 252 not out against Surrey and 191 against Hampshire and went in to bat against Hampshire on May 31 needing 46 runs to become the first tourist to amass 1000 runs before the end of May. There was some media criticism that when Bradman was on 38 it literally bucketed rain. Hampshire captain, The Hon. Lionel Tennyson kept his team on the ground in torrential rain to ensure Bradman was not robbed of the record. He belted the two fours and the fieldsmen sprinted for the pavilion.

All England knew this nightmare was here for the long haul. The cricket buffs searched for flaws in his make-up. They picked at his technique and questioned his ability on all types of wickets. Yet at the end of the day the truth was undeniable; he was the greatest striker of the ball the game had produced. His eye was uncanny, his timing supreme and his aggression allowed him to dominate all bowlers.

The *Daily Chronicle* declared the beauty of Bradman was "his use of the bat as a weapon of offence."

He was ready for the first Test. The English scribes while marvelling at the class of Bradman doubted the rest of the Australians contributed sufficient menace as to cause any great concern for the future of the Ashes. They suggested only Bradman and Clarrie Grimmett could find a place in the English team.

England was a raging favorite for the first Test. Sadly for the Poms, Grimmett played with Australia and wrecked the English first innings to have them 8-241 at stumps. After mopping up the tail next day for 270, the Australians went to bat and The Don was tumbled out by Tate for eight in a dismal Aussie batting collapse for 144. England was jubilant. The home side batted late into the third day to amass a huge lead.

In the second innings, Bradman went to the crease at 1-12 and accelerated to 31 in the first 35 minutes. He became the first Australian to score a century at Trent Bridge. He partnered Stan McCabe through the crisis and batted Australia to a position of needing 200 runs from the last seven wickets.

McCabe went to a brilliant catch and when Bradman fell at 131, Australia's resistance crumbled and it was beaten by 93. The Australians had to regroup for the second Test which was quickly upon them.

Playing at Lord's is the ambition of every batsman and the ultimate is to hit a century at your first Test appearance on the sacred ground. There was consternation when the Australians lined up to meet the Duke of York, who was to become King George V. No sign of Don Bradman. The future king was all but forgotten as panic set in and couriers flew hither and thither. Archie Jackson was told to strip to take Bradman's place. All of a sudden The Don arrived and there was a football roar of approval – he had slept in. That wasn't his first royal indiscretion; he was later to be damned by the English press for strolling with the King with his hands in his pockets.

Woodfull won the toss and sent England in. It was 9-405 at stumps and it seemed the Ashes were destined to stay in England. The one man being compared with Bradman made 173 – Kumar Shri Duleepsinhji. Known as "Ranji," he had scored 2124 runs to that stage of the season as against Bradman's 2156. The Don's average was 102.66. Ranji boasted 68. 51 but was more prone to sacrifice his wicket when the job was done. Bradman made the supreme effort to catch him on 173.

Australia's openers Woodfull and Bill Ponsford got the Aussies away to a magnificent start. They had 162 on the board when play was interrupted. Bradman was available to meet up with royalty this time as King George V visited Lord's during the game and shook hands with the players. His timing was superb for England. With concentration broken by His Majesty, the partnership was immediately broken. Bradman strode briskly to the wicket. He was in the mood for the challenge.

First ball he strode down the wicket to Jack White to get off the mark. He gave a spellbinding display of dancing footwork that took him to the pitch of every ball that fell short of the popping crease. With long backlift, superb stroking and a flowing follow through he gave a performance of such artistry that the English crowd willed him to keep his wicket.

He didn't batter or belt the bowling. He stroked it and whipped it as he drove Tate, Gubby Allen, White, Walter Robins and Hammond to all angles of the ground. He joined Ponsford at 3.30 p.m and was still there at stumps on 155. Next day he proceeded purposefully towards the Anglo-Australian record of "Tip" Foster – 287 in 1903. He was in total charge until Chapman took a diving left handed catch at extra cover to close the great hand at 254. Not only was it the best catch he'd ever seen, Don believed it was the best hand he ever played.

Chapman again caught Bradman brilliantly in the second innings, for just one. Australia levelled the series with a seven wicket win. Now it was on to the third Test.

England had never been so caught up in a sporting event; nor had Australia. The telegraph system was wiring instant match updates of the match to Australia where radio commentators simulated "live" reports. Woodfull again won the toss, this time he batted and the luckless Jackson who had lost his mantle as Australia's greatest batting prodigy was out fifth ball, caught Larwood bowled Tate.

Bradman was facing the fire early at 1- 2. Larwood delivered a blistering in-swinger. There was an immediate roar for an lbw – very close that one, but not out. Larwood thought otherwise.

The ball did not put The Don in awe of the bowler. Instead he crisply smacked subsequent deliveries to all parts of the field. The rabid English spectators could do nothing but marvel at the fluency of the great man's stroke play. He struck the ball with a batting rhythm not unlike the flowing strike of the greatest international golfers. It was unheard of in most forms of cricket let alone the first day of Ashes Test when a wicket has fallen in the first over. But then Bradman could do things nobody had ever heard of – he struck a withering hundred before lunch. Woodfull was out at 92.

Kippax and Bradman stayed together and at tea Bradman was 220 not out. Another century in a session. And off the last ball of the day he took his score to 309 in a day's play and his 2000 runs for the tour. It was the highest individual score by any batsman in a single day of Test cricket. He took his score to 334 next morning before falling to a catch behind off Tate.

What an ovation he received from the English crowd! The English players could only glower. There was a rich reward, too, waiting in the pavilion. An Australian businessman, Arthur Whitelaw, now settled in England, gave him a 1000 pound bonus in recognition of his feat. That was more than enough money to buy a quality home in depression-torn Australia.

Great as that innings was there were those who thought the highlight of the Test was Bradman throwing down Jack Hobbs' wicket and seemingly setting Australia on the way to an important victory. Rain intervened to save England and the match was drawn.

No celebrations for The Don. When the game was done Bradman simply retired from view to listen to classical music in his hotel room. His own players were critical of his refusal to interact with them away from the field.

They were reported to regard his retiring nature as snobbish, even elitism. There was a reaction to the media obsession and were particularly offended by posters and banner headlines suggesting it was Bradman alone playing the English. It was a media insensitivity beyond the young man's control but some of the ensuing jealousies and personal criticisms could have been curtailed had he been a more social animal and better mixer with his fellow players.

Bradman replied to his critics in his book *Farewell to Cricket*: "I was often accused of being unsociable, though I fear the charge was applied in a very loose sense. In substance it boiled down to my dislike of artificiality and publicity."

He added, "I did not think it my duty to breast the bar and engage in a beer drinking contest. I made no attempt to interfere with others." He said he had as much right as others to pursue his own interests.

"I well remember being accused of snobbery because in the evening following my world's record batting score, I stayed in my room listening to music. Was I expected to parade the streets of Leeds?"

He continued, "Any exceptional performance makes great demands upon the physical and nervous resources of the performer. Some people try to overcome the resultant fatigue by the use of stimulants – others by seeking counter excitement. I always obtained the best results by seeking quietness. Music is a tonic to the jaded nerves....."

The Don was quite right of course. You are either one of the boys or you are not. Who could argue his right as a virtual non-drinker to shun the boisterous after match festivities to wind down as best suited his own metabolism. The feeling prevailed that he took his isolationism much too far. Cricket is essentially a team sport and requires a considerable contribution of self- sacrifice to the common cause. Perhaps more so when captain than a younger member of the team. At this stage Don was not yet 22.

He became the first player in history to record centuries in four successive Tests.

Australia was moral leader of the series but went to Old Trafford for the fourth Test on level footing. This was regarded as the ultimate showdown for the two teams. Woodfull, as was his custom, won the toss. He batted and opened the innings with Ponsford. Although the wicket was cutting up from the first over they staged a grand partnership of 107 before Woodfull went. England had introduced Scotsman Ian Peebles into its attack and he had Bradman caught for only 14, prompting an English newspaper poster, HE'S OUT.

It was a great Test for the Australians morale. Without a contribution from Bradman, they battled hard to register 345 against a revitalised English attack. Rain again intervened and after a number of interruptions Australia was in the driver's seat having them 8-251 but the weather forced another draw and now Australia had to win the fifth Test to regain the Ashes.

Not the time for the world to open beneath The Don's feet. In those much-criticised private musings he had been writing his book. He delivered some chapters to the literary agent before the tour clash with Glamorgan. The agent, being an opportunist, had a winner on his hands in light of the great feats Bradman had performed on this tour, and had no difficulty selling the serial rights to the *London Star.* The first article was published on August 4 and was to cause the first of the great Bradman storms. Hitherto his headlines, although innumerable, were focused on the genius of his batting.

That was about to change. The fifth Test was at hand and for a change the weather was fine as the Australians arrived in London for the deciding battle for the Ashes at The

Oval. Bob Wyatt replaced Chapman as captain and at least won the toss and batted. A draw was sufficient for the English and they were very patient in compiling 405 with an ultra-cautious contribution of 161 from Sutcliffe.

Australia had to go on the attack and the Aussie openers Woodfull and Ponsford laid into the English bowling with murderous intent. It was 1-159 when Bradman joined Ponsford. Rain again brought proceedings to a halt. When play resumed next day Bradman went after the bowling between showers and Australia was 3-403 at the end of the day.

The wicket had degenerated and the ball was rearing. Larwood resumed the next day with some vicious bowling, short of a length and rearing dangerously at Bradman and Jackson. They were struck repeatedly and Larwood sensed a human weakness in Bradman. He saw the unflappable batsman grimace and wince in pain when hit near the heart. One English newspaper group reported spectators had tears in their eyes watching the assault. The young batsmen dug deep and kept the run flow going. Bradman brought up his double century as he added 98 in the morning session. He was finally out for 232, caught by George Duckworth off Larwood. The ball had flicked his shirt not his bat.

Bradman had won that battle but Larwood had come to a conclusion which was to bring forth bloodcurdling headlines and drive a wedge between the relationship of the two countries. A rift that would never be fully repaired. Bradman walked back to the pavilion knowing he was wrongfully dismissed but concealing the anger and pain of a body and mind racked with pain. He had taken one bad blow in the chest from Larwood and had a torso bruised and battered by the short pitched bowling. Jackson was no less wounded.

Australia's Percy Hornibrook ripped through the English batsmen for match figures of 7-92 and despite the rain interruptions England was out for 251. Australia had stormed to victory and regained the Ashes. Now the English selectors tormented by a carping local press and daunted by the invincibility of Bradman, decided to find a new leader and a more determined policy to tear the Ashes back from the colonials. They knew they had to do something to stop the flow of The Don who finished the tour with 2960 runs at 98.66 just 40 runs short of a century average.

Bradman didn't know it but war had been declared and he was the target. Cricket would never be the same again.

While the Australians had been on tour a mighty chestnut racehorse had carried the burden for them. Phar Lap and Bradman were the heroes of the nation and no amount of modesty or sensitivity could stop that.

Sensitivity wasn't in evidence when tour manager William Kelly made his tour report alleging The Don had breached his contract in publishing extracts of *Don Bradman's Book* while on tour. Bradman argued the section published was about his early life, whereas his contract precluded him from publishing anything about the tour. Nothing was published about the tour until the tour was over. Kelly was not the most diplomatic of tour officials and his report was petty in the extreme.

The Board of Control's decision making was petty and bureaucratic. They fined Bradman 50 pounds which made a small dent in his tour payment.

Fame had its price. Australia had never turned on such a display of affection for one individual. Everywhere he went he was swamped by crowds and the demand on his services for parades, public addresses, autograph sessions and special appearances was overwhelming. He was said to have hated every minute of it but the financial yield from all the promotion and publicity was to set him up for life. All the time the resentment of teammates intensified.

The English press made a welter of Bradman "stealing the thunder and plunder" of his mates. When the Bradman book controversy broke, they made a feast of it. Bradman was harvesting a fortune in benefits and the players who contributed heavily to the cause were being scorned. They received no fringe benefits and in the midst of depression this rankled even more. His fortunes were enhanced with major deals including a lucrative bat sponsorship with the Mick Simmons company and another deal on cricket boots. He stitched up a radio contract and in times of dark depression with his fellow players struggling for financial survival, the Bradman haul bordered on the obscene.

The wall between players and the star grew as some players spoke against him saying he had not shared in his new wealth with the team in any way. "He didn't even shout a round of drinks," said one. Soon the press was being fed stories of aloofness on the tour and not being part of the team fabric. "He wasn't one of us," they claimed.

The domestic season and a tour by the West Indies enabled the players to take out their frustrations on the field. Bradman became something of a cricket elitist as he spent his summer almost entirely focused on the internationals, playing his six matches against the tourists before finishing the season off with Sheffield Shield games against South Australian and Victoria. After the run feast in England his early performances were modest and his first Test performance an abysmal four runs.

The embarrassment of a static, careless performance in the Test recharged the batteries and he teamed with Jackson in a spectacular partnership against South Australia. Bradman struck a devastating 258 but he still could not strike it against the West Indies, making only 25 in the second Test. The Australian selectors had little concern as the Aussies cruised through the first two Tests proving they were an indomitable force even without The Don. That established, he proceeded to have his revenge on the Windies with 223 in the third Test, the double century being compiled in 251 minutes. He blazed 152 in the fourth Test again striking a century in the morning session. He had no need to bat a second time in any of the first four Test matches.

Don racked up a dashing 220 against Victoria in a run orgy that made him the first Australians batsman to exceed the 1000 runs in three domestic seasons. The fifth Test was an anti-climax with 43 and a duck, the first of his Test career. Late in the season he broke an ankle in Rockhampton and was in plaster for three months.

The calm before the storm prevailed while Bradman coped with the crisis over his book and isolation from his teammates. The South Africans toured Australia in 1931-32 as the spread of the Great Depression saw Australia remain at home for four years. Don was in love with the stunningly-attractive Jessie Menzies, a charming young lady with all the breeding and character integrity for which Bradman was acclaimed. They were the perfect couple and planned marriage. First they contemplated the future and agreed neither of them wanted to live in the turmoil of public and media intrusion that had marked the previous years. He was 22 and the broken ankle cautioned him that the end could be but a twist of fate away.

English Lancashire League cricket had cast its covetous eye on the skills of Bradman and made several monumental offers which further fanned the controversy of his putting money ahead of Australia although he rejected the offers.

While he pondered the problem he had dominated the Australian season. He batted the South Africans to oblivion with hands of 226, 112, 167 and 299 not out in four successive Tests. He batted five times to finish with a world record average of 201.5 for a series. He scored two other centuries against the South Africans, too, for NSW, again amassing well over the 1000 runs in a domestic season although he played only nine games. This included just four Shield games for a remarkable symmetry in scoring 0, 23,

167, 23, 0. That first duck came at the hands of aboriginal bowler Eddie Gilbert who bowled so fast that he smashed the bat out of Bradman's hand before having him caught.

Bradman said Gilbert's burst was faster than anything he had seen, Larwood included. Keith Miller was to comment later in the Bradman career that The Don had a weakness for declaring balls that claimed his wicket as the best ever bowled. Gilbert was to have a tragic career being called for chucking and snubbed by Australian selectors. Bradman said, "If he did not actually throw the ball then he certainly jerked it."

All England was in awe as Bradman went into recess to await the arrival of the Jardine-led MCC. He was about to face his greatest demon and cricket its darkest and most evil times.

Don Bradman looked at the list of English players named to tour Australia and made the observation, "A bumper attack seems imminent." The selection of Douglas Jardine as captain did not set off any alarm bells. Jardine was of public school stock, a lawyer and a strange man with strong beliefs. He was a student of mysticism and eastern philosophy and was a religious sceptic. Which made it easier for him to do what he had to do.

A few months earlier, English cricket authorities had sounded him out as a potential skipper of the Australian tour. They knew he was cold, calculating and ruthless. Bradman was the prime target but not the only target. To regain the Ashes he knew he had to break the back of the most formidable batting array the game had seen – Bill Woodfull, Bill Ponsford, Victor Richardson, Stan McCabe and Jack Fingleton. The aristocracy of world batting.

He conferred with former English pace bowler Frank Foster and they evolved the bowling strategy and field placements that were to shame their nation. Foster says he warned Jardine to direct fast bowling at the batsman was dangerous. No left-arm bowler should ever bowl legside theory, particularly over the stumps, because of the grave danger to batsmen. Harold Larwood and Bill Bowes were right-arm bowlers and Bill Voce a leftie.

Before he could turn loose his artillery they had to get Bradman to the wicket. The Australian Board of Control ordered him not to continue his writing career.

The regulations were clear cut, warned the Board. If he insisted on writing he would be ineligible for selection for the Ashes challenge. Bradman was defiant, "I will stick to my contract. If the Board will not allow me to carry out my contract then I will not be available for Test cricket."

The Board members were in the unenviable position of being losers whichever way they went. Moral cowards or stubborn fools. The controversy raged while Bradman greeted Jardine playing for the Combined Australian X1 against the MCC in Perth. Caught on the worst of sticky wickets Bradman succumbed for 3 and 10.

Jardine had no need to unleash the secret weapon he had trialed at various English county venues. His volcanic fire power remained plugged for then.

Smarting from that reversal Bradman made Victoria pay in the Sheffield Shield season opener. He hammered 238 in the first innings and 52 not out in the second. That put Australian minds to rest as he struck the first 100 in just 73 minutes. Then it was England again as an Australian X1 faced the MCC on the MCG. Bradman was in superb touch. The touring English press and their Australian counterparts didn't realise what was unfolding.

Bradman did. November 18, 1932 was the day Jardine and Larwood unveiled their secret weapon, one of those days that "live in infamy." The dress rehearsal of the real

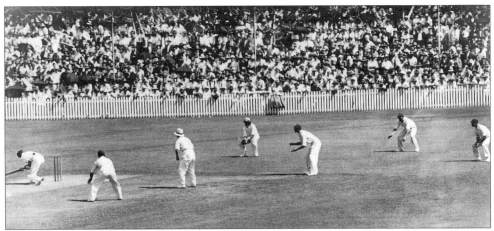

Bill Woodfull is struck during the infamous Bodyline series. With five close-in fieldsmen on the leg-side and several more patrolling the boundary, any sort of leg-side shot was hazardous.

thing. It was the Pearl Harbour of sport. A sneak attack unlike any other ever experienced in the noble game of cricket. Even the bible deplored it – the words of *Wisden* lashed out as the tour degenerated into a vicious blood-letting, venom-spitting feud that enraged both nations. All English sporting traditions went out the door.

When Jardine and Voce packed most of their fieldsmen in an intimidating circle of catching positions on the legside there was an uneasy hush in the Australian rooms. There was a muttering and stirring in the crowd as they sensed a bold new English fielding strategy was about to be unveiled. Little did they suspect the fastest and most menacing bowlers in the world were going to ignore the three upright stumps and direct their attack at the player not the wicket.

Not only would they bowl in the line of the body – "Bodyline" – but they would also pitch the ball so short that it reared directly at the chest, shoulders and heads of the batsmen. "We saved ourselves for this match because we wanted to get Don in strong company before giving him the full blast of our fast leg theory tactic," admitted Larwood.

Jardine hit the Australian X1 with the full force of his pace attack. He revealed why he had brought four speedsters to Australia as he flung all four against the Aussies and set the leg trap to the most fierce and menacing eight ball overs cricket had seen. Larwood admitted he pulled out all stops and delivered two vicious bouncers and a barrage of other short-pitched balls at the batsman in every over. The legside field was stacked with "catchers."

Larwood was delighted with what unfolded. "It was a refreshing sight to see Bradman clumsily waving his bat in the air. Bradman and Woodfull were out to strokes foreign to them." Larwood got The Don both innings, lbw for 36 and bowled for 13. Yet it is worth noting The Don had not holed out to the legside field. The English media was delighted and the *Evening Standard* told its readers, "The problem of Bradman has been solved."

Bradman knew the game was heading for crisis. He spoke to Victorian Cricket Association officials about the unorthodox tactics and predicted problems ahead unless there was some official intervention. But administrators declared the tactics acceptable under the prevailing rules. Larwood said, "I knew I had Don on the run."

The English speedster did note that very early in his counter attack, Bradman removed his body from the line even before Larwood delivered the ball. His incredible eyesight enabled him to smack superb and beautifully timed square cuts to the fence. Larwood admitted that Bodyline may have only a limited effect in stunting Bradman's scoring. Don failed again when NSW met the Poms and he was removed by Maurice Tate and Voce for 18 and 23, losing his wicket in orthodox fashion.

Bradman withdrew from the first Test because of illness rather than his unresolved dispute with the Board over writing, a dispute that was resolved when the newspaper released Bradman from his contract.

Bradman took a break and pondered the best way to combat Bodyline. Woodfull who was the other prime target of Bodyline was left to face the music alone – music that became a funeral dirge for the Australian team.

Jardine launched his obsession to win the Ashes back for England by having a private aside with Larwood. "You are my main weapon Harold, and I know you can help me."

He asked, "Are you prepared to bowl leg theory?" Larwood said Jardine had asked, rather than ordered. "I told him I wouldn't get wickets any other way and I was willing," he said. Had he been more skilled as a swing bowler, he said he may not have had to resort to Bodyline.

The first Test at the SCG, even without Bradman, was like Krakatau erupting. It was the calm before the storm when Jardine first used orthodox field placements in the early overs of Australia's first innings. He was simply baiting the hook. The Australian openers were going along quietly when Jardine tugged on his cravat and signalled the English players to move into their legside positions. Six players were grouped from the leg slip, square leg and two short mid-ons. Two others were on the fence for a hook, the wicketkeeper was 20 yards from the stumps. With Larwood bowling there was just one player to defend the rest of the ground. Larwood began his low, menacing cannonball roll to the wicket and delivered a sharp rising thunderbolt at Woodfull.

The crowd roared as the ball which all but ripped off Woodfull's unprotected ear flew to the keeper's upflung glove. The crowd and Woodfull knew the ball had gone precisely where Larwood wanted it to go – at his head. Ball after ball followed the same searing path. Nor was there any respite when Bill Voce took over at the other end.

Never before and never afterwards had Australian cricket crowds trembled so perilously to the edge of riot. Sydneysiders were belligerent and clearly outraged by the venomous bowling that crashed into the Australian bodies with no regard to their welfare. Voce sent Ponsford back to the pavilion for seven and Larwood rattled out Woodfull, Fingleton and Kippax.

The Australians now knew Jardine was prepared to take lives if that was required to win back the accursed Ashes.

Larwood was less austere than his skipper and countered the venom from the Hill with a two finger sign, intensifying the hatred. Threats of all kinds were made against the English camp – at best Jardine could expect to escape from Australia in tar and feathers. The media pondered the fate of the English monsters if an Australian batsman was actually killed at the wicket.

That didn't stop the English body assault and the wickets tumbled. Fingleton stirred the emotions of the crowd by taking the Bodyline on the body rather than yield his wicket to the legside piranha. He took blow after blow until his body was a mass of bruises, yet he refused to show his hurt. Every time he was pinged the crowd would howl abuse.

The Australian who looked comfortable was McCabe. He went for his shots, ignoring the packed legside field and was so successful that Jardine reverted to orthodox field placings.

His 187 not out was a towering performance that the English team used to plead the case. It was inept batting and not Bodyline that destroyed the other Australians.

It was during this Test that "Gubby" Allen told Jardine he would not bowl to Jardine's field if he set legside fieldsmen. He would bowl at the wicket and to hell with the consequences. Allen told Jardine, "You forget Douglas, I am an Australian." He had been born at Darling Point, Sydney. Allen challenged Jardine to send him back to England on the next ship.

"Gubby was an amateur and could afford to take that stand," said Larwood, "I know what would have happened to a Notts coalminer who gave Douglas Jardine a similar ultimatum."

In between taking the odd pinch of snuff from a pocket cache, Larwood had 5-28 and when the pacemen again ripped through the top order in the second innings the result was never in doubt. First blood to England – real blood!

Larwood said, "Had they hooked us, Bodyline may well have ended there and then. We gave them every chance to hook and they didn't." The crowd saw their Australian martyrs lining up one after the other to take the body shots until they were mercilessly cut down. The crowd counted out the English bowlers on each and every run to the wicket. England had a crushing 10 wicket win, Bodyline a runaway winner.

With five wickets in each innings, Larwood finished with match stats of 10-124. The newspapers were calling him "The King of Speed" and "The Silent Assassin."

There were 64,000 at the Melbourne Cricket Ground to see Bradman stride to the wicket in his return for the second Test. All Australia looked to Don as the man to save the situation and belt Bodyline to oblivion. No Australian sporting scene had ever heard an ovation such as the one that greeted him on his slow, measured walk to the wicket with Australia already two wickets down. Larwood said he'd never heard its like before and never heard it again. "It was a roar that came from 64,000 throats unleashing an unbridled release of emotion," he said. The acclaim reserved for a God.

The Don took strike to the bespectacled Yorkshireman, Bowes. "I saw The Don eyeing the changed field placements," said Bowes. "I asked my mid-on to move to silly mid-on. The noise was incredible. Three times I began my run and three times I had to stop until the noise died down. Each time I made a field change, each time Don took it in.

"I had a thought. 'He expects a bouncer – can I fool him?' I ran up with the most threatening expression I could muster. Don stepped across his wicket intending to hit the ball out of sight. But as the ball flew towards him, he realised it was not a bouncer at all. In a manner that only a really great batsman could achieve, he changed the elevation of his intended shot and got a very faint edge on the ball, but his defensive move was ineffective. He played it on. The crowd was stupefied."

Bowes said Jardine, normally a sphinx, couldn't help himself. "He clasped both hands above his head and was jigging around doing a war dance."

Bowes had bowled an innocuous delivery outside the off-stump and produced sport's greatest after shock. Bradman bowled Bowes nought. The first ball Bradman faced in Test cricket against Bodyline produced Bowes' only wicket for the Test series. Don threw his head back in shock and trudged to the pavilion in funereal silence. The world's greatest roar had turned to deafening silence in less than a minute, Bradman the victim of a rank long hop.

Larwood believed Bradman was the victim of the Melbourne curator. He suspected the wicket had been watered to slacken his pace and was so slow it upset Bradman's timing in taking that first delivery.

He made amends in the second innings with a spanking 103. Combined with Bill

The delivery which almost sparked a riot: Larwood to Bert Oldfield, Adelaide, 1932-33.

O'Reilly's 10 wickets, the Aussies were able to level the series with a 111 run win and head for Adelaide for the game that would undoubtedly decide the series. Larwood felt Bodyline was useless if the Australian curators continued to slow down the wickets. "None of our fast bowlers could perform on such wickets," he said.

"Don's innings was one of the greatest of his career. We gave him everything we had and he darted here, there and everywhere and I thought in the end he would surely tame Bodyline." Yet for all the majesty of that innings Larwood said it gave him hope, "As he darted about I said to myself. I've got you frightened. Wait 'til I give you this one "

Even Jardine admitted he was in awe of the Bradman century in Melbourne, saying The Don's innings was orthodox and correct, whereas in subsequent matches he took outlandish steps to counter Bodyline by darting to and fro across the face of his wicket. Jardine believed had Don relied on his natural gifts, he would have put an end to legside theory. "In Melbourne he obtained the complete mastery which so many Australians associate with his batting – why he ever deserted such methods will always remain a mystery to me."

The Adelaide curator prepared a hard, fast strip – just right for a full-blooded Bodyline assault. The Poms were back in business. Jardine after making 1 and 0 in Melbourne left the selection room after inviting his co-selectors to leave him out of the third Test. They called him back and said, "You're in."

One wonders how history may have changed had he been dropped.

Jardine won the toss and batted. England compiled 341. It was Saturday, January 14 and Australia's reply was just four overs old and Fingleton was already out. On the last ball of his second over, Larwood got a fast rising ball to thunder into the Woodfull chest, just above the heart.

As he dropped his bat and staggered from the wicket, Jardine walked across to Larwood and said loudly and clearly so as to be heard by Bradman, "Well bowled Harold!" The ball had been bowled to an orthodox field.

Grey-faced and obviously sick and distressed Woodfull set himself to face the first ball of the next Larwood over when the insensitive and imperious Jardine stopped play and signalled his players to move into a densely packed legside placement. It was the ultimate in bad timing, bad taste, bad sportsmanship and Jardine arrogance. Nor was Larwood sensitive to the situation – he hurled the next ball at the stricken Australian captain with all the venom he could muster. "It was my nature. I liked batsman well enough off the field but when we were out in the middle I hated them – they were my enemy."

Larwood and Jardine disagree on the circumstances of the fateful decision to attack the wounded Woodfull with legside after being so badly hurt. Jardine insisted it was Larwood's decision. "At the start of the next over Larwood made a sign to me he wanted a legside field. Had either he or I realised the misrepresentation to which we were to be subjected, neither of us would have set that particular field for that particular over." Larwood was furious that he was transformed into the villain and made the scapegoat on his return to England. Even in his final years, living in Australia, he was adamant Jardine made the decisions when he was to bowl Bodyline.

Larwood hammered Woodfull with rearing bumpers, the second of which reared and knocked the bat out of his hands. The crowd was in a paroxysm of rage. Bradman was soon out to Larwood. After weaving away from a few bumpers he popped a simple catch to short square leg. Woodfull held the Australian innings together with a stubborn 22.

The rage of the crowd was white hot. Blood-curdling threats were screamed from the pickets. Angry spectators lined the English race at the end of each session and hurled threats and menaces at the tourists.

English manager "Plum" Warner went to the Australian rooms to offer sympathy for his hurt and Woodfull responded with his famous declaration of contempt, "I don't want to see you Mr. Warner. There are two teams out there on the oval. One is playing cricket, the other is not. The game is too good to be spoilt. It's time some people got out of the game."

Woodfull's outburst was leaked to the press and created worldwide headlines. His words stirred the nation. But the worst was still to come.

It was Monday, January 16, 1933, when the English implemented the full force of the lethal weapon. Larwood had not bothered with legside theory in the early overs of the day as England had six key wickets for a little over 200. However, popular 'keeper Bert Oldfield had made 40-odd and was well set, leading a charge at England's total of 341. After Oldfield executed a superb leg glance off Larwood to the boundary, the next one was dropped short. Oldfield was beaten for pace and edged the ball into his temple, suffering a fractured skull. He was rushed to hospital by ambulance.

"Critics had been warning somebody would be killed. I thought the day had come," said Larwood. "Bert staggered and fell to his knees, I ran to the crumpled figure and said 'I'm sorry Bertie!' Oldfield mumbled, 'It's not your fault Harold.'"

It *was* Larwood's fault. He may have been under orders but he knew he was playing a sport that England had built its national integrity around. It was he who delivered the thunderbolts at the player and not the wicket. It was Larwood who struck Woodfull over the heart and then Oldfield in the temple. He thought he had killed Oldfield yet he continued to aim at the head.

"I was asked to bowl Bodyline and I carried out instructions," he said.

Woodfull bustled out to his 'keeper, still nursing Larwood induced bruises and thundered, "This isn't cricket. This is WAR."

Larwood was alarmed at the mood of the crowd. He expected the pitch would be

invaded and moved to a position to grab a stump to defend himself. Thousands chanted and counted him out as Oldfield staggered from the field. Jardine was as much a target for abuse as Larwood. There were mass screams of BASTARD... BASTARD... BASTARD. Even more roared, "Go home you Pommy bastards!" In the press box, side-on to all the action, Australian newspapermen were raging at their English counterparts.

Larwood claimed to be deeply concerned. "If just one person had jumped the fence I am certain the mob would have followed and they may well have lynched us."

Police reinforcements were called when rubbish was hurled onto the ground. As Larwood continued the attack

England, 1938: having twisted an ankle bowling at the Oval, Don Bradman is assisted from the field by Ted White and Chuck Fleetwood-Smith

against O'Reilly, the thunderous roar of anger only increased in volume. Australia was all out for 222 in reply to England's 341. The Englishmen ran a gauntlet of abuse to the pavilion.

Larwood protested the ball which struck Oldfield was bowled to a "normal" field. If it wasn't Bodyline it was Headline because it all but killed Oldfield.

In the England rooms, Jardine was unrepentant, "Listen to the bastards yelling. I think I'll go in myself and give the bastards something to yell at."

Larwood said the Australian hatred of Jardine was reciprocated. Jardine had worn the English cap while fielding but in an arrogant gesture of contempt for the mood of the crowd he took his striped Harlequin cap from his bag and fixed it on his head. The Australian barrackers had dubbed Jardine "Rainbow" because of that colorful cap. They sensed he resented the tag and howled it at him at every opportunity. The aristocratic Jardine did not like being derided by the colonial mob.

This day he wore that cap as an indication of his contempt for the Australian crowd. A brave but foolhardy gesture.

He changed the batting line-up, grabbed his pads and strode steely-eyed to the wicket to open the English second innings. He knew the crowd hated this symbol of English public school snobbery and would know why he wore it. At the sight of him, the masses erupted.

The crowd abuse of Jardine was extraordinary and there was blood lust that would not be satisfied short of the Australian pacemen killing him. There were howls, "Hit him in the bloody head Tim," to Australian pace bowler Tim Wall. But the Australians refused to retaliate and to the absolute aggravation of the crowd, Jardine struggled his way to 56 before losing his wicket. Larwood had to have a police escort from the ground. When drinks were taken during his innings, a spectator protested when Woodfull offered Jardine a drink. "Don't give him a drink. Let the bastard die of thirst!"

That night the Australian Board of Control sent their historic cable to the Marylebone Cricket Club protesting Bodyline was unsporting, was menacing and creating intense bitterness, threatening the relationship between the two countries. The MCC offered to cancel the rest of the tour if Australia was so inclined. Australia was not so inclined – the controversy was good box office. The English players passed a vote of confidence in Jardine at the end of the Adelaide Test. Jardine, in turn, threatened to withdraw his services as captain if the Australian Board of Control didn't recant its accusation of unsportsmanlike conduct.

Frank Foster, having helped Jardine orchestrate the plan, now turned on the austere English captain. In a bombshell denunciation in England, he made front page banner headlines as he decried the English Ashes triumph. His first words were repeated in huge type: JARDINE IS WELCOME TO THE ASHES, AT THE PRICE ENGLAND PAID FOR THEM.

He followed with: "Say this for me to the captain of the English Eleven in Australia – Douglas Jardine, I am ashamed of England's win. I will face you on your return with these words on my lips."

Foster demanded Jardine be dumped as English skipper and replaced by Allen. Manager Warner, a former English captain, never spoke out against Bodyline at any stage of the tour, yet privately he was understood to have rowed with Jardine over the tactics.

"I finished that tour with 33 wickets, an all-time record for a fast bowler," Larwood said. "I took a wicket every 40 balls. Bradman was my victim four times, twice his stumps rattled – whereas he was my boss in England, I called the tune in Australia."

On his return to England, Larwood had a stunning pile of hate mail. The barb that cut the worst was one note which simply said, "The Hangman's Name is Larwood."

Brisbane was the venue for the fourth Test where Australia batted first and made 340. England replied with 356 and then ripped Australia apart in the second innings, sealing a four wicket win. In the Fifth, Larwood damaged his foot and although he had broken some bones and was in agony, Jardine would not allow him to leave the field until Bradman was dismissed.

"Now you can leave," said Jardine after Bradman was bowled for 71. Larwood hobbled from the field alongside his arch enemy. Neither was to know that they'd never face each other again. He would be pilloried on his return to England and became so bitter and disillusioned that he migrated to Australia, where he was warmly embraced by the Australian community – the very same people who had screamed for his head back in Bodyline days.

Having won back the Ashes England moved into line with the international mood and supported the rule changes that outlawed legside field saturation. Bodyline was dead.

Years later, Larwood told Keith Miller and others during a Melbourne visit in the early 1980s that he'd been warned he could kill somebody. "There was a time I thought I had… Bertie Oldfield looked bad but the truth is he mishit a hook and hurt himself.

"I bowled in excess of 100 mph and from the time the ball hit the turf the batsman had only the blink of an eye to make a decision – Don had a little more than that, but at best, half a second."

University tests revealed that when his fast ball struck a batsman's ribcage or Oldfield's skull, it was the equivalent to being hit by a two ton force.

It is frightening to look back and realise Bradman and company faced this most vicious of all sporting onslaughts wearing just the soft baggy green Aussie cap.

With Bodyline behind him Don Bradman got on with life. He elected to study the rules and constitution of the game to better understand how such things as Bodyline could fester. Australia was invited to tour England in 1934 although five members of the pompous MCC opposed the invitation. King George V had a large input into settling soothing oils on the troubled waters.

Bradman prepared for the tour with a shortened Shield season and produced his sixth successive 1000 runs in a season. He averaged 132.44 and headed for England in the peak of his form.

There was a huge outcry when Bradman advised the New South Wales Cricket Association he was shifting to South Australia. He had been offered a position with an Adelaide sharebroking firm which would secure his future and relieve him of his diversified newspaper, radio and marketing commitments.

Many in NSW reckoned Bradman had sold out the interests of his home state. Malicious stories circulated and the English press carried front page stories that The Don was at loggerheads with the Australian Board of Control. That he refused to make the 1934 tour unless he could be accompanied by wife Jessie. The London *Daily Express* suggested Jessie Bradman was wielding the bat in these decisions.

The Don was totally unconcerned about the tour of England. He was unwell with a mystery illness, he was more than willing to miss the tour, recover his health and intensify his study of the stockbroking. A specialist described him as severely run down – he was advised a restful sea cruise to England with the Australian team was just what the doctor ordered, providing he didn't participate in any of the stop-over games on the way to England. The voyage should also settle a back problem which had been diagnosed as fibrositis.

On arrival in England, Bradman found the Brits filled with contrition. By now even the MCC Bluebloods accepted they had done cricket a great disservice and the Australian refusal to resort to Bodyline in retaliation had been commendable restraint. The diabolical duo, Larwood and Jardine had been jettisoned.

Bradman was still feeling unwell and asked Woodfull to excuse him from the first tour match but the skipper said this would only serve to give England's morale a boost. It would convince them something was wrong. Bradman played the opener against Worcestershire. His appearance created more spectator pandemonium than a personal appearance by the Loch Ness monster.

Although underweight and shaky, he repeated the performance of his precious tour, crafting a superb double century. It was a matter of guts for his next five matches saw only a shadow of the great stroke player. England headlines were now asking WHAT'S WRONG, DON? He gave them the answer when Australia was in strife against Middlesex. Woodfull and Bill Ponsford made ducks but Bradman blazed his way to a quick-fire century, including 76 runs in boundaries.

Australia won the first Test at Nottingham by 238 runs without a major contribution from The Don. This gave England more concern, what would happen when he struck form? He provided the answer to that in the second Test at Lord's. He strode to the wicket at first drop and immediately began to cart the English bowling to all angles of the field to race Australia's score to 1-141. His dancing feet and thrashing blade had the fieldsmen diving for cover. Concerned that his star was being too rash and likely to dance his wicket away, Woodfull sent out a message for him to cool down.

On his very next shot as he set himself to blaze the ball to the boundary he remembered his instructions and eased the power out of the shot and was caught. The rains came, the wicket turned sticky. Australia was bowled out cheaply and following on, lost the game outright.

Had Woodfull not cautioned Bradman, they would have averted the follow-on and the Poms would have batted on that bed of treacle. The third Test was drawn although England dominated the game. The Ashes looked like remaining in England with Bradman out of form and not scoring a century in two months.

The weight of Australia was on Bradman as Australia went into the fourth Test at Headingley – the scene of his world record. Australia whipped England out for just 200. The match was set up for the Aussies but Bill Bowes immediately struck, removing Bill Brown, Woodfull and Oldfield, the latter pair for ducks. Bradman joined Ponsford for the start on the second day. The great Neville Cardus cautioned him to take time and settle in."I'll kick your bum if you make more than four in the first half-hour," he said.

Bowes still had two balls to complete his over of the previous night. Bradman drove them both to the boundary.

Ponsford and Bradman were still together close to stumps when Ponsford fell. Bradman had amassed 271 in a single day's play. He went on to 304, Australia going on to score 584. The Don was so debilitated by his innings and illness that he had to be carried to the massage table. While fielding in England's second innings, he tore a thigh muscle and had to be helped from the ground. This time rain saved England. Which set the fifth Test at the Oval as the decider. There was even a call for Larwood to be brought back into the side, but there was no chance of a reprieve. Larwood was in Coventry.

They would have to save the series and the Ashes with traditional British bulldog grit.

As the Australians prepared for the finale, they were stunned when Bradman excused himself and was rushed to a private hospital to undergo a series of intensive tests. His damaged leg was immobilised and the surgeon, Sir Douglas Shields, took him to his home to rest.

Bradman was determined to play in the final Test and took his place, as usual, at No.3, being soon at the wicket with the Australians 1-21.

Partnered again by Ponsford, Bradman was incredible, slashing, pulling and driving the English pace attack to all points of the compass. Bradman hit 244 off 272 balls, for a tally of 548 in two hands. Ponsford went on to 266 and set Australia up for a compelling win.

The amazing batsman, now acclaimed as the greatest batsman who had ever lived, had created an aura of greatness no Commonwealth sportsman had ever accomplished. He was no longer his own man – he belonged to his adoring public.

Finishing the tour with 149 not out at Folkestone, he took 30 from one six ball over – 4,6,6,4,6,4 – his 50th century in 175 first-class innings. And he had turned 26 just eight days earlier.

As the Australians prepared for the voyage home, Bradman was suddenly stricken with severe abdominal pains. He was rushed to hospital where he was diagnosed as having a long standing and severe appendicitis – the cause of his mystery malaise revealed at last. There were serious complications and the hospital released bulletins that expressed their concern at his condition. Rumors of his death circulated.

Charles Kingsford-Smith volunteered to fly Jessie Bradman to her husband's side in his new aircraft, *The Southern Cross.* "Smithy" was to disappear soon after while competing in the London to Australia air race.

King George V asked he be kept informed of any changes in The Don's condition.

With hideously poor timing Jardine chose this moment to release his book on the 1932-33 tour in which he belittled Bradman's batting skills. Faced with the awareness that Bradman's illness was already racking his body during the Bodyline series, Jardine, was now deplored more than ever.

Bradman recovered but admitted he'd hovered on the brink of eternity as his body battled the two year-old condition. He was ordered to take six months to recuperate. Thus he missed the 1934-35 season which was intended to be his first for South Australia as well as the tour of South Africa.

Minus his appendix, Bradman took to the 1935-36 domestic season with a fresh spirit although still recovering his physical strength. He played only eight first-class matches. He made three figure scores in four of them. Playing his first season with South Australia, he aggravated New South Wales with 117 in his first Shield appearance and followed with 233 against Queensland and 357 in a demolition of Victoria – 707 runs in just three Shield hands. NSW had some revenge dismissing him for a duck after Queensland ended his century streak on 31. He wasn't out of touch for long as he posted 369 against Tasmania and finished the season with an average of 130.33.

Bradman had overcome his early establishment problems to become heir apparent to the throne of Australian cricket. He was named an Australian selector in 1936 as he prepared for England's quest for the Ashes. The Australian public had not forgotten the Bodyline saga and were anxious to see Bradman humiliate the visitors.

The master batsman produced his credentials as the 1936-37 first-class season opened. He captained the Rest of Australia against Australia and carted the cream of bowlers all over the field for 212 in the Bardsley-Gregory testimonial.

On October 28, 1936, Jessie Bradman gave birth to the Bradman's first child – a boy. This event came on the eve of South Australia's clash with the touring MCC.

That night Bradman asked Cardus if he could spend the evening with him. They discussed the upcoming tour at some length before The Don drove to the hospital to visit his wife and infant. He returned to Cardus deeply saddened. Doctors at the hospital had given him a disturbing prognosis on his baby son. "I'm afraid the poor little chap will not pull through," he said. The boy died on the day the match opened and although the tourists took the exceptional step of allowing Bradman's position in his team to remain open until after the first session of play, the grieving captain did not play and did not return to the field until mid-November when he captained the South Australians against Victoria.

The Vics had a notable attack but Bradman, having recovered from a gastric attack, savaged the bowling mercilessly as he ran up 192 before part timer Ross Gregory had with him caught. He followed this with an authoritative 63 against the tourists. He had made 567 in three hands leading up to the Brisbane Test – his first as Australian skipper.

He headed a rookie team with five players on debut. England batted first and Ernie McCormick did his captain proud with his first ball in Test cricket. He dismissed opening bat Stan Worthington and also saw Maurice Leyland and Charlie Barnett back to their rooms but England made 358.

Sadly for Bradman, on debut as captain, he failed in both innings with 38 and 0.

Australia was caught on a sticky wicket to be all out for 58 in the second innings to lose by 322. Misfortune followed misfortune for the new Australian skipper. England batted first in the second Test in Sydney and declared at 6-426 before torrential rain drenched the ground and produced another unplayable sticky. Bradman made another duck. Although he reached 82 in his second dig the Aussies were again beaten by an innings.

The Ashes looked to be heading back to London with the immortal Don having his worst start ever to a Test series. England needed to win only one of the remaining three Tests.

There were more sensations as the critics implied his team was not supporting him. There was a swelter of criticism of selection and tactics. He took a crippled team into the third Test but "Chuck" Fleetwood Smith was available again after missing the first two with injury. England was supremely confident until Bradman won the toss and batted, declaring at 9-200 with more rain expected and the prospect of a sticky wicket.

The Englishmen struggled to lay bat on ball on the mud heap – quite the worst wicket Bradman had seen. For a time England made a brave stand but three magnificent catches by Len Darling to snatch the wickets of Walter Hammond, Leyland and Barnett broke their back.

Now Bradman showed the depth of his cricket knowledge. He didn't want England dismissed before the wicket dried out a little. A stint on that wicket could destroy Australia. He stalled off the inevitable as long as he could, having his bowlers bowl too wide or too short so they'd delay England's dismissal. "Gubby" Allen woke up a little too late and declared at 9-76. Now Australia had to bat with the wicket still terrible but improving by the minute. He sent his worst two batsmen to open the innings: Fleetwood-Smith and Bill O'Reilly.

Fleetwood-Smith was joking referred to as the ferret of Australian batting – normally he went in after the rabbits.

"But why, Don?" he asked.

Bradman smiled, "Chuck, the only way you can get out on this wicket is to hit the ball. You can't hit it on a good wicket – you have no chance on this one."

The gamble only half-worked. O'Reilly actually laid bat on ball and was caught and bowled by Bill Voce. But Fleetwood-Smith survived and by the Monday when it was bright and sunny again, Bradman was confident that his key batsmen would bat on a much-improved wicket.

The first day attracted 78,630 spectators. On the Monday it was 87,798. Bradman joined Jack Fingleton at 5-97. Two rabbits and the ferret had lost their wickets in that scorecard so it wasn't quite as poor a scoreline as first indicated. The great concern was Bradman's ordinary form, the first sustained slump in his career. He soon put his faithful at rest. His innings had opened at 2.50 Monday and did not finish until the end of the first hour on Wednesday. In that time he amassed 270 in 478 minutes. The applause that greeted the century milestones for both Bradman and Fingleton was so raucous and sustained that it held up play for several minutes, Australia going on to win the titanic match by 365 runs in front of more Test fans than any assembled for a match Downunder in the 20th century.

Now for the fourth fateful Test with Australia fighting to stay alive. There was a vast hangover of emotion from the Bodyline series that would not be satisfied without reducing England to rabble. With Captain Don at the helm the Australia faith never wavered. But the Board of Control did their best to unsettle things. Without consulting Bradman, the Board carpeted four of his key players Fleetwood-Smith, Stan McCabe, O'Reilly and Leo O'Brien. Typically as a law unto themselves the Board gave no reason for putting the players before their tribunal. Wild speculations were screamed across the front pages. All four being Catholic, there was talk of sectarianism. Most prominent was that the quartet were rebelling against Bradman's leadership and would not play the fourth Test. A plague of rumor flooded across Australia – one given considerable credibility was that he lost a leg in a car accident – as with the report of his death in England it was a gross exaggeration. He had strained a leg muscle, but that in itself spelt disaster for Australia if he couldn't play in the decisive Test.

Australian hopes were dampened when they batted and were bundled out for 288 on a perfect wicket – Bradman failed again with 26, the fifth time in eight innings in this series that he failed to reach 40. The Poms replied with 330 to lead by 42. It was now or never for Australia as Australia lost Fingleton before erasing their deficit. McCabe joined Bradman and they faced a venomous spell from Voce but serenely built a partnership. Bradman batting to a negative boundary dotted field gracefully amassed his runs and the headlines in London postered the clash as BRADMAN v ENGLAND. He batted throughout the third day to go to stumps at 174 not out – the master had done it again. Next day he took his score to 212 and in the process England re-invented Bodyline; albeit it to the bowling of spinner Hedley Verity. Australia compiled 443. England dug deep, batted patiently and stoically with Hammond leading what looked likely to be a winning batting marathon into the sixth day.

Fleetwood-Smith, having been an unlikely batting hero in the third Test, was now handed the ball by Bradman with the words, "The match – and the Ashes – depend on you." Fleetwood-Smith bowled Hammond with an unplayable ball which spun back wickedly between bat and pad to take the great man's stumps. The rest was a formality and Australia levelled the series with 148 runs to spare.

Vengeance was at hand. Never had a team come from two down to win. Bradman kept in touch with a Shield century against Queensland before the Ashes decider in Melbourne. Every gate and turnstile of the great stadium saw queues stretching for a half-mile long before the gates opened. Many waited through the night to be certain of prime viewing positions. The toss was vital – Hammond lost and Australia batted.

The fiery footballer Laurie Nash was included in this crucial game. Nash had been spurned by Australian selectors because of his brash, confident and aggressive approach to the game. He first forced his way into the Australian team after taking 7-50 against South Africa in Hobart 1931-32. He blitzed the Springboks in his first Test when they made only 36 and 45, Nash taking 4-18 and 1-4. He was then ignored by the national selectors until recalled for this most historic of matches after taking 4-37 against the M.C.C.

There was early tragedy for Australia with both openers dismissed cheaply and Bradman at the wicket with the score at 42. Bradman was supreme and in under four hours had amassed 169, many with magnificent straight drives off England's greatest fast bowlers, who could only stop dead in their tracks and marvel at the hiss of the ball whistling past them and exploding into the pickets. On a sun baked wicket, Don led an Australian scoring frenzy that produced McCabe's stirring 112 and "Jackie" Badcock's stylish 118. They set a first innings score of 604 and were never going to lose from there. England were out in less than a day for 239. They followed on and fell over for 165. Australia had made cricket's greatest comeback and exorcised their demon without ever resorting to any but the most noble of tactics. His bowlers Fleetwood-Smith, O'Reilly and Nash had played central parts. Nash took 4-70 but the bombastic super hero of Australian Rules football was never selected again.

The Aussie summer was spent fine tuning the team to make the 1938 tour of England with the Poms grooming a young Yorkshire lad Leonard Hutton who they claimed to be good enough to take over the mantle of world No. 1 from The Don. Bradman batted 18 times in the domestic season for seven centuries which included one score of 246.

As Australian captain and a selector, Bradman was heading into troubled waters. His partners in selection were Bill Johnson and "Chappie" Dwyer. When they made their team selection for England '38, eight of the players were on their first tour. Badcock, Sid Barnes, Lindsay Hassett, Frank Ward, Fingleton, McCormick, Ted White and Merv Waite were all being blooded as tourists.

Bradman as the most significant member of the selection panel won no friends when Bert Oldfield, 40, was left out of the tour and the rising champion Don Tallon overlooked. However, O'Reilly and Fleetwood-Smith were included, ahead of Clarrie Grimmett, who was still taking wickets, at the age of 46. Bill Ponsford was outraged and declared his old mate's omission was "sheer lunacy." Years later Bradman claimed Grimmett was past it.

There was public outrage and most attacked Bradman because of his undoubted influence on selection. The icon had become an Australian Aunt Sally. The Don had begun Phase 2 of his stormy career – the phase that isolated him from players and public alike. Given their inexperience, many believed the Australian were on a hiding to nothing.

As usual Bradman opened the tour with a double century at Worcester – 258 in 293 minutes after taking 105 minutes to score his first 39 thus 219 came in 188 minutes. Rookie McCormack started atrociously, however, being no-balled 19 times in three overs for overstepping. It shattered his confidence for the entire tour. When he extended his run to 25 yards to compensate, it took him 19 strides to make the crease by which time a spectator at the sightscreen yelled, "Quick, shut the gate or he'll be out on the road."

The Poms were petrified by the time Bradman arrived at the crease for the Test series opener at Nottingham. He played seven tour matches for seven hands with two double centuries and three centuries. Scores of 258, 58, 137, 278, 2, 143 and 145 not out, total 1021, average 170.1. Again he posted a thousand runs by the end of May; the only player to accomplish the batting miracle twice. The English media were looking for scandal and could find none. England was fearing the worst as they lined up for the first Test at Nottingham, won the toss and declared at 8-658. Bradman scored 51 and 144 not out, but even his feats were surpassed by the great McCabe who produced the innings of a lifetime, 232 from 300 scored. "Come and watch this," Bradman told teammates at the back of the rooms. "You'll never see its like again."

Bradman marvelled at the majesty of McCabe's stroke play. "Towards the end I could scarcely watch the play. My eyes were filled as I drank in the glory of his shots." Thanks to McCabe, Australia made 411 and forced an honorable draw.

In the second Test at Lord's, it seemed neither McCabe nor Bradman could save the Aussies. England made 494 and had Bradman out early for 18. Australia still managed 422. Bradman had to bat out many hours to save the match. He held Australia together, compiled a patient 102 not out and saved the day. He had set a remarkable second innings record for Test cricket. His last four Tests had produced second innings hands of 270, 212, 144 not out and 102 not out – all against England, 728 runs for twice out. In the course of that final innings he passed Jack Hobbs' world Test record of 3638 runs. His past five Tests had produced more than 1000 runs – another record.

In the midst of these glories came a crashing bureaucratic nonsense from the Australian Board of Control. They told Bradman that Jessie was not allowed to join him at the end of the tour. It would create "an embarrassing precedent," thus ignoring the fact the precedent had been set with Mrs. Woodfull. Both Bradman and wife refused to be drawn into the controversy. An English newspaper offered to back the Bradmans to the hilt to pay all costs in flying Jessie to England, paying any fines imposed and even fund a lawsuit to prove the Australian Board had no authority to impose such bans. He was offered 4000 pound sterling per year sponsorship from a sporting goods company and unprecedented writing offers, but rejected everything including an offer to fund a Bradman led private cricket tour.

The stocks of the Australian Board hit an all time low. Bradman privately contemplated finishing the tour and handing his resignation to the Board on his return to Australia. He was talked out of it by Dr. Rowley Pope, the benevolent medicine man who toured with the Australians. The Australian players supported their captain to a man and instigated a private telegram to the Board telling them they supported their skipper's request and demanded it be granted. The Board was forced to rethink and announced "any" player's wife could join the party at the end of the tour – four wives took up the invitation, Mesdames Bradman, McCabe, Fleetwood-Smith and Jeanes.

The third Test at Manchester was a washout which meant the fourth Test at Leeds would decide the series. If Australia won they would retain the Ashes.

England started with 223. Australia's reply was built solely on the back of Bradman. While wickets fell around him in overcast conditions, conducive to swing, he refused to take a light appeal although the light was so bad spectators could not see the ball. He knew once the rain fell Australia was doomed. So he batted in the dark and put together one of the greatest back-to-the-wall hands of his illustrious career. Hammond had no qualms using his pace men to intimidate the Australian batsmen. He could not tame Bradman whose magnificent eyesight pierced the gloom long enough for him to post a great 103 before Bowes claimed his wicket. He had steered his team to 242 and a narrow lead of 19.

The Australians were greatly moved by his heroic performance in such dangerous conditions, they bent their backs and whipped England out for just 123. O'Reilly was magnificent. But Australia was soon in diabolical trouble with Bradman and the top order batsmen back in the pavilion well short of the 105 runs needed for victory. But the middle order rallied, held off the English attack and Australia took a series lead with a five wicket win.

The final Test at the Oval was more than academic. It was a mathematical nightmare. The new English superstar Hutton batted for two days in breaking the Bradman record and setting a new world Test record of 364. Bradman was furious that Hammond had not declared until his team reached 7-903. Bradman broke his ankle while bowling and was carried from the ground unable to bat and Australian was thrashed by an innings. The series was drawn but Australia still held the Ashes and would hold them for the duration of the war.

Because of the war Bradman's international career was put on hold for eight years. He turned 30 during the 1938 tour and was 37 when he next played in a bid to get cricket going again after the war. With the MCC touring in 1946, the batting legend was concerned about his immediate future as he suffered searing muscular pain in his comeback matches.

The love/hate relationship with England took an ugly turn during the first Test at the 'Gabba as Bradman returned to a Test pitch after an eight year break. Hammond was bitter in his criticism of Bradman not "walking" when England swore he was caught at 28, having edged a ball from Bill Voce that Jack Ikin took at slip. But umpire George Borwick said "not out" and his partner Jack Scott agreed, saying the ball was a "bump" ball, having struck the Bradman bat, and flew into the turf before being taken by Ikin. The Don went on to amass 187 to break England's back.

Hammond made an unpleasant aside to Bradman although publicly stating he would accept the umpire's decision. He didn't really. Nor did his former batting partner Fingleton who later said, "No harm is done in now admitting to posterity that Bradman *was* out." Fingleton was one of those Australian Test players with an intense dislike for The Don. O'Reilly was another. He said Bradman was clearly out and must have wondered how a bump ball could all but spin Ikin off his feet as he caught it chest high at great speed.

In the English camp, the awe of Bradman turned to hate. The English newspapers went on the attack and branded him a cheat. Yet Bradman did not believe he should capitulate when there was doubt about the catch. He left the decision to the umpire and the controversy that followed was remarkably bitter and prolonged. Hammond claimed it changed the course of the series. Many believe had he failed in this Test Bradman may well have retired. As it was he went to Sydney for the second Test, made 234 in a 405 partnership with Sid Barnes and Australia comfortably won the Ashes series although The Don's form waned over the final three Tests.

If his fade out against England early in 1947 buoyed English hopes that the Bradman menace was fading, they were dashed when India toured Australia for the 1947-48 series. He continued his domination and became the first Australian to 100 first-class centuries during the Australian X1 game against India in Sydney on his way to a season average surpassing 140.

Reaching his milestone in just 295 innings, he confirmed his standing as the finest batsman of all time with a century every three times at bat.

That set him up for his farewell to cricket – his tour of England and a determination to make it through the entire tour to be the first undefeated team in cricket history. He began that tour with the traditional century against Worcester, 107. While he believed his form inferior to his pre-war performances, he made four centuries before the first Test at Trent Bridge, narrowly missing three others in the seven match lead-up. The Australians swept all before them against the counties.

Come the Tests, English captain Norman Yardley unveiled a new legside theory he believed could subdue the 39-year-old batting master. Asking Alec Bedser to concentrate on swinging the ball across Bradman's body to limit his stroke play, Yardley believed it could frustrate Bradman into some injudicious stroke play. While he fell to the Bedser leg trap, he made 138, launching the Test series with his usual aplomb. In the second innings he was out for a duck, again via a Hutton catch from the bowling of Bedser.

Australia won again at Lord's but how the English writers chortled when Bradman was out for 38. The low score was not the cause of jubilation it was "caught Hutton – bowled Bedser" that had them so excited. In the second innings he made 83 before Bedser struck again; this time Bill Edrich picking him up in the legside trap.

The second Test at Lord's was his farewell to the game's celebrated shrine. How he wanted a century and an Australian triumph on this hallowed strip. He fell short of his ton but had one of his wishes fulfilled – the important one. Australia won and took a commanding grip on the series. The third Test was drawn and Australia, still unbeaten, retained the Ashes.

The fourth Test had sensational results for Bradman on the threshold of his final appearance in Test cricket against the old enemy. By now he had disciplined his stroke play so that Bedser's legtrap was rendered obsolete. England set Australia 404 in 345 minutes on the final day to win. Bradman and Arthur Morris came together after Hassett fell. Bradman instructed Morris to control one end while he controlled the other. They would pick the runs off with boundaries and twos. The pair set about the English bowling to set all sorts of records for the last day of play. They posted a stand of

305 and Bradman went on to win the match with 173 not out. That innings took his Test average over the 100-run mark with just one Test match left in his career. A simple four runs would ensure he finished his career with 7000 Test runs and a triple figure Test average.

Bradman's final Test was to be historic for a number of reasons other than the great man's retirement from Test cricket. Yardley won the toss and batted when he should have bowled. His penalty was to see his entire side back in the pavilion for 52 on the first morning .

This guaranteed Bradman a win for Australia and an unbeaten series almost certainly in the bag. Bradman also went to the crease for the final time in Tests. His all time Test average was 101.93. He had scored 6996 runs in 79 innings with 10 not outs. Tragically he made a duck, beaten second ball by a googly from Eric Hollies and returned to the pavilion with 6996 runs from 70 completed hands; average 99.94.

Bradman reflected, "The fieldsmen gathered around and gave me three cheers... I dearly wanted to do well, but it was not to be. That reception had stirred my emotions very deeply and made me anxious – a dangerous state of mind for any batsman to be in. I played the first ball from Eric Hollies though not sure I really saw it. The second was perfect length googly which deceived me. I just touched it with the inside edge of the bat and the off bail was dislodged."

He didn't get a chance to bat again to get the necessary runs because Australia swept through England again to win by an innings. Australia went on to accomplish Bradman's mission to be the only international team to go through an English tour unbeaten.

His last three hands on English soil as Australia wound up their tour produced 150, 143, 153. Who would retire on such a note? Who else could produce such first-class figures at 40 years of age? He terminated his career with a staggering first-class tally of 28,067 runs at 95.14 – having missed seven years of international cricket from 1939-46.

Bradman played only three more first-class games in Australia, two of these were testimonials and the third a farewell Shield appearance for South Australia against Victoria which produced 30 runs before being bowled by Bill Johnston. In his own testimonial he farewelled his fans with a spanking 123, but not before he'd been deliberately put down by Colin McCool when he was 97.

He was knighted in 1949 – the announcement made in the New Year honors list.

It was not long after retirement that Bradman moved into a position of influence within cricket administration. He served a marathon stint but in time the "essential" secrecy and "confidentiality" of Australian Board of Control and selection decision-making eroded some of his standing with players and the public at large. Where once he had taken his own stand against blinkered bureaucratic dictatorship, he now accepted the code of silence. It wasn't difficult for a man who had long since lost respect for large sections of the media and steadfastly refused to engage in any discussion on controversial issues.

The dumping of Keith Miller from South Africa, the Sid Barnes exile and the Ian Meckiff chucking controversy all intruded on his reputation for infallibility. He made all-too-rare defences of his position but usually allowed the wildest and widest of the mark to pass unchallenged. He was careful not to anoint too many of the men who served under him with the wand of friendship.

He retained friendships with many of his old teammates and contrary to speculation it does seem he had a warm regard for the wild child, Sid Barnes. Stan McCabe whose batting had so pleased The Don at Trent Bridge all those years ago was upset at being ignored by Sir Donald and complained the great man never bothered to drop in on him at his sports store, even though it was in the same building where The Don regularly visited NSW cricket authorities. It clearly hurt McCabe that a man with whom shared so many illustrious moments at the crease had so little time for him in later life.

Fellow greats O'Reilly and Miller were also labelled as being well on the outer for many years. O'Reilly went to the grave firing shots at The Don whereas if there was any direct friction between Miller and Bradman, it mellowed as the years passed and death thinned the ranks of players of the Bradman era.

O'Reilly never tempered his criticism of Bradman. He resented Bradman criticising his bowling ability before he ever played Test cricket. Bradman had written that O'Reilly might have been a success on matting wickets but would never make it on tour. O'Reilly accused The Don of setting a bad example by ducking and weaving during the Bodyline saga. He also blamed the great man for the premature end to Grimmett's career. A fiery Irish Catholic, O'Reilly felt his religion was a disadvantage with Bradman a Protestant conservative.

If there was a flaw in Sir Donald Bradman, it was his intense integrity. He never accepted there was a requirement for him to become one of the cricketing rat pack, that he had any obligation to change his quality of life away from the playing field. He clearly dedicated himself to his career as a cricketer and as in any business fame and fortune went to the performer.

That he applied himself better, worked harder and performed better than any other player in his field justified the financial benefits he accrued – that was business and cricket was his business.

He was accused of many things as player and official but because he never deigned or bothered to give explicit details of his involvement or non-involvement in such issues as the Miller sacking, the Meckiff controversy and even the final stages of the Barnes saga, debate remains clouded. Whatever history records, it should be tempered with the certainty that Sir Donald acted always with the best interests of the game at heart. – it's not as certain that he disdained the pain and suffering of the individual in the pursuit of "what was best for the game."

THE SUN & THE STARS
Legendary English cricket writer R. C. Robertson-Glasgow summarised the Bradman career: "He did not mean to be just one of the stars, but the sun itself."

Don Bradman THE MAN & HIS RECORD

Born: August 16, 1950
Teams: New South Wales, South Australia & Australia
First-class debut: 1927-28
First-class record: Matches 234. Batting — Runs 28,067, Average 95.14, Highest score 452*, 100s 117, 50s 69. Bowling — Wickets 36, Average 37.97, Best bowling 3-35. Fielding — Catches 131, Stumpings 1. Captaincy — 120 matches for 61 wins, 13 losses, 45 draws and 1 tie.
Test debut: 1928-29
Test record: Matches 52. Batting — Runs 6996, Average 99.94, Highest score 334. Bowling — Wickets 2, Average 36.00, Best bowling 1-8. Fielding — Catches 32. Captaincy — 24 matches for 15 wins, 3 losses and 6 draws.
Tours: England 1930, 1934, 1938, 1948.

Don Bradman's Test record series by series:

BATTING & FIELDING

Season	Opponent	Mt	Inns	No	HS	Runs	Ave	100s	50s	Ct.
1928-29	England (h)	4	8	1	123	468	66.85	2	2	3
1930	England (a)	5	7	0	334	974	139.14	4	-	2
1930-31	West Indies (h)	5	6	0	223	447	74.50	2	-	4
1931-32	South Africa (h)	5	5	1	299*	806	201.50	4	-	2
1932-33	England (h)	4	8	1	103*	396	56.57	1	3	3
1934	England (a)	5	8	0	304	758	94.75	2	1	1
1936-37	England (h)	5	9	0	270	810	90.00	3	1	6
1938	England (a)	4	6	2	144*	434	108.50	3	1	-
1946-47	England (h)	5	8	1	234	680	97.14	2	3	3
1947-48	India (h)	5	6	2	201	715	178.75	4	1	6
1948	England (a)	5	9	2	173*	508	72.57	2	1	1
Totals		52	80	10	334	6996	99.94	29	13	32

BOWLING

Season	Opponent	Mt	Balls	Mdn	Runs	Wick	Ave	BB
1928-29	England (h)	4	-	-	-	-	-	-
1930	England (a)	5	6	-	1	0	-	0-1
1930-31	West Indies (h)	5	54	1	15	1	15.00	1-8
1931-32	South Africa (h)	5	6	0	2	0	-	0-2
1932-33	England (h)	4	72	1	44	1	44.00	1-23
1934	England (a)	5	-	-	-	-	-	-
1936-37	England (h)	5	-	-	-	-	-	-
1938	England (a)	4	14	1	6	0	-	0-6
1946-47	England (h)	5	-	-	-	-	-	-
1947-48	India (h)	5	8	0	4	0	-	0-4
1948	England (a)	5	-	-	-	-	-	-
Totals			160	4	72	2	36.00	1-8

COUNTRY BY COUNTRY RECORD

BATTING & FIELDING

Country	Mt	Inns	No	HS	Runs	Ave	100s	50s	Ct.
v England	37	63	7	334	5028	89.78	19	12	20
v India	5	6	2	201	715	178.75	4	1	6
v West Indies	5	6	0	223	447	74.50	2	-	4
v South Africa	5	5	1	299*	806	201.50	4	-	2

HOME & ABROAD

Country	Mt	Inns	No	HS	Runs	Ave	100s
Tests at home	33	50	6	299*	4322	98.22	18
Tests abroad	19	30	4	334	2674	102.84	11

BOWLING

Country	Mt	Balls	Mdn	Runs	Wick	Ave	BB
v England	37	92	2	51	1	51.00	1-23
v India	5	8	0	4	0	-	0-4
v South Africa	5	6	0	2	0	-	0-2
v West Indies	5	54	1	15	1	15.00	1-8

HOME & ABROAD

	Mt	Balls	Mdn	Runs	Wick	Ave	BB
Tests at home	33	140	2	65	2	32.50	1-8
Tests abroad	19	20	2	7	0	-	0-1

HIS HIGHEST TEST SCORES

334	v England, Leeds, 1930
304	v England, Leeds, 1934
299*	v South Africa, Adelaide, 1931-32
270	v England, Melbourne, 1936-37
254	v England, Lord's, 1930
244	v England, The Oval, 1934
234	v England, Sydney, 1946-47
223	v West Indies, Brisbane, 1930-31
232	v England, The Oval, 1930
226*	v South Africa, Brisbane, 1931-32
212	v England, Adelaide, 1936-37
201	v India, Adelaide, 1947-48

HIS BEST TEST BOWLING

1-8	v West Indies, Adelaide, 1930-31
1-23	v England, Adelaide, 1932-33

BUCKING
THE
SYSTEM

"Stop the mowing or I'll take my team out of the game."
Hutcheon backed off but Sid had made a formidable enemy.

The angry provocateur fought officialdom to the end. He jumped
turnstiles, offended the King of England, and took the Australian
Board of Control to the Supreme Court and won. He clowned around at
Bradman's testimonial, inciting opinion everywhere he went.

T HE GREAT ENGLISH pace bowler Alec Bedser made an intense study of Sidney
George Barnes and passed judgment: "He is pure and simply a man on the back
foot." That was one thing you could never say truthfully about Sid Barnes, a point
he proved in the courts as well as on the cricket field.

Cricket is notorious for its bad judgment. Bedser was wrong as were many others
who passed judgment on Barnes, one of the great opening bats of international cricket.
No player fought officialdom as hard and as long as this pugnacious New South
Welshman. He fought them until he had them on their knees in Australia's Supreme
Court.

There is a propensity for sporting authorities to believe they are law unto
themselves. They make judgments in closed chambers and inflict their will on their
sporting industry without recognising there is an obligation to show that their
judgments and impositions are reasonable and just.

Such officials abound in many walks of sport. Harsh, punitive and discriminatory.
Their actions oft fly in the face of the common law rights of the individual, the
Constitution of the nation and the simple right of an individual or group to a fair go.

J Pollard

69

The Australian cricket scene boasts more than its fair and reasonable share of such autocratic injustice. Individuals have been banished in their prime for reasons the public and the individual have been left to guess at – and in the speculation the individual is done an even greater injustice. Wild, unfounded and totally untrue stories do the rounds and in the passing of time the lies often becomes truth.

Many of these exiles have been the result of players not yielding to the demand of the Board or selectors that they become cloned to the perception that all cricketers must conform to a rigid, robotic role model, strictly correct, totally colorless and as bland as the traditional white flannels they wore.

Sid Barnes was such a victim. After the job was done, he believed it was time to have fun and entertain. Cricket bureaucrats crushed him but he refused to yield.

There have been few more sensational upheavals in cricket than when Sir Donald Bradman and his selectors named Barnes in their team to play the West Indies in 1951. The Australian Board of Control summarily vetoed that selection and demanded they name another team, without Barnes. They refused to state their case other than he was being discounted "for reasons other than cricket ability." It was Star Chamber justice at its most arrogant. Barnes was forced to write to Sir Donald and obtain written confirmation there was absolutely no basis for a rumor circulating that he had stolen a car on an English tour and sold it for his own profit. Sir Donald wrote the letter and expressed his sympathy for his beleaguered batting mate: "It's one of the penalties of fame," he said.

Barnes was not appeased. A doctor friend had heard on good authority he had stolen the car and sold it. It was a widely spread story and Barnes said he was the victim of other smears including stealing money from players and insulting the Royal family.

The Board actions were outside the law of the land – Barnes resolved to bring them back within bounds. He took the cricket gods to the Supreme Court of Australia...

Yes, Bedser was very wrong about Barnes. Whether it was defending his wicket or his character, he was always on the front foot... whether the enemy be a Pom or the Board of Control.

There have been few more controversial and entertaining characters and the story is one that stirred a nation and created a chasm in cricket.

To some extent it was seen as a case of class distinction and bureaucracy gone mad. He was not born with a silver spoon or fashioned for cricket at one of the illustrious public schools. His claim to fame as a shoot from the Barnes family tree is that his grandfather was held up regularly by the bushranger Thunderbolt.

Barnes was a great cricketer and Australia was deprived of his services when he still had much to give. Sid was an individual who could not and would not be tamed. Yet his "incidents" would be regarded as trivial stacked up against the escapades of international cricketers a few decades on from when Sid bowled tennis balls at batsmen; took block with a 12 inch bat; jumped a turnstile or took a full blooded hook in his ribcage fielding at suicide short-stop.

There are those who believe Sid Barnes committed sporting suicide. Others believe he was murdered by the "big brother" syndrome of Australian cricket

The Sid Barnes story is about all that – his story moved the very upright and principle-motivated Labor leader Dr. H. V. Evatt to rally to his cause. Dr. Evatt, leader of the Federal Opposition in the Menzies era, was a distinguished lawyer and fighter for minority causes and a long term trustee for the Sydney Cricket Ground.

Wisden says Sid was born in 1916, but his mother says it was 1919, just before the death of his father. There'd been a mix up in the Queensland births and deaths records; but it didn't really matter.

His grandfather had driven a stagecoach for Cobb & Co and boasted of being held-up many times by the noted bushranger Thunderbolt – the grandfather insisted Thunderbolt was a gentleman bushranger who robbed only the rich and that he did with a certain courtesy and respect. But he did have one great resentment of Thunderbolt. He had a champion racehorse he had set for a big Queensland race.

Thunderbolt bailed him up at the Barnes farm on the eve of the race and took the horse, promising to return it before the race. The horse returned but had obviously spent a night on the tiles with Thunderbolt because he ran an inglorious last.

His grandparents, mother, brothers Horace and Alfred moved to Sydney suburb Leichardt while he was a baby. His mother bought some houses and young Sid became the rent collector. Collecting rent in the Depression days developed that hard hide. The family business developed an innate appreciation of squeezing every cent out of life – Sid was to be noted throughout his career as an avaricious money machine. At seven, he charged his 15-year-old brother Horace sixpence a session to bowl to him.

Despite the thoughts of a schoolmaster who didn't like Sid's correct technique, which flew in the face of his own untutored theories on how kids should bat, the younger Barnes boy blossomed as a cricketer – particularly street cricket. Street cricket was all the rage in the mid 1920s and some streets played a higher level of cricket than others. He was more than pleased when he graduated from his own street of Corunna Road to the neighboring suburb Cardigan Street which had a better constructed street and thus a more even pitch. It was a more well-to-do suburb which paid higher rates. Yes there was class distinction, even in street cricket. With his frugal ways and the only player with a bank account, Sid became the suburban treasurer, financier and organiser at no financial discomfort to himself. He bought, sold and financed everything on the understanding Sid got two innings to everybody else having one.

Some of the Asian members of his cricketing community objected to the exorbitant interest rates he charged for financing their cricket but reconciled themselves to the inevitable when he packed up the gear and went home. He acknowledged street cricket had its drawbacks. While the public school boys had a free range of shots playing cricket on traditional playing fields, house occupiers in the suburban streets took a dim view of hook shots and sixes that menaced and often shattered their windows. Police intervention was frequent and the cost prohibitive – so hook shots and lofted pulls were outlawed, instant dismissal to all offenders. They also introduced new fielding positions – two players were stationed in the adjacent laneways at "cockatoo point" to warn of police sneaking up the lanes to catch them in the act.

This introduced the batsmen to delicate cuts and powerful straight drives and a reluctance to hammer the ball to the off side of the street wicket. Grandad Barnes repaired the windows and absorbed the cost in a worthy cause.

Street cricket prepared many of these youngsters for the full playing fields that became available as they entered their teens. Suburban clubs were looking for boys with a cricket appetite and a keen eye. But once lorries started threatening to mould the players into their street pitch they were forced to take their team to the local tip where they cleared an area which they called the Pit Cricket Ground and played with more freedom and safety, albeit with a distasteful smell that permeated their new home ground. But everything has its price as Sid kept telling his team.

At least they had progressed to a "turf" wicket. The new location was now the "Pit team" which was a bit classier than their main rivals "The Sewers" gang who played along the local sewerage drains. Sometimes arguments flared into bloody war with shanghais and stones being used with reckless abandon. A catapult wound left Sid with a large permanent scar along his upper lip. His family decided Sunday school might introduce him to a more heavenly element. What it did introduce him to was organised cricket.

What a wondrous change came over his sporting life as he emerged from the sewers and rubbish dumps to play with St. Augustine's "C" Grade team. Anybody socially aware knows St. Augustine's breeds a rare breed of sportsmen – very competitive to say the least. Sid was yet to have any awareness that there was a world of cricket outside his own little sphere. He was aware Australia had a player called Charlie Macartney because the local girls called Sid "The Governor General" after Charlie who carried that tag.

He was soon putting up some impressive performances with bat, ball and wicket-keeping gloves. Such feats as 7-1 in an opposing score of four runs. He was elevated to "A" grade ranks and averaged 34 in his first season. His batting had him selected for the NSW schoolboys team in 1931 – so he virtually raced through the stages of progress that took most well schooled youngsters several seasons. He made a pile of runs and kept wickets brilliantly but nobody kept the records. His performances were good enough to be invited to join Sydney Petersham District cricket club as a 13 year-old.

His first appearance for Petersham drew a good roll-up of Pit and Sewer players keen to see if he would kick down his wicket when given out. Sid was third drop and instead of sitting with his clubmates he padded up and walked around to his mates. The wickets fell and when it was his turn to bat he simply hurdled the fence and strode to the wicket. The "Sewer" boys roared him to the wicket and thus flushed with the acclaim of his peers Sid compiled a masterly four before having his stumps scattered. He avoided the Sewer boys by returning to the pavilion by the orthodox route only to cop an horrific blast from his captain for his lack of class in the way he went to the wicket. An untidy mind makes for an untidy batsman. The Sewer boys had walked from the ground in disgust as soon as their hero's wicket fell. He was to find that was the norm in cricket. Shattered by the experience he went back to the junior competition.

His career may have taken a permanent downturn but a schoolteacher named Rose invited him to play with the Teachers X1 and eventually they played against Petersham seniors captained by Dudley Seddon who had been quite taken by the potential of Sid as a gloveman and even given him a green and gold Petersham cap. He urged Sid to return to the club but Barnes decided he would not return to grade cricket until he felt he would make his mark with the seniors. Seddon kept the pressure on him and with support from ex-international Tommy Andrews, he agreed to play a season with the reserve grade Petersham team. This came after he made 104 in the Poidevin-Gray Shield competition and then took 5-36 after taking the first five wickets as a 'keeper – possibly a record in itself.

Not knowing cricket had any great standing Sid said he was in no awe whatsoever when he played in his first competitive match. Nor was he ever to be in awe of huge personalities and puffed-up officials. Which may have been his ultimate undoing.

At 15, he had advanced to Poidevin-Gray Shield class and then into first grade cricket in Sydney. At that tender age he faced "The Tiger," the great Bill O'Reilly, the man they erroneously said made the great Bradman quake. Young Sid held out against O'Reilly until stumps on the first day. Tiger patted him on the shoulder and said, "Well played, lad." Sid took that accolade in his stride, "Yeah..." before adding his own compliment, "You bowled pretty well out there yourself." Barnes was a bit puzzled when the great man burst into a fit of laughter.

"I couldn't see what was funny. He had been the best bowler I had faced to that stage and I thought he deserved to be told." Well he was not to know the Tiger had just returned from a triumphant tour of England where the greatest batsmen in the world found they couldn't play him.

Barnes played his first full season of senior grade cricket at 16 and headed the batting averages with 500 runs at 40. A lot of it was due to Andrews' private coaching sessions and drilling him into a religion of treating net practice as a proofing ground and essential to the well being of a cricketer when he walked to the middle. Barnes said too many top ranking players suffered as a result of treating the nets as a bore and a waste of their talent. "They turn it into a farce with their lazy, casual attitude." In 1936, the year "Gubby" Allen brought the MCC tour to Australia, Sid decided he envied Don Bradman his headlines. "He was front page news whether he made a hundred or a duck. I wanted some of that recognition." He decided to make a study of the exciting young Australian – not Don's batting because he believed every player was unique to his own style – he wanted to study the mannerisms and professional techniques. Sid was a powerful build with strong forearms and big shoulders, totally different in physical character to that of Bradman. He was looked upon as a No. 4 or 5 batsman with a very sound defence and a strong, aggressive strokemaker.

He sat on the SCG Hill and watched Bradman compile a big innings. He noted Bradman had most of the strike and that it was calculated. He controlled the game and the scoreboard by taking two out of every three balls, taking the single off the last ball and then placing the ball to get twos or fours. This was the technique Barnes decided to copy. Control of the strike.

Now he was in dangerous territory as he made the state side. Sid was brilliantly fast between the wickets and frequently left his batting partners stranded as he ran to get the quick single off the last ball. NSW batsman Arthur Chipperfield was notoriously slow out of the blocks and was in line for a trip to England but suffered some dismal run outs in partnerships with Barnes. Sid was not considering the welfare of his running mate and Chipperfield complained to NSW state captain Stan McCabe. He even suggested Barnes was angling to run him out of the touring team to grab the berth himself. McCabe told the youngster to remember he was faster than his batting mates and it wasn't essential that he pinch the strike.

"Just remember lad, you've got 20 years left to make your mark. Don't HOG the strike." Sid heard him but didn't necessarily listen for he continued to dominate the strike. The youngster was always planning ahead because he had no doubt he was international bound and when he was invited to trundle a few balls to Walter Hammond and the other key English batsmen he agreed with alacrity. But when he was expected to practice with them for hours on end, he bridled. "When I come to play cricket against them I don't want them to know my bowling." He solved the problem by bowling nothing but slow, straight balls at the Poms, rather than his leg-breaks and wrong-uns.

By now Barnes was an accomplished and fierce batsman and a brilliant field, taking a big catch to help in Australian Test pace candidate Ginty Lush's 13/115 match analysis. On the eve of selection Lush faced Barnes in a grade match and when Sid had posted 113, Lush decided it was time to remove him. He took over the bowling and his eight balls found the boundary as Barnes smote four 6s and four 4s to take 40 runs off the over. Seddon had walked down the wicket to Barnes after the first two sixes and said, "Keep it going, this chap's lost his block against you."

The performance put him in the NSW state team for the final match of the season against South Australia where he was out twice lbw, for 31 and 44. That was his first match against Bradman. Sid always maintained he was in awe of no man yet in indiscreet moments he revealed he was in terror of Clarrie Grimmett in this match who beat him time and time again. McCabe solved the problem by taking the strike away from Barnes and belting Clarrie out of the attack. He noted McCabe played Grimmett off the front foot and thereafter he always adopted the same tactic and was not troubled by him again.

When he was overlooked for the 22 to play the Grimmett testimonial, he felt he had missed selection for the 1938 tour of England and gave thought to playing senior rugby. That clash between Australia's best cricketers was staged well before tour selection and Sid was having an impressive season, which included 97 in his maiden international, against the visiting New Zealanders.

A few days later he made 99 not out and 127 not out against Western Australia, which was still to become a member of the regular Sheffield Shield competition.

Before the second last match of the season against Bradman's South Australia, McCabe told him, "If you get a score in this match tomorrow I'm pretty sure you'll be packing your bags for England." McCabe's timing couldn't have been worse. Sid went to bed that night half-awake and half dreaming what he was going to do to Grimmett's bowling. "What I didn't do to his bowling was nobody's business. I was a lather of perspiration. I got up and had a cold shower and I didn't go to sleep for hours."

The nightmare took its toll. He batted like an old cow with arthritis, making just six runs in 90 minutes in front of Bradman who was a selector. The second innings was little better, just 21. it was inconceivable Bradman and his men could pick him for the tour after that performance.

He shut England out of his thoughts for the final game of the season and hammered the Victorian attack mercilessly. On 98 he hooked Ernie McCormick in the desire to finish the hand with a flourishing six over square leg. It caught the shoulder of his bat and flew into his face. Blood gushed everywhere as he reeled from the wicket. He was helped to the rooms where the doctor wanted to stitch the wound as McCabe sent a replacement batsmen to the wicket. Barnes wanted none of that. He chased after the batsman and sent him back to the pavilion. He went out and finished off his century. "Having got that close I wasn't going to let another one escape me," he said. His wicket fell at 110 and he returned to the doctor to have the stitches inserted.

He was now Scarface Barnes with a new mouth scar to add to his collection of a stiff upper lip and another under his chin from a bicycle accident. A couple of days later he was walking on clouds as he learned his ton against Victoria had lifted him into the touring side – in that state of euphoria he blindly walked into a telegraph post for another nasty head wound.

It may have been while he was in this dazed state that he made himself a personal vow. He had such immense self-confidence he not only determined to be a success on tour he set himself the ultimate target – he was going to eclipse Bradman and he would meet The Don at his own game of stealing the strike. "I was determined in the final wash-up not to yield ground to Don and if it came to the crunch we would have to agree to fair share of the ball. I had it in my favor that I was even faster between wickets than he and I could get a single just as easily as he."

There was a great bonding of players when they embarked on the great Orontes cruise to England with "Jackie" Badcock taking it on himself to look after Sid, the baby of the tour. Sid who was sartorial elegance itself couldn't come to terms with the sloppy appearance of the various state legislators of cricket. Tour manager Bill Jeanes was also secretary of the Board of Control. His first words to Barnes were, "Where did you get that hat. Throw it away."

Sid was proud of that hat, he'd just bought it from a fashionable Sydney store. When Jeanes went a step further and plucked the hat from the Barnes head and cast it to the crowd below. Sid was furious and rushed down the stairs and gangplank and recovered the hat from a curious wharfie who had stuck it on his well-oiled head.

His temper didn't improve when he was handed what seemed like a thousand autograph slips and a fountain pen. Sign them all, was the message. "It was just plain silly," said Barnes, "We called it our homework and sat down at the tables and swotted over these signatures." Barnes said the autograph hunters despised these slips.

"I decided never to be caught again," said Sid, "In Perth before the '48 tour I had a stamp made of my autograph." When team manager Keith Johnson told the players they had to sign 10,000 autographs before they left for England Barnes found a couple of kids. "My first 5000 autographs cost two bottles of ginger beer, the other 5000 cost one bottle."

Ernie Toshack was also carpeted for neglecting his responsibilities. He protested he had signed every slip. Johnson snarled, "I see that. But I note you no longer have a C in your name Toshak." Touche! Sid said his point was proven when they left their hotel in London at the end of the tour the porter asked what he was to do with the box full of autographs.

Back to the '38 tour, The tour cruise continued with the players exercising hard on the ship until one day as they approached Gibraltar, Sid fell and damaged his wrist but concealed the injury for fear of being sent home as unfit. He had broken the scaphoid bone and a doctor set it in plaster. There was a lot of mental anguish to go with the physical pain. The medical opinion was 13 weeks on the sidelines.

Australia was almost two players short as Barnes filled in his boredom by indulging in pranks. He had ordered a cricket bag to carry his gear and the bag that arrived was coffin size which encouraged his mate Jack Badcock to jump inside and stretch out. Sid promptly zipped the bag and snapped the lock shut – sadly the keys were inside and the bag was made out of stern stuff, designed to withstand the rigors of travel, flood and fire. With Jack breathing his last few pockets of usable air before expiring, Sid was able to cut a small air hole in the bag.

THE ROYAL SCANDAL

Sid filled in his spare time by trying his hand at producing a movie of the tour. He reasoned when he got back to Australia he and Bill O'Reilly could go on tour with the film. They would make a fortune addressing sports nights for the cricket-hungry masses who heard little and saw almost nothing of these tours. O'Reilly would deliver the lectures and Barnes would be the technician. In time to come, the Barnes films raised a considerable amount of money for charity. He became remarkably proficient at film making and his color study of Australia's tour in 1948 was a remarkable and successful cricket epic, shown all over Australia.

Knowing the Barnes penchant for turning everything to his financial advantage, he was accused of making the films for profit. He vehemently denied this, saying he maintained strict financial records of all the dealings with the films including taxation statements – "All I got from the films was my expenses," he insisted. The films were to lead him into troubled waters with the Australian Cricket Board in 1951.

He was accused of abusing his position of trust to take intimate pictures of the Royal family. The films were labelled a breach of royal protocol and the manner in which the film was taken deemed insulting behaviour to the Royal Family. The royal displeasure was rumored to be listed in the "secret" Australian Board of Control dossier on why Sid Barnes was finally deemed unworthy of further representing Australia.

When Barnes took the Board to court to disclose their secret agenda against him, Bill Jeanes was asked if he had evidence to prove guilt of discourteous behaviour towards the Royal Family. Jeanes stated at no time had the Board any such information or suggestion of conduct offensive or derogatory to members of the Royal Family.

Sid Barnes admitted trouble only once filming royalty. This was in '48 when King George and the Queen saw a match at Lord's. Barnes asked protocol controller Lord Gowrie, aide-de-camp to the King, for permission to take film of the Queen Mother at Windsor Castle when she was chatting to the cricketers. The Earl said the Queen Mother would be delighted if he did so. He again asked permission when the King and Queen met the players as they lined up on the ground before play began at Lord's. Earl Gowrie again told Sid he could film the meetings between the royals and the players. After the royals met Sid and passed down the line, he fell out of the line and took footage of their informal stroll and chats.

The Earl and Sid were unaware all the rights to film the Test had been sold. Sid fumed over that one, "The M. C. C. could sell the rights to film us yet we were not allowed to film ourselves. Nor do I see they had any rights to exclusive filming of the royals. "

Barnes lost the first 10 weeks of the tour to his broken hand and made his debut on English soil against Derby on June 29, 1938, by that time Bradman had totted up 1592 runs. He now set himself to match the master over the balance of the tour. The Don added another 837 runs while Sid made 1080, average 48.

His batting was instantly in tune with strong hands of 42 and 58 against Derby and Nottingham. It was his 140 not out at Durham which won him a berth in the fifth Test after Australia had already stitched up the series. That may have been touch and go because tour management was not impressed that Jack Badcock and Barnes had crashed a car into a ditch after the fourth Test celebrations. It was not their fault, Barnes was not a drinker and they were being chauffeured.

The driver was knocked unconscious in the accident and there was deep concern that both players could have been killed. When Bill Jeanes asked why he was arriving back at the hotel in a dishevelled condition he said he fell over a rake in the garden – he feared if he revealed the extent of the accident he may have been rested from the next day's game and he wanted to play to shore up his bid for Test selection.

He pulled up sore and sorry the next morning, stiff as a board. Badcock came out of the crash much better and belted 110 before being run out, Sid was missed twice before being lbw for an inglorious nine. Nevertheless he was selected for his first Test against England. It wasn't the most soul-stirring event as England and Len Hutton batted for three and a half days before declaring. Len Hutton had ground out a new world record score of 364 and the Poms declared at 7-903 – a slight case of overkill which Bradman swore he would never forget or forgive. Ben Barnett was in the horrors behind the stumps and dropped Hutton several times. England whipped Australia mercilessly but Sid on debut had 41 and 33 and was well pleased that he had met the best of English bowling and found they held no terrors for him.

Sid became known to his associates as BBB – Beau Brummel Barnes because of his fetish for fashionable clothes. The 1938 tourists insisted he was so impressed by King George and his superbly tailored suits that he asked the monarch for the name of his tailor and was politely ignored.

On return, he was NSW outstanding batsman with 650 runs at 46 in the absence of Stan McCabe, who was ill and Jack Fingleton and Bill O'Reilly who took a temporary break.

The outbreak of war in Europe brought uncertainty to the Australian scene but a full Shield season was again played, Sid again making 500-plus runs at almost 45.

As Germany launched its multi-fronted attacks in Europe, cricket continued in

Australia and Sid started the 1940-41 domestic season in Bradman-like form. He followed an opening duck against Queensland with 108, 133, 137, 132, 185 and 51 in successive hands.

At the end of the war Sid found himself playing for NSW in a hastily convened first-class cricket series that took in matches against other states and the Australian Services team. He proved early he had found touch of Bradmanesque as he batted for 200 out of 338 at the 'Gabba in Queensland on a slow ground that had ankle deep grass.

He had a very stormy relationship with the Queensland representative on the Board of Control J. S. Hutcheon. He was infuriated when he found ground staff cutting the ground to the bone after NSW had batted. He objected to this grossly improper action only to be severely reprimanded by Hutcheon and ordered to mind his own business. Sid instantly went on the attack. "Stop the mowing or I'll take my team out of the game."

Hutcheon backed off but Sid had made a formidable enemy. He put that experience behind him as he again rattled up the centuries: 115 against South Australia; a devastating 146 opposed to the Vics; more devastation with 156 off the Queensland attack and then a classical 102 against the all-conquering Australian Services team. He regularly threw his wicket away belting sixes after passing the century.

He was getting tons with greater efficiency and regularity than the mighty Bradman. He scored 11 centuries in 12 first-class matches; his one failure being 51. Barnes declared the Services team was over-boomed and bet Keith Miller five pounds he would score a century against them. Miller paid up and then the pair were teamed along with Ray Lindwall for the 1946 New Zealand tour which Bradman declined on ill health.

Just one Test was played. New Zealand batted first and made 42. Australian made 8-199 and the Kiwis lost by an innings and plenty when they made another 42.

They returned from New Zealand to meet the MCC tourists and his first encounter was a personal brush with Walter Hammond who he found ungracious. He consoled himself with a solid, familiarising knock against the Alec Bedser-led English attack. Bedser was also having a look at the Australian batsman and declared Sid essentially a back foot specialist.

The Australians were having trouble finding a settled opening combination. The job was offered to Barnes and it appealed. He would be in before Bradman and better placed to take control of the game. "Better to have the game by the throat before Braddles comes to the wicket than come after he's turned on the champagne and I look like flat beer." He was still making Bradman the driving force of his ambition and delighted when Bradman made himself available and was named, as captain, in Australia's first Test side for the first Ashes confrontation since 1938.

Barnes was 31 out of 46 when Bradman strode to the wicket in his normal No.3 spot. Sid received a short ball from Douglas Wright which he pulled ferociously and somehow Bedser dragged the catch of the year out of the air and his first innings as an opener ended at 45. Surviving a controversial appeal for caught before he was 30, Bradman made a century and the Aussies 645. Caught on a sticky wicket, England was never in the race and lost by an innings.

Bradman took Sid aside after the game and told him he was pleased with his performance as an opener before admonishing him for being too attacking. "You were looking for runs all the time," said Bradman. "I think what you want to watch as an opener is not getting out. A good start is vital and batsmen down the line can get all the runs when the edge is taken off the attack." The philosophy of an opening batsman was not to hook until you passed the half century – that was a test of the Barnes patience if ever there was one.

The one drawback in the Bradman instruction was that he knew he could no longer continue his duel with the wonder man. He had a lingering suspicion that Bradman knew of his not too secret agenda to eclipse his deeds. His game had been re-directed and Sid admitted he was going to miss those limelight days and newspaper headlines for a slashing innings. He said he was prepared to dress himself in the drudgery of being an Australian opener, if that's what Bradman required.

The second Test saw England grind out a first innings 255. Australia then went to bat and Morris was again out early in a stop-start rain interrupted innings. Sid expected Bradman to join him at the wicket and was stunned to see the low-order spinner Ian Johnson arrive at the wicket with instructions from Bradman he was to survive at all costs and appeal against the light at every opportunity until the umpires caved in.

He followed orders and wore the controversy that followed. The rules allowed the batsman to appeal against the light after every alternate ball and the opener followed his captain's orders to the limit and finally the umpires terminated play. After every appeal the umpires met in the middle of the wicket to discuss the light. The crowd became restive and the fieldsmen frustrated.

"Come on Barnes," said Hammond. "Why don't you get on with the game?" Barnes retorted, "Don't get upset Hammond. You'll be out here for hours." And it was hours before the umpires gave in and Barnes was hooted every step of the way to the pavilion.

Privately Bradman lauded his effort, "That 20 was worth more than a hundred to us today." That didn't spare Barnes being pilloried by the world press as he took the full brunt of the criticism.

The game resumed the next day and the wicket was still ordinary. Johnson went and so did his replacement Hassett. Miller entered. Where the hell was Bradman? Barnes was still being blasted by the Hillites for spoiling their entertainment the previous day. "Braddles" had turned him from hero to anti-hero with one change of the batting order. When Miller departed at 4-159, Bradman finally came to the crease whereas Barnes had been there for every run of the innings. They batted together to stumps. The next day proved to be the most divisive in the Barnes career.

He had a lot of gear to take into the SCG, having taken all his equipment home the previous night to clean. He parked alongside the Hammond Jaguar. A young constable moved over and ordered him to move the car 50 yards away. Sid was reasonable, if it was good enough for Hammond to park there, it was good enough for him. The constable was concerned only with the Barnes car. "Move it!" Sid offered a compromise. He had to go into bat, he would see the sergeant in charge and if he still had to move it, he would.

Barnes proceeded to have 10 minutes practice in the nets only to have the constable seize him by the arm, force him against a wall and warn him he was "booked". He demanded the opener's license and threatened him with arrest if he did not comply. Barnes described what followed, "I jerked free and the constable barged into a pressman, who dropped his camera on to the concrete path, and in the ensuing turmoil I hurried off and left them. My car stayed where it was, I stayed at the wickets for almost all of that day and I don't know what happened to the constable. I wouldn't exactly commend him for tolerance."

Barnes was front page news, particularly in England as their cricket writers ran riot with the story, hugely embellished. Another black mark in the Barnes dossier. The innings continued with Bradman instructing his partner to hold things together, he was unwell with pulled thigh muscles and a gastric upset. He doubted he could be relied on.

"Bradman is most encouraging when you bat with him. He keeps up a running commentary between overs and is full of information about what the other captain and his bowlers are thinking. And trying to do. He never misses a beat. He kept telling me throughout the partnership how the whole Test rested upon me. I began to feel after awhile I was carrying the House of Bradman as well as Australia's cricketing fortunes on my shoulders." He agreed he did not have Bradman's hunger for mammoth scores. A century was enough no matter what type of match. Once achieved, Sid felt a batsman had an obligation to entertain the public with some lusty hitting. With that attitude he had no chance of rivalling the scoring triumphs of the world's greatest batsman. Bradman was emphatic that the essence of the game and team success was never giving up your wicket.

Barnes likened this marathon innings as matching Hutton's record performance in boredom. Both he and Bradman amassed 234 as they set a new world record partnership of 405. The 234 was also an SCG record and Barnes says he threw his wicket away to share a record with Bradman rather than have it on his own. "I worshipped him," he explained.

The Don had fathered him throughout his first-class career. When he got back to the rooms Bradman smiled at him, "Well done 'Bagga' you have done a great job for Australia." Sid beamed back, "You didn't do so bad yourself." The tag Bagga was a nickname given to Barnes by Jack Badcock after the cricket bag incident in England.

He damaged his right hand between Tests and to protect his hand he dropped himself down the NSW batting list to No. 6 where he scored only five and was forced to hospital from the pain of the injury, unable to bat in the second innings. As a result he lost his captaincy although he probably set his execution in motion the match previously against England. A couple of the state selectors had been harassing young players and the skipper told them the team would be better served if they stayed away from the rooms – the rooms belonged to players, not officials. He told one selector if he wanted to get a message to a player he should go through the captain.

Everywhere he went this season he left spot fires that nobody bothered to put out. The press was having a field day as he blundered from confrontation to confrontation. The third Test in Melbourne gave him the biggest headline since Bodyline and a massive entry in the Board's black book.

The banner headlines said it all: Barnes Uproar! TEST STAR HURDLES TURNSTILE.

In half a season he had clashed with the English skipper Hammond; banned selectors from the NSW dressing rooms; accused of making a mockery of Test light appeals; broken away from the long arm of the law; refused to bat when his side was going down the gurgler; accused his Test skipper of grandstanding; threatened a walkout at the 'Gabba – even thrown away his Australian wicket to get in the record books with Bradman.

There was also a report he was not only disliked by the crowds because of light appeals, slow batting and mocking gestures, but also on the outer with a number of Australian cricketers. *Daily Express* writer Harold Dale claimed the Aussie players ignored Barnes when he split his bat when 71 not out against England. He signalled the rooms for a replacement but was ignored. He even walked to the shade of the members stand to wait for the bat but when no-one came on with a replacement bat, he went into the rooms himself.

The MCG gate incident remains one of the best-remembered incidents involving any of the cricket wildmen.

Players were given two guest tickets for each Test. He gave one to his wife, Alison, before a New Zealander who had befriended the Australians on the '45 tour arrived in Melbourne and asked Sid for tickets.

The Victorian Cricket Association refused to provide an extra ticket, as did all other contacts. He took the ticket back off his wife and gave his friend both. Now he had no ticket for his wife although he was 22 not out overnight.

In the panic over tickets, he arrived at the ground having forgotten his own pass and there was less than an hour to go before the start.

Those who knew the avaricious side of the Barnes character suggest he had sold all three admission tickets at a very handsome scalper price – a massive crowd had queued for hours for access to the ground.

Sid was confident the gatekeepers would realise they couldn't refuse entry to a not out Australian batsman, the crowd would lynch such officiousness. He quietly placed himself on the end of the queue for ticket-holders and when he got to the keeper of the turnstile he gave a disarming smile and drawled, "Look old chap, I'm Barnes, I've left my ticket back at the pub. It will be alright, won't it?"

"I'm sorry, I can't let you in. My instructions are to let nobody in without a ticket." Barnes asked him to send a messenger around to the rooms for the manager or Bradman. Not likely. "Stand aside sir, so I can attend to the people who do have tickets." Time was running out but Sid stood aside only to be totally ignored while the gatekeeper continued endlessly punching holes in tickets.

Barnes became extremely frustrated and agitated. "Look here," he snarled, "I've got to get into this ground. You known I'm Barnes and running late already. You're not sending for anybody so I'm coming in." With that he jumped over the turnstile and made haste to the Australian rooms. He was padding up as Board member Aubrey Oxlade stormed in and told him he had been reported and he wanted him to go and apologise to the president of the Melbourne Cricket Club. Barnes argued that he had to go out to bat and it had been bloody officious stupidity by the gatekeeper that had provoked the situation.

"I'd still be out there waiting if I did what he wanted. What would the Board have said if I hadn't been here to bat?

"I did break in, but I'M NOT APOLOGISING TO ANYBODY!"

Barnes liked Oxlade and didn't want to upset him but the administrator's timing was ordinary; Barnes was about to go out to bat. Somehow Sid regrouped his thought processes and added 20 more runs before being out for 42 in a haul of 365.

Extraordinary controversy raged over the incident. Calls for disciplinary action, sacking, fines and even public opinion polls taken across the land to see if the public had suffered enough of the exhibitionism and mouthiness of Sid Barnes. The English press went in harder. Sid was the traditional Aussie larrikin. The odd man out. The square peg in the round hole. Yet according to Barnes it was all a massive media beat-up. "I never heard anything further about the incident at an official level." Yet he never heard the end of it publicly.

He was annoyed by the carping English criticism; particularly as he held himself responsible for Denis Compton returning to form after a torturous beginning to the tour.

Playing for the Australia X1 against the MCC in Hobart, Sid deliberately grassed an edge off Compton when he was only 11. The Englishman smiled and said, "Thanks Sid." Sid had no regrets; Compton was a great fellow and a master stroke player. The Tasmanians were entitled to see more of him. Compton struck a resurrecting 124, the first of four tons on the trot. "If it had been a competitive match I wouldn't have turfed it. It was an exhibition game and I believe I did cricket a service."

Selection for the 1948 tour of England was automatic if you leave aside the hysteria over his various breaches of etiquette. It should be noted for all his eccentricities, which perhaps has some relationship to the Pit and Sewer arenas on which he honed his philosophies, Barnes had been very much a loyalist.

Before he could be selected of the 1948 tour of England the Board representatives brought up the ticklish problem of the Barnes eccentricity. They wanted assurances there would be no clowning, no jumping turnstiles, illegal parking, wheeling and dealing, breaching royal protocol, bowling tennis balls or batting with midget bats. Barnes told the sub-committee the game was about entertainment and he believed he knew what was acceptable, good taste showmanship. He assured them he would not stray outside these parameters. Of course his parameters were considerably wider than those of the Australian Board of Control. He was told he was in the side but the Board would take a dim view of any perceived "clowning."

So it was off to England by slow boat with the Barnes luggage traditionally larger than all others because he had so many trinkets to take abroad for horse trading. There was considerable concern on the Fremantle wharf when blood was seen seeping from his wardrobe trunk. A policeman located him and took him to the ghastly scene where alarmed stewards surrounded his blood drenched and dripping trunk. Sid produced his keys and opened the trunk to reveal what he knew had to be revealed.

Several bottles of cherry brandy he had packed for the tour had been smashed by the Australian wharfies, typical handling of anything marked FRAGILE. Dress shirts, suits, underwear and his favorite sharkskin mess-jacket were all a dripping mess. How would that look at Buckingham Palace — more like a losing duellist than a cricketer!

On arrival in England he set himself to make 1000 runs in May – hopefully beating Bradman to the objective. He set himself to develop a full head of steam and began the tour brightly, his 176 against Surrey a highlight.

Having made 560 runs early in the tour, Bradman rested him for the games against Cambridge and Oxford, games in which he could have expected to score heavily. In fairness to Bradman they were close mates and The Don took off the same games wherever possible so they could tour together. The Don bought himself a baby grand piano and Sid acquired the best of movie equipment which was to cause him all that drama with the royals and the Board of Control.

Bradman feared Hutton most and he feared the great Yorshireman might be thinking of another 13-hour batting stint. He suggested a daring experiment to Sid, "I have the feeling if you worry him by fielding up close, on top his bat almost, we might rattle him. What do you think?"

"It's fine by me."

"Do you mind how close you field."

"Not at bit. I doubt he'll knock my head off."

It was rare for Hutton to lift at a ball on the on-side. He seldom hooked. The theory was put to the test in the MCC match at Lord's. Sid was not in fear, although he knew a blow to the temple could see his carcase interred on English soil, perhaps alongside the Lord's wicket or perhaps cremation would provide genuine Ashes for the jousting.

"If your end comes, it comes," said Barnes.

Australia batted first and made 552, Jim Laker being extraordinarily expensive, having nine 6s hit off him over the short on-side boundary in the morning session. Hutton was decidedly uncomfortable to find Sid fielding almost in his pocket but looked in ominous form with 52 and 64. Barnes reported to Bradman that none of the English bats relished a close-in fieldsmen. They decided to extend the tactic.

Australian won the first Test with Barnes making a cavalier 64 from 98 to win the match. He then had a lean trot and felt powerless to do anything about it which took

Jack Pollard Collection

Manchester, 1948: Sid Barnes is helped from Old Trafford after being struck over the kidneys by a full blooded drive from Dick Pollard early on the second day of the third Test.

him into the second Test at Lord's a little on edge. He wanted a century in this Test as his two finger salute to the snobbish administrators who refused to allow him to use their nets a year earlier. He even had eight pounds on himself at 15-1 to score the century.

He batted himself in quietly and determined to watch the ball grow from a little red grape to a giant pumpkin. He was too cautious and popped a gentle catch to Hutton and his revenge on the aristocrats was a blob – a Lord's duck, the most unpalatable of all game birds. What made it worse was his wife had journeyed in for the match knowing how he had set his heart on making this *his* game.

He went back to his hotel with the sulks. He crawled into bed at 8 pm and churned through the grisly events of the day.

There was a knock on the door. He didn't want visitors unless it was wife – and she was banned. He threw the door open and there was the little champ himself, Norman Von Nida. He was a vinegary little cuss and snarled at the brooding batsman, "What's up with you. Mooning and moaning in bed? Get up and get your mind off things. You'll never do any good by going to bed early when you're failing. All you'll do is worry."

Von Nida hit the right button. Barnes jumped out of bed, called Alison who was a couple of miles away and they steamed off to a night club. It was great medicine, took his mind off the game until he strode out to the crease for the second innings. Again he elected to wait for the pea to become a pumpkin but made sure he punished the bad balls as his eye and brain dictated. He concentrated on locking his eye on the ball and never let one past as he closed in on his first 50 all the way through to the hundred barrier. He hadn't thought about the bet but only about getting control of his game again.

"The Von" had told him the betting was a good investment. It was wise to have faith in yourself and back your confidence with money. It was this time anyway the 128 pound return on his bet was close to a king's ransom in that era. He was so rapt on reaching the ton he blazed away and hit three 6s before donating his wicket to Norman Yardley going for another. His 141 was a great moment.

When England batted, Barnes took on the role of intimidating fieldsman. And he was aware that while taking strike Hutton was having furtive sideway glances to Sid who had positioned himself close-in legside. The selectors were not impressed and dropped Hutton from the third Test which the Aussies thought was a classic misjudgment. Much as they respected Compton, Hutton was the man they feared most. Compton batted brilliantly at Old Trafford despite taking a colossal blow in the head while hooking.

As the English innings fell apart, Compton strove to get the maximum score from what opportunity remained. Audibly he told No. 10 Dick Pollard to go negative and just hold up his end while Compton did the scoring. Armed with that knowledge Sid smirked and decided it was a great time to cramp Pollard by fielding in his hip pocket.

Sid Barnes took up position at what was described as "suicide point" – within breathing distance on the leg side.

Compton was already wounded in action with plaster covering a deep cut on his forehead induced by that searing Lindwall bouncer. Compton was batting courageously and stroking the ball brilliantly.

Knowing Pollard was just going to poke and prod, Barnes decided it was safe to crowd in even closer – you could say it was the death seat particularly as the Australian bowler was Johnson who was dropping slow off-spinners just short of a length to draw the mistake or a loose slog. Barnes edged closer....

No helmet, face guard or body protectors, just a baggy green hat and a huge heart.

Batting for England gave Pollard a rush of blood as he forgot all about Compton's instructions to just hang about. Johnson knew the essence of bowling when your mate is at short leg or "death gully" is not, under any circumstance, to bowl a ball so loose that the batsman can wallop a drive through that vulturous fieldsman.

Johnson bowled a rank long hop that even he called his "donkey-drop" and the beefy Pollard struck it with a full blooded pull that was on Barnes before he could twitch. He did plenty of twitching after the ball struck him amidships and did its level best to burrow between his ribs and out through his backbone. Sid went down in a heap, writhing in agony from what seemed to the hushed crowd to be a mortal blow. Miller was sceptical as the Australian fieldsmen carried the twitching Barnes body to the medical rooms, a huge red splotch deepening in the middle of his chest cavity – now a cavity so pronounced you could fit a cricket ball into it.

"Sid was a bit of an actor and the boys carrying him off said he even crossed his legs to be more comfortable in the transportation." The two doctors who examined him were far more concerned although a cynical Miller still insisted they found nothing wrong. This contradicted unofficial medical reports doing the rounds that claimed the blow could have been fatal, had badly bruised vital organs and had left an immense bruise and a considerable amount of agony. They said a little closer to the heart and it may well have killed him.

Barnes said, "I never saw the ball from the bat. All I knew was that I had received a terrific blow over the ribs on my left side. I suppose I was lucky it didn't kill me as some are killed from such a blow near the heart when playing cricket.

"My legs buckled under me and I collapsed. My first thought as I was hauled to my feet was that I had gone blind in the left eye. My whole left side seemed to be paralysed and I couldn't see from the eye at all."

He was taken to hospital for x-rays where the specialists made a discovery, Sid had extraordinary ribs and it took the full force of the gamma rays to penetrate ribs so thick they would have done justice to the super structure of a Spanish galleon – which may explain why the ball didn't pass through his body. He was held in hospital overnight. When he returned to the match his upper body was a massive black and blue bruise.

Knowing Australia needed him, he told Bradman he would take his turn at the crease and headed for the nets. "After having a hit I went out to the middle but felt groggy. I played a few balls then ran a single. I just collapsed again and was carried off by a group of Pommy bobbies."

That was the end of the Old Trafford Test for Barnes and the next Test as well.

Australia won the fourth Test to retain the unbeaten record.

Barnes the prankster: Taking block with a mini bat during the Bradman testimonial match in Melbourne, 1948-49. Wicketkeeper Don Tallon shares the mirth of the moment.

During the Surrey match at the Oval on this tour a little English mongrel ran on to the sacred turf. Sid caught him and handed the little canine to Umpire Alec Skelding. Skelding had a fear of dogs and ran away with Sid chasing after him with the dog in his outstretched hands.

The umpire with his arms full of Australian guernseys ran almost to the boundary to stay out of the reach of Barnes and the wriggling dog.

The final Test was to be historic for a number of reasons. Yardley won the toss and batted when he should have bowled. His penalty was to see his entire side back in the pavilion for 52 on the first morning. This guaranteed a win for Australia and an unbeaten series.

Bradman retired and Barnes was no longer chasing the Bradman shadow. Barnes decided to take a break from cricket declaring himself unavailable for the South African tour. He made an exception of Bradman testimonial. "I wanted to play in that and promised Don I would." He made 32 and 89 and in-between time took a small toy back out to the wicket. He handed his Test bat to the umpire and took block with the midget.

He also missed the Freddie Brown English tour of Australia but made himself available for the West Indies as Australia was struggling to find a reliable opening combination. Barnes had a nagging suspicion he had lost the plot with the Board of Control and at the beginning of the 1951-52 season he spoke to Board chairman Aubrey Oxlade concerning rumors the board was antagonistic to him. Oxlade told him he had the answer in his hands – the bat. "You know what I think of you as a cricketer and as a man."

His scores started to come as he made 57 and 28 against South Australia and back in harness with Arthur Morris as his partner he made 107 in a 200 run stand. Popular opinion was that performance combined with others would see the old firm reinstated for the third Test against the Windies.

Barnes got the shock of his life as he drove through Sydney anticipating the announcement of the Test team. His eyes popped at the newspaper poster: TEST SHOCK. BARNES IN, BARNES OUT.

He ran into the nearest newsagency and seized a paper. The poster said it all. Don Bradman and his co-selectors had picked him for the Australian Test team. They submitted 13 names to the Board of Control and subsequently the Board caused a stir by objecting to one of the players. No prizes for guessing who. The team was referred back to the selectors – this was unprecedented in Australian Test cricket.

The Board of Control tried to duck the issue by refusing to name the player who had been dumped, saying it was a policy not to identify players discarded for reasons other than cricket ability.

"It makes me feel like an unwanted cur," said Barnes.

There was a massive public and media backlash against the Board and one doubts that public respect for the Board and Australian Test selection criteria has ever been restored.

As national support welled behind him Barnes again went on the front foot and drove the Australian Board of Control into court as Board members ducked for cover in the face of this hostility.

Sid was angered that the NSW Cricket Association continued to appoint him state captain but would not demand an explanation from the Board as to his banishment from international cricket. Ironically Sid's daughter, Helen, came home from school one day and asked her father, "Daddy. Why can't you win?"

Why not indeed? The next day he saw Mr. J. W. Shand Q.C. and in February, 1952 the wheels began to turn.

Three months after the sacking on the advice of Shand Q.C. Sid went public to clear his name. In a media statement he expressed concern that the secrecy surrounding the Board action had led to disturbing speculation which was injurious to the well being of his family and himself. He invited the Board to publicly explain and justify their course of action. He disclosed a personal conversation with Oxlade and that gentleman's denial of any involvement.

Barnes said he had left the matter with Oxlade on his assurance that he was going to take it up with the Board and had told Barnes the final right of approval rested with himself. Later contact with Oxlade had run him into a brick wall as the official said he had no power to disclose any of the discussions that took place.

Barnes wrote individually to Board members asking them to state their position publicly. The Sydney *Truth* uncovered a startling notation in the Board of Control minutes: "Mr. Hutcheon sought permission to move the following motion: *The approval of selections of Australian teams shall be dealt with upon a confidential basis; no minutes shall be recorded in respect thereof and no publication shall be made of the names of any persons who may be disapproved or the reasons therefor.*"

The motion was carried by the necessary three-fourths majority. The newspaper blasted the Board decision and declared it was clearly designed to avoid leakage of information on the Barnes issue.

Subsequently Jeanes made a public statement on behalf of the Board saying that august body had never disclosed or named any players as being disapproved as a member of the Australian team. He said because of recent matters discussed the Board was prepared to state that at no time had it possessed any information suggesting dishonesty on the part of Barnes or conduct offensive or derogatory to members of the Royal family..... the Board was digging itself into a hole because when it finally emerged from behind its closed door mentality it didn't know how to go public.

Shand Q. C. described the Board's response as, "Grudging, ungenerous and unhelpful."

He also pointed out that three members of the Board, NSW delegates Oxlade, Frank Cush and Johnson repeatedly approved Barnes as NSW captain. It was their clear duty to make known why their player was rendered unacceptable for Australia. "It is clear the Board had no real reason for excluding Barnes and being aware of the arbitrary nature of their decision is studiously avoiding the disclosure of the insupportable reasons for its conduct."

Shand said the Board members had no excuse for not publicising their reasons as Barnes invitation to publicise their reasons granted them immunity. All members of the Board replied to the Barnes invitation with a curt notice they would not enter into correspondence on the subject matter set forth.

Then one day a letter appeared in the Sydney *Daily Mirror* letters to the editor column written by a Mr. J. L. Raith of Stanmore. The letter took the side of the Board of Control maintaining they could not clear themselves because their lips were sealed. The writer unequivocally declared the Board would not have excluded Barnes capriciously and would have done so only for some matter of a sufficiently serious nature.

Mr. Raith suddenly found himself the vehicle on which court action could drive the sorry business into the open. He was sued for libel and in his defence he would be forced to call the ABC to account. Raith served the Board of Control up to Barnes on a platter.

Sid either retired hurt or went on the attack. The next step was one giant step for cricket – straight into courts. Raith to defend himself was forced to subpoena Sir Donald Bradman, Oxlade and their fellow board members. Sir Donald justifiably avoided the hearing by forwarding an affidavit explaining for business reasons and a result of his son having polio he was unable to attend.

Board secretary and tour manager Jeanes quickly discovered he was no longer in cricket's Star Chamber but in the public forum where he and his Board members were on equal footing. "Take off your hat!" roared a court attendant as the jaunty Jeanes strode into Judge Lloyd's District Court with his hat perched on his head. Barnes couldn't resist a smile remembering when Jeanes had flung his hat over the side of the ship when Sid made his first international voyage. It was also something of a status reminder for the Board spokesman. Hatless Jeanes entered the witness box and was asked by Mr. Smyth Q.C. to produce Board of Control documents.

Jeanes cleared his throat and expounded his instructions. "Your Honor. I have brought certain documents with me under subpoena but I object to their production. They are the property of the Board of Control. I am the secretary of the Board of Control and I have no authority to produce them."

He learned very quickly the difference between the High Court of Cricket and the courts of Australia. Judge Lloyd said he did have the authority to produce the documents – that authority was the order of the court. What he didn't have was the authority *not* to produce them.

Jeanes was pragmatic and continued to object as each document was called. He continued to produce and the crowded courtroom had a very clear picture of "the law unto itself" mentality of the Board as it grudgingly yielded up its secrets which Jeanes insisted contained "certain confidential, personal and private letters." If they were good enough for the Board of Control to see they were good enough for the court of Judge Lloyd.

The Board was on very clear notice that there was nowhere to hide in a court of law. The barristers poured over the documents before Shand made an opening address to the jury in which he lashed tour manager Keith Johnson as Sid's "treacherous friend;" and soon it was Sid Barnes being called to the box.

Having seen the severe demands on witnesses under examination, Barnes was plainly nervous when he stepped into the box to launch the case to make the Board disclose its reasons for vetoing his selection. Mr. Shand Q. C. smiled as he took Sid through his evidence opening with the first headline: "Mr. Barnes, it seems you were put out of the Australian X1 for taking film during the 1948 tour of England."

That was it! That was the deep and dirty secret the Board had refused to divulge "in the best interests of Barnes." Shand Q.C. drew evidence from the Australian opener that established at the end of each tour of England he received the traditional 150 pounds "good conduct" money – clear evidence of the tour management's approval of the player's conduct. Jeanes and Johnson had been Barnes tour managers and Johnson in charge of the controversial 1948 tour.

Cross-examined by Raith's defence barrister Mr. J. W. Smyth QC, Barnes agreed he had launched the media examination of his case and the public was justified in joining in debate. He agreed Raith was entitled to believe the Board had acted properly. In other words Raith was the innocent dupe in the case.

Smyth then addressed the jury and it was clear he now realised how flimsy was the fabric around which the Board had dumped their star opener. Smyth said he found it amazing that the one person who publicly supported the Board action was denied any support by Board members and forced to compel their attendance and documentation by subpoena. He was severely critical of the Board's handling of the issue.

Next to the box was Oxlade who confirmed Bradman, Cush and himself had voted to keep Sid in the Test side – it was a telegraphic vote. He agreed there were factors detrimental to Barnes selection, jumping turnstiles and a Johnson report after the English tour of taking certain film footage. The Board also had other matters before that tour. Pressed by Smyth QC to explain the "others," Oxlade said Barnes had taken off his cap and bowed to the crowd. "Things like that," said Oxlade.

It was drawn from him that Johnson had made a report on return saying Barnes had taken Ern Toshack off to play tennis when Toshack was 12th man. Oxlade agreed that Toshack was over 21 and was responsible for his own actions and this was not a discredit for Barnes in any way. Although Barnes was not cautioned about taking film, Johnson had made a verbal report and a number of Board men had stated it was doubtful they would approve of Barnes as a Test player in the future.

Nobody had bothered to warn Barnes against taking the film or advised him it was a matter of report. He agreed Johnson's written report spoke glowingly of the exemplary conduct of the players and they behaved in a manner befitting worthy representatives of Australia. That was the written report – the verbal report had a secret sting in the tail.

Oxlade said he held a strong view Barnes should not have been excluded from the Test side. Johnson took the stand next. He acknowledged he was one of the Board members who voted against Barnes. He did so on the basis of sufficiently serious facts known about the player:

· Jumped the Melbourne turnstile.
· Asked for permission to sometimes travel alone through England. When permission was refused Barnes recognised his authority, albeit reluctantly.
· Taken movie pictures in England.
· Taken Toshack 300 yards away from the ground to play tennis when Toshack was acting as 12th man.

Even after Shand QC had discredited these "incidents" as being unproven and unpunished or the subject of any inquiry by the Board of Control, Johnson made the extraordinary statement to the court that even if Barnes was the best batsman in the world, he would not select him for future Australian Test teams because of these incidents. Mr. Smyth QC dropped his head into hands at the bar table. Johnson said he could not say how long the ban on Barnes would be enforced. The vote to exclude him had been 9-3.

Johnson said these points made Barnes unfit to represent Australia. He denied making statements to Barnes that he would be a certainty for the 1953 tour of England if he remained quiet.

Grilled by Shand, he agreed the worst thing that could happen to a cricketer was to be dismissed from a team on grounds other than cricket ability. He agreed the public could think the discarded player was guilty of dishonorable conduct. He agreed when he wrote his report the team was exemplary in England that the word "team" meant every player including Barnes. Then he recanted to say the report was true about every member of the team except the one – Barnes. He admitted that in fact his written report was false.

He was not aware Lord Gowrie gave permission for Barnes to take film of the royals. He admitted his report misled the state bodies who received his report. He admitted speaking to Board members reflecting on Barnes. He agreed Sir Donald Bradman sometimes travelled apart from the English touring party with approval and accompanied by Barnes.

Taken through the incidents that made Barnes unworthy, he agreed the turnstile incident was before the 1948 tour and certainly didn't make him unworthy of representing Australia on that tour.

In effect with Toshack responsible for his own actions with regard to the tennis, Barnes having been selected regularly after the turnstile incident which had never been raised against Barnes officially or unofficially and the fact he had permission from Lord Gowrie to take the films, the Johnson campaign against Barnes simply fell apart. Johnson was forced to admit at best he was a fourth grade cricketer who had never so much as played senior grade cricket. In fact there was only one member of the Board who had ever played first-class cricket and that was Sir Donald who had voted for Barnes.

Johnson said none of the incidents isolated justified exclusion from the Australian side; nor did two of the incidents but all three incidents did justify exclusion. Mr. Shand Q.C. said in fact not one of the three "incidents" stood up. Johnson said he opposed Barnes because he thought he was temperamentally unsuitable and had opposed him on the NSW board as state captain.

The judge made him answer when he declined after being asked if he would select Barnes if he became a world beater who could bowl slow and fast, never missed a catch and averaged 200 – if it meant the difference between winning and losing the Ashes. He said, "No, I wouldn't."

Shand Q.C.: "And you say you have a wide national outlook for the best of the game?"

"Yes."

"Do you still think you are qualified to be a member of the Board?"

"Yes."

The Board of Control was out of control as the farcical trial gathered momentum and roared towards the inevitable conclusion. "Chappie" Dwyer and Frank Cush gave evidence saying they could see no reasons why Barnes shouldn't represent Australia.

When Smyth QC made his final address to the jury for the defendant Raith he said it was his duty to prove truth and public benefit if he was to win the case for his client. He had to prove the Board had not acted capriciously.

"Seldom in the history of libel has such a plea failed so completely and utterly.....

"Neither my client nor myself had any idea what it was with which Barnes was charged, nor could we secure any information. You can see now why the Board was so reluctant to help us, why the Board was so anxious that none of its records should be available in the court for the purpose of assisting the defendant."

Thus he acknowledged Barnes had won the case. He turned to the question of damages against Raith. He asked the jurors not to award damages that would reflect what every decent citizen would feel those members of the Board who, upon such silly, trivial grounds excluded Barnes from the Australian X1...

"Did you ever hear such Tommy rot... my client foolishly, as it turns out, believed that this Board was an impartial body of cricket administrators. You can well imagine what Mr. Raith thinks of those gentlemen now."

He rounded off by saying Barnes had not set out in this case for financial gain but to clear his name. Barnes waived his damages claim of 1000 pounds and settled for the crushing moral victory over the Board. It seemed a tad unfair that Mr. Raith paid the costs and the Board members escaped with only their pride bruised.

Judge Lloyd accepted the settlement of the case. He said Barnes had cleared his name so there was nothing left for the jury to determine.

CASE SPLITS BOARD

Board of Control chairman R. A. Oxlade resigned soon after the Barnes case, but denied his decision had anything to do with the case. The main antagonist Keith Johnson resigned within a couple of months of the trial due to "business pressures." Former Board chairman Dr. Allen Robertson was disgruntled when Barnes won his case. "Only half the story had been told," he declared. Yet another unsubstantiated red herring.

Sid Barnes walked from the court with his name cleared. The battered members of the Board of Control left in tatters, one hoped a wiser and more judicious crew ..... but we may wonder if that battle changed anything.

It would be the fitting end to the clash between the battler and bureaucracy to record that Sid Barnes strode out to a standing ovation at Lord's crashed a brilliant double ton and secured the Ashes for Australia while the old Board members were tumbled out of office by an enthusiastic and "open" Board of Control inclusive of great cricketers who knew all the ropes.

Sid did his level best as the 1952-53 season opened with the stormy libel case several months in the background. He drew rave notices with a crashing and spectacular 156 against Ian Johnson's Victorians. He was in his mid-30s but stroked the ball with sharp-eyed precision and ran his hard singles and punishing threes with great speed and stamina. "He's a certainty for the first Test," declared the experts as the selectors set themselves to meet the South Africans.

There was a new selection panel Jack Ryder, Phil Ridings and Bill Brown. A number of Board members had resigned since the case. The Board said the three selector's initial list would merely be "preliminary" selection.

He displayed all his roguish humour as he belted the Vics and doffed his cap and bowed to the wildly applauding crowd as he posted his century. That crowd hosted three Australian selectors and his presence drew 17,407 spectators to the MCG. Some 40 years later VCA officials would have killed for that sort of attendance at a Shield match. He had completely won the Victorian crowd and one assumed he had proved all he had to prove to the selectors.

But had he? It did not appear so. He remained in exile when Jeanes announced the first representative teams of the summer. All Australia was outraged. Barnes was shattered as he pondered another long legal onslaught on the Board, well aware by now they would have shored up their legal defences and would fall back on the age factor.

"Bad luck, Sid, but I had nothing to do with it," said Bradman.

Sid tried to drown his sorrow in more pranks as he volunteered to act as 12th man for the NSW side in Adelaide and made a feature of his duties by walking to wicket in a suit and tie carrying the drinks to the players on trays draped with white towels.

He set up a portable radio near the wicket; combed Keith Miller's hair as part of the service; offered cigars to players; held a mirror in front of Miller so he could preen himself; sprayed scent over the boys and used a clothes brush to dust down their shirts and trousers; handed iced towels to the players

From there on he accepted the inevitable and retired to concentrate on writing. He died in December, 1973 aged somewhere between 54 and 57 years of age. Family members found him on the couch, having overdosed on tablets. He left a widow and three children.

Indian captain Lala Amarnath falls lbw for a duck to the Barnes toppie: MCG, 1947-48.

Sid Barnes THE MAN & HIS RECORD

Born: June 5, 1916 (according to Wisden)
Teams: New South Wales & Australia
First-class debut: 1936-37
First-class debut: Matches 110. Batting — Runs 8333, Average 54.11, Highest score 234, 100s 26, 50s 37. Bowling — Wickets 57, Average 32.21, Best bowling 3-0. Fielding — Catches 80, Stumpings 4. Captaincy — Matches 7, Wins 3, Losses 2, Draws 2.
Test debut: 1938
Test record: Matches 13. Batting — Runs 1072, Average 63.06, Highest score 234. Bowling — Wickets 4, Average 54.50, Best bowling 2-25. Fielding — Catches 14.
Tours: England 1938, 1948, New Zealand 1945-46.

Sid Barnes' Test record series by series:

BATTING & FIELDING

Season	Opponent	Mt	Inns	No	HS	Runs	Ave	100s	50s	Ct.
1938	England (a)	1	2	0	41	74	37.00	-	-	1
1945-46	New Zealand (a)	1	1	0	54	54	54.00	-	1	2
1946-47	England (h)	4	6	0	234	443	73.83	1	1	4
1947-48	India (h)	3	4	0	112	172	43.00	1	-	6
1948	England (a)	4	6	2	141	329	82.25	1	3	1
Totals		13	19	2	234	1072	63.06	3	5	14

BOWLING

Season	Opponent	Mt	Balls	Mdn	Runs	Wick	Ave	BB
1938	England (a)	1	228	3	84	1	84.00	1-84
1945-46	New Zealand(a)	1	-	-	-	-	-	-
1946-47	England(h)	4	56	0	23	0	-	0-1
1947-48	India (h)	3	280	6	100	3	33.33	2-25
1948	England (a)	4	30	2	11	0	-	0-11
Totals		13	594	11	218	4	54.50	2-25

COUNTRY BY COUNTRY RECORD

BATTING & FIELDING

Country	Mt	Inns	NO	HS	Runs	Ave	100s	50s	Ct.
v England	9	14	2	234	846	70.50	2	4	6
v India	3	4	0	112	172	43.00	1	-	6
v New Zealand	1	1	0	54	54	54.00	-	1	2

HOME & ABROAD

	Mt	Inns	NO	HS	Runs	Ave	100s	50s	Ct.
Tests at home	7	10	2	234	615	76.87	2	1	10
Tests abroad	6	9	2	141	457	65.28	1	4	4

BOWLING

Country	Mt	Balls	Mdn	Runs	Wick	Ave	BB
v England	9	314	5	118	1	118.00	1-84
v India	3	280	6	100	3	33.33	2-25
v New Zealand	1	-	-	-	-	-	-

HOME & ABROAD

	Mt	Balls	Mdn	Runs	Wick	Ave	BB
Tests at home	7	336	6	123	3	31.66	2-25
Tests abroad	6	258	5	95	1	95.00	1-84

HIS HIGHEST TEST SCORES

234	v England, Sydney, 1946-47
141	v England, Lord's, 1948
112	v India, Adelaide, 1947-48

HIS BEST TEST BOWLING

2-25	v India, Melbourne, 1947-48
1-51	v India, Adelaide, 1947-48
1-84	v England, The Oval, 1938

4

MILLER'S LUCK

"Moody Miller, Miller the so very, very magnificent, always pops up like a fifth ace, unexpected, and likely to disturb the balance of any game."

One of the most charismatic and universally-loved cricketers in the game's history, handsome allrounder Keith Miller ranks with Gary Sobers, Ian Botham and Imran Khan as post-war cricket's outstanding allround player. Flamboyant and anti-authoritarian and with a presence envied by even the greats, he mysteriously was omitted from a tour of South Africa when at the height of his powers. His provocative books and columns often included criticisms of Don Bradman with whom he had a love-hate relationship.

AN ENGLISH CROWD, steeped in tradition and love for all things British, stood to a man – all 30,000 of them and rent the air with the loudest and most sustained applause ever afforded a cricketer on English turf.

The man returning to the pavilion and raising his right arm to acknowledge the tribute was not Bradman, not Hammond, Hutton or Larwood. He was not an Englishman. Far from it – he was their most feared foe.

But so great was the performance, so memorable the moment that the crowd could not refrain from honoring Keith Ross Miller as he bid farewell to Lord's – the sacred home of cricket.

His farewell gesture to a country he had served as a bomber fighter pilot was the total destruction of their beloved Test side and they loved him for it.

Miller had gone to England under Ian Johnson's captaincy with a great black cloud over his fitness. Australian selector Sir Donald Bradman had sent him on tour declaring it would be unfair to ask Miller to be a key bowler. He was chosen as a batsman. Miller should not risk permanent injury, even for Australia. But Nugget Miller was a risk taker and there was nothing he wouldn't risk for Australia.

Sir Donald under-estimated the Miller grit. This was illustrated in the second Test at Lord's. The game was becoming an utter bore when the great Australian revved it to life.

Miller was simply awesome at Lord's as he was simply awesome throughout the tour and throughout his career.

Australia was struggling and losing control. Aged 36, with a back that belonged to a geriatric, he tore into the Pom top order and with a few murderous deliveries he had ripped through the cream of English bats to take 5-72.

After blasting England away for 171 to give the Aussies a first innings lead of 114, he made 30 vital runs as Australia's second innings collapsed to 6-115. With Australia back in the game he again decimated England with another stirring "five-for." It was spellbinding, inspirational, heroic stuff.

It was Keith Miller's match and the crowd thrilled to every moment of the drama. Keith could not have enjoyed it more because the English people were his people too.

For all that venom he fired at them he loved Britain. He relished their aristocracy, their horse racing, their sense of history, their landscape, their art, their music and their heritage. He just loved Australia more.

There could be no prouder moment in the illustrious career of Keith Ross "Nugget" Miller than his walk to the Lord's pavilion having inspired Australia to a devastating win that brought this sort of tribute from a besotted media. The London *Daily Sketch* was delirious in its praise of the mercurial Miller. The Sketch all but drooled, "Moody Miller, Miller the so very, very magnificent, always pops up like a fifth ace, unexpected, and likely to disturb the balance of any game."

Alex Bannister in the *Daily Mail*, "Doff your grey topper gentlemen, the greatest Australian fighter of the fighting race – Keith Miller."

Sir Leonard Hutton, "I cannot remember Miller bowling better or with more vicious purpose… no two balls were alike."

One English writer sighed, "If only Miller was an Englishman."

He wrote, "If this be his Test farewell to Lord's, he has on his three tours lit a lamp in England that will never be put out…."

And his captain Ian Johnson marvelled, "I asked more by far than any captain is entitled to ask of a player. He gave it to me in much larger quantities than I ever expected, let alone was entitled to receive."

It was a tad ironic that all England loved him to distraction yet some cad burgled his car while he was sunbaking on Brighton beach and made off with his wallet, diary and cheque book. Detectives attended Buckingham palace for the investiture of his MBE by the Queen – because the thief also stole his invitation to the palace.

Ah! England – the scene of most of the great moments of the Keith Miller story.

It was at Trent Bridge – the home of Larwood and Voce – where the charismatic and obscenely handsome Keith Ross Miller gave the ball a vigorous rub on his creams, licked a lip, flicked back his mane of black hair and ambled into his run to the wicket.

The run was fluent but ever so casual, picking up length of stride as he reached the point of delivery.

The target some 22 yards away was the ear of the world record holder Len Hutton.

There was nothing to indicate to Hutton this ball would be any different to a few dozen innocuous off-spinners and mild cutters already delivered off Miller's short run. Hutton was at ease, hadn't he just cracked 14 runs off the last half dozen Miller deliveries?

But there was a difference.

This ball, this delivery, contained the pent-up passion of a proud young Australian reared in the Bodyline Age and imbued in the deep spiritual bond for all Australians to call England to answer for that abomination of sportsmanship.

An uneasy truce had prevailed while the two nations united to hold off a greater evil. Keith Miller had put his life on the line more than once for these fellows. But that war was over and it was back to the old war with venom…

Miller took that last stride to the popping crease with a little more emphasis, the right shoulder swung in its arc with Tiger Woods ferocity. The long, whipcord arm had drawn back, so fully extended as to almost clip his back right heel. With rhythmic rotation of the hips the arm whipped forward with the shoulder turn cutting across his body and releasing the ball with a devilish snap of the wrist.

It hit the turf on a perfect length, on the spot just inches from the prodding forward defensive stroke of a batsman totally shocked by the speed of arrival … it was a brute of a ball. Having brought the ball down from the full height of the extended arm and upright frame with the lash of a stockwhip, the ball reared off a length and all but clipped the Hutton ear from its moorings. No helmets in those days.

The brave Yorkshireman's eyes stood out on his head. Not a word was spoken. The ground was hushed. The realisation hit the crowd and Hutton at the same time. That ball could have killed him. Harold Larwood never bowled a more lethal ball because with Larwood the batsmen at least knew what to expect.

A rumble ran through a crowd shocked by the unexpectedness of the delivery. The rumble became a roar as fellow Lancashire and Yorkshiremen remembered the wrath of Australians when their men delivered such thunderbolts at colonial heads. There was a gentle swell of catcalls and boos.

They had not noticed the difference between Larwood and the Australian – Miller was not bowling to a legside field, nor had he pitched the ball short. It was an exquisitely fair but spectacular ball. The swashbuckling Miller, with broad chest exposed as shirt buttons popped from stress, grinned roguishly as he wasted no time delivering the next thunderbolt that had Hutton falling away in confusion!

That did it! The crowd went bonkers. The roar was unprecedented in English cricket – it was more an outlet for their pent up frustration at the success of the barnstorming Australian tourists.

It was the first Test of the 1948 tour and it should be noted it was late in the day and Hutton had made 14 runs off a Miller off-spin over. Earlier Bradman had closed Australia's innings with a massive score and English wickets tumbled with Hutton playing a brave lone hand. But his onslaught on Miller was a tactical miscalculation.

The crowd roared and roared, forcing Miller to stop mid-wicket and wait for the hullabaloo to die down. It didn't so Miller continued the attack in uproar. Hutton passed that one explosive ball off as an accident caused by some unseen gremlin on the pitch.

Having seen the whites of Hutton's eyes Miller, however, sensed a breakthrough.

From the same amiable run-up the Australian fired four searing bumpers at Hutton in the midst of a dozen mundane spinners and cutters. The last over of the day caused greater uproar. A fourth bumper crunched into Hutton's shoulder which had an arm attached that had been shortened by a wartime mishap. The partisan crowd erupted and hooted abuse until the close of play when hundreds of the protesters stormed the field and formed a gauntlet of hate, abusing Miller as he passed between them to the gate. This despite Hutton square cutting the last Miller ball to the fence.

One spectator who abused him too vehemently was seized in one hand and lifted from the ground. Without raising his voice Miller pleasantly inquired, "Are you coming with me?" He then lowered him back to earth and the abuser fled. The English media, searching for new headlines since VE Day had a feast as they spread huge banner headlines across their front pages: BUMPER WAR.

The Australian media contingent defended their man to the hilt, some English writers also sprang to the Australian's defence but this was a great, new cricketing controversy to get their teeth into and the critics milked the controversy for all its worth. The English had endured the horrors of World War 2 and the Battle of Britain. This was a chance to let their hair down and stir up a sporting war with their arch enemy.

The London press wrote a spirited defence of Miller against the wrath of the Nottingham crowd. They described the crowd scene as disgraceful. The London *News Chronicle* declared, "If we squeal every time a fast bowler makes a ball rear, it's time we abandoned cricket and took up ludo."

Bannister wrote, "I wish England had a bowler who could do something similar. It is perfectly legitimate for a pace bowler to pitch the ball short so long as the batsman is not directly intimidated, Miller did not attempt intimidation; he struck Hutton on the shoulder, but this was accidental."

This led to anti-Miller forces scoffing, "Are the defenders of the bumper suggesting Miller was bowling at the stumps? The bumper is directed to fly as close to the point between ear and shoulder as to encourage an injudicious hook. It is an absurdity to suggest otherwise."

Everybody but the Sheriff of Nottingham had his say and Miller knowing his shock weapon was causing alarm amongst English batsmen simply went on bowling them within the prescribed boundaries of cricket law.

One of the English pace bowlers playing that Test laughed at the outrage, "Booed? – Any bowler getting bounce from this wicket ought to get a medal."

Thanks to the fear Miller struck in English hearts, Australia creamed England in the first Test and the ecstasy almost had disastrous consequences. Bill Johnston and Nugget hopped into a not so large steam bath to ease away the aches and pains. Big Bill was long limbed and double jointed. He could put his crossed legs behind his head which he proceeded to do while in the bath – unfortunately he lost control over his posterior and slid beneath the waves, in his own personal headlock.

It looked like a joke until the bubbles started to erupt from beneath the surface and it was soon a desperate struggle to right the angular body and extract the head from the trap. No success until Bill himself managed to disentangle himself to break the surface gasping for air and half-drowned.

He didn't learn a lesson from that escapade and soon after performed the same India rubber man trick at the top of a stairway, lost balance and bounced like a human rubber ball down to the bottom of the stairs. The double jointedness probably averted a broken neck.

The episode was typical of Keith Miller. Things happened to him and around him. He was a man with an aura. His commanding bearing and Hollywood looks made him the epicentre of public interest. He was news and he attracted trouble like a magnet. His career was one continuous headline.

"Trouble comes looking for me," he once declared.

"I gamble. I am quick tempered and not the most reliable man you would wish to meet. Yet whatever my faults I have no time for the half-truth. I like to call a spade a spade."

That is as fitting an introduction as one could imagine for the most charismatic cricketer the world has seen.

If you had to settle on one word to capsule the magnetism of the man it would surely be – presence.

When Miller strode to the wicket or was tossed the ball everything stopped and everybody watched.

Miller was the sportsman who had everything – he probably belonged in Hollywood except all he did in life was for real.

The perfect specimen – an outstanding student Miller had the vitality of Botham, the looks of Valentino, the physique of Adonis, the athleticism of Carl Lewis, the reflexes of Ali and the strength of Tyson. He had the style of Raleigh, the charisma of Flynn and the warmth of Cary Grant. Keith Miller remains a gentleman and good sport in every sense.

He was a heroic Battle of Britain fighter pilot and the most explosive sporting personality Australia has produced. He is still the companion of aristocracy, the guest of honor in the highest of society and a feted guest at any racetrack around the world. He has wined and dined with royalty and yet revels in a down-to-earth day in the pub with the crowd from the outer.

A man's man with all the airs and graces mixed with a devil-may-care nonchalance that sets him apart from the rest. A man for all and any company.

It is almost 50 years since Miller last fired a searing bouncer at an English opener or straight drove a swashbuckling six over the sightscreen. Those of us who saw Nugget Miller in action will never forget the sight and it is doubtful any one of us will ever accept the world has seen his equal.

Time dulls the memory and in time the teeming millions who saw Miller in action have fallen away to a minority. Fortunately there are great photographs and sufficient movie footage to acquaint the uninitiated with his grandeur

England great Denis Compton recalled his first encounter with Miller while playing for England against a combined Dominion side at Lord's. The match was a charity game to entertain the besieged 1943 Londoners. The dashing young Australian fighter pilot spent his leave time playing for the Australian Services Cricket team.

Miller was called to relieve the bowling after four others had failed to dislodge Compton. Denis asked wicketkeeper Stan Simsey what sort of stuff Miller bowled. The 'keeper suggested Keith wanted the exercise but could be a bit quick.

"A bit quick?" said Compton, "He came off a short run but when he let the ball go, my hair nearly stood on end. That was the fastest ball bowled against me since I played against Ernie McCormick in 1938." Simsey told the truth. Keith played for Victoria in all their 1939 matches but never bowled, not even in the nets.

It was while playing in the Victory Series to celebrate the end of global hostilities that the world discovered that Miller was an extraordinary bowler. The first ball he bowled at Lord's was a fast rising bumper at Bob Wyatt which caught his glove on the way through to slip.

The unofficial Test series with the Australian Services against England to commemorate the Victory in Europe resulted in the Miller figures of five matches for 10 innings (3 not out) 443 runs at 63.28. On debut as a bowler he took 10 wickets for 277 runs at 27.70. In the fourth Test he scored a scintillating 118. Top English scribes were in awe of his potential. He followed that with a magnificent 77 in the final Test at Old Trafford. England got up to level the series, the perfect result, Miller the best performer for the two teams.

Compton said he next saw Miller in East Bengal when Keith was playing for Australian Services and Denis for the locals. The game was stopped by a riot and the umpire said to Compton, "Mr. Compton – you very good player – but you must go."

Denis obviously thought he was being given out but the umpire was concerned as he saw the rioters pouring over the pickets, "No Mr. Compton, you very good player – but you must go."

He got the message and beat a hasty exit in company with Miller. They became great mates but when he toured Australia with the English team in 1946 and took block to face Keith Miller at the Sydney Cricket Ground, Keith polished the ball on his hip, flashed a wicked grin and drawled, "Now Mr Compton, you very good player – but you must go." Which he did soon after Nugget ripped a few holes in the space around his ears.

Ray Lindwall was unequivocal about Miller's prowess, "I've seen them all. The great Garfield Sobers at his best and I have no doubt Keith Miller is the greatest cricketing allrounder of my time. Keith had the ability to rise to the occasion when the team was up against it. If you were on top he would finish it off with flair – a wonderful mixer and huge personality."

Remarkable to believe this cricketing Adonis was a runt. So small as an early teenager that his cricketing coach had to have a special cut down bat made for him. They called him a dwarf and an ugly duckling but he always had ability even when he had to stand on the tips of his toes to see over the stumps.

Even so, a kid needs luck to be able to take the right path in sport. Fate was kind to the young Keith Miller, he was surrounded by the greats of Australian cricket.

Bill Ponsford – the prolific Australian opening batsman – had one fan he couldn't escape. The kid was outside his home day and night, day after day, week after week.

The youngster idolised Ponsford and was delirious at the nod of a head or a wave of the mighty arm that had smote so many courageous boundaries off that fearsome English Bodyline attack. Having sighted his hero the kid bolted back to his own home just 400 yards away where he would practise for long hours with his older brothers Les and Ray. They used an old bat and a soft tennis ball.

At brother Les' instigation they watched Ponsford bat at every opportunity. His brother insisted his style was the epitome of batting perfection. Young Keith did his utmost to master the Ponsford technique.

Keith Ross Miller was born in Sunshine on November 28, 1919. His parents Les and Edith, of Scottish origin, already had two sons and a daughter. His parents named him after two Australian aviators of considerable fame Sir Keith and Sir Ross Smith who flew a pioneer passage from London to Essendon in a Vickers Vimy bi-plane.

Although there was no great sporting heritage in the Miller family the youngster was blessed that his two brothers had an appetite for sport and played grade cricket in Melbourne. "I made my first strokes in the street defending a lamp post wicket."

Those were the days – the days when almost every suburban side street was a cricket or football field depending on the season. This practice stood him in good stead for the school cricket competition which led to selection for an interstate schoolboys competition. His school captain was Merv Harvey, the eldest of the famous Harvey cricketing brothers.

Keith Miller had that one big problem – dwarfdom. "I barely stood the height of the stumps."

But cricket was everywhere he went. A master at his school, Melbourne High, was Australian Test captain Bill Woodfull.

The young Miller tried his hand at District cricket but couldn't get a game even as low in the pecking order as the St Kilda fifths. He had serious ambitions to become a jockey – for apart from football and cricket he loved horses.

If ever a youngster had sport thrust upon him it was Keith Miller. The captain of his school team was Keith "Bluey" Truscott who was first a champion Melbourne VFL footballer and later a World War 2 fighter pilot hero who became a squadron leader, won the DFC and was killed in action.

A Victorian player and South Melbourne coach, Hughie Carroll gave the youngster free coaching. Carroll recommended South to give Miller a trial, which they did. His first game of senior cricket was against St Kilda and he played in short pants. "I never looked back – they did fundamental things that turned it all around for me. The first thing they did was measure me and supply me with a cut-down bat to compensate for my lack of height and weight. What a difference it made and I went straight into the firsts."

All of a sudden he was a first grade cricketer and his last game of the season was against Carlton captained by Woodfull. Keith went into bat when South was 5-30. The kid whipped the bowling to the tune of 61 runs that lifted his team back into the game. "It was my first thrill in cricket." Carlton awarded him a special engraved cup "for sterling performance." It was presented to him in his Melbourne High School class-room by Woodfull. Later he was to receive a clock as a trophy for heading the batting averages for the Melbourne Colts. " These are the only two cricket trophies I have bothered to keep," Miller said. "I treasured them."

Miller was also displaying considerable skill on the football field, mainly as rover – but two years after his initial cricket success he found himself playing senior League football for St. Kilda. "What a transition. In the time it took to age from 16 to 17, I grew a foot." He quickly furnished into a superbly proportioned athlete. He was selected for Victoria's B team against Tasmania and flayed the attack at the Melbourne Cricket Ground in making 181. This won promotion to the senior state side.

In November, 1939, he made his senior Victorian debut against Don Bradman's South Australia. He failed with the bat in both innings being efficiently removed by the great Clarrie Grimmett. The consolation was the thrill of a lifetime in running out The Don who rarely lost his wicket on a misjudged run. Bradman needed only 24 for his century when Miller fielding at square leg noticed out of the side of his eye that The Don was still short of his ground at the bowler's end. He hurled the ball to Maurice Sievers who was able to break the wicket leaving "Braddles" stranded.

Miller studied photographs of the fall of wicket and noticed all the routed Victorian batsmen had been playing back to Grimmett. When the return match was played a month later he decided to go on the attack and advance down the wicket. He scored his maiden first-class century – 108. Then he played at a ball from Grimmett which flew to Bradman's hands and The Don exclaimed, "Oh well bowled Clarrie."

The Victorian refused to walk believing it was a bump ball. The umpire hesitated but up went the finger. Next day he read in the media an inference he had been "cheated out."

Far too harsh a word for gamesmanship but it was persuasive evidence that life at the wicket is fickle and only fools "walk."

By the end of the 1939 season, Miller was the most exciting new cricket prospect on the Australian scene. His batsmanship was as spectacular as his appearance, long fluent strokes hit with superb timing and power. He had an awesome scoring rate and was fearless in his approach. He exuded the confidence of youth and refused to allow bowlers to hold him down.

All Australia knew Keith Ross Miller had arrived and would be in contention for the next Australian Test squad, to New Zealand in March, 1940. But it was never to eventuate. The warlords made sure of that.

THE FIGHTER ACE

It was 1944. The fighter bomber was gurgling in its death throes as it limped towards its bomb-cratered landing strip in southern war torn England, One engine burned out and the tail section a charred mess.

At its controls was a handsome grim faced pilot nursing the last few lurches out of his wounded, dying craft, weeping as much for the stricken plane as he was for himself.

The landing field came into sight and he gingerly went through the landing procedures – no under-carriage and the tail assembly shot. A belly-landing was the only option. He wobbled to the beginning of the strip, steady as possible, and then. . . touchdown. A screech of tortured metal ripping apart on concrete, fumes, heat, noise, dust and the endless skidding sensation with the tortured bodyworks the only brakes to stop the slide to total destruction. The skidding, scraping and screeching came to an end in a cloud of smoke, dust and flame. Flt. Sgt Miller was able to disengage his harness, clamber from the cockpit and jump safely down to Mother Earth.

The mechanics looked at the torn and twisted wreckage of what was left of the once magnificent Mosquito bomber. A mechanic marvelled, "A bloody miracle. "

"No!" grinned the pilot, "Millers Luck."

Cricket would not have been the same had probability taken its course that day.

When war broke he was the 19 year-old darling of Australian sport and a brilliant future lay ahead but he decided to enlist. There was Government pressure for him to stay at home and take the public mind off the mental and physical anguish of war. He would have none of that.

War! This was the greatest adventure of all – and so it proved. Cricket and football could wait. His country was at war and he was there to answer the call. There was something ethereal about the Air Force. Keith registered at the air force recruiting centre but the Air Force did not call him into service until January, 1942. He went directly into air crew and after an initial introductory course he was shipped to America to complete his training. While stationed at Massachusetts he met Margaret Wagner from Boston, the girl who was to become his wife.

Training complete, he was flown to New York and boated to Greenock, Scotland on the Queen Elizabeth. The great ship was crammed so densely with servicemen they had to sleep in relays. A train took him from Scotland to Bournemouth, England where he was immediately introduced to the "thrills" of war. German fighter-bombers made repeated daily raids on their south-coast base, hitting the area first with bombs, then strafing the area and township with machine-gun fire before streaking off for home.

He was soon to be dubbed Lucky Miller. His sporting prowess was well known and he was invited to play in a special cricket match at Dulwich College. Now called "Nugget" by his mates he left his base with a friend Bill Young. Young was to be killed in action. The game over they returned to base just after a raid had devastated the town area. Seven of his closest mates had been killed by a direct hit on their lunch time bar room. He would undoubtedly have been amongst the dead but for that cricket match. The next day when the roll-call of the "missing believed dead" was called he heard, "No. 41608 Miller K. R. Sgt." He realised he had not been given a leave pass for the cricket match and was assumed to have been killed.

Soon after he was flying a Beaufighter on a night exercise when he noticed the oil gauge drop to zero. He put it down to the usual gremlins who seemed to haunt this particular aircraft. Soon after another instrument went down with a "phutt". The weather was closing in and had degenerated to the worst kind of English pea-souper. Somehow he managed to find base and drop the plane on the landing strip.

Repairs and adjustments were made and within the hour the craft was back in the air with another pilot, Jock Meek flying. Jock was no sooner airborne than he realised something was wrong, he was recalled but it was too late, the plane crashed and Jock was killed. The grieving Australian could find no joy in his own escapes as tragedy stalked his mates.

Soon after he was returning from a night operation over France, gliding in for a landing when it appears he misjudged his touchdown. He hit the landing strip, bounced off the runway – he "gunned" the motors to get airborne again to make another landing. Only one motor caught and the craft skidded away sideways at high speed. He was slewing towards a hangar and total disaster. A fiery death loomed but somehow Nugget throttled back and managed to frog leap the building. He cleared the hangar by millimetres and the plane flopped back to earth and slid to a halt on the other side – a mangled wreck but the pilot escaped relatively uninjured.

The "Millers Luck" really stuck. He was flying Mosquitoes and attacking an airfield in Schleswig-Holstein near the Kell Canal. The Mosquitoes had drop tanks attached to the wings, filled with highly inflammable substances and Mills bombs.

As Miller dived for his run at the target, he was caught in the enemy searchlights at 900 feet. He threw the craft about wildly trying to escape the enemy before resuming his run. He pressed the bomb release. . . catastrophe!

Only one bomb dropped and exploded into a gigantic fireball. The out-of-balance Mosquito, lopsided with the bomb and fuel tank still stuck on one wing, weaved and lurched sideways as giant balls of flak hit the air.

The pilot gasped as he realised he had lurched miraculously away from a direct enemy hit. Shells exploded where he would have been but for the misfire. The luck had stuck but so had the bomb as he made a nerve racking trip back to base. The bomb would not shake loose. As he approached home base he radioed the control centre. The control command said there was nought else he could do but come in and land and "keep his fingers crossed" the jolt of landing didn't break the bomb loose.

The perspiration ran icy cold, the hair on the nape of the neck frozen stiff.

"I must have made it through. I can't remember the landing. My next conscious recollection was standing on the grass with a lot of figures running out towards the plane. I was shaking as somebody asked 'Where's the tank?'

"I answered, 'On the plane. ' It wasn't.

"They found it back on the runway where it had broken loose on impact. The officer who found it whistled quietly. " It's a miracle it didn't explode? I don't understand it." Miller's Luck!

Six years were chopped out of the Keith Miller career and apart from a brief flirtation with Victorian Shield cricket, the Services competition and the Victory series against England in 1945, he had missed the best years of a player's career.

Don Bradman who was now a powerful voice in Australian cricket deplored Keith's plans to play with an English club to secure his future. Bradman said Miller's departure would end his Test career and suggested Australian officials would have to consider inducements to keep such stars as Miller at home.

With his English trip aborted, he played cricket for South Melbourne and football for St Kilda making the state side at both. The Australian Services team also called him into action for a series against New South Wales. He won selection in the Australian team which toured New Zealand and despite continuing war-related back problems finished third in the batting with an average of 64.2 and taking 5-27, his bowling heavily curtailed by his injury. Returning to Australia, he won selection in the Bradman team to meet the Poms, Bradman having decided he would make a return to international cricket despite his own dodgy health.

Miller was restless, uncertain that he even wanted to play cricket. While he was uncertain off the field, he was totally positive on the field and now with swashbuckling batting and blazing bowling, combined with spectacular fielding he cut a magnificent figure on the playing field – so much so he was dubbed the Cricketing D'Artagnan.

On his return from overseas although short of match practice he played for Victoria against South Australia and carved out a first innings of 188 run out after taking 2-32. He made a quickfire 30 in the Vics 1-79 to help win the match by nine wickets. He was run out in the next Shield match against NSW, this time for 153.

Although he was to lose a number of Shield matches to his Australian duties he accumulated 667 Shield runs, including a double century to finish the season with an average of 133.40 and a bowling average of 21.

He was handed his baggy green for the first Test against England in Brisbane and was soon in the cricket hellfire as Don Bradman won the toss and batted. Everything went against the tourists. In a triumphant return to Test cricket, Bradman made 187 after England claimed he'd been caught before he'd made 30. Thunderstorms lashed the ground, wickets were not covered and after the Aussies amassed their runs on a perfect strip, England had to bat on the worst of "stickies" and were crushed as Miller raced through them with 7-60 and 2-17 following 79 with the bat.

It was a fabulous debut. Miller was fast and dangerous, his bouncer lethal.

On a rain-sodden wicket Miller had the ball rearing on its end, trimming the eyebrows of openers Bill Edrich and Cyril Washbrook before terrorising Walter Hammond, Denis Compton and the rest. Some English critics ignoring the field placement claimed he bowled Bodyline and said the cricket war between the nations had resumed.

Miller laughed off the criticisms. He had a rare gift to make the fast ball rise sharply off a length and he was damned if he was going to put aside this very lethal but legal weapon.

It was the start of a triumphant series in which he was to finish second to Bradman in the Test averages (384 runs at 76.80) and take 17 cheap wickets. It also brought the first signs of friction between himself and The Don.

It was a boiling hot day in Adelaide and Miller was sitting with Ray Lindwall having a beer after a tiring stint in the field. Bill Jeanes, secretary of the Australian Board of Control walked in and told them to get cracking as he had taxis waiting to take them to their next destination. The weary duo wasn't prepared to pull up stumps on instant orders and there were heated words. Jeanes reported Miller to Bradman and soon afterwards the former ace pilot received a message from The Don requesting his presence in Bradman's stockbroking office the following morning.

Bradman explained Jeanes had a recent illness and asked Miller to forget the incident, but Miller never did. "That peremptory summons irritated me. I had to walk from my hotel to his office and as I walked thoughts ran – here I am just back from a war, a war which had been dangerous for me in parts and I am sent for like an erring schoolboy called to the Head's study. He could have come to the rooms and spoken to me at the ground, but oh no, that wasn't good enough for The Don."

Australia won the series comfortably but Miller detested the spirit in which the internationals had been conducted. He was also peeved that his conduct in grabbing a souvenir stump on the winning hit was questioned by the Victorian Cricket

Association's disciplinary chairman Arthur Liddicut who claimed Miller had broken the rules.

A PRIZED POSSESSION
The sports master of Elsternwick State School found a neatly handwritten letter amongst his mail in November, 1946.

Mr. R. J. Gainey was surprised to say the least to read: "Dear Mr. Gainey:

Perhaps I will be a stranger to you, but I am Keith Miller, the boy you encouraged in cricket at Elsternwick State School.

After that I always said that if I should some day represent Australia in cricket, I would write to you. That explains this letter. It was always in my mind that I would try to do justice to the faith you once had in me, that I would prove your judgment true."

Gainey did recall the young Miller. "He was one of the smallest boys I had ever seen, defending his wicket from all comers with a broomstick, because he had such a quick eye." Gainey quickly moved the lad up a few rungs to play with the seniors although he was only 10 years old.

Needless to say that letter became the prized possession of the Gainey family.

There has always been a cloud of mystery over the supposed feud between Miller and Bradman. Keith says he's not vilifying Bradman in recounting various events. The Don was human and not a god. He cited a number of episodes that revealed normal human frailty in this larger than life personality.

There was the Cec Pepper case, a year before the Jack Ikin catching incident in Brisbane. An event that revealed the icon had his blind spots. Pepper returned from the war to play a services game in which Bradman was playing one of his comeback games. He had been discharged from the Army because of fibrositis and even though he was patently ill his greatness carried him to 112. Early in that innings Pepper, then considered the best allrounder in the world, deceived Bradman with a flipper. Everybody believed Don was plumb lbw. Yet the loud appeal was turned down.

Pepper, a fierce competitor who craved the great wicket, spun on umpire Jack Scott and snapped, "You're a ———— cheat." He was reported and Pepper was finished unless there was divine intervention. He was dumped from the tour of New Zealand and quit Australia to play professional cricket in England. Miller said, "I think Bradman should have realised that and intervened on Pepper's behalf. He could have done it so easily. It would have saved Pepper. As it was, a great cricketer was lost to Australia."

If those umpiring mistakes kept Bradman's cricket alive then they were the best umpiring mistakes on record. Miller had no argument with that but he mourned for Pepper the sacrificial lamb.

"It was inevitable I suppose The Don and I should clash," he says. "Our temperaments were so different.

"There was an Adelaide Test against India in 1947-48 where Vijay Hazare made a century in each innings. He repeatedly turned me off the stumps and hit me behind square leg. It was boiling hot and I asked Don for a man between square and fine leg. He refused to even consider it. I had been bowling flat out so I finished the over off with a couple of off-spinners. He promptly took me off.

"I regard it as an insult for a captain not to listen to his bowler but in fairness this was not the usual for Don. He could be very considerate to bowlers, more often than not. He just got the occasional bee in his bonnet."

There was another incident later the same day in this Test of wills between bowler and skipper. During a Miller over, Don fielded a ball and threw it to Miller. It landed short and Miller blocked it with his boot, looked across at his captain and soccered it back to The Don while 20,000 spectators gaped in amazement. Even if Bradman had made a mistake and that's all it was, Miller's actions were viewed as an extreme in confrontation. The ball was at Bradman's feet... so to speak.

Would he just boot it back, signal a nearby lackey to move across and give it to the recalcitrant speedster on the full or pick it up and walk over to Miller for a nose-to-nose rebuke? The Don displayed remarkable cool. He picked it up, threw it to Lindsay Hassett who was closer and the vice-captain lobbed the ball neatly to Miller – and the game continued. But it was in the Bradman memory bank.

For Miller it was a reminder to the skipper that he was not above the normal courtesies of the game. Perhaps it was the day frustration and petulance bubbled over for the Indian tour was not a highlight year in the Miller career. Although Australia swamped the series 4-0, Nugget compiled only 185 runs at an average of 37. Bradman, 40, scored 715 at an average of 178.75. Miller took only nine wickets in the five Tests.

There was one bright spot in the season and that came In November '47 when an Australian X1 played India on the Sydney Cricket Ground. Having scored 99 first-class centuries, Bradman was looking for the hundredth. The Don was efficiently but carefully grafting that century when Nugget came to the wicket and began to chop up the bowling. All of a sudden there was a risk that he was going to dance past Don and score a lightning century. He jammed on the brakes, farmed the strike to his skipper until the great man became greater. Then Miller made an extravagant play and threw away his wicket at 86. He believed it was The Don's day and a Miller century may have been a distraction to the big event. Bradman went on to make 172.

As the Australian team sailed to England for the 1948 Ashes tour it was clear great minds did not necessarily think alike. Don Bradman as captain of Australia believed Nugget was a more valuable bowler than batsman.

The Don's long term adversary Bill O'Reilly thought the opposite during the Indian tour of Australia in 1947. O'Reilly said Miller was being called on to do more bowling than necessary. "He has remarkable batting ability and my advice to Australian and NSW selectors is to relieve him altogether of this responsibility," said O'Reilly.

"His sort of bowling will surely cut short his batting career. Why take risks with a man whose batsmanship is something typical of our game at its very, very best. There surely has never been a fast bowler who can bat so well as Miller. His place as a bowler can be filled over and over again. As a batsman he is an ornament to cricket."

There you have the rub of it – two of the greatest minds in cricket were in total disagreement except for one point of view – they both conceded he was the finest slips fieldsmen in the world. Bradman the batsman believed Keith was one of the world's greatest bowlers and O'Reilly the bowler believed Keith was one of the world's finest batsmen. Compelling evidence that Keith Miller was and is the finest allrounder the game has seen.

Perhaps the enemy camp through the *News Chronicle* correspondent put his finger on the pulse when he said Miller was the difference between the two great teams in 1948. "If he fails with the bat he wins the game with the ball," he wrote.

During the tour the presence of aristocratic Keith Ross Miller and his fellow tourists was requested at Balmoral Castle for an informal afternoon with Her Majesty Princess Elizabeth, the future Queen Elizabeth.

Thereafter in 1953, Elizabeth now the Queen of England visited the Australian team while they were playing Middlesex at Lord's, she was accompanied by the Duke of

Edinburgh and in the spirit of Sir Walter Raleigh, Miller flourished his bat for the queen rather than his cape.

"I thought I would enliven their visit and when Johnny Young bowled to me I strode down the wicket and clouted him into the nursery for six." With a Miller sweep and flourish of his bat he was acknowledged by the smiling monarch.

A SHOCK FOR HUTTON

During the festival match at tour end at Scarborough, Miller opened the bowling to Len Hutton after lunch. He raced in at a furious pace and pitched the ball short of a length. It whizzed feet above the startled Hutton's head. Nobody had ever seen a bumper like that one and little wonder, he had used a colored tennis ball he had concealed in his pocket!

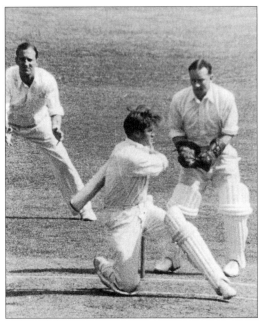

Keith Miller on the attack in England where his enjoys on-going popularity given his annual visits.

1948 – Having fought the great war in Britain and risked his life a hundred times for England, the flamboyant Australian was at war again – with England. No bomb laden fighter bombers at his disposal for this adventure – just a slither of willow and a small leather hand grenade. These along with a superb fighting spirit and unlimited athletic prowess were all that stood between Nugget Miller and the poison darts of a venomous press.

All England was anxious that their proud team would regain the Ashes from the colonials. They had enormous respect for Bradman and Miller but the first couple of matches of the tour alarmed them as The Don and Nugget tore their best county and student sides apart. Keith slammed a whirlwind 202 in just three sessions against Leicestershire – this included a 159 stand with Bradman. Next he bowled with venom against Yorkshire, collecting 9-91 and was also top batsman for the match. His 163 in 250 minutes at Lord's against the MCC sent the alarm bell jangling and the English presses spinning out their venom.

The Pommy writers had not forgotten the Miller bumper barrage in that controversial debut Test in Brisbane. Miller wasted no time giving them fuel for their fire.

Miller had returned for a renewal of hostilities in the same war zone where he served so manfully in World War combat. This time he was the invader and enemy, not the defender and hero as he was from 1943-45.

The scene of the first Test, Trent Bridge became the first war front as Vivian Jenkins in the *News of the World* set the public agenda when he headlined his verdict: BUMPER WAR..."If bumpers were not cricket in the case of Larwood, they are equally not cricket in the case of Miller."

By striking Len Hutton in the fiery closing, Miller stirred English emotion and revived the wartime passion of a united British bulldog.

The English press urged their bowlers to launch a bumper barrage at Bradman – "This would surely stop Miller." But Alec Bedser, the frontline English bowler was not equipped for such a role, he was a superb line and length bowler who could move the ball either way at will, but not at express speed.

Miller said bowling bumpers to Len Hutton was nearly always rewarding – he didn't have a clue how to play them. But Bill Edrich was different; you didn't bowl short to the English opener or he thrashed you to the fence.

Miller was the vital player in an eight wicket win in the first Test. He took seven vital wickets for 163. His batting in the Tests was not the all conquering feature it had been in the county clashes. He averaged just under 30 but the prolific scoring of the powerful Australian batting line-up made it more important that he take the wickets.

The second Test at Lord's stirred more controversy when Bradman handed the ball to Miller after Lindwall had bowled. Miller indicated his back was causing problems and declined to bowl. Ian Johnson immediately took the ball and bowled Hutton.

The vow of silence cricketers took with the ACB prevented Miller explaining he had a recurrence of the back injury from that Mosquito crash landing. "I told Bradman before we went out that I didn't think I should bowl because the back was painful. To my surprise after one over from Lindwall he tossed the ball to me and said 'Have a bowl.' I simply could not bowl and told him so before walking away."

Keith said Bradman wanted Johnson to do well on the '48 tour and dryly commented that Bradman gave him chance-after-chance of bowling at "nine-ten-jack." He said Lindwall, Bill Johnston, Ernie Toshack, Colin McCool and himself worked hard to get the first six out and then made way for Johnson to clean up the rabbits.

Australia won the second Test by 409 runs so it can be seen the friction between the two superstars did not undermine team morale or performance. As they left the field on the final day, victorious by eight wickets an angry crowd again gathered at the players race and one spectator personally abused and threatened Miller. He seized the man and carried him by the shoulders into the Australian rooms where he let him loose. He bolted.

Australia was lucky to draw the third Test. The team regrouped to win the fourth in magnificent style by seven wickets after England made 496 in the first dig. Bradman fell cheaply in the Australian first innings thus Keith Miller came together with the young Neil Harvey at 3-68. What a partnership they structured. They raced to 121 in 95 minutes where Miller fell at 58. Harvey made his century on debut and Australia trailed by 38 runs. England needing a win to stay in the Ashes battle went after the runs and set Australia a target of more than 400. Arthur Morris and Bradman had a mind boggling partnership that gave Australia a stirring seven wicket win. Mission accomplished they went on to win the Fifth by an innings and 149. Miller taking 4-27.

If he wasn't fit to bowl for much of that tour it wasn't affecting his batting. He smote 21 6s in 17 tour matches and was described as the only batsman in the world who could belt a six over the pickets one-handed and kneeling. His free hitting established a world record for first-class cricket

The philosophies of Bradman and Miller were very much at odds and Miller could never understand the relentless destruction of weak opposing sides in '48.

"I would say to him, 'Haven't we got enough now?' and he would give a crooked little smile and, in that thin, piping voice say, 'I remember when England made 900 against us and kept us in the field for three days.'"

1953 tour: Miller and Australian captain Lindsay Hassett share a joke with the Duke of Edinburgh during a charity one-day game at East Moseley.

As good as he was with his bouncer, Keith Miller also developed great variety, including several versions of a slower ball which often diddled the batsmen.

The Miller googly or leg-break were his secret weapons, so cleverly disguised and so disruptive to batting concentration that they joined his bouncer as a great partnership breaker. "I bowl to get people out, not to show off," Miller said.

"When I bowled I always tried to work out what the batsman was thinking – what I would be thinking if I faced myself. Some great bowlers just nag away bowling the perfect ball, ball after ball. When I was set, I loved to bat to the great Alec Bedser for that very reason."

Miller's greatest attribute was to produce the unexpected. He refused to allow batsmen to second guess him. If they expected a bumper they got a googly. If they braced themselves for a thunderbolt they would get a round armer, anything to ruffle the calm. He would call it his "mad five minutes" in which he used every ball in his arsenal and it didn't matter if this included long hops that were smote for four – bad balls got almost as many wickets as good balls. Even flicking back his hair or throwing his arm in the air in a gesticulation to tell the batsman only God's intervention had saved them, were part and parcel of the batsman ruffling procedures.

"And let's be honest," he says, "if it gets a wicket, it is not a bad ball, it's a damn good ball."

THE LAUGHING CAVALIER

On that tour of tours, Miller scored 1088 runs at 47.3. If Bradman believed the Victorian could have done much, much better had he been less cavalier, he was probably right. Although Nugget said he never worried about statistics he did have a big game attitude that saw him rise to magnificent heights when the challenge was on – but he could play and look the buffoon when his mind was elsewhere and the challenge beneath his level.

No win and no achievement was above or below The Don's ambitions. Miller liked and respected Bradman but at times he rankled. Keith

107

was opposing Bradman in the Alan Kippax-Bert Oldfield testimonial and thought it was high time he tested the great man's reflexes.

"I sent down a bumper which he hooked beautifully. The next one I sent down was a lot faster and Bradman was very nearly sconed. Only this time he didn't laugh. He looked daggers at me. So for devilment, I sent him another. He hooked it and was caught."

He was to play in another testimonial soon after – the Bradman testimonial at the MCG. "Bradman held me back in the batting order until the crowd turned up. When Bradman did send me in, I batted light-heartedly and got out trying to hit 6s. When I was out I saw him looking at me with disgust written all over his face and clearly he thought I had not concentrated and did not care.

"My reaction was that Bradman, like so many others, took the game too seriously. Cricket was meant to be enjoyed at all levels and I certainly played it as such. Whether my apparent couldn't-care-less attitude was responsible I don't know but I was not selected for the next tour, which was to South Africa in 1949-50." Worth noting that observation.

Miller's writing collaborator R. S. "Dick" Whitington suggests Bradman was responsible for the shock omission of the champion allrounder from the 1949-50 tour of South Africa. Bradman repudiated that charge declaring it ludicrous that one man made the decisions in Australian cricket – he was just one vote on a three-vote selection panel.

There was an extraordinary culture shock for cricket enthusiasts when the Australian selectors announced the Lindsay Hassett-led Australian team to tour South Africa in 1949-50. There was no Keith Miller.

The Australian Cricket Board of Control was its stoic, close-mouthed self. The selectors decisions were not to be questioned. The selection criteria was their business and they didn't have to explain it. The three selectors happened to be new cricketing knight, Sir Donald Bradman, Jack Ryder and "Chappie" Dwyer.

The outcry was instantaneous and explosive. Charismatic batsman Sid Barnes, who was unavailable for the tour, lashed the selectors in the Melbourne *Argus*: "If I were asked to select a world cricket team I would choose Miller in the first four. I regard him as the world's best allrounder." He accused the selectors of "betraying a trust" implicit in their charter. He said if any action was to be taken for reasons of temperament, behaviour on and off the field, deportment and tour habits, this was the responsibility of the ACB not selectors.

Barnes view was shared by cricket experts around the world. Australian cricket writers rated it the greatest selection sensation in cricket history. The provocative Barnes fueled the fire, "If Keith had the same outlook as Don Bradman or Bill Ponsford he would have made colossal scores. He could, if he desired, become the statistician's greatest customer."

Other great Australian players rallied behind Miller and almost to a man the cricketing world deemed the selectors were allowing personalities to cloud their judgment. Stan McCabe and ex-captains Victor Richardson and Herbie Collins deplored the omission as the heat became intolerable for the selectors who hid their reasoning behind a wall of silence.

The respected Jack Fingleton also bought into the dispute with criticism of the selectors and a pointed dig at Bradman. This drew a rebuke from Bradman, "Mr. Fingleton unduly flatters me by suggesting that I was the sole Australian selector. It's a pity he doesn't confine his remarks to something he knows something about."

The controversy took a dramatic turn in November, 1949 when the Australian Board of Control invited Miller join the South African tourists after South Africa made approaches for Australia to send an extra player. This combined with fast bowler Bill Johnston being injured in a car smash brought about the change of heart or mind. Miller was constrained, "Not at any time during last year's tour did my captain Sir Donald Bradman or the manager of the team Mr. Keith Johnson criticise my behaviour on or off the field."

So he hopped on the plane to Fremantle, stepped on to the good ship *Dominion Monarch* and sailed off to South Africa on November 21 in time to arrive and acclimatise himself for the first Test in Durban on December 2.

Nugget recorded that when Chappie Dwyer learned of Bradman's denial while managing the touring party in South Africa he was livid and declared he had nothing to do with the speedster's omission. This left Jack Ryder swinging the can. "So Ryder must have left me out – he must have had three votes."

Nugget made a slow start to the tour but the Springboks were seething with excitement at the very real prospect they had the team to beat Australia. A massive crowd crammed Ellis Park for the first Test and immediately Australia was 2-2 with both openers Morris and Jack Moroney out for ducks. Miller had been sent in by an ill Hassett at the first drop.

Miller and Hassett rescued the innings to some extent and when Keith fell for 21 they were 3-71. Hassett might have been small of stature but he was a giant in a dog fight. He was a mammoth in this innings as against all medical advice with flaring tonsils and extreme discomfort he batted to stumps, picking up a century on the way. The next day was a break for Christmas Day and the Aussie skipper spent the day in bed. He was out next day for a superlative 112. Australia with a century from Sam Loxton had rallied to make 413.

The discard Miller had a point to prove. He had already helped with the bat but now he lashed the South African batsmen with a magnificently sustained and venomous bowling spell that shot the Springboks back into the pavilion for 137, Miller 5-50. They followed on and Johnston 6-44 shot them out for 191 in the second. Ian Johnson had a total yield of 6-91 to complete the rout by an innings and 85.

The second Test was Harvey's match with an enchanting 178 of 7-526 dec. Miller with 58 nearly missed the middle day of the Test when he had a car mishap many miles from the venue. He made it back with the Australians out on the field and Hassett patiently placing the field for a bowler who wasn't yet on the ground. The great South African batsman Dudley Nourse helped out as much as best he could, taking block several times. Two minutes after the scheduled start of play Miller cruised on to the field and Hassett threw him the ball.

Two balls later Nourse was walking back to the pavilion, the victim of an angry, rearing steam ball flying at the Nourse armpit – he fended off an easy catch to Johnston. So much for sportsmanship. He took 3-54 and South Africa folded for 278. Nourse made 114 in the second innings but it was a lone stand against the rhythm and swing of Lindwall who took 5-32 for the Aussies to win by eight wickets. The fiery Australian was again under attack for pelting too many bouncers at the enemy.

The third Test at Durban was a tactical triumph for Miller who found the wicket had turned into a spinner's nightmare after torrential rain. He gave just one ball a tweak and it spun like a top. He contrived to keep the South African batsmen in rather than out by not spinning the ball when the opposition already had 250 on the board. Miller and Hassett knew if they declared with the wicket in that state Hugh Tayfield would spin them out quick smart. Nourse did not declare and were eventually all out for 311. Australia needed 112 to avoid the follow on. They scored 0-31 before Tayfield was introduced into the attack.

This was it! Australia knew more about the wicket than Nourse and well realised their hour of peril was at hand. Tayfield went as close as any bowler has ever gone to turning a ball 360 degrees. In the time it took Australia to prod and poke to 42 the rookie spinner had taken five wickets. Soon it was 7-46 and by some miracle of application the Australian's saw out an hour of play before the final wicket fell at 75 – right on 5.50 pm. Too late to bat again that day.

Next day Australia 236 behind and certain to follow on faced oblivion. But Miller declared Australia would win the Test and put his money where his mouth was. Believe it or not Nourse did not enforce the follow-on. He thought the wicket could only get worse – it did for him. The Australians ran through the Springboks for 99 and trailed by 335. Nourse was still at ease with the world and confident he would take the series into the final rubber.

Australia were soon a battling 4-95. Then Harvey took over and when he finished so were the South Africans. The dashing left hander rattled the pickets with a divine array of strokes that brought him 155 runs and with the support of Sam Loxton and Colin McCool, Australia moved from that perilous 4-95 to 5-336. The series was won.

The fourth Test at Ellis Park was a draw but it was memorable for an interlude between a tiny umpire and the provocative Miller. After two plumb lbs were turned down by the little fellow in a wide brimmed hat, Miller walked over, turned up the brim so the umpire could see and then proceeded to catch the batsman plumb again.

"How's THAT?" yelled Nugget. "That's Aht!" beamed the umpire with finger raised. Keith turned the brim back down again.

Harvey made his fourth century in five Tests when he compiled 122 in the final Test at Port Elizabeth as Australia won by an innings and 259 runs. Miller's parting gesture at the moment of victory was to rip the souvenir bails off the stumps, stride to the enclosure for non-whites and tossed the precious symbols to the delighted black throng.

THE NUGGET AND THE DON

The South African selection controversy brought a rumbling volcano out into the open.

Was there a feud between Bradman and Miller?

Although he was only one voice many people believed Sir Donald Bradman was the controlling force in Australian cricket and would not believe in his role as selector if he couldn't have swayed his fellow selectors to name Miller in the team. The controversy raged but Sir Donald refused to dignify the public rumor with any sort of reply.

Sir Donald and Nugget Miller strode two different roads on their journey through cricket.

Keith took the high road that had its dips and potholes. The Don simply started at the bottom and took the short uphill route to the top, never deviating off course and never missing a step. Whatever route they took they both arrived at the top.

One wonders if Sir Donald would like to review a judgment he made in 1968 when he declared his fellow knight Sir Garfield Sobers was "unquestionably the greatest allround cricketer of all time. " The Miller devotees were astounded.

Admittedly Sobers had a magnificent record to support Sir Don's assessment. He had a record 365 not out, 26 Test centuries, 8032 runs average 57.78 and 235 wickets average 34.03. Add to that 109 catches. It is perhaps not surprising the great man could be swayed by such figures, boasting as he did an incredible Test record batting average of 99.96 – an average that was in excess of 100 until that immortal "duck" at the hands of Eric Hollies in his final Test innings.

Sobers played 93 Tests. Miller played 55 Tests because World War 2 sliced what may well have been his six best years out of his playing life. Yet he was still able to amass 2958 runs at 36.97, capture 170 wickets at 22.97 although his Test career did not start until he was 27. He was also rated the world's best slips fieldsman and took some amazing catches.

Sobers began his Test career at 17 and was never interrupted and he had the luxury of playing 30 of those Tests against minority countries. His 365 was against Pakistan before it became a force in cricket. Likewise many runs were accumulated against India before they attained status as a cricket power. Thirteen of his 26 centuries came against New Zealand, Pakistan and India.

These figures should not be seen as an attempt to belittle the undoubted genius of Sobers but they serve to illustrate why statistics do not necessarily mirror the correct reflection of the dynamic duo's relative abilities.

Don Bradman was always a man who played his shots as he saw them but men who played under him for the baggy green cap were disappointed. To a man the Australian players of the Bradman – Hassett – Johnson era believed no man could be rated as a greater allrounder than Miller.

Ray Lindwall was something of an allrounder himself but rated himself as essentially a bowler who could bat a bit. Accordingly he was very jealous of maintaining his averages. "Keith never seemed to worry about averages," said Lindwall, a man who ranks with Denis Lillee as the greatest pace bowler the nation has produced.

The stylish speedster who so often shared the opening attack with Nugget, had no doubt his partner was a greater player than Sobers or any other allrounder. Lindwall freely argued that Miller was a man who "played" cricket. He wasn't obsessed by statistics. He did what was necessary and when it was done he had his fun.

"They said he was swashbuckling and that's what Nugget was. He did what had to be done to win but he never treasured his wicket so much that he wouldn't put it at risk to entertain the crowd. He threw it away many a time when there was nothing left but the entertainment of the public.

"He bowled the same way. We all have our days and sometimes I would do more with the ball than he did and other times he would move it all over the place and get life I didn't know was there. When wickets had to be taken he could produce the unplayable ball almost at will. I am biased because he is a friend but I have no problem rating him as the best cricketer allrounder I have seen."

R. S. Whitington was surprised when Bradman depreciated Miller to a lower rating than Sobers and set about finding out what Bradman's compatriots thought of the assessment. He found an ailing Stan McCabe only a few weeks before the master batsman died. It was McCabe who played what Bradman declared the innings of a lifetime. It was the 232 not out in 235 minutes at Trent Bridge.

McCabe was a man after Miller's own heart. When there was a challenge there was nothing he couldn't and wouldn't do. There are those who rated his 189 not out against South Africa when the fielding captain Herbie Wade appealed against the light because his players were endangered by the thunderous strokes of the McCabe bat. There were also those immortal Bodyline hands when he scored an heroic lone stand 187 not out against Larwood and Voce. The "not out" beside those three hands indicates how well he held himself together in the three great innings of his career.

McCabe expressed disappointment in the Bradman verdict in favor of Sobers, "I fancy Don has forgotten Keith Miller and Walter Hammond," said McCabe, "Wally was the greatest cricketer I ever played against and I'd have a bet on Keith Miller beating Gary in a solo, single-wicket match."

Cricket's bible Wisden described a Miller innings of 185 in 165 minutes for the Dominions against England in a Victory test at Lord's in 1945 the most masterly innings played for a generation. McCabe said Nugget was likely to lose interest in proceedings when his team was winning too easily. "Keith at his peak was the finest allrounder I watched and I do not under-rate Gary. The trouble with Keith was he needed a crisis to rouse his killer instinct. " McCabe said had Miller applied himself with the same fierce application as Bradman he would have scored 5000 runs and taken 300 wickets in Tests. "The trouble with Don is that seeing is believing and he never saw the best of Keith as a batsman. He didn't see the Services cricket which replaced international cricket in the wartime crisis. He didn't see the Victory innings or the Dominion matches. "The Don classed Keith as a great fast bowler who was apt to be over-rated as a batsman." McCabe died within a few weeks of making this judgment.

There was a strange reluctance in Bradman to mingle with the men who shared so many great moments with him. McCabe who supplied The Don with the spectacle of the greatest innings of them all told Miller that although he and Bill O'Reilly had a sports store next door to the NSW Cricketers Club, where Don often called in, he never made the short detour to see McCabe or O'Reilly.

Perhaps it was the simmering feud between The Tiger and The Don that kept the rather introverted cricketing statesman at arms length but McCabe responded to a Miller probe, "Have you seen the little fellow lately?" by saying, "Oh no. He won't bother to come and see me you know."

Miller thought it odd that Braddles and Tiger began their cricketing careers together in neighboring small communities in country centre NSW and played each other when champions of their country towns, yet were at odds with each other.

Bradman was a great admirer of O'Reilly's bowling and O'Reilly had nothing but regard for the Bradman greatness. Yet they had little time for each other. The green eyed monster and not the green cap was Miller's assessment as the underlying cause of friction. He confessed he had some difficulty deciding which of the two was the greatest Australian and international cricketer. Each was supreme in his own sphere. In his retirement year Keith Miller said Bradman was the greatest batsmen he had seen, O'Reilly the greatest bowler and Don Tallon the finest wicketkeeper. Neil Harvey was the most wonderful fieldsman.

All Australians – no doubt three of those greats would have nominated Keith as the greatest allrounder.

Of course there was much more empathy between Miller and O'Reilly. They came from much the same mould and enjoyed each other's company. Bradman liked his own company and that of people from outside the world of cricket. Media men in Sir Donald's later life were surprised at the reclusive nature of Australia's most sought after sportsman. They couldn't grasp that the man was probably sick to death of exposure. He had a life of his own he wanted to live without having hordes of newshounds constantly baying at his heels.

Nor could Nugget resist a little dig at the ego of Bradman. "In the Test series of '48 I recall Compton playing a magnificent hook shot against Ray Lindwall. Arthur Morris fielding at short square-leg, held a wonder catch. Bradman rushed up and called, 'Well caught Arthur. Now you know why I put you there. I remember him playing that shot in 1938. ' I thought that was taking egotistical captaincy too far. That was a rare touche from Miller who in the next breath commended the shrewdness of the Braddles captaincy.

"But he is no god. He is a human being with strengths and weaknesses but as a batsman he was on his own." Miller said Bradman would have mastered the bowlers of the 1950s and beyond but he doubted he would have amassed the huge scores that came his way pre-war.

"The man could be inconsiderate and irritating in secondary things yet could be splendid in other, bigger matters." He was particularly taken with Bradman's habit of receiving hundreds of letters while on tour and setting aside those from children which he would answer personally.

It seemed highly unlikely the pair could ever be really close after Miller's final tour of England in 1956. Sir Donald has always shown a disapproval of having unauthorised observations and speculations about his private life and dealings being aired in public. There is no way of knowing how he regarded a series of articles and a book written by Keith Miller in October '56 but it was unlikely he was amused.

Keith wrote, "I don't think Bradman has any cause to take exception to the criticism I have made of him. He is quick enough to point out any similar weaknesses he thinks he has found in anyone else.

"After the war Bradman by his own standard was not such a good player, but by the yardstick of any other batsman he was still great. He relished fast bowling. His talent and amazing co-ordination made him, as I say, a genius.

"I can think of at least two pace bowlers who had the shattering experience of seeing Bradman send the first three balls they bowled to him to the fence. Bradman just picked his place on the pickets. In one of the early games of my career in first-class cricket Bradman made a double century. When he was 196, I was in the covers. When the captain gave me a reinforcement, I thought to myself, 'No matter how hard this fellow hits the ball into the covers, one of the three of us is bound to cut it off.'

"I could move a bit in those days and I was determined to make Bradman get the next four runs in singles if I could. The next ball he drove past me like a rocket. It crashed into the pickets. I did not have a chance to move.

"The facet of his character which made him a man apart inevitably led him to do the odd, unusual things."

F reddie Brown led the MCC tour of Australia 1950-51 and he was selected for his captaincy rather than his cricket prowess, something akin to Mark Taylor's selection for the 1997 tour of England. Nugget Miller having been snubbed and reprieved for the South African tour now had a burning passion to prove Sir Donald and his co-selectors were wrong to slight him.

He opened the season with 201 not out against Queensland. He followed this with a succession of big hands of 63, 138 not out and 214 not out; all up 616 at an average of 308. With such a rush of runs the Bradman record of 1690 in a season in 1928-29 was very much at risk.

Keith Miller was in aggressive mood when he faced Victoria and hurled thunderbolts at the head of the diminutive Lindsay Hassett. The little Victorian was a magnificent hooker but finally appealed to the umpires to view the bowling as intimidatory. Miller barked at him to allow the umpires to form their own opinions and gave him a few more. Hassett played a stunning innings and Victoria won.

Hostilities were placed on hold while Australia faced England in Brisbane on another of those treacherous wickets. The Aussies scored 228 and 7-32 dec. bowling England out twice to win by 70 runs, Len Hutton making a superb 62. The second Test was also close with Denis Compton bravely wearing two black eyes which created much romantic rumor. Freddie Brown confounded his critics with 62 and 5-52 but they lost by 28 runs. Miller had a lean time of it in those two clashes.

On to Melbourne for the third Test where England had a solid start with 290 which was short circuited by Miller taking what many declared the greatest slips catch of all time to dismiss Cyril Washbrook in full cry. He then blasted out Hutton, Compton and Reg Simpson for four runs from five overs.

Now Australia batted and quickly lost their three top batsmen. Miller joined Neil Harvey and by stumps he was 99 not out and Australia 6-368. When play resumed the next morning there was no sign of Miller as the English players took up their positions. Nobody had ever heard of such a thing – 99 not out and no appearance. But as Ian Johnson began his walk to the wicket Miller slipped out of the crowd and strolled beside him to the crease. He had drifted through the crowd to escape the battery of pressmen swarming around the members gates. Australia made 426 and Nugget was 145 not out. The catch, 4-37 and an unbeaten 145 before the match was half over. Jack Iverson finished the game off tweaking the Poms out for 123 with spell binding finger spin that netted 6-27. Australia won by an innings and 13 runs.

The rest of the tour was formality with the champion scoring 44 and 99 in the Adelaide Test and winding up the series on top of the averages with 350 runs at 43.75. He did not beat the Bradman record but did amass 1332 runs at 83.25. His Test bowling resulted in 17 wickets at 17.82, second to Iverson.

There was no way that Braddles and Co. could leave him out of the next international tour by the West Indies in 1951-52. A challenging series if ever there was one as the West Indies began to come of age with the aid of magnificent three Ws – Worrell, Walcott and Weekes, Frank, Clyde and Everton. They also had the magnificent bowling talents of Valentine and Ramadhin.

Weekes was dubbed the black Bradman; a title that passed on to Brian Lara in later years.

Sonny Ramadhin and Alf Valentine had spun England to oblivion as a lead-up to this contest which was billed as a world championship. Ramadhin had taken 35 wickets on that tour and came to Australia with an enormous pre-series build-up. The West Indies played a dashing form of cricket that had them dubbed the Caribbean Cavaliers, their style was Calypso Cricket.

The Australians were on edge and in the first Test in Brisbane the duo began to topple the Australians batting super structure. It was Miller's turn at the crease and he had been in the doldrums. Never one to poke and prod his way back to form, he was joined by Ray Lindwall and both decided attack was the best means of defence.

"We didn't care if Ramadhin bowled off breaks or leg spin, googlies or flippers. We just advanced down the wicket and hit them where they landed and it paid off." Nugget belted up a quick 40 and Lindwall a spectacular 60 to give Australia an unlikely lead of 10 runs. They went on to win a low scoring match by three wickets although the two spinners took a dozen wickets.

With Miller having his own technique the scene moved to Sydney where he belted up another hundred as did Lindsay Hassett and from a precarious early beginning Australia was on top. Nugget found he could pick the Ramadhin spin and taunted him with jibes, "Well hello Shorty! You're a nice little chap but you haven't improved your bowling since last match, have you?" He would then slog him to the boundary.

Thereafter he had control of the record breaking spinner but found Valentine a more formidable opponent. "He never quit. He gave it everything, he showed me his fingers one night and they were red raw. I had some jelly that deadened pain and gave it to him. I admired the way he kept plugging on the unresponsive Aussie wickets."

Australia won that series although the Windies had a chance to level in the fourth Test until the Aussie tailenders knocked off an agonising 38 runs to turn defeat into victory. Nugget's bowling of 20-398; average 19.90 and with the bat, 337 runs at a modest 33.70 were still significant in the series win.

Keith was to make the return visit to the West Indies in 1955 where a huge crowd was waiting on Australia's arrival at Kingston Airport, Jamaica. He was amazed to see

Valentine standing in the crowd. It was a pathetic sight to see the great bowler treated like any other non-entity.

Keith Miller was appointed NSW captain in 1952 – no mean honor when one considers Arthur Morris was in the side and had held the captaincy for some years. The selectors wanted a more compelling and adventurous spirit in their side.

Speculation that he would also be appointed Australian captain was not taken seriously. It surprised nobody that the Australian selectors made Australian captaincy more improbable when they appointed Morris as vice-captain to Lindsay Hassett. Miller was keen to captain Australia but dare not show the selectors that ambition. As the South Africans headed for Australia, Keith trekked to Hong Kong for a bit of practice.

OUT "COURT"

In October 1952, playing an exhibition game in Hong Kong Keith Miller hit a prodigious six that zoomed out of the picturesque Hong Kong oval, very nearly smashing a window of the Bank of China skyscraper.

Another booming sixer landed on the second storey balcony of the adjacent Hong Kong Supreme Court.

He was out "court" for 25. Australian paceman Alan Davidson played with the Hong Kong team and hit 25 off one Miller over.

Miller went in against Jack Cheetham's Springboks with his eyes wide open but he was still amazed at what he saw. The South Africans who toured Australia in 1952-53 introduced spectacular new fielding techniques, including the sliding, diving boundary save and Aussie Rules leaps for spectacular catches. It was by fielding alone they forced a 2-2 drawn series on Australia and made cricket coaches and administrators aware that fielding was now a huge run saving, wicket taking factor.

Nobody appreciated the genius of the South Africans more than the brilliant slips fieldsman Miller albeit he became their star victim. He cracked an imposing 50 in the second Test at the MCG and a century was there for plundering. He smote another big hit off Tayfield that sent the ball soaring towards the boundary, well clear of Russell Endean and six written all over it. The crowd in the stand jostled to snatch a grandstand catch. But just inside the fence Endean launched himself high into space, flying higher than Joe Cocker he dragged down the unbelievable catch of catches.

Endean was to make three similar grabs to snare Miller's wicket this series and instead of 18 runs Australia lost three vital wickets and reduced the great batsman to only 153 runs in six hands; yet he saved the series with the top bowling average of 18.53 for his 13 wickets.

It was in this Test Keith passed the 100 wicket-1000 run milestone. He wasted no time advancing on the 2000 runs. Australia had a fight on her hands throughout every Test and it was the great allround ability of Miller in the Sydney Test that saved Australia's hide. He took 5-81 and clouted another half century with 55. But he was one of the walking wounded. He broke down in the Adelaide Test and was rested from the final Test which was won by the Springboks.

England licked their lips as the veteran Australian pace duo limped into the touring team with grave doubts about Miller bowling and Ray Lindwall reduced from a great speedster to a limping master of swing and swerve. It seemed to them the 1953 Ashes tour was theirs for the taking.

Miller launched into the English tour with customary flair. He had 421 runs on the board in the first seven days and had launched a book with R. S. Whitington that rocked the international cricketing world. He began the tour by giving his tour captain Hassett

With his Errol Flynn looks and charismatic personality, Miller was a fabulous drawcard everywhere he played.

a broadside for being negative.

The Australian selectors had chosen the '53 tour to blood a number of youngsters and a heavy burden of responsibility fell on the senior players of the tour. Miller being vice-captain was expected to lead by example through a series that was rain drenched, dour and at times frustrating. But it was that gut wrenching, unrelenting bitter fight for survival that the English loved – it mattered not that the first four Tests were fought to grim and controversial draws. That was gritty cricket the way it was meant to be played.

Miller and Hassett produced the batting that saved the first two Tests – Hassett getting a century in each and Miller featuring in vital partnerships and hitting a superb 109 in the fierce second innings conflict at Lord's. Miller's back was giving him hell and it was left to Lindwall to tear down the English castles with some great bowling stints.

Australia set themselves to win the fourth Test at Leeds. Australia as holders of the Ashes only had to win this Test to be certain to retain the trophy. But they had noted the Lord Chief Justice of English umpiring Frank Chester, once popular with Aussies was now a snarling adversary. If Australian fieldsmen appealed for sincere decisions he would snarl, NOT OUT! and when dubious English appeals rent the air, the Chester finger speared angrily upwards.

Miller was infuriated by some of the calls and told Chester to stop snarling at his players. Chester's response to Miller appeals and comments thereafter was to turn his back and walk away in silent contempt. This drew Nugget to snap at him, "Frank, I want an answer!"

It all boiled over in that fourth Test when Hassett flung the ball to Miller who easily ran out English batsman Reg Simpson – he did so by the proverbial street and to a roar from the Australians. No response from Chester. Keith Miller asked quietly, "How was that, Frank?"

He said the umpire seemed about to topple but replied "Naht Out" shaking his head in the process. Miller was flabbergasted, he appealed four more times in disbelief as Lindwall hurled himself to the turf in anguish.

"How was that!... How was that? How was that? How was that?...." Not out! Simpson batted on to the smouldering anger of the players.

Miller at a suitable time asked Chester how he made such a mistake. The umpire retorted, "You have to realise I have to move very quickly to position." Miller exploded, "God almighty, they were on their third run."

It only got worse. Australia led by 99 runs on the first innings and had England in a precarious position in their second innings just 140 ahead when an injured Denis Compton was given permission to return to the wicket to fight a rearguard action late in the innings. He was promptly caught by Graeme Hole at second slip. That was all but the end of the innings and the series was as good as won. But umpire Frank Lee had been unsighted and did not see the Hole catch. He asked Chester to adjudicate as that umpire had a clear uninterrupted close-up view.

"Not out!" snarled Chester. The Aussies were in shock – Compton battled on for a gallant 65.

Australia chased the runs but ran out of time with six wickets to spare and only 30 runs to get.

Hassett immediately wrote to cricket authorities and black-balled Chester from the final and deciding Test at The Oval. Chester had saved the day for England and in reality won them the series for England came out, won the final clash and regained the Ashes.

The final losing Test was a bitter one for the proud allrounder. He failed with the bat making one and nought and took just two wickets

One man stands out as the most liked man in cricket – great cricket raconteur and Victoria-Australian crafty pace bowler Bill Johnston. It was a source of endless amusement on the '53 tour that Bill topped the tour averages from No. 11. He had an amazing run of "not out" innings.

He maintained no English bowler ever mastered him, in fact he had to throw his wicket away to get an average after he had accumulated a hundred runs without having his castle disturbed. Hassett did his level best to preserve the Johnston wicket as with impish rather than vindictive guile he wanted Big Bill to surpass the Bradman tour record. He even asked Norman Yardley to ensure Bill's wicket was not taken in the final tour innings against the MCC at Scarborough. Such a calamity would cut Bill's average in half. Johnston's last wicket partner ensured the sanctity of his tour by swiftly getting himself out and Bill Johnston finished the tour with his "better than Bradman" batting average of 102.

The '53 tour was a disappointment to lose the Ashes series when it should have been won but there were compensations. The Miller tour produced 1433 at 51. 17 and 45 wickets at 22.53. His Test batting was 24.77 and bowling 10 wickets at 30.3.

The roguish and lovable Freddie Trueman crossed the Miller sights in 1953 and there was instant rapport. Freddie's affable and expressive story telling was punctuated with obscenities that his broad Yorkshire accent helped him escape normal censure in mixed company – he made luck sound like look and this seemed to soften the rough edge of his language in the ears of the fairer sex.

Keith Miller tells how Trueman won the Young Cricketer of the Year award in 1953. He had been well trained by his Yorkshire mates Len Hutton and Bill Bowes to hate all opposition. His award was made at the annual BBC dinner by Sir Norman Birkett and the BBC had a very strict time schedule and some very distinguished guests to go to air. The trouble was that when Freddie took over the microphone and regaled his world wide audience with a series of side splitting anecdotes that he batted out time and when stumps were pulled the main illuminaries were let speechless – speechless in "on air" time that is.

Trueman is without doubt the most entertaining of all after dinner speakers.

During the '53 tour Trueman was the new English rage although his rough edges rankled with officialdom and got him into considerable hot water. Nugget admitted he was less than impressed with his bowling although he enjoyed playing against the boisterous Yorkshireman On his return to Australia he described Freddie as "just another bowler."

Trueman had refined his act and lifted his performance by the time Miller returned for the 1956 tour of England. Playing at Lord's, Freddie fired in a sizzler that sent the Miller stumps cartwheeling in all directions. As the Australian began the trudge back to the pavilion a beaming Trueman sauntered alongside, "You must be 'just another' batsman Keith." Trueman had an exquisite capacity to give the snobbish and elite their come uppance. Representing The Players against The Gentlemen, a now defunct class distinction feature match for English players, Freddie was a little put off with the airs, graces, flourished and fidgets of an Oxford lad as he postured before taking first delivery.

It was a ripper that swung and ripped the middle stump out of ground and sent it cart wheeling to the sightscreen. The batsman marvelled at the ruin of his castle, carefully removed his gloves, placed his bat under his arm and began the long walk pavilionwards.

"A wonderful ball Trueman," he said airily.

By now Freddie had had enough, "Yeah it was and a pity to waste it on a bastard like you."

The gem of Freddie Trueman misadventures came at a very social consul dinner on an Indian tour. Freddie with napkin in collar called down the long table to one of his bejewelled Indian hosts, "Hoy! Sling down the salt Gunga Din." The Trueman stories do the rounds and the names and name places change but the stories are constant.

Len Hutton was knighted for his services to cricket and being a broad Yorkshireman it seemed to open the door for further cricketing knighthoods ... perhaps Sir Frederick Trueman. The ferocious Yorkshireman just laughed, "They don't knight bloody bowlers. ... only batsmen. The last bowler to be knighted was Sir Francis Drake."

Less humorous was Trevor "Barnacle" Bailey, cricket's equivalent of the tortoise – a dedicated but aggravating player. He had an annoying trick of straightening up and walking away from the wicket as a bowler began his run up. A little gamesmanship designed to break a bowler's rhythm. He did it once too often to Miller at Leeds.

Nugget simply smiled down the pitch and launched a furious array of bumpers that threatened to part his hair or give him an extra eye socket in the middle of his forehead. Trevor took it in good part – but not so the spectators who mobbed the Australian as he left the field – one strayed too close for safety and bellowed, "You bloody Australian bastard."

Miller made an instant citizens arrest, picked him up by the scruff of the neck and bundled the abuser into the rooms where he handed him over to the properly constituted British constable.

THE TYPHOON

Australia had a weather researcher who could look into the past to forecast the future. His name was Indigo Jones and his disciple was Lennox Walker. But neither of them could forewarn Australia of a massive Typhoon called Tyson that was to sweep across Australia.

Had they known the Australian selectors may well have brought Hurricane Miller to the fore.

As Australia prepared for the battle to regain the Ashes from England in 1954-55 the main concern was not the content of the English team but who should and would lead Australia into battle.

There was anger at losing the urn of Ashes in 1953 and a demand for a dynamic and aggressive leadership to restore Australia's ranking as the world's foremost cricketing power. The media took the great debate to the public. They asked "Who do You Want to Captain Australia?" The thunderous answer was KEITH MILLER.

Miller looked to be the man – he had captained NSW to a stirring

Sheffield Shield triumph in the 1953-54 domestic season with flair and daring, balanced by careful planning and a cricket awareness that enabled him to probe out and destroy the enemy through their weakest links. But to have Miller at the helm, his protagonists at Board and selection level had to have a change of heart.

They had to accept him for what he was. A man welcomed into the arms of royalty, favored by Prime Ministers, revered by his peers and respected by his opponents – an extrovert with a desire to entertain, to joust rather than resort to trench warfare but a killer when the war had to be won. He had flaunted his defiance in the face of authority but always rallied to the cause.

He was the man to captain Australia – but would he? Rightly or wrongly his friends saw Sir Donald Bradman as the stumbling block. The Don has always denied this by inference but not by defined statement. He was, he insisted, "but one voice." He did not say how he used that one voice – nor does he have to.

We all realise that his fellow selectors and the Australian Board of Control revered the man – as we all do. So what he said would have much import in what eventuated. . . and Keith Miller WAS cast aside.

The Australian public was looking to Miller for something special. Public opinion polls conducted by national media showed an overwhelming support for him to captain Australia now that Hassett had stepped down. He had very much taken over the public and on-field mantle of Sir Donald. But officialdom continued to shun him. NOBODY KNEW WHY. It was clear his peg did not fit the hole that was the Australian captaincy. Ian Johnson did fit.

If Keith Ross Miller was regarded as a hometown fool he was seen as an international genius. Cricket authorities everywhere made comparisons of the batting, bowling, fielding and captaincy records of Johnson and Miller. The latter won every category yet the former got the job. Johnson was to be admired for the way he handled the situation under the extreme and hostile pressure.

On this tour Len Hutton fell foul of some of his players when he dropped the great Alec Bedser in favor of a Brian Statham – Frank Tyson attack. Hutton produced "Typhoon" Tyson and it was a devastatingly winning production.

It was a strategy that worked and was responsible for England retaining the Ashes he won from the Aussies in his inaugural year of leadership. It may well have been that Bedser may been even more destructive – it is doubtful, but who can tell. Bedser was so disgusted he all but boycotted the English net practice preferring to stray to the Australia's nets and bowl to the Aussies. He sent some magnificent balls at Miller.

"Not bad for a Test discard," laughed the Australian, a ribbing Alec Bedser knew was an accolade not an insult.

But Bedser was a mere zephyr alongside the breathtaking speed of Tyson. In the early stages of the tour Tyson whipped through the Aussie bats and they were ducking and weaving as if Larwood had been reincarnated – in fact Larwood was chuckling in the grandstands, having emigrated to Australia where he was to become a regular drinking mate of Nugget's.

In the early exchanges Nugget was the only Australian X1 batsman who could cope with his pace. He made 86 in Adelaide while the other top bats fell around him but the first Test wicket in Brisbane, the home of cyclones, was very unfriendly for typhoons. Tyson took 1-160 and Australia declared at 8-601. Australia went on to win by an innings and 154.

The English chief Gubby Allen flew into Sydney demanding Hutton drop Tyson from the Sydney Test but Hutton played the speedster in defiance and blasted Australia away with Tyson taking a total of 10-130. It was a thriller that saw England win the match by just 28 runs after Miller withdrew with a recurrence of his back complaint. It was an irony that had he played he would have captained Australia as Ian Johnson was also forced out by illness. Both were out available for the important Melbourne Test on the understanding Keith was not called on to bowl.

Australia's batsmen were accused of giving ground in Sydney and Miller was expected to show them how the colonials handled naked aggression. Hutton won the toss and elected to bat first. Sir Robert Menzies had taken a stroll to the wicket and cast his keen eye over the strip. He collared Miller in the members enclosure and suggested he should try a few overs. "There's a ridge on that wicket and your back might stand up in the heat."

Miller had a word with skipper Ian Johnson and was given the new ball.

He bowled nine overs – eight of them maidens and dismissed Hutton, Edrich and Compton to have 3-5 off nine overs. His back compounded and England struggled to 191. The Aussies came back with 231 with the wicket falling to pieces.

Then an extraordinary thing happened. Somebody watered the pitch. First-class cricketer and noted sports writer Percy Beames actually spotted the strip being watered heavily by hose. Despite heatwave conditions Australia found when the match resumed after a Sunday break the wicket was greener than it had been on Friday and the cracks had closed and conditions were excellent for the English bats as they structured a lead of 239. The heat continued and soon the wicket was back in its state of collapse – just in time to welcome the Australian bats to a fresh round of hostilities from Tyson.

The ball fizzed wickedly off those huge cracks and he took 7-27 in blasting England to a 128 run victory. To his credit Johnson played splendidly and with great courage.

The Australian batting collapsed again in Adelaide and the series was lost when England recorded their third successive win. They needed only 94 runs in their second innings and had a heart flutter when a fired up Miller smashed down Hutton, Edrich and Cowdrey to have them reeling at 3-18 but Compton steadied England and helped them through the crisis. The fifth Test was a washout and the Ashes remained in England.

There was deep concern in Australia at the continued injury problems of Miller and Lindwall and the new pace menace that Tyson represented and the need to address the problem before the 1956 tour of England took shape.

The Englishmen had flown home and almost immediately the Australians, without taking time to lick their wounds, were en route to the West Indies. That tour provided plenty of salve for those wounds. It was a time to regroup and Ian Johnson proved a very worthy captain as he forced discipline and training on his players. He also called on Miller to head clinics to straighten out technique weaknesses so evident against the Poms. He played no favorites and he whipped his team back into shape. Resentment turned to admiration.

They needed this jolt. The Windies were a formidable crew with the three Ws, Valentine and Ramadhin. The tragic Collie Smith who was to be killed in a fatal English car smash involving Garfield Sobers, was also in the side with the young Sobers. It was a formidable assignment the Australians faced and Miller gave his team the leadership they needed. He dug in and amassed 147 in the first Test to make a 9-515 declaration possible.

Johnson had been injured by a bouncer and Miller took over the captaincy for the balance of the match not having the spin of Johnson or the medium pace of Ron Archer who was also injured. Miller bowling himself sparingly, ripped out the teeth of the Windies batting when they threatened in the first innings.

He forced the follow on and soon had the Caribbean warriors on the backfoot at 3-32. Then came the inevitable revival as Smith, in his first Test, headed for a century with strong support from Clive Walcott.

Miller played himself to a point of exhaustion but rallied for another onslaught that saw him remove Smith on 104 and help mop up the innings to return 5-98 and become the hero of an expansive win. Some said it was his greatest Test performance because his captaincy had also been outstanding and imaginative. That win set the stage for a magnificent and triumphant series. It came with plenty of fire as the rejuvenated Miller and Lindwall hammered bumpers, bouncers and lightning bolts at the West Indies batsmen. Johnson told them to cool things – to no avail. The heat was unbearable and in time it took its toll.

In later years when Wes Hall, Charlie Griffith, Curtly Ambrose and Joel Garner cut loose, Australia had little cause to protest. The West Indies crowds were outraged by the venom of the Australians and there were riotous scenes.

Magnificent batting by Walcott and Weekes created a 242 partnership in the second Test at Queen's Park which Sobers finished off. The Australians batted better and finished with a first innings lead of 218 after belting up 9-600. Such a game was always going to be a draw but the crowds had a great spectacle and their batsmen hooked an amazing collection of sixers into the surrounding trees which were encrusted with clinging multi-colored fans enjoying a free seat.

The series produced a record 21 centuries. The third Test in British Guiana was staged in an atmosphere of political rioting and the home side was bundled out for 182 after Miller blitzed the openers. Likewise Sobers ripped through the Australians but not before they established a meagre lead. The second innings saw the locals out again for a modest 207 and it was a formality for Australia to go two wins clear.

The Barbados Test was a duel between Weekes and Miller with honors even. Weekes made 132 out of 214 but Miller took 4-51 including the Weekes wicket. Australia won the match and stitched up the series. Miller made his third Test century of the tour in the final Test success at Kingston and took a total of 8-165. His Test average for the tour was 73.16 with the bat and 20 wickets at 32.45 against a magnificent West Indies combination was a proud achievement for the undefeated Aussies and the sort of form needed if they were to belt the Poms.

The team batting performance in the Tests was 3200 runs for 60 wickets; 53.33 per wicket. It was back home to prepare for England.

The Australian team travelled to England for the 1956 series with Miller doubtful he could bowl. He was convinced a bad knee and a chronic back had terminated his bowling career and from here on in he was a batsman only

He headed to a Harley Street specialist recommended to him by his Australian practitioner. It was amazing.... the Harley Street man fixed his back in five minutes – it had been hell for 10 years. His diagnosis being that a small particle of fractured vertebrae worked itself out of position from time to time and pressed against a nerve. Nugget cruised through the first two Tests without difficulty albeit he was over-worked.

By now Nugget was the elder statesman of Australian cricket and Australia led the series as the third Test began at Leeds. Australia had crushed England by 185 at Lord's before a draw at Trent Bridge. The second Test had flattened the Australian pacemen, Lindwall had been unfit and Pat Crawford broke down causing the burden of containing the Poms to fall on an over-worked Miller. Late in the match he felt his wobbly knee go on him but he still produced Trent Bridge figures of 6-127.

He was given 10 days rest but the knee was puffed up and the medics put a tap on it. The knee gave buckets of fluid and opinion was that he would stand up to the stresses of the five days – but when he struggled against Hampshire he knew he wasn't up to the challenge of the Leeds Test. The Australians did not realise how tough a test that was going to be.

DOCTORED WICKETS

Was there a doctor in the woodwork – a wicket doctor?

Australia were confident of taking the 1956 Test series by the throat at Leeds. Even more so when the English selectors named only four bowlers, Trueman, Bailey, Laker and Lock. It was a mystery selection manoeuvre. Did they know something the Aussies didn't?

The experienced Australians didn't like the look of the wicket from the outset; they would have liked it even less had they been able to see what lay just beneath the thin veneer of turf that coated the worst cricket strip in England. The critics said it looked a beauty, but beauty is skin deep and the skin had peeled before the game was a day old.

Miller couldn't bowl even after Ron Archer had England 3-17 in an inspired spell. Johnson had asked him to keep up the pressure. The temptation was there but the body wasn't. He argued the risk was too high and the probability would be to put himself out of the rest of the tour. May and Washbrook were then together and carried England to 204 before May was out for 101 – they went on to 325.

Australia was concerned about the wicket from day one. Richie Benaud was extracting amazing turn as bare patches appeared overnight. The Australian batsmen were caught in whirlpool as Tony Lock and Jim Laker began to tweak the ball and caused it to cavort at extraordinary tangents to the delivery line. The spellbound Australians were 6-96 with their eyes revolving from obeying the first principle of batting to keep their eye on the ball. Miller, Benaud and Burke with 41, 30 and 41 followed the other principle of laying their bat on the ball to carry Australia to 143. The follow-on saw them bundled out and losers by an innings and 42 runs. Laker and Lock took 18 of the 20 wickets.

Australian critics howled foul whereas the English critics and the English bowlers simply claimed Australian incompetence. Australia went to the fourth Test less than confident with the wicket tampering controversy commanding a world stage – but accusation and exposure didn't stop the doctoring. The series was all evened up on the scoreboard but on the surface – the playing surface that is – things were less than equal. At Old Trafford Ian Johnson lost the toss and walked out to the wicket. His face sagged.

The pitch was already showing cracks before a ball had been bowled. The Australians were outraged. . . but it was all too late. Major scandal hit cricket – there was no doubt about it . The Pommy curators doctored the wickets. Unabashed, unashamedly the curators conspired to swing the series England's way.

There were no admissions but th evidence was damning. England set a precedent which has infiltrated world cricket to such a stage that approaching the 21st century curators everywhere are "under orders" to prepare wickets to suit the strengths and frailities of the home side.

Miller, Lindwall and Johnson studied the cracks in the Old Trafford wicket and scratched their heads. A day earlier they had practised and batted on wet, dead turf that constituted the practice wickets. They looked at this 22 yards of dried out disaster and knew "the bastards had doctored it." Miller complained to umpires Frank Lee and Emrys Davies, both well respected by the Australians, "I think three days will see this through." They agreed. But for the intervention of rain a little over two days would have seen it all over.

The first ball produced a powder puff of dust. Australia had played on this strip early in the tour and Len Maddocks was jumping to take Alan Davidson balls chest high standing half-way to the fence. The Manchester wicket was always quick. This one was prepared was devoid of bounce, dry and crumbling.

The wicket was clearly poisoned. The strip was red and the surrounds were black. The artificial surface concealed a spinner's paradise from the first ball that cracked its surface. The groundsman made the world headlines and when Miller spoke to him about the trauma he all but sobbed, "I'm fed up with it. They won't even give me five minutes to cut my throat."

It didn't matter who won the toss, England was always going to win the match. Australia's bowlers were inept on turning wickets and well the English knew it. In the course of three days of spinning mayhem Yorkshireman James Charles Laker took 19 Australian wickets for 90 runs (9-37 & 10-53). He did not prepare the wicket but it does cricket and the history of the game a grave disservice that Jim Laker was hand-fed a record that is unlikely ever to be equalled, let alone broken. At least the remote possibility of removing his name from the record book with a "perfect 20" exists for some future champion.

It has been said from time to time that Laker's performance is one of the 10 greatest sporting feats of all time – how ridiculous! A record based on a false and dishonest premise is not a record of any merit. Taking other matches into consideration Laker had the most remarkable record of taking 29 of 30 Australian wickets to fall in successive games. He took all 10 Australian wickets that fell at the Oval when Australia played Surrey in May.

Obviously Australia lost the Manchester Test by an innings and then some. England 2-1 and the Ashes still in their keeping – not necessarily with any honor.

All that remained of the Test career of Keith Miller was one last fling at The Oval where he determined to level the series. England made 247 – Miller 4-91. Australia was soon struggling at 5-47 until Nugget dug in and steered the team to 9-202 before he fell for a determined 61 – one of the great cameo hands in extreme conditions aggravated by rain.

Thus far it was Miller's match. England declared at 3-182 setting Australia 227 on a treacherous track. Australia again tumbled until Miller strode to the wicket and after five wickets had fallen cheaply, he teamed with Richie Benaud to bat out the rest of the match to salvage a draw. It wasn't the way he would have wanted his Ashes career to end – not losing a series to England. But the crowd cheered him to a man as he ended his career at the wicket – unbeaten and defiant!

In 1956 a youthful Princess Margaret confided to her aides she found Keith Miller the most charismatic and engaging of all male personalities. Of course there was photographic evidence that she had met the Australian charmer at Balmoral castle in 1948 – there is a picture of the princess strolling informally around the castle gardens with Keith and Ron Saggers. Princess Margaret caused a serious flutter and flapping amongst royalty gossip columnists when her uncle Lord Louis Mountbatten extended an invitation for the suave Australian allrounder to be his guest at a private dinner and sat the princess and the cricketer together for a private film screening. Extremely titillating gossip seeing Keith had lovely wife back in Sydney, Australia.

Nugget accepted the invitation with great aplomb, not at all in awe of being entertained in a private suite at the Mountbatten estate. An insensitive media headlined the story and flashed the news to Mrs. Miller that her husband was having a private tete a tea with Her Royal Highness. Mrs. Miller gave off a little chuckle, "That's Keith for you – he gets all the women in."

---

*Keith Miller did make one last Test appearance on his way home from the '56 tour of England. He top scored for Australia against Karachi with 21 in Australia's first innings of 80. Injury prevented him playing in the three match series against India.

Keith Miller THE MAN & HIS RECORD

Born: November 28, 1919

Teams: New South Wales, Nottinghamshire & Australia

First-class debut: 1937-38

First-class record: Matches 226. Batting – Runs 14183, Average 48. 90, Highest score 281*, 100s 41, 50s 63. Bowling – Wickets 497, Average 22. 30, Best bowling 7-12, Five wickets in an Innings 10, Ten wicketsin a Match 1. Fielding – Catches 136. Captaincy – Matches 38, Wins 17, Losses 3, Draws 18.

Test debut: 1945-46

Test record: Matches 55. Batting – Runs 2958, Average 36. 97, Highest score 147. Bowling – Wickets 170, Average 22. 97, Best bowling 7-60, Five wickets in an Innings 7, Ten wickets in a Match 1. Fielding – Catches 38.

Tours: England 1948, 1953, 1956, New Zealand 1945-46, South Africa 1949-50, West Indies 1955, Pakistan 1956-57. He also toured with the Australian Services team to England, India and Ceylon in 1945.

Keith Miller's Test record series by series:

BATTING & FIELDING

Season	Opponent	Mt	Inns	No	HS	Runs	Ave	100s	50s	Ct.
1945-46	New Zealand (a)	1	1	0	30	30	30. 00	-	-	1
1946-47	England (h)	5	7	2	141*	384	76. 80	1	1	3
1947-48	India (h)	5	5	0	67	185	37. 00	-	2	5
1948	England (a)	5	7	0	74	184	26. 28	-	2	8
1949-50	South Africa (a)	5	8	2	84	246	41. 00	-	2	3
1950-51	England (h)	5	9	1	145*	350	43. 75	1	1	3
1951-52	West Indies (h)	5	10	1	129	362	40. 22	1	1	5
1952-53	South Africa (h)	4	6	0	55	153	25. 50	-	2	3
1953	England (a)	5	9	0	109	223	24. 77	1	1	2
1954-55	England (h)	4	7	0	49	167	23. 85	-	-	1
1955	West Indies (a)	5	6	0	147	439	3	-	1	-
1956	England (a)	5	10	1	61	203	22. 55	-	1	3
1956	Pakistan (a)	1	2	0	21	32	16. 00	-	-	-
Totals		55	87	7	147	2958	36. 97	7	13	38

BOWLING

Season	Opponent	Mt	Balls	Mdn	Runs	Wick	Ave	BB	5wI	10wM
1945-46	New Zealand (a)	1	36	2	6	2	3. 00	2-6	-	-
1946-47	England (h)	5	979	15	334	16	20. 87	7-60	1	-
1947-48	India (h)	5	576	14	223	9	24. 77	2-25	-	-
1948	England (a)	5	829	43	301	13	23. 15	4-125	-	-
1949-50	South Africa (a)	5	1080	17	390	17	22. 94	5-40	1	-
1950-51	England (h)	5	854	23	301	17	17. 70	4-37	-	-
1951-52	West Indies (h)	5	1027	16	398	20	19. 90	5-26	2	-
1952-53	South Africa (h)	4	728	17	241	13	18. 53	4-62	-	-
1953	England (a)	5	1116	72	303	10	30. 30	4-63	-	-
1954-55	England (h)	4	708	28	243	10	24. 30	3-14	-	-
1955	West Indies (a)	5	1136	37	640	20	32. 00	6-107	1	-
1956	England (a)	5	1231	44	467	21	22. 23	5-72	2	1
1956	Pakistan (a)	1	174	9	58	2	29. 00	2-40	-	-
Totals		55	10461	337	3906	170	22. 97	7-60	7	1

COUNTRY BY COUNTRY RECORD

BATTING & FIELDING

Country	Mt	Inns	No	HS	Runs	Ave	100s	50s	Ct.
v England	29	49	4	145*	1511	33.57	3	8	20
v India	5	5	0	67	185	37.00	-	2	5
v New Zealand	1	1	0	30	30	30.00	-	-	1
v Pakistan	1	2	0	21	32	16.00	-	-	-
v South Africa	9	14	2	84	399	33.25	-	4	6
v West Indies	10	16	1	147	801	53.40	4	1	6

HOME & ABROAD

	Mt	Inns	No	HS	Runs	Ave	100s	50s	Ct.
Tests at home	28	37	4	145*	1601	48.51	3	7	20
Tests abroad	27	50	3	147	1357	28.87	4	6	18

BOWLING

Country	Mt	Balls	Mdn	Runs	Wick	Ave	BB	5wI	10WM
v England	29	5717	225	1949	87	22.40	7-60	3	1
v India	5	576	14	223	9	24.77	2-25	-	-
v New Zealand	1	36	2	6	2	3.00	2-6	-	-
v Pakistan	1	174	9	58	2	29.00	2-40	-	-
v South Africa	9	1808	34	631	30	21.03	5-40	1	-
v West Indies	10	2163	53	1038	40	25.95	6-107	3	-

HOME & ABROAD

	Mt	Balls	Mdn	Runs	Wick	Ave	BB	5wI	10WM
Tests at home	28	4872	113	1740	85	20.47	7-60	3	-
Tests abroad	27	5589	224	2166	85	25.48	6-107	4	1

HIS HIGHEST TEST SCORES

147	v West Indies, Kingston, 1955
145*	v England, Sydney, 1950-51
141*	v England, Adelaide, 1946-47
137	v West Indies, Bridgetown, 1955
129	v West Indies, Sydney, 1951-52
109	v England, Lord's, 1953
109	v West Indies, Kingston, 1955

HIS BEST TEST BOWLING

7-60	v England, Brisbane, 1946-47
6-107	v West Indies, Jamaica, 1955
5-26	v West Indies, Sydney, 1951-52
5-40	v South Africa, Johannesburg, 1949-50
5-60	v West Indies, Melbourne, 1951-52
5-72	v England, Lord's, 1956
5-80	v England, Lord's 1956

Keith Miller's other internationals

BATTING (1) Australian services v England (The Victory Tests), 1945

Mt	Inns	No	HS	Runs	Ave	100s	50s	Ct.
5	10	3	118	443	63.28	2	2	1

BOWLING

Mts	Balls	Mds	Runs	Wicks	Ave	BB
5	726	19	277	10	27.70	3-42

BATTING (2) Australian services v India, 1945

Mt	Inns	No	HS	Runs	Ave	100s	50s	Ct.
3	5	1	82	107	26.75	-	1	-

BOWLING

Mts	Balls	Mds	Runs	Wicks	Ave	BB
3	378	15	162	4	40.50	2-60

BATTING (3) Australian services v Ceylon, 1945

Mt	Inns	No	HS	Runs	Ave	100s	50s	Ct
1	1	0	132	132	132.00	1	-	

BOWLING

Mts	Balls	Mds	Runs	Wicks	Ave	BB
1	102	4	37	2	18.50	1-14

THE
SPEED
KING

"If you're going to bowl fast, fear and intimidation are part and parcel of it. You cannot produce that effect by being a nice bloke." – DENNIS LILLEE

The most outstanding fast bowler in the history of the game, Dennis Lillee was a headliner with a capital "H" from the time he knocked Geoff Boycott's cap off in Perth through to the Javed Miandad, aluminium bat and betting controversies which soured cricket's good name.

IT WAS VERY nearly cricket's O.K. Corral. Never had there been a more provocative second or two in Test history, or as open a display of on-field aggression. As Javed Miandad menacingly brandished his bat, having been kicked in the ankle, Dennis Lillee clenched his fists and shaped up like one of the oldtime bareknuckle boxers. The cricket world held its breath.

Realising tempers were at a boiling point, Greg Chappell, at slip, yelled "Dennis" and sprinted down the wicket to intervene. Umpire Tony Crafter had already stepped between the pair, trying to shepherd Lillee away. It was an extraordinary, never-to-be-forgotten display of petulance and a long-term blot on cricket's good name.

Had it not ended there and tempers overflowed into open violence, the disgrace would have been permanent.

Lillee, the firebrand fast bowler with the savage streak, wasn't prepared to back off. Maybe Miandad was, but eye-witnesses remained unconvinced. Not only was Miandad known for his cheek and arrogance, he could be impulsive in an out-of-control way.

"I could tell by looking into Dennis' eyes that something was going on," said umpire Tony Crafter, who stepped in between the militant pair.

Crafter called "over" and tried to separate the players. "I wasn't aware of what was going on behind, but I could tell by looking at Dennis' eyes that something was happening," he said. "I wanted to keep them apart and get Dennis off to fine leg and away from the zone."

Pakistan threatened to go home unless Lillee was carpeted, its team manager Ijaz Butt claiming had Lillee been a Pakistani, he would have been banned for life. Furthermore, he said Lillee's antics of mimicking, clapping derisively and sitting on the pitch were totally outside the game's ethics. There was a touch of theatre about it all; the Pakistanis well knew they'd have a far better chance of resurrecting their tour with Lillee under suspension.

Claiming Lillee had only been retaliating, the Australians labeled Miandad the instigator and accused the Pakistani captain of deliberately walking into Lillee in mid-pitch and pushing his bat into his ribs while taking a single through square leg. It was Miandad who was at fault. He should apologise.

When Chappell, as captain, met with pressmen that night to explain the code of conduct findings, he expressed genuine surprise that Miandad's conduct hadn't also been questioned, before announcing that for his role in retaliating, Lillee's penalty was a $200 fine – one-fifth of his game wage.

There was widespread amazement at the leniency of the fine, as decided under the newly-implemented player's code-of-conduct system. Umpires Crafter and Mel Johnson immediately launched an appeal, saying the fine was not compatible with the seriousness of the offence. At an official inquiry in Melbourne, the Australian Cricket Board announced a further two-match penalty, applicable to Australia's following one-day internationals.

Adding to the furore, Lillee claimed he'd retire if suspended. As always he wanted the last word. But he back-tracked after being reminded that he was on the verge of 300 Test wickets and Lance Gibbs' all-time record.

Australia's easy win paled into insignificance as the local and overseas media went into overdrive against the latest Lillee indiscretion. Having seen television replays which showed that the volatile paceman had precipitated the collision by deviating off a straight line as he walked back up the pitch, many pressmen believed Lillee would be outed for the rest of the series. Some favored him missing the entire Test summer, including all three Tests against the West Indies.

Javed Miandad, a fiery customer who loved to incite the Australians.

Despite his apology, 24 hours later, his actions were widely condemned, former Test captain Richie Benaud advocating a more appropriate fine should have been $2000 and two Test matches. "It was one of the most disgraceful and humiliating episodes seen on a cricket field," he said.

Even some of his own teammates felt he'd gone too far.

Lillee said the incident was "unfortunate" but denied he'd triggered the initial contact. He was adamant that Miandad had provoked the clash by lunging at him with his bat.

"I was bowling from the northern end when Miandad played one away through the on-side and took off for a single," he said. "He could see there was going to be an easy one in it and had slowed to a walk about two-thirds of the way down the wicket. I had stopped in my follow through and also had noticed that

The Lillee comeback in 1974 was only possible after a committed seven day a week training program.

there wasn't going to be much of a continuation of the action and so turned to go back to my mark.

"I had just made the turn when I felt a sharp blow to my side ribcage area. I recoiled and realised that it had been Miandad striking me with what I presumed was his bat.

"He then continued on down to the crease at the bowler's end. I followed him down the wicket and just by the stumps tapped him on the pad with my boot as if to say, 'What do you think you're doing? You can't get away with that.'

"It was not, as described in the media, a 'vicious kick,' it was no more than a tap with my boot. That doesn't mean to say that I should have done what I did. "I'm certainly not proud to have been a part of it. However, I am upset that the fellow who actually caused the whole thing has escaped untarnished and unpunished."

The reaction in Pakistan, where Miandad was hero-worshipped, was predictably anti-Lillee. One critic accused the great fast bowler of having become "as cranky as an unpredictable racehorse."

"He seems determined to bring the game into disrepute," said Nadir Hussein in the *Pakistani Cricketer*. "The run-in with Javed Miandad was just the latest exhibition of an ego-inflated temperament that equates tantrums with combativeness. Playing hard and fair is one thing. Playing dirty is another.

Set 543 runs to win, Pakistan was bowled out for 256, Miandad's 79 being top score. The Australians also won in Brisbane, but lost in Melbourne to take the series 2-1.

With 15 wickets in three Tests, Lillee increased his career tally to 305, two behind Freddie Trueman and four behind the great West Indian Gibbs. In reality, he was lucky to still be playing.

Dennis Lillee's standing as the greatest fast bowler of all time is rarely questioned. He smashed opposing batting line-ups apart like a torpedo zeroing in on an unprotected frigate.

Few bowlers possessed his Exocet accuracy, his repertoire of deliveries or his devoted following. To hear thousands chant "Lil-lee, Lil-lee, Lil-lee" as he charged into bowl from the southern end in Melbourne, or the Hill in Sydney was always special.

129

EIGHTEEN MONTHS SIDELINED

When Dennis Lillee's back gave out in 1973, he spent six weeks in a plaster caste, hoping desperately that four stress fractures at the base of his spine would repair sufficiently for him to be able to play again.

He hadn't intended to bowl at all in 1973-74, but after his club, Perth, named him captain-coach, the urge to bowl was too great. After a committed training program and careful re-management of his bowling action, he helped his club into the grand final, making 654 runs and taking 48 wickets and gaining vital confidence for his comeback to first-class cricket the following October.

"My back was fully healed, my form and pace encouraging and I was keyed up about the prospects of the following season," he said. "I'd also learnt a lot about the art of bowling. I couldn't pace blast the batsmen out, so I had to concentrate on line and length which was a good lesson – and I learnt the importance of bowling to a field."

In all, he missed 18 months of topline cricket but returned a tougher and even keener athlete. "Having tasted the big time, I wasn't prepared to give up without a fight," he said.

"It meant a lot of exercise and running and a lot of mental preparation as well."

He was also to miss Australia's '77 tour to England. "The doctor said at some time or other I risked breaking down there and given what I'd gone through, I wasn't prepared to go through all that again," he said. "I was 27 and had done most of the things I'd wanted to do."

An inspiration for hundreds of young pace bowlers around the world, Lillee had it all: he could swing the ball away at pace, cut it either way and aim his bouncer straight at the throat. Later in his career, he was innovative, slowing down to bowl medium pace seamers interspersed with "change-up" deliveries at near express pace, just to keep opposing batsmen on the back foot.

By eclipsing the records of every bowler before him, despite a career-threatening back breakdown which forced him to play a season as a batsman in Perth grade cricket, Lillee became a cricketing immortal, a larger-than-life figure who cornered almost as many headlines as the great Don Bradman.

Lillee was never one to be intimidated by the formalities. He said "G'day" to the Duke of Edinburgh and during the Centenary Test in 1977, even asked Her Majesty, The Queen for her autograph. Months later, a personally-signed photo of The Queen, arrived from Buckingham Palace!

Intimidation and passion were central in his on-field psyche. He bullied, taunted and berated batsmen. Some critics considered him headstrong and even callous; but no-one dared say it to his face.

His partnership with Jeff Thomson in 1974-75 revived memories of Bodyline. It seemed inconceivable that any pair could have bowled faster.

Lillee with Jeff Thomson. It was inconceivable that any pair could have bowled faster.

In winning the Test series 4-1, Australia wrested back the Ashes in emphatic fashion, thanks mainly to their ferocious speedsters who bowled with sustained fire and pace.

The Englishmen were shell-shocked. After he was dismissed in Melbourne, opener David Lloyd got into the dressing rooms and started shaking uncontrollably, the effects of never having had to move around so quickly in his life.

The tourists were amazed how quickly Lillee bowled, considering his back breakdown in the Caribbean just 18 months previously. As for Thomson, he was the ultimate shock trooper, a Mad Max with a cricket ball who bowled at express pace and publicly admitted he loved to see blood on the wicket.

The tourist's senior batsman Denis Amiss, with five Test 100s already in the calender year, had privately discounted Lillee as being any sort of threat after seeing him in his comeback Shield game in Adelaide. He was just above medium-pace and while he may pick up occasional wickets, Amiss considered it unlikely that he'd be the physical threat of '72. Despite being hit in the throat first ball by Thomson in the pre-Test clash against Queensland, Amiss also doubted Thomson's right to a place in Brisbane. In his only Test two summers before, he'd taken one wicket at a cost of 100-plus. How wrong he was to be – on both counts.

From 2.02 p.m. on the second day of the opening Test, when England began the run chase for Australia's 309, Amiss and his opening partner Brian Luckhurst were the first targets of an unrelenting speed blitz which were to shatter both body and morale and within 18 months rocket Australia to world champion status.

On a 'Gabba wicket which was uneven and under-prepared, promoting steep bounce, the Englishmen soon realised the enormity of their challenge in defending the Ashes. Not since Lindwall and Miller at their fastest had Australia possessed as formidable or speedy a set of new ball bowlers.

"Lillee's first over was faster than anything he had produced in Adelaide in the Shield match," said Amiss. "He also managed to make the ball leave the bat and bounce a lot. I was glad to get off the mark with an edged four and then as Thomson started to steam in from the other end, we realised for the first time how difficult batting was going to be."

The tourists soon slumped to 2-10 with Amiss out for seven, shortly after having had his thumb cracked by Thomson. Captain Mike Denness was hit in the shoulder first ball. At 4-57, the innings teetered on collapse before the combative Tony Greig, who had bounced Dennis Lillee out late in the Australian innings, counter attacked with a blend of skill, good fortune and audacious shotplay, including deliberate back-cuts over the top of third slip *a la* fellow South African Eddie Barlow.

In scoring 110, he steadied England and brought Lillee's temper to the boil, beginning a series of confrontations in the mid-1970s, which broke into open warfare during World Series Cricket.

When Greig arrived at the wicket, he said, "Good morning Dennis," to which Lillee replied, "Get up there... now it's your turn."

His first delivery, a searing bouncer, cleared Greig and wicketkeeper Rodney Marsh and struck the sightscreen first bounce. Finding a willing ally in the courageous John Edrich, the pair added 73 for the fifth wicket, the biggest English partnership of the match.

Relishing the challenge, Greig cover drove Lillee to the fence and said, "Take that Lillee," before signalling the four himself. He also pretended to head the bouncers away. Lillee reacted with a spate of bumpers "He tried to kill me," said Greig. "I continued to play up to him and the more upset he became, the worse he bowled, for Brisbane was a sporty wicket on which the ball of fuller length was the danger delivery."

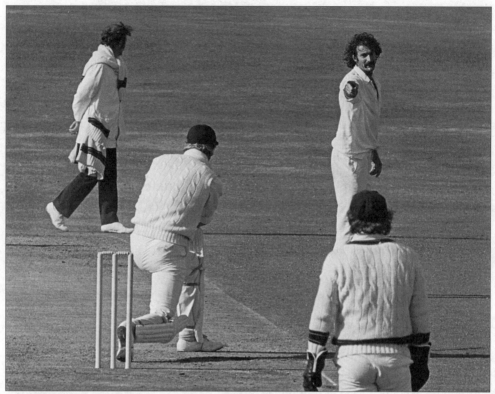

Old adversaries: Lillee and Tony Greig fire into each other during the '75 tour.

Patrick Eagar

"I began to exaggerate my follow through and signal my own fours, well aware that the rage would do nothing to help his length or direction. I reached my century with the aid of a good deal of luck, but the innings remained as memorable as any I have ever played, partly because it was my first 100 against Australia, partly because it had been a century in a crisis, but most of all because it was scored against the finest fast bowling combination I have ever faced."

Late on the fourth night, with England set 333 to win in seven hours, the initial onslaught from Lillee and Thomson was so threatening, Amiss genuinely feared for his safety.

"We were left with an awkward last hour in which I faced the most frightening fast bowling I have ever seen," he said. "Thomson and Lillee ran like madmen. They were not bowling bouncers but deliveries which lifted unpredictably from just short of a length. Three of them whistled by my chin and, because the light was poor, one of the umpires warned Thomson to pitch the ball up. Thomson clearly was not having any. The next four balls whistled past my face and off we went."

Edrich, with a broken finger, Amiss, broken thumb and David Lloyd, who hadn't played in Brisbane, were all enforced absentees from the second Test, forcing an SOS for 42-year-old former captain Colin Cowdrey for his sixth tour as a reinforcement.

Having triumphed by 166 runs in Brisbane, the Australians won by nine wickets in Perth in another virtual walkover, 24 of the 40 wickets in the opening Tests falling to Lillee and Thomson, the Australian close catching superlative especially the reflex catching of Ashley Mallett in the gully.

Lillee believed Thomson had terrorised the Englishmen in the opening Tests and as part of the psychological build-up to Melbourne, went into graphic detail via a television interview, how he aimed his bouncer directly at opposing batsmen, hoping to strike them in the rib cage and higher.

According to Greig, all the senior Englishmen felt frightened at some stage in the series, especially with curators around the country preparing green wickets with luxuriant grass covers.

At the prompting of the team's physiotherapist Bernard Thomas, the tourists started to wear made-to-measure protective armour of foam rubber across their chests.

"Never in my career have I witnessed so much protective gear applied to individuals before they went out to bat," said England captain Mike Denness. "On the plane flying from Australia to New Zealand, the players were clearly more than relieved that they had all left Australia intact and without fatal injury."

Cowdrey rated Lillee and Thomson the most difficult and unpredictable pair he'd ever faced, ahead of the very best from around the world he'd opposed in his prime years from Lindwall-Miller and Hall-Griffith to the Springbok tearaways Adcock-Heine.

Keith Fletcher said he tired of using his bat as a shield. One delivery from Thomson spat at his face in Perth with such venom that he only just got his gloves in line, the deflection being taken at the second attempt by Marsh.

"That ball was the fastest of my career and convinced me that Thomson must rank alongside the quickest of all Test bowlers," Fletcher said. "I had time only to get my glove in front of my face. The deflection was travelling so fast that it actually thumped the chest of Marsh standing more than 20 metres back, before he got his gloves to it."

Thomson was genuinely lethal, his bouncer slanting into the right-handers at high speed. Opposing batsmen found difficulty in getting into a rhythm against the devil-may-care Queenslander. If he didn't know where his deliveries were going, how could they?

With no head protection, the batsmen often seemed in danger of serious injury – against both the new and old ball. If anything, Thomson seemed more of a danger with the old one which he found he could grip better. With his ambling run-up and slinging action, he generated enormous speed and power which often saw Marsh and the slipsmen standing 25 and 30 metres back.

The Australians, particularly those who had been intimidated by John Snow in 1970-71, enjoyed their revenge.

Later in the tour, Lillee admitted to the Englishmen at an after-match gathering that he was surprised to get past the first Test. In his early comeback games he had despaired of ever again being able to bowl fast and harbored fears that if he broke down again he may finish as a cripple.

Buoyed by Thomson's outstanding performances, however, the further the series went the more confident and aggressive Lillee became. His on-field crankiness upset the Englishmen who believed his stares, gesticulating and habit of pointing batsmen to the pavilion was unnecessary.

In the New Year Test in Sydney, Greig struck Lillee on the arm and Lillee dropped the bat and started swearing. Fletcher at short leg picked it up and snapped, "Now you know what it's like to have a dose of your own medicine."

Despite the on-field heat the sides regularly mixed off the field, having drinks in the rooms of whoever was fielding. No matter what went on in the middle during that series, it was forgotten at the close of play.

Australia clinched the Ashes on the fastest SCG wicket for years. Following Ray Lindwall's practice of being fully warmed-up in the dressing rooms before walking out, Lillee's first ball to Amiss soared over his and Marsh's head before thudding one bounce into the sightscreen for four byes. Another bouncer, to tailender Geoff Arnold, just missed his ear and again soared out of Marsh's reach and careered to the boundary. Even Lillee looked relieved that the ball had missed Arnold. The Englishmen seemed frozen by fear and had hardly moved out of his stance.

In the second innings, Edrich, England's acting captain, had a rib broken by the first ball he faced from Lillee. With huge, black storm clouds gathering and Lillee charging in to chants of "kill, kill, kill," the atmosphere was electric. One hundred and eighty thousand attended the five days of the game, an SCG record.

Denness agreed his team had been unable to counter Lillee and Thomson's combined onslaught. "Bob Willis, flat out over five overs, is probably as quick as anybody, but the Aussies had two men of that calibre," Denness said. "It was no use thinking of taking a single off Lillee to get to the other end. You then had Thomson pounding in at you."

THE WILD ONE

Not only was Jeff Thomson the world's fastest and most explosive bowler, he was amiable, easy-going and likeable, as integral to Australia's world champion teams of the mid-'70s as any of his champion teammates.

Timed at 99.68 mph during the West Indian Test in Perth in 1975-76, Thomson's famed speed blitzes demoralised and intimidated opponents and accelerated the use of helmets by thousands of batsmen around the world.

When he struck Alvin Kallicharran on the back of the head causing the West Indian champion to drop his bat and vomit by the side of the pitch in 1975-76, even Australia's wicketkeeper Rod Marsh recommended the diminutive left-hander wear head protection.

The West Indies No.11 Lance Gibbs once took Ian Chappell aside on the morning of a Test, saying, "I don't want any bouncers from that madman Thomson. If you can't talk to Thomson, see if Greg (Chappell) can have a word to him. I'm only the No.11 bat and I've got a wife and kids."

For sheer awesome pace, Thomson was phenomenal, being able to command steepling bounce on the deadest of wickets. In combination with Dennis Lillee in the mid-1970s, the pair unleashed the fastest bowling seen in Australia since Frank "Typhoon" Tyson in 1954-55 and Harold Larwood in 1932-33. In back-to-back Australian summers which saw Ian Chappell's team win 4-1 and 5-1, Lillee and Thomson took more than half the wickets to fall – 58 out of 108 against England in 1974-75 and 56 of 105 against the Windies in 1975-76.

They would have had an even more impressive strike rate had "Thommo" not torn muscle fibres in his right shoulder and missed the 1974-75 Melbourne Test after a day of social tennis in Adelaide and Lillee not ricked his ankle having bowled only a handful of overs in the sixth and final match.

"It always meant a lot to me to have Thommo at the other end," said Lillee. "He took the pressure off me. With Thommo firing the way he did, the odd batsmen were inclined to take a few risks against me.

"There was never any rivalry between us because both of us were happy with the other's success and what it meant to the team."

Thomson's famous interview in "Cricketer" magazine in 1974 where he said he liked to see blood on the pitch, created worldwide attention and was the forerunner to his return to the Australian team after one unsuccessful Test when he took 0-110 bowling with a broken foot in Melbourne two years previously.

In the interview with the "Sydney Morning Herald's" Phil Wilkins, Thomson said:

- "Batsmen know I'll go for them if they get a run off me. I was real friendly for a season or two. I was not after them. But I get shitty real quick these days. That's the important thing in this game... lose your temper real quick."

Hot property: Thommo in his bachelor days during the '75 tour of England.

- "If I want to hit a bloke, I'll hit him. I really want to make it big next season."
- "I enjoy hitting a batsman more than getting him out. It doesn't bother me in the least to see a batsman hurt, rolling around screaming and blood on the pitch."

Thomson was so furiously fast at grade level that he caused ex-Test captain Ian Craig to give up the game.

With his slinging action, he initially had little idea where the ball was going, adding to the perils for the batsmen.

Unhappy at his exclusion from the NSW Sheffield Shield team, he went north, to Queensland. Within months, he'd reclaimed his Test place and a decade later become one of the elite Australian bowlers to take 200 Test wickets.

As a teenager from Sydney's Punchbowl High, he preferred lounging around on beaches to doing any serious study.

A self-confessed rebel who was banned for life from soccer after hitting a referee – he missed with his right and connected with a left, breaking the ref's nose – Thommo regularly brushed with authority

His anti-establishment and no-nonsense views were a feature of any conversation. The fact that he was made a bankrupt after a failed sports goods enterprise in 1981, showed that even sporting legends aren't necessarily assured of success off the field.

His financial future had appeared rosy, too, when he signed a 10-year $600,000 deal to work in publicity with Brisbane radio station 4IP. The agreement petered out within two years, Thomson having received nothing more than $320 in cash, each week. A Ferrari he was driving had to be returned as he couldn't afford the lease payments.

However, he fought his way back, coached the Queensland Sheffield Shield team for four years and now runs a flourishing gardening business.

During the Ashes tour in England in 1997, he teamed up again with Lillee in a double-act as luncheon and after-dinner speakers, the pair ripping into reputations as they had the world's best batsmen in the '70s and '80s.

Lillee described Thommo as "the Minister of Culture and Public Relations."

"I just clean up after him," he said.

Many believe Dennis Lillee's incomparable 355 wicket haul at Test level would have extended well beyond the magical 400 wicket mark, but for his entry into World Series Cricket ranks which cost him 24 traditional Tests.

In reality, it's doubtful if Lillee would have played much past 1977 under the old regime and the old set of payments, which saw even the topliners receive only minimal rewards. Test selection was by invitation only and if a player preferred not to play, there were 100s of others who would.

Lillee's enthusiasm and motivation for the game was clearly rekindled by the commercialism of Kerry Packer's breakaway troupe. While he loved cricket and in particular, bowling as fast as it was humanly possible, had World Series not evolved, there would have come a point, maybe even before his 30th birthday, where Lillee could easily have quit big cricket.

He'd been upsetting officialdom as early as 1972, when he claimed cricketers were playing for peanuts and should be receiving $25,000 a year, minimum. While the comments, made at the conclusion of the English tour, were intended to be off-the-record, he didn't back down from them when they were made public in Australian newspapers. The resultant "please explain" meeting with the Australian Cricket Board's Ray Steele was the first salvo in an on-going battle.

His run-ins and growing dislike of administrators were second only to his hatred of opposing batsmen. He had a maverick streak and even blued at times with his captains, especially if they happened to prefer someone else to bowl with the new ball!

As the all-star fast bowler of the '70s, he was feted virtually everywhere he went. He'd made such a remarkable recovery from his severe spinal injury of 1973 that officials allowed him to overstep authority even if it tweaked at the game's very fibre.

Unwittingly, those who tended to forgive and forget and gloss over Lillee's indiscretions, ultimately did him a disservice. From being shy, bordering on introverted, he developed a supreme ego. Had he been subject to discipline earlier, he may not have become quite as roguish the figure who so irritated authority. Then again, had the ACB paid Ian Chappell and Co. as well in the early '70s as they did at the end of the decade after the so-called compromise between the Board and Kerry Packer, much of the antagonism may have been avoided.

Traditionalists, however, point to Lillee's antics, saying they too often flouted authority. Central to their argument were Lillee's key involvements in:

- The kicking controversy with Javed Miandad;
- The infamous aluminium Combat bat affair;
- The Leeds betting furore, which saw he and Rod Marsh win $A15,000 after backing England to defeat Australia;
- And the vandalism of a dressing room at Launceston's historic NTCA ground during his comeback half-summer in 1987-88.

While universally respected for his unyielding commitment and unsurpassed wicket-taking talents, he's also regarded as the game's most notorious bad boy.

From the time he knocked Geoff Boycott's cap from his head with his first delivery in an international against the 1970-71 Englishmen at the WACA ground, Lillee was news.

His spitfire speed from a rocking, energetic run-up was timed at almost 90 mph, just fractionally behind Jeff Thomson.

His frank admissions that he bowled his short deliveries to scare and, if necessary, hurt opposing batsmen, were part of his intimidating persona. He revelled in his role as pace spearhead and would bowl until his captain took him off. He wanted wickets, first and foremost; and never worried about runs being conceded.

Ian Chappell said he'd never met a cricketer with such an iron will, or such a love of running in fast. "The stories of Lillee's ability to overcome pain and push himself to the limit are endless and I sometimes think that those people who criticise captains for overbowling the man, should be made to go out on the ground and physically take the ball from him," he said.

"In 1979 in Trinidad, on a hot, humid day when the dust from the dry ground filled your lungs everytime you tried to breathe, I'd bowled him for an extended spell as wickets were at a premium and runs precious. I hadn't realised how extended the spell was until I asked him how he was going. His mouth was working, but no words were coming out. He was exhausted, but he still took the ball from me and walked back to his mark. He must have bowled that last over purely on will power."

As Lillee's legend grew, so did the demands on his time.

He loved the actual cricket part of his life, but not the associated attention. "There are lots of times when I'd like to disappear off the face of the earth," he said, "or wear a mask that nobody would ever recognise me in."

The huge upswing in cricket's popularity led to new levels of hero worship in the mid-'70s. The anonymity Lillee so desired was impossible especially given his habit of rising so often from the dead.

In 1981-82, a Sydney newspaper claimed Lillee should retire after going wicketless against Pakistan in the Christmas Test in Melbourne. He bounced back with 16 wickets in three Tests against the West Indies to skip past Lance Gibbs' world mark. "People have been telling me to retire for a long time now," he said. "I've got news for them. I'll retire when I'm ready."

The stormiest fortnight of Dennis Lillee's career came early in the season of compromise, 1979-80, a summer in which he had once again been written off as a has-been. Just as a disenchanted Ian Chappell was being admonished for misbehaviour and subject to a six week suspended sentence, Lillee was accused of petulance and interfering with the spirit of the game.

The first black mark came as the opening West Indian Test in Brisbane ground to a draw. Relegated on the final afternoon to first change duties behind Jeff Thomson and Rodney Hogg, Lillee angered captain Greg Chappell and wicketkeeper Rod Marsh by deliberately sending down a bouncer while Marsh was standing over the stumps.

Having seen Lillee bowl a slow off-break from just three paces, Chappell called to Lillee, asking whether he was bowling fast or spin.

"Spin," said Lillee, riled at no-ball calls being made by umpire Robin Bailhache.

Chappell changed the field to suit a slow bowler, thinking Lillee intended finishing his over, which was to stretch to 11 balls, as quickly as he could.

Instead, from just five or six paces, he delivered a short-pitcher at close to top pace. It whistled past an astonished Collis King and was only just taken by Marsh, who'd come up to the stumps.

Marsh fumed and cursed at Lillee, who was already storming back to his mark, without even half an apology. Chappell was clearly unimpressed and strode 60 metres from slip to near the member's pavilion to admonish his fast bowler.

"He was such a strong-willed beggar and such a good bowler you had to accept that occasionally he was going to get pig-headed," Chappell said. "The adrenalin would pump so fast he'd go over the top."

Their confrontation was reported almost as widely as the centuries by Chappell and Kim Hughes which helped save the game.

Ten days later Lillee was headline news again, this time over his use of a revolutionary aluminium cricket bat in the opening Test against England at the WACA Ground.

Lillee had first used the bat, without even a ripple of protest, in the first Test of the summer, against the West Indies in Brisbane. Given that he batted just nine minutes and faced seven balls without scoring a run before falling lbw to Joel Garner, it was hardly surprising.

However, his continued use of the bat in the second Test of the summer against England caused a furore and resultant action from no less an authority than the game's rulemakers, the Marylebone Cricket Club.

In a bizarre start to Saturday's second day's play, Lillee, who was not out overnight, resumed with the Combat bat he'd been attempting to market into schools and at junior level. After four deliveries from Ian Botham, one of which Lillee drove through mid-off for three, England captain Mike Brearley complained to umpires Don Weser and Max O'Connell, precipitating an unscheduled break in play while Lillee argued the legality of the bat with the umpires and anyone else within range.

Play was held up for 10 minutes as Lillee first refused to replace the bat with one of two wooden ones offered by Australia's 12th man Rodney Hogg before marching off the ground, only to return minutes later with the same bat!

"I decided to use the Combat bat to introduce it to the public," Lillee said. "There was

Lillee and his infamous Combat bat, Perth Test, 1979-80.

no damage from the bat on the ball. We wanted the bat to get some exposure for Christmas sales. Mike Brearley stuck his nose in when he shouldn't have."

Lillee was hooted by sections of the crowd over his antics which included hurling his bat 20 metres towards the pavilion in apparent anger.

Many, like English wicketkeeper Bob Taylor, felt he was grandstanding. "No one could believe it when the cream-colored bat made a clanging sound when it hit the ball," he said. "Even Greg Chappell, his captain, was stunned and he came onto the pitch to make Lillee use a proper bat.

"Lillee made a complete fool of himself by trying to goad Mike Brearley, then flinging his bat away in mock temper. It was a totally theatrical performance for the benefit of the cameras and Lillee had the cheek to feign a loss of temper."

Chappell ended the fiasco by taking a conventional Duncan Fearnley out himself, the umpires having refused to re-start the game until Lillee swapped bats.

It was an extraordinary standoff, in which Lillee flouted rule 46 which states that umpires are the sole judges of any dispute.

Lillee escaped immediate censure having produced a letter from the Australian Cricket Board saying it neither approved nor disapproved of the revolutionary bat. At the time, the laws of cricket did not demand bats being made from wood.

But he was roundly lashed in the media, his behaviour being variously described, by Australian and English press writers, as disgraceful, unsavoury, petulant and intolerant.

Former Test captain Bobby Simpson accused Lillee of deliberately eroding cricket's spirit. "With the events of the past few years I wonder whether some of the present Test cricketers appreciate or understand their responsibility to the game," Simpson said. "In the two Tests this season we have seen Dennis Lillee breaching perhaps the most sacred code amongst cricketers by which the captain basically runs the team.

"In Brisbane, Lillee earned a public rebuke by Chappell when after allowing his captain to set a field for off-spinners to his bowling late in the Test match, he sent down a searing bouncer which almost decapitated 'keeper Rodney Marsh.

"Lillee also showed scant regard for the wishes of his captain in the aluminium bat incident. Chappell made it quite clear that he didn't want Lillee to use the aluminium bat by sending out Hogg with two wooden bats as soon as he saw Lillee was using the synthetic variety. Lillee publicly snubbed him by refusing to accept his instructions."

The English pressmen called for Lillee to be disciplined, John Woodcock from *The Times* saying that in just six eventful hours, Lillee's Jeckyl and Hyde personality had unfortunately showed "both the recalcitrant child and the great bowler."

John Thicknesse of *The Evening Standard* said Australian officialdom had allowed Lillee's undoubted playing importance to cloud their responsibilities. "Jeez," he wrote, "how can you suspend a man who's got three Pommie bastards out in eight overs? "

It was revealed later that his close mate Marsh, in a moment of mischief, had re-fuelled Lillee's anger when he returned mid-incident into the rooms. "When Dennis walked into the dressing room with Greg Chappell urging him to get onto the field and get on with the game, I walked past and said, 'They can't do that to you mate. You can use any bat you like.'

"Dennis looked at me and said, 'You're bloody right' and strode back onto the field with his aluminium bat.

"That was when all hell broke loose and Dennis tossed the bat in the air when Brearley complained again. It was quite funny really. I copped a decent old serve from Greg for egging Dennis on but it was worth it. Dennis was never going to get too many with it."

Greg Chappell had actually picked up the bat and given it an impromptu trial in the nets on the eve of the game. It was tinny and made a strange, clunking sound. Unless you hit it right in the middle, the ball went no-where. "You're not going to use *that* bat, are you?" Chappell said to Lillee in half jest.

Late in the Test, Lillee issued a statement saying he wouldn't be using the bat in the Australian second innings. His sole concentration was to help Australia win the match. "However, I would like to make the following two points," he said:

> "(1) Tests already carried out on the aluminium bat have produced excellent results, certainly with no more damage to balls than willow bats and I take great exception to anybody who says otherwise if they themselves have made no field tests;
> "(2) Saturday's incident was in no way a publicity promotion as was suggested. I admit to being very angry as the laws of the game permit me to use the bat as I did in the Test in Brisbane and the laws still permit me to use it."

Soon afterwards a Melbourne district batsman was told to replace his Combat bat in mid-innings after it caused a deep two and a half centimetres cut in a ball just eight overs old.

It took the ACB a fortnight to make official its misgivings at Lillee's actions. He was issued with a severe reprimand, "for general behaviour," a decision which re-opened the controversy, one English critic saying Lillee had been caned with the force of a feather.

"The umpires are reported to have said that they did not see the bat thrown," said Laurie Mumford from the *Evening News*. "Presumably the bat can only have finished where it did by remote control."

Lillee and a partner lost thousands over the ill-fated aluminium bats venture. What worked for baseball didn't necessarily work for cricket. Within six months, the bats had been officially outlawed, by decree of the MCC. Lillee had never intended their use for Tests or Shield cricket, but for practice and at backyard level. At a recommended retail of $72, the bats were 30 per cent cheaper than the most expensive English willow bats such as the state-of-the-art Gray Nicolls "Scoop." Now they are eagerly sought by memorabilia hunters.

As tour pranks go, it was the grand-daddy of them all. The 500-1 odds were irresistible; the only complication being that it meant backing England.

Most would have ignored the temptation, but not Dennis Keith Lillee

Ever since first sampling the English betting tents during Australia's 1972 tour, Lillee had been intrigued by the on-ground betting. He couldn't believe the latest odds flashing on the new Headingley scoreboard from Ladbroke's: "England 500/1"…and in a two horse race.

It was lunchtime on day four of the third Test at Leeds and England was slumping to what seemed to be a certain innings defeat. "Have a look at that," said Lillee. "Five hundred to one! Surely those odds can't be right.

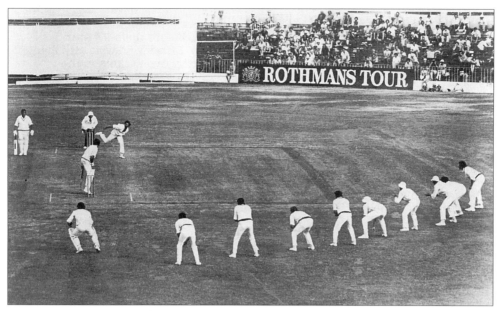

The most attacking field ever? Lillee bowls to New Zealand tailender Ewen Chatfield in the second and final Test at Eden Park in 1977. Next to wicketkeeper Rodney Marsh are Greg Chappell (first slip), Rick McCosker, Gary Gilmour, Doug Walters, Kerry O'Keeffe, Ian Davis, Gary Cosier, Alan Turner and Max Walker.

"I'm going to put 50 quid on that. I can't believe anyone would offer those sorts of odds."

England seemed that far gone that Lillee was ridiculed for even thinking about having an interest. But he still wanted in, even if it meant parting with just 10 pounds. "I went around to the others, asking if any of them also wanted to have a bit, but there were no takers. I got to Marshy and said, 'Look, you're silly if you don't... put 10 on.'

"He said he wouldn't, so I suggested five, 'just to be with me.' However, I couldn't talk him into it because he was convinced, like the others, that there was no way England could win."

Enlisting the team's bus driver, Peter Tribe to lay his bet, Lillee joined his teammates on the stairs ready to take the field. As Marsh walked past, he put his hand up to Tribe indicating he wanted a fiver on, after all.

Tribe thought the bet was almost too ridiculous to worry about, but placed the money anyway.

Having won at Trent Bridge, Australia was on the verge of regaining the famous Ashes urn, having outplayed England on the first three days at Headingley. Melbourne's *Sunday Observer* newspaper thought so and even issued a newsagent's banner, ASHES COME HOME.

Forced to follow-on, 227 runs behind, the Englishmen had collapsed to 4-41 in their second innings and it seemed inevitable that the game would finish well inside four days. But in a Boys' Own turnaround led by Ian Botham, who had resigned his captaincy after making a pair at Lord's in the previous Test, Engand not only set a small target, but in extraordinary scenes bowled Australia out for 111 to win by 18 runs in the closest and most gripping Ashes Test in 50 years.

Against all odds, Lillee had won $A10,000 and Marsh $A5000. Busdriver Tribe said he felt "sick, absolutely sick" as the Australians plunged to defeat.

BOB'S SCREAMER

The Australians had never seen the betting tents before their '72 tour.

In the game against Yorkshire at Bradford, Lillee, who was 13th man, found that you could get 5-1 about Australia taking five wickets in the session.

"We all put in heaps, because we believed we could do that," said Rod Marsh. "With about half an hour to go in the session we had our five wickets and Dennis was running around and jumping up and down with excitement. He went to the tent to collect and the bloke explained that the session hadn't finished and if we got any more wickets it would be a lost bet.

"Dennis yelled out that we couldn't take any more and we all acknowledged the fact and proceeded cautiously.

"We had Bob Massie at fine leg who wasn't the best of fieldsmen at any time, but sure enough a few minutes before the end of the session this bloke hooked one and Bob took a screamer. We all raced down to kick his backside in."

There were immediate denials about the bet, Lillee only admitting to it to his closest mates But it all became official 12 months later when Lillee declared in *My Life in Cricket* that he had in fact had a big win. He wished it was more and that he hadn't been talked out of his original 50 pound wager.

"I didn't regard it as betting against my team or my country," he said. "I just thought the odds of 500/1 were ridulous for a two-horse race.

"I'd flatten anyone who ever suggested I threw a game. I have a completely clear conscience over the betting incident. I believe my integrity, as far as playing to win every game I played, is unquestioned."

Marsh said both he and Lillee felt they were betting against the English bookmakers – "trying to show the Poms how silly they were for offering such stupid odds of 500/1." *

"I couldn't see the harm in having a bet," he said. "Nobody would have known or cared about the bet if we had won. It wasn't until after the game when someone said that we had won a quid that it dawned on us. But I don't believe we did the wrong thing because we didn't consider it a bet against Australia. That was never the intent."

The Australian Cricket Board moved to include a clause in all future player agreements under the heading BETTING:

> "The player undertakes that he will not directly or indirectly bet on any match or series of matches in which he takes part."

New South Wales captain Rick McCosker believed the bet reflected badly on cricket and was a poor example to the youth. Former Australian batsman Neil Harvey went further, saying Lillee should get out of the game.

Busdriver Tribe was happy though. For his part in laying the bets, he received a set of golf clubs and a return air ticket to Australia.

Mick Basile is a comparitive unknown outside Perth, where he played only a handful of first-grade games. But he left an indelible imprint on the psyche of the young Dennis Lillee. "Your first aim as a fast bowler should be to put the wind up a batsman," Basile, a left-arm fast bowler said. "Length and direction will come later as you gain experience."

Like all promising youngsters, the young Lillee was inundated with advice from the

* The odds weren't to be repeated until 1997 when the bookmakers again quoted an English victory, in the fourth Test at Leeds, as 500/1. Australia won this game by an innings.

time he was first selected, aged 16, after just six second-grade games in Perth's first X1 late in the 1965-66 summer. While all of it was well meaning, much was irrelevant. However, some key points, such as Basile's urging him to consistently bowl as fast as he could, were integral in the young bowler's development.

So was ex-England fast bowler Peter Loader's tip at State colt's practice for Lillee to focus on the base of the stumps and work out his ideal length and direction from there. Australian X1 swing specialist Ray Strauss assisted with swerve and variations, while Test pace bowling legend Ray Lindwall offered some technical advice as well as encouraging Lillee to be better balanced at delivery by slowing down the first steps of his run-up and gradually increasing his speed before reaching maximum pace just prior to release.

Lillee's education was further assisted when he spent a season with Haslingden in the Lancashire League. He further refined his run-up rhythm and learnt the importance of control. Twelve months later, having headlined against the Rest of the World, he returned with Ian Chappell's 1972 Australians one of the outstanding pacemen in the world.

It had been a rapid promotion for the rangy youngster from suburban Maddington, who as a kid had to wear ankle high boots to stop himself from falling over.

AN EXTRAORDINARY DAY

It took years for Dennis Lillee to learn to control his matchday nerves. His big breakfasts often included as many as 10 Weet Bix, but he'd still feel exhausted from pent-up nerves come 11 a.m.

His finest international performance, from a statistics point of view, came at the height of one of his nervous spells, while representing Australia against the 1971-72 Rest of the World team in Perth.

After five overs in his opening spell, he told Ian Chappell he was totally spent and needed a rest. Chappell asked him to bowl just one more over so he could organise a replacement.

By dismissing Tony Greig, Gary Sobers and Richard Hutton in the space of eight deliveries of his sixth over, Lillee, bowling at lightning pace, decimated the star-studded World X1, taking five wickets in nine balls on his way to an extraordinary analysis of 8-29 from 7.1 overs.

The World X1 was bowled out for 59 and opening batsman, Indian Farookh Engineer, dismissed a second time, before lunch in the same session!

The eldest of three children, Lillee was initially just as keen on swimming and Australian football, but cricket became more important, especially on the regular Sunday visits to the Jarrahdale home of his grandfather, Len Halifax.

Len was coach of the local cricket team and taught the fundamentals to Lillee and his younger brother, Trevor.

Just 18 months separated the boys in age and they were fiercely competitive. Lillee's father, Keith, also developed a keen interest and joined them in their backyard tests.

While Trevor concentrated on batting and was good enough to play first-grade cricket, Dennis' first love was fast bowling. "To get a turn with the bat meant that I had to get Trevor out and because he was so good, it was hard work," said Lillee. "It had a major influence on me bowling fast. There was no room in the backyard for the refinements of spin and swing.

"Dad was a truckdriver and often didn't get home until quite late on summer evenings, but there was always enough daylight left to squeeze in a game before he sat down to tea. There was always a scramble to set the game up as soon as we heard Dad arriving home. We always just 'happened' to be playing cricket when Dad came into sight around the side of the house. No matter how weary he was, Dad would always oblige us and play."

Among many heroes, all of whom were fast bowlers, West Indian tearaway Wes Hall was Lillee's greatest inspiration. He mimicked Hall's huge, extended run-up, if not his pace and revelled in his performances during his two seasons as an import with Queensland's Sheffield Shield team in the early '60s. One day at the WACA Ground, he and his brother jumped the back fence and were among a group of kids to talk to Hall for 10 minutes while he sat out in front of the player's pavilion.

"We clambered around him for what seemed like an eternity, firing questions like a machine gun," Lillee said. "Wes never tired of answering our questions, most of which must have been absolutely stupid. He seemed to love it and that personal touch made an everlasting impression on me. I floated home that night and the next time I bowled at the lads it was an inspired Dennis Lillee who let a few go at surprising pace."

From his early teens, Lillee was totally absorbed and obsessed by cricket. Leaving school after his third year of senior school, he worked as a storeman and then as a bank teller. He also moved from his junior club, South Belmont, to Perth Cricket Club, from where he was to launch his illustrious career.

An analysis of 9-35 for Perth colts against Bassendean-Bayswater and some more consistent first-grade performances in his third and fourth years with the team were important stepping stones in his elevation into WA's state side. He'd learned to bowl an out-swinger at pace and while he was terribly raw with his rocking run-up, the energy and power in his release made opposing batsmen genuinely jump around in their creases.

With the state's two senior pacemen Graham McKenzie and Laurie Mayne away with the Australian touring team, his timing was immaculate. WA captain Tony Lock needed a new pace spearhead and from his very first outing, against Queensland in Brisbane, gave him the new ball – and the choice of ends. "Just bowl quick son and the leave the rest to us," he said.

It took Dennis Lillee just 15 months* to break into the Australian team. His pace had been impressive and he was aggressive, as he proved when bombarding South Australian tailender Trevor Pearson with short deliveries at the WACA Ground.

Having finally bowled Pearson to end SA's innings late on the opening day, Lillee immediately went into the SA dressing rooms to apologise, realising in the heat of the moment, he had broken one of cricket's unwritten laws and bowled dangerously short at a fellow tailender.

The elder statesman of Australian cricket, Les Favell, was livid and after telling Lillee he was basically a young upstart, copped a return barrage, the fired-up tyro promising to sort him out in SA's second innings!

Having just finished kindergarten when the universally-popular Favell first played Test cricket 15 years before, Lillee was strictly out of line in answering back and received another blast, from his own captain Tony Lock, when he explained what had gone on in the next room.

But he was true to his word and 48 hours later, claimed 7-36, including Favell caught in the slips for single figures, as WA clinched a 10 wicket victory with a day to spare.

His WACA spree ensured his selection for the Australia "B" team's tour of New Zealand and while he played in only one of the three four-day internationals, on a batting paradise at Wellington, he was rapt to even be asked.

The opportunity to bowl in tandem with one of his heroes, Australian pace bowling

* And 20 matches

great Graham McKenzie from the start of the 1970-71 international summer, featuring a tour by England, added to his excitement.

But with only six wickets in four matches on tour and a thumping from Barry Richards in WA's first home game of the season in November, Lillee's momentum from the previous summer was missing and he was relegated to 12th man duties for the match against the MCC in December. "Things were going so badly," he said, "that I thought it was the end of a brief career for Dennis Lillee. I naturally thought the next step for me would be out of the 12 and perhaps the end of the road."

But when McKenzie dropped out of the game, Lillee was re-selected and given his normal with-the-wind duties, bowled with great pace from his first ball when he caused quite a stir by knocking England No. 1 Geoff Boycott's cap from his head.

With two second innings wickets, Boycott, for nine and Colin Cowdrey, six, he had been impressively fast and Jack Fingleton, one of Australia's most experienced cricketing journalists, said Lillee should be tried in the Tests.

In late January, with England leading the series 1-0, and Australia having to replace the injured Ross Duncan for Adelaide, Lillee became the fifth Australian new ball bowler to be named during the summer. His six wickets in the Queensland game in mid-December had been important, but the Boycott bouncer was the clincher.

Lillee was in Perth playing in a Sunday afternoon City v Country fixture when the news was broadcast. He was thrilled. It remains one of the highpoints of his career.

With 5-84 and 0-40 on debut, he made as impressive an entry into Test ranks as McKenzie, 10 years earlier during the '61 tour of England.

Not only was he to surpass McKenzie's record of 246 Test wickets, his wonderful durability and ability allowed him to become the world record holder at the Melbourne Cricket Ground in the 1981 Christmas Test when he took his 310th wicket, Larry Gomes caught at slip by Greg Chappell.

An inspiration to a whole generation of fast bowlers, Dennis Lillee was at his most irresistible in Melbourne where he claimed 82 wickets at almost six wickets per Test.

Several of his bursts were unforgettable, especially his Centenary Test heroics in 1977 when he took 11 wickets and his Christmas Test classic against the West Indies in 1981 when powering in from the MCG's southern end on the opening night, he bowled Viv Richards from the very last ball before stumps to see the Windies slump to 3-7.

Not as well known were his more private onfield battles, with some of his captains, particularly Greg Chappell. The pair were so alike in so many ways and while they became great mates, there were times when that friendship was tested. Their biggest run-in came in the fifth Test of the 1975-76 summer in Adelaide when Chappell relegated Lillee to first change duties behind Gary Gilmour and Jeff Thomson after Australia had started with 418.

"Stuff me, I thought, what had I done?" Lillee said. "My figures in the preceding Tests were fine (15 wickets in three Tests). I'd bowled well in the nets and I'd cleaned my teeth and gone to bed early the night before. What was going on?"

Lillee had never been anything but an opening bowler. Even in his first season with Western Australia, as a raw express, his captain Tony Lock had bowled him downwind.

After having missed the Sydney Test with pleurisy, his demotion rankled and for one of the only times in his career, he deliberately bowled badly and suffered accordingly.

His first five overs cost 39, including seven 4s, as Viv Richards launched into him, scoring at a run a ball. "Greg kept coming up to me and saying, 'What the hell do you think you're doing? I'm setting an off-side field and you're bowling down leg-side!'

"'Just leave me alone', I replied. 'I'm doing the bloody bowling. You captain the side.'"

It wasn't until Rod Marsh reminded him that his erratic performance was justifying Chappell's decision to relegate him in the bowling order that Lillee suddenly sparked.

Dennis Lillee's longevity was as striking as his wicket-taking ability. Despite his back breakdown at 23 and a deteriorating right knee which finally collapsed after years of wear and tear, his fierce determination to succeed and unrivalled competitive streak enabled him to keep going long after most of his contemporaries had settled for nothing more physical than an occasional stint of Saturday afternoon gardening.

An underrated factor in his "second-coming" after the turbulent World Series Cricket years, was his committed training regime under the expert eye of Austin Robertson snr., who in his prime in the Depression Years was the fastest runner in the world over 130 metres.

Lillee felt he was struggling with his run-up and wanted to learn to run smoother and quicker, so he could bowl longer, more effective spells with minimum risk of breakdown.

So chuffed was Lillee with the fine-tuning of his running technique he kept returning to Robertson for years right up until his much-publicised retirement from international cricket in 1984.

He ran in faster, felt more balanced and was just as successful as in his prime, continuing to average around five wickets per Test, despite being on the wrong side of 30.

Asked what had motivated him to continue into a second decade of international cricket, he said, "I kept going because I love cricket, the bowling and the involvement. Even if I had only 150 wickets I'd still be out there bowling because I love it. There are times when you get down in the dumps and don't even want to know about a cricket ball and I've had a lot of those times. Other times, there's nothing better..."

So good was he during the early '80s when he became the consumate, if controversial, allround fast bowler, many of his antics were either ignored or accepted, despite growing unrest at Board level.

He lost count of the times he was written off, even, on one notable occasion, when his knee finally gave out, by Richie Benaud. The maverick in him demanded he bow out on *his* terms, not anyone else's.

Even in his farewell international season when his habit of being last out of the dressing rooms caused ripples, Lillee was defiant and combative. Before the summer start, Kim Hughes, then only his state captain, suggested that Lillee should consider slowing down and bowling at first-change with Western Australia. Lillee's answer was to bowl more overs and take more wickets at Shield and Test level than anyone else in the country.

Controversial to the end, Lillee incurred a suspended $1000 fine for swearing in front of the South Australian Cricket Association members at the Adelaide Oval in a Shield game and had the fine imposed during the 1983-84 summer after a disagreement with umpires over the timing of a drink's break in Brisbane. When a two-match suspension was also included, he applied and was granted an injunction which allowed him to play in a grade match.

Even after captaining Western Australia in Hughes' absence and taking his 845th first-class wicket in the 1983-84 Sheffield Shield final, Lillee wasn't entirely finished, even if he had announced his retirement from all levels of the game.

While he substituted wind surfing at his family's coastal getaway at Margaret River, it was never going to be enough, not for someone who'd given a lifetime so passionately to cricket. He enjoyed the solicitude and extended time-off with his two boys, but a part of him also hankered for a return to the limelight. He'd retained his profile, chiefly through his Carpet Call advertisements, rather than his appearances at the cricket, which were scarce. He'd never been a great watcher or overly thrilled with commentating. But he loved coaching and seeing young prospects advance.

Allan Border had helped sow the seeds for a comeback during an impromptu coaching session Lillee was involved in with several of the Australian pacemen before a game in 1986-87.

With his fast bowling stocks dangerously low, Border asked Lillee if he would consider playing again. He'd watched him in the nets and was amazed how well he was bowling, even after three years off. Flattered by the invitation, Lillee didn't make any commitment, but did have an elbow operation in the New Year which allowed him to fully extend his right arm for the first time in years.

The time away from the game had been invigorating and by July he confirmed the newspaper rumours. He'd been in training down south and was as fit as any 38-year-old had a right to be. Yes, he would be coming back, but only at grade level. He loved the game and wanted to again have a bowl. Nothing more, nothing less.

In the first weekend of October he re-launched his career with Scarborough, taking 4-70 from almost 30 overs, including the wicket of Kim Hughes. He was still bowling at good pace, too and with excellent control. One well-credentialed club cricketer, Doug Harris, said he was the fastest he'd faced in Perth grade cricket for five years.

With 40 first-grade wickets in half a season, including 10 in one weekend, Lillee suddenly found himself in demand. Publicly, his ambitions started and finished at grade level, but having worked so hard and seen the fruits of his success, he wanted more.

Tasmania was without a big-name overseas player and was keen to continue talks which had started in October. England swing bowler Richard Ellison hadn't been invited back for a second summer, while West Indian Eldine Baptiste, its favored import, had touring commitments in India. Would he be prepared to come and play?

Having gained an exemption from the usual three-month residential requirements, Lillee was happy to accept, even though many wondered at his motivation. What could be prove? Even his old pace partner Jeff Thomson remained unconvinced, comparing Lillee's leaving WA for Tasmania as like going from Malibu to Alcatraz!

With hair considerably thinner, but torso tight and willing, Lillee took his place at the head of Tasmania's attack as if he'd never been away from the game. It was no publicity stunt. Showing a continuing brilliant sense of occasion, he took a wicket with his first ball, South Australia's Andy Hilditch caught behind on his way to 4-99 from 45 overs.

Despite his time away from the game, his classic action remained, as did his superb fitness which allowed him to bowl long spells. Border said he could even be a valuable standby player at international level in case of injuries to his senior pacemen.

There was one hiccup, however, after the Tasmania-Queensland McDonald's Cup game at Launceston's NTCA Ground when the visitor's rooms, used by the Old Scotch Collegians during the summer, were badly damaged, glasses broken, light fittings shattered and an honor board damaged. Lillee and Queensland's high-profile import Ian Botham were said to be squarely at fault, the Tasmanian Cricket Council lodging an official complaint, resulting in an $1800 fine, which Lillee appealed.

His latest brush with authority didn't worry his sponsor, AAMI, which had largely funded his time in Tasmania. "Dennis is an individual, a very high-powered sportsman," said a spokesman Graham Dobson. "He can't go in second gear, he's flat out in everything he does, whether it's bowling or celebrating. He doesn't do anything at half pace."

With 16 wickets in six first-class games, Lillee had exceeded expectations, given his time away from the game and he fielded further offers to continue playing in the English winter. The most attractive was from Northamptonshire, looking to replace new signing Curtly Ambrose after his inclusion in the 1988 West Indian touring party. "I'd got myself fit, so thought why waste it," Lillee said.

He arrived in May to front page headlines and while an ankle injury was to restrict him to just seven of the 22 championship games, he made an immediate impression with 1-39 and a county-best 6-68 to set up victory against Gloucestershire on his debut.

While it was to be his playing highpoint, his mere presence and active coaching of the Northant's speedsters such as David Capel and West Indian Winston Davis was invaluable, as was his appeal, which was squarely reflected via increased membership.

While his playing commitments since have generally included only the traditional international tour opener at Lilac Hill, a gentle-paced game he has always approached with total commitment, one memorable testimonial match in Melbourne to benefit Dean Jones provided a delightful insight into his competitiveness, even at the age of 45.

He opened the bowling from his favorite southern end to young Victorian Brad Hodge. The first delivery, just a warm-up, was unceremoniously whacked over the top of point by an advancing Hodge. The second, about five yards quicker, was aimed straight at Hodge's ear and just flicked his armpit as he retreated before ending with Rodney Marsh, who burst out laughing. "No once charges the great D.K.," said Marshy.

THE STORMY PETREL

Just as important as the Lillee/Marsh link in Australia's rise to unchallenged world supremacy in the 1970s was the inspiring presence of Ian Chappell, the team's trailblazing captain who fought for his players like they were brothers and in return received unstinting loyalty.

Chappell was a stormy petrel of the game, a rough diamond who bared his buttocks in mid-pitch, fought officialdom and led the breakaway Australians in Kerry Packer's World Series movement. The handsome rewards elite cricketers enjoy today owe much to Chappell's determination in refusing to accept what had been. He was suspicious of cricket officialdom and demanded a more generous share of the lucrative monies the game was generating.

Administrators regarded him as a renegade, but the same ones who bad-mouthed him in the corridors of power loved the way he batted and basked in the success of his teams.

His career may have ended in a flurry of searing headlines, but nothing could detract from his sterling contributions from No. 3 which in his best years, on all wickets, saw him ranked ahead even of his brother, Greg. The West Indians prized his wicket above everyone else's and when he retired, in 1980, only two other Australians had amassed more Test runs: Sir Donald Bradman and Neil Harvey.

Chappell's tumultuous final 12 months saw him:
• Charged with assault after punching a Guyanese public relations man in the stomach;
• Suspended from Sheffield Shield duty for three weeks having abused umpires;
• And suffer a further suspended sentence after an ugly set of incidents in Sydney when he repeatedly clashed with fast bowler Len Pascoe, backing himself into such an indefendable position that even brother Trevor and close mate Doug Walters were among the NSW players to rebel.

Attending the disciplinary meeting with Bradman with a beer in his hand, he said he didn't care if he never played again.

Soon afterwards, having just retired, Chappell was suspended from commentary duties at Channel Nine for using a three-word expression: "Jesus .... Christ" during a luncheon break.

While the incidents on and off the field, temporarily clouded his overall contributions in lifting Australia to world championship status, happily they weren't enough to cause him to sever his connections with the game. His deep insights as a commentator are now widely recognised.

His Chappell-led teams of the '70s were dubbed "The Ugly Australians," their win-at-all-cost philosophies being damned by traditionalists. Disinterested in the game's delicacies, they sledged opponents and triggered the drafting of new code of conduct laws.

Viv Richards and the West Indians said the "verbals" they received as Australia won the 1975-76 series 5-1 hardened them against the Australians and with

Ian Chappell: constantly flouted convention. His last seasons were particularly controversial.

their growing battalion of fast bowlers emulating the deeds of Lillee and Thomson, served as an on-going blueprint for success.

Chappell condoned the sledging and in fact, was a ringleader, all the time looking for an edge. He made no apologies, his teams playing and partying just as hard. Rod Marsh said he learnt more chatting about the game over a beer, Ian Chappell style, than through any extra hour in the nets.

Dennis Lillee was another disciple, whose antics Chappell condoned, realising a fired-up, hostile Lillee was a priceless asset.

"You chaps are a very good team," said one Englishmen at the conclusion of Australia's '75 tour, "but on the field you're a bunch of bastards."

The steamrolling success of the Australians under Chappell saw the team win 15 and lose just five Tests in 30. But it left scars which are still keenly-debated today. "Ian Chappell was responsible for orchestrating the verbal intimidation. I think it was much worse on that '74-'75 tour than I have ever known it either before or since," said English batsman Keith Fletcher. "It has long been considered part of the game in Australia, but Chappell and Dennis Lillee took it to unfortunate extremes."

Bob Taylor accused Chappell of "ugly histrionics" while Tony Greig openly blued with him, proving that their much publicised feud was far more than just theatre.

During a World Series game in Perth, Greig, who had been in poor form, went out to run for West Indian Gordon Greenidge, who had a leg injury. Greig wasn't wearing a helmet which he usually did when batting so Chappell immediately demanded he wear one.

Rodney Marsh quipped that the original was at the panel beaters, a reference to Greig having been struck while batting earlier in the innings.

Chappell eventually agreed for him to stay, minus the helmet, saying, "Oh well, let him do it. He's never out here long enough when he bats anyway."

Dennis Lillee THE MAN & HIS RECORD

Born: July 18, 1949
Teams: Western Australia, Tasmania, Northants & Australia
First-class debut: 1969-70
First-class record: Matches 198. Batting — Runs 2377, Average 13.90, Highest score 73 not out. Bowling — Wickets 882, Average 23.46, Best bowling 8-29, Five wickets in an Innings 50, Ten wickets in a Match 13. Fielding — Catches 67.
Test debut: 1970-71
Test record: Matches 70. Batting — Runs 905, Average 13.71, Highest score 73 not out. Bowling — Wickets 355, Average 23.92, Best bowling 7-83, Five wickets in an Innings 23, Ten wickets in a Match 7. Fielding — Catches 23.
Tours: New Zealand 1970, 1977, 1982; England 1972, 1975, 1980, 1981, 1983; West Indies 1973; Pakistan 1980; Sri Lanka 1982-83. Also toured with the International Wanders in South Africa in 1975-76 and NZ and the West Indies with Ian Chappell's WSC Australians in 1979.
One day international debut: 1972
One day international record: Matches 63. Batting — Runs 240, Average 9.23, Highest score 42 not out. Bowling — Wickets 103, Average 20.83, Best bowling 5-34, Five Wickets in an Innings 1. Fielding — Catches 10.

Dennis Lillee's Test record series by series:
BATTING & FIELDING

Season	Opponent	Mt	Inns	No	HS	Runs	Ave	50s	Ct.
1970-71	England (h)	2	3	0	10	16	5.33	-	2
1972	England (a)	5	7	4	7	10	3.33	-	-
1972-73	Pakistan (h)	3	4	1	14	18	6.00	-	2
	West Indies (a)	1	-	-	-	-	-	-	-
1974-75	England (h)	6	8	2	26	88	14.67	-	2
1975	England (a)	4	4	2	73*	115	57.50	1	-
1975-76	West Indies (h)	5	6	3	25	77	25.67	-	1
1976-77	Pakistan (h)	3	4	0	27	47	11.75	-	1
	New Zealand (a)	2	2	1	23*	42	42.00	-	2
	England (h)	1	2	1	25	35	35.00	-	-
1979-80	West Indies (h)	3	5	0	16	28	5.60	-	1
	England (h)	3	4	0	19	50	12.50	-	-
	Pakistan (a)	3	4	2	12*	18	9.00	-	1
1980	England (a)	1	-	-	-	-	-	-	-
1980-81	New Zealand (h)	3	4	0	27	67	16.75	-	-
	India (h)	3	5	1	19	40	10.00	-	1
1981	England (a)	6	10	3	40*	153	21.86	-	1
1981-82	Pakistan (h)	3	5	1	16	39	9.75	-	1
	West Indies (h)	3	5	0	4	8	1.60	-	2
	New Zealand (a)	3	3	0	9	21	7.00	-	2
1982-83	England (h)	1	1	1	2*	2	-	-	-
	Sri Lanka(a)	1	-	-	-	-	-	-	1
1983-84	Pakistan (h)	5	4	2	25	31	15.50	-	2
Totals		70	90	24	73*	905	13.71	1	23

BOWLING

Season	Opponent	Mts	Overs	Mds	Runs	Wicks	Ave	BB	5wI	10wM
1970-71	England (h)	2	62,3	5	199	8	24.88	5-84	1	-
1972	England (a)	5	249,5	83	548	31	17.68	6-66	3	1
1972-73	Pakistan (h)	3	96,1	19	353	12	29.42	4-49	-	-
	West Indies (a)	1	32	5	132	0	-	-	-	-
1974-75	England (h)	6	182,6	36	596	25	23.84	4-49	-	-
1975-76	West Indies (h)	5	129,3	7	712	27	26.37	5-63	1	-
1976-77	Pakistan (h)	3	130,2	16	540	21	25.71	6-82	2	1
	New Zealand (a)	2	83	13	312	15	20.80	6-72	2	1
	England (h)	1	47,7	9	165	11	15.00	6-26	2	1
1979-80	West Indies (h)	3	120,1	24	365	12	30.42	5-78	1	-
	England (h)	3	155,1	41	399	23	16.87	6-60	2	1
	Pakistan (a)	3	102	19	303	3	101.00	3-114	-	-
1980	England (a)	1	34	9	96	5	19.20	4-43	-	-
1980-81	New Zealand (h)	3	106	27	245	16	15.31	6-53	2	-
	India (h)	3	148,3	33	452	21	21.52	4-65	-	-
1981	England (a)	6	311,4	81	870	39	22.31	7-89	2	1
1981-82	Pakistan (h)	3	104,3	22	332	15	22.13	5-18	2	-
	West Indies (h)	3	121,3	26	317	16	19.81	7-83	1	1
	New Zealand (a)	3	79	23	183	7	26.14	3-13	-	-
1982-83	England (h)	1	71	25	185	4	46.25	3-96	-	-
	Sri Lanka(a)	1	30	6	107	3	35.67	2-67	-	-
1983-84	Pakistan (h)	5	230,3	51	633	20	31.65	6-171	1	-
Totals		70	18471*	652	8493	355	23.92	7-83	23	7

* denotes balls bowled

COUNTRY BY COUNTRY RECORD
BATTING & FIELDING

Country	Mt	Inns	No	HS	Runs	Ave	50s	Ct.
v England	29	39	13	73*	469	18.04	1	6
v India	3	5	1	19	40	10.00	-	1
v New Zealand	8	9	1	27	130	16.25	-	4
v Pakistan	17	21	6	27	154	10.27	-	7
v Sri Lanka	1	-	-	-	-	-	-	-
v West Indies	12	16	3	25	113	8.69	-	4

BOWLING

Country	Mts	Balls	Mds	Runs	Wicks	Ave	BB	5wI	10wM
v England	29	8516	361	3507	167	21.00	7-89	11	4
v India	3	891	33	452	21	21.52	4-65	-	-
v New Zealand	8	1774	63	740	38	19.47	6-53	4	1
v Pakistan	17	4433	127	2161	71	30.44	6-26	5	1
v Sri Lanka	1	180	6	107	3	35.67	2-67	-	-
v West Indies	12	2677	62	1526	55	27.75	7-83	3	1

HOME & ABROAD

	Mts	Balls	Mds	Runs	Wicks	Ave	BB	5wI	10wM
Tests at home	44	11534	341	5482	231	23.73	7-83	15	4
Tests abroad	26	6937	311	3011	124	24.28	7-89	8	3

HIS HIGHEST TEST SCORES
73*   v England, Lord's, 1975
40*   v England, Lord's, 1981

HIS BEST TEST BOWLING
7-83   v West Indies, Melbourne, 1981-82
7-89   v England, The Oval, 1981
6-26   v England, Melbourne, 1976-77
6-53   v New Zealand, Brisbane, 1980-81

HIS HIGHEST ONE-DAY INTERNATIONAL SCORES
42*   v West Indies, Perth, 1981-82
21   v England, Edgbaston, 1980

HIS BEST ONE-DAY INTERNATIONAL BOWLING
5-34   v Pakistan, Leeds, World Cup 1975
4-12   v England, Sydney, 1979-80
4-28   v West Indies, Sydney, 1979-80
4-32   v India, Sydney, 1980-81
4-56   v England, Sydney, 1979-80

Dennis Lillee's World Series Cricket Supertests record
BATTING & FIELDING

Season	Mt	Inns	No	HS	Runs	Ave	Ct
1977-78 (h)	5	9	2	37	97	13.85	2
1978-79 (h)	4	7	3	20*	51	12.75	-
1979 (West Indies)	5	8	1	30	78	11.14	4
Totals	14	24	6	37	226	12.55	6

BOWLING

Season	Mts	Overs	Mds	Runs	Wicks	Ave	BB	5wI	10wM
1977-78 (h)	5	152,4	10	765	21	36.42	5-82	1	-
1978-79 (h)	4	189,3	68	387	23	16.82	7-23	2	-
1979 (West Indies)	5	180,4	26	653	23	28.39	6-125	1	-

HIGHEST WSC SCORES
37   v WSC West Indies, Melbourne, 1977-78
30   v WSC West Indies, Port of Spain, 1979

BEST BOWLING
7-23   v WSC West Indies, Sydney Showgrounds, 1978-79
6-125   v WSC West Indies, Antigua, 1979
5-51   v WSC World XI, Sydney Showgrounds, 1978-79
5-82   v WSC World XI, VFL Park, Melbourne, 1977-78

Dennis Lillee's other internationals
BATTING (1) v Rest of the World, 1971-72

Mt	Inns	No	HS	Runs	Ave	50s	Ct.
4	5	1	11	19	4.75	-	2

BOWLING

Mts	Overs	Mds	Runs	Wicks	Ave	BB	5wI	10wM
4	117,4	20	482	24	20.08	8-29	1	-

BATTING (2) For the International Wanderers in South Africa, 1975-76

Mt	Inns	No	HS	Runs Ave	50s	Ct.
2	4	1	22*	22	7.33	-	-

BOWLING

Mts	Overs	Mds	Runs	Wicks	Ave	BB	5wI	10wM
2	70,4	22	180	15	12.00	7-27	1	-

OLD
IRON
GLOVES

"Right you bastards, you're going to pay for this. You don't want me but you're not going to get rid of me." – ROD MARSH

Rod Marsh, the combative wicketkeeper with the billiard-table legs and Groucho Marx moustache endured Australia-wide ridicule after his nightmarish first Test. Now he's regarded as one of the game's living legends and the nickname he initially found so distasteful a term of endearment.

WHEN ROD MARSH cracked his own beer drinking record by downing 45 cans between Sydney and London in 1983, he could hardly walk or talk and was wheeled around Heathrow airport by teammates in a motorised luggage trolley. It's a world record which never made Wisden but cemented Marsh's reputation as one of cricket's lovable larrikins – and one helluva drinker.

He has also been forgiven for his famous 500/1 bet against Australia at Leeds in 1981, when he and Dennis Lillee had a landfall $15,000 win after the Australians inexplicably slumped to a humbling third Test defeat.

Drinking to excess on long plane trips and betting of any description now are subject to misconduct clauses, offenders risking heavy fines and suspension.

At the time, the drinkathons were considered harmless pieces of fun, by the immediate team officials anyway.

Marsh had never been able to resist a challenge. It's why he and the perenially-thirsty Doug Walters had more than 40 cans each on the way to England in 1977. When Marsh was told their record had since been broken, he resolved to have one more dash at it, realising it was likely to be his last opportunity, on a major tour anyway.

With Lillee acting as the initial pacemaker on the Singapore leg and others substituting after that, Marsh had downed 15 cans by Singapore, another 15 by Bahrain and went at it unabated until he'd passed Walters' mark of 44 from 1977.

Even the Qantas captain joined in the fun, saying the plane was on schedule and so was Australia's vice-captain Rodney Marsh! Had Marsh known that his impetuosity was to rebound on his ambitions of captaining Australia, he would have settled for a quiet novel or two and a few rounds of whist. But that had never been his style.

As the plane, a Boeing 747, taxied into Heathrow, the purser thanked everyone for flying Qantas before congratulating Marsh on a job well done. The last of his 45 cans had been duly downed and he was the new trans-Continental champion!

As soon as the plane doors opened, Marsh breathed in the crisp English air and suddenly felt wobbly – the combined affect of little sleep and the considerable amount of alcohol he'd imbibed. "If there'd been a hole available, I would gladly have climbed into it and slept for 24 hours," Marsh said. "The brains kept sending messages to the limbs, but the limbs refused to obey, or perhaps they simply didn't hear.

"Dennis Lillee and Graeme Wood were well aware I was in no condition to negotiate the long walk across the Heathrow tarmac under my own steam so they helped me get out of my drinking clothes and into my team uniform, then propped me up as we negotiated the aircraft steps. They also showed enormous initiative by flagging down a motorised luggage trolley to carry me most of the way to the terminus building. Still the English press managed to find us. The photographs they took were less than flattering and they did my image no good at all. Then again, perhaps the image wasn't all that good beforehand."

Lillee says it was hilarious watching Marsh attempt his last cans. "No. 44 was your standard-sized can, but to Rodney it must have looked as big as a bucket," he said. "With some difficulty he focussed on it, somehow guided it to his mouth and sipped, sipped, sipped. Time was running short and there was still a can to go after this one.

"With only minutes to go, he downed the last of No. 44 thereby equalling Walters' record – and braced himself as best anyone in that besotted state could – for the big one, No. 45. The clincher.

"The can was broached and Rodney raised it ever so wonkily to his lips. He must have wished he'd never seen a beer, but he soldiered on. Time, however, was ticking away. We were well on the descent path to Heathrow and still the best part of a can to go.

"'I can't make it,' Rodney pleaded in a voice which sounded like he had a mouthful of marbles.

"'Bullshit!' we chorused. This challenge had by now assumed almost the significance of an Ashes series. There would be no capitulation. We tilted Rod's head back and literally force fed him. He gurgled, he gargled, he grunted and he groaned. But by God, he drank it!"

There was wild cheering from his teammates and fellow passengers who had been geeing him on since Bahrain.

Despite the best efforts of Lillee and Wood in trying to steer him away from any English press representatives, they rounded a corner and bowled straight into a band of photographers. The newspapers enjoyed themselves enormously at Marsh's expense the next day and word of his escapade filtered back to Jolimont, the headquarters of the Australian Cricket Board. While nothing was ever said officially, the maverick in Marsh which had so often seen him publicly flaunting authority, was to cost him the greatest prize of all: the Australian cricket captaincy.

Patrick Eagar

Sharing a beer with his golfing brother, Graham, 1975 Australian tour.

The only time Rod Marsh captained Australia was by default, in mid-match during his recordbreaking 80th Test appearance in Adelaide in 1981-82 when the designated leaders Greg Chappell and Kim Hughes was both off the field injured.

With Dennis Lillee also sidelined early in the match, the Australian attack was reduced to just three major bowlers, Jeff Thomson, Len Pascoe and Bruce Yardley.

Marsh fought bravely to keep the West Indians in control. "I have never been so proud," he said of his high-performing trio – and of his new, elevated role.

After having Australia 4-17 in the first hour on day one, it took the Windies until late on day five to win the game. Marsh's leadership and pride in leading his country was immense and some who had disregarded him previously now warmed to his credentials.

Many considered the captaincy was his right, given his extra experience, even though only one 'keeper in 80 years, South Australia's Barry Jarman had ever led at Test level and then for only one match as a substitute.

After Chappell withdrew from the 1982 Pakistan tour, the 14-man Australian Cricket Board executive had been split between Marsh and Hughes as his replacement, until chairman Phil Ridings voted for Hughes. Marsh had in reality missed the job by only a vote or two.

Former England captain Mike Brearley later noted that Marsh's exclusion had been more to do with his association with the maverick Ian Chappell than any of his own leadership shortcomings. "For them he was tarred with the same brush as Ian Chappell...or revolution and extremism," Brearley wrote. "This was a major mistake; he might well have proved a more imaginative Test captain than Greg."

A young Rod Marsh: he kept wickets from the age of eight.

Marsh had refused to be Hughes' deputy for Pakistan, the job going to Allan Border with Bruce Laird as the third selector.

Marsh (and Lillee) had also declined to act as Hughes' vice-captain from the start of the 1980-81 Sheffield Shield season. He regarded Hughes as an upstart and saw his appointment as politically-motivated from within the WACA hierachy who wanted Hughes as WA's first-ever captain of a full-strength Australian X1.

Marsh had openly lobbied for the leadership and believed his seniority should be the clincher, even when Hughes was re-named WA's captain at the start of 1983-84.

When Hughes was again preferred as Chappell's successor, even after losing all three Tests in Pakistan and heading the disastrous World Cup campaign which saw the Australians beaten by lowly Zimbabwe – then only an associate member of the ICC – it freshened a feud which had festered for years.

On the eve of the internationals, during what should have been a friendly and convivial yacht cruise as part of the season launch, Marsh and Hughes became involved in a searing argument, which while kept quiet at the time, quite a feat considering the bevy of pressmen aboard, was indicative of the heat between them.

Marsh had been openly critical of Hughes' captaincy for years, considering him brash and impetuous. He believed him too headstrong to learn from his mistakes and far from the ideal choice to continue to lead the national side. Hughes traditionally tended to forfeit his wicket through his own doing rather than through the skill of the bowler. How could he command respect when he played so recklessly?

The senior WA players had constantly been urging him to gradually build an innings. "Okay," said Marsh, one day. "You've batted 240 minutes. How many are you?"

"Eight hundred!"

When Hughes recklessly ran himself out in the McDonald's Cup final, Marsh took him aside and said as captain he had to lead by his example. Instead, he was tearing the team apart.

Ian Chappell was typically provocative about the Board's decision to retain Hughes and at one of Marsh's Australia-wide testimonial dinners, in Sydney, said he thought the ACB had given Hughes the goldmine and Marsh the shaft.

In a famous interview story in *Playboy* magazine, Marsh was openly critical of Hughes and officially censored by the Australian Cricket Board.

Claiming Hughes was naive and too immature for the captaincy, Marsh said he could tell Hughes something and a week later he'd be making the same mistake again.

"I want to make it quite clear that I'm very proud to be playing for Australia and I will play under anyone. But I'd honestly prefer to play under several other players who I think would do a better job," he said.

He said Hughes was "bloody good company" but "liable to do silly things, whether he has a bat, a golf club or cards in his hand. He's that sort of guy. Many times Kim has walked out to bat and the rest of the players have looked at one another as if to ask: what's he going to do today? It's irrelevant if he succeeds or fails but it's important to feel he's going to play the right way every time."

Marsh claimed to have been Australia's defacto captain for years, especially in the field where he'd helped the Chappell brothers and Hughes with subtle fielding changes and strategies. "I'm in the best position to see and I can work out the angles better than anyone from behind the stumps."

Ironically the fallout from his candid comments rebounded directly at Marsh, rather than damaging Hughes' on-going captaincy chances. "Obviously a lot of people don't believe you should be honest when you discuss your teammates and the fact that I served it up to Kim Hughes was resented in some quarters," Marsh said. "Kim has always respected me and the article incensed him enough to make him want to prove me wrong."

Marsh's 24 hour beer-drinking blitz in 1983 and his decision to join his best mates in the breakaway World Series Cricket movement damned his long-term ambitions. "I firmly believe I would have captained Australia if I hadn't played World Series," he said. "The fact that I crossed the line and deserted the establishment lingered, despite the fact that I was one of the last Australians to have signed up."

Marsh says the ACB was prepared to pardon Greg Chappell, who was made captain again after the compromise was agreed and Kerry Packer closed World Series.

"I'm not suggesting that I'd have been as good a captain as Greg," Marsh said. "What I'm saying is that while the establishment was prepared to forgive Greg Chappell, it was not prepared to show me the same generosity.

"If captaincy had been foremost in my mind when the Packer people approached me, the best thing I could have done was say 'no thanks' and stuck with the conformists. How could the Board have then refused me, after I'd turned my back on a good quid for the sake of purity and the establishment? Who knows, I might have been recommended for a knighthood!

"But I didn't say no and if that's what was to eventually cost me cricket's ultimate honor, then that's too damned bad."

Rodney William Marsh was one of cricket's foremost playing personalities of the '70s and early '80s, at international and state level. Along with John Inverarity, Ian Brayshaw and Dennis Lillee, he was a magnetic force in enabling Western Australia cricket to mature and prosper.

While he never fulfilled his ambition to captain Australia, he was frequently the tactician behind Australia's success.

Colorful, charismatic and loyal, Marsh had a devil-may-care attitude and a rebellious streak which struck a chord with the man in the street. He mightn't have always been diplomatic, but no one was more popular, not even "Thommo" or Lillee.

Fiercely supportive of those he admired, Marsh could also be abrasive and intimidating, particularly if he felt a batsman should have "walked." Universally recognised as one of the great characters of the game, Marsh wasn't averse to a well-chosen word or two, particularly if he felt it would unsettle an opposition batsman.

Under the Ian Chappell regime, he developed a wall of silence to certain batsmen, even his chirpy and much-admired English counterpart Alan Knott who loved to say "hello" and chat. Generally, however, his zestful and often irreverent humor bubbled close to the surface.

LILLEE ON MARSH

"When he was a youngster, Bacchus looked bloody dreadful. He opened the batting in those days and when I ran in to bowl the first ball, I couldn't help but wonder how a bloke so slovenly could get a game of cricket in a top grade side.

"Then again, it was University, so he must have some talent. They let beatniks in, so why not this fella?

"I made a classic mistake that day. Keep in mind I was young and raw, concentrating only on bowling fast. The words 'line and length' had been mentioned to me, but hell, speed was my go. Well that slob Marsh started to carve me up. He despatched my shorter, faster balls to all points of the boundary. I kept thinking to myself that surely a bloke who looked as bad as he did couldn't keep playing shots like that. But he did. I wished I'd never laid eyes on Rodney Marsh, whoever he was." – DENNIS LILLEE.

His determination and natural skill saw him become the game's most successful wicketkeeper, despite his chequered start when his Billy Bunter-like physique was as big a discussion point as his agility. He wasn't particularly polished, but he was highly effective and so wide a span did he cover behind the wicket, that his captains consistently enjoyed the luxury of employing wider catching arcs, first slipsman Ian Chappell, for example, invariably standing where most other countries would position their second slipper. For extra speed in sprinting to the wicket to take returns, he was the first at international level to use cut down pads, trimmed above the knee.

Marsh's rise to fame coincided with Australia's acceptance as the unoffical champions of the world after its pace-led defeats of England and the West Indies in consecutive summers in the mid-1970s.

His competiveness was legendary. Greg Chappell said only one other player in his memory, Victorian Ian Redpath, played with equal passion. "Those two blokes would have died for the green cap," Chappell said. "Rod would have taken it a step further. He would have killed for it."

Incredibly durable, he retired in 1984, having hardly missed an international since his rocky Ashes beginnings in 1970. Now he's helping nurture Australia's next set of stars, via his fulltime coaching role at the Commonwealth Bank Cricket Academy in Adelaide.

Patrick Eagar

So wide a span did Marsh cover that first slip invariably stood wider. Here he catches Bob Woolmer for a duck, Trent Bridge, 1981.

Originally from Armadale on the fringes of Perth, Marsh played his first competitive games as an eight-year-old and immediately began keeping wickets. His mother wanted him to be a concert pianist and most days he was made to practice for up to two hours before being allowed outside to play with his mates.

His most memorable birthday present was a pair of wicketkeeping gloves for his 11th birthday. He'd practise throwing a ball against the cylindrical upright of the family clothes line and dive after the ball as it rebounded at unpredictable angles.

At 13, he represented the West Australian schoolboys in Sydney before captaining the team the following summer in the carnival in Brisbane, a year in which he also claimed his most prized teenage scalp, international Neil Harvey stumped in a semi-serious game at the WACA Ground.

His first grade debut, at 16, with West Perth – the first of his seven Perth grade clubs – was as a substitute for WA and Australian tourist Gordon Becker. When Becker returned, Marsh held his place as a high-order batsman.

From his earliest days, Marsh was noted for his billowing cheeks and chubby legs which saw him pack safety pins in case his trouser seams split. At 174 cm (5ft 8½ in), he appeared as wide as he was tall. Dennis Lillee reckoned one look at Marsh and you would have sworn he'd been on a diet of cream pudding and dumplings for most of his teenage life.

159

But his enthusiasm for cricket was boundless. He dreamed of being his country's wicketkeeper in the mould of polished Australian Testman Wally Grout, who he had seen and studied as a schoolboy. Like the legendary Queenslander, Marsh was an enterprising and swashbuckling batsman who cared little for reputations and scored runs at pace, especially delighting in lifting the ball high and hard on the legside.

During one of the teenage carnivals, he made 50 on his first appearance on the Sydney Cricket Ground. He revelled in the atmosphere and sense of history and vowed he'd be back there some day.

Fun-loving and adventurous, he was a popular team player even then and would go anywhere for a game.

He was 17 when he first first brushed with authority, being fined one guinea when playing as a fill-in for Ongerup, a southern wheatfarming town, during Perth's annual Country Week carnival. The farmers had arrived in the Big Smoke with only six players and rather than forfeit their place altogether, bolstered their ranks by including five locals, including Marsh. After winning the first two games, Ongerup had all its points cancelled when someone recognised Marsh during the third match. The eligiblility clauses had been breached and Marsh and his four young West Perth teammates were each reprimanded and fined.

His first fulltime senior wicketkeeping duties coincided with his move to the University of Western Australia in pursuit of his teaching qualifications. He played in University's first-grade side and was considered such a promising allround player that he was also included in the WA State Colt's squad.

His cricketing priorities, however, were frowned upon by the university's scholastic staff. After continually absenting himself from geography tutorials in favor of practising cricket on Tuesday and Thursday nights, he was summoned to the college professor.

"My dear boy," said the professor, "what can you possibly hope to gain out of cricket?"

"I believe I can play the game a bit, I love it and I wouldn't be happy if I didn't go to

training because of geography lectures."

The professor admonished him and advised him to reconsider, as "you'll never do any good at cricket."

There was one on-going benefit from his first-year geography unit. He met his wife-to- be Roslyn Wilson.

Under the expert tutelage of ex-Test man John Inverarity, one of his major career influences and a person expert in communicating with the young, Marsh's cricket accelerated at a rapid rate. The presence of budding Test leg spinner Tony Mann in University's first X1 gave Marsh an early opportunity to consolidate his technique for taking qualty wrist spin.

The teenage Marsh... when Dennis Lillee first met him he joked he'd been on a lifetime diet of cream cakes!

Just one week before his 21st birthday, having scored several "A" grade centuries and played in two premierships, Marsh debuted as a specialist batsman in the international against Gary Sobers' visiting West Indians and scored 0 and 104, becoming only the fourth West Australian to make a century in his maiden first-class match.

Only once did he have a chance of keeping wickets in his debut year, in Adelaide when Becker was indisposed in the South Australian second innings.

Replacing Becker as WA's fulltime 'keeper the following summer, Marsh took five catches in WA's opening game of the season against Queensland in Brisbane, further alerting the national selectors of his emerging abilities. His haul included the entry, c. Marsh, b. Lillee, the first of 223 victims the famous pair were to share at State and Test level.

His State captain, famed Englishman Tony Lock, had encouraged him to set no limits and while he'd arrived on the scene too soon to seriously consider making the major tour of Ceylon, India and South Africa from October, when Queensland's John Maclean, an old schoolboy adversary, was chosen ahead of him for the Australian "B" team tour of New Zealand at the end of the season, Marsh was genuinely disappointed and vowed to improve in every area. That winter, he lost 20 pounds through an exhaustive exercise and diet program and had to completely refashion his wardrobe.

Having been trounced 4-0 in South Africa, the Australians were clearly looking to rebuild and Marsh's wintertime dedication was to pay a handsome and immediate dividend.

No-one could have predicted, however, just how quickly he was to be catapulted ahead of his fellow contenders, especially the incumbent Brian Taber.

Taber, 30, was captain of New South Wales and had kept in all nine Tests in India and South Africa. While he had struggled on the last leg of the extended tour and dosed himself up daily against a growing bronchial asthma concern – which he kept private – he was expected to retain his place for another Ashes tour.

His touring deputy, colorful Victorian Ray Jordon claimed to be 33, but in actual fact was 34 and past his best, though on eve of the selection, in the Victorian-South Australian game in Melbourne, complicated matters by taking 10 victims in a career-best performance. He was in reach of Taber's record-equalling nine catches and three stumpings amassed in a Shield game in Adelaide just 12 months previously when to his chagrin, Ian Chappell declared the SA second innings with seven wickets down.

The third contender, Maclean, was just 24 and like Marsh, a well-rated middle-order batsman and future Shield captain.

Marsh had started the new season exceptionally well and with Western Australia on tour for the entire first month playing games in each of the eastern capital cities, he'd had extra games in which to impress before the first Ashes squad for Brisbane was announced.

Marsh had played on four consecutive weekends, while Taber, Maclean and Jordon had played only twice. Their respective performances were:

	BATTING	*KEEPING*
Marsh	20,59,53,0,64,32,39	14 victims;
Taber	19,39*,12*	10 victims;
Maclean	0,27,0	2 victims;
Jordon	1,3,5*	12 victims.

Marsh was in Brisbane and dined with Maclean the night the team was decided. Both felt Taber would be retained. There was no hint of him being made victim of the

South African disasters. The two friends and rivals chatted mainly about old days and the match just completed. At 6.45 a.m. the following day, Marsh was awoken at the team motel by his wife, Roslyn, calling long distance.

"Congratulations," she said.

"What for? We didn't do too well yesterday, did we?"

"No, no," she cried. "You're in the Australian team."

There was a pause before Marsh, still half asleep, said, "What are you talking about?"

"They've picked the Australian side. You're in it."

Hardly believing he had leap frogged over three players for the position, Marsh whooped with delight and immediately opened a celebratory beer for himself and his roommate Derek Chadwick. Roslyn had heard the announcement late the previous night, but the motel switchboard closed at 10 a.m. and she hadn't been able to raise anybody until the next morning.

She had no idea she'd be breaking the news of a lifetime.

Marsh had made 39 and taken six catches against the Queenslanders. He'd wondered why Sir Donald Bradman had bothered to come all the way from his home town Adelaide to see the game. Within days, his wife had provided the answer. At 23, he'd just become Australia's youngest-ever wicketkeeper.

A SLUG IN WAITING

Raymond Clarence "Slug" Jordon was one of three senior 'keepers to be overlooked when Rod Marsh was surprisingly named for his Test debut in 1970-71.

Slug had kept wickets for a decade for Victoria with a secret known only by his mother and closest mate Bob Cowper.

Street smart way beyond his years, when he debuted for Victoria in February, 1960, he deliberately put his age back, thinking it may one day help him into representative ranks.

"Barry Jarman had just played for Australia for the first time. We are the same age and when I got my chance and was asked my date of birth, I just put it back a bit, " he said.

Jordon debuted two days after his 24th birthday, but told everyone he'd only just turned 23. And in 1969-70, after a decade of service, he made his one and only international tour as the No.2 'keeper with Bill Lawry's Australians to Ceylon, India and South Africa.

His selection was more a reward for services rendered and an acknowledgment of his expertise in standing over the stumps to the former firebrand turned seam bowler Alan Connolly.

While he was officially listed as being 32, Jordon was actually a year older, and celebrated his 34th birthday late in the South African leg.

"I was an old dog for a hard road type selection, " Jordon said. "There was talk that I went on the tour because I was an old stager who'd paid his dues. Standing up to Alan Connolly probably gave me the nod.

"We'd heard of Rod Marsh, but at that stage he wasn't even keeping regularly for WA so there was no way known he would have gone.

"I was sure Brian Taber would be retained for the Ashes Tests. He hadn't been too bad in India when conditions were quite harsh but he was terrible in South Africa where I felt he'd kept like a dog.

"Coming into the third Test in Johannesburg, I believed I was a genuine chance of finally getting a Test. 'Phanto' (Bill Lawry) pumped up that I should replace Taber. Chappell and Taber stuck with each other. Chappelli was one of Tabbsy's greatest mates and that was that. I missed out.

"There were a few murmurings and come the player's meeting before the opening day of the Test, I went to Fred Bennett, the manager, and said, 'Do you mind if I go out Freddy, because something might be said which I might regret. I went out to the movies and saw The Battle of Britain which was ideal. It went for three hours. The meeting was over by the time I came back, Phanto later explaining that he was only one vote of three.

"Even though Tabbsy had had an awful series, I never even expected him to get the arse for the Ashes. When they brought in Marshy it was like a complete cleaning out of the dead wood which went to South Africa.

"Graham McKenzie was almost finished and Bill Lawry himself was soon to be sacked. After another 12 months with the Victorians, I was out too. No-one bothered to ring me and I was really dark about it. I said to Phanto at a Shield reunion why hadn't he shown me the decency of a phone call given that we'd played 10 or 11 years together? 'I never rang you when you were picked,' he said, so I smacked him in the mouth.

"I would have liked to have played at least that Johannesburg Test. But I knew I was always a long shot. During that game in Melbourne when I was on course to break Tabbsy's Shield record, I dislocated a finger late in South Australia's innings and just taped it up.

"Sam Loxton who was on the national panel came into the room and asked me how it was.

"'It's okay,' I said. 'Just a bit of tape will fix it up.'

"He insisted that I get it x-rayed and I thought that was a bit funny, especially when he came in the cab with me. 'This is not like Sam Loxton,' I thought to myself. 'He's being too nice.'

"He even came in with me and stayed as I saw the doctor. As I had suspected there was only a dislocation and definitely no break. I'd be able to play on, no worries.

"Sam immediately left and I had to take my own cab home! I knew then that things weren't looking too good. I was never going to play for Australia."

Rod Marsh's initial joy at his selection soon soured. Having dropped three catches in a nightmarish baptism, he felt deflated and uncomfortable about his lofty new status. He may have been representing his country, but didn't know if he truly deserved it.

Trying to settle his nerves, Ian Chappell, Australia's vice-captain, advised him to forget about what had been and focus on the next catch. "You're due to take one soon," he said, a one-liner which a sensitive Marsh initially took the wrong way until Chappell explained it was a long-standing team joke.

Replying to 433, England took almost two days in making 464. The three Marsh grassed were all frontliners, John Edrich, Keith Fletcher and Basil D'Oliviera and all came on the Sunday. Marsh was shattered and that night flung his Australian cap into his locker, saying, "You don't deserve to wear it." Only his captain Bill Lawry felt sicker; any hopes Australia had harboured of winning after Keith Stackpole's double century had vanished.

While Marsh took four catches for the game and kept tidily, despite some erratic throws from the outfield – the Englishmen thought Australia a poor fielding side – he feared the three muffed chances would almost certainly cruel his ongoing selection hopes. One had been from the bowling of mystery spinner John Gleeson, who the deposed Brian Taber could pick in his sleep. "Deep down, I knew I hadn't kept really badly," Marsh said. "The catches I dropped had been three stiff chances, but I felt sure that others, particularly the selectors, would have put black marks next to my name big enough to rule me out for a long time."

Several eastern States cricket writers called for Marsh's immediate sacking. A cartoonist depicted him as an overweight burglar, slipping on a rug, grabbing for the curtains and bringing the sideboard and the silver crashing down on himself.

The most biting criticism came from a hostile Sydney cricket writing sect which backed Taber in most vitriolic fashion. Marsh was dubbed "Iron Gloves" or "Fat Rodney" and told an Ashes Test was no place for an overweight and cumbersome rookie. Even the esteemed English writer John Woodcock recommended Marsh be dumped, especially after he grassed another important wicket, Geoff Boycott in Perth.

The crowds in Brisbane and Sydney were particularly caustic, hooting even when Marsh was walking to the wicket. "As I neared the crease and the booing still continued I said aloud, "Right you bastards, you're going to pay for this. You don't want me out here but you're not going to get rid of me."

He felt angry and disappointed, but never wavered from his resolve to prove himself. "The criticism certainly hurt," he said. "I felt I always had the ability. When I first started playing cricket, I was always going to play for Australia. That was in my mind anyway. The easy part was being chosen. The hard part was staying in the side."

One of Marsh's four debut catches had come from an acrobatic leap from the bowling of his WA colleague Graham McKenzie and was probably enough to keep him in the side. His batting, too, was a bonus. In South Africa, where the Australians were beaten 4-0, it had often been a case of five out, all out.

No-one doubted his enthusiasm – particularly his appeals, which were full-throated in that's-got-to-be-out fashion, or as veteran writer Dick Whitington described, "a cross between a Dervish dance and a stamping Flamenco."

But clearly there was a school of thought which believed he had been fast-tracked into the job and may not necessarily have been the right man.

Marsh described his first Test series as "a mind-shattering experience."

"It was probably my batting more than my 'keeping which got me the spot," he said. "When I dropped a few catches, they started screaming because they'd never seen an Australian 'keeper drop so many catches. It all made me determined to work harder. I was fairly agile for my bulk, but I got fitter later on."

Mentally, he also improved, learning to relax in-between deliveries.

Ian Chappell was a particularly motivating influence, especially during his days of self-doubt. "Things didn't go my way in those early Tests, I wasn't batting as well as I should have been and I wasn't getting the rub of the green when I had the gloves on," Marsh said. "Ian was at my side both on the field and off. He really let me know where I stood. He never actually gave out praise, that wasn't his job, but if I did do something well, which wasn't too often, he'd say briskly 'well done,' or nod his head. That was enough to give me a considerable lift. Everytime I did something bad I could feel his disappointment and that spurred me on to do better."

The pair had an instant rapport. They'd played golf with Doug Walters the day before Marsh's debut Test in Brisbane before dining with legendary Ray Lindwall that night. Marsh had no time to be nervous – he'd had too much of a good time.

Not only does Marsh regard Chappell as the finest captain of his time, he was one of the outstanding batsmen and tacticians. "Ian taught me more about cricket than anyone," he said. "I got to know the game under him. I was around him so long, a lot of his views rubbed off. Any guy who ever played under him had so much respect, even if Ian didn't always have the respect of all the officials, the establishment or the press. If Ian asked you to jump, you'd say, 'How high?' "

Despite another missed opportunity in front of his home crowd in Perth in the second Test, Marsh held his place all summer, his highlight being an innings of 92 not out, the highest score by an Australian wicketkeeper, in the drawn fifth Test in Melbourne. In his penultimate Test as captain, Bill Lawry was condemned for not delaying his declaration longer to allow Marsh time to make a few extra blows for his historic

100. Marsh felt it was a bonus to even make it that far given that he'd originally believed Lawry would declare at tea on the second day when he was 60. "I wasn't at all upset," he said. "In fact, I was so delighted to have at least done something worthwhile in the series that I couldn't have cared less. I knew I'd get a game in the next Test and that's all that worried me, particularly with all that bloody flak flying around me as to how bad I was."

With 10 victims for the series and a batting average of 26, Marsh realised he'd have to work doubly hard to even hold his place. Possession was only nine-tenths of the law.

The backlash at Taber's omission was to continue for some time and was at its fiercest in Sydney for the fourth international against the Rest of the World in January.

In a reception Richie Benaud described as the most miserable and bad-mannered he'd heard in years, Marsh was jeered all the way to the wicket and booed again 10 minutes later as he came off for tea.

"I really believed that if I failed I was finished as a Test cricketer," Marsh said.

Some consoling and complimentary words from his fallen adversary Taber at the tea interval lifted his spirits and the jeers turned to cheers as he twice swiped Intikhab Alam over the infield to reach his half century. When the Australian innings closed, he was 77 not out and had convinced even his critics on the Hill who accorded him a rousing reception. The tide had turned; never again did he ever enjoy anything but total crowd support.

In six tours to England, including five for the Ashes, Rod Marsh never missed a Test. He believes his career turning point was the 1972 tour in which Australia, with 10 first-time Ashes tourists, fought back to tie the series 2-2.

Marsh hit the series-squaring runs at The Oval and jumped onto the dressing room table and joyfully recited the Australian battlecry:

> Under the Southern Cross I stand
> A sprig of wattle in my hand
> A native of my native land
> Australia, you %#$*& beauty!

After the hiccups of his maiden Ashes series, this had been like heaven. Twice he'd snared five catches in an innings, at Manchester and Nottingham and also batted boldly, lifting slowman Norman Gifford for four 6s on his way to a buccaneering 91 in the opening Test at Old Trafford.

Australia was glorious in defeat, but Marsh was devastated and still regards it as one of his few career regrets. "That tour, being my first to England, remains something special," he said. "But I wouldn't have minded being able to get us over the line at Old Trafford. Had we won, I'm sure we would have won the series. I got 91 and we fell 80-odd short. John Gleeson (30) wasn't going to get out while I was there. But the minute I got out, so did he and it was all over."

Dennis Lillee had been a revelation against the Rest of the World the previous summer and was outstanding throughout '72 with a record 31 wickets. Marsh says Lillee bowled consistently fast, especially in mid-tour when he was in full rhythm. "He bowled a few overs against Leicestershire which were as quick as I ever saw him bowl," he said. "He'd bowled bloody fast a week before at Lord's and was in good rhythm. 'Garth' McKenzie (the West Australian pace bowling legend) was playing for Leicester. That might have had something to do with it."

Having established himself as a key member of the side, Marsh's blossoming

Golf has always been one of Rod Marsh's favorite sporting diversions.

confidence and friendship with Ian Chappell saw him frequently involved in team strategy. Chappell regarded him, like Lillee and his brother Greg, as a kindred soul.

At Manchester on a seamer's paradise, Chappell was persisting with his spinners, John Gleeson and John Inverarity, in much the same style as he used to bowl Ashley Mallett and Terry Jenner in tandem back in Adelaide.

"You're a bloody idiot, you know, " said the straight-shooting Marsh. "This is a seamer's paradise and you've got two spinners on. Get Greg (Chappell) and 'Beatle' (Graeme Watson) on. Anyone that bowls seam is going to have a picnic."

When Doug Walters was dropped for the final Test, for the first time in Ashes history, New South Wales did not have a representative in the Australian Test team. Western Australia, however, had six: Lillee, Marsh, Massie, John Inverarity, the Victorian-born Watson and Ross Edwards.

While Marsh lacked Taber's polish and often seemed more like a soccer goalkeeper as he flung himself around to intercept wayward Lillee deliveries, he was unerringly effective and with 23 victims in five Tests, created a new record for an Australian wicketkeeper in England.

Ten of his catches came from Lillee's bowling, including four at Old Trafford and three at The Oval. In 69 Tests together, they were to become Australia's most successful bowler-wicketkeeper combination, sharing 95 wickets, including Tony Greig five times, Deryck Murray and Ian Botham, four.

Marsh was also expert in predicting the banana-like swing of Bob Massie, who created a sensation by taking 16 wickets in his fairytale debut at Lord's. The English batsmen were all at sea deciding between the inswinger and outswinger. Because he'd kept so often to him for WA, Marsh could tell three yards before the popping crease what Massie was about to bowl. "This gave me a tremendous advantage. Bob sent both his inner and outer down on the line of the off-stump and if I knew it was going to be the outer I would start moving early to cover the extra ground needed in case the batsman snicked the ball even wider than it would have swung. If it was an inner I'd be down the leg side to cover the extra yardage."

Marsh's footwork became sure and polished and he was rarely wrong-footed after his initial series, bar for the occasional Test when the wickets had deteriorated badly, as on a frightful turner at Headingley in 1972, when there were 19 byes. A year later, at Port-of-Spain, he allowed 17 byes in the first innings and 19 in the second and was relieved to emerge from the game without serious injury. Standing up even to a bowler of Greg Chappell's gentle pace was fraught with danger, several deliveries exploding on landing and soaring over the head of first slip for four byes. Marsh maintains that Ian Chappell's

Marsh was a regular fixture in England, making six tours, including five for the Ashes. Here he catches Geoff Boycott, at Edgbaston, 1981.

97 in that game was one of the finest innings he ever saw, right up there with Barry Richards' 356 in Perth in 1970-71 and Gary Sobers' 254 at the MCG a year later.

If the 1972 Ashes trip was the most memorable tour of all, 1977 remains the most nightmarish.

The Australians had a poor side which lacked unity, especially after news broke of the breakaway internationals, funded by media mogul Kerry Packer and involving all but four of the touring Australians.

For the first time since 1954-55 and "Typhoon" Tyson's outstanding speed blitz, England won three consecutive Ashes Test matches, a young Ian Botham taking five wickets in an innings in each of his maiden Tests, at Trent Bridge and Headingley.

With Dennis Lillee unavailable, ostensibly because of a stress fracture, it broke up the notorious and formidable pace partnership with Jeff Thomson which had so unsettled the top-order English in 1974-75 and again in the Tests following the World Cup in 1975. The pair took 58 wickets at home and 37 away, bowling at a breakneck speed which often saw Marsh leaping for the ball, well above his head. As the deliveries thudded into his gloves, he said to the Chappells, standing in the slips, 'Christ that hurt. But I love it!'

Marsh developed a series of signals with the pace pair as they reached the top of their marks. He'd throw a glove in the air for a bouncer; or grab his boot for a yorker.

With Lillee back in Australia resting his back, the Australian attack, outside the intimidating Thomson, was pedestrian while the batting was weak, starting from the top where Rick McCosker had three different opening partners, none of whom were particularly successful.

The older players, Greg Chappell, vice-captain Marsh and Walters were accused of not relating sufficiently well with many of the rookies. After a promising start, Chappell failed to make a 50 in any of the last three Tests, while after Lord's, Walters' technique was

ROD MARSH HISTORY

1969: Marries Roslyn Wilson, a physical education graduate who he'd met at University.

1970-71: Debuts for Australia, ahead of NSW captain Taber. After an inauspicious debut, is dubbed "Irongloves" by Sydney pressmen hostile at their man's omission. Makes 92 not out in the fifth Test before Bill Lawry's controversial declaration.

1971-72: Is again named in Australia's team ahead of Taber for the hastily-scheduled internationals against the Rest of the World. Test legend Alan Davidson is just one of the critics saying Taber "is by far the best wicketkeeper in Australia and should have been selected ahead of Marsh."

1972-73: Amasses his highest first-class score, 236 for WA against Pakistan in Perth. Makes history by scoring 118 not out against the Pakistanis in Adelaide, the first century by an Australian 'keeper in Test cricket.

1973-74: Makes a Test-best 132 against New Zealand in Adelaide, sharing in a late-innings stand of 168 with Kerry O'Keeffe; Takes the catch of his career: NZ's Bevan Congdon, caught down the leg side, from Max Walker's bowling in Auckland.

1974-75: Snares six catches in an innings for the first time, against NSW in Perth, having hit 168 against NSW in the earlier game in Sydney.

1975-76: Is warned by the ACB on the eve of the Tests not to wear pads bearing the trademark of the manufacturer... Ian Chappell is also warned for field advertising; Publishes his first book, "You'll Keep;" Takes 67 wickets for the season in 15 matches with WA and Australia, breaking his own national record. Eleven of the wickets come in the Shield game against Victoria at the WACA Ground and 26 in the six Tests; Hits a half century in just 11 scoring shots (three 6s and eight 4s) against the West Indies in Perth.

1976-77: Makes 104 and takes 10 catches against SA in Perth, the first time in Australia a 'keeper has achieved the "double;" Is hit above the eye while trying to hook Imran Khan, the ball finishing 30 metres away at backward square; Becomes the first Australian keeper to score an Ashes century: 110 not out from 173 balls against England in the Centenary Test; Also creates a new Australian wicketkeeping "high" for most dismissals in Tests, surpassing Wally Grout's record of 187.

1977: Joins World Series Cricket on a three year $105,000 guarantee, trebling his previous cricketing wage of less than $15,000; For the first time in his career, starts to regularly bat in a helmet. Before using the Australian-made prototype from Albion, he borrows the crash helmet version from World X1 opener Dennis Amiss. During his innings he is hit on the head and when he suddenly remembers he's wearing a helmet, his relief at having emerged unscathed is comical.

1980: Tours Pakistan for the first time and says he learns more on one trip, keeping on the slow-turning wickets, than in any of his previous Australian seasons.

1980-81: Lifts Lance Cairns for 26 runs in five deliveries in a tumultuous finish to an Australian one-day innings against NZ in Adelaide; Takes 35 victims at Sheffield Shield level for WA to to earn a $5000 bonus from team sponsors, Channel Nine; Is the first cricketer reported by umpires under the new player code of behaviour. Peter McConnell claims Marsh had sworn at him after the first ball of the WA-NSW game, a wide delivery from Dennis Lillee, which was called four byes.

Marsh's on-field apology is taken into account by his teammates, who under the newly-implemented rules, judge the misdeameanour and issue a $25 fine.

A full throated stumping appeal against New Zealand, 1980-81 World Series.

At the Commonwealth Bank Cricket Academy headquarters in Adelaide.

1981: Overtakes Alan Knott during the Headingley Test as the most successful wicketkeeper in Test history when he catches Ian Botham from the bowling of his great mate Dennis Lillee. This is the game in which the pair take bets on an English victory at 500/1... and collect.

1981-82: Breaks Neil Harvey's Australian appearance record when he plays his 80th Test for Australia, in Adelaide.

1982-83: Is fined $200 for breaching the player-writer rule and commenting on selection in two newspaper articles; Takes 28 catches in the Ashes series, including six in an innings in the first Test in Brisbane. His nine wickets for the match equals the Australian record.

1983: Is awarded an MBE for his services to Australian cricket; Drinks 45 cans of beer on the flight from Sydney to Heathrow; Has a song, "Hero of the West," dedicated to him by legendary country singer Smokey Dawson as part of his Australia-wide testimonial.

1983-84: While farewelling big cricket along with close mates Greg Chappell and Lillee, during the 1983-84 Sheffield Shield final in Perth, Marsh is severely reprimanded for showing dessent against umpire Peter McConnell after he claimed a Jeff Thomson delivery which bowled Geoff Marsh was a no-ball. He angrily thumps his bat into the ground and hurls it 15 metres, before telling McConnell how far he believed Thomson had over-stepped. He'd played in the game despite a broken big toe suffered on the eve of the McDonald's Cup final in Adelaide in which he made 54 from 38 balls; Earlier in his final summer he boycotts the final session of the WA-Victorian game on a cracked and badly-worn Melbourne pitch saying there is too great a risk of injury with the second Test starting the following Friday. Greg Shipperd substitutes behind the stumps.

1984: Releases another book, "Rod Marsh, Gloves, Sweat and Tears... the final shout."

1991: Is dismissed from radio 2UE's international cricket panel, after previously seeing Geoff Boycott awarded his Channel Nine contract; Becomes head coach at the Commonwealth Bank Cricket Academy in Adelaide, his team successes including consecutive victories against four touring teams.

1994: "Stumped Marsh, bowled Marsh" appears in the family scorebook for the first time during a charity game at Melbourne Grammar, between an Australian X1 and a touring Indian X1. The batsman is Ravi Shastri and the bowler Marsh's second son, Daniel, who had just played his initial first-class games with SA.

again exposed on wickets which seamed and allowed maximum movement for even the most-pedestrian medium-pacer. Had he not been the third selector, he may have well been stood down.

First-time tourist Kim Hughes confronted Marsh before the fourth Test at Leeds and said the side needed a technician capable of grafting and wearing the Englishmen down. He volunteered as the man for the job, but the Australian hierachy disagreed, Hughes not playing until the final Test at The Oval when the series had already been decided.

The team which had been split since day one, was dangerously separate as it slid to a succession of defeats.

Enjoying old times with Jeff Thomson in a charity game, Melbourne, 1995.

At a meeting in Leicester in mid-tour which Chappell called to remind everybody of their prime responsibility, to defend the Ashes rather than worry about any side issues, particularly World Series, Marsh reinforced the determination of the players, saying his commitment to the Australian cap was total and he would punch the nose of anyone who disputed it.

A fortnight later, while sitting among a small group of players at the team's hotel in Leeds, Marsh was accused of siding with Victorian

Richie Robinson, who had opened in the first Test as a specialist batsman and played again in the third, this time as a No.6.

Despite a top score of just 34, Robinson had been picked again for the fourth Test, ahead of batting specialists Hughes, Gary Cosier and Craig Serjeant, who coincidentally, were three of the four not to have signed Packer contracts. After a nice old barney, Marsh left misty-eyed, deeply upset that his loyalty had been questioned.

Having lost the Ashes, Chappell wrote to the Board, advising that he had offiically retired from Test cricket. For months he'd parried talk that external problems had crippled the Australians. Now he no longer had the energy to deny it.

Marsh, who had been one of the last to sign with World Series, took only nine catches behind the stumps and at Trent Bridge, collected the first pair of his Test career. While he finished strongly with the bat with 63 at Headingley and 57 at The Oval, it was a mediocre return from one of the foremost stars of the international game. Had it been a happier, more successful tour, Marsh may have had regrets at leaving the traditional fold. Given the acrimony in England, he was glad to be out of there.

The widespread player unhappiness at a declining split of the record profits had spilled irretrievably towards revolution. Marsh's endeavours for the top 15 players in the country to gain base contracts and for a provident fund rewarding those who had given long service had both been rejected. When Austin Robertson, acting for Kerry Packer, approached him at teatime on the final day of the Centenary Test, he couldn't help but say yes.

"Who have you got," he asked and on being told that all his old mates had already committed, he agreed, virtually on the spot. He felt badly let down. Guarantees on Test-eve over improved benefits had not been met and he was fighting mad. "I went off my brain completely," he said. "There was only one bloke responsible and that was Bradman. How else could it have happened."

By signing with Packer, Marsh felt he was gaining the long-term security not available through the ACB. He'd be paid handsomely whether he played or not. He'd also be performing at an elite new level, a challenge he was to find as motivating as any he'd ever had.

Many of the signing on fees were handed over during the Centenary Test. To avert suspicion, Robertson mingled with the players and handing them envelopes, said, "Here are your theatre tickets, boys."

Had World Series not emerged, Rod Marsh says he was seriously considering retirement at the end of the '77 tour. He'd become a fulltime cricketer only that year, but was becoming ill at ease with the pay and travel demands and increasingly mindful of his family responsibilities.

Two summers of Packer cricket, which included tours to New Zealand and the West Indies, guaranteed the elite cricketers a new elevated presence in the game. If they had complained previously they were playing for peanuts, they weren't now. Greg Chappell, for example, had a five year contract guaranteeing him $50,000 a year initially, rising to $70,000 in his final year.

Marsh was on a three year, $105,000 minimum and like Chappell, at last had the opportunity to set himself up for life.

The new lucrative rewards, which in the 1990s now see half a dozen of Australia's best cricketers well on the way to milllionaire status were central, too, to keeping the stars of the Packer era involved long after a compromise had been negotiated. Dennis Lillee and Greg Chappell each played their last Tests at 34, while Marsh was 36, the "big

Dr. W. G. Grace dominated the game for almost half a century. With his high-pitched chuckle and unquenchable zest for everything cricket, he was a true giant of the game.

Sid Barnes was a provocative, outspoken opening batsman whose career would have been even greater but for the war.

The legendary Don Bradman at
a cavalcade of champions
during Sydney's Bicentennial
Test. Now in his 90th year, he
doesn't make public
appearances.

Don Bradman's most famous
dismissal, bowled first ball by
Bill Bowes, Melbourne, 1932-
33. He responded with an
unbeaten century in the second
innings, Australia winning its
only Test of the most
acrimonious summer of all.

Patrick Eagar

No-one plundered bowling quite like Ian Botham, England's devil-may-care allrounder who single-handedly won the Ashes in 1981 with some breathtaking allround performances.

Provocative Victorian Merv Hughes intimidated batsmen with his hostility and onfield aggro, becoming the darling of the Melbourne outer in the late '80s.

Ken Ramsbury

Imran Khan's allround abilities made him Pakistan's leading player. In 1995 he caused a stir by marrying Jemima Goldsmith, the daughter of a wealthy Anglo-French financier.

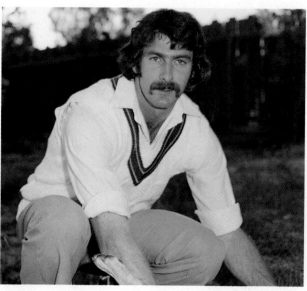

The infamous Lillee-Miandad incident, Perth, 1981-82. "I knew something was happening," said umpire Tony Crafter, "by looking into Dennis' eyes."

First steps for the emerging fast bowler: a young Dennis Lillee at Australian practice, 1971.

Viv Jenkins

SPORTS NOVELS

FOR AUGUST 1948

1/-

Registered at the General Post Office, Sydney, for transmission by post as a periodical.

The great Keith Miller was a front-page personality for many sports magazines of the '50s.

KEITH MILLER
(Brilliant all-rounder)

Rodney Marsh on his way to a century in the memorable Centenary Test, Melbourne, 1977

Viv Richards was an awesome, intimidating batsman who endangered even opposing bowlers with his savage hitting.

Shane Warne, the '90s showman, having some fun in a one-day international in Perth.

Sergio Dionisio

A full-throated Warne appeal during the 1997 Texaco Cup games which the Australians lost 3-0 before retaining the Ashes with three straight victories in mid-tour.

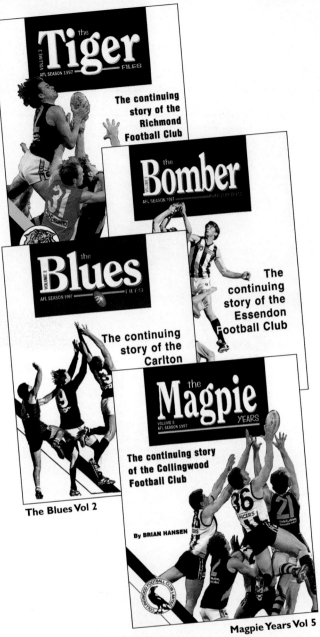

The continuing
story of the
Richmond
Football Club

The continuing
story of the
Essendon
Football Club

The continuing
story of the
Carlton

The Blues Vol 2

The continuing story
of the Collingwood
Football Club

By BRIAN HANSEN

Magpie Years Vol 5

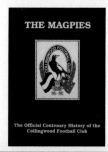

THE MAGPIES

The Official Centenary History of the
Collingwood Football Club

Special Investors Edition THE MAGPIES
Catalogued and numerically registered.
Priced $250.00 Special $175.00

The Blues Vol 1

Bomber Missions

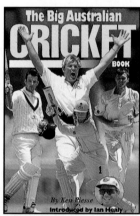

The Big Australian Cricket Book

ars Vol 1   **Magpie Years Vol 2**   **Magpie Years Vol 3**   **Magpie Years Vol 4**   **Tiger File Vol 1**   **Tiger File Vol 2**

Vol 1   **Wildmen Vol 2**   **Wildmen Vol 3**   **Mal Brown**   **Percy**   **The Centurions**

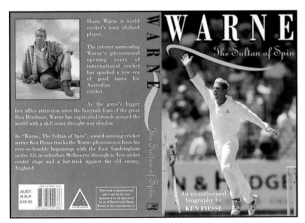

WARNE The Sultan of Spin

The Jack Dyer Story

POST TO: B.H.P. P.O. Box 698 Mount Waverley 3149

☐ CHEQUE   ☐ M/ORDER   ☐ VISA   ☐ BANKCARD   ☐ MASTERCARD

CARD NO ☐ ☐ ☐ ☐ ☐ ☐ ☐ ☐ ☐ ☐ ☐ ☐ ☐ ☐ ☐ ☐

SIGNATURE _____ EXPIRY DATE _____

NAME _____

ADDRESS _____ POSTCODE _____

PHONE (BUS) _____ HOME _____

*CREDIT CARD ORDERS CAN BE PROCESSED SAME DAY FAX (03) 9557 3503

PLEASE INCLUDE $5.00 FOR POSTAGE AND PACKING

The Greatest

HOOKESY IS STILL HITTING VICTORIA FOR SIX.

Hear Hookesy and Healy (the footballer, not the cricketer) talk cricket on Melbourne's leading sports radio station.

3AW
NEWS · TALK · 1278
Talking Melbourne

three" retiring within weeks of each other at the conclusion of the 1983-84 season, five years after returning to traditional ranks.

A RECORD RUN
When Rod Marsh broke Alan Knott's world record of 263 dismissals at Headingley, in 1981, appropriately with a catch from the bowling of Dennis Lillee, the Englishman sent him some champagne with a handwritten note: "Well played, hope you don't drop the bottle."

The record coincided with Lillee's 32nd birthday. "I am very proud that I am part of the record, " Lillee said. "Rod has been a great wicketkeeper, mentor and friend for more than 10 years."

Wise-cracking Doug Walters quipped that Marsh would have broken Knott's mark years previously, "if he'd accepted all those chances in his first Test!"

Rod Marsh's years of keeping wickets to some of the fastest bowlers in history brought a painful legacy. Not only were his hands chipped and bruised, his knees were too, triggering early arthritis and several wear-and-tear operations.

In 1976, he had the cartilage removed from his right knee. and despite a 10 week lay-off before he recovered anything like his normal mobility, it would still swell appreciably.

In his later years it was commonplace after a day's play to see him stretched out in the dressing rooms with huge ice packs on his knees.

His hands first became sore halfway through the 1974-75 summer during a Shield game in Sydney. The balls used were harder than normal and Marsh's hands so bruised and battered, he'd bandaged them before and sometimes after each day's play, making him look more like a prize fighter than a wicketkeeper.

Only rarely, however, did he ever use more than one pair of inners. The English custom was to use two, but Marsh liked to be able to "feel" the ball better, even if it meant his hands taking more of a pounding.

His acrobatic leaps became a highlight, but weren't always guaranteed to stop a Jeff Thomson bouncer, even if he was standing 30 metres back. When "Thommo" was at his fastest in the 1974-75 Ashes summer, bowling at more than 90 mph, some of his short deliveries not only cleared the batsman but Marsh as well. He stood almost as far back for Lillee, who broke John Edrich's ribs in his fastest spell of the summer. The Sydney wicket was lightning fast, rivalling Perth's glassy WACA pitches for pace and 28 byes were recorded against Marsh, 15 in England's first innings and 13 in its second.

Marsh's hands took a particular pounding that season and each morning he'd carefully tape elastic bandage around each of his fingers with extra protection for his knuckle pads.

Despite the wear and tear Marsh didn't miss any international game in Australia until a badly bruised finger forced him out of a one-dayer against the West Indies in his final season in Melbourne in 1983-84. By then he had made the decision to quit big cricket.

While he was grossly overweight early, fueling the criticism of his first up performances in Australian colors, he trimmed his weight to just 80 kg (12st. 8 lb.) in his final seasons.

In his farewell summer, he continued to play despite suffering a triple fracture of the cheekbone after deflecting a bouncer from Pakistan's Azeem Hafeez into his face in Adelaide in early December. He wasn't wearing a helmet.

He also carried a broken toe into his farewell game, the 1983-84 Sheffield Shield final against Queensland.

Jumping to take Thommo at Melbourne, 1974-75. "Christ that hurt, but I love it," he told the Chappell brothers.

THE GREATEST OF THEM ALL

"Despite his grizzly bear physique, Marsh hurled himself vast distances to make catches with prehensile ability. Hard though he strove to conceal it, he possessed a teddy bear amiablity. His language could be aggressive but he liked to be liked and made far more friends than some of his associates, " – JOHN ARLOTT

"Rod Marsh is one of the greatest Australian cricketers ever to set foot on the field. A wicketkeeper fit to rank with Wally Grout who was the best of my playing time. He has a deep knowledge of cricket and like Grout, would always be useful to a captain from the angle of giving advice different from the observations of the skipper, " – RICHIE BENAUD

A not-so-friendly welcome to Trent Bridge, 1977.

"Of all the players I have met, Marsh was the most competitive. You could almost feel how much he cared when you were out in the middle. Rod never knew when to give up. No cause was altogether lost while he was out there fighting. I remember when he played Test cricket with a broken toe and I had to ask him, 'Are you all right, Rod?' 'I will be if we win,' he replied, " – DICKIE BIRD

"Had it not been for World Series Cricket, Rodney Marsh would have captained Australia at some stage during his career. In fact, Marsh has probably forfeited more than any one of the 60 players who signed their names to a new way of life for cricketers," – IAN CHAPPELL

Until Ian Healy's sustained brilliance as a wicketkeeper-batsman in the 1990s, Rod Marsh was clearly Australia's best-performed wicketkeeping allrounder with a dozen first-class 100s.

If anything, however, he under-achieved as a batsman. Having posted his 10th first-class 100 against Essex in 1977, it took him another seven years to make two more.

By his own admission, the continual confrontations with the West Indian speedsters affected his confidence and exposed his technique.

"I became shellshocked from the continual barrage," he says. "Anyone who says they like playing fast bowling is either a liar or an idiot. There is no real joy in having the ball bounce around your throat all day long. I just don't know how to combat it really. You spend a lot of your time just trying to stay in and only some of it trying to score runs. I've never got to the stage where I have been too frightened to go out and bat against them but I have been frightened batting against them – perhaps more frightened of losing my wicket than of getting hit."

Without his unbeaten century in the very last Supertest at St John's in 1979, his average would have been closer to 15 than 20 in his World Series appearances, compared with his overall Test average of almost 27

"World Series Cricket was a helluva experience," said Marsh. "Playing against the best players in the world every day...it was the toughest and best cricket I ever played in. It seemed like there were six bouncers an over!"

Centenary Test salute: Marsh is applauded from the field by teammates Gary Cosier, Doug Walters, captain Greg Chappell and Max Walker after breaking Wally Grout's record of 187 dismissals.

He tended to be dismissed to chancy shots far more than earlier in his career when his batting was good enough to go in at No. 4 for WA and on one notable occasion, at Leeds in 1975, even to open for Australia. His close mate Ian Chappell often called him "George the Gorilla," a not-too-subtle dig at his liking for the big shot.

In a one-day international in Sydney in 1981-82, Marsh made such an almighty swipe that he was left holding only the handle of his Gray Nicolls bat, the blade finishing somewhere near mid-on and the ball at the mid-wicket boundary!

On song, he was responsible for some of the fastest scoring of his time, at first-class and international level. In 1975-76 in the WA-West Indies game in Perth, he reached 50 with just 11 scoring shots, the least amount of scoring shots for a half-century in Australian first-class history.

His most acclaimed hitting, outside his heroics against Norman Gifford at Old Trafford in the 1972 tour, came in 1980-81 on the short square boundaries of the Adelaide Oval, when he lifted New Zealander Lance Cairns for 26 runs (three 6s and two 4s) in the final five deliveries of Australia's innings. One of his 6s landed on the bonnet of a luxury car on display as part of the International Cricketer of the Year promotion.

With three Test centuries, the first by an Australian wicketkeeper, Marsh's credentials as a free-scoring and dangerous opponent are well known. The only wicketkeeper-batsman of his time with a superior record is England's Alan Knott who made five 100s in 95 Tests at an average of 30-plus.

When the mood suited, Marsh could be just as gritty a defensive player. At Melbourne in 1974-75, Marsh's tactics against the dual spin of Derek Underwood and Fred Titmus when Australia needed 55 in the last 15 overs were questioned. With just three wickets in hand, he believed his caution was justified. Along with Max Walker, the pair took just seven runs from the first seven overs of the final hour, Australia eventually falling eight runs short in a go-slow against an under-manned attack. *Wisden* described the tactics as "defying explanation."

There had been a flurry in the end against the second new ball, but it was still an anti-climax, especially for the huge crowd which over five memorable days had broken the 250,000 attendance mark and had keenly anticipated Australia's third consecutive win.

Previously, in Dunedin, his batting tactics were also questioned, this time in the game against Otago when he became

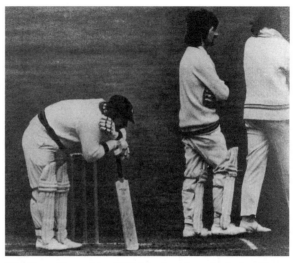

The Dunedin go-slow, 1974. Marsh rests on his bat waiting for Otago wicketkeeper Warren Lees and slipsman Robert Anderson to settle in-between overs.

frustrated by the opposition's defensive tactics and closed up a game. Otago captain and off-spinner Gren Alabaster bowled his medium pacers almost exclusively and an unimpressed Marsh dawdled to 31 in three hours, blocking half volleys, leaning disinterestedly on his bat in-between overs and warring with Alabaster when he suggested Marsh show the same aggression as Gary Gilmour, who made a breezy 34 in less than an hour.

c MARSH, b LILLEE

The most satisfying wicket Rod Marsh and Dennis Lillee shared outside the international arena came in 1976-77 in a Gillette Cup semi-final in Perth.

Having been dismissed by Queensland for just 77, it seemed Western Australia had no chance before Lillee, having started with three consecutive bouncers to star import Viv Richards, bowled him for a duck.

Realising the importance of dismissing Greg Chappell, then universally regarded as the game's No.1 batsman, Lillee was bowling at his quickest, when at the top of his mark, he saw Marsh standing yards outside leg stump, the tip-off to try and have Chappell caught down the leg-side.

Bowling a bouncer straight at the Queenland captain, Chappell went for the hook, but the extra pace surprised him and he gloved the ball to leg slip where a jubilant Marsh accepted it.

Had he been in his usual spot, outside the off stump, the ball would have flown harmlessly to the fine-leg boundary. The two old friends were as ecstatic as Chappell was amazed.

In the most dramatic one-day game in Australia in the '70s, the Queenslanders were bowled out for just 62, Lillee taking 4-21 from 7.3 overs. He later admitted he'd risked a breakdown by bowling so quickly, but once roused, he had no intention of slowing down.

"The day was as cold as sin and the dressing room was only one step removed from a cowshed so when I went out to bat, I decided it was better out in the middle than freezing in the rooms," Marsh said. "When I went on strike, I jacked up against Alabaster's tactics and refused to risk my wicket for runs. I simply blocked every ball. If he had brought on a spinner I would certainly have played a few shots but until then, I

Maiden Ashes tour: David Hookes pictured during the 1977 England tour.
Patrick Eagar

WHEN THE TRUTH HURTS...

When charismatic South Australian David Hookes dared suggest that
Rod Marsh and not Kim Hughes should be Australia's cricket captain, all
hell broke loose at Australian Cricket Board headquarters in Jolimont.

It had been the most tumultuous period ever in Australasian cricket,
with the fallout over the underarm incident, the diabolical behaviour of the
West Indians in New Zealand, the Dennis Lillee-Javed Miandad kicking
controversy and confirmation that Lillee and Rod Marsh had bet against
Australia on the '81 tour.

As vice-captain under Hughes of Australia's World Cup team in 1983,
Hookes not only should have known better, he should have kept any
grievances he had about Hughes' leadership skills to himself.

His frank interview with Adelaide radio personality Ken Cunningham
at the conclusion of the '83 tour was to cost him $1200, almost 25 per cent
of his touring fee. It ensured national headlines, especially after Hookes
paid for the taxi fare from Sydney airport for the man who tried him, ACB
cricket co-ordinator Bob Merriman!

It also soured Hookes' attitude towards officialdom which had been
tested from the time he joined Barry Curtin and Jeff Crowe in smoking

cigars at the tea interval of a grade game involving his club, West Torrens and the "non-smoking" club, East Torrens. Within 24 hours, what was meant to be a harmless prank cost him a "please explain" phone call and the vice-captaincy of South Australia that season.

Given his outstanding debut in the Centenary Test when he was hailed as the new wonder kid of world cricket after striking five 4s in a row from Tony Greig's bowling, some felt he'd under achieved in playing only 22 more Tests.

Ian Chappell felt he was never quite the same batsman again having been floored by an Andy Roberts bouncer which broke his jaw, at the Sydney Showgrounds during the first year of World Series.

However, he proved his mettle with continuing outstanding form at Sheffield Shield level and his seasons as an Australian Test regular, including another summer as national vice-captain in 1985-86. And he did make 143 not out in his last Test innings!

Not only was he noted for his record runmaking, however, but for his acid tongue and temper. With administrators having implemented a new code of behaviour aimed at roping in the number of growing cases of extravagent player behaviour, Hookes was among the first players disciplined.

He forfeited his entire Sheffield Shield playing fee ($130) having being found guilty of abusive language after a charge of "showing resentment" against the umpires when light rain triggered a premature close to the Shield game against New South Wales with South Australia just 11 runs short of victory in Sydney in 1981-82.

Three years later in Brisbane, he marched furiously off the 'Gabba after just seven overs of the match seeking to have the umpires replaced after Robbie Kerr, who'd edged a catch to third slipsman Michael Haysman, remained at the wicket.

"We fielded with 10 blokes as I went off to find Tom Veivers (from the Queensland Cricket Association) to find some umpires who could see," said Hookes. "Tom smoothed things over and told me how I knew it couldn't be done and that it would be best if I went back on the ground and got on with it.

"He was right of course, but I had a lot of satisfaction in giving that particular umpire minus 2000 out of 10 in the end-of-game report."

His run-ins with NSW captain Geoff Lawson and abuse of Australian spinner Peter Taylor, when he declared he shouldn't be be in the "F...ing Australian side" during another heated moment of a Shield game at the SCG were further pointers to a temper which sometimes ran out of control.

David Hookes – In brief

Born: May 3, 1955

Teams: South Australia & Australia

First-class debut: 1975-76

First-class record: Matches 178. Batting – Runs 12,671, Average 43.39, Highest score 306 not out, 100s 32. Bowling – Wickets 41, Average 58.02, Best bowling 3-58. Catches 167.

Test debut: 1976-77

Test record: Matches 23. Batting – Runs 1306, Average 34.36, Highest score 143 not out, 100s 1. Bowling – Wickets 1, Average 41.00, Best bowling 1-4. Catches 12.

One-day international debut: 1977

One-day international record: Matches 39. Batting – Runs 826, Average 24.29, Highest score 76. Bowling – Wickets 1, Average 28.00, Best bowling 1-2.. Catches 10.

Tours: England 1977, 1983; Pakistan 1980; Sri Lanka 1983; West Indies 1984.

determined to remain motionless. The crowd went berserk, but I didn't budge and had a running verbal battle with Alabaster. Unless he brought on his spinners, I said, he would see no shots from me.

"As my protest progressed a wicket fell and Gary Gilmour came out and messed it up by whacking a couple of sixes off the medium pacers. I rapped Gary over the knuckles and Alabaster wasted little time in telling me that's how I should be putting my bat to use. 'I'll tell you what I'll do with this bat in a minute,' I said. 'Perhaps I would be if you'd only have a bowl.'"

Ian Chappell had encouraged his team to bat for as long as they could, given the freezing conditions. The game was eventually abandoned through bad light with Otago 6-39 having been set 201 to win in 145 minutes. As Alabaster walked onto the ground and glanced at the grey skies, the umpires conferred and raised the bails, believing the light too bad to continue even though the Australian spinners were operating. Chappell was unimpressed by the umpire's promise that play would recommence immediately the light improved. He said the Australians were heading back to their hotel to get warm.

The "Ugly Australian" tag, invented during Ian Chappell's reign as captain, was never stronger than during the 1975 tour of England, when Jeff Thomson was accused of poor sportsmanship and of being one of the prime "bad boys" among the touring Australians.

Rod Marsh was also a target, especially after he slammed the dressing room door and broke a window having been dismissed in the first Test at Edgbaston. "It was a simple accident for which Rod apologised to the ground authorities," said Chappell. "But when it appeared in the papers the next day, readers could have been accused for thinking Marsh had hurled a hand grenade through the door."

Marsh had made a gutsy half-century, before being dismissed first ball after a break in play as the umpires searched to replace a ball which had gone out of shape.

ONE REGRET

Rodney Marsh's mastery standing back from the stumps is unrivalled; however, with just one stumping every eight Test matches, he believes others, particularly England's Alan Knott, were more adept against spinners.

For the record, his stumpings came from Ashley Mallett (seven times), Ray Bright (twice), John Gleeson, John Inverarity and Jim Higgs.

"The best thing I could have done for my keeping is to have spent a couple of years in England playing county cricket," he said. "To have stood up over the stumps – the way 'keepers judge 'keepers – on uncovered wickets for example, would have been a great education."

While he had forcibly opened the door with his bat, the window had shattered only after the door inadvertently slammed. A month later, having been involved in another flare-up, in the members' stand at Northampton, he was accused of "rampaging tantrums" by former England captain Ted Dexter.

Marsh never minded the "Ugly Australian" tag believing it went with Australia's territory as the world's leading cricket team.

Despite his run-ins with authority, there was a softer side not often portrayed.

One of the often-forgotten highlights of the Centenary Test was Marsh's honesty in recalling Derek Randall late on the final day when he was 161 and England within sight of a what would have been a magnificent victory. Randall had walked on seeing Tom Brooks' raised finger, believing it to be a regulation caught behind, but Marsh, who had dived forward almost a metre to make up ground, immediately called a "no-catch" and intimated to captain Greg Chappell he'd scooped the ball on the half-volley.

"Have you gone all religious?" asked Chappell, who had been fighting desperately to retain control of the game.

Had he not owned up, Marsh said he wouldn't have been able to live with himself. "If I hadn't done it, I would have been the biggest bastard on this earth. I could never sleep at night if I knew I caught someone on the bounce. I can be as hard as anyone on the field, but cheating just isn't on."

Several years later, again in Melbourne, as Trevor Chappell advised the umpires he was about to deliver his infamous underarm in a dramatic finale to a one-day final against New Zealand, Marsh shook his head and called to Greg Chappell, "No mate, don't do it."

Despite his misgivings, Marsh remained loyal to Chappell, as did Dennis Lillee and continued to back him during his difficult period when his form slumped so badly in 1982-83 that he seriously considered stepping down from the captaincy. While initially Marsh was more Ian Chappell's mate, in the end it was The Three Musketeers, Greg, Lillee and Marsh. Their decision to retire within weeks of one another sent Australian cricket into a tail spin from which it took years to recover.

Rod Marsh wanted to be sure that he'd finally had enough. It was the only reason he didn't join Ian Chappell and Dennis Lillee in announcing his retirement in after the Sydney Test in early 1984.

He wanted to play the World Series internationals and judge if his hunger was still there. While he only had to put his hand up to have been an automatic selection to the Caribbean, thereby passing the 100-Test mark, he said records had never been a priority and remained of little consequence.

"It's only how your teammates judge you that deems you a good or an ordinary player. All it boils down to really is the fact that my desire to play first-class cricket is no longer there.

"I came to the decision some time ago but I had to confirm it in my own mind by playing the one-day games to make sure I wasn't kidding myself."

Marsh said it wasn't as much fun without his old mates Greg Chappell and Dennis Lillee in the dressing room. "After all, there is a hell of an age difference between me and most of the other players."

THE ORIGINS OF 'BACCHUS'

Rod Marsh's nickname "Bacchus" comes from the Victorian country town of the same name.

The West Australian team was en-route, by train, from Adelaide to Melbourne when they stopped at the Bacchus Marsh station.

"This is your station, one of the boys said to me. That's how it all started."

On announcing his retirement, he wrote in his column in *Truth:* "Cricket fans Australia-wide just don't realise how hard it is for a player to combine a Test career with family life. That's why I am quitting. You could say I'm doing it for love. In 15 years I've been home for Christmas twice, I've missed countless birthdays and I've shared just one wedding anniversary with my wife, Roslyn."

He said Roslyn Marsh was not only a tower of strength, she was his harshest critic. "She actually gets me out of a slump. Although she hasn't played cricket and knows little about the game, the fact that she's got the guts to stand up and tell me how badly I'm playing is the one thing that motivates me above all else I do."

Rod Marsh THE MAN & HIS RECORD

Born: November 4, 1947

Teams: Western Australia & Australia

First-class debut: 1968-69

First-class record: Matches 257. Batting — Runs 11,067, Average 31.17, Highest score 236, 12
100s, 55 50s. Bowling — Wickets 1, Average 84, Best bowling 1-0. Wicketkeeping — Catches
805, Stumpings 65.

Test debut: 1970-71

Test record: Matches 96. Batting — Runs 3633, Average 26.51, Highest score 132, three 100s, 16
50s. Bowling — Wickets 0, Best bowling 0-3. Wicketkeeping — Catches 343, Stumpings 12.

Tours: England 1972, 1975, 1977, 1980, 1981, 1983; West Indies 1973; New Zealand 1973-74,
1976-77, 1981-82; Pakistan 1980, 1982. Also toured NZ and the West Indies with Ian
Chappell's WSC Australians in 1979.

One day international debut: 1970-71

One day international record: Matches 92. Batting — Runs 1225, Average 20.08, Highest score 66,
four 50s. No Bowling. Wicketkeeping — Catches 120, Stumpings 4.

Rod Marsh's Test record series by series:

BATTING & WICKETKEEPING

Season	Opponent	Mt	Inns	No	HS	Runs	Ave	100s	50s	Ct.	Stmp
1970-71	England (h)	6	9	1	95*	215	26.88	-	1	11	3
1972	England (a)	5	9	2	91	242	34.57	-	2	21	2
1972-73	Pakistan (h)	3	5	0	118	210	42.00	1	1	16	-
	West Indies (a)	5	7	1	97	297	49.50	-	3	17	-
1973-74	New Zealand (h)	3	3	0	132	148	49.33	1	-	16	1
	New Zealand (a)	3	6	0	47	173	28.83	-	-	13	-
1974-75	England (h)	6	11	2	55	313	34.78	-	1	18	1
1975	England (a)	4	5	0	61	133	26.60	-	1	14	1
1975-76	West Indies (h)	6	8	0	56	236	29.50	-	1	26	-
1976-77	Pakistan (h)	3	6	1	41	119	23.80	-	-	11	-
	New Zealand (a)	2	2	0	4	6	3.00	-	-	13	-
	England (h)	1	2	1	110*	138	138.00	1	-	5	-
1977	England (a)	5	9	1	63	166	20.75	-	2	9	-
1979-80	West Indies (h)	3	6	1	23*	57	11.40	-	-	11	1
	England (h)	3	4	0	42	70	17.50	-	-	11	-
	Pakistan (a)	3	5	0	71	106	21.20	-	-	4	1
1980	England (a)	1	1	1	16*	16	-	-	-	1	-
1980-81	New Zealand (h)	3	4	0	91	100	25.00	-	-	10	-
	India (h)	3	5	0	45	83	16.00	-	-	15	1
1981	England (a)	6	11	0	52	216	19.64	-	1	23	-
1981-82	Pakistan (h)	3	5	0	47	142	28.40	-	-	11	-
	West Indies (h)	3	5	0	39	117	23.40	-	-	10	-
	New Zealand (a)	3	3	0	33	59	19.67	-	-	5	-
1982-83	Pakistan (a)	3	6	0	32	72	12.00	-	-	3	1
	England (h)	5	7	0	53	124	17.71	-	1	28	-
1983-84	Pakistan (h)	5	6	2	33*	75	18.75	-	-	21	-
Totals		96	150	13	132	3633	26.51	3	16	343	12

COUNTRY BY COUNTRY RECORD

BATTING & WICKETKEEPING

Country	Mt	Inns	No	HS	Runs	Ave	100s	50s	Ct.	Stmp
v England	42	68	8	110*	1633	27.22	1	9	141	7
v Pakistan	20	33	3	118	724	24.13	1	2	66	2
v West Indies	17	26	2	97	707	29.46	-	4	64	1
v New Zealand	14	18	0	132	486	27.00	1	1	57	1
v India	3	5	0	45	83	16.60	-	-	15	1

HOME & ABROAD

Country	Mt	Inns	No	HS	Runs	Ave	100s	50s	Ct.	Stmp
Tests at home	56	86	8	132	2147	27.53	3	6	220	7
Tests abroad	40	64	5	91	1486	25.19	-	10	123	5

HIS HIGHEST TEST SCORES

132	v New Zealand, Adelaide, 1973-74
110*	v England, Melbourne, 1976-77
118	v Pakistan, Adelaide, 1972-73
97	v West Indies, Jamaica, 1973
92*	v England, Melbourne, 1970-71
91	v New Zealand, Perth, 1980-81
91	v England, Old Trafford, 1972

MOST CATCHES IN AN INNINGS

6	v New Zealand (1), Christchurch, 1973-74
6	v England (2), Brisbane, 1982-83
5	v England (2), Old Trafford, 1972
5	v England (1), Trent Bridge, 1972
5	v New Zealand (1), Sydney, 1973-74
5	v West Indies (2), Melbourne, 1975-76
5	v New Zealand (1), Christchurch, 1976-77
5	v West Indies (1), Brisbane, 1979-80
5	v India (1), Sydney, 1980-81
5	v Pakistan (1), Perth, 1981-82
5	v Pakistan (2), Perth, 1983-84
5	v Pakistan (2), Sydney, 1983-84

MOST DISMISSALS IN A MATCH

9	(9 c), v England, Brisbane, 1982-83
8	(8 c), v West Indies, Melbourne, 1975-76
8	(8 c), c New Zealand, Christchurch, 1976-77
8	(7 c, 1 s), v India, Sydney, 1980-81
8	(8 c), v England, Adelaide, 1982-83

MOST DISMISSALS IN A SERIES

28	(28c), v England, 1982-83 (five matches)
26	(26c), v West Indies, 1975-76 (six matches)
23	(21c, 2s), v England, 1972 (five matches)
23	(23c), v England, 1981 (six matches)
21	(21c), v Pakistan, 1983-84 (five matches)

HIS HIGHEST ONE-DAY INTERNATIONAL SCORES

66	v Pakistan, Sydney, 1983-84
54*	v Pakistan, Sydney, 1981-82
52*	v West Indies, The Oval, World Cup 1975
50*	v Zimbabwe, Trent Bridge, World Cup 1983
49	v New Zealand, Sydney, 1980-81
44	v New Zealand, Adelaide, 1980-81
42	v England, Manchester, 1977
41	v England, The Oval, 1980

MOST DISMISSALS IN A MATCH

5	(5c), v England, Leeds, 1981
4	(4c), v England, Birmingham, 1972
4	(4c), v England, Birmingham, 1977
4	(4c), v India, Sydney, 1980-81
4	(4c), v New Zealand, Perth, 1982-83
4	(3c, 1s), v Pakistan, Sydney, 1983-84

Rod Marsh's World Series Cricket Supertests record

BATTING & WICKETKEEPING

Season	Mt	Inns	No	HS	Runs	Ave	100s	Cat.	Stmp
1977-78 (h)	6	12	0	59	194	16.	16	23	-
1978-79 (h)	4	7	0	23	91	13.	00	11	-
1979 (West Indies)	5	9	1	102*	252	31.50	1	18	-
Totals	15	28	1	102*	537	19.88	1	52	-

HIGHEST WSC SCORES

102*	v WSC West Indies, St John's, 1979
59	v WSC West Indies, Sydney Showgrounds, 1977-78
49	v WSC West Indies, Guyana, 1979

MOST CATCHES IN AN INNINGS

5	v WSC World XI, VFL Park, Melbourne, 1977-78
4	v WSC West Indies, Jamaica, 1979

MOST DISMISSALS IN A MATCH

7	(7c), v WSC World XI, VFL Park, Melbourne, 1977-78
7	(7c), v WSC West Indies, Jamaica, 1979
6	(6c), v WSC World XI, Sydney Showgrounds, 1977-78

Rod Marsh's other internationals

v Rest of the World, 1971-72

Mt	Inns	No	HS	Runs	Ave	100s	50s	Cat.	Stmp
5	7	1	77*	186	31	.00	-	2	11

THE
LION OF
LAHORE

"We're coming to get you!" roared the Lion of Lahore... and the West Indies licked their lips at the challenge.

A champion with an indomitable spirit, a winner of lost causes, Imran Khan made his downtrodden people proud. He always believed he was under the direction of God, that he was to lead his people. He led Pakistan to its proudest sporting moment, the 1992 World Cup. Now he has a greater vision.

THE STORY OF Imran Khan Niazi with its Eastern mystiques and culture is a story apart from all others who have played the game of cricket with international distinction.

Imran is the product of another world. He is moody, calculating, handsome, complex, wealthy, a man of destiny.

He is a superior being, particularly in his own eyes. Which is not to demean the man for he refuses to be demeaned. Imran believes there is more to his life than hurling a little leather missile at three upright sticks.

Yet cricket established him with his Muslim race as a leader of commanding presence. He was Pakistan's most outstanding sportsman. In the Western world he was seen as wickedly wanton, courts ruling he'd sired a child out of wedlock. He was a God to one nation and sinner to the other.

In time he was to give away hundreds of thousands of dollars to build a hospital for the poor of Pakistan. But in his other world he was branded a playboy, a drug user, a cheat and a manipulator. He became the male sex symbol of the Western world, pursued and caught by desirable women. He was the centre of scandal after scandal on

183

and off the sporting field. Much that was written about him was lies; much was truth.

Teammates said he used them to conceal drugs. One accused him of smuggling women into his rooms, breaking the taboos of his people. Many believed he cheated on and off the field. Imran vehemently denied the charges.

Cricket did more for Imran that put him in sporting record books – it was far more important than that. Cricket gave him a vast following in his own strife-torn country as his incredible sporting feats lifted the spirit of his struggling nation. He became a leader who understood their problems and had the resolve to put things right. His success was their success.

Imran is the product of high-profile parents, an Oxford graduate, a socialite of commanding presence and the associate of tycoons, royalty, politicians, entertainers, media and sporting icons. Imran believes he discovered the real purpose of his life as his mother died. The proud, charismatic personality quit cricket and embarked on a new mission; one that many believe will see him one day rule Pakistan.

Cricket was a means to an end for Imran. His agenda was undoubtedly set for him by his mother - which is where the Imran Khan story really begins...

Shaukat Khan sat opposite the mystic and asked what the future held for her son. The visionary closed his eyes, sent his inner self in search of the spirit of the future and told the mother of Imran Khan: "Before you die, your son Imran will be a great man."

Thirty years later, the mystic's vision had become reality. Imran the Warrior chief sat opposite his own clairvoyant and asked, "What is my destiny?" This mystic was less reassuring and decidedly more alarming. "Imran Khan – if you enter into politics you will be assassinated."

Imran rejected three grand political appointments but finally sought the counsel of his socialite friend, the Marchioness of Worcester. She said, "Imran knew that if he went into politics he would have to change a whole class of rulers. He believes in revolution. There would be violence and it would be frightening."

The Marchioness told him: "You had better be prepared to die for your country if you want to enter politics."

Imran replied: "I will go into politics when I am ready to die."

In 1988 President Zia-ul-Haq offered him a political post which he declined. Six days later Zia was blown up in his private plane. Zia was a man to be feared; he was the leader who organised the widely condemned hanging of political leader Ali Bhutto on a spurious murder charge in 1979.

In 1993, Imran knocked back a post with the Pakistan interim government and instead took over a position as Ambassador for Tourism. But in 1996 Prime Minister Benazir Bhutto, the daughter of Ali Bhutto, was sacked and Imran decided his time had come; he'd make his play for power and via his Movement of Justice Party, contest the February elections. While he lost, he saw it only as a beginning.

The Marchioness of Worcester, better known as actress Tracy Worcester said, "I think he should go into politics. He should be prepared to put up with the threat to risk his life for the justice of his country."

Cricket had led to Imran Khan to what he believed was his destiny. If it also led him to his death, so-be-it.

The career of Imran Khan was to have many pitfalls. His career was a never-ending story of confrontation, headlines and scandal.

He was to fight an eternal war within his own ranks as he fought with Javed Miandad for captaincy of Pakistan. He was accused of using his wealth and powerful family and political influences against his lowly-born adversary. He brought about a civil war in Pakistan cricket.

His players sold stories to newspapers claiming their skipper was a womaniser, drug smuggler and hash smoker. He committed so many breaches of team discipline on his first tour he lost his entire pay packet to fines – calculated at 38 penalties for indulging in late night social activities when he should have been resting. Strange to say Imran did not drink alcohol.

His own national papers delighted in scandalising the champion's activities. One said a stress fracture of the leg attributed to cricket attrition was in fact the legacy of a beating by two brothers of a Lahore beauty queen he had been dating. It was also attributed to a curse placed on him for striking a young autograph hunter with his bat.

There was international scandal in 1992 when he confessed to have begun tampering with balls in first-class matches 10 years previously when he first used a bottle top to lift the seam of a ball. He saw no wrong in lifting the seam or scratching the surface of the ball. "That has gone on ever since the game began," said Imran.

Superstars Ian Botham and Allan Lamb became associated in a massive court confrontation with Imran when they sued him for libel. They lost in the court and at great personal expense; the court costs massive.

Imran became embroiled in the 1995 controversy when Australian cricketers Mark Waugh, Tim May and Shane Warne alleged the Pakistan captain Salim Malik had offered them bribes to throw the first Test in Karachi in 1994. Malik denied the claims and there was massive friction when he toured Australia with Pakistan after the three Australians made the allegations.

Imran said the scandal should not be swept under the carpet. "These are the most serious allegations I have heard in 20 years of cricket... Salim Malik should be taken to task if he has done it. Or those cricketers who have accused him should be taken to task. It should be brought out into the open."

Imran said a prominent bookmaker had told him a number of times that he had "bought" Indian players. He revealed a plot supposedly uncovered by Javed when Pakistan played Australia at Sharjah in 1990. "Javed called me and told me that four Pakistani players had been bribed to throw the match."

Imran called a player's meeting and told the team he was betting the $30,000 prize-money on Pakistan to win. "There was no evidence of anybody throwing the game. They played brilliantly and we won our bet at even money."

The anger of his victorious players in the World Cup of 1992 forced him to quit cricket. They claimed he directed a fortune in donations away from his players into a fund for his own personal monument.

The colorful career of the handsome and alluring giant reached its climax when squillionaire television tycoon Kerry Packer made him the "sex bait" to snare millions of women as followers of World Series Cricket. Packer's marketing men made Imran the sexiest man on earth.

His career embraced some of the worst incidents in cricket including riots, ball tampering, bribes and plotting.

Of course there was the other side of the controversial Pakistani. He never backed away from a fight and undertook a remarkable one-man war against the deadly West Indies pace attack. When Andy Roberts headed up a brutal bouncer barrage against the Pakistani batsmen, Imran struck back. He hammered the West Indies batsmen from No. 1 to No. 11, answering the thunderous bouncer barrage with venomous deliveries of his own. It the end it was the West Indies who backed away.

When India and Pakistan were on the brink of war, Indian spectators pelted the

Pakistan outfielders with rocks during the fourth Test of 1987. Imran advised the umpires he was removing his players from the field. When order was restored he returned to the field with his six outfielders wearing metal helmets.

Such was his status in Pakistan that when he retired, students across the nation went on hunger strikes and others threatened to riot, demanding he continue. Finally President Zia ordered him to resume playing cricket. An offer he couldn't refuse...

The Pakistan nation was created when independence was proclaimed in 1947. It hosted its first Test tour when the West Indies visited in 1948-49 followed by an English tour in 1950-51.

The Khans were a proud family, bound by honor. When he was only 13, Pakistan traffic police caught Imran driving his father's car, clearly without a licence. He bribed his way out of trouble but when the family chauffeur reported the incident to Shaukat, she was furious. "You should have gone to gaol rather than stoop to this," she blazed at her son...."And you, a Pathan."

His mother had an overwhelming influence on young Imran's development as she filled in many hours telling him romantic stories of the great cricket matches played in Jullundur between members of her family. These cricket traditions continued when they moved to Lahore. With cricket the sporting focus of the rich and influential Khan family, Imran was to have the best foundation possible for a youngster. His mother also imparted a passion for animals, the mountains and wild life. Ironic that one of his favorite recreations became hunting and shooting.

Imran's mother and her two sisters were to give birth to three sons, each of whom captained Pakistan: Imran, Javed Burki and Majid Khan. Imran attributes this to the quality of cricket and coaching at Zaman Park rather than family influence. As soon as a youngster was old enough to hold a bat he was assured of assimilation into the cricket activities of even the greatest of Zaman Park players. Players in any given team could range from 10 to 30 years and the matches were always full-blooded and serious. The kids grew up fast in that make-or-break cauldron.

His uncle Ahmad Raza Khan was a national selector and boasted that Imran would play for Pakistan. It was a comforting feeling to know the selectors had a favorable eye on you. "To me his words were gospel," said Imran.

Throughout the next few years his mind was filled with the exploits of Javed Burki and Majid Khan. They were his inspiration. Majid was the greater inspiration as he was a devastating allrounder with incredible stroke play and destructive medium-fast bowling. He was Imran's idol and when they ultimately played together, Imran felt more despair when his cousin was out than when he lost his own wicket. They were to become bitter enemies.

By 14, he was the youngest member of the elite Aitchison College team. In those beginnings he was essentially a batsman and rarely bowled. When he took up the ball to hammer a few overs he found more amusement in slinging short-pitched balls at the batsmen than he did in getting wickets. "I enjoyed watching them hop out of the way." Being the best batsman in the best school in Pakistan led him to believe he must be the best batsman in the land. Finally he was selected in the squad for Lahore's under 19s against a visiting England under 19 team. "I strode out to bat, wearing my newly acquired spikes and ready to unleash a glittering array of strokes; but the spikes upset my footwork and the first few deliveries beat me completely . The harder I tried, the worse I became. I was soon told to go and stand in the outfield." He began to appreciate a place in international cricket was not a birthright. Despair set in and finally the selectors tossed him the ball to roll his arm over. This wasn't his perceived strength. he felt he'd blown his chance. After just a few deliveries a selector stopped him and observed, "You have the perfect action for a fast bowler." To his amazement he made the team as a fast bowler and was listed No. 10 in the batting order.

Playing with a Pakistan team was a new life. He met up with cricketers who had come up the hard way. "They came off the streets, they played by the roadside or any flat piece of land where matches could be played.

"They treated me with a certain amount of hostility. My teammates thought I did not deserve my place in the team. They thought I was there because of my connections." Perhaps he was – selection as a bowler certainly was a remarkable stroke of good fortune.

He didn't speak the same language as his fellow Pakistanis. The others spoke Punjabi, Imran spoke Urdu and his Punjabi was halting at best. He was the butt of their jokes and sarcasm and it took time for him to win their respect. He soon realised he had too high an opinion of his batting. His under 19 captain Wasim Raja made him realise he was light years away from being a master bat. He was shell-shocked by the abilities of Afzal Masood and Azmat Rana and realised he was out of his league and lucky to be playing for Lahore at a time when they were lacking pace bowlers.

He made his debut against Sargodha and instantly blew it. His selection was described as nepotism. The chairman of selectors was his uncle, the captain and the club's most senior player were his cousins. He was selected as opening bat and opening bowler.

Rain delayed the start of the game so he went back to his room for the weather to abate. When he returned, the game had started and another batsman opened for him. His clubmates were far from impressed with his spoiled, precocious disdain for the disciplines of the game. His skipper Hammayun Zaman gave him a lashing and accused him of being spoilt and unworthy. "I did behave as though I was doing them all a favor by gracing the occasion" he said.

Humility was bred out of the fighting Khans by more than 500 years of tribal command. He continued his first-class career under the guidance of his cousin and team captain Javed Burki.

Javed guided him carefully and he became Pakistan's second highest wicket taker for the 1970-71 domestic season. His bowling was erratic but virile. He had a charming knack of getting everything right in big games. This won him selection for Pakistan against an International X1 captained by Micky Stewart – he was just 18.

This is when William Shakespeare came into his life. Imran performed well against the international side which led Wing Commander Bill Shakespeare of the Worcestershire county club to invite him to play for the county. They would arrange to continue his schooling at Worcester's Royal Grammar School. His performance also brought him selection in Pakistan's team to tour England.

Imran Khan was on his way but from here on in, the silver spoon was in storage and he was on his own. Mothers, uncles, cousins and position cannot make you competitive on the international cricket scene.

The image of Imran Khan being a rich, spoiled product of the Pakistani upper class had not been dispelled although many times he asserted he has never been rich nor a playboy.

The spirit of Imran Khan was not to accept mediocrity and to always believe in one's "self." He was concerned in 1971 to see the Pakistani tourists accepting they were inferior cricketers. They were "always" thrashed by England and acted at though they accepted they would always be inferior – a hand-me-down to their days of colonial servitude. That offended Imran's anti-colonial sensitivity. Unlike many of his teammates he came from a tribal instinct that never yielded to the British rule. They did not kneel to the sahibs.

The Pakistan tourists went to England to face the invincible and the inevitable. Imran said the players were filled with the wrong advice. "We were told it was impossible to see the ball once it left Alan Ward's hand, the English never drop a catch. I would not be able to take a wicket because the English were technically perfect. Our back lift was too high so we would not get runs."

The team manager angered Imran at the MCC dinner reception. Imran believed his speech on behalf of the tourists was snivelling, servile and weak. "He declared the English had taught us discipline through cricket and how to eat with a knife and fork."

Imran said he was acutely embarrassed. He was to be offended again and again. He was told it was not permitted to rebuke a rude waiter but had to accept churlish insults. He was warned to get wickets he would have to fortify his body by drinking beer like Freddie Trueman. Instead he took to drinking milk and said his players followed his example and also turned to milk.

He had weaknesses on this tour, not the least that his bowling which worked so well in Pakistan was treated with disdain by the English batsmen. He was too young and inexperienced to make the necessary adjustments. He played the first Test against England and his bowling cost Pakistan a certain win, forcing them to settle for a draw. He couldn't control the huge swing he was gaining. Off the field he built an immediate reputation for being wild, undisciplined and arrogant.

Imran and a couple of the younger players fell foul of officialdom by breaking curfews which brought a string of fines. Fines were two pounds an offence and at the end of the tour his breaches cost him dearly. He received only two pounds from the player payment of 80 pounds that would have been due had he toed the line. The Pakistan manager did not keep the statistics, he simply kept his money and money was scarce for Imran in his early county days.

He ran foul of teammate Saeed Ahmed who started the tour sharing a room with Imran. Saeed urged the youngster to enjoy life and attend the local discos but then reported the youngster for disturbing his sleep by coming home late from discos at 3 am. Saeed claimed this was the reason he wasn't scoring runs. Imran was almost sent home whereas Saeed was given the room to himself, which was what he had been after.

Imran had no time for the veteran who he accused of crying like a baby during a match when several catches were dropped off his bowling. He bawled his eyes out in the middle of the pitch. Imran, Ali Tallat and Raza Azmat burst into a fit of giggling and were dragged before captain Intikhab Alam who also broke into laughter. "The more they treated us like schoolboys the more we acted like schoolboys," said Imran.

For all the mischief making, Pakistan was competitive and although Imran was dumped after the first Test, England only just scrambled home by 25 runs in the deciding third Test. While Imran had been banished from the team as an cocky upstart, he desperately wanted to be a part of his country's No.1 side and learned if he wanted to be respected, his game would have to improve. "I learned to curb my pride and started doing things like filling a bath for weary bowlers in order to prove that one was part of the team."

Had he not agreed to play for Worcester, his international career may have ended with his return to Pakistan. Instead his next season saw him stationed in England as a school boarder and county cricketer. He was a moderate student but brilliant cricketer – a quality that was not evident on his first international excursion. His skills later won him the captaincy of Oxford, where he studied politics and economics from 1973-76.

He subsequently shifted counties to Sussex so he could pursue the London nightlife.

He had been lonely and bored at picturesque Worcester. The change of county was not without its acrimony and in subsequent years led to racist taunts at Worcester and legal action from Imran.

His Oxford friends and the nightlife of London took precedence over cricket management but his development continued never the less. He capably mixed the exciting swirl of nightlife with his sport continuing to refrain from alcohol, smoking and drugs.

On the basis of his outstanding form with Oxford, Imran was selected for the three Test series against England in 1974. Again he had a modest series which saw all three matches drawn yet he showed sufficient for Wisden to suggest he would be a force in Pakistan cricket. He was not popular with the Pakistan team who saw him as an Oxford snob. Most of the team came from the lower levels of Pakistan society and were poorly educated. On that tour the Pakistan players were censured by press and umpires alike for their attitude towards umpire David Constant. They believed Constant was unfair when he insisted that the Pakistan players continue matches on rain-affected wickets that were unplayable.

These jealousies and resentments were short term – his teammates returned to Pakistan while he remained in England for four years of county and University cricket. He enjoyed life around Oxford but not the isolation and unfriendliness of Worcester.

He relished his change to Sussex as it meant he was now a clubmate of famed English speedster John Snow.

Unfortunately Snow left virtually immediately, but Sussex remained a strong unit, winning the 1978 Gillette Cup with Imran taking the key wicket of Ian Botham in the final. He teamed many times with Javed Miandad while the flamboyant Javed was at Sussex. His Sussex days ended when he arrived late from London for a Sunday League match.

Racism was ever an aggravation to Imran. He was disturbed by the volume of vitriolic taunts against his race both on and off the field. Although he abhorred racism and apartheid, he forged a great friendship with the Afrikaner Garth Le Roux at Sussex and on tour with the Packer caravan.

Color distinction was distasteful particularly when racial insults are generally hurled at the victim by a person or persons of inferior breeding, education and culture. Typical of which was the herd of illiterates who showered him with Pakistani taunts when he was batting for Sussex against Worcester. He became so enraged he played into the hecklers hands. They wanted to distract him into making a rash error of judgment.

Imran charged down the wicket, smashed a mighty six into their midst and gave a derisive signal with his bat. He had registered his contempt but in so doing had breached the mental discipline he required of himself. He could so easily have lost his wicket. He later commented that if he did have children he would not raise them in a racist environment such as existed in England.

Before all this took place he returned home to play a series against New Zealand in 1976 where the aggravation between himself and Sir Richard Hadlee germinated. Imran paid scant regard to the ethic that you don't bounce tailenders – besides Hadlee prided himself on his batting technique. Imran hit the New Zealander with two ripping bouncers before the umpires issued a warning. Khan promptly fired another at Hadlee's head and the umpires ordered him out of the attack. He then travelled to Australia where a new world opened to him. He regarded Australia as a cricket heaven and easily the world's best set-up for cricket. It was here the doors to World Series cricket swung open. A quiet development suddenly gained extraordinary momentum.

Unlike some international cricket powers, including Australia which fought Packer, Pakistan embraced World Series Cricket under the firm orders of Pakistan's leader, General Zia. Zia made Imran his own personal ambassador of cricket – much to the chagrin of Javed. But Imran was no man's puppet.

He now became embroiled in the financial disputes of the Pakistan players who were getting less for their tours than were the cricketers of other nations – a miserly 50 pounds for touring New Zealand. Six players including Imran stood their ground and the fee was raised to 250 pounds. But dissatisfaction had been created. This made him susceptible to an approach by South African and English icon Tony Greig, who was buying cricket mercenaries for breakaway cricket.

Greig offered Imran a lead role in World Series. The fee was a King's ransom and he would play in a world team against Australia. His cousin and idol Majid Khan would also be in the team along with another Paki, Asif Iqbal. It meant Khan missing Test cricket for at least 18 months but the bait was irresistible. This brought about an impasse and General Zia intervened, ordering the Pakistan selectors to include the World Series players in their official team for the 1978 series against India.

Prior to joining World Series, Imran had played 11 Tests, including three on tour to Australia where his vicious in-swing saw him making breakthroughs and being compared with the celebrated speedster Dennis Lillee. He took 18 wickets in the three games including five in an innings in Melbourne and a dozen in Sydney. Pakistan drew the series and it was in no small way due to Imran's input.

The plotters of World Series jotted down his name after the Sydney performance which lifted Pakistan to a memorable first Test win on Australian soil. He gave the Aussies a blaze of bouncers, a preview of what he was to unleash against the World Series Australian team. Both Lillee and Imran were severely reprimanded and warned by the umpires for abuse of the bouncer. Rodney Marsh gesticulated at him with the bat when he was almost nailed to the sightscreen. The Packer men had a dream enemy warrior. His glamor and color drew a vast feminine support.

It was the animal attraction of Imran Khan that captured the attention of the Packer marketeers. He was rare box office material, opposed to Dennis Lillee, he was sensational confrontational and gladiatorial fare. That he was handsome with all the class, grace and mystique of an Indian maharaja made him the essential centrepiece of the World X1.

RATING THE QUICKS
In 1979, the University of Western Australia conducted scientifically-controlled camera tests to assess the speed of the game's leading pacemen.

Imran Khan was rated the third quickest bowler at 86 mph, just behind Michael Holding (87) and the No.1, Jeff Thomson (91).

His new ball teammate Sarfraz Nawaz was timed at 78 mph.

Make no mistake about Imran Khan – he is proud of his heritage and can drift from the cultures East to West as Clark Kent can transform from mouse to Superman. To belittle his people is to belittle him. He can be cutting and harsh with critics of his country, its traditions and its people. He is intolerant of people who do not comprehend the historic struggles of Pakistan or the reasons for conflict amongst their tribes. He resents touring spectators who are ignorant and breach the traditions and taboos of his nation's sacred institutions, both physical and spiritual.

After the 1976-77 tour of Australia, he headed for Pakistan's tour of the supposedly

Imran rebukes wicketkeeper Salim Yousuf after he'd cheekily claimed a catch behind against Ian Botham during the third Test of the 1987 tour. Botham reacted angrily and had to be separated from Yousuf by umpire Ken Palmer.

invincible West Indies. His batting had not yet consolidated but his bowling was magnificent.

The quality of "The Lion of Lahore" was his refusal to knuckle under. Confronted by the might of the West Indies when Pakistan could not unearth world class pace bowlers, Imran took up the challenge personally.

He traded bumper for bumper with the West Indies and took 25 wickets for the series. Although out-gunned he never wavered. He hurled bouncer after bouncer at the Calypsos and didn't spare the lower-order. He didn't segregate the enemy – they were all there to be brought down. He felled tail enders with his bouncers including vicious bouncer sharpshooter Andy Roberts. He collected Roberts with a riveting ball that very nearly decapitated the West Indian.

The Windies came back, launching a fusillade that threatened to nail the handsome Imran Khan head to the sightscreen. That didn't faze him, he returned the barrage. The Windies pace bowlers started to worry about their own welfare. Imran was without fear.

He fought the West Indies to a standstill and there was profound lessening of the ball assault on his players in future encounters. Imran had a huge advantage over the West Indies pace attack. He could do what their pace bowlers couldn't do – he could handle a searing bouncer. They were terrified when he unleashed his weaponry against them whereas he was fearless when he took the best they could sling at him.

Pakistan went down narrowly in the five Test series 2-1 with two drawn. Imran's batting was now coming together and he was prominent in the world rankings as an allrounder. His 57 wickets and blazing bat in those 11 Tests secured him an invite into the Packer extravaganza.

Packer was also packaging his series for television and satellite coverage across the world. He wanted a super sex symbol to put the icing on the package. Imran Khan was his man. They didn't come any sexier than this tall, athletic Pakistani. Packer had the magazines and television outlets to flog Imran's sex appeal. The publicists went to work and Imran became the most glamorous sportsman the cricket world had ever seen.

Billboards, magazine covers and television screens projected the Imran Khan profile until his face was indelibly set in the minds and hearts of women throughout the cricketing world. His penetrating eyes had smouldered their way into the minds of a besotted feminine following.

Centrestone of the World X1, even Australian women deserted the Aussie X1 in their tens of thousands to follow the husky hunk all the way to his harem – if they were that lucky.

An Australian national womens magazine conducted a poll that overwhelmingly labelled Imran the sexiest man in the game.

The World Series was the making of Imran as a cricketing personality. It brought him together with the undoubted cream of world cricket. It set him a standard. He had to prove he was the equal of the best of them; even more, he wanted to be the best of the best.

World Series was a winner for Kerry Packer. It took the grand old game out of its staid and dreary traditionalism and gave it an infusion of new blood. The one-day concept became enmeshed in traditional cricket and modernised the game with the marriage of the traditional Test cricket to the adventure and guaranteed results of one-day cricket. The two camps jumped into bed together and had the best of both worlds.

In the Packer revolution, Imran was closely associated with Sarfraz Nawaz, the colorful master of swing and soon to produce the most devastating Test bowling spell seen in Melbourne. A bowler who was accused of ball tampering by Northamptonshire teammate Allan Lamb. Sarfraz said Lamb's accusations were unfounded and emphasised English bowlers polished both sides of the ball in the course of the game whereas Sarfraz polished only one side – thus the variation through the air and off the pitch. He taught Imran his tricks, including wearing cotton cricket clothing instead of polyester, taking advantage of natural oils secreted by the body. Brief input by Snow and considerable support from Sarfraz and Garth Le Roux transformed Imran into one of the world's greatest bowlers.

Sarfraz was sufficiently incensed by Lamb's accusations to hit the English skipper with a writ for libel after an article was published in 1992. When it came to his defence Lamb accused his English teammates of deserting him and lacking "guts" in not supporting his claims that Pakistan bowlers tampered with the ball to get their match winning "reverse" swing which confounded the textbooks.

Without their help, the case collapsed, costs in excess of $200,000 being awarded.

Combined with his great batting prowess, Imran became the world's outstanding allrounder. His belief in his destiny made him an inspiring, almost invincible leader. He was fiery and dangerous. One ball he rocketed at batting rabbit Ashley Mallett put the Australian spinner in hospital for a week. "He ducked into one of my bouncers. I took one in the neck myself and I was lucky to escape with bruising.

"With such a battery of great fast bowlers about, it was inevitable batsmen would be the victims. The worst was David Hookes who had his jaw broken in three places by West Indian Andy Roberts. The element of danger appealed to the spectator."

World Series brought the best together and Imran had no doubt the best batsman of them all was Viv Richards, "He was head and shoulders above all the others. Bouncers were wasted on him because he had the reflexes of a gunslinger – the best way to get him out is to bore him."

He also had immense respect for the courage of Ian Chappell. "In WSC he played some amazingly gutsy innings. In the super series final, they had no way of saving the match and Andy Roberts hit him on the hand – breaking it. Yet he refused to come off and stood there batting one-handed for an hour. No wonder he was such a great captain. His team would follow him anywhere because he would lead by example and expected others to reach his standard."

It is Dennis Lillee who he set above all others with an admiration that borders on hero worship. "He was a tremendous bowler and entertainer. I believe he has done more for cricket around the world than anyone else in his decade. He was a trump card and everybody loved him. Dennis Lillee told me his best performances were in WSC because he was amongst the best and had to bowl his best for every moment of play – he fought all the time and never shirked a responsibility. Dennis never gave up and made things happen by sheer will power. With a superb action he was really quick for a long time."

Imran said the World Series tour of Australia 1976-77 made him the cricketer he was.

"It was the most exciting cricket I have ever undertaken and I've never felt an adrenalin flow like that before or after."

On his President's orders, Imran led the 1978 Pakistan team against India for their first meeting in 18 years. They had drawn their previous 13 Tests as Imran took over leadership from the provocative Javed who had changed character with the responsibility of captaincy.

Previous to being appointed to the role aged only 22, Javed had been the spark of the team, a lively and humorous individual who lost his charm with the captaincy. Despite their battles later, Javed respected Imran and made many personal and career sacrifices for him.

Imran never doubted he had made the right decision in accepting the captaincy despite the sad history of past Pakistan captains. None, including Javed, had left the post happy or voluntarily, generally the victims of the spite and self serving egotism of their Pakistani players.

Imran wasn't interested in history. He was a forward thinking individual, supremely confident of his capacities. He soon found he had more enemies at home than abroad. Particularly in the media. "They were standing over me with knives raised," he said.

Javed had plenty of media sympathy. He had been an outstanding performer and came of age much quicker than his more privileged rival. Javed was a man who rose from humble beginnings and limited schooling of Karachi, the wrong side of the track. Imran was from the influential gentry of Lahore and was one of the plotters who would not play under Javed. He could expect no more loyalty and support than he had given Javed.

The first Test against India was drawn but Pakistan played inspired cricket to win the remaining two matches. Imran, determined to prove Pakistan had finally found fire power with the new ball, launched a blazing attack against the pride of Indian batsman. He rained bouncers at the diminutive master bats Sunil Gavaskar and his brother-in-law Gundappa Viswanath. Initially these actions were deemed unworthy of Pakistan against such respected batsmen. Imran ignored the critics – he was a man on a mission. He had a point to prove. First he proved it with the venom of his somewhat erratic and disconcerting bowling, then he delivered the coup de grace with his bat.

It was at Karachi in hostile Miandad territory that Imran's leadership was put to the test. Pakistan needed 164 runs in the last 100 minutes of the final session of the match to win. Imran led the run race and when Pakistan were flagging he hit two 6s and a 4 off a Bedi over to win the match with seven balls to spare. That led to an incredible wave of emotion across Pakistan – the exultation of the crowd at Karachi at the nail-biting conclusion of the Test was the most euphoric sporting scene ever witnessed in Pakistan. And the centre of attraction was Imran Khan – the Star of Pakistan.

Even his worst enemies – the Pakistani press – sang his praises. He was the nearest to Allah a mortal could be.

"Overnight I became a star in Pakistan," said Imran. The magnificent storming win sealed the series and confirmed his leadership qualities. All thought of plotting the demise of Miandad and being "bred" into his position of power demolished with his commanding play and leadership. Now he was their leader, the most popular man in the nation.

This series and the outstanding global success of the Packer inspiration launched Imran's career into the stratosphere. He became a cult figure and found himself the target not only of adoring cricket fans but also adoring women from both the East and West.

He was to be criticised many times for associating himself with the dregs of English society. Life wasters who clutched to his slipstream and gave nothing in return. It seemed he was at home with the pseudo intellectualism of London's social set and far from comfortable with the many and varied lifestyles that cricket embraced. Throughout his career, Imran never socialised with English cricketers and minimised association with his own.

In looking at the wild side of Imran Khan and how he was perceived by the public, keep in mind at no stage did he consume alcoholic drinks, experiment with drugs or smoke. Which might explain why he ignored after the match bonding with teammates.

Whereas some of his associates said he was innately shy, others said he was vain and disdainful, easily bored by the conversational limits of many sporting associates. He thought Ian Botham was a bully and David Gower too slick. He had respect for the knowledge of Sir Garfield Sobers and Australia's Ian Chappell although neither would describe themselves as intellectual giants, they had his respect.

The most charismatic cricket personality since Keith Miller caught the eye of all major international women's magazines. He was the epitome of ideal bachelorhood. That he had the aura of the East around his handsome features and tall lithe, athletic body made him the stand out from all glamor men in sport.

In the romance and matrimonial field he came from a background of arranged marriages in which he was deemed not to have sufficient breeding to marry a young princess who took his eye. His preference for pre-nuptial association seemed to have a definite bias to Western women, one author suggested this was because he would be shot had he trifled with the daughters of proud Pakistani parents. In 1997, a Los Angeles court decreed Imran was the legal father of four-year-old Tyrian Jade White, born out of wedlock to American Sita White, who'd first had a relationship with Imran when he was Pakistan's captain in 1987 before meeting again in 1991.

Imran admitted his parents would be shocked and upset if they learned he consumed alcohol and had intimate relationships – he was emphatic he had not consumed alcoholic beverages.

He had reconciled himself to eventually accepting an arranged marriage.

Despite his university studies, Imran was a palpably poor businessman and even the grandiose project of funding and developing his massive hospital project stalled. He had to fall back to his father and other advisers to salvage the project from his own managerial inadequacies.

The character of Imran Khan came under scrutiny as he passed from puberty to manhood – just when and where that happened nobody is quite certain but he did revel in the disco and social swirl. Pakistanis are fastidious about the moral behaviour of their people and they were soon aware that the young cricket prodigy and social swinger was being exposed to the wild life of London.

It ill behoves a male to make a sensual evaluation of Imran but even the most macho of us can perceive the fellow has considerable animal appeal and would probably appeal to the basic instinct of women. One woman's magazine drooled: "Imran is masculine, athletic, handsome and intelligent. He has the face of a good man. His skin is sufficiently touched by the East to be exotic; his body, unpolluted by alcohol or cigarettes retains its condition. Khan has an Oxford drawl of the English upper class tinged by his native accent... There is a feline ease of movement and an edge of arrogance... Throw in his love of women, his politeness, intellect, outstanding cricket ability, he has a reputation for having an entourage that is the very stuff of gossip columns."

A friend Sarah Crawley describes him as a rare mortal, "No man looks as devastating as Imran," she said.

Top model Marie Helvin agreed. "Everyone falls for him. He has a scent that is very attractive to women."

It is interesting to note that one biographer who pondered the marital prospects of Imran Khan in 1993 doubted he would be married having escaped the net for several decades. He suggested Emma Sergeant had been his one great love but there were certain protocols that forbade the relationship going to the altar. She married somebody else. He made the observation that if Imran did go to the altar the bride would need a massive dowry.

In time he did break the barrier and married an attractive heiress Jemina Goldsmith who adopted the Muslim faith and satisfied the Pakistan nation. Politically and diplomatically, he had transformed a delicate situation into a triumph.

It took Kerry Packer just two years to bring traditional cricket to heel and by 1980 Imran had nine more Tests squeezed into his busy schedule, as well as the 1979 World Cup, when Pakistan was led by Asif Iqbal.

The Cup was a mediocre chapter in Imran's career. He was injured or ill for most of the tour and the Pakistan players returned home to face accusations of debauchery.

For a young nation in terms of international competition Pakistan now found itself being saturated by Test cricket. Imran returned home in broiling heat for a rare Australian tour of Pakistan in 1979-80.

The Australians were beaten 1-0, Imran taking six wickets at 24 and averaging 22.50 with the bat. In the return matches in 1981-82, Javed was captain and the tour a rabble, the Australian dominance not reflected by their 2-1 winning margin. The World Series tournament was not without incident. An adoring Imran fan, 27-year-old Balmain nurse Sheree Mackay, made sure she had bail money when she attended the day-night match between Pakistan and the West Indies at the Sydney Cricket Ground.

Wearing smart Bermuda shorts and form-fitting top she waited until 9.15 pm when Imran was at the wicket smiting mightily. She herself was smitten. At the right moment, with no security guards on the alert, she hurdled the pickets and streaked fully-clothed towards Imran. At the wicket she handed him a rose and bestowed a kiss on his cheek before jogging back to the boundary. Imran followed and placed the rose just over the boundary rope, retrieving it at the end of the game.

The Pakistan Board of Control linked Pakistan's failure in the Tests with the player's unhappiness at Javed's leadership. Subsequently eight players, including Imran and Majid Khan refused to play under Javed against Sri Lanka.

The dispute was eventually resolved after they missed two Tests. They agreed to play in the Third under Miandad on the undertaking Javed would step down as captain for the tour of England.

Imran won that third Test at Lahore almost on his own with bowling stints of 8-58 and 6-58. That performance set him up for the captaincy of the 1982 English tour and again led to accusations that he had undermined his skipper to get the job. He entered the 1982 series against England with three brooding former captains serving under him Miandad, cousin Majid Khan and Wasim Bari. They served him as best they could. His personal support of the spinner Abdul Qadir won him the almost dog-like devotion. "He's my greatest friend and Allah," said Qadir

The English tour drew enormous criticism. His players were accused of squealing against the umpires, appealing to ridiculous extremes with Imran fostering the umpire dissent with his own belligerent approach. Off the field his cousin Majid was trying to have him change his lifestyle to that expected of men of the Muslin faith. The bond between them was irrevocably severed when Majid made a duck in the first Test against

England. He believed he was entitled to see out the series but Imran dropped him from the second Test which Pakistan won.

Although he was recalled and failed in a losing third Test, Majid felt he'd been disgraced by Imran. Their relationship was irrevocably destroyed. Imran conceded he handled the dismissal of his legendary cousin very badly but no amount of remorse could repair the wound. Apparently pride was more "relative" to selection than form as Majid had failed in four hands in a week before being dropped.

With 21 wickets in three Tests at 18.57 and a batting average of 53, *Wisden* named him among its top five Cricketers of the Year. Despite Pakistan losing the series, Imran was headlined everywhere.

London *Daily Mirror* writer Noreen Taylor had a subtle dig at the glamor man when he granted her a private audience in his London hotel room. Her opening two paragraphs said it all: "Imran Khan is worried in case I portray him as a sex symbol. This is possibly why Imran is stretched across his hotel bed wearing only a petulant expression and a pair of tiny, black satin shorts."

An added touch was that he gave Ms. Taylor "a smoulder over the shoulder" as he confided the attentions of the Australian women had left him exhausted when his fellow players were totally relaxed.

Imran was shedding relationships, both male and female, at an alarming rate. His close friend Sarfraz hung up in his ear over another minor altercation and like Majid turned his back on Imran, refusing to talk to him ever again.

His relationship with Javed, his constant rival for Pakistan captaincy, was also strained, as was his friendship with Qadir. However, his popularity and influence at home was so immense that even the Prime Minister Nawaz Sharif was resentful of his popularity.

Perhaps these upheavals were a consequence of his powerful personality. His conviction that he was right – the inner belief he was somebody special – The Chosen One. Certainly he was the Gifted One and the one the Pakistani public rallied behind.

"Why be jealous of Imran?" asked wicketkeeper Wasim Bari. "He will say he was led by God. Imran is God-gifted. He has worked hard and is fair."

Imran had a fixation about cricket and on getting results. He was emphatic that his team attack at all times.

It seems remarkable Imran played in 10 Test series before scoring his first Test century against the West Indies in 1981. His second Test century came two years later.

In 1983, he took 10 wickets and scored 117 against India – a batting-bowling feat only Ian Botham had accomplished. His 8-60 against the Indians was a Pakistani record.

Always volatile, he blew up storms wherever he played –1983 was a year of cyclones for the fiery Pakistani. Australian skipper Kim Hughes clashed with Imran during a one-day international at the SCG.

Imran was furious when his sparring mate Javed Miandad was given run out at 67; he thought it was too close to call. He also claimed he was not out when Australian umpires raised the finger against him at the vital stage of the decisive fifth Test of an earlier tour. Hughes accused him of having a blinkered view highlighting a number of dubious decisions given against Australia throughout past series.

Later in the same year Imran was reprimanded while playing for Sussex. The umpires accused him of continually abusing opposition players after being hit on the chest by a short-pitched ball. He apologised.

In the same week the Pakistan Cricket Board selection committee quit in protest when Imran was named captain of the team to tour Australia in 1983-84. The committee opposed his appointment because of a stress fracture of the shin which was threatening his career. It was little wonder he'd broken down. He'd played in 20 Tests from 1981-83; opposing Australia, West Indies, Sri Lanka, England and India. By not being able to bowl for 12 months, he was once again able to devote himself to his batting.

He temporarily lost the captaincy to Zaheer Abbas after he missed the early part of the Australian tour. There was great controversy over the captaincy with Imran on the outer with the Pakistan Cricket Control Board. Again political influences moved in on Imran's behalf. The dictatorial Pakistan president Air Marshall Nur Khan was very hands on with his cricket ambassadors. He sacked the Board and reinstated Imran as captain. It didn't save the series which was won by Australia.

Imran played the final two Tests, in the first of these scoring heavily with 83 and 72 not out to hold Australia to a draw. They lost the final Test and then the one-day series. Back in Pakistan, the new-look Board was dismissed and Zaheer reinstated!

Having lost the series Imran was told by medical men his career was over. It wasn't until October 1984 that he put his leg to the test and medical men pronounced him cured.

He rehabilitated by playing a season with New South Wales, the team winning the one-day series and the Shield. Imran vowed to quit the game at his peak and not fall victim to selectors as had been the fate of a number of earlier Pakistani greats. "I had promised myself I would leave cricket when I was still at the peak of my form and still enjoying the game. Above all I vowed that I would never be at the mercy of the selectors, or face the prospect of being kicked out in an undignified way like so many Pakistani greats."

He made his return to Test cricket after a two year absence with quality performances in a short series against Sri Lanka in Pakistan and found himself back as captain when the much-maligned Javed stepped down as captain Imran led the return tour of Sri Lanka which was as bitchy and unpleasant a series that could be imagined. He scrambled out with a draw and considerable shame. His team then played a one day series for the Asia Cup which it lost.

The first Test had Pakistan players yelling at Sri Lanka's Arjuna Ranatunga that he was a "cheat" which led to the umpires taking the players from the field. His players were in trouble for arguing with the umpires who they also claimed were cheating. Javed had an explosive flare-up with a spectator after a rock was thrown at him in the second Test. Imran wanted to call the series off. The manager Salim Asghar Mian took a copy of *Wisden* onto the ground to show the umpires they didn't understand the rules. It was bordering on war and there was an ominous edge of menace in the crowd feeling. General Zia intervened and ordered the tour to continue. Tormented by the death of his mother, the unrest in his ranks, the hatred of the opposition and seeking his purpose in life, Imran did not enjoy the tour.

His mother's death from cancer filled his life and all his thoughts. It was a harsh and lingering passing that seared the soul of her son. From the time the dread disease had her in its grip, he had vowed he would devote his life to the fight of cancer. It inspired him to conceive, promote and generate the funds to build the Shaukat Khanum Memorial Hospital in Lahore, a shrine to his mother's memory.

Imran was profoundly affected and influenced by his inability to do anything to reverse the effects of the dread disease and save his mother. It was with the Shaukat Khanum Memorial Hospital that he found perspective and purpose. On the cricket field he could turn adversity into triumph by his own personal dynamism. He did the impossible and his devout following in Pakistan saw him as a symbol and force who could reverse their catastrophes.

A TIME TO DIE

Imran's people are great believers in prophesies dispensed by mystics –
Imran describes them as guides to destiny. Which helps explain why he
turned down several political appointments offered to him after a mystic
warned him if he entered the political scene he would be assassinated.

"I'll decide when I am ready to die," he said.

One assumes he decided it was time to die in 1996 when he entered
politics.

Every dollar he earned was donated to the appeal. He contributed more than
$500,000 of his own earnings but he needed millions. He knew he couldn't build this
hospital on his own. This had to be the ultimate team effort. He dedicated himself to the
project. He also had to dedicate himself to recovering his fitness. His sporting prowess
would play a major role in getting the hospital built and if he could not play again, the
dream would fail.

General Zia organised subsidies to cover the medical costs of Imran's treatment and
he went into plaster for six months. Fortunately the operation was a success and his
rehabilitation put him back in the game as good as ever.

Pakistan had the ultimate in cricket box office – Javed and Imran were a superb
combination and lifted Pakistan to the top of the cricket world. Their on-going feud
made their cricket even more compelling, particularly as the captaincy kept flying from
one to the other throughout a decade of turmoil.

Imran was a more popular leader than Javed yet he also had his critics and enemies.
The bitterness between the factions of Lahore and Karachi dominated the media and
public thinking. Imran was accused of playing favorites giving his Lahorite friend Qadir
priority over Karachi's Iqbal Qasim.

Qasim Omar, a leading batsman who distrusted Imran described him in the English
People publication as "a negative, arrogant, spiteful leader who picks on players for no
reason."

Great scandal erupted in the English media as Pakistan players went on the attack
against their skipper. He was accused of actions totally unacceptable to Pakistan
culture of drug taking and womanising. Although he denied the charges they made
huge headlines.

Omar caused a sensation when he wrote to the Pakistan Board claiming Imran
made him carry drugs for him inside his batting gloves. President Zia imposed a seven
year playing ban on Oman as a reprisal. Omar never played for Pakistan again. In the
same publication, another frontline Pakistani Younis Ahmed accused Imran of openly
smoking pot and taking girls to his room while on tour. Younis had also played for
Pakistan for the last time. Younis claimed Imran had used Vaseline, a bottle top and a
screwdriver to roughen the ball.

In time these scandals died away as Pakistan and the cricketing world accepted the
smear was scandal sheet rubbish. Yet the two players had given the media the story at
great personal cost.

Imran was thirsting for the clash with the Windies on Pakistan soil. He regarded them
as the world power and to beat them was to put Pakistan at the top of the world. To make
the triumph complete, he wanted international umpires for no other reason than to
dispel all doubt about the integrity of the series. This time he was backed by a dynamic
20-year-old paceman, Wasim Akram who he believed was destined to replace him as the
world's best allrounder. With considerable input from Qadir, Pakistan won the first Test
at Faisalabad, despite a frightening barrage by the Windies. Imran was struck by a fierce
bumper on the first day – he knew it needed medical attention but the Pakis had

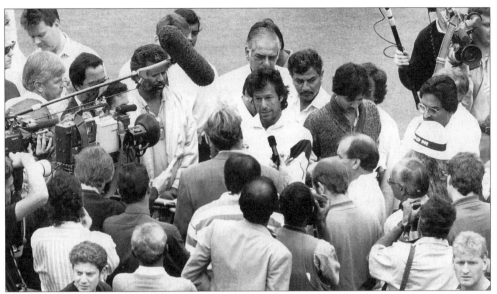

Hail the World Cup heroes: Imran went on the political trail just minutes after leading Pakistan to the 1992 World Cup triumph.

already lost five wickets for few runs. If he left for treatment the innings would fold. He stayed on and made a defiant 61 of a total of 159. Only then would he have stitches inserted in his hand. Salim Malik had his arm broken but batted in a cast.

With Akram taking 6-91, the Windies' first innings lead was restricted to less than 100. Qadir mesmerised them in the second, the Windies plummeting to 53 all out – a record low.

A great series followed. The Windies won the second Test in Lahore, despite Imran's 5-59, the Third at Karachi was drawn, Imran taking 5-11 and 6-46 and making a gutsy 11 not out at the close when bad light ended the drama.

He hadn't won the series but sharing the title was a satisfying outcome.

Then came an astounding series against India with the two countries trembling on the brink of hostilities on their border. He led his team to victory in the Test series 1-0 and then enjoyed a 5-1 slaughter in the one-dayers. There was very nearly open warfare on the cricket pitch for the third Test of the series when Imran noted sawdust on the pitch. He accused India of tampering with the wicket, trying to dry it out contravening the rules. Indian groundsmen claimed the sawdust had been blown there by the wind. Imran said his players would not bat on the wicket and the umpires abandoned play for the day. Friction built as the series hung in the balance for the fourth Test. His outfielders were pelted with rocks large enough to kill. He took his players from the field and when they returned, six of the outfield fieldsmen wore helmets on Imran's order. The gesture was treated as Imran's macabre sense of humor. He kept the Pakistan spirits high and led them to victory in the decisive fifth Test at Bangalore.

Although Imran gave his friend Qadir precedence in his teams over Qasim, he preferred Qasim in this crucial game. In the final innings Sunil Gavaskar looked likely to take the game away from Pakistan yet Imran bowled Qasim unchanged throughout, Qasim taking nine wickets in the match to spearhead a 16 run win which clinched the series. Yet he never played under Imran's leadership again which intensified the friction between Lahore and Karachi. But not right there and then – with the man from Karachi and the Lion of Lahore national heroes, 200,000 delirious fans turned out to welcome their team home to Lahore.

Nawaz Sharif who was soon to become Prime Minister was angered that the masses not only totally ignored his presence, but knocked him down and battered him in their eagerness to greet Imran Khan.

Pakistan, led by Javed, won the Test series against England the following year. He took 21 wickets at 21.67 and averaged 47.75. Whereas the day would come when some English media would scream that Imran was a self-confessed cheat there was considerable evidence to the contrary during the English tour. He severely censured his own wicketkeeper for falsely claiming a catch off Ian Botham during the third Test at Headingley. Salim Yousuf grassed an edge by Botham but in the blink of an eye snapped it up again and appealed. Botham was livid as he gesticulated and swore at the 'keeper.

Imran cancelled the appeal and rebuked the 'keeper but later criticised Botham for his reaction. "If people start using expletives on the pitch it shows a deficiency."

Imran had been eyeing retirement for some time and felt he could quit on a winning note with the 1987 World Cup. His plan was brought undone at Lahore when Australia unexpectedly won the semi-final.

Imran promptly retired and Miandad also quit as captain in the face of team unrest. Without the leadership of the dynamic duo the nation's cricket future looked bleak.

If Imran thought he could quietly retire to pursue his personal ambitions his fanatical followers soon disabused him of such notions. The nation demanded his return. "People demonstrated outside my house, some threatened a hunger strike, my mailbag increased to more than 100 letters a day, the phone never stopped ringing," he said. "I avoided crowded places after being warned I would be mobbed by people demanding my return to cricket.

"Most pressure came from the boys in the Pakistan team – especially the young ones. They pleaded with me to take them to the West Indies... I never realised how much personal pressure I was going to face."

There was no such pressure for Javed to review his resignation as skipper. He had lost the support of many of his players. They were so frustrated by his captaincy and style that they had threatened to withdraw from the West Indies tour. Imran felt he owed the players support because of the way had supported him "through thick and thin".

While the Pakistani nation staged protests and students went on hunger strikes, the ultimate persuasion came from Pakistan's President Zia. He summoned Imran and the players to a banquet on January 18, 1988 and told Imran in front of the players that he must return to cricket for the good of the nation. "One has to rise above the self," said General Zia when Imran told him he wanted to finish on a high. His protests were brushed aside and he announced his return to international cricket. Imran's family and friends advised him against the return, cautioning him that Pakistanis were a volatile and emotional people. If he lost the West Indies tour he would lose his standing in the community.

In return for his return to cricket general Zia offered Imran a cabinet post in his government – he declined, no doubt recalling the clairvoyant's prediction he would be assassinated if he entered the political scene.

No visiting team had won in the West Indies since 1973, very few had lost with honor, most visitors being totally humiliated by the venom of the bowlers and the brilliance of the batting. The last visiting team to the Carribean had been England and they were shattered 5-0.

"All my career I had taken risks. Playing it safe with no risks taken was not for me. If I could win this series on their soil I would have established Pakistan as the No.1 cricket power in the world," said Imran.

He offered a challenge to the Windies. "We're coming to get you!" roared the Lion of Lahore... and the West Indies licked their lips at the challenge. And get them he did. In the first Test at Guyana, although almost crippled by an infected toe, Imran ripped through the West Indies taking 7-80 and 4-41. The Windies had a four man pace attack and Imran warned his batsman than any man backing away from the short ball would be sent home. Javed set the example and belted his first ever century against the Windies pace attack and Pakistan's 435 gave them a first innings lead of 143. Imran, an inspired man of the match, led Pakistan to a stirring win.

The second Test at Port-of-Spain saw him play with a strained thigh and the toe condition but they whipped the Windies out for 174. A great battle was drawn with Pakistan finishing just 31 runs short of victory when time ran out. Now they need only draw the final Test in Barbados. They set the Windies 266 for the final innings and finally it was down to two wickets remaining and the Indies needing 59. Gutsy batting won the day and the series was drawn. In the tension of the finish Qadir struck a West Indies spectator and had to settle the damages out of court.

The Miandad-Imran Khan rollercoaster continued with the baton of captaincy passing from one to the other in a never ending two man relay. Miandad was ever reluctant to captain when confronted by likely defeat such as a tour of the West Indies and he was ever stridently opposed to Imran's desire to retire. Pakistan needed Imran and that was Javed's concern. What's more their rivalry brought the best out of them. Imran took so much advice from Javed in the fury of battle that nobody was ever quite certain who was the leader. The might of Imran's captaincy came from his prowess – he led by example. He stood with Keith Miller and Sir Garfield Sobers as the greatest allrounders the game had produced.

After a tour of New Zealand, Imran embarked on his last round of Test engagements in Pakistan and Australia. Pakistan hosted three tours from 1989-92: India, West Indies and Sri Lanka. His other tours were in Australia in 1989 and 1992 for the World Cup. He was burning with zeal to perform in these farewell encounters but it was no longer cricket ambition that drove him. He knew the success of his hospital building project hinged on his and Pakistan's success. The 1992 tour of Australia was the ultimate crusade and crowning triumph of his career but in many ways it was his ultimate blunder in team diplomacy.

Imran again quit after the Australian tour of 1989-90 when he performed brilliantly in his nation's narrow loss. But the hospital cash crisis forced another comeback in 1991 for the series against West Indies and Sri Lanka leading up to the 1992 World Cup series in Australia.

Pakistan and Australia were locked in battle for the right to challenge the West Indies for the title of world's No.1. Having failed to beat Australia, Imran believed beating the Windies would be an alternative path to world leadership. He refused to take part in a tour of New Zealand where Miandad took over and Pakistan were again accused of ball tampering and cheating after Waqar Younis took 29 wickets in three Tests. Javed willingly stepped down for Imran to captain the side against the Windies.

The cheating controversy was raging across the world and for the third successive series, the result was drawn. It was an arm wrestle they seemed unable to end but he derived some consolation from winning the one-day series although his team had to weather another storm as Desmond Haynes accused Pakistan of tampering with the ball. The branding of Pakistan as a nation of cheats had Imran on the verge of retirement – only his obsession to fund the hospital kept him going.

Imran had made a solemn vow that he would fight the cancer that took his mother from him. The best way to accomplish this was to build a significant hospital for the research and treatment of cancer victims. A hospital for the poor not the rich.

This gave added impetus to his drive to win the 1992 World Cup – the most spectacular of all cricket competitions with nine nations in contention for the title. To win would provide an incredible launching pad to fulfil his dream. He was supremely confident and spent months resurrecting his bowling arm and style to his glory days. He persuaded Pakistan authorities to arrive in Australia a month before the Cup to get everything just right.

Then on the eve of the first Cup match against the West Indies he ricked his shoulder and was unable to play. The Pakistanis lost by nine wickets. Specialists warned him his cause was hopeless; if he played, the injury would only get worse. They had to win the next round or they were out of the Cup. He played but didn't bat or bowl, fortunately the opposition was Zimbabwe and they won easily. As a last resort he subjected his shoulder and its stress tears to electrolysis and magnetic currents. It was agony but it enabled him to roll his arm over and if he bowled his 10 overs without a spell he could survive, just.

He was treated constantly throughout the opening series of eight matches. To make the finals they had to fly to New Zealand and beat the unbeaten Kiwis. Inspired captaincy and naked aggression won through and they were into the second round with just four wins from eight games.

New Zealand as top team met Pakistan as worst qualifier. And this time the Kiwis rattled on 7-262 to have the game by the throat, Martin Crowe smashing a superb 91. Imran made 44 but after he fell Pakistan needed 123 from 15 overs to make the final. Javed smashed 60 from 37 balls and with the help of Moin Khan won the match to keep Imran's dream alive.

"I knew God was on our side," said Imran. God knows he was lucky he also had Javed on his side. Against all odds they were in the final against England.

There were more than 87,000 spectators at the MCG for the final, the opening of the Great Southern Grandstand having preceded the game.

Imran won the toss and batted. Pakistan struggled for 2-113 from 35 overs and were in danger until Imran and Javed took over with 136 coming from the next 16 overs, Imran making a compelling 72. With a batting burst from Wasim Akram, Pakistan finished at 6-249. Ian Botham was the bogeyman for Pakistan and the bogeyman was removed with one ball from Akram and the great bowler brought Pakistan home by 22 runs. The game was telecast to a billion viewers and they saw the massive crowd erupt into a frenzy when Imran bowled Richard Illingworth to seal the win.

The emotional outpouring made the setting for Imran's victory address to those billion viewers. He had led Pakistan to the World Cup triumph and immediately estranged himself from his players. As he stepped onto the victory dais to accept the cup, the cheque and the accolades of the international cricket world, Imran overlooked the traditional words of praise for his team's great effort. They had lifted their nation to this, their proudest moment in international cricket. Their skipper addressed several hundred million viewers around the world. Instead of acclaiming his players he devoured the moment for his own purposes and used this international stage for an extraordinary free commercial. Totally dismissive of his team's stunning success he used the precious minutes of satellite television to beg alms. He flogged the appeal to set up the Shaukat Khanum Memorial Hospital in Lahore. A worthy cause but there is a time and a place for everything.

Many of his players were enraged. Minutes earlier they had visions of a grateful Pakistani nation showering them with gifts that would secure their future. In a few short minutes Imran had redirected all that generosity towards his hospital. Bundles of money were left at Australian hotel reception desks obviously intended for Imran's appeal – but try and tell the Pakistan cricketers this was the case.

There was a time the money-conscious Javed Miandad collected $ US100,000 for hitting six off the last ball to win a one day match for Pakistan. Although his teammates had played their part, Javed, declined to share the money. Imran persuaded the players to cop it sweet. Their turn would come. They thought the World Cup was their chance for wealth. Instead much of the flood of donations went to the Imran Appeal. Imran had failed to understand his teammates came from impoverished backgrounds. The incensed players demanded their Board reinstate Javed as captain for the tour of England.

In reality the players had little cause for complaint. Imran inspired and united them for that triumph and eventually, each player received an estimated $A678,000 from Government and non-Government sources. Each player was also given a prime block of land; a far cry from those early Imran days when he received the equivalent of $A5 (after fines) for a tour of England and offered $A120 for a tour of New Zealand.

The pain in his shoulder was now matched by the pain in his heart. The aggravation was the final straw. Imran withdrew from the tour of England and announced his retirement – this time there was no General Zia to convince him to put Pakistan above "self."

Javed was back at the helm but soon pleading with Imran to take charge again, even if it was as team manager. He declined.

Imran now acknowledged his cancer crusade was more important to him than cricket. He would raise more than $25 million by the end of 1995. He accepted his World Cup speech was flawed in its failure to acknowledge the importance of the sporting feat and the performance of the Pakistan players but he was jubilant he had the stage that made it certain the hospital would be completed. That was the important issue.

He had captained Pakistan in 48 Tests for 26 drawn, 14 wins and eight losses. He averaged 52.34 batting and took 187 wickets at 20.26. It says something of his competitive juices that in the 40 Tests he was not captain he averaged 25.44 and took 175 wickets at 25.53. He made 3807 Test runs at 37.69 including six centuries and took 362 wickets at 22.81, pushing him to the forefront of the greatest of all-rounders.

Thus irrevocably retired he now devoted his energies to the foundation of the cancer hospital which was to win him worldwide publicity and incredible acclaim. Imran now pursued his destiny with a religious fervor. He studied the Koran, prayed devoutly every day and interpolated quotations from the Koran into his conversations. In following the teachings of the Koran he satisfied his basic needs and gave away surplus money to worthy causes – in this case, his mother's hospital.

The hospital opened in 1995 and Imran decided to further consolidate the image of a statesman by putting aside his playboy lifestyle to marry English heiress Jemima Goldsmith.

Retirement from cricket did not mean he had retired from notoriety and controversy. The international media indulged itself in an orgy of recrimination of Pakistan's determination to win regardless of honor and ethic. Imran in retirement and steeped in fund raising tours found himself defending his countrymen at the same time. Now the feud between Javed and Imran deepened as the unsettled Javed accused Imran of using his influence of having him sacked first as captain and then as a player.

Imran Khan THE MAN & HIS RECORD

Born: November 25, 1952

Teams: Pakistani International Airlines, Dawood Club, Oxford University, Worcestershire, Sussex, New South Wales & Pakistan

First-class debut: 1969

First-class record: Matches 382. Batting — Runs 17771, Average 36.79, Highest score, 100s 30, 50s 92. Bowling — Wickets 1287, Average 22.32, Best bowling 8-34, Five wickets in an Innings 70, Ten wickets in a Match 13. Fielding — Catches 117.

Test debut: 1971

Test record: Matches 88. Batting — Runs 3807, Average 37.69, Highest score 136, 100s 6, 50s 18. Bowling — Wickets 362, Average 22.81, Best bowling 8-58, Five wickets in an Innings 23, Ten wickets in a Match 6. Fielding — Catches 28.

One day international debut: 1974

One day international record: Matches 175. Batting — Runs 3709, Average 33.41, Highest score 102 not out, 100s 1, 50s 19. Bowling — Wickets 182, Average 26.62, Best bowling 6-14, Five wickets in an Innings 1. Fielding — Catches 37. Captaincy — 139 matches for 75 wins, 59 losses and one tie. Four games were abandoned.

Tours: Australia 1976-77, 1978-79, 1981-82, 1983-84; England 1971, 1974, 1982, 1987; New Zealand 1978-79; India 1979-80, 1986-87; Sri Lanka 1985-86; West Indies 1976-77, 1988. Also toured Australia with the WSC World XI in 1977-78 and 1978-79.

Imran Khan's Test record series by series:

BATTING & FIELDING

Season	Opponent	Mt	Inns	No	HS	Runs	Ave	100s	50s	Ct.
1971	England (a)	1	1	0	5	5	5.00	-	-	1
1974	England (a)	3	6	1	31	92	18.40	-	-	2
1976-77	New Zealand (h)	3	4	1	59	105	35.00	-	1	1
	Australia (a)	3	5	0	48	86	17.20	-	-	2
	West Indies (a)	5	10	0	47	215	21.50	-	-	2
1978-79	India (h)	3	4	2	32	104	52.00	-	-	-
	New Zealand (a)	2	3	1	33	63	31.50	-	-	-
	Australia (a)	2	4	0	33	90	22.50	-	-	1
1979-80	India (a)	5	8	1	34	154	22.00	-	-	-
	Australia (h)	2	2	0	56	65	32.50	-	1	-
1980-81	West Indies (h)	4	7	0	123	204	29.14	1	-	-
1981-82	Australia (a)	3	5	1	70*	108	27.00	-	1	1
	Sri Lanka (h)	1	1	0	39	39	39.00	-	-	1
1982	England (a)	3	5	1	67*	212	53.00	-	2	-
1982-83	Australia (a)	3	3	2	39*	64	64.00	-	-	1
	India (h)	6	5	1	117	247	61.75	1	-	4
1983-84	Australia (a)	2	4	1	83	170	56.67	-	2	-
1985-86	Sri Lanka (h)	3	2	0	63	69	34.50	-	1	-
	Sri Lanka (a)	3	4	0	33	48	12.00	-	-	4
1986-87	West Indies (h)	3	6	2	61	115	28.75	-	1	1
	India (a)	5	7	2	135*	324	64.80	1	2	-
1987	England (a)	5	5	1	118	191	47.75	1	-	3
1988	West Indies (a)	3	5	1	43*	90	22.50	-	-	1
1988-89	New Zealand (a)	2	2	1	71	140	140.00	-	2	-
1989-90	India (h)	4	5	2	109*	262	87.33	1	1	3
	Australia (a)	3	5	1	136	279	69.75	1	1	-
1990	West Indies (h)	3	5	2	73*	151	50.33	-	2	-
1991-92	Sri Lanka (h)	3	3	1	93*	115	57.50	-	1	-
Totals		88	126	25	136	3807	37.69	6	18	28

BOWLING

Season	Opponent	Mts	Balls		Mds	Runs	Wicks	Ave	BB	5wI	10wM
1971	England (a)	1	168	9	55	0	0-19	-	-	-	-
1974	England (a)	3	672	26	258	5	52.60	2-48	-	-	-
1976-77	New Zealand (h)	3	908	15	421	14	30.07	4-59	-	-	-
	Australia (a)	3	964	13	519	18	28.83	6-63	3	1	-
	West Indies (a)	5	1417	54	790	25	31.60	6-90	1	-	-
1978-79	India (h)	3	973	42	441	14	31.50	4-54	-	-	-
	New Zealand (a)	2	663	17	255	10	25.50	5-106	1	-	-
	Australia (a)	2	752	23	285	7	40.71	4-26	-	-	-
1979-80	India (a)	5	914	38	365	19	19.21	5-63	2	--	-
	Australia (h)	2	336	14	144	6	24.00	2-28	-	--	-
1980-81	West Indies (h)	4	540	13	236	10	23.60	5-62	1	--	-
1981-82	Australia (a)	3	902	38	312	16	19.50	4-66	-	--	-
	Sri Lanka (h)	1	314	11	116	14	8.29	8-58	2	1-	-
1982	England (a)	3	1069	48	390	21	18.57	7-52	2	--	-
1982-83	Australia (h)	3	620	35	171	13	13.15	4-35	-	--	-
	India (h)	6	1339	69	558	40	13.95	8-60	4	2-	-
1983-84	Australia (a)	2	-	-	-	-	-	-	-		
1985-86	Sri Lanka (h)	3	724	37	271	17	15.94	5-40	1	--	-
	Sri Lanka (a)	3	696	27	270	15	18.00	4-69	-	--	-
1986-87	West Indies (h)	3	638	23	199	18	11.06	6-46	2	--	-
	India (h)	5	739	21	392	8	49.00	2-28	-	--	-
1987	England (a)	5	1010	33	453	21	21.67	7-40	2	1-	-
1988	West Indies (a)	3	779	16	416	23	18.09	7-80	2	1-	-
1988-89	New Zealand (a)	2	620	35	198	7	28.28	3-34	-	--	-
1989-90	India (h)	4	1113	47	504	13	38.78	4-45	-	--	-
	Australia (a)	3	420	16	167	4	41.75	2-53	-	--	-
1990	West Indies (h)	3	114	5	54	4	13.50	2-22	-	--	-
1991-92	Sri Lanka (h)	3	54	1	16	0	-	0-16	-	--	-
Totals		88	19458	728	8258	362	22.81	8-58	23	6	-

COUNTRY BY COUNTRY RECORD
BATTING & FIELDING

Country	Mt	Inns	No	HS	Runs	Ave	100s	50s	Ct.
v Australia	18	28	5	136	862	37.47	1	5	5
v England	12	17	3	118	500	35.71	1	2	6
v India	23	29	8	135*	1091	51.95	3	3	7
v New Zealand	7	9	3	71	308	51.33	-	3	1
v Sri Lanka	10	10	1	93*	271	22.29	-	2	5
v West Indies	18	33	5	123	775	27.67	1	3	4

v HOME & ABROAD

	Mt	Inns	No	HS	Runs	Ave	100s	50s	Ct.
Tests at home	38	47	13	123	1540	45.29	3	7	11
Tests abroad	50	79	12	136	2267	33.83	3	11	17

BOWLING

Country	Mts	Balls	Mds	Runs	Wicks	Ave	BB	5wI	10wM
v Australia	18	3994	141	1598	64	24.96	6-63	3	1
v England	12	2919	116	1158	47	24.64	7-40	4	1
v India	23	5078	217	2260	94	24.04	8-60	6	2
v New Zealand	7	2191	67	874	31	28.19	5-106	1	-
v Sri Lanka	10	1788	76	673	46	14.63	8-58	3	1
v West Indies	18	3488	111	1695	80	21.18	7-80	6	1

HOME & ABROAD

	Mts	Balls	Mds	Runs	Wicks	Ave	BB	5wI	10wM
Tests at home	38	7673	312	3131	163	19.20	8-58	10	3
Tests abroad	50	11214	416	5127	199	25.76	7-40	13	3

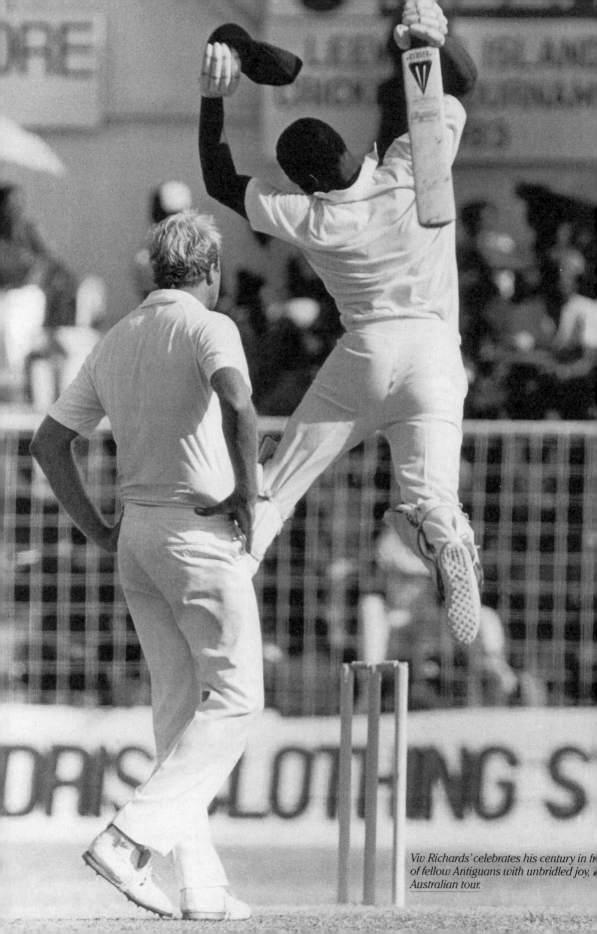

Viv Richards' celebrates his century in fr[ont] of fellow Antiguans with unbridled joy, [during the] Australian tour.

THE MASTER BLASTER

Richards immediately transferred his attack to Border,
inviting him around the back of the SCG stand at stumps.

Vivian Richards would have been in his element in the Wild, Wild West; a
six-shooter on either hip; those chilling eyes, menacing black pinpoints,
flashing white teeth, the cocky killer smile. Viv Vicious is ready for the
roll of the dice. The most intimidating bat slinger a man could face.

T HEY CALLED HIM "The Master Blaster" because he was batting's Top Gun. He was
also "King Viv" and "Smokin' Joe." He liked the homage attached to those tags.
Yet Viv Richards insisted he hated pseudonyms. Once, when he was called to the
victory dais introduced only as, "The greatest batsman on earth," he refused to budge.

"My name is Vivian Richards – that is who I am and who I want to be remembered
as," he told the host.

"Ladies and gentlemen – I give you the greatest batsman on earth: VIVIAN
RICHARDS! ..." and Richards duly stepped on to the stage to receive his due.

Richards is a proud man, very proud. He rankled at being dubbed "The Black
Bradman," not because of the color implication, but because he wore the mantle of no
other man – Don Bradman included.

In the sheltering palms of the Caribbean they admire and respect the great deeds of
Sir Donald Bradman – so much so that many call him "The White Richards." There is
no rancour or racism involved. The West Indies have a vastly different priority to most
other cricket connoisseurs. They rate two of their own ahead of the magnificent Don: Viv
Richards and Sir Garfield Sobers.

At some time or other both have been referred to as *Black* Bradmans but they were unique. Yet Viv Richards, like India's run machine Sunil Gavaskar, lived in the shadow of Bradman, both in their time being described acrimoniously as colored versions of the great man. What was intended as the ultimate compliment was in fact condescending and unwittingly racist.

Richards was an entirely different performer to any other cricketer. He exuded arrogance, confidence, menace and pride. He had the swagger of a prize fighter who knows he is indomitable. This was a man who thrived on challenge. Unlike other ego-driven super players who offered only lip service to lesser levels of cricket in return for massive salaries, Viv Richards gave it his all.

When he was sacked from county side Somerset he took the first professional offer that came his way – from Rishton in the Lancashire League – for chicken feed at a time he refused a million to play in South Africa. Yet he played for Rishton and gave it as much as he would have given had they been the West Indian Test team.

It didn't worry him that he played on poorly prepared, almost makeshift wickets against local butchers, plasterers, plumbers and like, snatching a few hours off to play against the world champion. The ball was hurled with furious intensity and according to what piece of wicket it struck the ball shot along the ground or flew at a dangerous tangent, threatening to remove his head if ever his reflexes deserted him. The 3000 residents of Rishton loved him and he them.

But Richards was not the casual, unruffled and nonchalant being that his on-field demeanour generated. At times the facade cracked, he threatened and intimidated sports writers, he allowed his players to bombard lower-order batsmen with bouncers and insults of cowardice, he abused Australia's coach and leading batsmen, he invited its captain behind the grandstand... he even labelled fellow West Indians as Judas players and set out to destroy opponents who had belittled him.

He was accused of being more racist than the white racists he hated. He created a riot, copped two year's suspension and then played through and ran away from more riots. His playing life was a cauldron of great cricket and passionate incidents. There was never a dull moment when Viv was around.

Like the time he abused Steve Rixon, Australia's wicketkeeper for daring appeal a bat-pad catch from Murray Bennett's bowling at the Sydney Cricket Ground in 1985. Richards, who had been frustrated by Bennett's tight spell, told Rixon it was a ridiculous appeal, only to be told that he couldn't bat and umpire the game as well. Rixon would appeal whenever and as often as he pleased.

The two engaged in a good old-fashioned barney, neither prepared to back down. Enter Allan Border, Australia's newly-appointed skipper, who told Richards to stop whingeing and get on with the game.

Richards immediately transferred his attack to Border, inviting around the back of the SCG stand at stumps for a round or two; and he wasn't talking a friendly sherbet. All three players were reported, but no action taken, the administrators ruling that the altercation be left on the field.

Richards under pressure behaved badly. Fortunately the likeable and genius was much more often on display than his darker side. History remembers him as a true great, perhaps the greatest entertainer the game has produced.

Isaac Vivian Alexander Richards was born into a middle-class Antinguan family at St. John's on March 7, 1952. He could always play cricket be it on the Caribbean beaches or the traditional ground. He captained the school team and when he played his initial first-class game in a Leeward Islands cricket tournament in 1968 he started a riot that drew a two year ban from cricket – two wasted years that delayed his advance.

He admits he did the wrong thing, disputed an umpire's decision when given out caught off his pads for a duck. The umpire was in error but the first rule of cricket is that you abide by the umpire's decision. Richards didn't and elected to put on a tantrum for his home crowd. He glared, stood his ground, stamped his foot and banged the turf with his bat. Steam was gushing from his ears when he finally stomped to the exit gate. His petulance and anger caught fire in the crowd who had rolled up in their thousands to see the exciting local boy's maiden match. The crowd reaction was so violent and threatening the umpires left the field. The game was going to have to be called off unless officialdom backed down.

After a conference and the passing of almost two hours Richards was told by authorities the umpire had been over-ruled. He was told him to go back and finish his innings. The crowd having won the backdown then decided they were wrong. The mood swung against the youngster. He was ill at ease and immediately out for a duck. No tantrum this time as he trudged back to the pickets.

When he made a duck in the second innings he claimed a record surely unique of three ducks in the same match! The powers to be wasted no time holding an inquiry and banning young Richards from all cricket for two years. The feeling was so high in his own community that he became an object of abuse which forced him into seclusion. He saw out his two year ban boxing, playing soccer and basketball.

He also realised there was no gain in allowing his temperament to rule commonsense. He had a fiery temperament and his own fierce beliefs in the quality of the African ancestry in his West Indies breeding. He was prone to dismiss the considerable Indian influence. He now knew better than to allow his emotions to take charge of him again. It could end his career.

He was back to play for Leewards in 1972. The teenager displayed great flair but not great durability although he did spank a quality 82 against the visiting New Zealanders. His first 19 first-class matches in the West Indies from 1972-74 revealed considerable promise but no centuries – there were seven half centuries in 35 hands. That wasn't surprising as the nature of the beast was to launch aggressive assaults on the front foot. He was easy prey to some of the cagey veterans of West Indies cricket until he became more worldly and shot selective. He came with a rush in the finish with 42 and 52 not out against the touring MCC.

As 18-year-olds, he and pace prospect Andy Roberts had been sent to England for cricket schooling and the experience vastly improved his technique. He drilled himself to attack on the front foot at every opportunity whereas the hard surfaced West Indian wickets had transformed most of the Caribbean batsmen into back foot stroke players.

He won his cap to play county cricket with Somerset in 1974 where he teamed up with a young Ian Botham. He made a strong impression in one-day fixtures winning man-of-the-match honors with 81 not out on debut against Glamorgan. He was again man-of-the-match next-up with 71 against Gloucestershire.

His inaugural first-class appearance for Somerset produced just seven runs against India, but by the fourth game he had found his feet and clouted 74 against Sussex. The next match saw him finally reach his maiden first-class century when he crafted a polished 102 against Gloucestershire.

He was named in the West Indies touring side of India in the same year and knocked up 102 in his first hand against North Zone at Pune.

His Test debut, aged 22, in India was less than impressive with innings of four and three. "I was distraught and immediately decided I was not up to the Test level," he said.

Clive Lloyd disagreed. He was given another chance and this time settled in determinedly before scoring a punishing 192 not out in the second Test in Delhi. Despair turned to jubilation as he tasted success and victory but there was still more drama ahead.

After winning the first two Tests the West Indies lost the next two and were in danger of forfeiting a series in India for the first time, only to win the deciding fifth Test which went into a sixth day after riots on the second afternoon.

Then followed two draws in the two-Test series in Pakistan which left Richards pondering the safety of Test cricket. In the second Test at Karachi, the exuberant Pakistani fans invaded the pitch to congratulate local hero Wasim Raja on a century. They were followed by the police on a baton charge. The West Indies players had seen it all before and bolted for the pavilion as pandemonium reigned. "The spectators went wild," said Richards. "It was absolute chaos and I wouldn't like to guess how many people were hurt." This time 150 minutes were lost, the deadpan National Stadium wicket being the ultimate winner.

It wasn't until 1975 that Richards was seen, in full cry, in the Caribbean. His first home century came for the Combined Islands against Guyana at St. George's Park. Back in England with Somerset, he thrashed his first double century, against Yorkshire. He was by then a national hero. His proud bearing when he stalked to the wicket won him the accolade of King Viv but there was only one nickname he ever accepted – he didn't mind if you called him Smokin' Joe.

World heavyweight champion Smokin' Joe Frazier was Richards' hero. Viv was known simply as The Man in the Leeward Islands but Smokin' Joe almost everywhere else.

Richards relished that accolade for he admired enormously the colorful, bustling, ever-forward aggression of Frazier. He played cricket the same way, always on the front foot, slugging it out. He took on the mannerisms of the heroic fighter, thick beard, extravagant but expensive clothes, jaunty trilby hats with flashy bands.

He cut a stylish somewhat extravagant figure – but if it came to a confrontation he could handle his fists as well as any man. He also chewed gum murderously, chomping on his gum as if it was a Shane Warne spin finger. He chewed continuously, many believe it was through many hours of watching Viv at the crease with open-mouthed amazement that Australia's captain Mark Taylor developed his gum chomping technique that is as much a feature of Taylor's psyche as his flicks to slip.

The little-known West Indian joined Somerset in 1974 and made a mating that may well have historic significance. He shared an apartment with Ian Botham for 10 years but never his habits. They did, however, form a mutual admiration society and became the firmest of friends. A strange bonding of the world's two most charismatic cricketers – Botham the world's most controversial allrounder and Viv the outstanding batsman and fieldsman; the best of friends and the worst of enemies depending on where their paths crossed.

There is no evidence the two pugnacious, hard-muscled friends ever became physically aggressive to each other. Had they done so, Botham may well have met his match. Both's recorded physical encounters were invariably with less impressive physical beings than Richards.

With considerable immodesty, Botham lines himself alongside the great Viv Richards in cricket talent although he was quick to concede Richards was without peer as a batsman.

When England's Ken Barrington died, Botham turned to Richards for solace. "Since Ken died the only person whose opinion I seek is Vivian Richards," he said. "I don't think it is easy for anyone less than Viv to help me in any way, because they have not experienced the same things. It is difficult to talk to anyone about cricket unless they have played the game to a similar standard."

Botham says his friendship with Viv was born of physical respect. "Viv is the only bloke around, apart from Peter Willey, who is as strong as I am. He is not intimidated by me, which is why we've never had a serious row."

Some may view this comment with a raised eyebrow. It certainly develops the impression there is a bully boy mentality to the respect (or was it fear) for each other. "We respect each other as men, as fighters. His power is awesome...Viv is as brutal as I am, or he could be, if ever either of us choose to use force. In the end, especially in sport, things do come down to brute force."

While conceding English cricket did much to further his cricket education, Richards hated many aspects of it, particularly detesting the snobbery and superiority many in the England X1 exuded in the face of failure they chose to ignore. He was targeted for racist abuse and criticism. While he made bosom friends like Botham, he also had many enemies. He also had a chip on his shoulder but there was nobody in English cricket big enough or good enough to knock it off.

Not even his great mate Botham could subdue Richards and Botham readily acknowledged it. Botham had a remarkable adulation for Richards, "From the start, I regarded Viv as the only fellow with as much pride, ambition and confidence as me. He can be ruthless and kind; humble and arrogant at the same time. He is a big man, as was Brian Close, as are all men with great qualities and great faults. Viv is totally independent, never drops his head, never admits he may be beaten. He has the courage to back himself against anyone. He's a hell of a competitor." Richards was also a batsman who scorned extra protective equipment. He faced the mercurial Jeff Thomson and blistering Dennis Lillee wearing no more protection than his West Indian cap during the rip-roaring 1975-76 series.

Despite his blood curdling introduction into Test cricket Aussie style, it remained that way too. He regarded his non-use of helmets as a strength, a sign that he wasn't going to be intimidated by anyone.

Lillee and "Thommo" were at the height of their venom, as was Australia which won 5-1.

It was a tough learning experience for the West Indians, Richards regarding it as the "hardest, meanest cricket tour" he'd ever been involved in.

"It changed my whole concept of Test cricket," he said. "Nothing could have fully prepared any of us for what we were to experience."

Richards admits he admired and respected the ability and determination of the Australian pacemen but all too often, they were over the top. "We had to take so much," he said. "The verbal abuse was particularly stunning. West Indian people are in general mild, good mannered folk and we had anticipated an atmosphere of friendly rivalry. But as soon as we wandered out on that field, we had to face their taunts. It did not prove easy to concentrate when somebody was snarling at you, 'You —— off, you black bastard.'"

The West Indies fought fire with fire, bouncers for sledges.

Richards was really Smokin' as he recalled his team's fightback after that drubbing: "I would like each and every one of those persons who have knocked us in our rise to power to remember the kind of savagery we faced on that Australian tour. We came up against extreme savagery in that series, what many people would call extreme racism. Now what is a West Indian bouncer compared to that?"

He had a stunning finish to the Australian tour, launching himself into 1976 with a breathtaking 101 in the fifth Test in Adelaide followed by 98 in Melbourne. Both hands were in the second innings as the Windies went down fighting.

He insists the murderous West Indian attitude towards cricket evolved from that tour. To survive in the international jungle, Clive Lloyd realised the Windies would have to give up their cavalier image and go for the jugular with all the weaponry they could muster. Their stock arsenal was the sharp eye, flashing bat and tall, lithe and powerful bowlers who could rip a ball at a batsman from greater height and with more fizz and venom than any other nation on earth.

It was just a matter of attitude. And his attitude over the next six years would transform him into the most devastating batsman on earth.

Australia had created a monster. Having been thrashed in Australia, the wounded West Indies limped home to meet India in the Caribbean.

India bitterly resented the bouncer barrage that came their way as the Windies sought to redeem their status.

The teams were locked 1-1 when they came to the fourth and decisive Test on a relaid greentop at Kingston, a Test that left Indian bodies strewn about the wicket, cut down by the most withering, sustained pace attack the world had seen – more venomous and dangerous than the Bodyline barrage, this was Bodyline played to an orthodox field with the ball coming on to the batsman too quickly to be avoided.

There was no need for a packed legside. Anger flared when the Indian key batsmen were physically felled by the fierce bumper barrage. Brijesh Patel had a ball smash into his mouth and Anshuman Gaekwad fell as if dead when hit above the left ear. When Gundappa Viswanath was hit and forced to retire, the Indian innings was a shambles. The innings finally ended at 5-97 with the other five batsmen "retired hurt" or "absent hurt." Needless to say the West Indies clinched the series 2-1 with Indian skipper Bishen Bedi declaring the West Indian bowling the worst form of intimidation imaginable and condemning the umpires for not intervening.

While India hated the tour it was the start of a remarkable year for Richards. The 1976 calendar year stamped him indelibly as the best batsman in the world, even ahead of the great Greg Chappell. Smokin' Joe really blazed in the series against India as his flashing bat struck three successive Test centuries; it was just a warm-up as he was to prove during the Windies' triumphant British campaign, made even sweeter by England captain Tony Greig's infamous verbal blunder that he intended to make the West Indies grovel.

It stirred a fury he wasn't capable of controlling. That a South African would dare tell a black cricket side he wanted to make them grovel was the ultimate of insensitivity. The big, blond South African had jagged hard on a raw nerve. The Greig sledge came on the eve of Richards' debut Test against England at Trent Bridge. He was proudly African/West Indian – a Rastafarian. Greig's boast made Richards flare with rage and he vowed he would teach Greig and all England a lesson at Nottingham.

England saw the new Viv Richards, the man who used the bat as bayonet – a weapon to punish, insult and humble his enemies. He used hate and contempt to fuel his batting which now took on an unprecedented venom. He was in a killing mood as he strode aggressively to the wicket. He never doubted that day he would tear Greig's England apart. He took block, one look around the field and then made baleful eye contact with the bowler. The message was in the eye and he immediately was all over the Englishmen savaging their bowling to all points of the compass with fierce hooks and thumping drives. He was 143 not out at stumps.

When he gave up his wicket soon after lunch next day he had plundered 232 supreme runs from the devastated English attack and hit 34 4s and four 6s in 450 minutes of batting bliss.

While that Test was drawn, the Windies went on to crush England 3-0. Greig was humiliated and Richards triumphant.

He made 828 runs, average 118, with a further double century (291) at The Oval.

His seven Test centuries in the calendar year were a world record and gave him a record Test aggregate of 1710 runs with an average of 111 in his first innings and 60 in his second. His overall average of 90 could only be described as Bradmanesque.

The remarkable aspect of his feat was that at no stage did he grind out his runs or bother about long stretches of consolidation. The eye was right and he struck the ball with venom. The world's finest fieldsmen acknowledged many shots were past them and breaking the pickets before they had taken a step to intercept. He added to the lustre of this season by belting his first century in a one-day international against England at Scarborough.

Eleven years later, as captain, Viv invoked the memory of Greig's infamous one-liner to motivate and drive his men from the Caribbean to a slashing 3-0 series win.

The Greig taunt became his creed to convince his players there may be times when they were "down" but they were never "out."

He rounded off his memorable 1976 by signing on with Queensland in Australia's Sheffield Shield competition, a stint memorable by one straight drive against Tasmanian Kevin Badcock which was hit with such velocity that Badcock had his skull smashed.

It was understandable that Richards was top of the Kerry Packer shopping list when his World Series was launched in 1977, ironically with Tony Greig doing most of the recruiting. Along with Imran Khan, "The Master Blaster" was the centrepiece of the World X1 to compete against the Australians.

He performed to the billing of the greatest showman on earth, too, his lightning strikes with the bat, his nonchalant athleticism in the field and his ability to send down some sneaky overs of orthodox spin transforming him into an outstanding allrounder in the new cricket concept.

His fielding was excitement itself. Having figured in three run outs to effectively end Australia's World Cup final hopes in 1975, few risked taking a second on his arm. He could intercept the firmest struck balls, gather and hurl down the stumps in one fluent motion. His catching was also acrobatic and sure.

Richards was the mood and the man of the World Series. The publicists flogged Imran Khan as the world's most eligible and desirable bachelor, but it was Richards who pumped the adrenalin into the series. He had the most positive approach. He wasn't concerned that wickets were difficult and scoring low. He didn't care that he wasn't smashing centuries on featherbed wickets. "Cricket isn't about having bowlers slaughtered on flat wickets," he said.

The West Indies officialdom decided to run in tandem with Packer rather than sever ties with their greatest drawcards. Yet when Australia toured the Caribbean in 1978 without the so-called Packer rebels, there was ill feeling that the Windies selectors threw their Packer men against the weakened Australians.

After winning the first two Tests, they dropped two of their Packer players Desmond Haynes and Richard Austin. Clive Lloyd supported the rebels as Richards and seven others walked out in sympathy. Viv played only two Tests, for scores of 39 and 23.

After basking in the two years of extraordinary exposure and hype of the rebel cricket movement, the cricket powers struck a deal with Packer. He got the television rights he'd been seeking all along and the right to promote the game, while they got their players back.

The game would never be the same again but Packer had what he wanted – high voltage entertainment married to the traditional warfare of five day Test cricket. The subsequent boom in the game proved he had given the public what it wanted.

Part of that settlement saw the continuance of the one-day World Series Cup concept and Richards, although declaring his on-going support for Test cricket as the only true measure of a player, set his sights on winning as many one-day titles to establish the Windies as masters of all forms of cricket.

The final of the 1979 World Cup in England was everything he expected it to be. Wildly exciting with an adrenalin pump in every player and every spectator. What a stage for Smokin' Joe. He blasted 138 not out to win the final off his own bat. It remains the record score in a final and among his fondest memories – if he could only remember.

After the Windies won the game, he admits going on a champagne binge. "Perhaps some reporter might like to tell me," he quipped.

Richards didn't overly like reporters. He was known to have thrown one out of his dressing rooms although he worked for the reporter's paper on contract. He regarded many journalists as hypocrites.

He was in his prime when he visited Australia in 1979-80 for a short Test tour and the World Series Cup, facing the fire of Dennis Lillee, Len Pascoe and Rodney Hogg in the process.

Richards took fiendish delight in punishing the Australian pacemen who dared to think their ear ripping bumpers at the Richards head would force him to wear a helmet. To Richards the baggy cap was a symbol of his contempt for the decapitating head ball. Nor did he bother about protective body gear. He played much of his early cricket without the essential box to shield his groin and even in the full fury of Test and one-day cricket wore only a thigh pad, box and pads.

In one Test, Pascoe opted to give Richards a lethal serve of bouncers and was infuriated to see the West Indian flashing a brilliant white toothy smile down the pitch at him. Pascoe came in harder and pounded a ripper rising above the middle stump only to watch Richards crash it to the fence and chirp back at the furious bowler, "Butter, Lennie, Butter!"

Pascoe came back harder, faster and sent the ball rising viciously at the Richards ear, he swatted it over the boundary as he would a fly. As the umpire extended his arms skywards to indicate six runs, Viv said, "Marmalade, Lennie, Marmalade!"

Michael Holding, the outstanding Jamaican, developed a habit of not having any eye contact with Richards if he happened to be bowling to the master bat. "Whenever I bowled against him, I would either ignore him completely, not even looking at him, or else go to the other route and applaud any good shots. But he upset a lot of bowlers who got uptight at his antics."

Richards was so in charge of his game that he couldn't resist the gentle banter in the midst of the most furious combat. It was when his eyes glinted and his mouth set and he said nothing that bowlers needed to fear him most. That was when the great man was setting himself to kill off an enemy that he didn't like. If he didn't like you, he probably hated you. That was the Smokin' Joe streak.

He was hit of course – nobody's perfect. Hogg sconed him in Melbourne one day. Pascoe finally took him under the ear with a fierce rising ball. It stung and blew his neck up like a goitre but he didn't fall and Pascoe, a friendly companion off the field snarled,

"The next one will put you in hospital." Viv flicked it off his ear for four more. That was his answer to everything.

He was the craftsman who set up a mighty West Indies triumph in the Australian Tests that saw them take the Frank Worrell Trophy home to the Caribbean. Australia scrambled out of the first Test in Brisbane with a draw despite the champion blitzing the much-vaunted Aussie attack for a glorious 140. The Windies dominated the second Test – again he only needed one innings, this saw him out for 96.

He was man of the match in all three Tests and naturally man of the series. The Windies won the final Test by 408 after he scored 76 and 74 – 386 from four hands at 96.5. Then came the World Series Cup against England and Australia. After Australia won the Sydney one-day international, Richards blasted the Windies back on top with an unbelievable 153 not out off 131 balls at the MCG. His next five hands of 62, 85 not out, 88, 23 and 65 were stunning performance in the context of one-day internationals. He was also the man of that series, having fulfilled his wish to conquer in both cricket arenas.

With the emergence of television, cricket had become an extraordinary money-making vehicle not only for television moguls but also cricket authorities around the world. They couldn't pack enough cricket into a year. Everybody wanted non-stop tours. Crowdpleasers like Viv Richards, Imran Khan, Ian Botham, Dennis Lillee and Kapil Dev were in demand, which meant their teams were in demand.

Playing endless cricket 12 months a year began to take its toll. Richards was starting to develop some nagging injuries, including a sore back, but had no choice but to keep touring and following the sun.

There was little rest on returning to the Caribbean from Australia. Soon he was into a five Test and a one-day series in England. The Windies won the first Test at Trent Bridge where he scored 64 and 48. He followed with a smashing 145 at Lord's.

Then came the third Test and there was vicious intent in his batting as he set to humiliate English pace bowler Bob Willis. Willis had been an arch protagonist ever since giving him an unprecedented barrage of bumpers early in his career. Back then he got the Richards wicket cheaply; King Viv was rankled and promised himself he would avenge that attack one day.

That day had come. When Willis was imprudent enough to declare he had a secret weapon to demolish the Master Blaster, he sealed his own fate. It is folly to make boasts that you cannot fulfil – particulary when 22 yards away is a man with a deadly eye and the most vicious hook in cricket. And a memory to match.

Richards selected the third Test at Manchester to rule over Willis. First England was bundled out for 150 to set the stage. The Windies lost instant wickets of Desmond Haynes and Gordon Greenidge to be 2-1 when Viv strolled languidly to the wicket – but it's the eye you watch not the walk.

First he played out a quiet over waiting for Willis to appear at the other end. Then it was Willis measuring his run and fixing his focus on the West Indian. Willis was supremely confident, England had its Caribbean rival on the ropes.

Willis powered in for his first delivery only to watch it disappear to the fence in the twinkling of an eye.

In a rare display of savagery, Richards batted quietly when facing England's alternative pace bowlers, hardly bothering about runs, before launching into Willis.

He was positively murderous as he hooked and pulled the lanky paceman to oblivion and had plundered 53 of his 65 runs from Willis before Ian Botham came to the rescue and took his wicket. Some critics saw Richards determination to kill his enemies with the bat as a weakness that drove him to lose his wicket making audacious and rash strokes.

As it transpired the first Test win clinched the series; the other four being drawn. In between time he hit four centuries against the counties and in one over against Warwickshire hit 4-6-6-4-4-6-4 (34) off Chris Clifford. His fielding was equally impressive, his catching and throwing worth the admission charges alone. He snapped the ball out of the air with nonchalant ease. Even the greatest players fell into his deadly web. Consider Mike Gatting at Lord's when he stood close to the boundary with the ball at his feet inviting Gatting to sprint for a second run. The English star took three paces and before he could retreat to safety saw his stumps shattered.

BLACK IS BEAUTIFUL

Famed author Jeffrey Archer recalled addressing his young son during the Brixton riots. He asked the boy how he felt about the National Front's view that black people were inferior:

"Pathetic," snorted Master Archer, "None of them have ever seen Viv Richards at the crease."

The Tests of 1981 confirmed Viv Richards' standing as the most feared batsman in the game. After the first scheduled Test at Guyana was abandoned, the result of the Robin Jackman affair, the Windies won two and drew the other two to take the series 2-0.

Again it was the dominant Richards who took centre stage. The Windies won the second Test in Port-of-Spain and then King Viv made a certainty of the series. After making a duck in his first innings he struck a superb 182 not out to win the third Test at Bridgetown.

Viv was the hero of the Caribbean, the idol of Antigua. He was a proud man when cricket authorities bestowed Test status on his home island. Viv strode to the wicket to bat in the first ever Antiguan Test – he was swelling with pride when that innings concluded. He had set out to show his people what he could do for them at the highest level. He struck a memorable 114 against the Englishmen at St. Johns to trigger a set of island parties which lasted for weeks.

Viv also married his childhood sweetheart Miriam during this period. He was lionised by his countrymen, his face was on West Indies stamps and he was accumulating wealth like no other West Indian before him.

Most believe his glory years as a batsman were from 1976-81. Injuries affected his reign but he was still a formidable opponent, especially in the shorter one-day game where he'd crash opposing attacks with ease.

In the Tests against Australia in 1981-82, he had only a modest series with just one 50 in six hands. But he was brilliant in the one-dayers, firing a number of brilliant hands at the business end of the series.

He'd continued to spend his off-seasons in England with county team Somerset, swelling the gates whenever he was due to bat like a Bradman in the '30s.

As the most-publicised player in world cricket, outside the headline-hunting Ian Botham, he was in demand wherever he played, receiving a "name your own price" offer from South Africa, despite his well-known dislike of apartheid. He could have made a fortune had he signed a contract to play in the Republic in 1983. But he said he'd shoot himself before selling himself to that deal and becoming an "honorary white." He branded the West Indians who did accept the big money on offer as "Judas" players.

An angry exchange between King Viv and Steve Rixon, Sydney, 1984-85, after Richards had abused Rixon for appealing for a close-in catch from the bowling of Murray Bennett. When Allan Border joined in, telling Richards to stop whingeing, the angry West Indian invited him around the back of the grandstand at the conclusion of play!

Richards would never sell his soul and made it clear he was insulted for negotiators to believe he would.

His judgment was confirmed when West Indies teammate Colin Croft, who did join that tour, reported back that he had been turned out of a "whites only" railway carriage during the visit. Although he was a guest of the South African government and an honorary white the ticket collector had told him to move to a suitable non-white carriage.

"How could I play for money in a country like that? Where I and all my friends would be treated like second-class citizens. It would be immoral for me to go to South Africa," he said.

After a mediocre couple of years by his own lofty standards, Richards was desperate to set the record straight. He was a long way from over the hill. He had to get something going. The mundane was unacceptable. He lived and died by the willow blade. He firmly believed the strong inherited the earth and he would never die wondering if a red hot go would have turned defeat or a tame draw into victory.

This spirit was best illustrated in the first Test against India at Kingston in 1983. The fourth day was a washout and a draw was unavoidable as India crawled to 6-167 at tea on the final day with the West Indies still to bat. India had an overall lead of 164 with one session to play and four wickets in hand.

One blazing over from Andy Roberts removed three of those wickets. Within half an hour they had the last wicket and were faced with getting 172 runs in half an hour plus 20 overs...one-day cricket without the fielding or bowling restrictions.

Gordon Greenidge and Desmond Haynes started with a brisk 46, but 106 were still required when the last 15 overs began. Richards went for the bowling with gay abandon, lashing 61 from 36 balls including four 6s and five 4s to set up a memorable win.

Just 16 runs were required from two overs, Jeffrey Dujon striking the winning six in the last over. It was the most entertaining final session in Test history.

Although he had a couple of mediocre Tests with scores of one and two, he interspersed these with hands of 109 and 80 to help his team win yet another Test series.

There were so many magnificent batting feats already on his sheet that it seemed one more would scarcely be noticed.

Well they hadn't seen anything yet!

In 1984, he sauntered to the middle with his team needing quick runs against England at Old Trafford to win the first one-day international. His cocksure strut, a measured tactic, was on show that day. Many critics and opposing players found his air offensively arrogant. In essence, it was a ploy by Richards to assert his authority on the game. Of course he believed in himself but he wanted his opponent to believe in him as well. He walked to the wicket with an air of a supreme commander – and why not? It was theatrical and posed, but it was effective.

In that international against England he made 189 not out in a score of 272, the finest one-day innings ever played.

Bob Willis couldn't believe it when he fired a great ball, full length on his leg stump and Richards swayed onto his back foot and smashed it over the long-off fence. Willis had never seen that shot before and he only saw it once more during his career, when Richards repeated the identical cut shot at Hove against John Snow. That time he not only cleared the boundary off the back foot, but landed the ball into the wall of some flats outside the ground.

The Windies won the three-match series with Richards scoring 84 not out in the third international. In three hands he was once out for 276 runs.

The Master Blaster was justifiably proud of what he had accomplished although he swore he never reflected on his achievements or was interested in what had been. Pride all but overwhelmed him, however, when Clive Lloyd retired and the great man bestowed his mantle of leadership on Richards. Succeeding Lloyd as captain of the world's greatest ever cricketing force was indeed an honor.

He was to have his knockers from within and from without – but when he was finished his tour of leadership, his record was unequalled as the most successful cricket captain in international history.

Richards was on top of the world and he made his feelings profoundly evident when he made Somerset's and his own highest-ever first-class score of 322 in one remarkable day's play against Warwickshire at Taunton.*

It was one of his stellar moments, to rank with his incredible century from only 56 balls in his native Antigua several months later, in April, 1986.

In previous Tests against David Gower's visiting Englishmen, he had been criticised for throwing his wicket away in cavalier nonchalance. He took to the crease for his second innings of the fifth Test with 28 minutes to the tea break. Facing 15 balls in that period, he raced to 28. That was an appetiser.

After tea, he pounded 50 in 46 minutes from just 35 balls, crashing drives and pulls that left the fieldsmen rooted to the spot as the ball smashed into the pickets. The final stroke sent the ball soaring high over long-off for six. It kept going, clearing the ground and landing outside the St. John's Recreation Reserve.

He was in no mood to be contained but John Emburey saw him hop down the wicket before he had released the ball. Emburey had him dead, dropped in a slower, wider one which was going to leave him stranded and stumped. Viv improvised, let go with his left hand to get more reach. One handed he clouted the ball over long-on for a stunning six – a shot beyond the recall of all the cricket connoisseurs lucky enough to behold that one handed six.

* Only six others have made more runs in a day's play: Brian Lara 390, Charlie Macartney 345, Bill Ponsford 334, Kumar Sri Duleepsinjhi 333, Jack Robertson 331 and Barry Richards 325. Eddie Paynter also made 322.

He was on his way towards Jack Gregory's record century from 67 balls. Botham tried a yorker and Richards drove the ball straight back down the wicket, sizzling a path through the Botham hair and all but leaving a burn welt on the scalp. There was no stopping this surge and he crashed through the century barrier between tea and stumps from just 56 balls, this second 50 having come from just 21 balls. In all he batted just 83 minutes, hitting seven 6s, as the Windies charged to a resounding 240 run win to complete a 5-0 wipeout.

MR 100 PER CENT

On leaving Somerset, Viv Richards said: "I have always given 100 per cent whether it was playing for the West Indies or Somerset. What these committeemen have said about Joel and myself being selfish – no way! If I was a selfish man I would have the most centuries in the world today. It's more a matter of different cultures. There are times when I like to go to my room and have a couple of beers and watch television.

"I can't sit at the bar drinking 10 beers a night, that's not just my line. So if that makes me not a team man then I think it's sad and unfair."

Having seen the West Indies taken to the brink of defeat by Pakistan in 1986, Viv Richards argued there was no need for rival nations to target the West Indian pace attack. "Pakistan and Imran Khan proved we could be beaten," he said. "To try and deter our bowling is only sour milk. Very, very sad.

"I'm severely critical of all those people who have been calling our fast bowlers murderers and all that. What is the matter with these people? Don't they remember the Larwood's or the Thomson's and Lillee's?" He believed everybody was looking to gun the Windies down; not that he resented that cooker pressure. "It makes it interesting playing when there is always a gun pointing at you."

The gun was pointed at him by Somerset when they handed out one of the greatest ever shocks in county cricket by sacking both Joel Garner and Richards. Ian Botham was also about to be axed but he beat them to the punch by quitting in sympathy with the West Indies champions.

Richards said his departure from Somerset was the result of "lies and deceit." He was bewildered. He had given Somerset everything – that was the way he was. He was the captain of the world's greatest cricket team. He had just led a 5-0 win over England and was the most sought-after player on earth – yet he wasn't worthy of his position in the Somerset side. That hurt!

It should not have surprised for there was considerable jealousy among the Somerset players. When Viv belted a sizzling century for Somerset a year earlier – off only 70 balls – the crowd rose to its feet and roared football crowd applause as he brandished his bat. Instead of applauding, one sour Somerset batsman snarled, "How am I supposed to play with that kind of thing? That's not batting, that's just slogging." Richards smiled when he heard that. "I call it talent. God gave it to me and he don't give it to many people."

Richards wasn't a slogger. Like Bradman, he had a remarkable eye and with the power of his forearms, could unleash the most powerful strokes imaginable.

He was a master batsman with every batting skill in the book. With a few exceptions, he believed every ball could be spanked.

His loyal Somerset supporters couldn't believe what happened. They loved Richards and Garner and worshipped Botham. In one fell blow the county had given away the three greatest drawcards in cricket – the world's best bowler, best batsman, best fieldsman and best allrounder. The club fell apart.

Viv took his Somerset sacking like a man. "You love a place. You give it your heart and soul and suddenly they take your legs off."

Unheralded Lancashire League club Rishton won his services because no county club bothered to approach him.

There were strong overtones of racism in the shut-out of Richards. "A lot of people, a lot of cricketers, resent West Indians coming here to make a living," he said.

Richards was becoming tired of his frequent globetrotting and in 1987 said he would take a year's absence from touring. His magnificent career was drawing to a close and he wanted to ensure his final years of cricket would not diminish his hard won reputation of being one of the world's greatest cricketers.

He felt he needed a year off to replenish mind and body. He said he would take the break after the World Cup in Pakistan and India. He had made 10 tours of Australia.

The weariness didn't show out in his batting in that World Cup series and he carved another niche in cricket records when he struck a withering 181 against Sri Lanka at Karachi.

He led the Windies to a drawn series against Pakistan 1-1 in 1986 before drawing with New Zealand 1-1 in 1987.

The once-great Windies appeared to be wobbling a little.

The ferocity of their pace attack and majestic batting of their stroke players had made them the world's cricket power for almost two decades.

But the rule-makers were making it harder for the Windies to dominate. Much to the Windies' disgust, they outlawed more than one bouncer an over. Richards was furious, "It sickens me," he said. "When we get beaten it is the best thing in the world – the headlines go – 'Bang! Bang! Windies Go Down! But if we win, they say: 'Yah, I Told You So!'

"You just can't win. Everyone is looking to gun you down."

Given Lloyd's outstanding record, Richards was on a hiding to nothing when he took over the captaincy. When he led his team to victory he was accused of inheriting greatness. When he lost, he was a flawed leader unable to win with the greatest force on earth.

When the Windies got away to a slow start in the 1987 World Series, Richards and the Windies were written off. But, typically, they came back hard, winning the competition and Richards the player of the one-day international series. The Australians were enraged. "It was a shocking decision," said Border. "Richards is a great player but he had had an ordinary series. Steve Waugh had a magnificent series as did Dean Jones. Viv should not have got within a bull's roar of winning this trophy."

Richards had made a habit of scooping the pool of massive individual prize money and trophies. He won three International Cricketer of the Year titles from 1979-85.

"It has got to the ridiculous stage," said Border, "I am sick and tired of him winning prizes. He just has to turn up and he wins something. Most of the time he doesn't deserve it." England's skipper Mike Gatting agreed with Border and Richards response was typical – he gave the presentation ceremony a miss.

THE KING & I

Some said it was cricket vaudeville at its worst when Ian Botham and Viv Richards renewed their Somerset partnership by creating a sports show, "The King and I" and going on tour.

It featured plenty of footage of the two dynamic batsmen crashing 6s which, after an hour of hooks and drives, became a crashing bore. They compensated for that tedium with racy anecdotes that defied protocol.

Their criticism in questioning the courage of Allan Border who believed he was a close friend of both players not only upset Border but also Australian cricketers. It might have made money but it tarnished their image with their supposed mates Downunder.

It wasn't a happy period for Viv. The Windies were less than impressive and he had been dumped from Somerset. He was 35 and beginning to feel it. He wanted a break. It took only one call from Rishton to secure Viv's services for $35,000 to play a 21-week season.

He arrived by helicopter at Rishton for his first game – right in the middle of a snowstorm. But the show had to go on because there was a crowd of 3000 packed into the little ground as he winged his way from Antigua and strode to the wicket in inclement weather. The first ball looked dead on line and the bowler roared for an lbw as the great man missed and brushed a hailstone from his eye.

"Howzat!" roared the bowler.

"Not out!" snarled the umpire, equally aggressively. The bowler, a local laborer was flabbergasted that he could never boast that he got the world's greatest batsman first ball. In fact he could never boast that he got Viv at all. This was Lancashire League and they still had their scaffold for hanging highwaymen and umpires who made unpopular decisions. The umpire scowled at the bowler, "OO d'you think they've come to watch laad, him baat or me umpire? Not Oot – That's it and don't be so daft."

Viv belted 87 from 92 balls – six 6s and nine 4s. "It's the first time I've made runs in a hailstorm," he said.

Viv, Miriam and their two children lived in a pleasant rustic pub while he saw out this stint. It was just the break he needed. He enjoyed the step-back in intensity and was genuinely chuffed when the locals erected a sign at the ground – "The Home of Viv Richards."

ABILITY SHOWS THROUGH

Viv Richards captained the West Indies for the one-day international series in Australian in early 1987 and was almost instantly dismissed as on the decline when he lost successive matches to England and produced four innings of 19, 43, 13 and 0. Richards remained unconcerned. "I know how my cricket works. I believe if you have some kind of ability, it's going to show through sometime. I wouldn't say I'm hungry, but if I ever do get loose I know I'm going to enjoy it thoroughly."

Like his mate Ian Botham who organised highly publicised walks to raise money for cancer research, Richards had his altruistic side.

He was to devote considerable time to the Antiguan Blind Society of which he was patron and associated himself with Amnesty International. "I have a strong affection for troubled people," he said.

The World Cup in India 1987-88 saw Viv Richards desperate to establish his credentials as a captain. He had been lampooned around the world as being technically unsound. The Windies had won the first two World Cup titles and lost the third in the play-off with India in 1983.

Richards had convinced at least some of his detractors that he was a fine captain when he led the Windies positively against the Pakistani tourists in 1988. Unavailable for the first Test, which the Windies lost, Richards saved them with a powerful century in the second Test in Port-of-Spain despite Imran Khan claiming he twice had him out lbw. Imran again claimed an umpire foul in the decisive third Test but the Windies won and Viv was a national hero for having helped tie the series.

He was a grim and focused cricketer when he took his team to England in 1988. His team was united and focused and Richards keen to impose discipline on the younger players, in particular.

"It was one of the hardest things in life to follow a man like Clive Lloyd but I have always been happy in this job. It is other people who haven't always been happy with me," said Richards.

The series was a triumph as he swept to a 4-0 whitewash and headed for an Australian tour looking to play his 100th Test. At 36, he had a chronic ankle complaint but wasn't too short of his best when he became the first West Indian and the 22nd overall to post 100 first-class centuries in the match against New South Wales. It was his 421st game and his 658th innings. His first century had been scored for Somerset 15 years earlier against Yorkshire.

Richards scored the two runs needed for that famous century from the same end where 39-year-old Don Bradman had scored the runs to reach his 100th 100.

That cricketing eccentric Greg Matthews bowled the ball and immediately shouted, "Man, I've made history again. The man who bowled the ball..."*

A week later in the Test, his 100th, he claimed his 100th Test catch and was happy for the Windies to win by nine wickets, maintaining their ascendancy over Australia.

With 68 batting from No.5 he was in good form and maintained his touch for Perth with 146, his 23rd Test century and fifth against Australia.

The Windies won the first three Tests on a set of fast and bouncy wickets to ensure the Frank Worrell Trophy, but there was controversy when he lost his control mid-tour and berated umpire Tony Crafter. Crafter said he had never experienced a blast like this from any cricketer.

Richards was reprimanded by his board – he hated taking a backward step on or off the field. Almost as much as he hated being lectured.

By January, Richards had extended his winning run to 18 wins and four losses in 30 Tests since taking over from Lloyd. He was anxious to maintain his unbeaten record and was unhappy when the Sydney curator prepared a spinner's paradise for the fourth Test which Australia won decisively. He congratulated the Aussies on their win, but suggested they could expect similar treatment when they toured the West Indies in 1991. His criticisms were again branded arrogant and belligerent.

He had his critics but Richards had not yet lost a series and that was what he believed his duty to be. He wanted the West Indies to remain unchallenged as the greatest force in cricket. If he stood on toes in protecting his arsenal, so what?

RE-BORN AT GLAMORGAN

Yorkshire broke with tradition when it invited Viv Richards to join its staff in 1989. The proud and dour club had never taken an international on board before. The offer was even more out of character as the Yorkshire club had a the history of a small hard core of supporters regularly taunting black cricketers who opposed their famous club.

Ultimately tradition prevailed and discussions broke down and Richards joined Glamorgan instead. He made his point with his first visit to the wicket for his new county – 119 against Leicester. He followed with a century in each innings against Essex and another century against Notts.

---

* Bradman took only 295 hands to complete his ton of hundreds. Only Denis Compton (552) Len Hutton (619) and Boycott (645) took fewer innings than Richards to reach that target. There can be no argument that Bradman compiled his record against the best of first-class competition, the three Englishman had the advantage of playing against the lower end of first-class cricket – county cricket. When assessed in that light, the Richards' effort would be second only to Bradman.

Richards runs out Carl Rackemann to trigger the first tied result in one-day international cricket, Melbourne, 1983-84.

Richards was becoming increasingly moody and at times seemed to lose his renowned composure during the English tour of the Caribbean.

First he upset his own supporters and some players by suggesting West Indians were basically of African origin. In fact there is a very strong Asian influence in their breeding and that element was angered at being summarily dismissed by their skipper.

England won the first Test at Kingston before the second, at Guyana was abandoned, the third Test at Port-of-Spain was all but in England's keeping. However, Richards forced the game to a draw with his slowdown tactics, ensuring himself a fearful blast from the English press. He was off the field for much of the controversial final day because of illness, Desmond Haynes standing in.

The West Indian bowlers sent down just 16.5 overs in almost two hours as England, five down, finished 31 runs short of victory. Richards was castigated for his direction in slowing his pace bowlers to a rate of eight and nine overs an hour. Unrepentant, he declared he was there for West Indian cricket, not England nor the English press. Certainly he would not allow the media to captain his side for him. Now the press was thirsting for his blood. He gave them the opening and they didn't miss him.

The fourth Test at Bridgetown was in the balance, with England holding the Windies out. Richards badly needed a wicket. There was one of those close things, the ball hit the pad and was snapped up by the close-in fieldsmen. The appeal went up. The batsman Rob Bailey scornfully stood his ground dismissing the suggestion he had brushed the ball with his bat. Umpire Lloyd Barker seemed to ponder but his finger remained in his pocket and, according to the English press would have stayed there.

But Richards made his move. According to Fleet Street he charged up the wicket from the cordon of fieldsmen "like a whirling Dervish." He was screaming the appeal and waving his arms in the air. Mike Tyson would have backed off and belatedly umpire Barker made the most hurtful of all finger gestures at Bailey. The fury of the English press and the English camp was turned against Richards. He was accused of intimidation and the headlines, posters and television replays screamed foul.

Richards didn't have to front the media until his triumph was complete. With the breakthrough effected, Curtly Ambrose took 5-18 with the second new ball to mop up the English second innings and ensure a 164 run win. Richards denied he had intimidated the umpire. He said his gesture was "excitement" at knowing his team had captured a vital wicket when time was running against them.

Now Viv was really in the English gun but he wasn't an easy target to find as they lined up their sights on the fifth Test.

Something was amiss when the West Indies team walked out on to the field for the start of the second day's play in the fifth Test at St John's but the skipper didn't lead his team onto the field. There were only 10 West Indians. Richards was missing. All of a sudden the English media spotted him – and heard him. He was right there amongst them in the press box. Very, very angry.

Dressed in a black T-shirt and waggling a threatening finger under the nose of English *Daily Express* writer James Lawton. It was Viv's response to a front page story by Lawton over suggestions he had administered a finger sign to the crowd on the first day of this Test. "You wrote bad things about me," Richards raged, "Watch it, you have got to be careful. People get hurt and when they get hurt they get angry. I'm in an angry mood right now – anyone who gets in my way must be careful."

Pressmen said he threatened to whack anybody who wrote derogatory articles about him. Play had been in progress five minutes before Richards made it on to the field and eventually led his team to a 2-1 series win.

England believed the series may have swung the other way but for the Richards histrionics and gamesmanship. Of course a Gordon Greenidge-Desmond Haynes opening stand of 298 at Richards Antigua home ground helped immensely.

Viv was now Public Enemy No. 1 with the media, particularly as another member of the touring English press complained Viv had threatened to whack him, too.

PROTECTING ITS OWN

The English media is prone to be protective of its own and Richards became a prime target of the Anglican press box and sufficient hostility towards the West Indian captain had been aroused to justify an armed police guard when he flew into London to join Glamorgan when the English tour ended.

He was surrounded by six uniformed and armed police when he arrived at Heathrow Airport after reports there could be an unpleasant reception committee waiting on him following reports alleging bad sportsmanship in the Tests had cost England rare success.

Richards was at ease with the situation. "I've got a job to do. I am a guy who plays cricket pretty hard and I'm not to worried about what people think of Viv Richards at this particular moment."

At least he was taking some of the heat away from his great mate Botham who had been copping most of the broadsides of the media.

But this aggravation and unusual testiness in Viv Richards had an explanation.

"He's got the Gomer Pyles," explained a teammate. Yes, Richards had been keeping a painful personal problem hidden for several months. He had piles of trouble with haemorrhoids which is why he had various absences from the playing field during the English tour of the West Indies and why he was so testy during the Tests.

Once Viv could sit down comfortably and reflect on his stormy behaviour he apologised to the journalist he had threatened during the Caribbean tour. He was reprimanded by his own board and said it was "not something I am ever likely to do again."

With Richards now 38 the media played the great prediction game of when Richards would quit.

He missed the Pakistan tour while he had an operation to cure his seating problem and the West Indies were beaten. That led to speculation he had played his last Test and media pestered him for an announcement.

"I'm not going to let anybody make up my mind for me," said Richards. "I didn't announce my coming, so why should I announce my going?"

He added, "Nobody is going to hurry me along that path. I'm wise enough to know when I'm not wanted and when I can do enough and when I can't."

Against all forecasts he was appointed captain to host the Australian visit, a tour that was mooted throughout the world as "The Championship of World Cricket." That was the sort of title bout Smokin' Joe Richards relished.

"I think we can do it one more time against the Aussies before we have to make changes." The changes were imminent with some of the great Windies players, including Richards, deep into their 30s.

Richards lost many Australians during this tour as he waged an unprecedented war against the Australian players, attacking star paceman Craig McDermott both physically and verbally. The ill feeling that was generated still festers in Australians who took part in that tour.

Richards was right, even if his method was wrong. He led his team to an invincible 2-0 lead after four of the five match series. Smokin' Viv celebrated his defeat of the Australian tourists of 1991 with an incredible broadside for the Australian team manager Bob Simpson.

Frustration had been burning deeply within him for several seasons. He believed Australia's coach Bob Simpson was a leading figure in the campaign to undermine the might of West Indies pace attack. Anything that hurt Caribbean cricket hurt Viv Richards. He believed in black power and in his own way he maintained a color conflict – usually he fought his cause with the bat.

This time having won on the field he could not contain his venom in his moment of triumph on his home soil of St. John's. Simpson, he declared, was a moaner and a bad loser. "He's a very sour sort of loser and I hope he changes," Richards asserted. This followed a dig by Simpson that the Indies batting had become brittle – this after the Windies had won the fourth Test by 343 runs.

Simpson took Viv's remarks badly and moaned, "I'm amazed, disappointed and a bit shocked. I'll be looking further into it to see what action I might take."

Richards had said, "I've seen him over a number of years and seen the way he operates. I may say I'm not the greatest lover or admirer of Bobby Simpson."

The eruption came after he was asked to rate the Australians. "The Bobby Simpsons – have been shouting their mouths off. I've never been in the business of shouting my mouth off about what we're going to do. I dismiss anything that 'Simmo' says. I'm not a guy that listens too much to Bobby Simpson because I don't think we have the greatest respect for Bobby Simpson."

When Australia protested the Simpson blast, the English press swung their allegiance back to Richards, scoffing at Australia complaining about sledging – "The Australians started sledging. They are the masters of the art. But they can't take it themselves."

Richards subsequently withdrew the comments at Board instruction but did not apologise. Although Australian players sprang to Simpson's defence, Richards did have one champion amongst the Australians. Ian Chappell, ever practical, suggested Richards had been deeply wounded by Simpson's declaration that the Windies batting was fragile.

Richards pulverised opposing attacks into submission. with a stunning array of pull and hook shots against the fastest bowlers, Dennis Lillee included, Melbourne, World Series Cup, 1979-80.

Chappelli scoffed, "The West Indies fragile? This by the coach of a seven-man batting side that had just collapsed twice, thus losing the series comprehensively."

The fifth Test saw Australia doing some squaring of accounts. Again McDermott was taunted when he batted in Australia's first innings and suffered a fearsome attack that saw him take a smashing blow on the arm – Richards didn't appear over-concerned about his team's sledging. But there were plenty of angry words in the first West Indian innings.

McDermott ripped through the top order and words flew with every wicket. It was explosive when Gordon Greenidge looked plumb lbw but survived only to be caught dead in front again. McDermott then skittled Richards for a duck and words were exchanged as McDermott indicated the way to the rooms. McDermott had the first four West Indies back in the pavilion for 46. They were bundled out in the day and when Australia took a 189 first innings into their second innings they were greeted by a hailstorm of bumpers. The umpires stopped play when nightwatchman Ian Healy received four successive bouncers in fading light.

Next day with Mark Taylor amassing 144 out of 265, Australia stitched up their first Caribbean win in 13 years but lost the series 2-1. The two teams were now bitter enemies, so much so that few of the Windies players attended the victory ceremony. Richards came in for a lot of flak that his pride in his color and African background had caused him to lose sight of the values of the game. He should have maintained better control on his players and it was deemed unacceptable that a bowler should be singled out and repeatedly struck in a bumper blitz.

McDermott said the taunts applied to him had been outrageous and had failed to daunt him. He said he was called a coward repeatedly and there were calls to "break his arm" and "hit the coward." He accused the West Indies of trying to nail him with the ball thus eliminating Australia's main bowling arm. "It's the most aggressive cricket I've ever been involved with," said McDermott. He believed the attack on him came in response to his opening salvo of the Test series when two West Indies batsmen had to go to hospital for x-rays after being hit by McDermott searers.

It was very much a bad taste tour and finished on just the right note – both teams were reported by the umpires for abusive language and behaviour in the final Test. Australians were also accused of kicking in their dressing room door during the third

Test when denied access to their equipment for a training session. Ironically that was at Richards' home ground of St. John's making the insult double jeopardy. The Australians said they had to break the lock to get on with their job. Merv Hughes later admitted being the culprit along with fellow paceman Terry Alderman.

It was in these months the West Indies branded Craig McDermott a "white coward" setting an all time low in relationships between two nations who prided themselves on tough, harsh but manly conflict. There was nothing manly, or fair about that lie and it made Richards accusations of racism by Australians look feeble by comparison.

Richards was scathing after this tour. He railed against the Australians claiming the West Indies had turned to four pace bowlers in their team because Australia had started it in the first place. He said he had friends in Australian cricket, Ian Chappell and Rod Marsh being notables, but he was resentful of the "little" guys in the latest Australian side.

Of Lillee: "I don't mind him being like that because I knew he had character. He was tough, he was a good bowler. But you get some Mickey Mouse, like – I won't name names, but a few who toured the Caribbean recently – and they're not fit to lace that man's boots.

"That's why I was so pleased with the way that particular tour worked out. Those guys had to be put in their place."

It was clear Viv wouldn't be making the next tour of Australia.

During his farewell tilt against the Aussies, he became only the seventh batsman to score 8000 Test runs, this milestone occurring during the first Test in Kingston. He also overtook Sir Garfield Sobers as the greatest West Indian run scorer, a target he achieved when he passed 8032.

His tour of England in 1991 was the series where Viv decided to end it all. He captained his 49th Test at Edgbaston and made a certainty that he would be the only West Indian never to lose a series by belting a six straight back over Richard Illingworth's head to win the match. He was immediately rushed by West Indian players who carried him triumphantly to the pavilion.

For once in his life the jaunty, proud and disdainful Vivian Richards was swept up in the emotion. Instead of brandishing a bat and flashing a massive grin – he cried. Really cried. His cricket days were coming to an end.

Although his team had clinched the series, there was still the fifth and final Test to be played at the Oval and he could go out of that one on the attack. There was nothing to lose and in a way that was anti-climatic for Smokin' Joe Richards. Which might be why England won that Test – Botham's only success against the Windies as a player. England thus levelled the series and denied Richards a final triumph.

Throughout his reign as captain Richards had been accused of creating animosity and low morale in his dressing room. Yet the bonding and strength of the Windies was never as strong as it was under his leadership. He is the only captain in Test history who five times trailed 1-0 in a series and every time came back to draw or win that series. His was the most successful reign in history with 27 wins, 14 drawn and nine lost.

NOT ONLY FOR THE ENGLISH

Some of the bitterness Richards nurtured through his cricket career surfaced in his book "Hitting Across The Line" which was released after his last Test appearance. He penned such bitter comments as "some people think that cricket is a game only Englishman can really play."

"I still hear that even now – 'Oh you only have to bowl outside the off stump and they hit across the line... they can never play properly in England' – all that crap. I still come across it. These guys still believe in their country's innate superiority – it is pathetic. They think they are strong but they are not. They are weak, fatally weak."

Which outpouring reaped Viv the wrath of the press who said his problem was his skin – a dual edged problem "It's black and dreadfully thin," spat one writer.

While he had farewelled Test cricket in England, he desperately wanted to play one last World Cup tournament, in Australasia in 1991-92.

The West Indies selectors shattered his dream by leaving him out of the tour. There was outrage of course.

In the eyes of the West Indies officialdom he had become too angry. He had been too rude to the media, too testy out there in the middle. Haemorrhoids may have been at the seat of the problem but that didn't sit well with the selectors.

Supporters of Richards sprang to his defence. The media had been bitchy and witch-hunting the Black Bradman for years. They read racism into every twistable comment. Richards appealed to the selectors to consider his record which made him unequivocally the best batsman in the world over a 15 year span and his worst breaches of cricket etiquette had been uttered and executed in protection of West Indies cricket.

He was passionate and unrelenting on issues close to his heart. He claimed the British media had betrayed a confidential trust which provoked his controversial raid on the press box. The fall-out with Simpson had led to Australian manager Colin Egar demanding an apology from Richards. The English press on the Viv Richards see-saw said it was ludicrous that Australians were wounded by verbal attacks, this flew in the face of the reality that Australian cricket was the breeding ground for sledging and cruelly based insults.

In the finish and it was the finish, Viv was left home and said a sad and lonely farewell to a career that deserved an exit on the World Cup stage. "I made myself available but I don't think I was wanted by some of the players."

They could leave him home but they could never take his name from the pages of cricket history.

A DEEP ROOTED ANTAGONISM

The deep rooted antagonism of Richards for Australian cricket surfaced again in 1995 when he made a sneak attack on Steve Waugh on the eve of the second Test. After Australia had won the first Test in three days at Barbados, Richards was in a mud slinging mood.

No doubt it was designed as a distraction to unsettle the confident Aussies. He claimed the controversial Waugh catch of Brian Lara had hit the ground and Australia's win was "hollow." He said Waugh must have known the ball hit the ground and added, "If I see him around I'll let him know what I think in no uncertain terms."

Waugh said he believed the catch had been taken and had discussed it with Lara who had no problems with the situation. "Relations with West Indies were at their worst when Viv captained the side, that might explain something. He's finished now so I suggest he keeps his nose out of it and goes fishing or whatever he is doing now," Waugh said.

Viv Richards THE MAN & HIS RECORD

Born: March 7, 1952

Teams: Leeward Islands, Somerset, Queensland, Glamorgan & West
Indies

First-class debut: 1971

First-class record: Matches 507. Batting – Runs 36212, Average
49.33, Highest score 322, 100s 114. Bowling – Wickets 223,
Average 45.15, Best bowling 5-88, Five wickets in an Innings 1.
Fielding – Catches 464, Stumpings 1.

Test debut: 1974-75

Test record: Matches 121. Batting – Runs 8540, Average 50.23,
Highest score 291, 100s 24, 50s 45. Bowling – Wickets 32,
Average 61.37, Best bowling 2-17. Fielding – Catches 122.

One day international debut: 1975

One day international record: Matches 183. Batting – Runs 6526,
Average 46.28, Highest score 189*. Bowling – Wickets 117,
Average 35.83, Best bowling 6-41, Five wickets in an Innings 2.
Fielding – Catches 97. Captaincy – 108 matches for 70 wins
and 36 losses. Two games were abandoned.

Tours: Australia 1975-76, 1979-80, 1981-82, 1984-85, 1988-89;
England 1976, 1980, 1984, 1988, 1991; New Zealand 1986-87;
India 1974-75, 1983-84, 1987-88; Pakistan 1974-75, 1980-81,
1986-87; Sri Lanka 1974-75. Also toured Australia with the
WSC West Indians in 1977-78 and 1978-79.

*Viv Richards is acclaimed by fellow Antiguans after
his century against the 1984 Australians at St.
John's. He made 178 and shared a stand of 308
with Richie Richardson (154).*

Viv Richards' Test record series by series:

BATTING & FIELDING

Season	Opponent	Mt	Inns	No	HS	Runs	Ave	100s	50s	Ct.
1974-75	India (a)	5	9	2	192*	353	50.43	1	1	5
	Pakistan (a)	2	3	0	10	17	5.66	-	-	3
1975-76	Australia (a)	6	11	0	101	426	38.72	1	2	6
1976	India (h)	4	6	0	177	556	92.66	3	1	3
	England (a)	4	7	0	291	829	118.43	3	2	2
1977	Pakistan (h)	5	9	0	92	257	28.55	-	2	4
1978	Australia (h)	2	2	0	39	62	31.00	-	-	3
1979-80	Australia (a)	3	4	0	140	386	96.50	1	3	3
1980	England (a)	5	6	0	145	379	63.16	1	2	6
1980-81	Pakistan (a)	4	6	1	120*	363	72.80	1	3	9
1981	England (h)	4	5	1	182*	340	85.00	2	-	3
1981-82	Australia (a)	3	6	0	50	160	26.66	-	1	1
1983	India (h)	5	6	0	109	282	47.00	1	2	8
1983-84	India (a)	6	9	0	120	306	34.00	1	1	8
1984	England (a)	5	7	1	117	250	41.66	1	1	5
1984-85	Australia (a)	5	9	1	208	342	42.75	1	1	3
	New Zealand(a)	4	6	1	105	310	62.00	1	2	2
1986	England (h)	5	6	1	110*	331	66.20	1	2	2
1986-87	Pakistan (a)	3	5	0	70	175	35.00	-	1	1
	New Zealand (a)	3	4	0	38	77	19.25	-	-	5
1987-88	India (a)	4	6	1	109*	295	59.00	1	2	5
1988	Pakistan (h)	2	4	0	123	278	69.50	1	1	6
	England (a)	5	6	0	80	223	37.16	-	2	3
1988-89	Australia (a)	5	9	1	146	446	55.75	1	4	3
1989	India (h)	4	5	0	110	135	27.00	1	-	10
1990	England (h)	3	5	0	70	141	28.20	-	1	4
1991	Australia (h)	5	8	1	69	174	24.85	-	2	1
	England (a)	5	8	1	80	376	53.71	-	5	3
Total		121	182	12	291	8540	50.24	24	45	122

BOWLING

Season	Opponent	Mts	Overs	Mds	Runs	Wicks	Ave	BB
1974-75	India (a)	5	7	2	10	0	-	0-10
	Pakistan(a)	2	9	2	17	1	17.00	1-17
1975-76	Australia (a)	6	8,1	0	44	0	-	0-2
1976	India (h)	4	6	0	17	0	-	0-17
	England (a)	4	31	12	56	1	56.00	1-11
1977	Pakistan (h)	5	40,3	11	91	2	45.50	2-34
1978	Australia (h)	2	-	-	-	-	-	-
1979-80	Australia (a)	3	2	0	7	0	-	0-7
1980	England	5	36	12	85	0	-	0-1
1980-81	Pakistan (a)	4	26,2	6	61	4	15.25	2-20
1981	England (h)	4	100	35	206	5	41.20	2-24
1981-82	Australia (a)	3	49	13	109	0	-	0-17
1983	India (h)	5	36	9	87	1	97.00	1-14
1983-84	India (a)	6	3	1	8	0	-	0-8
1984	England (a)	5	1	0	2	0	-	0-2
1984-85	Australia (a)	5	16	4	32	1	32.00	1-7
	New Zealand (a)	4	39	7	89	1	89.00	1-34
1986	England (h)	5	20	7	29	0	-	0-3
1986-87	Pakistan (a)	3	5	2	9	1	9.00	1-9
	New Zealand (a)	3	67	19	147	2	73.50	1-32
1987-88	India (a)	4	50	11	103	3	34.33	1-28
1988	Pakistan (h)	2	17	6	44	3	14.66	2-17
	England (a)	5	10	1	28	0	-	0-2
1988-89	Australia (a)	5	117	12	299	3	99.66	1-12
1989	India (h)	4	51	8	128	1	128.00	1-28
1990	England (h)	3	28	10	47	0		0-11
1991	Australia (h)	5	23	2	101	0	-	0-5
	England (a)	5	5	1	6	0	-	0-1
Total		121	856	201	1964	32	61.38	2-17

COUNTRY BY COUNTRY RECORD

BATTING & FIELDING

Country	Mt	Inns	No	HS	Runs	Ave	100s	50s	Ct.
v Australia	34	54	3	208	2266	44.43	5	14	24
v England	36	50	4	291	2869	62.36	8	15	29
v India	28	41	3	192*	1927	50.71	8	7	39
v New Zealand	7	10	1	105	387	43.00	1	2	7
v Pakistan	16	27	1	123	1091	41.96	2	7	23

HOME & ABROAD

	Mt	Inns	No	HS	Runs	Ave	100s	50s	Ct.
Tests at home	48	67	4	182*	3136	49.77	11	14	50
Tests abroad	73	115	8	291	5404	50.50	13	31	72

BOWLING

Country	Mts	Overs	Mds	Runs	Wicks	Ave	BB
v Australia	34	268,1	44	694	7	99.14	2-26
v England	36	231	78	459	6	76.50	2-24
v India	28	153	31	353	5	70.60	1-14
v New Zealand	7	106	26	236	3	78.67	1-32
v Pakistan	16	97,5	24	222	11	20.18	2-17

HOME & ABROAD

	Mts	Overs	Mds	Runs	Wicks	Ave	BB
Tests at home	39	1846	28	795	11	72.27	2-21
Tests abroad	36	1027	57	521	9	57.88	2-91

HIS HIGHEST TEST SCORES

291	v England, The Oval, 1976	182*	v England, Bridgetown, 1981
232*	v England, Nottingham, 1976	178	v Australia, St John's, 1983-84
208	v Australia, Melbourne, 1984-85	177	v India, Port-of-Spain, 1977-78
192*	v India, Delhi, 1974-75		

HIS BEST TEST BOWLING

2-17	v Pakistan, Queens Park, 1988
2-20	v Pakistan, Lahore, 1980-81
2-24	v England, Kensington, 1981
2-34	v Pakistan, Queens Park, 1977
2-65	v Australia, Queens Park, 1984

HIS HIGHEST ONE-DAY INTERNATIONAL SCORES

153*	v Australia, Melbourne, 1979-80
189*	v England, Old Trafford, 1984
181	v Sri Lanka, Karachi, World Cup 1987
149	v India, Jamshedpur, 1983-84
138*	v England, Lord's, World Cup 1979

HIS BEST ONE-DAY INTERNATIONAL BOWLING

6-41	v India, Delhi, 1989-90
5-41	v New Zealand, Dunedin, 1986-87
4-45	v India, Port-of-Spain, 1988-89

Viv Richards' World Series Cricket Supertests record

BATTING & FIELDING Season	Mt	Inns	No	HS	Runs	Ave	100s	Ct
1977-78	6	11	1	177	862	86.20	4	8	
1978-79	3	6	0	46	116	19.33	-	3	
1979 (h)	5	8	1	54	303	43.28	-	4	
Totals	14	25	2	177	1281	55.69	4	15	

BOWLING

Season	Mts	Overs	Mds	Runs	Wicks	Ave	BB	5wI	10wM
1977-78	6	-	-	-	-	-	-	-	-
1978-79	3	-	-	-	-	-	-	-	-
1979 (h)	5	15	1	40	0	-	0-2	-	-

HIGHEST WSC SCORES

177	WSC World XI v WSC Australia, Gloucester Park, Perth, 1977-78
170	WSC World XI v WSC Australia, VFL Park, Melbourne, 1977-78
123	WSC West Indies v WSC Australia, Football Park, Adelaide, 1977-78
119	WSC World XI v WSC Australia, Sydney Showgrounds, 1977-78

David Bairstow is run-out in Melbourne as Richards celebrates the West Indies' two run win, 1979-80.

BULLDOG OR BULLY

"Botham's been bowling rubbish for the past 10 years. I don't think he can bowl a hoop downhill," – FREDDIE TRUEMAN.

He was England's most colorful and charismatic player since Dr. W. G. Grace; a man used to living on the knife edge. Driven by a heart that pumped adrenalin like an oil gusher and triggered by a mind that revelled in brawling, Ian Botham was a headliner with a capital "H."

He was to be a man of many indiscretions – the first in Australia before he'd even raised a bat or a bouncer against the enemy. Before making his mark in internationals, Ian Botham spent a season in Melbourne, a very dismal season in which he played poorly for Melbourne University and a mediocre, motley media team named the Plastics in Melbourne's mid-week cricket competition. Not much lustre there either. But he did meet important people.

Ian Botham was sitting in the bar of the MCG Hotel with ex-Australian captain Ian Chappell when "Chappelli" supposedly made a remark which raised "rude doubts" about the quality of English cricket. England had only recently been slaughtered by the West Indies. Australia had previously beaten the Windies 5-1.

Botham told Chappell he was wrong. Chappell insisted he was right. The story goes that Botham told Chappell to shut up. Ian wouldn't.

Botham stood up and with one swipe of his fist belted the Aussie skipper off his stool and flat on his back on the bar floor. Botham one for none!

Chappell maintained his dignity. Stood up, dusted himself off and conversation resumed along a different route. Finally the Australian captain took his leave, strolled to the hotel door, made a remark about English cricket in line with his previous sentiments. Botham roared like a bull and took off after Chappell.

The skipper had a head start and a lot of traffic to run block for him. Chappell vaulted over the bonnet of a car and before Botham could find a clear passage the Australian had vanished into the snarl of Melbourne traffic.

It would have been a great finale to their confrontation if their next meeting was at Botham's Test debut against Australia the following year. Instead Chappell and Dennis Lillee had joined World Series Cricket.

It was brother Greg who had to restore the family honor. Greg faced Botham in that maiden match, the third Test of the 1977 tour of England. Botham skittled his second Chappell when he shattered Greg's stumps at 19 on his way to a stunning debut of 5-74. Chappell dismissed the delivery as the worst to ever take his wicket. He now led the Chappell brothers 2-0.

Back home in Australia the Plastic men couldn't believe it. They remembered Botham as anything but a world class cricketer. Mind you, he was their sort of bloke, hard drinking, hard playing and full frontal.

Botham was an extremely rough and ready character. Imran Khan said he was a bully. Ian Chappell had the jaw to prove it. Allan Border wished Botham was an Aussie. Ian Chappell said, "I'm bloody glad he wasn't."

All this was typical of the man they called "Both" – nobody was ever quite sure what he was – a bully or a bulldog.

Ian Botham is an enigma. His wife, Kath, wrote a book about living with him and apart from him. She said it was at its worst when he was on tour and rumors were flying of sex orgies and drug abuse. She was besieged by media seeking her story while hubby Ian was in the West Indies in 1985. She knew something was in the air and her panic phone calls to Botham and associates did nothing to allay her fears. She was told a pack of lies was being circulated and Ian insisted she fly to Barbados with the kids to present a united front.

"I'm damned if I'll be seen as the distressed wife flying in to save her marriage," snapped Kathy, "I'll go when *I'm* ready."

Then came the headings: I LAID OUT COKE . . . BEAUTY QUEEN'S NIGHT OF PASSION WITH BOTHAM.

It was claimed beauty queen Lindy Field and Botham had engaged in such energetic sexual gymnastics that they broke a bed. He emphatically denied the allegations.

And another: TEST ACE IN SEX AND DRUGS SCANDAL.

The tabloids carried five pages of banner headlines and shock allegations. Kathy took it all in, assessed it and decided Ian Botham, her husband, was the victim of publicity-crazed extrovert women who preyed on sporting and political legends. "Living apart from each other as much as we do, we have to trust each other."

She finally flew to the West Indies as per an original schedule; the Botham's were reunited in front of a mass of journalists, flashbulbs transforming the scene into a pyrotechnical spectacular. Back in their hotel room Botham told her the stories were lies. She heard him out, believed him and stood by her man.

To read her account of events Kathy Botham is a foolproof shock absorber for the emotions of her husband. Within 24 hours of her salvage mission, Ian had run amok in their hotel room, flung pizza and wine bottles at the walls, stormed off and drank himself to oblivion, declaring their marriage over and attributing all blame to Kathy for not having faith in him. Extraordinary stuff because Kathy had remarkable faith in her husband and done nothing else but support him – albeit tearfully. "Yes, I believed Ian, I still do," she said.

But living with the pain and degradation of being headlined in the world press was often hard to take. Their two young children, a son Liam and daughter Sarah, were also wounded and were subjected to schoolyard taunts and abuse. Botham's reaction to accusation was to become belligerent. He was never one to play off the backfoot when naked aggression might win the day. He played life like he played his cricket.

Few wives, if any, have suffered the torment that was to fall the way of Kathy Botham – hers is the story of the cricket victim. The story of her husband is that of a sporting icon devoid of a safety valve. His life is such a wild roller-coaster that it needs to be broken into fragments to be digested.

There is a message in there somewhere for cricketers on tour. Two wives, Kathy Botham and Lindsay Lamb, were thrown together by cricket. They became firm friends and were then divided not by their own actions but by the supposed off-field exploits of their husbands.

Kathy Botham wrote in her own book that she believed in Ian Botham. Lindsay Lamb was less trusting but was allowed her own chapter in Allan Lamb's book – sub-titled "The Silence of the Lambs is over." It certainly was.

Allan Lamb must have wondered at the wisdom of offering his spouse uncensored space in his biography. Lindsay was not as easily placated as her co-sufferer. She took advantage of her place in hubby's book to issue a philosophy, a warning and an ultimatum.

Lindsay Lamb strikes one as a pretty smart female. She says she loves Allan warts and all – she just doesn't like seeing his warts flashed all over the headlines of the world tabloids – which is exactly what happened. "I'm not stupid," said Lindsay, "I know that cricketers are no different from other young men on the loose."

Lindsay said she went on seven cricketing tours and would tell every other cricketers wife to get out on those trips. "If you don't keep your husband's bed warm at night, then someone else might. That's not being cynical, just realistic."

She said she was shattered when all sorts of rumors came out of Pakistan. "Never mind the drugs, because I knew Allan dabbled as a kid and he told me that he was amazed to find what a socially acceptable thing it was in New Zealand. It was the sex stories that tore me apart. In my view, there's no smoke without fire.

"I knew I loved Lamby. Still do. But I don't trust him ... I would take Lamby to the cleaners if it happened again, he wouldn't know what happened."

Kathy Botham revealed in her story that she had a falling out with Lindsay after the New Zealand-Pakistan scandal of 1984 broke. She said she suddenly realised in the midst of her own problems that Lindsay Lamb must have been going through similar anguish. She phoned, all too late. She copped a blast for not making earlier contact and at the end of the day the wives were estranged and the husbands still bosom pals.

Ian Botham comes from English North county stock. He was to become known as "Beefy", "Both" or "Guy the Gorilla." His forebears were his father, Leslie, a naval man, his grandfather an inventor and his mother Marie Collett a Yorkshire girl. He was born on November 25, 1955 in Heswall, Cheshire and by the time he was two was already a menace to the local surrounds, particulary household windows. He developed a penchant for throwing his favorite hammer through them.

At four he was bowling cutters at the nearby Yeovil Boys Grammar School. He loved cricket and when the local teams were short on players, he was given a game. By nine he was in the school football and cricket teams. There was never any doubt in his mind that he was going to be a professional sportsman. Although outstanding at soccer, he intended to make his living playing cricket.

At 13, he was captain of his school's under 16 team and already under national scrutiny playing junior cricket with Somerset county. Aged 15 he was offered a professional opening – in soccer. He was a hard, punishing soccer player but believed he was a better cricketer. "What I liked about cricket was that you were a member of a team but could play as an individual." He also liked the deadly nature of batting – one mistake and you're out! Living on the knife edge was to be his way of life. But he liked bowling as a support system. If he missed with the bat he would recover lost ground with the ball.

He made his decision to go the way of professional cricket, left school and took up a job with the Lord's ground staff. He missed out on joining Middlesex and remained with Somerset and while he made the Somerset county team in September 1973, his performances were less than outstanding.

He was back in 1974 facing international cricketers and made his mark when Somerset played Hampshire in the quarter final of the Benson & Hedges series. After four mediocre first-class appearances, he faced West Indies and was handed the ball by skipper Brian Close and immediately took two wickets, including Barry Richards.

In reply Somerset were in deep strife at 8-113 needing 70 runs from 15 overs. Botham clouted a huge 6 which brought Andy Roberts back into the attack. The West Indian fired a devastating bouncer at the Botham head. He hooked fiercely, missed and the ball crashed into his mouth - he was spitting teeth all over the ground but refused to go off. "I shook myself and felt fine," he said. "It seemed to relax me."

Botham took to the bowling and with an over to spare, smashed Roberts to the fence for victory, unbeaten on 45. He'd arrived. England was about to unveil the most colorful and charismatic player since Dr. W. G. Grace. By no means Mr. Nice Guy, either of them. He trekked overseas to Australia where his playing stint with University and mid-week cricket was lamentable. On return to England, he played county cricket and caught fire. He took 75 wickets and was selected to play against the touring Australians in the 1977 Tests. He'd gone from Chump to Champ in a few short months.

Coinciding with his first Test selection, at Trent Bridge, was the imminent birth of his first child. He celebrated with a rout of Australia on debut with 5-74, five wickets being the accepted bowling "century," he was back home looking after Kath.

Botham's next Test at Headingley produced a duck, but revealed the other side of his quirky cricket nature. Wound him when he bats and he will tear you apart with the ball. He took 5-21 as Australia was forced to follow-on on its way to an innings loss.

Greg Chappell was not in awe of Botham on debut, in fact he was all but in contempt of him, "We had looked on Ian Botham not so much with disrespect as without respect," admitted Chappell who was to become Ian Botham's first victim in Test cricket – clean bowled for 19 by what he described as "a crap ball."

"Crap" balls were to get Ian Botham many a prized scalp because he experimented as he bowled. He used the full width of the crease to change the angle, he slowed the ball, tossed them high or slung them low. "Expect the unexpected," he said. He decided what he was going to bowl only as he loped to the point of delivery. If he didn't know what he was going to bowl, how would the batsman know?

He followed his two Tests against Australia with a tour of New Zealand under the methodical, run-grinding machine Geoff Boycott and the Kiwis were easy picking as Botham's stature continued to build. In his first five Tests Botham had one batting century and four bowling "centuries."

New Zealand caused a major upset by winning the first Test at Wellington – Botham had a poor match with the bat but took an aggregate of 4-40 with the ball. In the second Test he cracked his first international century, a stunning 103 after England had been rocked at 5-128. He also dominated the bowling with 5-73.

This was the Test England had to win. Time was the enemy. England had a lead of 183 and Boycott told his batsmen he was going to get quick runs and declare so that he could level the series. "Throw the bat at everything," he ordered.

Boycott opened with Brian Rose who was quickly out for 11, then Derek Randall was run out for 13. England 2-47. Boycott stagnated and with the declaration imminent, quick runs were imperative. "I don't know what's wrong," Boycott complained as Botham joined him at the wicket. "I can't seem to get the ball off the bat."

He'd scored 10 runs in 20 overs according to Botham. "Don't worry about it Fiery, I'll take care of it," he said.

Botham decided England wouldn't get quick runs while Boycott was there and the rookie decided to sacrifice his skipper. He waited until he had the call, stroked the ball for a suicide single and called his skipper through. Boycott started off but yelled "NO!"

Botham snarled "YES!" and kept running, making sure he got safely past Boycott. The wicket was thrown down and Boycott, who wouldn't give his wicket away in a church social, went scowling off to the pavilion, muttering obscenities.

Botham crashed a rapid fire 30, Boycott declared overnight and with 3-38, Botham helped rout New Zealand for 105.

There are not many cricketers who have deliberately run their skipper out in a vital Test and survived to boast about it. Then again consider the build of the man. 188 cms. A bulky 95 kgs. Huge thighs, the torso of a gorilla and extraordinary arm strength. Wrists that Mike Tyson would give an ear for. All this driven by a heart that pumped adrenalin like an oil gusher, triggered by a mind that revelled in brawling. England drew the series and Botham saved Boycott from acute embarrassment.

He followed the booming debut against Australia and New Zealand with a spirited series against Pakistan which saw him belt a century in the first innings of the first Test at Edgbaston to head up an innings win. He clouted 108 in the second Test at Lord's and then ripped through Pakistan to take 8-34 to rout the tourists again as England clinched the series with one Test to play. He was the first to score a century and take eight wickets in an innings. In one 65 ball spell, he took 7-12.

With 24 wickets in the three following Tests against New Zealand, his position as a Test player of note was cemented. By the time he'd played 11 Tests, he'd taken 64 wickets at an average of 16.39, including eight five wicket hauls as well as scoring more than 500 runs at 41.66.

In February, 1980, he became the first player to score a century and take more than 10 wickets in a Test. He decimated India in the Golden Jubilee Test at Bombay, taking six wickets in India's first innings, making 114 before routing the Indians with 7-48.

You wouldn't slash your wrists with a record like Botham's yet mystery surrounds a dash to hospital on the eve of the 1978-79 tour of Australia.

He had a gashed wrist sewn and a spokesman for The Doncaster Royal Infirmary said they had been ordered not to discuss the incident. His father said the gash was caused by a door. "I don't know which door, where or why." There was, however, a broken glass door at a local pub where his mates organised a Botham send-off. He couldn't bowl for three weeks after that incident.

During his maiden tour of Australia, he was dubbed The Miracle Man. Having recovering from the gashed wrist he was struck down by food poisoning, but continued to capture the headlines and perform like a seasoned campaigner.

A DOG OF A NIGHT

Having already gashed a wrist in a night out with the boys, Both struck more trouble at a stag night in Somerset during the 1979 season.

It was a night to raise money for a Taunton Town soccer goalkeeper. Apart from Botham, two strippers were the star attraction and spectators climbed into the rafters to get a decent or indecent view depending on your perspective.

A spectator said tables and chairs collapsed and the scene was something out of a wild West movie.

Botham played cricket the next day with an abrasion obvious on his nose. "I was not involved in a fight – I got that mark from a dog." Police attended but said no action was taken.

Botham couldn't resist sounding off in the Melbourne media. He drew the wrath of English cricket officialdom when he warned Australia in his $35 a week *Sporting Globe* column, "After we finish with your lot this weekend, you will need a completely new side. I'm here to firmly shove that not-good-enough tag firmly down your throats."

Australia made a mockery of Botham's threat by winning the third Test by 103 runs, but it was its only win of the series, England taking the Ashes 5-1.

In Adelaide, his sportsmanship was queried by Australia's opening bat Graeme Wood, claiming Botham had interfered with him after he'd been run out in Adelaide.

It was a furious exchange, Wood charging for a single only to see Botham block his path while Geoff Boycott threw his wicket down. Wood angrily protested to umpire Robin Bailhache he would have made his ground but for Botham forcing him to run wide. "I don't know whether it was deliberate or not. He just kept moving across me forcing me wider and I had no chance of getting there."

Umpire Bailhache refused to discuss the issue, but Botham denied all impropriety.

From his earliest days, Botham had been regarded as one of the most fiercely honest players to have graced the field. He played by the rules to the limit of the rules, he had too much faith in his own abilities to bring himself into disrepute, which is why he took Imran Khan to court in later years.

But he was also known to stand his ground.

On August 6, 1979, Ian Botham took his 100th Test wicket – and what a wicket it was: legendary Indian Sunil Gavaskar.

Taking that historic wicket in only his 19th Test set a new world record for the fastest 100 wickets, just 739 days. He did have the advantage, however, of playing more Tests per year than his predecessors.

His skipper Mike Brearley wasn't too impressed, however, with Botham's bowling performances against the Indians. He accused him of showing off by bowling too many bouncers which were easily punished.

"He's trying to show the world he can bowl bouncers better than Mohinder Amarnath can hook them. He did the same against Peter Toohey in Perth and against Rodney Marsh at Lord's in 1977 – if I could have taken him off mid-over I would have done so," said Brearley.

Two Tests later, he completed the 1000 Test runs and 100 Test wickets milestone, eclipsing the feat of India's Vinoo Mankad who completed the double in 23 Tests.

As one of world cricket's brightest new prospects, speculation mounted that he would join World Series Cricket. But he told reporters Kerry Packer could offer him one

* England's George Lohmann took his first 100 wickets in just 16 Tests and Australia's Clarrie Grimmett did it in 17. Another Australian, Charles "The Terror" Turner also did it in 17 Tests.

million dollars and he still wouldn't join. Asked if Ian Chappell's frontline presence in World Series had anything to do with it, he said, "Ian who?"

Old wounds re-opened when England toured Australia in the first compromise season in 1979-80. Ian Chappell had returned to official cricket after a colorful couple of years with WSC. Australia had won the first Test without Chappell. They wanted to win in Sydney to take the series, even though England had refused to put the Ashes on the line, given that it was only a three-Test contest.

Australian cricket was back to full strength and confident of victory. Botham had his own ideas. Chappell's pride demanded he take the English bully down a peg or two. Botham batted first and well aware a hungry Ian Chappell was waiting in slips. Instead it was Greg Chappell who gleefully grabbed the catch to terminate "Both's" innings at 27. He was top score in a miserable England collapse to be all out for 123. The broad smile on Chappelli's face telling Botham he had not changed his opinion of English cricketers.

Botham was champing at the bit to get at the Australians and bowled at Ian Chappell with venom in every ball. He ripped through the heart of Australia's batting to take 4-29 to gut Australia for just 145. Botham was denied the ultimate satisfaction as Chappell bravely held Australia's innings together for a top score of 42, ensuring the Aussies a narrow lead. Botham realised there was a lot more guts and fight in Ian Chappell than he suspected. Thus the two antagonists had dug deep and top scored for their teams.

Now Botham batted a second time and he came to the wicket with David Gower on his way to a brilliant 98. Greg bagged Botham for a duck and the first hug came from brother Ian as Botham stormed to the pavilion.

The Aussies needed to get 216 on a treacherous wicket and were soon in trouble at 1-31 when Ian Chappell strode to the wicket. On nine, he edged a ball and the big palm of the bearded Botham snatched up the catch as he bellowed his delight. However, Greg Chappell took over, matching Gower's 98 and leading Australia home.

Australia made a white-wash of the series by winning the third Test but not before Botham had smacked an unbeaten 119 in the second innings, Ian Chappell amassing 95 runs for the match for once out, including a share of the match-winning partnership with Greg.

The series only served to intensify the feeling between the two Ians. The animosity lingers, but brother Greg will give Botham the accolades that brother Ian declines.

"I should have known by the way he walked out to bat that day at Trent Bridge in 1977 that we were looking at a man of the future," said Greg. "Botham is a lucky player, but in this game you make your own luck. Botham is that kind of player. He doesn't know how to contain a batsman, he only knows how to try and get him out and he spends every moment trying to get wickets. And he always tries to make quick runs when he's batting. When it comes off it wins Test matches and when it doesn't the critics easily find room to hammer him. He is far and away the cricketer with the most charisma in English cricket."

Adding to his allround skills was his brilliant catching at slip or fearless fielding at suicide point. During the tour he encroached as much into the batsman's territory as the umpires would permit and the grinning, aggressive head was such a torment to the Aussie bats that they did their level best to blast him out of position.

They crashed their drives at him, bruising his feet and forcing him into the x-ray theatre. But still he'd only move closer. It was all part of the challenge. Why back off?

W ho would dare tantalise the most vicious pace bowler the world had seen? Simple – Botham would.

A war of words erupted between Australia's most aggressive fast bowler Jeff "Tommy-Gun" Thomson and the belligerent Englishman. The murderous and unpredictable slinging action of "Thommo" had been terrorising international batsmen for years.

Thommo reacted to a Botham boast that England would sweep the three-Test series by retorting, "Botham can't bat." The arrogant Pom would be cannon fodder for the Australian pacemen.

The allrounder smirked, "With every word of Thommo's philosophy, the smile on my face grows bigger and bigger." Thommo reflected that the Botham mouth was bigger than his bat and did his level best to fill the gap.

Botham's first two tours of Australia were little better than mediocre and despite his impressive early Test figures he wasn't rated particularly highly, not Downunder anyway.

However, back in character-less England, he was looked upon as a favorite son, someone who could lead English cricket out of the wilderness.

Early in 1980, he led the English X1 against county champions Essex. That was the stepping stone to leading England for the first two Tests of the summer against the West Indies. At 24, he was the youngest English captain in almost 100 years. He cleared the first hurdle and his captaincy was extended to cover the remaining three Tests.

After losing the first Test at Trent Bridge he was saved by rain in the second when England was on the ropes. He was then appointed for the remaining three Tests against the Windies, but lost the series 1-0.

General consensus was that England had done themselves proud and could easily have won the series. He was then appointed captain for the next Test series – against the West Indies in the Caribbean. A traumatic and controversial tour that saw England thrashed.

Leaving aside the one-off Centenary Test against Australia at Lord's late in 1980, Botham's first 10 Tests as captain were against the world champion West Indies at their murderous best. You wouldn't give that assignment to your worst enemy – or would you?

Having carried England on his back for several seasons it was not surprising he was now plagued with the all rounder's curse – a chronic back condition. He celebrated his appointment by belting 228 in 184 minutes for Somerset against Gloucestershire, his innings including 27 4s and 10 6s.

But captaincy took its toll on his performances. He tried to do the work of three men as the West Indies toured England: captain, lead bowler and strike batsman. As a result he took only 13 wickets for the series at 29.61 and averaged just 18.77 with the bat and also failed in the one-off Test against Greg Chappell's' Australians.

However, he was confirmed as captain for the return series with the West Indies and nobody envied him the assignment.

New scandal was soon to befall him. The British media had another Botham headline. BOTHAM CHARGED: ASSAULT IN CLUB ALLEGED.

Scunthorpe police charged the English Test captain with assault following an incident outside a nightclub on Christmas Eve. Police said Botham had been drinking with Scunthorpe United footballers in a South Humberside nightclub. He played third division soccer with the club. When reports first appeared in the tabloids, Botham responded, "I didn't lay a finger on anyone – the last thing I want to get involved with is something like this."

Chairman of selectors Alec Bedser said Botham's position as captain could be reviewed if he was charged.

It was next revealed a sailor had laid a complaint. Because the case would not be heard until after the West Indies tour, the England selectors took no action and the tour proceeded with Botham in charge. The English court's Sword of Damocles left swinging over his head.

Botham said, "I'm putting all this out of my mind. All I am going to concentrate on now is the West Indies."

Before he could do that he had to face committal proceedings in the lower court where the case against him was outlined. A fellow soccer player lined up with him in court: Joseph Patrick Neenan, 31, goalkeeper of Scunthorpe United. He pleaded guilty to the charge of assaulting Steven Robert Isbister, 19, occasioning him actual bodily harm and was fined $200 with $200 costs.

He was already a cricket rebel when Bedser, England's seam hero in the immediate post-war years, told Botham if he wanted to retain his captaincy he would have to lighten off. He was more than 30 kgs overweight.

Perhaps the English cricket management should have pressed the issue harder. He was allowed to roll on his rotund way claiming the bulge around his midriff was where he stored all that fuel and energy. If he was any lighter he might not be so strong.

His flirtation with the captaincy was never destined to go the distance. Too much an individual who wanted to do the individual thing was what made him a failure as captain.

He made early mistakes in diplomacy. It was the mouth that got him into trouble after the first two days of the first Test against the West Indies at Port-of-Spain. He threatened his team: "A few heads will roll if the West Indies bowl us out twice in three days."

The Windies had amassed 7-365 in the first couple of days. Three days later he was the anti-hero. England had compounded to lose 20 wickets in the three days – worst of all, Botham had failed personally. A year to the day since he became England's greatest sporting hero with 13 wickets and a century in the Jubilee Test in Bombay, he was called a "traitor" in his homeland.

The game was in its fifth and final day. Geoff Boycott had played with dogged British bulldog courage and Yorkshire grit to make it possible for England to salvage a tough draw. Captain Botham came to the wicket with all England expecting him to do his duty. If he could match Boycott's determination, England may save the game. It didn't matter if Botham didn't score a run. Staying there was what a captain was expected to do.

Botham's response was to lash at a ball from his Somerset clubmate Viv Richards. The ball went soaring into space and fell into the hands of a fieldsman in the deep. Botham was out and England doomed. With the captain throwing it away, discounting Boycott's valiant 70, England fell in a heap to be all out for 169.

Extraordinary criticism flowed through the wounded, bleeding English press: "Like a village green lunatic," one described the shot. "Almost criminal," quoth another. "Stupid and irresponsible," was one of the kindest criticisms. "This was the last sort of example required from their leader" and "an outrageous act of irresponsibility."

The tour of the West Indies went from bad to worse with an abandonment at Guyana and another loss at Bridgetown.

News of the World writer Paul Weaver summed up the 10 week tour with a plea for England to sack Botham as captain before the 1981 Ashes tour, saying Botham was "likeable, strong and talented" but "a disaster as captain."

The last thing Guy the Gorilla needed on return to England was another headline – yet there it was screaming at him from the news stands: Botham Assaults Writer.

Botham was in the firing line again, accused of assaulting Henry Blofeld, the colorful BBC commentator known as "Hatfield" for all the media outlets he serviced.

The assault according to Blofeld who initially decided not to publicise the altercation, was more verbal than physical and took place at the Bermuda Airport after he dared suggest that it was time Botham was dumped.

Blofeld was standing with about 10 colleagues at the Airport when a flushed Botham approached him loudly saying he wanted a word. It was suggested the Airport was not the appropriate place for the discussion but the English skipper persisted. "He then abused me strongly for what I had written about him. He became extremely personal and several times jabbed me forcefully in the chest," said Blofeld.

He recounted how another journalist had suffered similar reprisals and made the comment to Botham that he had a perfect right to express his opinions. Botham had replied – "And I have the right to punch you between the eyes if I wish." This, said Blofeld, was the law of the jungle and it was Botham's character that dictated his reactions. "There is a pig headed obstinacy not to change his mind on almost any subject."

Botham was soon saying, "Some jerks seem to think I'm the fastest gun around and need to be shot down." This followed an early morning incident when he was thrown into a swimming pool by an irate guest at a benefit for Viv Richards. Leamon Bent, 30, a mechanic was reported to be annoyed by Botham's behaviour. The argument was settled out of court when Leamon paid the English star $400 for ruining his suede jacket. The mechanic said he responded to an angry guest's urging for somebody to throw Botham into the pool. "I just snapped, got hold of him and chucked him in. He came up drenched and very uptight."

AN UGLY BIG BRUTE

Guy the Gorilla hired a gorilla of his own. It was reported he took a look-alike rugby mate Andy Withers on tour with him to Australia as a protector.

Andy laughed at suggestion he was an Al Capone style gorilla. "I'm an easy-going guy and I'm just going along because I like cricket and I'm a pal of Ian's. Besides if he gets into trouble he's an ugly big brute who will probably look after it himself."

It was a relieved Ian Botham who learned of his re-appointment to captain England in a one-day series against Australia at the start of the Aussies 1981 tour. After that it was one Test at a time.

He still had his assault trial to come and this would not have eased the tension. He emerged from the first Test with his pants around his knees and being soundly spanked by the ever critical British press. Australia won the match and skipper Kim Hughes felt sorry for Botham as he copped a media pounding. "They're treating him like he's a for-eigner," said Hughes, "Its not just the media, the public is at it too. I feel sorry for the guy."

At Trent Bridge, he had a horror match dropped three catches, scored one and 33 and bowled sloppily when he was required to be tight. The selectors decided the appalling wicket contributed to the failure and reappointed him for Lord's.

The critics howled, pointing to his statistics since being appointed captain – 12 Tests without a win, 276 runs at 14.53 and 32 wickets at 33.59. This compared with a pre-captaincy average of 40.48 with the bat and 18.52 with the ball.

England escaped Lord's with a lucky draw and this time Hughes turned on Botham, saying he had let Australia off the hook.

Kathy Botham had cried when her husband was out for a duck in England's first dig. When he was out first ball in the second innings for a golden duck, she left Lord's and went shopping with the kids. Relief didn't come until a few days later when she heard that Ian had quit as England's captain after being told the selectors would not reappoint him long-term. "Thank God," she sighed.

Explaining his resignation, Botham said, "I did so because I could see the disastrous effect the public examination of my ability to lead was having on my family and on the team. I was supposed to inspire and command."

His replacement, Mike Brearley had previously won 15 and drawn eight of his 27 Tests as captain. It was a wonder he'd ever been sacked.

Botham had captained England 13 times – 10 against the Windies and three against Australia without a win. Brearley said he was confident England could make a comeback and win the series. He described Botham as a colossus, a cricketing genius.

But how would he respond to the humiliation? Brearley asked him if he wanted to play. Bloody oath he did. Those who knew him best – the Australians – feared the worst. Feared the worst for themselves and the best from Botham. They knew if he got bowled over he would back as a fighting fury with the ball. He said it himself, "I'd like to captain England again one day and prove I can captain."

He had a point to prove and the challenge was there in front of him. The third Test against Australia at Leeds.

Wasn't it Test No. 3 against Australia at Nottingham in August 1977 that he made his fabulous debut? A touch of deja vu. Here he was meeting Australia in the third Test of 1981 with his career again on the line. Just the setting for some heroics.

First Australia got away to a magnificent start. Kim Hughes and Graham Yallop batted Australia into a powerful position. Then Botham stepped up and bowled superbly and with incredible variation. At one stage he took 5-25. He stopped Australia dead in its tracks when he took 6-95 off 39.2 overs. All this with a damaged right arm. The last time he had taken five wickets in an innings was the Test before taking over as captain. Australia declared at 9-401.

Dennis Lillee and Terry Alderman all but stitched up the match as they waltzed through the English first innings forcing a follow-on with England 227 in arrears. Only Botham stopped a rout with a fighting 50.

England was not only on the ropes but through the ropes. In the second innings it was reeling as Lillee made it 1-0 when he snared Graham Gooch. Brearley followed at 18 and Gower at 37. Mike Gatting went and England was 4-41. Peter Willey made a dogged stand with Boycott before he went at 105.

Botham, who had some claims to being a Yorkshire breed joined Boycott but after 214 minutes of valiant resistance Boycott succumbed and England was 6-133, still 94 runs from forcing Australia to even bat again. Worse was to come when wicketkeeper Bob Taylor went for one. England was 7-135.

What would you expect from Botham?

With five sessions of the game remaining, Botham was faced with the ultimate and impossible challenge. Still 92 runs behind Australia's first innings total and partnered by bowler and batting rabbit Graham Dilley.

It was a million to one against England winning. Ladbrokes offered 500-1. Dennis Lillee thought the odds ridiculous and suggested the team put 50 pounds from the Players Fund on England as a "saver." He was told not to be so stupid.

Botham had swaggered to the wicket at 5-105 and once again he did it his way. He didn't hold back, crashing drives which almost knocked the pickets off the fence. One of his sternest critics who damned him in the West Indies swore Botham batted like a clap of thunder – his bat was the lightning rod and the sparks flew.

At first the Australians on and off the field were captivated. Australia seemed headed for an easy win, no matter what. In the process they were being treated to a devastating display of power batting. They hoped Dilley could hang around a little. He did, batting for 80 minutes and catching the mood of Botham. The echo of Botham's cracking bat resounded around the ground as the minutes churned by and the scoreboard continued to tumble. He battered the ball rather than stroked it. Here was a one-man show of biblical proportions, only the hero was no David, this man was Goliath with an incredible eye that Cyclops would have envied.

The first milestone came when his 50 was on the board – it included 10 clubbing 4s taken contemptuously from the pride of Australia's pacemen Lillee, Geoff Lawson and Alderman. It wasn't an easy strip, not by any imagination. The struggle of England's other bats was evidence of how great a hand Botham was playing. When Dilley helped him bring up the 100 partnership, England still had three wickets standing and Australia had to bat again.

A few overs later Dilley was out for an invaluable 56. England was 25 runs ahead, two wickets in hand as batting rabbit No.10 Chris Old joined Botham. Australia was reeling and Botham urged his partner to have a crack.

He took only 35 minutes to slam his next 50 and race to one of the most gallant tons of all time. Forty-two of his second 50 had come with boundary shots; and 82 overall.

The roars of the crowd would have done the great MCG proud on Grand Final day. The British Bulldog was on fire and the pride of a nation stirred. The British press declaring of all cricket hours this was England's finest.

Botham was the first player to hit a century and take five wickets in an innings against Australia. He claimed the Australian bowlers became frustrated and Lawson bowled two despised "bean" balls at him. The Australians vigorously denied the allegation although Botham hinted he would "square up" on his next visit to Australia.

Old went with him as he crashed four boundaries to the fence – they raced on a lightning partnership of 67 in just 56 minutes before Old was out for a powerful 29. Hadn't the stubby Bulldog tail wagged proudly this day!

England was 92 runs in front and Kim Hughes deeply concerned – the Poms were now a winning chance and Botham in the final 15 minutes smashed another 31 runs while Bob Willis hung on grimly for one. Botham had clobbered 106 runs in the session from tea to stumps. He left the oval unbeaten on 145 with England 124 runs clear and very much back in the match.

Spectators, English and Australian alike, gave him a hair raising, spine tingling ovation as he stomped from the ground with that huge right fist brandishing his bat. A bat that had a chunk missing. He had clouted one ball so hard a chunk flew off the back of his bat – he disdained the wound, handed the lump of willow to the umpire and batted on.

Rightly so, because that bat deserved its place in that swagger to the pavilion. The bat, in fact, belonged to Gooch who'd made just 2 and 0 for the match. Botham borrowed it on the assumption Gooch had left a lot of runs in it.

The critics who branded him traitor and irresponsible in the West Indies had been shown what Botham believed cricket was all about. An indomitable spirit. This was what he had in mind in the Caribbean.

He was the Botham of old – but a wiser, harder man for the experience.

It was the Australian captain Hughes who put his moment into perspective "This will go down as one of the great innings in cricket history. The big thing about Botham is that he never changes his game. He is the sort of bloke who brings people to cricket and he is the type who can win matches – and he is the only one England has got. Anyone who tells him to change should be lynched."

England added only five runs the next morning and Botham with 149 not out finished just one run short of another world first of 200 runs and six wickets in an

Patrick Eagar

Botham's counter attacking after the Ashes seemed lost in 1981 was an alltime highlight. With centuries at Headingley and Old Trafford, he was instrumental in some astonishing English victories.

innings in the one Test. Australia needed 130 to win and only a few doubted they would accomplish the target with ease. One was Botham. His first two balls were crashed for four but in his next over he took Graeme Wood out of the game. It opened the gate and raised doubt in the Australian batsmen. They floundered as big Bob Willis charged in, decimating the Australian batting with 8-43. Australia made just 111 to lose by 18. Botham was the hero of the nation.

He wasn't finished yet. That win simply levelled the series. Botham was acclaimed as Phoenix – rising from the Ashes. On the eve of the fourth Test at Edgbaston, Prince Charles married Lady Diana Spencer and Botham pledged victory in the Test would be his wedding present to the greatest mating since Romeo and Juliet.

In its two innings in Birmingham, England made 189 and 219 leaving the Australians 151 to win. They were again sailing towards a comfortable victory at 4-105 when Allan Border lost his wicket to John Emburey. Brearley tossed the ball to Botham with Australia five down and needing just 46 runs Botham bowled 28 balls taking 5-1. Australia had again snatched defeat from the jaws of victory.

"The balls hit the wicket and weren't doing much," said Botham. "They were pretty straight. The Australians bottled out. I don't think they could handle it. It was lions and Christians stuff. Suddenly instead of Lillee running in at Melbourne and 90,000 bloody dingoes yelling, 'Lillee, Lillee, Lillee' or 'Kill, Kill, Kill,' it was me going at them with the crowd roused and urging me on."

SAYING NO TO SOUTH AFRICA

Both was No.1 on the shopping list for the renegade international tour of apartheid-torn South Africa in 1982.

Dubbed "The Dirty Dozen" the rebel tourists led by Geoff Boycott were poised to make an announcement that the key man of their tour was about to join – Ian Botham. He was offered $60,000 and bonuses to make the one-month tour. He declined and was then told he could name his own price.

It was a different story late in 1989 when he spoke to Dr. Ali Bacher, chief executive of the South African Cricket Board. This time Bacher told him to name his own price for a tour of South Africa and was assured things had changed and apartheid was on the way out. Botham put a million dollar tax free price on his joining the team for two tours. There was great falling out in the English camp as players manoeuvred for positions on the tour. When the first squad was announced, the Botham name was missing. The negotiators contacted him with a three-year offer which he rejected. Instead he wanted finally to play for England and prove himself against the West Indies. He was shattered a few weeks later when Ted Dexter phoned him and told him, "Hello Ian, I'm afraid we are not taking you to the West Indies."

Botham blew up! England had asked him to keep himself available. It was too late to rekindle the South African deal. He admitted a few bottles of brandy were required to soothe his fury.

A hurricane called Ian hit India in January, 1982. He made a blinding 142 at Kanpur, sharing a fourth wicket stand of 127 of which Gatting made just 10.

The return Tests, in England saw him make 128 at Lord's, batting with a suspected broken toe. Gower was his runner as he registered his 10th Test century. His 11th followed immediately, 208 at The Oval in the third and final Test, many acclaiming him the greatest batsman in the world.

He ridiculed the suggestion saying that title belonged undoubtedly to Viv Richards. "Viv is in a league of his own. I would never compare him to anybody else. Just look at his record. He has only been playing since 1974 and has already amassed 20,000 runs."

The London Sun went even further in its accolades declaring Both the player of the century "as good as W. G. Grace." Don Bradman wasn't mentioned.

The adulation of the Indian crowds during England's winter tour was such that they massed in their thousands outside Botham's hotel just for a glimpse of the great man.

Sometimes a glimpse wasn't enough. One day a spectator jumped from the crowd and in a flash the Beefy family jewels were in his clutch and the Indian was kissing him on the cheek. Botham didn't know what to do so he knocked the fan out.

As Botham continued to dominate home and away, a fierce rivalry developed between Pakistan's Imran Khan and the English superstar. The world was divided over which was the greater player, the three-Test series in 1982 an ideal chance to compare the two champions directly.

Imran fuelled the fires by rating Botham inferior to Keith Miller and Garfield Sobers. "Both" was not interested in comparisons. He let his deeds present his case.

The Pakistanis made the mistake of getting Botham for two and a first ball duck in the first Test at Edgbaston. He was a little off color with a suspected broken toe, his bowling hand was also bruised and swollen and his mouth aching and swollen from stitches in the gums. In the second innings when England needed a big effort, he bowled 21 overs and took two wickets in his first over as England took a 113 run victory. Skipper Bob Willis was profoundly moved. "I had to order him away from the ball when he was too exhausted to argue."

No doubt at all Botham won that series for Willis 2-1. He scored 100 runs for the game in the losing second Test before taking a match winning haul of 9-144 in the Third.

With 21 wickets, Imran had also been magnificent; the critics were again divided.

England now led the series 2-1 and the banner headlines screamed IT'S THAT MAN BOTHAM. He was the most popular man in England but still due to face the courts on criminal assault.

How could they find an English jury who would convict him?

Botham, true to his word gave no thought to the court action, he wasn't finished with the centre stage of cricket just yet. In some ways he was still at the helm for England. Leading by deed and whereas the selectors opted to make sure they saved the fifth Test and safeguarded the Ashes, Botham was in a winning mode.

The fifth and decisive Test at Old Trafford was in the balance with England 5-104 in its second innings and leading by 205 when Botham joined Chris Tavare at the wicket. He had already taken five wickets and held four magnificent catches. But the pendulum had swung and now Lillee and Alderman were in total charge, no matter how good the wicket looked. Botham thought likewise and batted accordingly. His batting was now being described as akin to a powerful blacksmith swinging a heavy hammer. Lillee threw down the gauntlet, placed two men on the long leg boundary and sent two sizzling bouncers at the Botham head – inviting him to hook.

The broad-shouldered powerhouse hooked three 6s off Lillee, pulled one off Alderman and swept another from first-series spinner Ray Bright to bring up his century off only 86 deliveries. He pulverised the Australians with a whirlwind 118 and when he departed, the Test and the Ashes were secure. He had struck a record six 6s.*

Australia fought to the finish with a remarkable fourth innings score of 402, but England still won, Botham picked up his third successive "man of the match" award.

There was a little light relief between Tests as he played in a John Player League match scoring a century in 67 minutes – the second 50 in nine minutes!

There was one Test remaining and he set England on the way by knocking over Australia's first three wickets but the match was drawn and having inspired England's 3-1 triumph Botham was a unanimous "man of the series."

Now Botham could relax – well not really. His next test came a week later at the Grimsby Crown Court. Her Majesty the Queen v The Hero of England, Ian Terrence Botham, charged with assault. He packed his wife and kids off to America while he faced the ordeal. The prosecutor, Graham Richards, claimed the attack on the young rating was "persistent, long and cowardly."

With Botham's trial under way the media that sang his praises was again filling its front page with allegations of assault and painting the prosecution story of two men belting and kicking a teenage rating. The case went two days, Botham denied the assault, the jury failed to agree on a verdict and the prosecution declared they would not present the matter again. No verdict meant he was judicially "not guilty." Botham said he had learned a lesson. He added, "I would rather face Dennis Lillee with a stick of rhubarb than go through that again."

During the 1982-83 tour of Australia, the mandatory scandal broke. The London *Sun* headlined a story alleging Botham had been in a New Year's Eve bar room fight with Australian pace bowler Rodney Hogg. Botham wasted no time taking out a libel writ, claiming heavy damages. He won a settlement.

* The most ever in a Test against Australia.

Heavy was an apt word for the allrounder. His critics lampooned him over his bulging waist line and questioned his fitness. Beefy Botham became the byword for newspaper headlines. One suggesting he was more the shape of a beach ball than an athlete.

Although he had a woeful series, Botham became the first player in history to reach 250 wickets and 3000 runs in Test cricket. It wasn't a glory tour for Botham although he had his moments. Australia careered away to a 2-0 lead after three Tests and needed only four runs in their final innings to take an unassailable three game lead after the fourth Test.

Botham had the ball and was bowling to Australia's last man Jeff Thomson. Thommo needed to nudge just three runs to level the match. "I was scared out of my life," said Botham. He bowled the ball, Thommo caught it with the edge of his bat and the ball flew to slip where it was juggled and finally caught. England and Botham had won the closest Ashes match since 1902.

The Englishmen could still save the Ashes if they won the last Test. "I wouldn't have missed the final moments of that Test for all the gold in the world," said Botham as he predicted a strong showing.

He was wrong, the game was drawn, giving Australia the Ashes 2-1.

His cricket went through a trough as he followed that Australian tour with four Tests in England against New Zealand and a return series of three in New Zealand 1983-84. England won the home series 3-1 with Botham having a modest input, highlighted by his only century 103 in the final Test. Perhaps the challenge wasn't enough to stir his competitive juices.

When critics suggested it was time to drop the moody champion, skipper Willis said, "Name the three players I have to pick to take his place."

For many, England's New Year tour of New Zealand in 1984 was meant to be an enjoyable interlude before having to face the world champion West Indians at home. But the holiday became a nightmare as the English team was branded undisciplined and unworthy as it lost the series 1-0 with two draws. Botham had four hands: 138, 18, 9, 70 while his bowling: 5-95, 1-137, 1-88, 0-70 was also unexceptional for the man toted as the greatest allrounder since Sobers.

Having been beaten by a second class cricket nation, there was worse to come. All hell broke loose as Botham and his mate Allan Lamb were caught up in great scandal emanating from their tour of NZ.

Journalist Mary Burgess swore an affidavit to the *Mail* on Sunday, saying she had been taken to a room in the James Cook Hotel in Wellington by a non-cricketing Englishman who was introduced as Dickie Dirt.

She claimed she came across Botham and Allan Lamb in the room in which drugs were present. Dickie Dirt had offered her some. She said she was not interested and left the room. She alleged one player, Botham, had been "spaced out." The newspaper claimed other girls told them of pot smoking and wild parties during England's disastrous tour of the Shaky Isles.

Donald Carr of England's Test and County Cricket Board applied the gag to Botham and Lamb declaring the allegations were so serious the Board would conduct an investigation. Botham is not easily gagged.

When confronted by two score of reporters on arrival in England from Pakistan, he was asked if he smoked marijuana and indulged in wild parties on the New Zealand tour.

There had been an earlier complaint from an English businessman Ian Brooks who named Botham and Lamb as having behaved "boorishly" in their Auckland hotel during the tour. He alleged drunkenness and surly behaviour. Team manager Alan Smith said the complaint was without justification Botham exploded: "All the drug allegations are lies, bloody lies.

"These stories are farcical and I intend to nail them as quickly as possible."

The media had a field day. Botham seethed, "Enough is enough. Everybody has a breaking point. I've got to point where I ask myself why the hell I should carry on."

One media outlet suggested he was making $600,000 a year, which was a very good reason for continuing his cricket career. The scandal escalated as reporters headed to New Zealand to quiz drug squad police over their probe of the allegations. Even rock star Elton John bought into the scandal. A close friend of Botham's, Elton said it as ridiculous to suggest the cricketer had smoked pot backstage at one of his New Zealand concerts. "With police every six foot how could anyone have a pot smoking party?" Yet Lamb in his biography acknowledged, without naming names, that there *had* been pot smoking at pop concerts.

The reports now flooded back that NZ police in Hamilton had interviewed Lamb and Botham about a broken window in their motel room and reported Chief Supt. Barnie Kelly as saying the player claimed the window had been broken by burglars, "We considered laying charges against one or the other of these men relating to a false complaint of burglary." They decided not to proceed along this line when $220 was forthcoming for the repairs.

Botham diverted attention from the New Zealand uproar by lampooning Pakistan on the BBC. He described Pakistan batting as being "like 11 women tearing each others eyes out" then fled back to London mid-tour for knee surgery. Botham said, "I hope I never have to go to Pakistan again. I think it's a place to send your mother-in-law for a month, all expenses paid."

Drugs and parties in New Zealand were forgotten as the press sunk their teeth into this one. Botham wasted no time in apologising to the Pakistan Board of Control for his remarks. He said he made the remarks at a time when he was feeling the effects of the knee operation and was in a low mood.

This controversy was exacerbated by Pakistan pace bowler Sarfraz Nawaz claiming one English player had been under the influence of drugs during the first Test in Karachi when Pakistan beat England for the first time. Nawaz said the player had been supplied with hash during the Test. "How could he perform well when he was drugged most of the time."

Sarfraz comments were seen as a reprisal for a new Ian Botham controversy. Sarfraz said Botham's comments were a poisonous utterance against Pakistan. On the issue of the drug taking he did not provide details but added, "Some friends told me they knew who supplied the hash in Karachi. I will be prepared to give the name of my informant if I am forced to." Botham moved quickly on any implication that he was the player involved in drug taking in Pakistan – an inference that could have been drawn because of the manner in which Sarfraz drew Botham's name into his criticisms. Botham took out a High court writ against the Daily Express who published the article under a heading BOTHAM ACCUSED BY TEST RIVAL IN NEW POT STORM.

Before he raked in the libel money, he had to spend a bit of his own. He was fined $1530 by the TCCB for his Pakistani insults which penalty the media deemed laughable and weak.

* In his book, *Botham My Autobiography* Botham published details of a New Zealand police investigation that dismissed many of the accusations posed by the media and concluded the release to the media saying there was insufficient evidence to charge any person with an offence.

A RUDE, ARROGANT MAN

The Botham public relations in his benefit year lacked a certain charm.

He attended a benefit dinner staying just long enough to pick up an $8000 cheque. He made a 60 second acceptance speech at the start of the dinner and then walked out leaving the 400 guests with mouths agape – not necessarily for the intake of food. When he heard one of the guests "boo." Botham responded with a snappy encore, "I usually get cheered when I say I'm going to piss off. Cheerio, I hope you don't get too pissed."

His next exercise in public relations to raise eyebrows was a claim that he ruined a village benefit match raising money for him. Botham's county team Somerset played Sparkford. Sparkford's skipper Graham Reeve said afterwards, "Botham is not welcome at the club any more. And from now on we will not play Somerset. It had always been such fun in the past and now Botham has ruined it. He is a rude, arrogant man who didn't have time for us."

The Sparkford supporters said Botham arrived an hour late, refused to sign autographs and poked his tongue out at spectators. He banned Sparkford chairman Murray Corfield from the changing rooms, played half-heartedly and failed to turn up at the barbecue and disco.

It was little wonder he turned sour on the press. Consider some of the banner headlines on the front page of the world's leading newspapers: Botham In Bother at Pub – Botham on the Mat – World Record to Botham – Bravo Botham! – Botham's Bother – Botham New English Skipper – Botham Quits! – Pub Brawl 'Botham Charged' – Botham and Wife in Drug Raid – Botham Guilty – Botham Sent for Trial – Botham Cleared – Botham Belts Chappell – Botham Crashes at 160 mph – Botham Attacks Media Man – Botham Sues Khan – Angry Mechanic Dumps Botham in Pool – Botham insults Pakistan – Botham insults Mothers'-in Law – Botham Apologises – Botham Rises – Botham Falls – Botham Pulls Out – Amazing Botham – Botham Turns Series – Botham "It's All Lies."

This was the player who admitted he deliberately ran out batting legend and English skipper Geoff Boycott because he was batting too slowly. That's what we call a Wildman.

The euphoria of Botham's return to omnipotence against Australia, India and Pakistan from 1981-83 had long since dissipated and a wave of scandal sent his career tumbling again. The timing couldn't have been worse as England geared up for a five-Test visit by the West Indies. With England's morale a shambles, they were white-washed losing all five Tests by massive margins, Botham's form sporadic at best. He had glory at Lord's with a first innings haul of 8-103 and another bowling highlight of 5-72 in the first innings at The Oval. He made three half centuries but his burning ambition to prove his greatness could never be satisfied until he performed a dominating role against the world's best. "I've never made a century against them or won a series. Until I do I am not fulfilled," said Botham.

In the process Botham passed more magical milestones. At Lord's against the Windies he reached his 4000 runs in Test cricket which attached to his 300-plus Test wickets in 69 Tests made him statistically the greatest allrounder the game had seen.

But he shocked English cricket authorities by suddenly pulling out of the tour of India and Australia to "take a break after eight years of solid cricket." He should have gone, because while England was away all hell broke loose at the Bothams.

They were all set to enjoy an English New Year at Epworth when there was a hammer on the door and in marched the British drug squad. The police searched the premises, seized some substances and arrested Ian and Kathy Botham. Their world was again shattered as they were released pending investigation.

From the time he entered Test cricket, Ian Botham was a headliner with a capital "H."

This was his worst nightmare – now his wife, an innocent victim, was embroiled in the affair and one thing that could be said about Botham was that he had stoically shielded his family as best he could from the glare of the media spotlight.

Ironically the raid came on the final day of his benefit year which raised $140,000 tax free for the Bothams. The media hounded the Bothams into sanctuary. For that he was greeted with a heading BOTHAMS IN HIDING.

Soon after Botham's lawyers announced Mrs. Botham would be cleared of involvement and Ian would plead guilty to being in possession of 2.19 gm of cannabis. He was charged with possessing drugs and fined $148 in the Scunthorpe Court. He said the pot was given to him during a West Indies tour and had been in his bedroom draw for up to three years – it had a street value of $6.

Botham was available when Australia toured in 1985 and despite the conjecture he was one of the first players chosen. England salvaged some pride and took the Ashes although Botham was again disappointing with the bat. He did exercise considerable control over Australia with the ball.

England won the 1985 series 3-1 and Botham had another controversial season, warned for intimidating bowling against the Australians and carpeted for seemingly dissenting with expletives the judgments of umpire Alan Whitehead. It all blew over with a mild rebuke but not before Botham threatened to sue if the TCCB punished him.

Sticking up for mate Viv Richards also landed him in hot water after he referred to Yorkshire fans as "arrogant, bigoted, biased and a bunch of racial idiots." He was angered by racial taunts directed at Viv during a one-day county game between Yorkshire and Somerset. "Yorkshire crowds seemed to taunt every player who is black."

He was again in the headlines when he did not sign an agreement to random dope-testing. He was joined in refusal by Viv Richards and Joel Garner who claimed it infringed their civil rights.

Botham also upset Yorkshire legend Fred Trueman suggesting Freddie spoke twaddle. The fiery Yorkshireman spat back, "He says I talked twaddle and that his teammates are with him. I can only assume they are as daft as he is. Botham's been bowling rubbish for the past 10 years. I don't think he can bowl a hoop downhill."

Botham redeemed himself in many eyes when he undertook the 1400 kilometre walks for John O'Groats in Caitness, Scotland to Land's End in Cornwall. The walk was aimed at raising money for leukemia research. His effort was inspired by one-legged cancer victim Steve Fonyo raising $7 million by running across Canada.

Patrick Eagar

Botham the bogeyman dismisses Wayne Phillips, Old Trafford, 1985.

The walk took 34 days and while he was the 454th person to complete the feat in 1985, he's the only one remembered for the feat. He raised $865,200 for the appeal, eventually passing two million. Again a casual walk through the English countryside had its moments. As he neared the end of his marathon he was alleged to have punched a motor cycle policeman three times. In view of the event, no action was taken.

Doing mileage for cancer became a worthy obsession with Botham. He walked dangerous territory in Ireland, he walked anywhere and everywhere raising millions. He even found some elephants and with Aussie mate Greg Ritchie duplicated Hannibal's 800 km trek across the Alps. He set himself a $7.8 million target on that one.

Occasionally he admitted he made mistakes. It was in 1984 he ran across Lord "Tim" Hudson who took over as his agent and turned his world upside down in a wave of promotional ballyhoo in which he had Beefy convinced he was going to be a Hollywood movie great, a fashion leader and multi-millionaire.

The association all but made him an international fool and nearly wrecked his marriage. The one blessing was Botham was color blind and never quite realised how garish were the clothes Hudson cloaked him in.

In a whirl, he quit Somerset after Viv Richards and Joel Garner were dumped. He blamed Peter Roebuck for their removal. Some said he beat the Somerset axe by 24 hours.

The stage was then set for the 1985-86 tour of the West Indies and if Botham was to prove himself against his nemesis he got off to an awful start. He arrived in the Caribbean having played the West Indies in three series for no wins, six draws and eight losses. He had not scored a century in 14 games and only two hauls of five wickets in an innings.

He was soon calling home and warning wife Kathy there was a new scandal alleging womanising and drugs involving a beauty queen and a socialite. It was little wonder England suffered another towelling by the Windies, losing the five match series 5-0 by massive margins. This made 10 straight defeats by huge margins and an unhappy Botham could not lay his ghost.

Ten hands produced a tour high of just 38 runs, an aggregate of 168 at 16.80. He took

11 wickets at 48.63 and only one haul of 5-71. It was the low point of his career, even worse than when he lost the captaincy for this time his fierce spirit had not been able to arrest the downhill toboggan that had become his career.

Later that year, the old stories came back to haunt him. Headings relating to the old New Zealand scandal surfaced, Botham displayed them in his own autobiography: I SAW IAN BOTHAM TAKE HEROIN and POT, COCAINE, HEROINE AND PETHIDINE.. TEST STAR TOOK THE LOT

The allegations had been made by Australian society figure Vivien Kinsella who had since died. Botham decided to drop his libel action against *The Mail on Sunday* rather than have people hurt by raking over the material again. That publication then ran a story headed: BOTHAM: I DID TAKE POT. A long article followed as part of an agreed compromise with Botham. The article acknowledged he had lied when he denied using pot. He also acknowledged in the article that *The Mail on Sunday* was not a paper that printed scandal for the sake of scandal. His back off was "one of the most difficult days of my life."

The TCCB acted swiftly, conducted a hearing and found him guilty of bringing the game into disrepute and not clearing *The Mail on Sunday* article with the Board. He was given a two month suspension from all cricket. A much shorter sentence than "life" demanded by Denis Compton. He did his time and came back to first-class cricket knowing his neck was on the block. He belted 175 not out in a county one-day match, hitting 13 6s.

Then came the third Test against New Zealand. England had to win to save the series. First ball he dismissed opener Bruce Edgar which equalled Dennis Lillee's record wicket haul of 355. Second ball snicked by Jeff Crowe through slips. In his next over he took Crowe out to become the new world record wicket taker. He was back in style and knocked up 59 not out in his only innings.

Getting selected is a cricketer's first requirement. Which made it hard to comprehend Beefy's blast at selectors during a Manchester dinner address. He described the English selectors as a "bunch of gin slinging old dodderers."

When a spy recorded his after-dinner jibe and released it to the media Botham was forced to make hasty repairs suggesting the dig was done in jest.

The selectors blushed and accepted his assurances, they knew they had to have him in Australia for the 1986-87 tour.

He, too, wanted to get at Australia. It rankled that he was regarded as a failure on Australian wickets and a failure against the West Indies on all wickets. He had won more Tests for England by individual effort than any man yet his triumphs were not on the toughest and most demanding of enemy soil.

He set himself a target in Australia:
· 30 Test wickets
· 400 runs
· Five catches

This would eclipse Sir Garfield Sobers' Test treble of 2000 runs, 200 wickets and 100 catches. He would have more than 350 wickets, 4000 runs and 101 catches. And still only 31 years old. He fell well short of his target with 189 runs and nine wickets, missing one Test with injury. He did take 10 catches which put him ahead of Sir Gary anyway.

His performances removed one of the monkeys from his back although the greatest surgeon and psychiatrist on earth couldn't remove the chip from his shoulder.

He proved he was still great and could play cricket Downunder even if he didn't live up to his own high expectations. He helped win the series for England. He set about that on the first day when he plundered a century from the Aussie attack. His 138 and bowling aggregate of 3-92 set up a seven wicket win. He failed in Perth and missed the third with injury. He stepped up again with 5-41 and three superb catches to set up an innings win in Melbourne. He failed with bat and ball in the fifth which Australia won.

Arriving home in England to a forgiving media, he was hero material again and if he'd blotted his copybook at any time on the Australian tour nobody heard about it. He had won the series with saintly decorum.

A CONTROVERSIAL FAREWELL
Flight 55: Beefy's Crash Landing! The headlines roared again –
BOTHAM FLIGHT DRAMA

The bully boy was at it again. The English dynamo had been grabbed by Federal police after urgent calls from the captain of Ansett's flight 55 from Brisbane to Perth. Australian cricket lovers, officials in particular, were horrified.

Botham was on two charges of passenger assault and another of disorderly conduct. Australians Greg Ritchie and Allan Border were also grilled by Federal Police about incidents on the flight. Botham's first statement was that he had not been "directly involved."

There was grave concern as rumors flew that Border would be charged. He was proved blameless other than a verbal exchange with Botham. Ritchie was also facing charges

It took time for the full details to emerge through the courts and cricket's Book of Revelations – the media. More scandals came to light. Dennis Lillee and Botham had been involved in a late night escapade at the Launceston cricket ground which resulted in $1800 damage to the dressing room. The Australian Cricket Board fined them over the incident and paid for the damage out of the fine.

One report said Botham had gone with the Australian skipper to Border's room to thrash out a dispute. Botham was said to have kicked at a door until the pain to his foot made him stop. There was some damage to furniture but Border thought it best not to take the matter further.

The mateship of Border and Botham, which later regenerated, had worn very thin over issues of leadership and Ritchie. Ritchie was about to join with Botham in Italy to take some elephants for a walk, Botham thought Border should have given his mate more support to keep his place in the Australian Test side.

The Queenslanders flew into Tullamarine from Brisbane to board the flight 55 to Perth. It was clear Botham was in one of those moods and had an early altercation with a female attendant in the Tullamarine bar. In the plane Ritchie took over Botham's seat next to Border and began talking to his skipper about Greg's demise on the international scene. Ten minutes before arrival at Perth, Botham took back his seat and abused Border for not including him in team discussions. Border said they were not discussing the team and Botham should mind his own business.

Passengers said the expletives flew. Perth Magistrates Court was told a passenger had asked the cricketers to "turn it down." Botham's defence lawyer John Staude conceded Botham's conduct was offensive and obscene. Staude said Botham's response to the passenger request was "to lean forward and put his hand on both sides of the passenger's head and tell him 'to mind his own business.' " At this stage another passenger, Allan Winter, told Botham, "Come on fella, keep it down, it's becoming a bit common in here." Winter said Botham gripped him by the scalp and hair, proceeding to shake his head from side to side forcefully on several occasions and called Winter an obscene name.

Botham told a startled passenger, "You! Eyes to the front. Shut up, otherwise you will be next." After the plane landed Botham approached Winter to apologise but it was too late for that. The prosecutor, Jeff Schools, said throughout the flight Botham had used obscene language which frightened passengers and he became worse when he began arguing with Border. Botham was fined $500 on a charge of assaulting Winter and $300 for offensive behaviour – he pleaded guilty to both charges.

Air stewards industrial officer Maurice Alexander said if the ACB did not give guarantees about cricketers behaviour in the future, a ban would be considered. "They can transport them by train or in a cargo hold, or separate aircraft as the VRC did with Bonecrusher."

It was no surprise that the shell-shocked Queensland team capitulated in Perth and missed its chance to win a first Shield. Greg Chappell headed a push for the Queenslanders to use a clause in its contract to sack Botham – which they did. There were headlines across the world as the English giant was sacked for breaching the code of conduct. In his cricket death throes Botham lashed about. He questioned Chappell's right to accuse, bringing up the underarm tactics used to beat New Zealand. Chappell stood his ground saying at least underarm was within the rules even if it was against the spirit of the game.

The ACB also fined him $5000 for two breaches of the code of behaviour – the flight 55 and Launceston outrages. Lillee was fined $1800 for his part. Botham retorted, "$5000 is about fifty quid sterling so I'm not really too bothered." In fact his behaviour put more than $1 million at risk as sponsorships wavered and Botham's career tottered.

No doubt with some input from wife Kathy, he announced he was finished with touring.

Both met up with the Pakistani team and they were not great friends. There was plenty of fire during and after a one-dayer at Edgbaston four Pakistani spectators complained to police the English allrounder had smashed their rear car window after he was caught in a traffic jam. Police said they were preparing a report and Botham made allegations against the fans.

England lost the five Test series 1-0, Botham didn't bowl because of his back condition, he batted moderately with the exception of a second innings 51 not out in 253 minutes that saved the fifth Test. In the course of the series he made his 5000th Test run. When he hit that run he had 14 centuries, 373 wickets and 109 catches

Botham struck a three-year deal to play Sheffield Shield cricket for Queensland which had never won the Shield. Against the earnest advice of Greg Chappell, Queensland decided Botham was the man to help get them there. So he came to Australia for the 1987-88 season and was greeted with unabashed joy by the Queensland skipper and friend Allan Border. How Border wishes he hadn't made that visit.

The trouble with Ian was that although he was larger than life he couldn't accept his behaviour matched the profile. He was constantly over the top as his trip to Australia for the 1986-87 tour was to show. Once again he claimed the media exaggerated his deeds. That line of defence was palpably wearing thin and the general consensus was that he was a bully-boy who refused to believe the greatest showman on earth had to yield to basic rules of conduct.

It was at this stage Botham almost became an Australian. To have Viv Richards join Queensland as their allowed international, Beefy was prepared to take out Australian citizenship. "Technicalities" such as residential requirements blocked the move.

Botham would not accept that being blessed with remarkable sporting talent was not a licence to ride rough shod over the meek who were entitled by the protection of

THE INCOMPARABLE FREDDIE TRUEMAN

Ian Botham took up the baton for England's most revered post-war pace
and seam bowlers from the lionhearted Alec Bedser through to
"Typhoon" Tyson, Brian Statham and the larger-than-life Frederick
Sewards Trueman.

A BBC special: Fred Trueman – This Is Your Life magnified the problems of globetrotting professional cricketer.

What was intended as a celebration turned sour when Mrs Enid Trueman told of her anguish in living with England's cricketing icon. It was impossible, she said, to have any home life married to Freddie Trueman. He'd been unfaithful while on tour and even when he was home, the intrusions on his time made it impossible for them to have any sort of privacy. They fought often and Trueman spent countless nights in his car outside his house in the Yorkshire Dales.

Twelve hours before his fabulous 6-1 spell against the 1961 Australians at Headingley, they'd had another fearful row and he'd spent the night with an overcoat for a blanket in his car in a Leeds car park before arriving early at the ground for a wash and a shave.

So tunnel visioned was The Stainton Express, however, that he refused to allow his much-publicised marriage breakdown and subsequent divorce to affect his performance.

He defied constant put downs from the cricketing establishment to become one of post-war cricket's mightest players.

After falling foul of authority during the 1953-54 tour of the West Indies, he was subsequently omitted from England's next two winter tours, to Australia and South Africa. His crime? To bounce a West Indian and break his jaw after he'd twice been called a "white bastard."

Trueman was so mad he refused to apologise. He went back to his mark and sat down. It was one of the few times he intentionally hurt a player. He seldom bowled a deliberate bouncer at a tailender, even when requested to by his captains. He said it stemmed back to the only man he was ever afraid of, his father,

If he happened to accidentally injure a rival, his father would be waiting at home and announce, "You've been at it again have you?" before pointing out the fellow professional Trueman had injured probably had a wife and a family to support.

"In my prime I could have hit anybody I wanted," said Trueman. "Those I did, apart from three exceptions, happened either accidentally or in the heat of the moment."

In a topline career spanning 20 years, Trueman was acclaimed as the world's fastest bowler for 10, being timed as a 30-year-old at 92 mph and even faster off the pitch.

"I bowled faster over a longer period than anyone else," he said.

An authentic eccentric, he became the first man to 300 Test wickets and announced anyone who followed would be "bluddy tired."

Fred Trueman – in brief

Born: February 6, 1931
Teams: Yorkshire & England
First-class debut: 1949
First-class record: Matches 603. Batting – Runs 9231, Average 15.56, Highest score 104, 100s 3. Bowling – Wickets 2304, Average 18.29, Best bowling 8-28, Five wickets in an Innings 126, Ten wickets in a Match 23. Fielding – Catches 439.
Test debut: 1952
Test record: Matches 67. Batting – Runs 981, Average 13.81, Highest score 39 not out. Bowling – Wickets 307, Average 21.57, Best bowling 8-31, Five wickets in an Innings 17, Ten wickets in a Match 3. Fielding – Catches 64.
Tours: Australia 1958-59, 1962-63; West Indies 1953-54, 1959-60; New Zealand 1958-59, 1962-63. He also toured South Africa in 1960-61 and the West Indies in 1963-64 and 1964-65 with the International Cavaliers; India in 1956-57 with C.G. Howard's XI; and represented a Prime Minister's XI in India in 1967-68.

the law to their share of this earth. Botham came to Australia and did magnificent things, he also did rough, outrageous things and embarrassed the game, his country and his friends in the process.

In the beginning Ian Botham was good for Queensland. They won four out of their first five matches and their crowds trebled – then the inevitable. Queensland had to beat Victoria to host the Shield final at the 'Gabba, where victory would all but be assured. Victorian skipper Dean Jones said he wouldn't be doing Border and Botham any favors. He would try to avoid outright defeat. When Botham toiled in vain for 17 overs and 1-53 he cut loose with the mouth. This led to umpires Robin Bailhache and Darrell Holt putting him on report for swearing. Dean Jones and the Vics held the Queenslanders out and they were forced to fly to Perth and more trouble leading into the final.

His farewell Ashes year against Australia in 1989 opened typically. A hotel security officer took out a summons for assault alleging he had been head-butted by Botham in a row over a taxi. Police agreed with Botham there was no case to answer and the security guard withdrew his summons. Botham claims to have received an out of court settlement for a Sun article headed BOOZED BOTHAM NUTTED HOTEL'S GUARD.

Police said they would take no action over another incident at the Britannia pub, Northampton. The publican said Botham roused jealousy when he began talking to some women at a barbecue, three of their boyfriends threw him into a toilet.

A broken cheekbone in a county match kept him out of the first two Tests against Australia. He was recalled for the final three matches and performed poorly as England lost the Ashes series. He averaged only 15.50 with the bat and took three wickets at 80.33

It seemed to surprise him that having put aside his decision not to tour again, he was not selected for the tour of the West Indies. It seemed Botham's Test career was over without one last shot at the Windies.

But two years later he was recalled for the 1991 series against the West Indies only to injure himself before the first and unable to make it to the crease until the fifth Test. He knew this was the last traditional crack at the world champions and finally he played with a winning England Test team. He went in at No. 7 and stood on his wicket at 31. He took 3-67 and was five not out when the winning run was struck that gave England a win by three wickets.

That was good enough to get him a Test against Sri Lanka, a trip to the Southern Hemisphere for the World Cup and a tour of New Zealand followed by two home Tests against Pakistan in 1992. Although he measured up to the slather and whack of the one day matches, his Test appearances only served to prove that the great cricketer had gone well beyond that "use by" date. He made his retirement official on July 18, 1993. He had set himself a target of 6000 Test runs and 400 wickets and finished only marginally short with 5200 runs and 383 wickets and 120 catches

The cricketer might have been finished but not the controversy. He was still destined to make headlines and not the least of these came with the ball tampering scandals that broke over Pakistan and ultimately led to the court confrontation with Imran Khan as Beefy and Lamb sued unsuccessfully for libel.

"I wouldn't change a thing," said Botham when asked if he would make any adjustments if he had his career over again. At the time the question was posed he was a millionaire, had a loyal and devoted family, was statistically the world's greatest ever allrounder and boasting a host of equally raucous and outrageous personalities as friends. Why would he change?

Ian Botham THE MAN & HIS RECORD

Born: November 24, 1955

Teams: Somerset, Worcestershire, Queensland, Durham & England

First-class debut: 1973

First-class record: Matches 402. Batting — Runs 19399, Average 33.97, Highest score 228, 100s 38. Bowling — Wickets 1172, Average 27.27, Best bowling 8-34, Five wickets in an Innings 59, Ten wickets in a Match 8. Fielding — Catches 354.

Test debut: 1977

Test record: Matches 102. Batting — Runs 5200, Average 33.54, Highest score 208, 100s 14, 50s 22. Bowling — Wickets 383, Average 28.40, Best bowling 8-34, Five wickets in an Innings 27, Ten wickets in a Match 4. Fielding — Catches 120. Captaincy — Matches 12, Wins 0, Losses 4, Draws 8.

One day international debut: 1976

One day international record: Matches 116. Batting — Runs 2113, Average 23.22, Highest score 79, 50s 9. Bowling — Wickets 145, Average 28.54, Best bowling 4-31, Four wickets in a Match 3. Fielding — Catches 36. Captaincy — Matches 9, Wins 4, Losses 5.

Tours: Australia 1978-79, 1979-80, 1982-83, 1986-87; West Indies 1980-81, 1985-86; New Zealand 1977-78, 1983-84, 1991-92; India 1979-80, 1981-82; Pakistan 1977-78, 1983-84; Sri Lanka 1981-82.

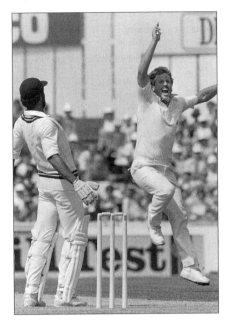

Ian Botham's Test record series by series:

BATTING & FIELDING

Season	Opponent	Mt	Inns	No	HS	Runs	Ave	100s	50s	Ct.
1977	Australia (h)	2	2	0	25	25	12.50	-	-	1
1977-78	New Zealand (a)	3	5	1	103	212	53.00	1	1	5
1978	Pakistan (h)	3	3	0	108	212	70.66	2	-	4
	New Zealand (h)	3	3	0	22	51	17.00	-	-	2
1978-79	Australia (a)	6	10	0	74	291	29.10	-	2	11
1979	India (h)	4	5	0	137	244	48.80	1	-	10
1979-80	Australia (a)	3	6	1	119*	187	37.40	1	-	3
	India (a)	1	1	0	114	114	114.00	1	-	-
1980	West Indies (h)	5	8	0	57	134	16.75	-	1	2
	Australia (h)	1	1	0	0	0	-	-	-	-
1980-81	West Indies (a)	4	8	0	35	108	13.50	-	-	5
1981	Australia (h)	6	12	1	149*	399	36.27	2	1	12
1981-82	India (a)	6	8	0	142	440	55.00	1	4	3
	Sri Lanka (a)	1	1	0	13	13	13.00	-	-	-
1982	India (h)	3	3	0	208	403	134.33	2	1	1
	Pakistan (h)	3	6	0	69	163	27.16	-	2	1
1982-83	Australia (a)	5	10	0	58	270	27.00	-	1	9
1983	New Zealand (h)	4	8	0	103	282	35.25	1	1	3
1983-84	New Zealand (a)	3	4	0	138	226	56.50	1	1	3
	Pakistan(a)	1	2	0	22	32	16.00	-	-	4
1984	West Indies (h)	5	10	0	81	347	34.70	-	3	5
	Sri Lanka (h)	1	1	0	6	6	6.00	-	-	-
1985	Australia (h)	6	8	0	85	250	31.25	-	2	8
1985-86	West Indies (a)	5	10	0	38	168	16.80	-	-	4
1986	New Zealand (h)	1	1	1	59*	59	-	-	1	-
1986-87	Australia (a)	4	6	0	138	189	31.50	1	-	10
1987	Pakistan (h)	5	8	1	51*	232	33.14	-	1	3
1989	Australia (h)	3	4	0	46	62	15.50	-	-	3
1991	West Indies (h)	1	2	1	31	35	35.00	-	-	3
	Sri Lanka (h)	1	1	0	22	22	22.00	-	-	2
1991-92	New Zealand (a)	1	2	0	15	16	8.00	-	-	1
1992	Pakistan (h)	2	2	0	6	8	4.00	-	-	2
Totals		102	161	6	208	5200	33.54	14	22	120

BOWLING

Season	Opponent	Mt	Balls	Mdn	Runs	Wick	Ave	BB	5wI	10wM
1977	Australia (h)	2	438	16	202	10	20.20	5-21	2	-
1977-78	New Zealand (a)	3	808	17	311	17	18.29	5-73	2	-
1978	Pakistan (h)	3	455	19	209	13	16.07	8-34	1	-
	New Zealand (h)	3	853	42	337	24	14.04	6-34	3	1
1978-79	Australia (a)	6	1268	25	567	23	24.65	4-42	-	-
1979	India (h)	4	1074	49	472	20	23.60	5-35	2	-
1979-80	Australia (a)	3	1039	14	371	19	19.52	6-78	2	1
	India (a)	1	293	14	106	13	8.15	7-48	2	1
1980	West Indies (h)	5	786	41	385	13	29.61	3-50	-	-
	Australia (h)	1	188	3	132	1	132.00	1-43	-	-
1980-81	West Indies (a)	4	872	31	492	15	32.80	4-77	-	-
1981	Australia (h)	6	1635	81	700	34	20.58	6-95	3	1
1981-82	India (a)	6	1443	52	660	17	38.82	5-61	1	-
	Sri Lanka (a)	1	149	2	65	3	21.66	3-28	-	-
1982	India (h)	3	561	16	320	9	35.55	5-46	1	-
	Pakistan (h)	3	905	33	478	18	26.55	5-74	1	-
1982-83	Australia (a)	5	1283	35	729	18	40.50	4-75	-	-
1983	New Zealand (h)	4	677	27	340	10	34.00	4-50	-	-
1983-84	New Zealand (a)	3	658	25	354	7	50.57	5-59	1	-
	Pakistan (a)	1	180	5	90	2	45.00	2-90	-	-
1984	West Indies (h)	5	980	30	667	19	35.10	8-103	2	-
	Sri Lanka (h)	1	336	12	204	7	29.14	6-90	1	-
1985	Australia (h)	6	1510	36	855	31	27.58	5-109	1	-
1985-86	West Indies (a)	5	809	12	535	11	48.63	5-71	1	-
1986	New Zealand (h)	1	156	4	82	3	27.33	3-75	-	-
1986-87	Australia (a)	4	638	24	296	9	32.88	5-41	1	-
1987	Pakistan (h)	5	807	30	433	7	61.85	3-217	-	-
1989	Australia (h)	3	480	15	241	3	80.33	2-63	-	-
1991	West Indies (h)	1	162	8	67	3	22.33	2-40	-	-
	Sri Lanka (h)	1	96	5	41	1	41.00	1-26	-	-
1991-92	New Zealand (a)	1	132	5	76	2	38.00	2-23	-	-
1992	Pakistan (h)	2	144	8	61	0	-	0-9	-	-
Totals		102	21815	736	10878	383	28.40	8-34	27	4

COUNTRY BY COUNTRY RECORD

BATTING & FIELDING

Country	Mt	Inns	No	HS	Runs	Ave	100s	50s	Ct.
v Australia	36	59	2	149*	1673	29.75	4	6	57
v India	14	17	0	208	1201	70.64	5	5	14
v New Zealand	15	23	2	138	846	40.28	3	4	14
v Pakistan	14	21	1	108	647	32.35	2	3	14
v Sri Lanka	3	3	0	22	41	13.66	-	-	2
v West Indies	20	38	1	81	792	21.40	-	4	19

HOME & ABROAD

	Mt	Inns	No	HS	Runs	Ave	100s	50s	Ct.
Tests at home	59	88	4	208	2930	34.88	8	13	63
Tests abroad	43	73	2	142	2266	31.91	6	9	57

BOWLING

Country	Mt	Balls	Mdn	Runs	Wick	Ave	BB	5wI	10WM
v Australia	36	8479	249	4093	148	27.65	6-78	9	2
v India	14	3371	131	1558	59	26.40	7-48	6	1
v New Zealand	15	3284	120	1500	63	23.80	6-34	6	1
v Pakistan	14	2491	95	1271	40	31.77	8-34	2	0
v Sri Lanka	3	581	19	310	11	28.18	6-90	1	0
v West Indies	30	3609	122	2146	61	35.18	8-103	3	0

HOME & ABROAD

Tests at home	59	12243	475	6226	227	27.42	8-34	17	2
Tests abroad	43	9572	261	4652	156	29.82	7-48	10	2

HIS HIGHEST TEST SCORES

208	v India, The Oval, 1982
149*	v Australia, Leeds, 1981
142	v India, Kanpur, 1981-82
138	v New Zealand, Wellington, 1983-84
138	v Australia, Brisbane, 1986-87
137	v India, Leeds. 1979

HIS BEST TEST BOWLING

8-34	v Pakistan, Lord's, 1978
8-103	v West Indies, Lord's, 1984
7-48	v India, Bombay, 1979-80
6-34	v New Zealand, Trent Bridge, 1978
6-58	v India, Bombay, 1979-80
6-78	v Australia, Perth, 1979-80
6-90	v Sri Lanka, Lord's 1984
6-95	v Australia, Leeds, 1981
6-101	v New Zealand, Lord's, 1978
6-125	v Australia, The Oval, 1981
5-11	v Australia, Birmingham, 1981
5-21	v Australia, Leeds, 1977
5-35	v India, Lord's, 1979
5-39	v New Zealand, Lord's, 1978
5-41	v Australia, Melbourne, 1986-87
5-46	v India, Lord's, 1982

HIS HIGHEST ONE-DAY INTERNATIONAL SCORES

79	v New Zealand, Christchurch, World Cup 1992
72	v Australia, Manchester, 1985
71	v Australia, Melbourne, 1986-87
68	v Australia, Perth, 1986-87
65	v New Zealand, Adelaide, 1982-83
60	v Sri Lanka, Colombo, 1981-82
60	v West Indies, St Vincent, 1980-81
53	v Australia, Sydney, World Cup 1992
52	v India, Cuttack, 1981-82

HIS BEST ONE-DAY INTERNATIONAL BOWLING

4-31	v Australia, Sydney, World Cup 1992
4-45	v West Indies, Birmingham, 1991
4-56	v India, Leeds, 1982
3-16	v Australia, Melbourne, 1978-79
3-23	v Zimbabwe, Albury, World Cup 1992
3-26	v Australia, Sydney, 1986-87
3-29	v Pakistan, Perth, 1986-87
3-29	v Australia, Brisbane, 1982-83
3-33	v West Indies, Melbourne, 1979-80
3-33	v West Indies, Devonport, 1986-87

Beating the cold in Melbourne, 1982-83

10

TORMENTED GENIUS

"He is not mature enough mentally. He is flying off the handle when he shouldn't be. I know he has a great cricketing brain, he knows the game and is a great batsman, but to lead a nation you have to be more than that." – MICHAEL HOLDING

West Indian virtuoso Brian Lara enjoyed 50 days of colossal scoring in 1994 which surpassed even the deeds of Bradman. It was like walking on the moon. No wonder he cracked up.

You can't expect brilliance without flaws. Sporting starlets blessed with uncommon skills invariably walk a tightrope. Their natural genius commands adoring audiences, but temperamentally many struggle to handle the resultant wave of recognition.

As cricket's first truly international megastar, Brian Lara, the ultimate flat wicket bully with the pop star following, became a prisoner of his fame.

He didn't set out to cause trouble; it followed him. He had any amount of time to play his shots; but no time to live his life. His astonishing runmaking feats of 1994 and resultant adulation led to worldwide acclaim, but complicated his life forever.

He couldn't cope and with West Indian cricket in decline, became so sensitive to the internal politics within and around the team that he withdrew from the 1995-96 Australian tour, temporarily abandoning the game he'd played with irresistible charm and skill since he was in three-cornered pants.

In the cricket-crazy islands of the Caribbean, his boycott was like a death in the family. As the proud holder of the most illustrious run records of them all, his life was a fairytale. He had his own brand of jewellery, a line of 501 jeans, unlimited free air travel, luxury accommodation and was generally feted like a visiting royal. Even his deadliest opponents called him "Prince."

Patrick Eagar Photography

263

FIFTY DAYS OF GREATNESS, April-June, 1994

Game	Date	Score	For	Against	Venue	Balls	4s	6s
1	April 16-24	375	West Indies	England	St. John's	538	45	-
2	April 28-May 1	147	Warwickshire	Glamorgan	Edgbaston	160	20	2
3	May 5-9	106	Warwickshire	Leicestershire	Edgbaston	136	18	-
	May 5-9	120*	Warwickshire	Leicestershire	Edgbaston	163	22	-
4	May 19-23	136	Warwickshire	Somerset	Taunton	94	14	2
5	May 27-30	26	Warwickshire	Middlesex	Lord's	48	3	-
	May 27-30	140	Warwickshire	Middlesex	Lord's	147	22	1
6	June 2-6	501*	Warwickshire	Durham	Edgbaston	427	62	10

Seeing Lara strike his cover drives with a full, uninhibited swing of the bat had become as great a joy as watching any of the champions of the generation. No-one could open and close the face of his bat in mid-stroke quite like him, his ability to improvise and find the gaps unequalled. He may not have had the violence of Viv Richards, but he possessed more shots.

His absence may have been blissfully brief, but his frequent blow-ups on and off the field a constant reminder that even the greats have their weaknesses.

Instead of celebrating his career and revelling in his masterly batsmanship, some regard him as a cricketing renegade whose good name has been scarred forever.

A fiery and unhappy 1995 tour of England in which he was accused of disloyalty by his captain Richie Richardson was the catalyst for his withdrawal from the Australian World Series.

One of four West Indian tourists fined 10 per cent of their tour fees after he briefly left the tour in the first week of August, Lara apologised to the Board and pledged his total commitment to West Indian cricket. It was an unreserved apology and he was livid when still subject to a fine.

In a press conference which triggered headlines around the world, Lara said he needed a break from the pressures of international cricket and from the West Indian team itself. Voicing his own personal protest after a meeting with a fully-supportive Trinidad & Tobago sports minister Pamela Nicholson, he announced his withdrawal from the squad to Australia:

"It's not only my cause. It's West Indies cricket. We are going through a period where a lot of questions are flying around about the future of West Indies cricket.

And I see my issue as a very small issue in the entire scenario. I assessed my situation and I thought I could not continue playing cricket under the problems that kept coming up.

It's nice to see that people vent their feelings, some in my favor, some not. But they also went on to broader things and I appreciate that. I'm happy to see that West Indies cricket means a lot, not only on the field, but off the field, to the people of the West Indies.

It's very hard to know what's going to result from the matter. At this point in time, I need a break away from the team because of the stress and pressure and, if allowed back into the team, whenever, I will just assess the situation and see if I could play under the same environment.

I don't know about the World Cup, that's left to be seen. I have opted out of the Australian World Series so far, that's the only series I'm going to miss. I don't know what's going to happen after that. I just have to play it as I see it. The main issue is that West Indies cricket doesn't belong to the Board. It doesn't belong to the players. It belongs to the West Indies people and they are now coming forward, maybe because of my issue and speaking out and that's very good for West Indies cricket.

The West Indies Board has got to account for whatever they do. The players now have got to account, for they represent the people. That's most important."

The English tour had effectively split West Indian cricket. Given their long-running supremacy against England in winning 27 and losing just four of their previous 43 Tests, it was a genuine surprise when the West Indies were beaten at Lord's and Manchester and could only draw the series 2-2.

While they had forfeited their world champion's mantle earlier in the year to Mark Taylor's visiting Australians, the nucleus of a great side remained. They had been expected to defeat England easily.

Despite a slow start which included his first ever "pair" in one of the leadups, Lara was the dominant batsman of the summer, amassing 765 runs at an average of 85 in the Tests and 1126 at almost 60 in all the first-class games.

The morale of the tourists was clearly tested by their Test defeats and at a meeting convened by manager Wes Hall at the conclusion of the fourth Test in Manchester, Lara amazed everyone present by walking out after a war-of-words with Richardson.

Accusing his captain of not imparting enough discipline within the team, Lara said he was retiring and heading to Birmingham, rather than travelling with the team to Somerset. Later, as the West Indian management tried valiantly to make Lara re-consider, he told Hall that cricket was "ruining his life" and he wouldn't be returning. The fame game had claimed another victim. It took a meeting with West Indian board chief Peter Short to remind him of his obligations; he was fast backing himself into a corner which he'd regret for the rest of his life.

Persuaded to return to the fold having missed just one match, Lara finished the Test summer with back-to-back centuries, scoring his runs at 80 runs per 100 balls in true Bradmanlike fashion. The fireworks were only beginning, however, especially when his mid-tour walkout was made public, Hall's apparently-confidential report being leaked to the *Trinidad Guardian:*

"On July 31, the last day of the fourth Test, we held a team meeting to address the unacceptable behaviour of some members of the team.

I spoke of the issues of players taking drinks in their hands from the dressing rooms onto the coach, wearing sponsors caps with peaks behind in public and in hotels.

The general loud talk in the dressing room which seemed to upset players who have remained silent about it and Ambrose's refusal to sign autographs for the sponsors' Cornhill.

Ian Bishop felt that during the last few years, management had been soft on some issues. He accused Ambrose and Benjamin of distracting the team with their noise and said that Winston Benjamin should have been sent home a long time ago.

He said it was difficult to concentrate at practice because of the disruptions Benjamin and Ambrose caused and he was quite prepared to suffer the consequences for speaking out.

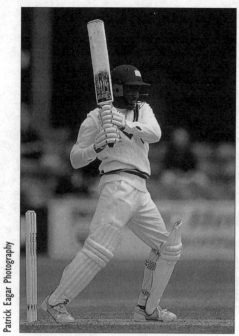

Lara's controversial English tour begins, Worcester, 1995.

Patrick Eagar Photography

Brian Lara said the same fast bowlers had worked hard and that the real problem was that the captain should be blamed for all the indiscipline, simply because managers and coaches come and go, but the skipper was there all the time these things were happening.

Furthemore, he said, he was not alone with that view since most of the players felt the way he did.

Captain Richardson replied that he had known Brian Lara for a long time and was very sorry that he felt that way about him. He was also sorry to hear that some of the players felt as Lara did. He said that he never asked anyone to be captain and although he was proud to be captain, if the players were to tell him to his face that they were of the same views as Lara, then he would let the Board know he would resign immediately from the captaincy.

Having said that he was not prepared to bow to any egotistical people with agendas and ambitions. As he said those words, Brian Lara jumped up and said, "I retire," and stormed out of the meeting.

I telephoned Lara after the meeting and asked him to report to my room. He came to see me. I listened to him and tried in vain to get him to change his mind. He kept saying that cricket was ruining his life. I had arranged to meet him the next morning, having advised him to sleep on it and let me know his final decision. He met me in the foyer of the Holiday Inn hotel and told me he had not changed his mind.

He knew that the team was leaving for Somerset at 11 a.m. and told me he was going to Birmingham and gave me his mobile number in case I wished to contact him. I hugged him and wished him goodbye.

I immediately contacted Stephen Camacho in Barbados, Peter Short in London and Pat Rousseau in Durham and gave them Brian's mobile number.

The team arrived in Somerst without Lara – I instructed the team not to whisper a word to anyone about Lara's departure. It is still the best kept secret of the year.

The president telephoned me on Wednesday, August 2, informing me that Stephen Camacho, Pat Rosseau and he had phoned Lara. The president also said that Lara had repeated what he told me.

The president wanted to know if it was okay for him to come to Somerset since Lara had requested to meet him and the committee. I agreed. I arrived in Somerset for the meeting on August 3, 1995. The meeting was convened in my room at the Castle Hotel. After the usual pleasantries, I asked Brian to explain his position as he had requested the meeting. He repeated all that he had told us before and added that management had censured him for abusing (Keith) Arthurton yet when Ambrose did the same to him in the captain's presence, no-one did anything about it.

Secondly, he said that Ambrose behaved badly on the coach after he did not get a hot meal at Paul Getty's game and again nothing was done. I told Lara that I was hearing about Ambrose's abusing him for the first time and I could not adjudicate on matters which weren't brought to my notice. Captain Richardson said that he was of the opinion that Ambrose and Lara were skylarking so he never paid much attention. I then explained I had asked for hot meals for Ambrose, Benjamin and Bishop but there were no heating facilities at the ground.

I had seen Ambrose throw a pack of cards across the bus but he certainly didn't utter any obscene words in my presence but I was sure when I went to the front of the bus he would have taken the cowardly way out and sworn in my absence.

When everyone else had spoken, the president told Brian that from all appearances he seemed to be imagining things. The president stated further that from what he had heard the management dealt wth all the issues which were brought to its attention and that it was not customary to divulge the contents of such discussions in all instances.

President Short told Brian that he noticed that at first he said he had retired. But now he was saying that he was "taking a break."

He said that would be a serious breach of his contract with the West Indies Cricket Board of Control and it would be viewed very seriously. The president explained to Lara that all the things about which he had complained were off the field matters and were, therefore, not the responsibility of the captain, but were squarely in the hands of the tour management committee.

He told Lara that his reputation was based upon cricket and that it would be the greatest mistake of his young life if he was to now throw it all down the drain since he could not take a break whenever he liked.

Lara's demeanour changed alarmingly and he said:

"What are you going to do with me? Please be lenient with me; Cricket has ruined my life."

At that moment, I realised that Lara needed all the help he could get. It was decided that he should rejoin the team and play in the match against Gloucestershire commencing on Saturday, August 5 – if that was okay with the tour committee and the members of the team.

There were a few rumblings but I spoke to all members of the team before the game at Gloucester and all was well.

The tour committee meeting was held to discuss the matter, bearing in mind that players had been previously fined for leaving a team meeting. It was agreed that players left the team and returned on their own violition to play and were fined, but when Brian left it seemed to be for good.

The committee felt that since it took the intervention of the president to arrange the meeting, even though it was at Brian's request, it was analogous to the Low Court superceding the High Court and that the matter would be referred to the Board in report form who should then deal with it as they saw fit."

In addition to Lara being fined 10 per cent of his tour fee, Curtly Ambrose, Kenny Benjamin and Carl Hooper were also subject to fines:

- Ambrose, for flaunting the team's dress code, both during the tour and the flight home when he wore a sports shirt and slacks. A further recommendation was made to the Board with respect to discipline;
- Benjamin, for dress code charges and for showing disrespect towards manager Wes Hall. He'd already been fined twice earlier in the tour for disciplinary breaches;

- And Hooper, for absenting himself from the tour without permission and not attending the farewell function held by the tour sponsors. He in fact was not seen after the penultimate match (at Scarborough).

Earlier, Winston Benjamin had been sent home on disciplinary and fitness grounds.

Having apologised for his walkout, Lara was aggrieved to be bracketed with the others. He believed the cleansing late-tour meeting with Board president Peter Short, who was in England on holiday, had resolved the matter and there should be no fine.

"Brian is a very sensitive young man, very intelligent and he takes things to heart," Short said. "He feels that his image as a cricketer and a person has been tarnished and he has felt that very keenly. It came as a severe blow to him (to be fined) especially after he considered he had reason to believe the matter was indeed resolved."

Short, however, was overruled by fellow board members. They demanded that Lara also be penalised. Effectively they catapulted West Indian cricket into its biggest controversy since Clive Lloyd and Co. signed with World Series Cricket almost 20 years before.

The day after the fine was imposed, an angry Lara told the *Trinidad Daily Express* that he found it very difficult to come to terms with the fact "that the management of the tour looked at me as one of the guys who tried to create disharmony in the camp."

His friend and confidant Joey Carew, the former Trinidad & Tobago captain and West Indian opener, said Lara was emotionally and physically tired. "A lot of people would venture to say that he is a spoilt brat but that is not the case at all. Brian is a very sensitive person and a lot of things have happened to him over the last five or six months that have emotionally disturbed him."

As the Windies team flew out to Australia without their star batsman, reactions raged for and against Lara. Former West Indian batsman Maurice Foster, a Jamaican delegate to the West Indian board, accused Lara of being spoilt; fast bowler Colin Croft called for an immediate two year ban; while legendary Michael Holding recommended a psychiatrist!

"I was not in any way suggesting Lara was out of his mind. That would obviously be ridiculous," Holding said in the *Caribbean Cricket Quarterly.* "But psychiatrists are there to help get people to concentrate properly on exactly what they're about. Leading business executives regularly see psychiatrists for this very reason and this is what Lara needs now. He needs someone to help him understand and deal with the pressures that his phenomenal success in the past two years has brought on him."

Noted West Indian cricket writer and commentator Tony Cozier blamed Lara's walk-out in part on the "debilitating amount of cricket that has been forced on Lara and his West Indian teammates."

In a 20 month period the Windies' schedule included 17 Tests and at least 45 one-day internationals in eight series in six different countries. "They have been on the move virtually non-stop, shuttled between venues with a frequency that international sportsmen should not be subjected to," Cozier said.

Brian Lara may now be a cricketing millionaire and an idol for thousands, but his beginnings were basic. Like most Caribbean youngsters from a humble village background, he was unable to afford cricket gear and would use makeshift bats and balls roughly fashioned from wood and play street tests all Saturday and on Sundays, too, if his parents hadn't marched him and his brothers off to church!

Other than the opportunity for regular coaching, he had to make his own way and as the 10th of 11 children and the youngest of seven boys, there were few other handouts. He'd hide his transistor radio under his pillow when Test series were on and listen in the middle of the night to the doings of his heroes Gordon Greenidge and Viv Richards.

Dashing West Indian opener Roy Fredericks was another of his earliest cricketing heroes and for years Lara would button his shirts at the sleeve *a la* Fredericks. He'd also practice the more flamboyant of Fredericks' shots in front of a mirror, all the time imagining he was on centre stage at Queen's Park, lifting the English or Australian fast bowlers all over the ground.

Born in May, 1969, in the village of Cantaro in the Santa Cruz Valley, north of Port of Spain, Lara was a favorite with his father, Bunty, who soon recognised his talent for sports. Like his brothers and cousins, he'd play "pass-out," a street version of cricket where you're out if you miss the ball. One of his Mitchell St. neighbours immediately noticed young Brian's potential and offered money to the other boys if they could get a ball past him. After everyone had gone home, Lara continued his own personal test matches until nightfall, using a broom handle or a ruler as a bat and marbles or small limes for a ball. He'd position his mother's verandah pot plants as if they were fieldsmen and try and find the gaps as he played his shots against a garage wall. If he missed the rebound, that was a wicket. He'd play four innings test matches, invariably between England and the West Indies, batting in turn for each of the 11 players.

At six, he was enrolled in the Harvard cricket coaching clinic at Port of Spain after his sister Agnes had seen an advertisement in a local newspaper. She bought him some whites, a green cap and a single-scoop bat and accompanied him to the first clinics. His father was also very supportive and rarely missed a practice session, let alone a match.

The West Indian way was to play daring, flamboyant cricket and even in his first years of competitive cricket, Lara played with an attractive, free-flowing style. His timing was also a talking point – as was his height. Until his mid-teens, he was only five feet tall and the borrowed pads he'd use seemed to reach almost to his thighs.

Accepted into Trinidad's Fatima College after the principal learned he was a cricketer, Lara's teen years were studded with outstanding achievements. While he was keen scholastically and bright enough to consider a career in accountancy, his driving force was cricket and it was clear that for one so young, he had extraordinary talent.

Sir Garfield Sobers was so impressed when he first saw him play in a schoolboy's tournament in Barbados, he declared him the brightest talent he'd seen in years.

His College headmaster, Mervyn Moore, said Lara not only possessed rare batting gifts, he shaped as a natural leader, having a calm authority and ready smile. "When Brian first came to us, he was so small and that used to frustrate him at times," said Moore. "But we soon knew that we had a great little batsman playing for us. We have an under 14s Giant's League and he dominated it."

Another memorable early match was against St. Anthony's when Lara, fiercely competitive even then, cleverly farmed the strike and helped Fatima to a narrow victory despite batting with the tail.

Shortly after arriving at the school, one of Trinidad's finest, Lara had announced his career goal to be the world's greatest cricketer! His enthusiasm for the game was clearly evident, and from his early teens, he'd analyse his every dismissal and invariably be his own harshest critic. He also earnestly discussed the game with his friends, plotting field placings and batting orders.

One of his junior coaches, Francisco Garcia, was taken by his ability to hit boundaries with the minimum of effort. "He never seemed to hit the ball hard to the boundary – he just stroked it and was a sheer delight to watch."

As a 16-year-old, he toured India with a Trinidad and Tobago secondary school's team, having been presented with a new bat by West Indian Testman Carlisle Best. At 17, he made two centuries in the Northern Telecom youth championships in Jamaica to

Retiring hurt against Pakistan in the 1992 World Cup, Melbourne.

assure his maiden first-class appearances soon afterwards.

It was clear that he had been ear-marked as a young player of extraordinary potential when he was named the West Indian under 19 captain ahead of more experienced players and visited Australia for the Bicentennial youth championships. Not only did he steer his team into the semi-finals, he also led a 172 run victory in the one-off test, in Sydney.

Jimmy Adams was one of the many future internationals who participated in the tournament. Others included Wayne Holdsworth and Alan Mullally for Australia, Mike Atherton, Nasser Hussain and Chris Lewis (England) and Inzamam-el-Haq, Mushtaq Ahmed and Basit Ali (Pakistan).

On his return to the Caribbean, Lara, a natural leader, was named the West Indies' under 23 captain for a representative game against the touring Pakistanis – even though he was the youngest player in the side. Later, he was to also lead West Indian "B" to Zimbabwe. Approaching his first-class debut for Trinidad and Tobago in January, 1988, he'd already made 12 representative centuries at under-age level. A stellar career was beginning.

The sure signs of a future champion on the rise came in only Brian Lara's second major match against a formidable foe in Barbados when he defied an attack which included Joel Garner and Malcolm Marshall for almost six hours in making 92 at Queen's Park. While he hit only six 4s, he impressed with his courage and clearly had a technique to match.

He was soon to be named Trinidad's Red Stripe Cup captain and make his first appearances for the West Indies, during the tour of Pakistan. Many of the team's most celebrated players including Viv Richards and Gus Logie were in their final international seasons. Youngsters such as Lara, Jimmy Adams and Carl Hooper were seen as the new breed, capable of preserving the West Indies' proud world champion image.

His joy at his rapid rise was temporarily forgotten when his father died from a heart attack on the third day of the Test against Pakistan in Trinidad. Lara, who was 12th man, left the game immediately. Six years later, he was to dedicate his mega Test innings to his late father.

When there's an 18 month gap between a cricketer's first and second Test matches, it's usually compelling evidence that a selection panel is far from unanimous in its approval.

Brian Lara had to wait a year and a half in-between Tests, but only because of the log-jam at the top of the West Indian batting order. In essence, the waiting made him hungrier to succeed but didn't lessen his disappointment after he strained ankle ligaments late in the 1991 tour of England and missed the final Test.

With Viv Richards and Gordon Greenidge making their farewell international appearances and Gus Logie still an integral part of a champion team, there was simply no room for Lara, despite his precocious talents.

With Richards temporarily unavailable because of an abdominal operation, Lara was lifted into the team for his first Test, against Pakistan at Lahore and scored 44 and five on debut before serving as the West Indies' permanent 12th man for the entire five Test series against Australia and filling that role for much of the tour of England as well. He felt it an honor to be around such great names as Richards, Greenidge, Desmond Haynes and Marshall and while impatient to play, knew his time would come.

But for torn ankle ligaments sustained at fielding practice at Edgbaston, Lara would have made his English debut in the sixth and final Test of the summer at The Oval after Logie was sidelined by a knee injury. Instead, the West Indies called up Clayton Lambert, who had been playing in the Yorkshire leagues, as their new No.6.

Of some consolation was Lara's string of one-day internationals, including the only time he batted with Richards in England in 1991 and his selection for the 1992 World Cup tournament in Australasia, where he made 333 runs at almost 50.

With an imposing strike-rate of more than 80 runs per 100 balls, he was scoring quicker than almost all of his Test contemporaries.

On return to the Caribbean, he was re-included in the West Indian Test side for the one-off Test against South Africa at Kensington Oval, where his second innings 64 was crucial in his team's narrow victory. At 50, he trod on his stumps, but neither umpire, D.M Archer on Steve Bucknor had seen the bail fall and allowed him the benefit of the doubt. Television replays showed that Lara had clearly dislodged the bail while playing his shot.

His imposing form for Trinidad & Tobago had seen him create a new record of 627 runs for the Red Stripe Cup competition, including a masterly double of 122 not out and 87 against Jamaica at Sabina Park. He'd been relieved of the leadership duties by Gus Logie and seemed far more relaxed, despite a relatively-minor incident involving Logie when he was subject to a $130 fine for criticising one of his bowling changes during a one-day game against Jamaica.

Clearly he had a sense of occasion and seemed to reserve his best for matches against touring teams. He made centuries in his only matches against the 1989 Indian and 1990 English touring teams. His 182 for West Indian Under 23 against the Indians at St Kitts featuring such a stunning array of off-side shots that Test selector David Holford said it was the finest display he'd ever seen from a teenager.

His arrival in Australia with Richie Richardson's 1992-93 touring team was eagerly awaited and while he made four 50s in his first eight major innings, there was no hint of what was to come in the New Year Test in Sydney, only his fifth in Test cricket.

Having won in Melbourne thanks to Shane Warne's last day heroics, the Australians had taken a 1-0 series lead with three Tests to play. Without Richards and Co., the momentum appeared to be swinging against the long-time world champions, especially when Allan Border won the toss on yet another docile wicket and batted late into a second day until the Australians had made 500-plus.

Needing 304 runs to even avoid the follow-on, the Windies slumped to 2-31 early on the third morning before Lara and Richardson emphatically resurrected their team's fortunes with an exhilarating 293 run partnership.

While rain hampered the Australian bowlers, especially spinners Greg Matthews and Warne who found difficulty in gripping the ball, the crispness and assurity of Lara's strokeplay was a wonderful reward for the spectators who remained despite the frequent rain breaks.

In the greatest innings he believes he's played, the bantamweight left-hander made 277 before being run out by Damien Martyn from cover, having called for a sharp run only to be sent back by Carl Hooper. He'd struck 38 4s and given only one chance, against Merv Hughes and the second new ball at 172, when Steve Waugh dropped a reflex catch at gully.

Against an attack which included Craig McDermott, Hughes and Warne, in only his second Australian series, it was a supreme display, Lara's runs coming in less than eight hours at a personal run-rate of 4.5 runs per six balls faced.

His first 100 came in just 125 balls. It was a glorious fightback, Lara outscoring his three partners Richardson, Keith Arthurton and Hooper by two to one. West Indian coach Rohan Kanhai said it was the best innings he'd ever seen and given the Windies fresh hope after the demoralising final sessions in Melbourne.

Having made 35 in brisk style, Lara was relaxing back in the dressing room during a rain delay when he received a phone call from Sir Garfield Sobers, in Sydney for the game. "This is your day, son. Just keep on batting."

Lara was flattered and honored, given Sobers' standing as the greatest player of his era. He resolved to make the biggest score he possibly could and ensure the draw.

"It was a great feeling to know that he believed in me," said Lara. "I have so much respect for him."

Some of his shots, particularly the square drive against Matthews for his 150 and a pull shot past mid-on against Hughes and the second new ball were among the finest of the memorable summer in which the Windies fought back to take the series with wins in Adelaide and Perth.

"I was amazed at my timing and strokeplay from the very start," Lara said. "What stuck me most was when Richie Richardson came to congratulate me (after he'd made 100). He said to keep going, get a big one and make up for the times when you don't get any. That was my intention, to continue batting for as long as possible. We were still in a bit of danger and the team needed me to stay out there."

Only for one brief period, before he reached 250, did he look like losing concentration, playing and missing several times outside his off stump.

The innings drew unanimous acclaim. It was Lara's personal best score, the highest by a West Indian against Australia and also the fourth-highest maiden century in Test history behind Sobers' world record 365, Bob Simpson's 311 and Reggie Foster's 287.

Claiming it to be the finest innings played in Australia for decades, Peter Roebuck said, "overnight, the youth had become a man."

Richardson's century paled into insignificance. "I can hardly remember my innings," he said. "I remember more the shots Brian was playing. It was kind of difficult playing and being a spectator at the same time."

At 23, Lara had established himself as Test cricket's new batting starlet. Consecutive 100s in the one-day internationals in South Africa and a third in the opening one-dayer against Pakistan back in the Caribbean highlighted his advancement and in the next 18 months he was to create a staggering array of new batting records which left even the greatest in his wake.

His feats were to also bring a burden of public expectation he'd never experienced before. As Sobers said, "There will be those looking to pull him down for whatever reason. In fact, I've already been told that Brian Lara is big-headed, that he doesn't listen to anybody, that he thinks he'd God's gift to the game and that sort of thing. "I know what it's like. I went through the same thing... having got to know Brian Lara, I think he's intelligent enough to take that sort of thing in his stride and accept it for what he is."

AMONG THE FINEST

Brian Lara's 180 in the Red Stripe Cup game against Jamaica at Queen's Park Oval in 1993-94 deserved to rank among the finest ever played in a first-class match in the West Indies. It was the highlight of his new record 715 run aggregate for the tournament.

In scoring 180 of 219 runs while he was at the wicket, he lifted Trinidad from 2-38 and 6-103 to 257, a first innings lead of 51. "When they set the fielders out to block the fours, he was still hitting boundaries," said Joey Carew.

"When they brought them in to keep him on strike, he chipped the ball over their heads and took a single, like a golfer would do. It was pure genius."

Never has there been 50 days of batting brilliance to equal it. By amassing colossal new Test and first-class batting records, Brian Lara ensured the birth of Lara-mania and his standing among cricket's alltime elite.

Not only did the 24-year-old crack Sir Garfield Sobers' long-standing Test record of 365 not out, but weeks later in England, he became the first player to score 500 in a first-class game.

In the closest any of us might get to seeing cricket perfection, Lara's extraordinary run of tall scores included five 100s in a row and an unprecedented seven in eight innings.

Incredibly on the very day he passed 300 on the way to 375 at the Recreation Ground in St John's, he rose at 5.30 a.m. for a game of golf!

Using a favorite Gray Nicolls bat which had been returned to him after being stolen several months earlier in Port of Spain, Lara was 164 not out at stumps on day one and 320 at the close on day two. When Angus Fraser beat an outside edge early on the third day, he stopped and smiled. "I don't suppose I can call you a lucky bugger when you are 340!"

On a slow and true wicket, he took particular toll of Chris Lewis, striking him for 15 4s and 105 runs in all. He also struck Fraser for 11 4s, Caddick for nine, Phil Tufnell six and Graeme Hick, four.

Batting with teenager Shivnarine Chanderpaul, who constantly urged him to settle and not take unnecessary risks on the third morning, Lara cover drove Andy Caddick to go past Sir Len Hutton's 364 and equal Sobers' 365.

Mike Atherton had the field set up to stop the short single and when Lewis dropped short, Lara instinctively went for the pull shot and hitting it cleanly watched it disappear in the direction of the Cathedral for four. The record many, including Sobers, said was unattainable was now his. But he was fortunate that it wasn't a deadheat. Television replays later showed that in making the shot, his front pad had just touched the stump dislodging the off-bail, without enough force for it to fall.

"The moment for me was indescribable," Lara said,* "a moment in my lifetime maybe never to be repeated – elation, wonderment, pure joy – the ultimate pinnacle in my career. Everything that happened was like a dream. My bat held high, cap in hand and in the distance hundreds of spectators racing in my direction. Suddenly I felt a hug. It was Chanderpaul and before I knew it we were surrounded by numerous police trying their best to keep the spectators away.

"A path was cleared for Sir Gary to come to the middle and congratulate me. He clasped me and said how proud he was. 'I'm very happy for you. I knew you could do it son. You were always the one.'"

*In his autobiography *Brian Lara, Beating The Field.*

As Sobers left the pitch, Lara bent down and kissed the pitch. Later he dedicated his mega-knock to his late father, Bunty, saying his love and support meant everything to him. "My father really believed in me and always told me that one day I was going to do just this," he said. "I remember him saying that achieving anything great would not be possible without dedication, discipline and determination. Our relationship was what every young boy should have with his father and such bonds are critical for the youth of Trinidad and Tobago these days. "I had some bad influences in my time and, if my parents weren't there to straighten me out, things might have gone haywire."

By becoming the first batsman in the series to score a double-century, he claimed a $100,000 bonus which went into the team funds. All around the Caribbean life stood

Some mid-innings adjustments to his protective gear, World Series Cup, Melbourne, 1992-93.

still, cabinet meetings and High Court cases being adjourned as people crowded around television sets and listened to the radio.

As in Sydney 15 months earlier, Lara had helped rescue the Windies from 1-10 (and then 2-12) to 5-593 declared. While he was at the wicket, 581 runs were scored of which just 180 came from his three partners Jimmy Adams, Keith Arthurton and Chanderpaul.

When Courtney Walsh declared, the West Indian players lined up in formation on the ground, bats high in the air and crossed to salute Lara as he entered the pavilion. It was an unforgettable send-off. "I think the public will put a lot of pressure on me and I'll have to live up to what I have done today and what I've done in the past. That is enough inspiration to keep going," said the young star. "Because I have the world record, people will be expecting a lot and I can't afford to disappoint them.

"There are times when I shall fail and I hope that people understand that I'm just a human being and it takes one ball to get you out."

A whole array of gifts were bestowed on him, from cash, free travel and complimentary airtime on his mobile telephone. He was even promised a house, courtesy of the Trinidad and Tobago's Minister of Sport, Jean Pierre. A street, Brian Lara Promenade was also named in his honor.

All schools in Trinidad were given a day off to watch Lara lead a motorcade tour of the island. The following day, at a Prime Minister's reception, he was awarded the Trinity Cross, Trinidad's highest honor.

Within days he left the celebrating all behind to fulfill his first county season engagement, with Warwickshire. It was a case of jumping from one party to another...

Brian Lara was considered such an important signing by Warwickshire that county chiefs broke tradition and awarded him his county cap even before he'd played a game. When negotiations with the Australian David Boon lapsed and Indian allrounder Manoj Prabhaker was diagnosed with long-term ankle problems, Lara was targeted and duly signed on an $80,000 contract on the eve of the fourth West Indies-England Test in Barbados.

It proved to be the signing of the century as within weeks Lara had made his world record Test score, prompting a flood of new memberships which added $100,000 to the Warwickshire coffers within weeks of the new season start.

There were just 11 days gap between Lara's epic 375 and his English debut against Glamorgan at Edgbaston. While it took him seven deliveries to score, once he middled the ball for his first boundary from the bowling of off-spinner Robert Croft, he showed himself to be a class above the rest.

Lara unmercifully punished anything fractionally off line, 104 of his 147 coming in boundary shots. It was the start of a brilliant month of May in which he was to re-write the record books with five 100s in a row and seven in eight innings, including the piece de resistance, his fabulous 501 not out against county newcomers Durham.

In a game destined to be a draw after rain washed out the third day, Lara began the fourth and final day on 111 not out. By lunch he was 285 and shortly before 2 p.m. had amassed the 107th triple century in major cricket.

Warwickshire's No.5, Trevor Penney made just 44 of a third wicket partnership of 314. Another triple-century stand was shared with wicketkeeper Keith Piper.

As Lara sailed past Bradman and many of the other epic runmakers, Durham captain Phil Bainbridge's field placings became so ultra defensive that he'd forfeit singles to Lara just to get Piper back on strike.

When the final over began at 5.28 p.m., two minutes before the designated close, Lara was 497, just two runs short of the world first-class record of 499 held for 35 years by the Pakistani Hanif Mohammad and a boundary from cricket's first quintuple century.

With fans roaring like a football crowd, the first three deliveries from John Morris were blocked and the fourth, a slow bouncer, struck him in the helmet as he tried to run it to fine-leg. When told by Piper that he had just two balls in which to score a boundary for his 500, he hit the next through the covers and raised his bat in triumph.

For the second time in 49 days he had cracked one of cricket's most unattainable records. With 62 4s and 10 6s, he'd handed out one of the greatest thrashings ever, having taken just 116 balls to move from 350 to 501.

The only time he appeared in any danger of losing his wicket was at 413 when he skied a pull shot over square-leg which the fieldsman, Michael Burns, failed to pick up.

Brian Lara's 1994

February 7: Ends the Red Stripe Cup competition with a record 715 runs, beating Desmond Haynes' 654 in 1991;

April 13: Surpasses Lawrence Rowe's 1117 runs in 1974 as the highest first-class aggregate by a West Indian in a domestic season on his way to 1513 runs at almost 90;

April 17: Passes the previous highest individual Test score of 178 at Antigua, by Carl Hooper (v. Pakistan, 1993) and Viv Richards (v Australia, 1984) on his way to 320 not out at stumps on day 2. Also beats Lawrence Rowe's 302 at Bridgetown in 1973-74 as the highest Test score by a West Indian against England;

April 18: Extends his triple-century to 375, a new individual high for Test cricket batsmen, before being caught at the wicket. Gary Sobers, who had held the old record of 365 not out since 1957-58, is one of the first to congratulate him;

May 23: Equals Everton Weekes' West Indian record of five centuries in consecutive innings (during the New Zealand tour, 1956) with 136 for Warwickshire against Somerset at Taunton;

June 3: Becomes the first batsman to score seven centuries in eight first-class innings when he reaches 100 for Warwickshire against Durham at Edgbaston;

June 6: Not out overnight, he passes a host of records, including the world's highest first-class score of 499 held by Pakistan's Hanif Mohammad (in 1959) on his way to 501 not out, cricket's first quintuple century;

June 23: Equals Sir Donald Bradman's record of eight centuries in 11 first-class innings, in 1938-39, with 197 for Warwickshire against Northamptonshire at Northampton.

*The controversial Ian Healy stumping, Brisbane, 1992-93. Umpire Terry Prue is about to give Lara out,
even though Healy had failed to take the ball.*

Not only was 501 the new high for one innings, it broke Graham Gooch's match
record of 456 (333 and 123) for England against India at Lord's in 1990.

Hanif Mohammad sent a telegram saying, "I'm happy to see him take my record. All
records are made to be broken and it is good for cricket. I think one of his secrets is his
height. He is very short and many other short players have scored lots of runs, like me,
Sir Don Bradman and Sir Len Hutton."

Warwickshire made 4-810 from 133.5 overs, Lara's last day share, 390! As in Antigua
two months previously, the players formed a guard of honor, bats held high and Lara
enjoyed a champagne toast as the county's player of the month. After a brief press
conference in which he reiterated that his recordbreaking ways didn't make him a great
player, Lara showered and headed outside to a massive reception where he signed the
first of 100s of autographs.

After a break back home in Trinidad, where he was joined by a bevy of journalists, he returned to England for the game against Kent, scoring 19 and 31, before making 197 against Curtly Ambrose and Northamptonshire at Northampton in a contest billed as a head-to-head between the world's greatest batsmen and bowler.

Ambrose had not dismissed him in nine previous meetings and was clearly keen, on a fastish wicket, to make amends. One delivery smashed into Lara's helmet and he was

375 – THE MEGA TEST SCORE

Score	Mins	Balls	4s	6s
1st 50	150	121	7	-
2nd 50	78	61	9	-
3rd 50	96	60	6	-
4th 50	112	71	5	-
5th 50	75	66	5	-
6th 50	99	55	6	-
7th 50	111	79	4	-
375	**766**	**538**	**45**	**-**

501* – THE MEGA FIRST-CLASS SCORE

Score	Mins	Balls	4s	6s
1st 50	97	80	6	-
2nd 50	47	58	8	-
3rd 50	57	55	8	-
4th 50	23	27	8	2
5th 50	22	25	7	3
6th 50	34	33	7	2
7th 50	39	33	5	1
8th 50	48	39	4	-
9th 50	63	48	2	1
10th 50	44	29	7	1
501*	**474**	**427**	**62**	**10**

501 not out – the details

Friday, June 3, 1994

100*   Brian Lara completes his seventh century in eight consecutive innings, a unique achievement in first-class cricket. No-one else had scored six centuries in seven county championship innings;

Saturday, June 4, 1994

No play, rain.

Sunday, June 5, 1994

111*   Resumes innings on final day;

148*   Reaches his highest score for Warwickshire;

248*   The new highest score in any first-class match against Durham;

278*   Highest score at Edgbaston; highest score for Warwickshire by a left-hander, beating Roger Twose's 277 not out against Glamorgan in 1994;

185*   Lunch. His 174 for the first session is a new Warwickshire record and only six short of K.S. Ranjitsinjhi's 180 in the pre-lunch session in 1902;

297*   The third wicket stand of 314 in 55 overs with Zimbabwean Trevor Penney is the best for any wicket against Durham in first-class cricket. Penny's share? Forty-four!

301*   First triple century at Edgbaston;

306*   New Warwickshire individual record score, beating Frank Foster's 305 not out against Worcestershire at Dudley in 1914;

323*   Highest score by a West Indian in England, beating 322 by Viv Richards, Somerset v Warwickshire, at Taunton in 1975;

325*   Reaches 1000 runs for season in seventh innings equalling Don Bradman's 1938 record. By scoring his 1000th run on June 7, he creates a new Warwickshire record, beating Bill Stewart who reached his 1000th run milestone on June 12, 1962;

367*   Highest score by a left-hander in England, surpassing Neal Fairbrother's 366 for Lancashire against Surrey at The Oval in 1990;

376*   Highest score by a West Indian, beating his own 375 for West Indies against England, at St John's, Antigua in 1994;

386*   Highest ever score by a left-hander, surpassing Bert Sutcliffe's 385 for Otago against Canterbury, at Christchurch in 1952-53;

406*   Highest score in England this century, surpassing Graeme Hick's 405 not out for Worcestershire against Somerset at Taunton in 1988;

413*   Nineteenth player to score 300 runs in a day;

418*   Tea. Makes 133 in the middle session, the first Warwickshire player to score 100 runs in two consecutive sessions in a day's play;

425*   Beats Archie Maclaren's 424 as the highest ever score in English first-class cricket;

458*   Breaks Charlie Macartney's record of 345 runs for the 1921 Australians against Nottinghamshire, at Trent Bridge;

475*   69th hit worth four runs or more (60 4s and nine 6s) beating the previous record of 68 (all 4s) by Percy Perrin (343*) for Essex v Derbyshire at Chesterfield in 1904;

501*   From the second-last ball of the match, scores a boundary off John Morris to set a new first-class individual record score, beating 499 by Hanif Mohammad for Karachi against Bahawalpur at Karachi in 1958-59.

eventually out for 197, having been dropped at slip off Ambrose at 170. While he scored at a run a ball, he made only 12 runs from 45 deliveries against his West Indian teammate. With his eighth 100 in 11 innings, he'd equalled Don Bradman's world record – yet another milestone in his incomparable summer.

His record-breaking displays were clearly having an affect on his health, however, and he was criticised for spending lengthy periods (16 hours in all) in the dressing rooms while his teammates were in the field. He also clashed with his captain Dermot Reeve, who called him a "prima donna" after an umpire's decision had been questioned.

Complaining of exhaustion, as well as a nagging knee problem, Lara played only three more championship games for the season, his absences becoming a national talking point, especially when coach Bob Woolmer accused him of lacking team spirit and thinking only of himself.

Lara had found the six day a week commitment of professional cricket physically demanding, but the standard had disappointed; it certainly wasn't as competitive as Australia's Sheffield Shield or the West Indies' own Red Stripe Cup. Realising he'd be committed to the West Indian national team the following English summer, Warwickshire wanted to know if he'd be back to continue the fairytale in 1996. Given the fabulous season he'd had, it was a case of naming your own price

"Before April," said Lara, "I was just a cricketer trying to establish myself, trying to get recognised on the international scene. I did not have a county contract and would not have had one but for the injury to Manoj Prabhakar. I was trying to get in there, get as many runs as possible and get people to notice me. Within two months I was propelled into a situation where you are compared ridiculously with people who have done the business for 10 to 15 years and become great cricketers. It is something you can't get caught up in because you have got a whole career ahead of you.

Welcome to life in the fishbowl. Even Brian Lara hadn't realised just how debilitating cricket could be 11 and 12 months of the year. Not only was there a huge burden of expectation to repeat his mastery of '94, he found he was working to exhaustion off the field meeting sponsor and media demands.

Having been fined by the West Indian board for his late arrival for the short tour of India from October to December, the first genuine cracks in his demeanour occured at Goa, in the one-day game against New Zealand when he was fined 50 per cent of his match fee and banned for dissent for one match by International Cricket Council referee Raman Subba Row. "I could have done without losing my earnings but at that time I was already completely exhausted and didn't mind the match off," he said.

Fulfilling a promise to play in a charity match at the Sydney Cricket Ground for the Bradman Foundation on the way home to Trinidad for Christmas, 1994, Lara's last public appearance in his extraordinary calendar year saw him caught behind for 23 from the bowling of Australian women's allrounder Zoe Goss.

He appeared jaded and clearly was wrestling with the demands of being cricket's most-celebrated personality. After all the hype of his English summer – and the associated spin-offs which had ensured his status as cricket's latest millionaire – he was looking for a rest rather than preparing for another home season.

His average had slumped to 33 in three Tests against the Indians and he missed out in the opening Test against New Zealand in Christchurch before rebounding with 147 in the second and final Test in Wellington. The long-awaited world Test championship with Mark Taylor's visiting Australians and his own head-to-head with Shane Warne was an anti-climax. From the opening Test in Bridgetown in April when Glenn McGrath produced the ball of the tour and induced a tickle to a searing off-cutter, Lara struggled for touch and found unusual difficulty in combating the Australian pacemen.

McGrath, who changed his line and went around the wicket, captured his wicket twice, as did left-armer Brendon Julian. Lara's highest score in four Tests was 88 at St John's when he fell to a miraculous one-handed catch by David Boon fielding at a shortish mid-on. The world-renowned leg-spin of Warne was not as menacing as expected, although he did dismiss him once, to an overspinning leg-break in the fourth and final Test at Kingston.

Lara had dominated in the one-day internationals, but his Test average of 44 was considered to be a virtual failure, given the peaks of his previous summer.

The stormy English tour added to his woes. More often than not he felt he was shouldering the blame for the Windies' stuttering form and when he made a pair against Kent and its novice pace bowler Dr. Julian Thompson, on summer leave from his duties at the Royal Berkshire hospital, Lara found than even old friends like Sir Garfield Sobers were becoming a little impatient.

Speaking early in the tour on the BBC, Sobers said that 60s and 70s were no longer good enough for a batsman of Lara's quality. He needed to concentrate more and work harder. Michael Holding believed he had to graft more and focus on crease occupation, rather than brilliant cameos. The most stinging comments came from within the team, veteran fast bowler Curtly Ambrose accusing Lara of no longer giving the impression that he wanted to work for his runs. After the pair against Kent, Lara said, "Everyone expects me to go out and at least get close to breaking those records every time I bat," he said. "I have an incredible level to live up to."

Even the everyday requests for autographs were gettting him down. After reading an article in which the acclaimed golfer Nick Price explained the difficulty he'd found in coping with the limelight, Lara was able to re-focus all his attentions on his batting and not allow anything extracurricular to intervene.

Having missed a century at Lord's, one of his greatest ambitions, he finished the series with three consecutive 100s. While some believed it inevitable that he regain his habit for heavyweight scores, it was a remarkable finish considering his emotional late-tour walk-out after criticising Richie Richardson over the everyday running of the team.

Fined 10 per cent of his tour fee for briefly withdrawing his services after the fourth Test, Lara's boycott of the one-day internationals in Australia showed just how tormented he'd become since his 50 days of fame in 1994.

It was feared that he may withdraw, too, from the next tour, to the World Cup on the sub-continent in early 1996. However, having announced his availability for selection, he helped the Windies into the semi-finals and was also in rampaging form against the visiting New Zealanders.

While there were one or two flashpoints during the World Cup, his break away from the game seemed to have freshened his attitude and dulled none of his skill.

Leading into the 1996-97 re-matches in Australia, the "Warne versus Lara" theme was again as prominent a talking point as Australia's defence of its world Test championship. Others were to play more important roles, however, with Warne still regaining confidence after surgery to his spinning finger and Lara playing without his normal fluency until the series had been decided.

Ever since his first Test in Australia in 1992-93, when he'd been controversially stumped by Ian Healy in Brisbane, it seemed his Australian appearances, in particular, were invariably incident-packed.

At Wangaratta in a game against Victoria leading into the 1996 Christmas Test, he was heading for his maiden century of the tour when given out hit wicket, by the third umpire Geoff Morrow, on the evidence of television replays. It seemed he had completed his shot and had only set out for a run after being called by partner Sherwin Campbell.

A bigger controversy broke in Sydney when Lara was judged caught behind from an attempted pull shot against McGrath. After seeing replays of the decision, he stormed into the Australian dressing room and told coach Geoff Marsh Ian Healy was a cheat and would not be welcome in the West Indian dressing rooms again.

Healy had dived forward and caught the ball so close to the ground that umpire David Shepherd sought the opinion of square leg umpire Darrell Hair in making sure the ball had carried. After receiving Hair's confirmation, Shepherd gave Lara out.

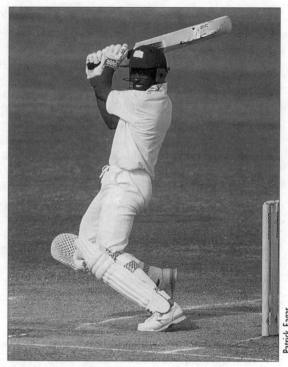

Patrick Eagar

On the attack against England, Trent Bridge, 1995. He averages more than 90 against the Englishmen.

West Indian manager Clive Lloyd tendered his own apology to the Australians and said Lara had been censored by management. "It's no big thing," he said. "There was no animosity. We had a chat and there is no problem. Brian realises he stepped out of line. As vice-captain he knows he must play by the rules. It was not in his jurisdiction to complain, but we'll deal with it. It's an on-tour situation."

The Australians admired Lara's ability and many liked him as a friend. But all disliked his histrionics. His Sydney blowup just reinforced their opinion that Lara, as fine a batsman as he was, was also one of the most mercurial superstars in the game, whose fragile temperament often let him down.

Healy is the hardiest of souls, but was stunned by Lara's outburst. "I'm glad we do live in a technological age, as all the replays showed the catch had been taken," he said in *Australian Cricket* magazine. "Brian didn't have a problem with it on the ground. No-one in our team did either – myself, 'Tubby' Taylor at slip or anyone else.

"Frankly I couldn't understand the fuss. It was all unnecessary from my point of view though I can understand the pressure Brian obviously felt under. He and all his supporters wanted it to be his day. When it wasn't, you can't help but be disappointed."

In the Caribbean, the latest Lara controversy again dominated the headlines. Everywhere but in Trinidad, opinion was divided. Back at home, however, the loyalty to Lara was overwhelming. One letter to the editor of the *Trinidad Express* summed it up: "Rather than criticise the young man for being intemperate," wrote Peter Minshall, "we should express our sympathy, our love, our support and a degree of admiration that at least one young man from the West Indies still cares passionately about the standards of gentlemanliness, honour and essential fairness that once were the hallmarks of the game of cricket."

Another letter writer commented, "To Brian Lara, I say continue to walk as you have done in the past and show your integrity from both sides. Walk out and speak out and to hell with the captaincy and cricket if you cannot call a cheat a cheat."

The Australians had expected a personal apology from Lara, but when one was not forthcoming, the wound were allowed to fester, one Australian player saying, "leopards don't change their spots."

Months later on the acrimonious final days of the series in Perth, the ill-feeling broke into open antagonism when Lara accused the Australians of "all day sledging" on tour rookie, Jamaican-born opening batsman Robert Samuels. On the last day of the game, he further inflamed tempers by coming out as a runner for his injured captain Courtney Walsh.

Tempers reached boiling point when Lara was accidentally tripped by Australian fieldsman Matthew Hayden and fell on to his back. The Australians felt he was over reacting and told him so, sparking more ill-feeling and an extraordinary mid-pitch conference between the two umpires Peter Willey and Darrell Hair and rival captains Mark Taylor and Courtney Walsh. The umpires demanded the two teams immediately settle their differences and when Taylor and Walsh shook hands, play re-started.

The normally mild-mannered Taylor later accused Lara of being "an antagonist" and initiating the new round of ill-feeling between the sides. "I found it very strange to see the vice-captain as the runner," Taylor said. "Brian came out as the runner and fell over. A few of the guys asked him to get up and he didn't like it. He said a few things back and the umpires didn't want it to go any further."

Taylor said Lara had provoked the only two incidents in the series. "He looks for things out there which get him going and get other people away from their game. He's a good player who plays it along the lines of (Sri Lanka's) Arjuna Ranatunga who puts opposition players off."

If Lara's motive was to create a division, it worked, Shane Warne branding Lara's behaviour a disgrace. "I was friends with Brian before the Perth Test, but he lost big points with all of us," Warne said. "They also said things to us but you didn't hear us saying, 'they got stuck into a young bloke playing his first couple of games.'

Gordon Brooks.

A narrow escape against Glenn McGrath during the 1995 Test series in the Caribbean.

281

"You just don't do that. It's sport. If you think the odd jibe can help a guy out, well fine. It's part and parcel of the game. Everyone who has played sport knows it happens. If you have a problem with it, or you think someone is going too far, well have a beer with them. You don't have to use the press as a tool to say 'everyone is ganging up on us.' That was disgraceful. Brian lost a lot of demerit points, not just with all of us but the public and everyone concerned. The biggest disappontment about the whole series was that he still hasn't apologised to Ian Healy."

After a disappointing summer by his own lofty standards, Lara had freewheeled back into form with back-to-back centuries in the Carlton & United series, as well as a classic 100 in Perth. Privately the Australians claimed he'd made all his runs after the series had been decided and the pressure was off. He remained suspect on bouncy wickets and was inclined to take unnecessary chances, especially early in an innings, as on the opening day in Adelaide when he self-destructed in Warne's first over.

Unimpressed by the Australian jibes, Lara claimed he'd make the Australians "pay" in the Caribbean in the home series in 1999.

RAISING THE TITANIC

Setting a field for him is always a nightmare. Getting rid of him cheaply alters everything," – MIKE ATHERTON.

"West Indians, both fans and his fellow players, accord him a Bradmanesque status and he has now come to appreciate why they regard a score of 80 a failure," – WES HALL.

"Brian Lara has become the most important figure in world cricket. The game may have provided him with a platform for fame and fortune, but cricket needs assets like Lara and it is no exaggeration to assert that its popularity into the 21st century depends on his continuance as a colossus," – ROBIN MARLAR.

"Brian Lara's innings of 501 against my old county Durham is so unbelievable that I wouldn't be more dumbfounded if they raised the Titanic and found 1515 survivors," – DEAN JONES.

The origins of the hostile relationship with the Australians stemmed back to two incidents which still rankle with Lara:
- In Brisbane, in 1992-93, Lara, having made 58, was given out "stumped" when television replays showed that Ian Healy had inadvertently broken the wicket with his glove and not the ball;
- In Barbados in 1995, again in the opening Test of the series, Lara (65) was given out caught in the gully by Steve Waugh when replays showed that the juggled catch may have been grassed.

Both incidents caused a storm of protest, especially the Waugh catch, criticism of the Australians intensifying after a particularly scathing attack from West Indian cricket great Viv Richards.

Richards claimed the catch had cost Lara his century and the Windies the game. In the Caribbean, Richards' word is gospel and for several days after the Test, which Australia had won, Waugh was virtually under siege. "I claimed the catch obviously thinking it hadn't touched the ground," he said. "The couple of the slips and the keeper were 100 per cent sure I caught the ball. I didn't even think twice about it until after the game when coach Bob Simpson said there was a bit of a stink about it.

"I said, 'what are you talking about?' It came as a shock to me that people said I didn't

At Tussauds' waxworks, 1995.

catch it. I juggled it a few times but I was sure the ball popped out of my right hand and landed on my left wrist."

Waugh had three grabs of the ball and it appeared to touch either his wrist or the ground before he claimed the ball in his left hand. Lara walked off, but not before giving a quizzical look to umpire Lloyd Barker, a West Indian, at square leg. Later, Srini Venkatagaharavan, standing at the bowler's end, said neither umpire had actually raised his finger.

The Windies started disastrously, losing 3-6 in the opening overs to Paul Reiffel and Brendon Julian before Lara and Carl Hooper added 124 at almost a run-a-ball in a thrilling counter attack, both being dismissed in their 60s.

West Indian captain Richie Richardson said replays of the catch had raised doubt that the catch had in fact been taken. "Most of the boys who saw it in the dressing room throught it was a bit dubious," he said. "But that's cricket. If Steve thought he caught it, there is no problem."

In his tour diary, Waugh accused Richards of trying to stir up bad blood between the teams which was at its peak when he was the West Indian captain. "It was absolutely none of his business to comment on the validity of my catch, which I still believe was out," Waugh said.* "I really find it hard to believe a cricketer of the stature of Richards would create tension in this way. He played the game at the highest level for a long time and should realise you don't need unwanted and unwarranted negative press if it can be avoided. The news of the attack shook me for a couple of hours until I came to realise that it had come from someone who was probably struggling to come to terms with the fact that he is no longer the centre of attention. I used to have great respect for the man but not any longer."

Waugh used the intensity of the backlash against him as personal motivation in averaging 107 for the series, including a series-clinching double century in the final Test in Jamaica.

The earlier controversy in Brisbane, involving Ian Healy, was clearly a case of Lara being wronged when umpire Terry Prue, at square leg, gave him out stumped late on the second day of the opening Test, just when the Windies, at 3-170, were building strongly towards Australia's 293.

Later describing it as the worst moment of his cricket life, Healy threw himself at the stumps, breaking the wicket with Lara short of his ground, having over-balanced against a curving Greg Matthews "arm" ball. Replays showed the ball had dislodged from his gloves *before* the wickets were broken. Lara was not out.

"The whole episode became instantly dramatic," said Healy, "with Prue walking in

* In Steve Waugh's *West Indian Tour Diary*

from square leg to chat with us while Lara, quite theatrically, stayed lying on the pitch with his bat outstretched into the crease as he looked up in hope for a reversed decision. He was eventually helped to his feet by Keith Arthurton.

"Lara looked at me and said, 'C'mon.'

"I said, 'Look where I am. I haven't got a clue.'

"I knew my gloves had brushed the stumps, but as I tumbled, I lost sight of the ball and probably closed my eyes.

"I had not appealed, rather I held out my arms in a gesture of bewilderment as if to say, 'I don't know what happened.'

"Mark Taylor, who was at first slip said the ball had not hit the stumps, information which was relayed to umpire Prue who said, 'I saw the ball hit the stumps.'"

Lara was dumbfounded to be given out. He implored Healy, "Tell the umpire what happened."

With the decision standing, Lara trudged off, saying he felt like crying. It was the turning point in what was shaping as a healthy West Indian reply.

At the time, the Australian Cricket Board was not using an off-field camera to help judge run outs, stumpings or hit wicket decisions. "Maybe if they were, I would not have been given out," said Lara.

Healy was also repentant. "If only we could go back in time. On reflection I would overrule the umpire 10 times out of 10 – even if there was only a modicum of doubt. Unfortunately I didn't do so and have had to live with the consequences."

Healy said his relationship with the West Indian team – and particularly Lara – was never the same again. "I spoke with Lara briefly during the 1995 tour there, but he no longer seems comfortable in my company. He does not warm to me."

Two Tests, later when Healy joined the Ausralians in trailing into the West Indian dressing room to congratulate Lara on his 277, he said the atmosphere was "sub zero."

"Do you want your arse broken, man," said Arthurton.

Healy hasn't been into a West Indian dressing room since.

FLYING OFF THE HANDLE

Not everyone agreed that Brian Lara should have been captain of the West Indies, in the absence of the injured Courtney Walsh against Sachin Tendulkar's touring Indians in 1997.

In an interview in the "Jamaican Gleanor", fast bowler Michael Holding said Lara was not mature enough to lead the team. "No, no," Holding said, "Write that in red letters and underline it five times. He is not mature enough mentally. He is flying off the handle when he shouldn't be.

"I know he has a great cricketing brain, he knows the game and is a great batsmen, but to lead a nation you have to be more than that."

Lara's leadership duties were restricted to the low-scoring third Test in Bridgetown, which the West Indies won by 38 runs, the only result of the five-Test series. His field placings and handling of his bowlers was impeccable, while his second innings 45 on a wearing wicket showed great innovation and flair.

He'd always been excited by the prospect of being the West Indies' fulltime captain, believing his leadership could become just as valuable as his runmaking abilities. However, his habit of irritating authority was to continue and having arrived at Antigua 36 hours after his teammates for the first of the two Tests with Sri Lanka in June, he was fined half his match fee of $US4000. His excuse to West Indian tour manager Clive Lloyd, that he'd had a flat tyre on the way to the airport and the spare malfunctioned was not accepted, the matter being referred to WICB president Pat Rousseau.

His reply, a match-saving century in the second Test, the first ever at Arnos Vale, showed he had fully accepted the reprimand and fine. Reverting to his normal No.3 position, in the absence of Shivnarine Chanderpaul, he batted for almost four and a half hours in a tensely-fought encounter eventually left drawn by poor weather.

Holding remained a critic, saying Lara had consistently repeated his mistakes, rather than learning from them.

"Lara has to show us that he is willing to accept that responsibility and behave accordingly before he can be given the captaincy," said Holding. "Yet he keeps on having these hiccups in his career. He keeps on being warned and fined by authorities. It is about time this sequence stopped."

Stephen Laffer

Brian Lara batting against Australia in the 1996-97 World Series.

Lara needs psychiatrist: Holding

Cricket has ruined my life, says upset Lara

Grow up, Brian, you're not yet great

Exhausted Lara pays high price for fame and fortune

Brian Lara THE MAN & HIS RECORD

Born: May 2, 1969

Teams: Trinidad & Tobago

First-class debut: 1987-88

First-class record: Matches 128. Batting — Runs 10978, Average 65.34, Highest score
501*, 100s 31, 50s 48. Bowling — Wickets 2, Average 153.50, Best bowling 1-14.
Fielding — Catches 161.

Test debut: 1990-91

Test record: Matches 45. Batting — Runs 4004, Average 54.10, Highest score 375.
Bowling — No wicket for 44. Fielding — Catches 59.

One-day international debut: 1990-91

One-day international record: Matches 118. Batting — Runs 4881, Average 46.93,
Highest score 169. 11 100s, 31 50s. Bowling — Wickets 2, Average 11.00, Best
bowling 2-5. Fielding — Catches 59.

Tours: Australia (with West Indies youth) 1988, Zimbabwe (with West Indies B) 1989;
Pakistan 1990-91; Australia 1992-93 & 1996-97; Sri Lanka 1993-94; India
1994-95; New Zealand 1994-95; England 1995.

Brian Lara's Test record series by series:

BATTING & FIELDING

Season	Opponent	Mt	Inns	No	HS	Runs	Ave	100s	50s	Ct.
1990-91	Pakistan (a)	1	2	0	44	49	24.50	-	-	1
1991-92	South Africa (h)	1	2	0	64	81	40.50	-	-	5
1992-93	Australia (a)	5	8	0	277	466	58.25	1	3	6
	Pakistan (h)	3	5	0	96	216	43.20	-	2	3
1993-94	Sri Lanka (a)	1	1	0	18	18	18.00	-	-	3
	England (h)	5	8	0	375	798	99.75	2	2	9
1994-95	India (a)	3	6	0	91	198	33.00	-	2	3
	New Zealand (a)	2	2	0	147	149	74.50	1	-	3
	Australia (h)	4	8	1	88	308	44.00	-	3	5
1995	England (a)	6	10	1	179	765	85.00	3	3	4
1995-96	New Zealand (h)	2	3	0	74	149	49.66	-	1	3
1996-97	Australia (a)	5	9	0	132	296	32.88	1	1	8
	India (h)	5	8	0	103	391	48.87	1	2	4
	Sri Lanka (h)	2	4	0	115	120	30.00	1	-	2
Totals		45	76	2	375	4004	54.10	10	19	59

BOWLING

Season	Opponent	Mt	Balls	Mdn	Runs	Wick	Ave	BB
1992-93	Australia (a)	5	12	0	4	0	-	0-4
1994-95	New Zealand (a)	2	24	0	8	0	-	0-8
1995	England (a)	6	6	1	0	0	-	0-0
1996-97	India (h)	5	18	0	16	0	-	0-16
Totals		45	60	0	44	0	-	0-0

COUNTRY BY COUNTRY RECORD

BATTING & FIELDING

Country	Mt	Inns	No	HS	Runs	Ave	100s	50s	Ct.
v Australia	14	25	1	277	1070	44.58	2	7	19
v England	11	18	1	375	1563	91.94	5	5	13
v India	8	14	0	103	589	42.07	1	4	7
v New Zealand	4	5	0	147	298	59.60	1	-	6
v Pakistan	4	7	0	96	265	37.85	-	2	4
v South Africa	1	2	0	64	81	40.50	-	1	5
v Sri Lanka	3	5	0	115	138	27.60	1	-	5

HOME & ABROAD

Country	Mt	Inns	No	HS	Runs	Ave	100s	50s	Ct.
Tests at home	22	38	1	375	2063	55.75	4	10	31
Tests abroad	23	38	1	277	1941	52.45	6	9	28

BOWLING

Country	Mt	Balls	Mdn	Runs	Wick	Ave	BB	5wI	10WM
v Australia	14	12	0	4	0	-	0-4	-	-
v England	11	6	1	0	0	-	0-0	-	-
v India	8	18	0	16	0	-	0-16	-	-
v New Zealand	4	24	0	8	0	-	0-8	-	-

HOME & ABROAD

	Mt	Balls	Mdn	Runs	Wick	Ave	BB	5wI	10WM
Tests at home	22	18	0	16	0	-	0-16	-	-
Tests abroad	23	42	0	44	0	-	0-0	-	-

HIS HIGHEST TEST SCORES

375	v England, St John's, 1993-94
277	v Australia, Sydney, 1992-93
167	v England, Georgetown, 1993-94
132	v Australia, Perth, 1996-97

HIS HIGHEST ONE-DAY INTERNATIONAL SCORES

169	v Sri Lanka, Sharjah 1995
153	v Pakistan, Sharjah, 1993
146*	v New Zealand, Port-of-Spain, 1996
139	v Australia, Port-of-Spain, 1995
128	v Pakistan, Durban, 1993
114	v Pakistan, Kingston, 1993
111*	v South Africa, Bloemfontein, 1993
111	v South Africa, Karachi, World Cup 1996
104	v New Zealand, Arnos Vale, 1996
103*	v Pakistan, Perth, 1996-97
102	v Australia, Brisbane, 1996-97

Brian Lara: averages just 44 against Australia, despite his mega 277 at the SCG in 1992-93.

WORKING **C**LASS **H**ERO

"The trouble with Merv Hughes, is that he thinks he's a fast bowler." – IAN CHAPPELL

For a big, playful kid who didn't go past year 10 at Werribee High, Merv Hughes made a triumphant career choice...

MERV HUGHES had never been more dispirited. After swearing off alcohol for almost a year, settling some long-running back problems and temporarily winning his personal battle of the bulge, he felt he'd made the sacrifices to finally cement his Test place and that he'd only have to say, "Open Sesame" to once again be walking out with Australia's elite.

But his mediocre returns in Victoria's opening Sheffield Shield games of the 1988-89 season floored him like a Joe Frazier left hook. For one of the few times in his life, he lost his zest and personal drive. The rebels to South Africa had been forgiven and the competition for places suddenly at a premium, especially amongst the fast bowling fraternity.

His morale slumped so alarmingly that he seriously considered retirement. Only a heart-to-heart with one of his bosum buddies Tony Dodemaide rekindled his spirits. Dodemaide reminded him of what he had already achieved, the opportunities ahead and how he'd never forgive himself if he backed off now.

"I was nearly ready to give the game away," Hughes said. "I felt like I was bowling well but I wasn't getting any wickets. At the start of the summer, when I was injured, I thought, 'I've been busting my gut for so long to play for Australia...stuff it, this year I might as well turn around, relax and enjoy myself.'"

He was ready to forget his new healthy diet, go drinking again and abandon all thoughts of anything more serious than Saturday club cricket with his mates at Footscray.

He'd tried to maintain his cheery exterior, but after taking only one wicket in Adelaide and none in Sydney, knew he had no hope of a recall, at least for the first Test of the Frank Worrell Trophy series at the 'Gabba.

Dodemaide, his club, state and national teammate, couldn't remember Hughes ever being as dejected. "At that stage, Merv was unproven at Test level. He didn't really know whether he could do it or not," he said.

"The season before, we'd played the last game together against Sri Lanka in Perth. It was a poor wicket and cracked up badly. Merv took five wickets but was very overweight and 'AB' (Allan Border) came out and gave him and 'Deano' (Dean Jones) a blast, saying they both wouldn't make Test cricketers unless they both pulled their heads in and did a helluva lot of hard work.

"Deano had made a century, but in the rush to get there before stumps one night, had taken unnecessary risks and was lucky to make it. Once he did, he'd thrown his wicket away. AB wasn't impressed and said so. Merv did all this work pre-season but it just wasn't happening for him. It all culminated in the game in Sydney when a caught behind against Greg Dyer wasn't given. Merv couldn't believe it and just about went over the edge. He was trying to so hard, yet nothing he could do seemed to be making any difference. All the negatives came down on top of him. He was as upset in the rooms afterwards and as low as he could have been. The team travelled back to Melbourne that night and the next day I went around to his place and talked about a few things, how I'd never seen him give up before and didn't expect to see him do it now. He had a lot to play for. But it was up to him. The key was to keep boring in regardless. He had to take things back to square one and turn the negatives into positives. We worked off each other a little bit and it turned around for him."

Victoria's following Shield game, against the Queenslanders at St Kilda, was scheduled at the end of the week and suddenly the wheel turned. Sent into bat, the Vics were bowled out for 103 in under three and a half hours. The importance of early breakthroughs were crucial and Hughes responded by dismissing Queensland opener Peter Cantrell first ball and Stuart Law fourth ball on his way to a Shield-best analysis of 7-60.

Set 125 to win a low-scoring game, Queensland lost six wickets with Hughes snaring another three, to give him 10 wickets for the match for the first time since blasting in the big-time virtually from nowhere.

It was his career turning point. "Swervin' Mervin" was back and three weeks later, responding to Australia's SOS in Perth when Geoff Lawson had his jaw broken and was unable to bowl, emphatically answered the critics who had made him a prime target since his topsy-turvey beginnings in international cricket.

By taking 13 wickets, including a hat-trick, Hughes became a favorite son virtually overnight and with his larger-than-life moustache and a succession of lion-hearted performances at home and away, ensured his on-going status as an Australian frontliner for as long as his knees could support him.

For a big, playful kid who hadn't gone past year 10 at Werribee High and been described by several of his schoolteachers as menacing and downright dangerous, he made a triumphant career choice, despite the hiccups along the way...

It was the supreme motivation. "The trouble with Merv Hughes," said Ian Chappell, "is that he thinks he's a fast bowler."

Merv's Charge Sheet

1988-89: Is fined $750 by the Victorian State Commissioner Gordon Lewis for misconduct during the Shield game between Victoria and South Australia in February, 1989; $500 for disputing the umpire's decision and $250 for crude and abusive language.

1989: Is warned by Dickie Bird for intimidatory bowling after repeated short balls to England's Robin Smith.
An Alice Springs magistrate accuses Hughes of "homosexual-type behaviour" and "unmanly activities" in that he dared to kiss his teammates on the field after a wicket.

1989-90: Snatches his jumper from umpire Steve Randell after a caught behind appeal against Sri Lanka's Asoka de Silva is rejected, during the second Test in Hobart. Randell does not make an official report.

Exchanges angry words with Wasim Akram after the Pakistani cannons into him while trying to take a quick single in Adelaide. The "right of way" dispute is quickly settled by umpire Tony Crafter. "It was a clash of the heavyweights," said Crafter. "Merv had completed his follow through and Wasim in running through didn't deviate an inch. There was a collision and lots of words. That was pretty provocative. I was stuck in the middle of them."

1991: Admits to breaking down a dressing room door, with Terry Alderman at St. John's in Antigua during the tempestuous '91 tour of the Caribbean. "Gentle persuasion by both our shoulders did the job nicely," he says. "We had no idea though that when we broke in (after the key had broken and the team was locked out) it would cause such an an international outcry."

1991-92: Earns a warning from International Cricket Council match referee Peter May during the third Test in Sydney when he kicks a stump from the ground after Steve Randell rejects a run-out appeal.

Escapes censure despite kicking a stump and sending a bail flying after the final ball of the fourth day's play of the fourth Test in Adelaide on January 29. Umpires Peter McConnell and Darrell Hair say Hughes was only joking.

1992-93: Is fined $400 having been reported by Steve Randell for dissent and abusive language after the final day's play of the drawn first Test against the West Indies in Brisbane. Captain Allan Border is fined $2000 at the same ICC end-of-match inquiry, which he boycotts.

Is reprimanded by the ICC's referee Donald Carr after being found guilty of dissent and abusive language charges brought about by umpires Randell and Col Timmins on the third and final day of the

Merv: constantly at odds with officialdom.

fifth Test. ACB executive-director Graham Halbish says the report is for Hughes' "quiet comments following the rejection of a close lbw appeal."

Escapes any official complaint despite appearing to elbow and spit in the direction of NZ opener Mark Greatbatch on the fourth night of the third Test at Eden Park.

1993-94: Is fined $450 for swearing at South African opener Gary Kirsten during the first Test at Johannesburg. The ACB considers the fine too lenient and adds another $4000 for "breach of contract."

Receives a $2000 suspended fine and is again severely reprimanded for acting under provocation when he brandishes his bat at a spectator while leaving the field on the last day of the first Test at Wanderers. Television footage is shown around the world of Hughes wheeling around in the player's race, banging his bat angrily on the side of the fence and poking it at a spectator who had been abusing him.

1994-95: Is fined and reprimanded by the Victorian Cricket Association for undisclosed offences during Victoria's one-day game against Tasmania at Hobart on October 29.

1995-96: Is issued with a suspended fine of $1000 by the Victorian Cricket Association for publicly criticising Victorian coach Les Stillman after the axing of wicketkeeper Darren Berry from the State side in December.

1996-97: Bristles at criticism by Victorian chairman of selectors John Grant that he'd never play for Victoria again.

While he says he's past four-day cricket, he firmly believes he could have been promoted back into the one-day side, given his excellent season start with Footscray.

1997-98: Joins the ACT one-day team on a "fly-in" basis for its opening year of Mercantile Mutual Cup cricket.

Unimpressed by the boisterous Victorian's wayward Australian debut, Chappell felt Hughes was downgrading a great Aussie tradition of quality opening bowlers from Lindwall to Lillee. He'd bowled too short and too wide and his pace wasn't that good anyway, maybe only a touch above Max Walker at his top.

Chappell reckoned he needed only half his 40 metre run-up, he stuttered at its start and almost shook hands with mid-off as he was taking off. He might be big and intimidating, but on batting paradises like the Adelaide Oval, when confronted by elite players such as Sunil Gavaskar, the sooner he concentrated on line and length the better.

It was the most biting broadside, especially coming from a former Australian captain and frontline television commentator.

Hughes dismissed most criticism, especially if it was levelled by anyone who hadn't played the game at the highest level. But this was something else. Chappell was an acclaimed leader and Hughes deeply wounded.

From his very first game, when he averaged 123 with the ball, made a duck and upset Australian officialdom by being seen in a hotel bar at midnight the night before the game, Hughes developed a rip-roaring habit of alienating opinion.

His forgettable debut not only included a thumping from the Indian batting maestro Gavaskar, he also had to answer a stern "please explain" from officialdom for hanging out pre-match with a bunch of rowdy mates from Melbourne.

Hughes had dared leave his room for the more congenial surroundings of the Hilton hotel's downstairs bar and nervously downed soda waters while doing his best to relax.

"All I had was two stubbies and a mountain of soda water in Charlie's Bar," Hughes said, "But I got hauled over the coals for that; apparently one of the Australian selectors spotted me. It was my first Test. I didn't know if we were going to be batting or bowling. I get bored silly just staying in my room. I like getting downstairs and talking to people. It's my way of relaxing. If you can get out, it takes your mind off the game. I copped a lot of flak over that. But if I'd taken five-for or six-for, no-one would have said a word."

Sharing the new ball with Craig McDermott, also in his debut Test in Adelaide, Hughes' elongated, angled run-up from deep mid-off caused as much comment as his wayward first seven overs late on the Saturday night.

When he broke through for a wicket with his fourth ball just after noon on the third day, he was so elated he raced past the fallen batsman, Indian No. 4 Dilip Vengsarkar and smothered wicketkeeper Wayne Phillips in a bear-hug.

While it was to be his only success, he did have Chetan Sharma, India's night watchman, dropped at third slip, despite David Boon's acrobatic dive to his right.

He also had his first mid-pitch run-in, with India's captain Kapil Dev, when the bails flew after Dev had played a pull shot. Hughes felt he'd trodden on his wicket, but Dev claimed the wind was responsible, sparking renewed volleys of invective.

The Australians fielded for almost three days and Hughes missed his two chief Victorian motivators, especially Tony Dodemaide who'd invariably pump him up from mid-off and wicketkeeper Michael Dimattina.

The Indians took 202 overs to make 520 and Hughes' maiden analysis was an unflattering 38-6-123-1. He'd bowled at full throttle, but after the initial overs with the first and second new ball, the bounce which threatened to worry the Indians was no longer a factor and Gavaskar, who had to retire hurt in mid-innings, was unhurried in making his 31st Test century.

Hughes expected to be dropped and he was. So disillusioned was he that he doubted that he'd ever get another chance. When the next Test side was announced, he still remembers the deep feeling of emptiness when his name was missing. He'd had a taste of the big-time and he wanted more.

His first Victorian captain John Scholes had told him to play every game like it was his last. From that day, he resolved to be the best he could be, train like he never had before and and prove his knockers wrong.

Dropped after his first, second and sixth Test matches and belittled by his captain Allan Border, even after his first "five-for" haul in Test cricket, it was a tough trail to the top, but Hughes made it and in the process bowled far above even his own expectations.

With 212 Test wickets, Hughes deservedly rates with some of Australia's finest. His strike-rate of 57 balls per wicket is superior to Ray Lindwall (59) and only just behind Dennis Lillee (52) and Jeff Thomson (52). No-one has shown more spirit or been more popular with his teammates. Allan Border called him "Gronk" (after the caveman) or "Fruit Fly" (the great Australian pest), but when the wicket was flat and a huge opposition score beckoning, knew who to turn to.

Few bowlers had superior ability to make it happen on the deadest of wickets. Hughes may have come from nowhere, but he was the consumate partnership breaker with a heart like a lion.

With his flowing moustache and gregarious ways which prompted unique crowd reactions, especially in his hometown Melbourne, Hughes became Australian cricket's new cult hero.

While he limped out of Test cricket, having signed his own death certicate by continuing to bowl on a badly deteriorating knee in the final weeks in England in 1993, his enthusiasm for cricket remained and he continued with his mates at Footscray long after the State and national selectors considered his "use-by" date had passed.

He'd been responsible for some of the sharpest and most intimidating spells since Lillee and Thomson were in their pomp. His exuberance and bristling, on-field demeanour sometimes spilled beyond the realms of decency, resulting in a spate of umpire warnings, reprimands and fines. But there were few smarter operators or anyone better suited for the big occasion.

When he was dumped for the last time from the Victorian pre-season squad, after failing to attend training and address his ballooning weight problems, batsmen around the country breathed a collective sigh of relief. No longer would they be subject to the Hughes stare or the change-up bouncer invariably aimed straight between their eyes.

Sad as they were to be without his wicket-taking abilities, many of his old Test teammates were also relieved on one score. Not everyone appreciated Merv's old "tongue in the ear" party trick whenever a big wicket fell!

BACK TO SCHOOL

MERV HUGHES said he was destined to be a sports person from a very early age.

After taking a week off to play Country Week cricket, early in his only term of year 11, one of his teachers at Werribee High asked about his priorities.

"The teacher really hopped into me. 'You took five days off to play sport?'

"That's right."

"Do you think sport is more important than your education? I looked at her and thought, "What a bloody stupid question."

"Well Mr Hughes," she said, "You'll have to be a very good footballer or a very, very good cricketer to make anything of your life."

The son of a schoolteacher renowned for his love of square-dancing, sport and readiness in adapting to his numerous Education Department postings, Merv Hughes was born in Euroa in north-eastern Victoria and at various times lived in Baddaginnie, Apollo Bay, Violet Town, Myrtleford and Euroa. His most permanent base was Werribee in Melbourne's unfashionable west where he spent the majority of his primary and secondary school years before leaving soon into year 11, after a series of run-ins with his teachers.

Hughes always preferred sport to his studies and being big for his age, played open-age cricket in Myrtleford from the age of 14. In those days he went in at No.3 and had an ambition to open the batting for Australia.

An early analysis of 6-1 for Lara against Sunshine was an indication that he may be better off specialising as a bowler, but he never lost his own high-opinion of his batting!

Ironically, a harmless practical joke triggered his move, aged 16, from sub-district into district cricket and into state selection focus. He and a mate were dropped from the firsts to the seconds by Werribee captain, Paul Maloney. Their crime? Stealing the skip's sock after a long day's play while the owner was taking a shower!

By Christmas, 1978, Hughes was at Footscray, the closest of three zoned clubs which, after a month-long study of the weekend's District minor X1 results, appeared to be least-equipped for emerging bowlers.

After taking eight wickets on debut in the third X1, Hughes was immediately promoted to the seconds, where he played in a premiership under the captaincy of ex-Australian Testman Ken Eastwood. The following year he played in another, at first X1 level and was judged to be the Australian Cricket Society's Young Cricketer of the Year. Former international, Ron Gaunt, was one of his earliest coaches at Footscray and along with captain-coach Lindsay James, advised Hughes to concentrate full-time on his bowling, rather than toying with the idea of being a batting all-rounder.

"From the first night when I paced out my long run-up, they told me that's what I'd be doing every practice night," Hughes said. "You had to bowl fast if you were to play in the senior side at Footscray. It wasn't a batting-friendly environment. You'd get to training and try and bounce the poop out of everyone."

With 9-25 in the semi-final against Melbourne and 6-57 in the final against Carlton seconds, a team which included a teenage Dean Jones, Hughes was suddenly being talked of as a budding State bowler. He'd bypassed most of the normal teenage selection processes and came from the unfashionable west, but there was no denying his sheer presence, or pace.

Jones remembers him most for his huge run-up. "He seemed to run in from the sightscreen," said Jones. "He would have been a good 40 yards back and he bowled good pace every ball."

The pair made their senior club debuts in the same match the following season and within two years – on New Year's Day, 1982 – were both named for their maiden Victorian games, a one-dayer, against South Australia in Adelaide.

While Hughes snared the wickets of Rick Darling and Jeff Crowe with successive deliveries, he also conceded almost six runs an over. It took him years to realise control was as important as sheer pace, especially at one-day level and was rarely an automatic selection for limited-overs cricket, even in his headiest international days.

A fortnight later, he also made his Sheffield Shield debut. Remarkably it was only through chance that he even found out about his selection. He was holidaying with mates at a beach-house at Ocean Grove when he went shopping and was congratulated by the wife of one of his old coaches at Werribee.

"I had just turned 21 and was having a ball," Hughes said.* "We didn't read newspapers or listen to the radio and we didn't have a television. We just ran and swam and generally had a totally relaxing time away from it all, not wanting to know anything about cricket except what we could do next to have more fun.

"Then we went shopping one day and we ran into Geoff Bean's wife, Sandra, as we walked down the street. She congratulated me on being in the Victorian side and I thanked her and started to rattle on about Adelaide and the good win in the match on New Year's Day.

"Suddenly she interrupted and said: 'Oh no. I read in the paper this morning that you have been picked for the next Sheffield Shield game.'

"What! I picked myself up, dusted myself down and left everybody standing in the street as I raced to the newsagents and grabbed a paper...sure enough there I was. I was picked to play against South Australia in Geelong. And it was just three days away!

"I jumped on the phone to Mum and Dad and was informed I had received a couple of phone calls. The bottom line was that I was due at training at the Albert Ground that night.

"I raced home as if my life depended on it, grabbed my cricket gear and scooted to Melbourne. I arrived late for training, which didn't please the bosses, but only if they'd known. If I hadn't gone shopping that morning and fluked bumping into Sandra, I may have spent a week lounging in the sun and surf and missed my first Shield match for the Big V!"

From his earliest Victorian matches, Hughes was lively in pace and personality and his dressing room antics amazed and entertained his new teammates.

As a joke, before his debut match in Adelaide, captain John Scholes told the score-board attendant, who'd come to check on the names of the Victorians, that Hughes' surname was in fact, "Hill" (after hillbilly). Sure enough, on the famous old SACA scoreboard, the name "Hill" rather than "Hughes" appeared, much to the merriment of the Victorians, bar Merv, who said his mother would be disappointed. He vowed immediate revenge and Scholes says Hughes is now so far in front, it's not funny!

Scholes had immediately warmed to his talent and endearing ways. He liked the fact that Hughes had even agreed to take the single bed when they roomed together for the first time on tour.

Scholes also liked Hughes' raw aggression and purpose. He had a twinkle in his eye and an infectious enthusiasm for the game and his mates. And if you asked him to bowl all day, he'd do it, no questions asked.

In his debut games of Sheffield Shield, Hughes operated into the wind behind the more-experienced ex-Testman Ian Callen. When Scholes gave him a chance downwind late in the match against the Queenslanders at Kardinia Park, Hughes reverted to his 40-metre run-up which he had temporarily abandoned at Footscray to help accelerate the over rate.

With six wickets for the game, including three of the top five in the first innings, he'd immediately justified his promotion.

Injuries to his hamstring and ribs restricted him to just four games in 1982-83, but he was impressive enough to earn an Esso scholarship to England, along with other Shield hopefuls, South Australian Michael Haysman, Queensland's Robert Kerr and NSW's Greg Matthews.

As part of a very sociable summer playing mainly for Essex seconds – where he claimed a season-high 60 wickets at an average of 18.65 – Hughes also represented Essex' No.1 team against the touring New Zealanders, but strained his back late in the year and was restricted upon his return. He'd also cashed in on the renowned English

*In Merv, Merv Hughes by Rod Nicholson.

hospitality, eating and drinking as he pleased. Tony Dodemaide, who was touring with an Australian youth team, met up with him at Chelmsford and was staggered by his friend's larger-than-life figure. Taking Dodemaide's advice to find a set of scales, fast, Hughes found his weight had ballooned from 92kg to 109kg!

He went on an immediate diet but was still grossly overweight on his return to Australia and given his nagging injury problems, under performed, playing only four games in 1983-84 and five in 1984-85. According to Dodemaide, one of his closest mates, Hughes developed stress fractures to his back "every other year."

"He was forever taking painkillers and anti-inflammatories after Christmas to get through the games," he said.

It wasn't until 1985-86, when Australia's cricket depth was ravaged by the first of the two rebel tours of South Africa, that he finally enjoyed an injury-free season. The absence of Messrs Hogg, Rackemann, McCurdy and Alderman, who had all joined Kim Hughes' controversial squad, was fortuitous From being a rank outsider for representative honors just 12 months earlier, he was suddenly in frontline contention, especially after taking six wickets against reigning Shield champions New South Wales in the second game of the summer. A fortnight previously, in Brisbane, he'd bowled 34 overs and taken 3-116, troubling everyone bar Allan Border who made 194.

It was the start of his most impressive season in which he captured 34 wickets and proved how a little commitment could open new doors. Instead of playing football in the off-season, he opted to rest his back which had been troubling him for some time and headed to the Top End for a three month holiday, which also included some body-trimming work in 40 degree conditions in a Darwin warehouse.

On return he'd grown a beard so luxuriant that even his mates at Werribee football club struggled to recognise him.

"You could hardly see my eyes for all the hair," he said in his autobiography, *Merv – My Life and other Funny Stories*. "I thought I had to do something if even the football club boys didn't know who I was. As I was getting it all cut off, the hairdresser asked me if I wanted to keep a moustache. We tried it, I liked it and it's been there ever since. Now it's my trademark."

On the opening day of the NSW game on a helpful wicket in Newcastle, he grabbed five wickets for the first time at major level and with his new walrus-like moustache, was described by one local journalist as a Mexican bandit from south of the border. A month later against the touring Indians in Melbourne, he claimed 3-42 from 26 hostile overs and when an injured David Gilbert withdrew and Geoff Lawson dropped after Australia's humiliating defeat in the Trans-Tasman Trophy series, Hughes and giant West Australian Bruce Reid were both named for their debut Tests against Kapil Dev's touring Indians in Adelaide. In the biggest selection shake-up since World Series Cricket, Geoff Marsh was also included for the first time.

Border was clearly becoming dissatisfied with Australia's mediocre performances and within weeks, in the return Tests in New Zealand, offered to relinquish the captaincy, saying, "I've said everything I can say to that lot."

Every boy who dreams of playing cricket for Australia wants it to be against England. There is no greater interest in any series.

Merv Hughes was like a young, excited pup when he heard of his selection for the first Ashes Test of 1986-87 against Mike Gatting's Englishmen. He might have missed the tour of New Zealand, but he was back in favor and even going a little easier on the takeaway food including his all-time favorite Aussie pizza with prawns!

The omission of Lawson, Australia's most experienced fast bowler, on the first morning in Brisbane was greeted with surprise, especially in the English camp. Having won the Ashes convincingly in 1985, the tourists had stumbled badly in 1986, losing eight of their 11 Tests for the calendar year, including a 0-5 drubbing by the West Indies. Many thought its Ashes squad to be the weakest ever to tour downunder, one journalist saying the team "can't bat, can't bowl and can't field!"

Gatting expected Australia to field its best and most experienced line-up. Instead, the new-ball attack consisted of Reid, who had played eight Tests, Hughes who had played one and debuting West Australian left-arm swing bowler Chris Matthews.

As so often happens, the early fortunes dictated the whole series trend. Allan Border sent England in, but the Australians bowled erratically on the first day, wasting the early life in the wicket. On the second they ran headlong into Ian Botham, in irrepressible mood, who made 138 as England amassed 450-plus.

"The inexperience of the Australian faster bowlers clearly showed, fortunately for us," said Gatting.* "Nerves must have played a part as well but none of them bowled a consistent line although Reid improved as the day wore on. Chris Matthews was never sure where the ball was going. Hughes was little better although clearly the fastest bowler and when he did get it right, produced a very good ball."

Gatting said Hughes' moustache made him look 35, rather than 25, and he wasn't backward in offering an opinion about a player's ability, especially when they fanned injudiciously outside the off-stump.

"He's quite an aggressive character on the field as all fast bowlers should be, with a habit of glaring at the batsman, hands on hips, at the end of his follow through when he has bowled a good ball. He also mutters a few words suggesting the batsman is the luckiest human being in the world."

Hughes had started in tandem with Reid, into the wind and had two of the top five, but couldn't remove obdurate Yorkshireman Bill Athey, with whom he engaged in a running war-of-words. On the second afternoon he was treated in cavalier fashion by Ian Botham, one of his overs going for 22.

"My first ball to him – a good one just short of a length outside off stump – was deliberately sliced over third man for six. I can't let him get away with that, I thought," Hughes said.

"Not wanting to be taken lightly I let him have a bouncer next ball. He hooked it for another massive six. Twelve off two balls. Not good for the figures, Stay cool and whatever you do, don't bowl another short one, I muttered to myself. I bowled a bouncer and he pulled it through mid-wicket for four. The ball struck the fence with such force that it bounced most of the way back to the middle. Well done Merv, nice thinking, I screamed silently to myself. For God's sake, pitch the next one up. I did and he crashed it through the covers for four.

"He had an enormous heave at the next ball and missed (thank heavens) and scrambled a two off the last. Twenty-two off the over. Well bowled Merv, have a rest. Good game cricket."

Botham had so often been a colossus in Ashes battles and was clearly tuned in to achieve. When Hughes opened with the second new ball, Botham hit three blazing 4s in a row. Writing in *The Age*, Trevor Grant dubbed him King Kong with a cricket bat.

His teammates were similarly impressed. "His attitude was unrecogniseable from that of the last time I had been with him in an England dressing room," said opening bat Chris Broad. "Gone was the bored, crabby teammate of 1984; instead he was tremendously supportive, continually positive and resolutely determined to come out

In "Triumph in Australia."

on top. When you graft such attributes on to his great natural talents you have a wonderful cricketer and an invaluable teammate."

Hughes had taken three first-up wickets, but conceded 134 runs. His nightmare at top level was continuing.

"How quick we have been in this series to write this mob (England) off as a crowd of no-hopers," said Bill O'Reilly in the *Sydney Morning Herald*, "just because they began as if they had a lot of bad blood to get out of their veins before the real cricket began."

Just after lunch on the fifth day, England had completed a convincing win. Border bypassed the television presentations and barely kept his cool with the press, delivering his answers with a snap and a snarl in true Captain Grumpy style. Only a fortnight previously at the 'Gabba, he'd sent Tasmania into bat in a Shield game and they'd made 526. His latest gamble had also backfired.

His captaincy and general demeanour took a terrible caning. "Look at him," said the legendary Keith Miller in the Melbourne *Truth*. "Sleeves rolled down, scruffy beard. Hand on his chin. He looks more like an escapee from a Ned Kelly gang movie."

Botham was man of the match, starting a memorable triple-win for England. Not only were the tourists to retain the Ashes, they won the Challenge Cup in Perth as part of the America's Cup bicentennial race-off and the World Series.

Despite their inglorious start to the Test series in Brisbane, the Australians made only one change, dropping Hughes for Peter Sleep and including Lawson for Perth.

Big Merv had been dropped after each of his first two Tests. While he was recalled for the third Test in Adelaide and held his place for the remainder of the series, he took only five more wickets to finish with just 10 in four Tests at an unflattering average approaching 45. "You think you're doing the hard work and all the right things at Shield level and you go up to the next level and find out what you're doing is no-where near enough," Hughes said. "The jump from club cricket to Shield level is a giant step. But the next step is twice as big. I don't know how players can go from Shield cricket straight into the national team and perform well."

Despite his lack of success, the Englishmen had rated Hughes ahead of the emerging Reid. He was awkward and always "at them," whether it was his first, second or third spell. However, there were too many "gimme" balls where he tended to slide onto leg stump. He also tended to bowl too short and not give his underrated outswinger full scope.

The Victorians qualified for their first-ever Shield final that summer and while they were outplayed by champions Western Australia and in particular, Mike Veletta who made 262, Hughes refused to buckle on a batting paradise which even saw a frustrated Ray Bright resort to bowling one delivery right-handed to Reid, WA's No. 11.

Despite the effects of an aching back, Hughes bowled 42 big-hearted overs and even after Veletta had passed 200 on the way to amassing the biggest score by a West Australian, was still going at full throttle on the fourth day. He was fast enough to make Veletta play and miss three times. Another delivery in the same over spat into his ribs.

Given his mountainous efforts, his figures of 2-113 were a travesty, but he'd outbowled everyone else in the match, a feat not lost on the national selectors, given Australia's growing commitments, both home and overseas.

The message was increasingly clear, however. Control the ballooning waistline and become fully committed, or forever remain on the fringes. At 26, Merv Hughes was at the crossroads as he approached the 1987-88 Trans-Tasman re-matches.

He'd missed selection for the Indian tour and the momentous World Cup victory on the sub-continent and despite five wickets in the first Test in Brisbane, including New Zealand's star batsman Martin Crowe in each innings, had again been axed.

When a hamstring strain kept him out of the Melbourne Test and opened the door for his Footscray teammate Dodemaide to make a dream entry, it seemed others were passing him in the battle for a regular new ball berth.

Even a big finish in the one-off Test against the Sri Lankans in Perth was little consolation, especially after Allan Border went public on what previously had been an "in-house" conversation topic.

After the Australians had won by an innings in little over three days, Border scoffed at Hughes' contribution, saying he'd been flattered by his figures (a Test-best 5-67) and remained grossly overweight. "If he's going to be fair dinkum, he should look at this very carefully," said Border. "I think he's got a long way to go. He's got tremendous pace, but he doesn't maintain a pressurised attack on the batsmen. To develop as a bowler, he's got to find better line and length."

There was little doubt that Hughes was bowling with more variety. He supplemented his natural in-swing with a slower ball, sometimes bowled from 23 yards and other times bowled with a leg-break action which tended to skid through. He also had learned to angle the ball nicely across the left-handers. But just when it seemed he'd straightened his line, he'd spray the ball wildly down leg. Something was amiss and after the Perth Test, it was revealed he had been bowling since Christmas with a stress fracture of his back.

FUN & GAMES WITH DEANO

One of few highlights for Australia during the one-sided 1988-89 summer came in Adelaide, when the Frank Worrell Trophy had been decided. Dean Jones made 216 and Merv unconquered on 72 not out, a very courageous hand considering the punishment he took from the West Indian fast bowlers.

Merv was hit twice in the groin and again in the stomach but soldiered on manfully, trying to ensure Jones his double century.

When struck on the back of the head by a bouncer, he wandered down the wicket to Jones and snarled, "if you don't get your 200 in a minute, I'll knock your head off."

With one ball remaining before the tea interval, Hughes was 49 not out and Jones suggested to him that he block it and wait until the final session to reach his milestone.

"I felt contented that I'd done the right thing and I was also sure that Merv had matured a lot since those early days when advice went in one ear and out the other. So I was almost heading to the pavilion when the bowler delivered the final ball of the session.

"Whack! Straight over the mid-wicket boundary for six to bring up his 50! He sure knows how to take advice."

The Australians were given a standing ovation as they left for tea. "Isn't that nice," said Hughes, conveniently forgetting Jones' double-century. "So much applause just for my 50."

Ever since Max Walker's defection to the ranks of World Series Cricket, Melburnians, especially those who frequented the infamous bay 13 area, had been searching for a new hero. Walker's popularity ballooned to extraordinary heights, especially after he became the first Australian in 50 years to take eight wickets in an innings against England, at the MCG in 1974-75.

His endearing grin and affable manner made him a favorite with thousands. In between overs, he'd field at fine-leg and sign autographs, accept drinks and generally play up to the crowd.

Only one of Hughes' first seven internationals, the fourth Ashes Test in 1986-87, was in front of his home crowd and while he made only two and eight and took 1-94 against Mike Gatting's Englishmen, as one of only two Victorians in the match, his mere presence guaranteed standing ovations.

It wasn't until two years later that Merv Mania really took off, when Melburnians paid tribute to him after his astonishing efforts earlier in the month at the WACA Ground.

Having been bypassed by the selectors in Brisbane, Hughes had fought his way back into the squad for Perth and on the morning of the match was preferred to Craig McDermott who was made 12th man.

He was well aware of his chequered record of seven Tests in three years and realised he had to take the next step, or be discarded permanently.

Buoyed by his previous successes in Perth – just 10 months earlier, he'd taken a Test-best 5-67 against the Sri Lankans – Hughes, bowling in tandem with Geoff Lawson, was soon rewarded for a blistering opening spell when Desmond Haynes missed an in-swinger to be lbw. His illustrious partner Gordon Greenidge could also have been out cheaply to Hughes, but for a dropped catch by Steve Waugh before he'd reached double figures.

Bowling unchanged for the first 90 minutes, Hughes returned immediately after lunch and so discomforted Carl Hooper with his extra bounce that the West Indian called for a chest pad.

For years the Windies had rarely been challenged at Test level. A breathtaking Viv Richards century, coupled with 93 from Gus Logie, ensured an impressive first innings score of 449. Hughes finished with 5-130 having taken the last two wickets in successive deliveries, Curtly Ambrose caught with the final delivery of his 36th over and Patrick Patterson caught from the first of his 37th.

Merv's good humor bubbled close to the surface, even under duress. After one of Richards' imperious drives, he stopped play and asked umpire Robin Bailhache to have Richards' bat tested for steroids!

"Even though he was at the end of his career, Viv was still an awesome player," Hughes said. "He was such an intimidating man to come up against. He really believed in his own ability. It helped make him such a fantastic player."

In reply, Australia was resolute in reaching 8-395, before Allan Border declared, protecting his No.11 Hughes from the volley of short deliveries from Malcolm Marshall and Curtly Ambrose, one of which had shattered Lawson's jaw and forced him to be carried from the field.

Hughes, who was sitting nervously in the rooms, having strapped on every possible piece of protective equipment, including David Boon's helmet with full grille, was about to hop up when Border said, "I think I'll declare."

Merv's reaction was precious. "I looked at Allan and thought, "I love my captain!' "

From a comfortable 4-367, the Aussie lower-order had tumbled, the last four wickets adding just 28 against the second new ball.

Seeing Lawson carried off, sections of the WACA crowd heckled the West Indians and particularly Ambrose. They considered it unsporting for a tailender to receive a bouncer second ball and roared like a football crowd as a fired-up Hughes paced out his mark to begin the West Indian second innings.

When the ball, which was full and straight, thudded into Greenidge's pads, trapping him lbw, the crowd, still hyped after the Lawson k.o., joined in the celebration. In the rarest of all hat-tricks, Hughes had three wickets in three balls, all in different overs.

In the drama and high emotion of the moment, even Hughes hadn't realised his feat and it was only a public address announcement several minutes later which alerted the

Australians. Steve Waugh, who'd been boundary riding, approached Hughes at the end of an over and said, "You've taken a hat-trick."

"No, I haven't."

"Yes, you have."

According to umpire Terry Prue, who had given Greenidge out, the Australians were naturally excited at getting a first ball wicket – "but no-one was aware that it was a hat-trick or that something special had happened."

Within half an hour after stumps that night, the Australians hopped into a mini-bus and went to visit Lawson. Asked about his hat-trick, Hughes told newspapermen, "That will look good on my record, but there are more important things to worry about. There is a teammate in hospital."

Lawson's enforced absence robbed Border of his most experienced strike bowler in mid-match. With spinner Tim May unsuited to the conditions, the attack was virtually carried by Hughes, Tony Dodemaide and Steve Waugh, who attempted to arrest the scoring by bowling tightly from the member's end.

Hughes shouldered greatest responsibility and responded magnificently, taking the first six wickets to fall on his way to a career-best 8-87. MARVELLOUS MERV BAGS A RECORD, *The Age* headlined after his 35 over, fourth day marathon.

After years of trying, the 27-year-old finally proved himself a Test-class bowler with enormous capacity. He started running in at fearsome pace at 11 a.m. and was still going strong at 6.24 p.m. when stumps were drawn.

After spells of seven and 10 overs in the first two sessions, he sent down 16 overs after tea, bowling unchanged from the River End in a remarkable display of stamina.

With five wickets in the final session (Haynes, Hooper, Richards, Logie and Jeff Dujon), he passed 10 wickets in a match for the first time in his international career. Each wicket was celebrated with gusto, particularly when Richards was so plainly leg before that he walked before Prue had time to even raise his finger! An ecstatic Hughes threw his arms in the air and hugged each of his teammates. It remains one of his alltime favorite wickets. "It gave me a lot of confidence to think I could mix it with the very best," he said.

Prue, in his first Test match, had never had to give an easier lbw. Richards took three steps before taking a cursory glance back at Prue just to confirm the inevitable.

Prue was amazed as everyone else by Hughes' efforts in bowling unchanged. "He just kept on going and going. That was the remarkable part of the whole thing," he said.

His partner Bailhache, in his 27th Test, said it was Hughes' finest moment of an illustrious career. "His speed and aggression was there throughout that entire day. It was pure aggro, in the nicest sense. The longer he bowled the more aggro and competitive he became. It all stood on his shoulders and he responded superbly."

As was to occur so often in following years when Hughes shouldered extra responsibility when others were injured, the burly Victorian cornered one end and refused all invitations to take a rest. "There was no chance of anyone getting the ball off me – and the way things were, no chance of me giving it away anyway," Hughes said.

"I was thrilled to get five wickets in the innings. I didn't really appreciate the significance of the 12 (when he surpassed the all time best match figures of an Australian against the West Indies.)* It wasn't until I got off the ground that I found out."

It was the first hat-trick by an Australian against the Windies while his match tally of 13 for 217 off 73.1 overs was a career-best analysis by an Australian against the West Indies.

While the Australians tumbled to a comprehensive 169 run defeat, Hughes'

* Bert Ironmonger took 11 for 79 against the West Indies in Melbourne in 1930-31.

Celebrating a wicket against the West Indies, World Series, 1988-89.

mountainous feats ensured peak publicity for days. Ian Chappell's famous quip, guaranteed to send any self-respecting fast bowler over the edge, was resurrected, Hughes admitting he'd used it constantly for extra motivation. "You take those criticisms on board and go away and work twice as hard," he said. "My motivation was to prove a point to Ian Chappell that I could play cricket. Hopefully over a 10 year period, I did that."

Ironically, Hughes hadn't even been sure that he'd play in the game, given the presence of a four fast bowlers in the Australian squad. "A lot of the time I've gone away thinking I'm going to be 12th man and just trained that way," he said.*

"This time I went away with a more positive attitude and had a real dip in the nets."

During his marathon final session spell, Hughes remained an intimidating presence, his never-say-die spirit lifting the Australians. Writing in *Merv*, Rod Nicholson said Hughes' capacity for "seemingly endless labour" enthused sports lovers around the country, Channel Nine reporting near-record ratings in the eastern states.

"Merv had the same pained expression on his face as a cyclist or a rower pushing to the limit to reach the finish line. The same dazed glare as a boxer fighting from memory, knowing that failing to go the distance is all that can beat him. Border kept asking if he wanted a rest. A stubborn shake of the head on a racked body was the only acknowledgement."

Far from believing he had established a permanent place in Australia's best X1, Hughes said he couldn't afford to relax and needed to keep bowling consistently if he wanted to play in the remaining three Tests against the Windies and make his maiden tour of England the following winter.

*In an interview with Greg Baum in *The Sun*.

"There are a lot of blokes who come and go and the people who are remembered are the greats," he said. "They put in consistent performances for 10 years, people like Desmond Haynes and Gordon Greenidge, Malcolm Marshall and Allan Border. I've still got a long way to go."

His next match figures proved how cricket can be a great leveller:

- Melbourne 0-123,
- Sydney 1-57,
- Adelaide 0-106.

He'd tried to bowl too fast and become frustrated when he didn't enjoy the same success. Life off-the-field had become overly complicated, too, with many new demands on his time, especially via media requests and public appearances.

He'd played his first World Series games, however, including the finals and been an immediate hit with the crowd, taking 2-34 in the first final in front of 73,000 adoring MCG fans. He'd even been entrusted with the responsibility of bowling the last over with the Windies needing nine to win. They scored only six, the Australians winning by two.

Two days later in the second final, in Sydney, he took 4-44, his best-ever one day figures which consolidated his English touring place.

He arrived with the 30th Australian team at Heathrow with fresh ambitions, not only hoping to build on his record, but to help Australia re-wrest the Ashes after the ignomony of dual defeats in 1985 and 1986-87.

THE GREAT AUSTRALIAN PEST
GEOFF Lawson was only half-joking when he dubbed Merv "Fruitfly" ...
the great Australian pest.

Merv Hughes admits to having more nerves than most waiting for the 1989 Ashes party to be chosen. Seasoned campaigners Geoff Lawson and Terry Alderman were automatic selections as new ball partners, but the battle was keen for the three back-up places between seven or eight players including Carl Rackemann, Hughes, Tony Dodemaide, David Gilbert, Greg Campbell, Michael Whitney and Craig McDermott. The rookie South Australian allrounder, Joe Scuderi, had also made a late charge and appeared in the Sheffield Shield final.

McDermott whose form had been as patchy as his attitude was left out, as was Scuderi, who was said to have time on his side. Dodemaide and Gilbert were also passed over, along with Whitney, whose non-selection was greeted with widespread dismay. The gregarious NSW left-arm paceman missed a place despite taking 7-89 and 2-60 in the final West Indian Test of the summer in Adelaide. With 58 wickets, Whitney had been the outstanding NSW cricketer of the summer.

Despite having been outplayed by the world champion Windies, Australia's victory in Sydney and their dominance of the drawn final Test in Adelaide had lifted expectations that the team was slowly building into a combination of substance. With only one series win in eight, Allan Border was thirsting for success, especially after successive defeats by the Old Enemy. Under Bob Simpson, the Australians had shocked the cricket world by winning the World Cup in 1987 and their work ethic, athleticism and running between wickets was soon a much-discussed feature.

Every touring team has a character the English media fraternity gravitate towards and in the boisterous, free-spirited Hughes, they reckoned they had an obvious choice. They were alert to his cult image in Australia and portrayed him as the great Australian yobbo who delighted in his capacity for food and lots of Aussie beer.

They also warmed to his obvious zest for life and his frequent one-liners, which on arrival included,"They throw rocks at me back home if I don't take wickets!"

For weeks he was the most photographed of all the Australians. Many regarded him as a comic first and totally under-estimated his fast bowling gifts. One Sunday tabloid tried to set him up with a buxon blond, but dropped the story when they learnt he was single and that the wedding ring he was sporting was in fact a gift from his parents.

Hughes played up to the press, but didn't allow the huge media focus to undermine his on-field ambitions or after the first frenetic weeks, to cut into his training. He worked hard in the nets, enjoying the regular tuition from Alderman and Lawson, who could make the ball swerve and cut seemingly at will.

Despite the warmest English summer since 1976, the Australians struck a set of sub-standard wickets leading into the Tests and after losing a one-dayer against Sussex being beaten inside two full days by Worcestershire at New Road were dubbed BORDER'S PUSSYCATS.

With just seven wickets in three first-class games, Hughes was only an outside chance for Test selection, before Rackemann, the popular choice as first-change, withdrew with injury and subsequently had to undergo a knee operation.

The promise of a lively Headingley wicket prompted both captains to play four fast bowlers, Campbell making his Ashes debut and Hughes being included for the unlucky Rackemann.

It was the start of a glorious campaign for the Australians, who adopted an uncompromising win-at-all-costs attitude from the start. It was also the making of Hughes as a Test cricketer. He took the deciding wicket (Phil DeFreitas, bowled) at Leeds among some very important wickets crucial to Australia's success.

By capturing 19 wickets in the six Tests, Hughes was a fast and hostile back-up to Alderman, who took 41 wickets, including 19 lbw and six bowled and Lawson, 29.

He cornered most of the publicity, too, especially after an Alice Springs magistrate accused him of "homosexual-type behaviour" and "unmanly activities" in kissing his teammates after a wicket!

"Up to that '89 tour, I'd been in and out of the Australian team," Hughes said."I might have taken 13 wickets in one Test but I took only 14 for the series. It was a nervous wait to hear the side selected for England. When I got on that tour, the turning point for me was to spend four and a half months with Terry Alderman and Geoff Lawson.

"To be selected for Australia is fantastic but the greatest honor an Australian cricketer can get is to be selected for an Ashes tour in England. The history and the tradition is fantastic. Terry and 'Henry' (Lawson) did the bulk of the work. I was just the understudy. We'd arrived as the underdogs and weren't expected to do well. To come back with a 4-0 win was sensational."

Hughes' initial tactics were simple, to bowl as fast and short as he could, trying to intimidate the Englishmen at every opportunity. Always vocal, his confidence soared the further the tour went and he started to take wickets with an occasional outswinger and leg-cutter. At Leeds, he bowled a bemused Chris Broad with a leg-break.

His most-satisfying wicket, however, came in the second Test at Lord's when David Gower, having made 106 and shared in a near 150 run stand with Robin Smith, was caught by opposing captain Border in the leg gully, trying to fend a lifter away from his rib cage.

" 'AB' suggested we try and get Gower caught in the leg trap and it worked. I tried to bowl as fast as I could and make life as uncomfortable as possible. Alderman and Lawson were used as the pitch-up bowlers to get the nicks, while I was used as the bloke

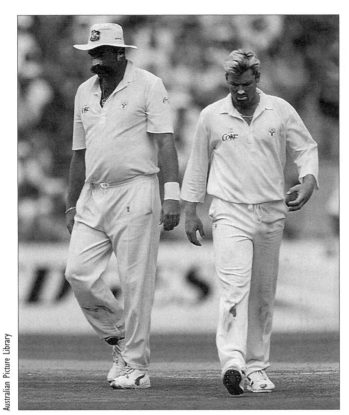

Australian Picture Library

Trouble at The Wanderers: Hughes with Shane Warne in mid-Test, 1993-94.

to come in, bowl short and intimidate the batsman. That Gower wicket is the one I like to remember most along with my first (Dilip Vengsarkar) in Adelaide and Viv Richards (lbw) in Perth a few months earlier."

The effervescent Hughes was fierce on the field and gentle off it, and integral in Australia regaining the Ashes 4-0. No-one partied like Merv. After one victory, he drank the entire cocktail list before it took three teammates to carry him off to bed! At Nottingham when he asked a young lady to join him for a drink, he picked up the stool with the lady still on it and carried it (and her) the length of the room before starting the conversation. His Indian rain dance the day after the Ashes win at Trent Bridge, complete with face smothered in sun cream, was another highlight, even if it failed to bring the desired rain!

At the conclusion of the tour, having played in the entire series for the first time, he told Rod Nicholson, "This tour will be hard to top, ever. It is like a dream come true. Every red blooded Aussie kid wants to play for his country and especially to play against England in England. Just being on this trip was something special. Then to play in the Tests was great. But to win 4-nil, the same margin as Sir Donald Bradman's 1948 Invincibles and to regain the Ashes in England for the first time in 55 years, well that's heaven."

In the final Test at The Oval, he was warned by Dickie Bird for intimidatory bowling after repeated short balls to England's Robin Smith, with whom he'd waged a running battle throughout the tour. In reality, he'd received as good as he'd given.

After Smith had played and missed, Hughes had yelled, "You can't #$%&*# bat Smith."

When the next ball went for four, Smith said, "Well we make a good pair, don't we? I can't #$%&*# bat and you can't #$%&*# bowl!"

Only a month previously, at Lord's, the International Cricket Conference had ruled that umpires must be stricter when interpretating intimidatory bowling. Given the flatness of the wicket, Hughes was far from impressed by his warning.

It was to be the first of a series of run-ins with umpires which were soon to make him the most controversial cricketer in the world.

Patrick Eagar

A beer shampoo as part of Australia's Ashes win, 1989.

When you're Australia's heaviest player since "The Big Ship," 21 stone Warwick Armstrong and bowl fast for a living, something has got to give. At 17 stone-plus, depending on the time of the year, Hughes found himself succumbing to more injuries than most and in 1989-90, on the eve of the World Series finals, had the first of numerous knee operations, which eventually were to hasten his demise from big-time cricket.

The constant impacting at the popping crease had taken its toll. Experts reckoned that fast bowlers' leading knees were particularly susceptible, having to cope with pressure six times a player's bodyweight on delivery. Their back knees were also constantly under stress, having to absorb up to three times a player's bodyweight.

Two days before the first Test against Sri Lanka in Brisbane, Hughes' right knee swelled so appreciably that he bowled just two deliveries at practice before entering hospital for exploratory x-rays. While being cleared of any bone or cartilage damage and being able to take his place in the Test, he knew he'd have to restrict his workload, particularly at training to allow his knee to settle.

From bowling at an express speed for much of the time in England only months before, he deliberately slowed his pace and worked on variations. With eight wickets in the second of the two Tests against the Sri Lankans in Hobart and six against the Pakistanis in Melbourne, he was in the outstanding form of his career.

The Australians went unbeaten in the Tests and won the World Series Cup, but several key players, including Hughes and batsmen David Boon and Geoff Marsh were casualties. Having taken 5-111 and 2-63 against the Pakistanis in Adelaide, Hughes played the final rain-ruined Test in Sydney, before having a cyst removed from behind his knee. His form in Adelaide had been a revelation, despite an erratic start when his first seven overs went for 43. Not only did he bowl at brisk pace, he swung the ball more in this game than at any other time in his career.

Trailing by almost 100 runs on the first innings, the Pakistanis seemed headed for a humbling innings defeat when they lost 4-22, all to Hughes, who was bending his in-swinger like a banana and so successfully running the ball back the other way that the top four, all right-handers, were caught in an arc from gully to wicketkeeper Ian Healy.

THE PEOPLE'S FAVORITE.
The MCG crowd drew Merv Hughes to its breast like no other.

On football's Grand Final day, 1989, when the victorious Australian cricketers were feted in open cars by almost 95,000 fans, hundreds of Merv face masks were distributed in a radio promotion, the deafening cheers for Hughes and another returning local hero, Dean Jones, rivalling the roar at the first bounce of the actual match.

Hughes' maiden Test runs came at the MCG, via a thick edge, and the accompanying roar of approval made him wonder what the reception would be like if he ever scored a 100!

During the 1988-89 season after his career-best 13 wicket haul in Perth, Merv Mania was its pinnacle and when he started to warm-up for a new spell in a one-day game against the Pakistanis, 100s in the crowd mimicked his every action. For several overs, he was unaware that his stretching routine was being copied, before Dean Jones could keep a straight face no longer and informed him as to what was happening. "From then on we tried some more difficult routines. It was great fun and both relaxing and motivational as it was great to know that the crowd was behind me," Hughes said.

Photos of Hughes in his canary yellow Australian uniform, stretching in unision with 100s of fans appeared on the front pages of most Australian newspapers and also on the front cover of a book about one-day cricket.

Not only was Merv an outstanding fast bowler... he was the people's favorite.

"I've never swung the ball more than on that fourth day in Adelaide," he said. "But suddenly it stopped swinging and Akram came in and smashed us (scoring 123)."

With captain Imran Khan also breaking through for a debut century against Australia, Pakistan made almost 400 before declaring, the game being drawn.

By taking seven wickets for the game, which was played in heatwave conditions, Hughes had again served above and beyond the call of duty. He'd taken his place in the side only minutes before the toss, having had a painkilling injection an hour earlier. His knee had been too painful to allow him to bowl more than a couple of warm-up deliveries on the morning of the match. But with Terry Alderman having withdrawn at the 11th hour and Carl Rackemann also nursing injury problems, Hughes reckoned he had to play and once again was superb given the senior role as Australia's No.1 bowler.

With 16 wickets in three Tests against Pakistan and 18 in three before Christmas, Hughes had become Allan Border's breakthrough bowler. His strike-rate of one wicket each 52 balls against the Pakistanis compared favorably with the world-ranked Akram, whose 17 wickets in three Tests came at a rate of one every 47 balls.

It was only following great debate and an interrupted training schedule after his knee operation that he missed selection in Australia's side for the one-off Test in New Zealand. Until then, he'd played 17 consecutive Tests.

He was philosophical about his knee problems and believed, given his family history, that at some stage he'd have to have remedial surgery. His father, Ian, had had numerous knee operations, his mother Freda had had one knee reconstruction and his sister, Peta, two.

A BINGE EATER

MERV Hughes' eating habits are legendary.

In Barbados in '91, Merv and Craig McDermott were feeling particularly hungry one day and went into a Kentucky Fried Chicken shop near the team's city hotel.

Not only did they have a 21-piece bucket of chicken, they each also had a large milkshake, large chips, some coleslaw and finished with a large Coke!

F ew fast bowlers with model actions and rigid and disciplined lifestyles rule for more than 10 years. Merv Hughes had never considered himself classical or conservative, but after his shaky entry into Test cricket, he was determined to make the most of his opportunity, knowing that one day it would end.

Competition within the Australian team was intensifying, with Bruce Reid defying surgery and a metal rod in his back to return for his first Tests in two years. A revitalised Craig McDermott had refound his purpose and was to return in the New Year, while a third highly-credentialed fast bowler Carl Rackemann had overcome knee surgery to also be a frontline selection.

The pace pivot, Terry Alderman, remained and with eight wickets in the first 1990-91 Test against England, continued to weave an amazing mastery in Anglo-Australian Test cricket. Hughes' Brisbane contribution was five wickets, but after taking only two in the second Test in Melbourne, was made 12th man in the third in Sydney, where England displayed its best form of the summer to force a draw.

Chest to chest with Mark Taylor after the dismissal of Ijaz Ahmed, one of three catches taken by Taylor at first slip from Hughes' bowling during the first Test against Pakistan, MCG, 1989-90.

After the game, Allan Border conceded that Hughes' demotion had been a mistake and he'd badly lacked his "make it happen" abilities on a batsman-friendly wicket.

Returned immediately into the X1, in Adelaide, Hughes took two wickets before finishing the series gloriously in Perth, grabbing six wickets and reaching the 100 wicket milestone in his 27th Test.

He increased his reputation even more in the West Indies in autumn, Border continuing to use him as a hostile first change bowler, behind Mike Whitney in the first and second Tests, Reid in the third and fourth and Alderman in the fifth.

McDermott was the lynchpin of the attack and took more wickets, 24, than anyone on either side.

The Australians were unlucky not to unseat the world champions, but the series was an acrimonious one, being characterised by ill-feeling which often spilled into the public arena.

With 37 wickets for the tour, Hughes was Australia's most successful bowler. Nineteen came in the Tests. It was significant in the two

Patrick Eagar

On his way to 4-37 in the Perth Test, 1990-91.

Tests Australia lost, the second at Georgetown and the fourth at Bridgetown, that Hughes struggled to effect the breakthroughs of the other Tests.

He was to again succumb to injury, having a groin operation, but not until after another highly-successful return season in Australia, where he was one of only five to take 50 or more first-class wickets, including 22 in the Tests against India. For the first time in his Australian career, he played the entire home series, his best figures coming in the opening international in Brisbane when he claimed seven wickets, including Indian No. 3 Sanjay Manjrekar caught and bowled from a full-pitched leg-break early on the the first afternoon.

The Indians crumbled in three and a half days, Hughes taking 4-50 in the second innings, featured by three catches to short-leg fieldsman David Boon. At one stage Hughes had 4-14 in his first six overs, before McDermott and Whitney wrapped up the tail.

His continuing good performances saved him from censure, but not from an in-house fine, team physiotherapost Errol Alcott being unhappy that his weight continued to hover up to and over 110 kg.

At the end of the summer he married kindergarten teacher Susan Kelly.

With South Africa's long-awaited return to the Test fold, Zimbabwe's admission as a full Test-playing member of the ICC, the continuing Australian push for two countries to tour each summer and the eagerness of cricket authorities worldwide to cash in on the popularity of one-day cricket, international itineraries were becoming complicated like they never had been before.

Australian players could count on playing and travelling for at least eight and nine months a year and sometimes longer. More than 20 were on base contracts with the Australian Cricket Board, half a dozen having the capacity to earn upwards of $100,000 per year. To reduce against burn-out, selectors were urged for the first time to alternate their fast bowlers, especially at one-day level, so they could be at their fittest come the Tests.

The prospect of almost 12 months of non-stop cricket, a full home series against the Windies in 1992-93, followed by three Tests in New Zealand and a full-scale Ashes tour, was enough for the national selectors to exclude Hughes from Australia's touring party to Sri Lanka in August-September. They believed he'd be better advised training back in Melbourne with the Victorian state squad and being spared bowling on the slow, often-heartbreaking tracks of the sub-continent.

Hughes was unimpressed, regarding his omission as an old-fashioned "kick in the guts." It rankled with him that despite his successes, he still wasn't an automatic selection. He wanted to play every possible game for Australia and used his omission as extra motivation for the season and with 6-83 against NSW in the Sydney in the opening round of Sheffield Shield, was clearly committed to regaining his place.

For the first time in almost two decades, the West Indies were without master batsman Viv Richards, but retained their formidable fast bowling depth, bringing six pacemen and no specialist spinner.

After rookie Shane Warne, in his Melbourne debut, spun the Windies to defeat in the second Test, expectations were high that the long-time champions were about to forfeit the Frank Worrell Trophy. But they hit back superbly, winning by a run in Adelaide and blitzing the Aussies in just 14 hours in Perth to take the series 2-1.

For the first time in his career, Hughes was accorded new ball responsibility, in tandem with Craig McDermott. He again responded to captain Border's every call and with 20 inexpensive wickets and an impressive strike-rate of a wicket each 43 balls, was even more effective than McDermott, with 18 wickets and a strike-rate of 55.

His on-field behaviour, which had been questioned previously, resulted, however, in two official reports; after the first and final Tests.

Umpire Steve Randell reported

His wickets were always celebrated with gusto, no matter if it was an opening bat or a No.11...

both Hughes and Allan Border for dissent and abusive language after the final day's play of the Brisbane Test which ended in a dramatic draw, Hughes copping a $400 fine.

Border was ropable that several lbw shouts against Richie Richardson were not upheld. Needing 231 runs to win in 65 overs, the Windies lost 4-9 in a sensational collapse before Richardson (66) ensured the draw. With three wickets in his first four overs, McDermott was magnificent, but Hughes went wicketless.

In Perth at the end of the Windies' tour, Hughes was again reprimanded after being found guilty of dissent and abusive language.

All summer he'd returned the fire of the West Indies, but his battle-scarred knees were deteriorating rapidly and insiders wondered if his renowned durability and courage could see him emerge unscathed through the twin tours of NZ and England.

With 13 wickets in the three NZ Tests, a recall for the one-day internationals and a fiery tilt at Kiwi opener Mark Greatbatch, Hughes maintained the highest-possible profile, but endangered a few friendships along the way,

NZ captain Martin Crowe describing Hughes behaviour, particularly at Eden Park, in the third Test, as reprehensible. "Watching his antics to the crowd, his constant spitting at the batsmen and his childish sledging made me feel sorry for the bloke. He's a good bowler, no question. but he acted disgustingly on the field and did nothing but place the game in disrepute," Crowe said. "Merv could be good fun off the pitch, but his behaviour while he was playing had me wondering why it took so long for a code of conduct to be invoked... I could never understand why Allan Border condoned Hughes' actions as they encouraged newcomers such as Shane Warne to start acting like idiots as well."

Late on the fourth day as NZ gradually gained ascendancy of a low-scoring, series deciding Test, Hughes extended his follow through, on one or two occasions almost finishing side by side Greatbatch. "I can still remember his dodgy breath, which gives you an indication of how close he was," said Greatbatch. "If it was within the rules to get physical Merv would have been into it." *

OLD HABITS DIE HARD

DURING the 1993 Ashes tour, coach Bob Simpson was hitting fly balls, calling out a player's name and thumping the ball as hard and high as he coud.

One by one he called the player's names, then he said, "Deano" meaning Dean Jones. No-one moved .

Simmo hit another. "Deano," he said again.

Again no-one moved, before Merv yelled out, "He's not here Simmo. You didn't pick him!"

Within days of returning to Australia, Hughes had a knee arthroscopy before a fortnight's rest when the touring party left for Heathrow. Craig McDermott was also under a fitness cloud, having had a double hernia operation, which forced him out of the one-day component of the NZ tour.

So confident were the Australians of continuing their mastery against England that when McDermottt was forced to fly home after a month and a half with a twisted bowel, he touring selectors decided against asking for reinforcements.

In conjunction with the Australian physiotherapist Errol Alcott, Hughes carefully managed his rehabilitation and didn't play until the fifth game at Taunton and didn't bowl even 20 overs in an innings until the first Test at Manchester, six weeks after the Australians' arrival. That was the game in which Shane Warne produced his immortal leg-break which castled Mike Gatting and gave Australia an immediate edge.

Having won the Texaco Cup matches 3-0, the Australians enjoyed a triumphant time in the Tests, winning four of the first five, before losing momentum and dropping the final Test at The Oval.

"It was disappointing to lose that final Test. Our motivation was to win 6-0, " said Hughes. "When we drew at Trent Bridge (after back-to-back wins at Old Trafford and Lord's), we lost that opportunity and towards the end of the tour, the boys didn't have that 6-0 result to drive towards. We didn't play as hard as we could but England did play particularly well and did pick their best side."

Two nights before the final Test, the Australians, still celebrating their Ashes victory, partied long and hard at Planet Hollywood, a clear indication that they had relaxed their earlier ruthlessness.

While Warne cornered most of the publicity from the first days of the tour, his performances in the Tests being unapproached by an Australian since the halcyon days of Grimmett and O'Reilly, Hughes was also superb, enjoying his best-ever series, with 31

* From Mark Greatbatch's autobiography, *Boundary Hunter.*

wickets – eight at Manchester, four at Lord's, seven at Nottingham, six at Leeds, none at Birmingham and six at The Oval to join the elite band of bowlers to take 200 wickets in Tests. Those who has branded him an imposter in the early weeks of the 1989 tour had been silenced forever. His 200 wickets had come in 49 Test matches, two less than Jeff Thomson, Australia's fastest ever bowler.

MAD ABOUT MERV

"The transition from unthinking tearaway, come number 10 or 11 batsman, to valued fast bowling allrounder is testimony to Merv's hours of hard work. For all the antics and frivolity, Merv is very dedicated to improving his game. A captain couldn't ask for a better team man." – ALLAN BORDER in "Merv, My Life & Other Funny Stories."

"Merv is one of the great triers in the game. Even when he's not bowling well, he's yelling encouragement to the other guys, often from way down at fine-leg. He's always good for a laugh at serious moments, team meetings or at the fall of a wicket.. I don't drink and I suppose lead a quieter life than some of the blokes and Merv is forever telling me to loosen up, to live a little. If Merv was any looser, he'd fall apart." – GEOFF LAWSON, from his 1989 Ashes diary.

"I would pick Merv in my team before anybody else. He's a bullock and just keeps charging in. Apart from his skills as a bowler, he's a terrific team man and while the style might look bull-at-the-gate, he's a fast bowler of skill and variety. He bowls with genuine pace and never lets a batsman relax for an instant. Swervin' Mervin has been a fantastic performer for his State and his country... and he's a good bloke to boot. To hang out with Merv is to be part of a cultural experience. Apart from being a top bowler, Merv is particularly famous for what he can eat. He is the only guy I know who can fit a whole Big Mac in his north and south. All in one go! I went to Darwin with him in 1987 for an exhibition match and they took us to this place where there was a sensational smorgasbord, at $20 a head. Merv was a revelation. He went back there four nights in a row and they reckon it was costing the little Japanese owner $100 a night to get Merv's $20. Merv wore a track to the food. I'd never seen anything like it." – MIKE WHITNEY, in "Quick Whit, the Mike Whitney Story."

In an interview with the *Herald Sun*'s Robert Craddock, Hughes said few players were instant successes at Test level and he hoped he had convinced his early detractors that he could play. "It has been a great motivation for me to succeed because of those things written early in my career about Merv Hughes the imposter," he said.

"You try and turn people around and hopefully I have gone a long way towards doing that over the last couple of years. You have a lot of blokes who criticise you and I don't mind copping it from blokes who have played a lot. I have copped a bit from Ian Chappell, Jeff Thomson and Richie Benaud and I hope I have turned them around. Test cricket is a very hard game. Once you get there it makes you want to be there and work harder. The media controls a lot of what you do. When they write you up there is a lot of pressure on you to perform and I have not had that pressure to take wickets. If I take wickets it always seems as if it is a bonus."

Hughes defended himself against persistent charges of sledging, saying he'd played the same way since his days of sub-district cricket at Werribee. "If it is not accepted by people then bad luck," he said. "It is a tough game and that is the way we play it."

Until the last month when he was clearly below his best, Hughes' injured knees lasted remarkably well. The only scare came at Northampton just eight games into the tour when his right knee locked up. Specialists diagnosed some roughage behind the

Clowning around during an impromptu soccer match at Wanderers, 1994.

kneecap and recommended an arthroscope operation, but Hughes refused, saying he'd play with painkillers.

"It did lock up a couple of times but Errol would fiddle with it and 15 minutes later, it'd be right. He watched it closely and would put ice on it whenever it got sore."

He was also sore at Trent Bridge, having to have treatment for a groin complaint which forced him to pull up so suddenly after one delivery that captain Allan Border sprinted from slip, only to receive a "thumbs-up" from Hughes who carried on to take 5-92, his best analysis for the series.

Just as the West Indian fast bowlers had done for years, Hughes revved himself up against the key opposition batsmen. Graeme Hick, who had made a superb century against the Australians at Worcestershire, was a particular target and after Hughes took his wicket three times in a row in the opening Tests, was discarded until The Oval.

So aggressive was he against Hick that umpire Dickie Bird intervened at one stage, asking Hughes, "What unkindness has this man done to you, Mr Hughes?"

If Englishmen hadn't taken him seriously on his touring debut in 1989, they certainly were now. Allan Border couldn't speak highly enough of his efforts. Whenever Hughes entered the rooms, his face would crinkle in appreciation.

Along with the magnetic Warne, Hughes was named one of the *Wisden* Five Cricketers of the Year, a just reward for his resiliance and big-hearted endeavours.

"In '93, I was the second-string bowler to Craig McDermott. He was going to be the No.1 bowler," Hughes said.

"It's a great honor to be regarded as Australia's No.1 bowler. People who get that responsibility lift an extra cog as Glenn McGrath did in the West Indies in 1995 when Craig came home."

Warne was Australia's most-used bowler, sending down 439 overs, or almost one in three. However, Hughes was only marginally behind him with almost 300 overs, or one in four. Spinner Tim May and seamer Paul Reiffel also played important, if underrated roles.

Asked about his motivation in continuing to bowl long spells despite his declining fitness, Hughes said, "It's disappointing to miss out with injury, but you don't bale out halfway through a tour because you're a little bit sore.

"People said I really struggled in the last Test, but had there been another Test, I would have got through that. It wasn't a matter of scraping to the line. I just had to pull up the reins a little bit knowing it was the last Test. I didn't carry the attack. The workload was pretty well shared. It was a great team effort by everyone. When you have 500 odd runs on the board with a day and a half to bowl the opposition out, you've really got nothing to lose."

Hughes' knee required more surgery than originally anticipated and it was uncertain how much cricket he'd play in the 1993-94 Australian season.

"The nurse told me, 'how does it feel not to be playing cricket until Christmas?' I didn't think too much about it... when the specialist told me later I was stunned more than anything else."

SHEER HABIT
Merv's only superstition other than a dislike of black cats, dietitians and anyone who dares talk when his favorite television programs the Simpson's or Seinfeld are showing was always to put his left boot on first before he went out to bowl.

As hard as he worked, Merv Hughes soon had to face the realisation that his knees would never be the same. Australian team physiotherapist Errol Alcott likened the task of supervising his rehabilitation to "having a big road train in the pits."

Hughes hated being on the sidelines, but he had no choice if he wanted his career to extend towards his last remaining ambition, of making a third Ashes trip in 1997.

He was ruled out of all cricket until January, when he played the first of two comeback games with Victoria, taking 5-70 and 0-66 against Queensland in Brisbane and 2-116 and 0-67 against South Australia in Melbourne.

Merv's clash with Wasim Akram: Tony Crafter is once again caught in the middle.

The Australian selectors were yet to be convinced by either of Hughes' new ball replacements, NSW rookie Glenn McGrath or the more experienced Paul Reiffel, who shared the drinkwaiting duties all summer.

Craig McDermott had made a strong return and was an automatic selection for South Africa. Hughes was more of a risk, considering his limited preparation, but was glad to be chosen.

Australian captain Allan Border said Hughes had been considered for selection in the third South African Test in Adelaide in late-January, but selectors felt it would be better to save him for the actual tour. "He's probably got two good years left in him," said Border. "It's best not to rush him."

Doubts remained that his knees, the right one in particular, had suffered irrepairable damage and could no longer sustain his huge weight.

Overlooked for the first four one-day internationals, Hughes' form in the lead-up games to the Tests had been far from flattering. Hansie Cronje punished him unmercifully in the game against Orange Free State, at one stage striking four 4s in five balls, all to the legside, on his way to a double century. Hughes' angry response at the end of the over was to throw down the stumps at the striker's end, even though Cronje hadn't attempted a run.

Named for his first Test for seven months, at Johannesburg, Hughes was clearly keen to make an immediate impression, but was wise enough to bowl a full length, relying on rhythm and accuracy, rather than sheer speed. He took two early wickets on the opening day, just before and after lunch, but was also placed on report for his "send-off" of Gary Kirsten after bowling him, for 47.

Writing in *The Sydney Morning Herald*, Phil Wilkins said Kirsten's wicket, in his final over before the main break, was "accompanied by the ugliest snarl into his ear as the bails fell."

Hughes was clearly heavier than during the Ashes tour, but with four wickets had made a reasonably successful comeback. However, his Kirsten sledge was to have an immediate backlash, with a $450 fine, 10 per cent of his match fee, being ordered by International Cricket Council referee Donald Carr. Within days, the ACB had added a further $4000 penalty, saying Hughes was in breach of his contract. His list of previous misdemeanours had clearly counted against him.

It was the third time Hughes had pleaded or been found guilty of abuse in 15 Tests.

Shane Warne was also condemned for his abusive language after he'd dismissed South African opener Andrew Hudson in the second innings. He, too, was to be heavily fined as the Australian administration cracked down on on-field behaviour.

Writing in *The Australian*, Malcolm Conn said, "It is no surprise that these two players have been brought to account because Sunday's immature performances were not far removed from the way they conduct themselves at various stages during many matches they play."

Peter Roebuck, in *The Age*, said, "Hughes had been in a filthy mood all afternoon ... usually he is the least grudging of cricketers. Here he seems mean and was continually posturing."

Adding further to the controversial opening Test was Hughes' $2000 suspended fine for angrily brandishing his bat at a spectator while leaving the field on the last day of the Test, which the Australians lost by 197 runs. Television footage showed Hughes wheeling around in the player's race, banging his bat angrily on the side of the fence and poking it at a spectator who had been abusing him. But for the undoubted provocation, Hughes was told he would have been in deeper trouble.

In a stormy exit from Test cricket, Hughes was to play only one more Test, at Cape Town, where he failed to take a wicket before being discarded for the last time, missing the third Test and being overlooked for the one-day tournament in Sharjah.

He was to play only four further Shield games with Victoria (for nine wickets at 40-plus) at the start of the 1994-95 season before being injured again and failing to regain his place.

He didn't declare himself officially retired from international cricket until he was 35 and the '97 Ashes squad had been chosen. In a letter to the Australian Cricket Board's acting chief executive Richard Watson, dated April 23, he wrote:

Dear Richard,

It is with great regret and overwhelming disappointment that I write these words.

Since my last appearance for Australia in 1994, I have been working extremely hard (and hoping for some other rival fast bowlers to retire gracefully, injure themselves or burn out) in my aim of securing a third Ashes tour in 1997.

However, after being constantly overlooked by the Victorian selectors, it dismays me greatly to have to similarly be overlooked by the national selectors.

It is obvious with the departure of Lawrie Sawle (chairman) and Bob Simpson (coach) from the selection panel, two of my greatest supporters, that my time is up.

The decision by the national selectors to overlook me has embarrassed and hurt me deeply.

I had felt that the new panel's decision to name Mark Taylor as captain offered me some hope but the recent demise of another fat boy in David Boon has indicated there are limited positions available for overweight cricketers.

With great regret (and overwhelming relief), I must announce that I have now officially retired from international cricket, unless you need me in the next month...

He kept his options open, however, for State cricket and finally said yes, to Mike Veletta's ACT X1, as part of the team's inaugural year of Mercantile Mutual Cup cricket in 1997-98. He still wanted to settle a few old scores. And the money was good, too!

THE BEST OF THE BEST

In 1997, the Australian Cricket Society asked Merv to name his best Australian team, in batting order, from all his Test teammates over a decade. he named:

Mark Taylor, Geoff Marsh (v-c), David Boon, Allan Border (c), Dean Jones, Steve Waugh, Ian Healy, Shane Warne, Craig McDermott, Tim May and Bruce Reid. His 12th man was Mark Waugh.

Asked about the best ball he'd ever bowled, he said, "That's easy... it was in the 1996-97 summer at Jubilee Park for Footscray against Ringwood. I was bowling to Darren Dempsey, a right-hander. It pitched outside leg, just missed the off bail and was taken by our 'keeper Rainor Reber in front of second slip. While I didn't get him out, it was the greatest ball I'd ever bowled. It was bloody well wasted on Jack (Dempsey). I told him so too!"

Merv Hughes THE MAN & HIS RECORD

Born: November 23, 1961

Teams: Victoria, Essex & Australia

First-class debut: 1981-82

First-class record: Matches 160. Batting — Runs 2569, Average 17.47, Highest score 72 not out, seven 50s. Bowling — Wickets 580, Average 28.92, Best bowling 8-87, Five wickets in an Innings 21, Ten wickets in a Match 3. Fielding — Catches 53.

Test debut: 1985-86

Test record: Matches 53. Batting — Runs 1032, Average 16.64, Highest score 72 not out, two 50s. Bowling — Wickets 212, Average 28.38, Best bowling 8-87, Five wickets in an Innings 7, Ten wickets in a Match 1. Fielding — Catches 23.

Tours: England 1989, 1993; India 1989-90; New Zealand 1989-90, 1992-93; Sharjah 1989-90; West Indies 1991; New Zealand 1992-93; South Africa 1993-94.

One day international debut: 1988-89

One day international record: Matches 33. Batting — Runs 100, Average 11.11, Highest score 20. Bowling — Wickets 39, Average 29.07, Best bowling 4-44. Fielding — Catches 6.

Merv Hughes' Test record series by series:

BATTING & FIELDING

Season	Opponent	Mt	Inns	No	HS	Runs	Ave	50s	Ct.
1985-86	India (h)	1	1	0	0	0	-	-	1
1986-87	England (h)	4	6	0	16	31	5.16	-	2
1987-88	New Zealand (h)	1	1	0	5	5	5.00	-	-
	Sri Lanka (h)	1	1	0	8	8	8.00	1	-
1988-89	West Indies (h)	4	5	2	72*	109	36.33	1	3
1989	England (a)	6	5	0	71	127	25.40	1	-
1989-90	New Zealand (h)	1	1	0	16	16	16.00	-	-
	Sri Lanka (h)	2	4	1	30	105	35.00	-	-
	Pakistan (h)	3	4	2	32	48	24.00	-	1
1990-91	England (h)	4	5	0	30	44	8.80	-	3
1991	West Indies (a)	5	8	0	21	41	5.12	-	2
1991-92	India (h)	5	8	0	36	154	19.25	-	4
1992-93	West Indies (h)	5	9	1	43	118	14.75	-	5
	New Zealand (a)	3	4	1	45	117	39.00	-	-
1993	England (a)	6	5	0	38	76	15.20	-	-
1993-94	South Africa (a)	2	3	1	26*	33	16.50	-	1
Totals		53	70	8	72*	1032	16.64	2	23

BOWLING

Season	Opponent	Mts	Overs	Mds	Runs	Wicks	Ave	BB	5wI	10wM
1985-86	India (h)	1	38	6	123	1	123.00	1-123		
1986-87	England (h)	4	136,3	26	444	10	44.40	3-134		
1987-88	New Zealand (h)	1	35	12	97	5	19.40	3-40		
	Sri Lanka (h)	1	39	9	128	5	25.60	5-67		
1988-89	West Indies (h)	1	63,1	41	503	14	35.92	8-87		
1989	England (a)	6	189,2	41	615	19	32.36	4-71		
1989-90	New Zealand (h)	1	56	15	143	7	20.42	4-51		
	Sri Lanka (h)	2	92,2	22	279	11	25.36	5-88		
	Pakistan (h)	3	140	51	357	16	22.31	5-111		
1990-91	England (h)	4	142,1	38	365	15	24.33	4-37		
1991	West Indies (a)	5	172,3	33	589	19	31.00	4-44		
1991-92	India (h)	5	199,3	46	511	22	23.22	4-50		
1992-93	West Indies (h)	5	145,2	30	432	20	21.60	5-64		

	New Zealand (a)	3	132,2	38	349	13	26.84	4-62
1993	England (a)	6	296,2	78	845	31	27.25	5-92
1993-94	South Africa (a)	2	70	13	237	4	59.25	3-59
Totals		53	2047,3	499	6017	212	28.38	8-87

COUNTRY BY COUNTRY RECORD
BATTING & FIELDING

Country	Mt	Inns	No	HS	Runs	Ave	50s	Ct.
v England	20	21	0	71	278	13.23	1	5
v India	6	9	0	36	154	17.11	-	5
v New Zealand	5	6	1	45	138	27.60	-	-
v Pakistan	3	4	2	32	48	24.00	-	1
v South Africa	2	3	1	26*	33	16.50	-	1
v Sri Lanka	3	5	1	30	113	28.25	-	1
v West Indies	14	22	3	728	268	14.10	1	10

HOME & ABROAD

	Mt	Inns	No	HS	Runs	Ave	50s	Ct.
Tests at home	31	45	6	72*	638	16.35	1	20
Tests abroad	22	25	2	71	394	17.13	1	3
Totals	53	70	8	72*	1032	16.64	2	23

BOWLING

Country	Mts	Overs	Mds	Runs	Wicks	Ave	BB	5wl	10wM
v England	20	764,2	183	2269	75	30.25	5-92	1	-
v India	6	237,3	52	634	23	27.56	4-50	-	-
v New Zealand	5	223,2	65	589	25	23.56	4-51	-	-
v Pakistan	3	140	51	357	16	22.31	5-111	1	-
v South Africa	2	70	13	237	4	59.25	3-59	-	-
v Sri Lanka	3	131,2	31	407	16	25.43	5-67	2	-
v West Indies	14	481	104	1524	53	28.75	8-87	3	1

HOME & ABROAD

	Mts	Overs	Mds	Runs	Wicks	Ave	BB	5wl	10wM
Tests at home	31	1222,2	296	3382	126	26.84	8-87	6	1
Tests abroad	22	825,1	203	2635	86	30.63	5-92	1	-
Totals	53	2047,3	499	6017	212	28.38	8-87	7	1

HIS HIGHEST TEST SCORES
72* v West Indies, Adelaide, 1988-89
71 v England, Leeds, 1989
43 v West Indies, Adelaide, 1992-93
38 v England, Birmingham, 1993
36 v India, Melbourne, 1991-92

HIS BEST TEST BOWLING
8-87   v West Indies, Perth, 1988-89
5-64   v West Indies, Adelaide,1992-93
5-67   v Sri Lanka, Perth, 1987-88
5-88   v Sri Lanka, Hobart, 1989-90
5-92   v England, Nottingham, 1993
5-111   v Pakistan, Adelaide, 1989-90
5-130   v West Indies, Perth, 1988-89

HIS HIGHEST ONE-DAY INTERNATIONAL SCORES
20 v England, Manchester, 1993
13 v West Indies, Sydney, 1988-89

HIS BEST ONE-DAY INTERNATIONAL BOWLING
4-44   v West Indies, Sydney, 1988-89
3-30   v Pakistan. Adelaide, 1988-89
3-33   v West Indies, Georgetown, 1991
3-36   v New Zealand, Hamilton, 1989-90
3-28   v West Indies, Sydney, 1988-89

POOR BEHAVIOUR, 1992-97

INTERNATIONAL CRICKET CONFERENCE,

Player	Country	Details of incident
TEST CRICKET		
1992		
1. Aaqib Javed	Pakistan	Failed to keep control of Aaqib Javed on the field
2. Javed Miandad	Pakistan	Violated Code 8 by speaking to the press
3. Intikhab Alam	Pakistan manager	Showed dissent at umpire's decision
4. Rashid Latif	(emergency fieldsman)	Showed dissent
5. Manoj Prabhakar	India	Showing dissent to umpire
6. Allan Border	Australia	Violated Code 3 & 5 by showing dissent to umpire and abusive language to umpire
7. Merv Hughes	Australia	Violations of Code 3 & 5
1993		
1. Allan Border	Australia	Violations of Code 3 & 5
2. Merv Hughes	Australia	Dissent against his dismissal
3. Vinod Kambli	India	Dissent against rejection of bat/pad catch
4. Andrew Jones	New Zealand	Dissent against teammates' lbw decisions
1994		
1. Peter Kirsten	South Africa	Dissent against his lbw decision; second offence for match
2. Peter Kirsten	South Africa	Verbal abuse of SA batsmen
3. Merv Hughes	Australia	Verbal abuse of SA batsman Andrew Hudson
4. Shane Warne	Australia	Breach of Article 2 for knocking a stump out of the ground after being bowled
5. Curtly Ambrose	West Indies	Showing dissent against umpires after lbw decision
6. Michael Atherton	England	Showing dissent against umpires after caught behind appeal rejected
7. Fanie de Villiers	South Africa	Dissent against rejection of lbw appeal
8. Jo Angel	Australia	Showing dissent against umpires after being given out caught behind
9. Guy Whittal	Zimbabwe	Clear dissent at umpire's decision after being given out lbw.
1995		
1. Ken Rutherford	New Zealand	After dismissing Craig McDermott, he "gestured" him to the pavilion four times
2. Chris Lewis	England	Public comments made against umpires and conduct of Pakistan team on the field
3. David Houghton	Zimbabwe	Abusive language and snatching hat from umpire after lbw appeal is rejected
4. Wasim Akram	Pakistan	Suggested that Ian Robinson, the local umpire, had interfered with the ball during Zimbabwe's first innings
5. Salim Malik	Pakistan	Similar comments against umpire Ian Robinson
6. Aamir Sohail	Pakistan	Audible bad language on field of play
7. Kerry Walmsley	New Zealand	Throwing his bat after being dismissed
8. Aamir Sohail	Pakistan	Made a statement which brought the game into disrepute in that he publicly criticised the dismissals of three playe
9. Bob Woolmer	South African coach	Asked umpire to consult technology after decision had been made
1996		
1. Hansie Cronje	South Africa	Breach of advertising code
2. Adam Parore	New Zealand	Excessive appeal
3. Chris Cairns	New Zealand	Sank to knees and hit wicket after lbw appeal rejected
4. Danny Morrison	New Zealand	For wearing a logo on an arm guard
5. Herschel Gibbs	South Africa	For wearing a logo on his pads
6. Vangipurappu Laxman		Showing dissent at an lbw appeal being rejected and engaging in conduct unbecoming an international player
7. Chris Cairns	New Zealand	Showing dissent after being given out lbw
8. Ijaz Ahmed	Pakistan	Quoted in press as saying he was given latitude by umpire for not calling wide deliveries
9. Heath Streak	Zimbabwe	Stood his ground rubbing shoulder after being given out caught behind
10. David Johnson	India	Continued and aggressive appeal after bat/pad catch rejected

INDIVIDUAL PLAYER BEHAVIOUR BREACHES

Action	Game	Match referee
Reprimand	v England, third Test, Old Trafford, July 2-7	Conrad Hunte
Reprimand	v England, third Test, Old Trafford, July 2-7	Conrad Hunte
Fined 40 per cent of match fee	v England, fourth Test, Headingley, July 23-27	Clyde Walcott
Fined 10 per cent of match fee	v South Africa, third Test, Port Elizabeth, December 26-30	Mike Smith
Fined 50 per cent of match fee	v West Indies, first Test, Brisbane, November 27-December 1	Raman Subba Row
Fined 10 per cent of match fee	v West Indies, first Test, Brisbane, November 27-December 1	Raman Subba Row
Severely reprimanded and warned as to future conduct	v West Indies, fifth Test, Perth, January 30-February 1	Donald Carr
Severely reprimanded and warned as to future conduct	v West Indies, fifth Test, Perth, January 30-February 1	Donald Carr
Severe reprimand	v Sri Lanka, second Test, Colombo, July 27-August 1	Peter Burge
Severe reprimand	v Australia, first Test, Perth, November 12-16	Srini. Venkatagharavan
Fined 25 per cent of match fee	v Australia, third Test, Adelaide, January 28-February 1	Jackie Hendriks
Fined a further 40 per cent of match fee	v Australia, third Test, Adelaide, January 28-February 1	Jackie Hendriks
Fined 10 per cent of match fee; severe reprimmand	v South Africa, first Test, Johannesburg, March 4-8	Donald Carr
Fined 10 per cent of match fee; severe reprimmand	v South Africa, first Test, Johannesburg, March 4-8	Donald Carr
Fined $US1500	v England, fourth Test, Barbados, April 8-13	John Reid
Fined 50 per cent of match fee	v South Africa, third Test, The Oval, August 18-22	Peter Burge
Fined 25 per cent of match fee	v England, third Test, The Oval, August 18-22	Peter Burge
Severe reprimand	v Pakistan, first Test, Karachi, September 28-October 2	John Reid
Fined 25 per cent of match fee	v Sri Lanka, first Test, Harare, October 11-16	Peter van der Merwe
Fined 75 per cent of match fee and two-match suspended sentence	v South Africa, fourth Test, Cape Town, January 2-6	Peter Burge
Fined 30 per cent of his match fee	v Australia, fourth Test, Adelaide, January 26-30	John Reid
Fined 10 per cent of his match fee and reprimanded	v Pakistan, second Test, Bulawayo, February 7-12	Jackie Hendriks
Severe reprimand	v Zimbabwe, second Test, Bulawayo, February 7-12	Jackie Hendriks
Fined 50 per cent of match fee, 2-Test suspended sentence until Dec 31 and severe reprimand	v Zimbabwe, third Test, Harare, February 15-20	Jackie Hendriks
Severe reprimand	v Zimbabwe, third Test, Harare, February 15-20	Jackie Hendriks
Reprimand	v Sri Lanka, first Test, Napier, March 11-15	Barry Jarman
Fined 50 per cent of match fee and a two-Test/ODI suspended sentence for six months	v Australia, second Test, Hobart, November 9-14	Raman Subba Row
Fined 10 per cent of match fee	v England, 2nd Test, Johannesburg, Nov 30-Dec 4	Clive Lloyd
Fined 50 per cent of match fee	v England, fifth Test, Cape Town, January 2-4	Clive Lloyd
Fined 20 per cent of his match fee	v Zimbabwe, second Test, Auckland, January 20-24	Nasim ul Ghani
Fined 10 per cent of match fee	v Zimbabwe, second Test, Wellington, January 20-24	Nasim ul Ghani
Fined 10 per cent of match fee	v West Indies, second Test, Antigua, April 27-May 2	Mike Denness
Fined 15 per cent of his match fee	v India, second Test, Calcutta, November 27-December 1	John Reid
Fined 15 per cent of his match fee	v South Africa, 2nd Test, Calcutta, November 27-December 1	John Reid
Fined 50 per cent of his match fee	v Pakistan, 2nd Test, Rawalpindi, November 28-December 2	C. W. Smith
Fined 50 per cent of match fee	v New Zealand, 2nd Test, Rawalpindi, Nov 28-Dec 2	C. W. Smith
Fined 15 per cent of match fee	v England, first Test, Bulawayo, December 18-22	H. Singh
Severe reprimand	v South Africa, third Test, Johannesburg, December 26-28	Barry Jarman
Fined 25 per cent of match fee	v South Africa, third Test, January 16-20	Barry Jarman

321

Player	Country	Details of incident
1997		
1. Pankaj Dharmani	India	Continued and aggressive appeal after bat/pad catch rejected
2. Saurav Ganguly	India	Continued and aggressive appeal after bat/pad catch rejected
3. Mohammad Azharuddin	India	Remained at crease for period of time after being given out
4. Ian Healy	Australia	Remained at crease for period of time after being given out. Also mouthed words of dissent

ONE DAY INTERNATIONAL CRICKET

Player	Country	Details of incident
1992		
1. Peter Kirsten	South Africa	Showed dissent after he was run out. Also used offensive language
2. Aaqib Javed	Pakistan	Violated Code 2 & 3
1993		
1. Desmond Haynes	West Indies	Showing dissent at umpire's decision,
1994		
1. Nayan Mongia	India	Dissent against a catch not given
2. Dion Nash	New Zealand	Breaches of Codes 2 & 5
3. Brian Lara	West Indies	Showing dissent against umpires after being given out stumped
4. Arjuna Ranatunga	Sri Lanka	Showing dissent after being given out caught behind by indicating thet the ball had come off his pad
5. Ken Rutherford	New Zealand	Attempting to intimidate umpire by moving towards him with hands raised saying, "That's out."
1995		
1. Dave Richardson	South Africa	Hit a stump out of the ground after being given out run out.
2. Brian Strang	Zimbabwe	Pointed batsman to pavilion
3. Greg Blewett	Australia	Breach of ICC regulation 7 (c) (ii) for wearing logo on wristband
4. Ricky Ponting	Australia	Breach of ICC regulation 7 (c) (ii) for wearing logo on wristband
5. Shane Warne	Australia	Breach of ICC regulation 7 (c) (ii) for wearing logo on wristband
6. Aamer Nazir	Pakistan	Offensive gesture after dismissing Sanath Jayasuriya
7. Nayan Mongia	India	Dissent and attempted intimidation of umpires after appeal turned down
8. Ajay Jadeja	India	Dissent in that he made a sign requesting a television replay
9. Roger Twose	New Zealand	Verbal abuse of Sanjay Manjrekar after he claimed a catch after appearing to cross a boundary
10. Ajit Wadekar	Indian team manager	Disclosed to media contents of report lodged by him to referee
11. Aaqib Javed	Pakistan	Offensive gestures to dismissed batsman.
12. Mushtaq Ahmed	Pakistan	Asked umpire to consult technology on stumping decision
1996		
1. Asanka Gurusinha	Sri Lanka	Comments made to opposing player on field
2. Phil Simmons	West Indies	Attempted intimidation of umpire
3. Steve Waugh	Australia	Breaches (dissent and disrepute) towards umpire calling wide deliveries
4. Gary Kirsten	South Africa	For fearing a colored bandanna during his innings
5. Mike Doherty	South African team manager	For not responding to referee's request to have Kirsten remove bandanna
1997		
1. Aamir Sohail	Pakistan	Lingered at crease after being given out. Twice asked umpire to look at replay screen. Swore as he passed umpire and threw his bat
2. Aravinda de Silva	Sri Lanka	Lingered at crease after being given out; showed dissent
3. Ijaz Ahmed	Pakistan	Crude and abusive language to outgoing batsman, Arjuna Ranatunga

OTHER ICC GAMES

Player	Country	Details of incident
1. Phil Tufnell	England	Bringing game into disrepute by throwing ball in aggressive manner after a caught behind appeal had been rejected

Poor Behaviour

Action	Game	Match referee
Fined 25 per cent of match fee	v South Africa, third Test, January 16-20	Barry Jarman
Fined 25 per cent of match fee	v South Africa, third Test, January 16-20	Barry Jarman
Severe reprimand	v South Africa, third Test, January 16-20	Barry Jarman
Suspended from two one-day internationals	v South Africa, third Test, Centurion Park, March 21-25	Raman Subba Row
Fined 50 per cent of match fee	v India, Port Elizabeth, December 9	Clive Lloyd
Suspended one match at Auckland (30-12-92)	v New Zealand, Napier, December 28	Peter Burge
Fined 50 per cent of match fee and warned as to future conduct	v Australia, Brisbane, January 10	Donald Carr
Fined $US750 & one match suspension	v Australia, Sharjah, April 19	A.M. Ebrahim
Fined $US350 and one match suspension	v Pakistan, Sharjah, April 20	A.M. Ebrahim
Fined 50 per cent of match fee, suspended for next match and severe reprimand	v New Zealand, Goa, October 26	Raman Subba Row
Fined 25 per cent of his match fee	v New Zealand, East London, December 18	Peter Burge
Fined 50 per cent of match fee	v Sri Lanka, East London, December 18	Peter Burge
Severe reprimand and 20 per cent suspended match fee for remainder of series	v Pakistan, Newlands, January 10	Peter Burge
Cautioned	v Pakistan, Harare, February 25	Jackie Hendriks
Fined 15 per cent of match fee	v India, Dunedin, February 22	Peter van der Merwe
Fined 10 per cent of match fee	v India, Dunedin, February 22	Peter van der Merwe
Fined 25 per cent of match fee	v India, Dunedin, February 22	Peter van der Merwe
Severe reprimand	v Sri Lanka, Sharjah, April 11	Clive Lloyd
Fined 10 per cent of his match fee	v Sri Lanka, Sharjah, April 14	Clive Lloyd
Fined 10 per cent of his match fee	v New Zealand, Pune, November 24	Peter Burge
Fined 50 per cent of his match fee	v India, Nagpur, November 26	Peter Burge
Reprimanded. Mattered referred to BCCI	India v New Zealand, Nagpur, November 26	Peter Burge
Fined 50 per cent of match fee	v New Zealand, Wellington, December 20	R. Madugalle
Fined 10 per cent of match fee	v New Zealand, Wellington, December 20	R. Madugalle
Reprimand	v Australia, January 12	Raman Subba Row
Fined 10 per cent of match fee	v New Zealand, Guyana, April 3	Mike Denness
Fined 30 per cent of match fee, suspended for three months	v India, Colombo, September 6	John Reid
Fined 10 per cent of match fee	v Pakistan, Nairobi, October 6	Mike Denness
Fined 10 per cent of match fee	South Africa v Pakistan, Nairobi, October 6	Mike Denness
Suspended for next game, against the West Indies 18-1-97	v Australia, Melbourne, January 16	Raman Subba Row
Severe reprimand	v New Zealand, Wellington, March 27	Peter Burge
Fined 20 per cent of match fee, plus a suspended fine of another 30 per cent if another breach occurs, to run for five months	v Sri Lanka, Colombo, April 26-May 1	John Reid
Fined 30 per cent of match fee	v Australia "A," MCG, December 13	John Reid

INDEX

FURTHER READING

Allan Lamb, My Autobiography, (CollinsWillow, 1996)

Allan's Australian Cricket Annual, various editions, edited by Allan Miller

Always Reddy, Ian Redpath with Neill Phillipson (Garry Sparke & Assoc., 1976)

Australian Cricket magazine

Ball of Fire, Fred Trueman (J.M. Dent & Sons, 1976)

Beating the Field, My Own Story, by Brian Lara with Brian Scovell (Partridge Press, 1995)

Brian Lara beating The Field, with Brian Scovell (Transworld, 1995)

Brian Lara the story of a record-breaking year, (Stanley Paul, 1994)

Botham, My Autobiography, (CollinsWillow, 1994)

Captain's Innings, an autobiography, Keith Fletcher (Stanley Paul, 1983)

Cricket Rebel, John Snow (Hamlyn, 1976)

Cricket Year, annual, various editions, edited by Ken Piesse

Cricket Yearbook 1994, edited by Richie Benaud (Hamlyn Australia, 1994)

Cricketer magazine

Farewell to cricket, Don Bradman (Hodder & Stoughton, 1950)

Fred Trueman's Cricket Masterpieces, classic tales from the pavilion, Fred Trueman with Peter Grosvenor (Sidgwick & Jackson, 1990)

Frindall's Scorebook, Jubilee Edition (Lonsdale Universal, 1977)

G'day ya Pommy b......! & other cricketing memories, David Lloyd (Weidenfeld & Nicolson, 1992)

Geoff Lawson's *Diary of the Ashes* (Angus & Robertson, 1990)

Gloves, Sweat and Tears, Rod Marsh (Penguin, 1984).

Greg Chappell, Adrian McGregor (Collins, 1985)

Henry, The Geoff Lawson Story, (Ironbark Press, 1993)

Howzat, Sixteen Australian cricketers talk to Keith Butler, (Collins, 1979)

Imran Khan, Ivo Tennant (H. F. & G. Witherby, 1994)

In Search of Runs, Dennis Amiss with Michael Carey, (Stanley Paul, 1976)

Inside Edge magazine

It's Knott Cricket, the autobiography of Alan Knott, (Macmillan, 1985)

Lambs to the slaughter, Graham Yallop & Rod Nicholson (Outback Press, 1979)

Lillee, My Life in Cricket, (Metheun, 1982)

Merv, Rod Nicholson, (Magenta Press, 1990)

Merv – My Life and other Funny Stories, (Pan Macmillan, 1990)

McGilvray, The Game Goes On, by Alan McGilvray, as told to Norm Tasker (ABC, 1987)

Mike Denness: I Declare (Arthur Barker, 1977)

Over and out, by Dennis Lillee (Metheun, 1984)

Oxford World Cricketers, a biographical dictionary, Christopher Martin-Jenkins (Oxford University Press, 1996).

Masters of Cricket, from Trumper to May, Jack Fingleton (William Heinemann, 1958)

Shane Warne, My Own Story, (Swan Publishing, 1997).

Shane Warne, Sultan of Spin, Ken Piesse (Modern Publishing, 1995)

My Story, Tony Greig with Alan Lee (Stanley Paul, 1980)

Standing up, standing back, Bob Taylor with Patrick Murphy (Collins Willow 1985)

Steve Waugh's West Indian Tour Diary (HarperCollins, 1995)

That's Out, Dickie Bird (Arthur Barker, 1985)

The Glovemen, the world's finest wicketkeepers, Jack Pollard (Kangaroo Press, 1993)

The Cricket Statistician, various publications produced by the U.K.-based Association of Cricket Statisticians.

The Gloves of Irony, Rod Marsh (Lansdowne Press, 1982)

The Grand Old Ground, a history of the Sydney Cricket Ground, Phil Derriman (Cassell Australia, 1981)

The West Indian Cricket Annual, various editions, edited by Tony Cozier

The Wisden Book of Test Cricket, various editions, edited by Bill Frindall

Test Cricket, Australia v Pakistan & West Indies, edited by Richie Benaud (Lansdowne Press, 1982)

Triumph in Australia. Mike Gatting (Queen Anne Press, 1987)

Thommo, Jeff Thomson, the world's fastest bowler tells his own story to David Frith (Angus & Robertson, 1980)

Under the Southern Cross, the autobiography of David Boon (HarperSports, 1996)

Viv Richards, the authorised biography, Trevor McDonald (Pelham Books, 1984)

Wisden Cricketers' Almanack

Whispering Death, Michael Holding & Tony Cozier (Andrew Deutsch, 1993)

You'll Keep, by Rod Marsh, as told to Ian Brayshaw (Hutchinson, 1975)